Favorite Brand Name™

365 PASTA RECIPES

Publications International, Ltd.

Favorite Brand Name Recipes at www.fbnr.com

Copyright © 1997 Publications International, Ltd.
All rights reserved. This publication may not be reproduced or quoted in whole or in part by any means whatsoever without written permission from:

Louis Weber, CEO
Publications International, Ltd.
7373 North Cicero Avenue
Lincolnwood, Illinois 60712

Permission is never granted for commercial purposes.

365 Favorite Brand Name is a trademark of Publications International, Ltd.

All recipes and photographs that contain specific brand names are copyrighted by those companies and/or associations, unless otherwise specified. All photographs *except* those on pages 25, 29, 35, 39, 41, 49, 112, 115, 128, 135, 136, 139, 143, 145, 151, 155, 165, 167, 171, 175, 179, 183, 185, 189, 191, 195, 197, 233, 245, 255, 267, 279, 285, 291, 293, 311, 313, 315, 319 and 325 copyright © Publications International, Ltd.

The *365 Favorite Brand Name* series is a collection of recipes from America's favorite brand name food companies and food associations. In addition, a selection of the most popular recipes owned by the publisher has been included.

DOLE® is a registered trademark of Dole Food Company, Inc.

LOUIS RICH® is a registered trademark of Oscar Mayer Foods Corporation.

Some of the products listed in this publication may be in limited distribution.

Pictured on the front cover: Fajita Stuffed Shells *(page 86)*.

Pictured on the back cover *(left to right):* Ravioli with Homemade Tomato Sauce *(page 294)* and Sweet Dijon Pasta Salad *(page 4)*.

ISBN: 0-7853-9144-4

Manufactured in China.

8 7 6 5 4 3 2 1

Microwave Cooking: Microwave ovens vary in wattage. Use the cooking times as guidelines and check for doneness before adding more time.

The HEALTHY CHOICE® recipes contained in this book have been tested by the manufacturers and have been carefully edited by the publisher. The publisher and the manufacturers cannot be held responsible for any ill effects caused by the errors in the recipes, or by spoiled ingredients, unsanitary conditions, incorrect preparation procedures or any other cause.

Favorite Brand Name™

365 PASTA RECIPES

SUPER SALADS & SOUPS	**4**
OUT OF THE OVEN	**54**
FROM THE BUTCHER SHOP	**106**
CATCH OF THE DAY	**144**
FRESH FROM THE GARDEN	**180**
ASIAN FARE	**220**
NEW CREATIONS	**252**
OLD FAVORITES	**286**
SPECTACULAR SAUCES	**306**
ACKNOWLEDGMENTS	**326**
INDEX	**327**

SUPER SALADS & SOUPS

1 SWEET DIJON PASTA SALAD

8 ounces tri-color rotini
¾ cup plain nonfat yogurt
¼ cup reduced-fat mayonnaise
2 tablespoons honey
1 tablespoon Dijon mustard
¼ teaspoon ground cumin
¼ teaspoon salt
1 can (15 ounces) black beans, drained and rinsed
1 medium tomato, chopped
½ cup shredded carrot
¼ cup chopped green onions

1. Cook pasta according to package directions; drain. Rinse under cold water until cool; drain.

2. Combine yogurt, mayonnaise, honey, mustard, cumin and salt in small bowl until well blended.

3. Combine pasta, beans, tomato, carrot and onions in medium bowl. Add yogurt mixture; toss to coat. Cover and refrigerate until ready to serve. Garnish as desired.
Makes 6 servings

2 MEXICAN TURKEY CHILI MAC

1 pound ground turkey
1 package (1¼ ounces) reduced-sodium taco seasoning mix
1 can (14½ ounces) reduced-sodium stewed tomatoes
1 can (11 ounces) corn with red and green peppers, undrained
1½ cups cooked elbow macaroni, without salt, drained
1 ounce low-salt corn chips, crushed
½ cup shredded reduced-fat Cheddar cheese

1. In large nonstick skillet, over medium-high heat, sauté turkey 5 to 6 minutes or until no longer pink; drain. Stir in taco seasoning, tomatoes, corn and macaroni. Reduce heat to medium and cook 4 to 5 minutes until heated throughout.

2. Sprinkle corn chips over meat mixture and top with cheese. Cover and heat 1 to 2 minutes or until cheese is melted.
Makes 6 servings

Favorite recipe from **National Turkey Federation**

Sweet Dijon Pasta Salad

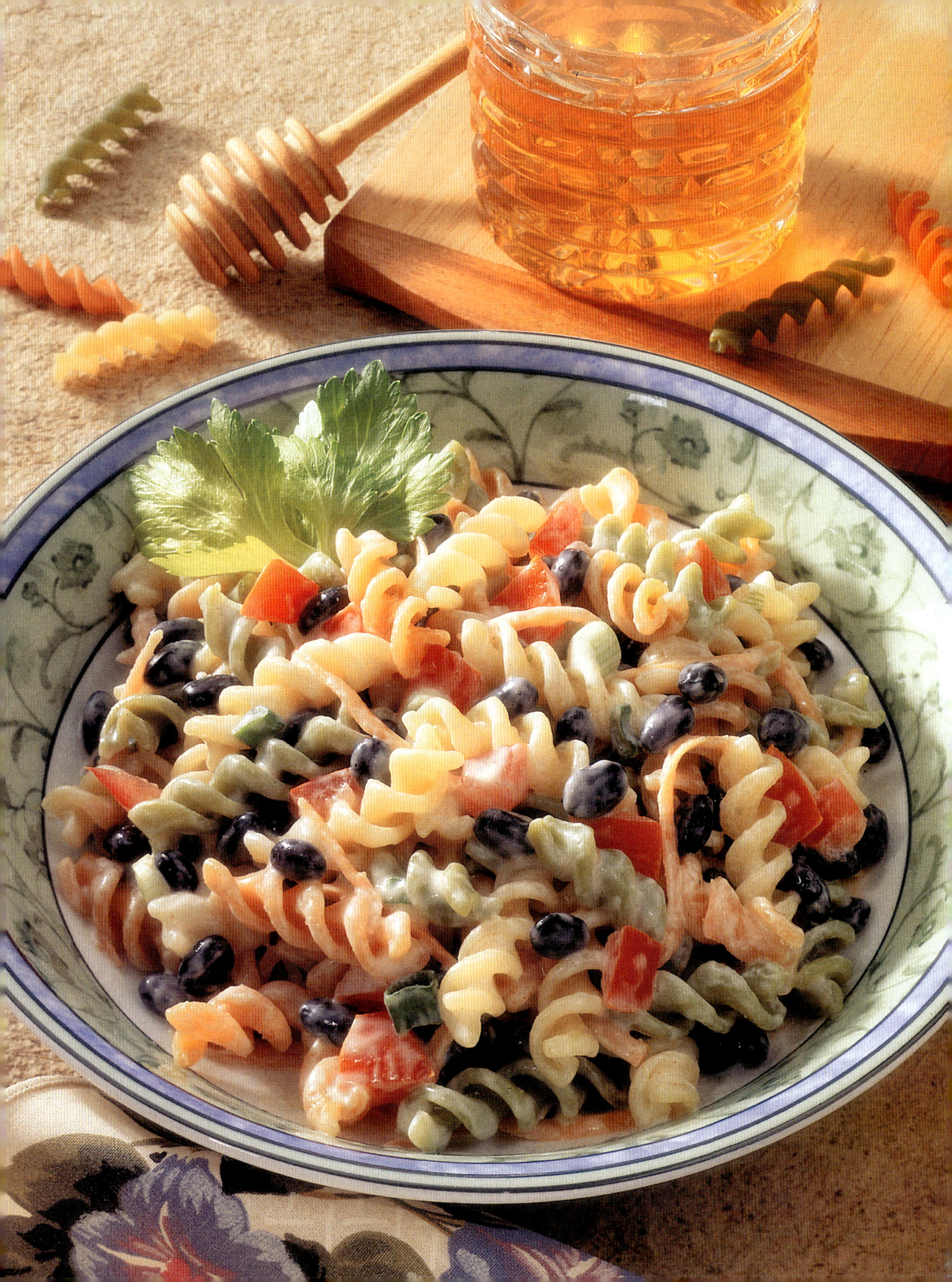

SUPER SALADS & SOUPS

3. PASTA SALAD IN ARTICHOKE CUPS

- 5 cloves garlic, peeled
- ½ cup white wine
- 6 medium artichokes
- 1 lemon, cut into halves
- 6 cups chicken broth
- 1 tablespoon plus 1 teaspoon olive oil, divided
- 1 package (2 ounces) artichoke hearts
- 8 ounces corkscrew pasta or pasta twists
- ½ teaspoon dried basil leaves
- Basil Vinaigrette Dressing (recipe follows)

1. Place garlic and wine in small saucepan. Bring to a boil over high heat; reduce heat to low. Simmer 10 minutes.

2. Meanwhile, prepare artichokes. Cut bottoms from artichokes so that they will sit flat; remove outer leaves. Cut 1 inch off tops of artichokes. Snip tips from remaining leaves with scissors. Rub ends with lemon.

3. Bring chicken broth to a boil in Dutch oven over high heat. Add artichokes, wine mixture and 1 tablespoon oil. Reduce heat to low. Cover; simmer 25 to 30 minutes or until leaves pull easily from base. Drain.

4. Cook artichoke hearts according to package directions. Drain well. Cut into slices to make 2 cups. Set aside.

5. Cook pasta according to package directions; drain. Place pasta in large bowl. Sprinkle with remaining 1 teaspoon oil and basil.

6. Prepare Basil Vinaigrette Dressing. Add artichoke hearts and 1 cup dressing to pasta; toss gently to coat.

7. Carefully spread outer leaves of whole artichokes. Remove small heart leaves by grasping with fingers, then pulling and twisting. Scoop out fuzzy choke with spoon; discard.

8. Fill with pasta mixture. Cover; refrigerate until serving time. Serve with remaining dressing. Garnish as desired.

Makes 6 servings

BASIL VINAIGRETTE DRESSING

- ⅓ cup white wine vinegar
- 2 tablespoons Dijon mustard
- 3 cloves garlic, peeled
- ¾ cup coarsely chopped fresh basil leaves
- 1 cup olive oil
- Salt and black pepper to taste

1. Place vinegar, mustard and garlic in blender or food processor. Cover; process using on/off pulses until well mixed. Add basil; continue to pulse until mixture is blended.

2. With motor running, slowly pour in olive oil. Season to taste with salt and pepper.

Makes about 1½ cups

Favorite recipe from **Castroville Artichoke Festival**

Pasta Salad in Artichoke Cup

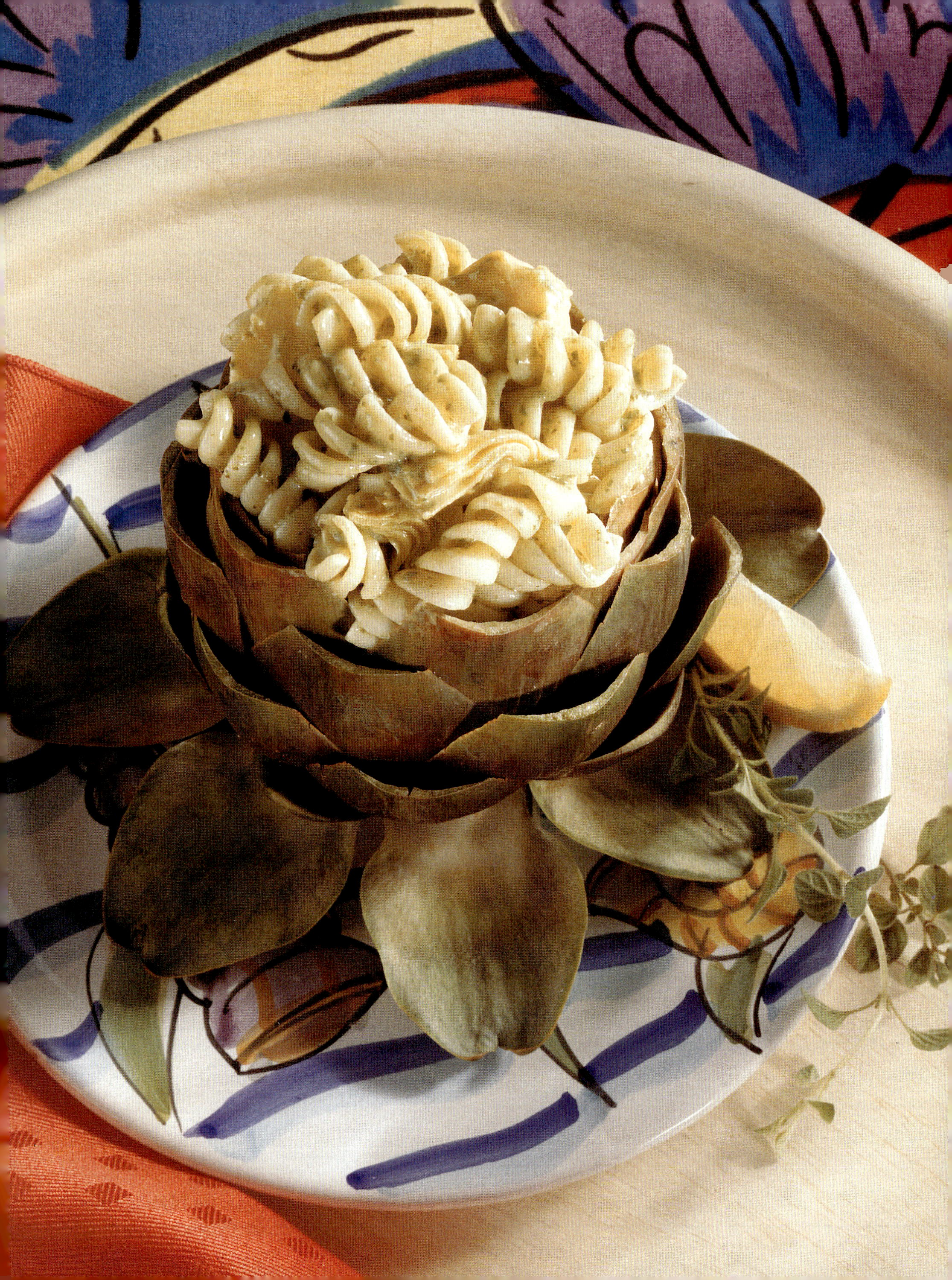

SUPER SALADS & SOUPS

4 ZUCCHINI–TOMATO–NOODLE SOUP

- 10 cups cubed zucchini
- ¾ cup water
- 4 cups chopped onions
- ½ cup butter
- 8 cups quartered tomatoes
- 4 chicken bouillon cubes
- 3 cloves garlic, chopped
- 1 teaspoon Beau Monde seasoning
- 1 teaspoon salt
- 1 teaspoon black pepper
- 4 cups uncooked 100% durum noodles, hot cooked and drained
- Garlic bread (optional)

Combine zucchini and water in Dutch oven. Cook over medium heat until partially done. Cook and stir onions in hot butter in small skillet over medium heat until tender. Add onion mixture, tomatoes, bouillon cubes, garlic, seasoning, salt and pepper to zucchini mixture. Simmer until tender. Add noodles; heat through. Serve with garlic bread, if desired. *Makes 8 servings*

Favorite recipe from **North Dakota Wheat Commission**

5 WARM PASTA AND SPINACH SALAD

- 1 package (10 ounces) fresh spinach, washed, stems removed and torn into bite-size pieces
- ½ pound mushrooms, sliced
- 8 ounces MUELLER'S® Twists or Ziti, cooked, rinsed with cold water and drained
- 1 medium red onion, sliced
- 6 slices uncooked bacon, coarsely chopped
- 1 tablespoon ARGO® or KINGSFORD'S® Corn Starch
- 1 tablespoon sugar
- 1 teaspoon salt
- ½ teaspoon black pepper
- 1 cup HELLMANN'S® or BEST FOODS® Real or Light Mayonnaise or Low Fat Mayonnaise Dressing
- 1 cup water
- ⅓ cup cider vinegar

In large serving bowl, toss spinach, mushrooms, pasta and red onion. In medium skillet, cook bacon over medium-high heat until crisp. Remove with slotted spoon. Pour off all but 2 tablespoons drippings. In small bowl, mix corn starch, sugar, salt and pepper. With wire whisk, stir corn starch mixture into drippings in skillet until smooth. Stir in mayonnaise until blended. Gradually stir in water and vinegar. Over medium heat, bring mixture to a boil; stir constantly. Boil 1 minute. Pour over spinach mixture. Add bacon; toss to coat well. Serve immediately. *Makes 8 to 10 servings*

Zucchini-Tomato-Noodle Soup

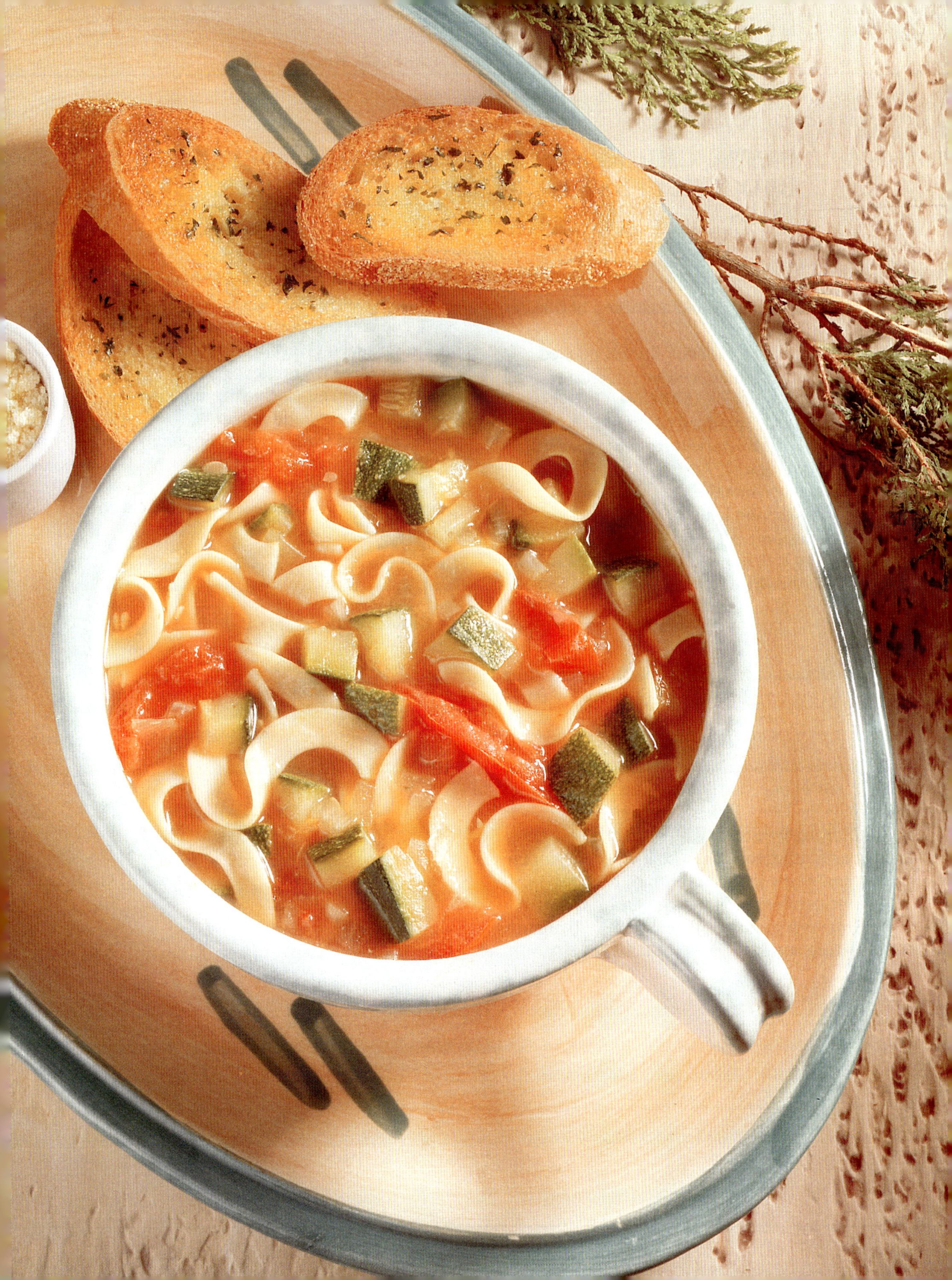

SUPER SALADS & SOUPS

6 PASTA, CHICKEN & BROCCOLI PESTO TOSS

4 ounces (about 2 cups) uncooked vegetable spiral pasta
2 cups cubed, cooked chicken or turkey breast meat
2 cups small broccoli florets, cooked crisp-tender, cooled
1½ cups (6 ounces) SARGENTO® Light Fancy Shredded Mozzarella Cheese
⅔ cup lightly packed fresh basil leaves
2 cloves garlic
1 cup mayonnaise
1 tablespoon lemon juice
½ teaspoon salt
½ cup (1½ ounces) SARGENTO® Fancy Shredded Parmesan Cheese
½ cup pine nuts or coarsely chopped walnuts, toasted

Cook pasta according to package directions until tender; drain and cool. Combine pasta, chicken, broccoli and mozzarella cheese in large bowl. Process basil and garlic in covered blender or food processor until finely chopped. Add mayonnaise, lemon juice and salt. Process to combine thoroughly. Stir in Parmesan cheese. Add to pasta mixture; toss to coat well. Stir in pine nuts. Serve immediately or cover and refrigerate. For maximum flavor, remove from refrigerator and toss gently 30 minutes before serving. *Makes 8 servings*

7 FRUIT AND PASTA REFRESHER

3 cups (8 ounces) rotini, uncooked
1 can (20 ounces) DOLE® Pineapple Chunks in Juice, drained
2 cups cubed assorted melon
1 cup seedless red grapes, halved
1 cup sliced celery
1 cup low-fat vanilla yogurt
¼ cup reduced-calorie mayonnaise
½ teaspoon ground ginger
Chopped fresh parsley (optional)

• Cook pasta according to package directions; drain. Rinse with cold water to cool quickly; drain well.

• In large bowl, stir together pasta, fruit, celery, yogurt, mayonnaise and ginger.

• Garnish with parsley, if desired. Cover; chill. *Makes 8 servings*

Prep time: 20 minutes
Cook time: 12 minutes

SUPER SALADS & SOUPS

8 AMISH VEGETABLE AND NOODLE SOUP

- 1 PERDUE® OVEN STUFFER® Roaster or turkey carcass with neck and giblets (except liver), chopped into large pieces
- 3 medium celery ribs, cut into ½-inch slices
- 2 medium carrots, cut into ½-inch rounds
- 1 large onion, chopped
- 1 can (46 ounces) chicken broth (about 6 cups)
- 1 tablespoon chopped parsley
- 1½ teaspoons salt
- ½ teaspoon dried thyme leaves
- 1 bay leaf
- ¼ teaspoon black peppercorns
- 2 medium boiling potatoes, scrubbed and cut into 1-inch pieces
- ½ pound wide egg noodles
- ¼ teaspoon crumbled saffron threads (optional)
- 2 to 3 cups coarsely chopped cooked PERDUE® chicken or turkey

In large stockpot or Dutch oven over high heat, combine carcass pieces, celery, carrots, onion, broth and enough water to cover carcass; bring to a boil, skimming off foam. Reduce heat to low; add parsley, salt, thyme, bay leaf and peppercorns. Simmer, partially covered, 2 to 3 hours; if not using carcass, reduce to 30 minutes.

With tongs, remove pieces of carcass; cut off meat and add to soup; discard bones. Increase heat to medium; add potatoes and cook about 10 minutes or until almost tender. Add noodles; cook about 10 minutes longer until noodles are tender. Add saffron, if desired, and chicken; cook 2 minutes longer or until chicken is heated through.
Makes 6 to 8 servings

9 TANGY TORTELLINI SALAD

- 1 (8-ounce) can HUNT'S® Tomato Sauce
- ½ cup vegetable oil
- ⅓ cup red wine vinegar
- ½ teaspoon seasoned salt
- ¼ teaspoon *each* garlic powder, celery seed, black pepper and dried oregano leaves
- 1 (7-ounce) package uncooked tortellini, cooked according to package directions, rinsed and drained
- 1 cup julienned salami or ham
- 1 cup julienned red bell peppers
- 1 (2-ounce) can pitted sliced ripe olives, drained
- ¼ cup chopped red onion
  Lettuce leaves

In medium bowl, whisk together tomato sauce, oil, vinegar and seasonings. Cover; refrigerate until ready to use. In large bowl, combine tortellini, salami, bell peppers, olives and onion. Arrange on lettuce leaves. Whisk dressing again; pour over pasta mixture. *Makes 4 to 6 servings*

SUPER SALADS & SOUPS

10 SESAME PASTA SALAD

- 1 small eggplant, unpeeled
- 1 large sweet potato, peeled and cut into ¼-inch slices
- 4 ounces portobello mushrooms, cut into ¼-inch slices
- 2 red bell peppers, cut into 1-inch strips
- 8 ounces thin spaghetti, cooked and cooled
- 8 ounces cooked shrimp
- ¼ cup sliced green onions
- 3 tablespoons finely chopped fresh cilantro or parsley
- Sesame Vinaigrette (recipe follows)
- 2 teaspoons toasted sesame seeds

1. Line jelly-roll pan with aluminum foil and spray with nonstick cooking spray. Preheat oven to 425°F. Cut eggplant into ½-inch-thick slices; cut slices into ½-inch strips. Arrange eggplant, sweet potato, mushrooms and bell peppers on prepared pan. Bake 20 to 25 minutes or until vegetables are tender. Cool.

2. Combine vegetable mixture, spaghetti, shrimp, green onions and cilantro in bowl; drizzle with Sesame Vinaigrette and toss. Sprinkle with sesame seeds.

Makes 4 main-dish servings

SESAME VINAIGRETTE
- 2 tablespoons reduced-sodium soy sauce
- 1½ tablespoons dark Chinese sesame oil
- 1 tablespoon red wine vinegar
- 1 tablespoon water
- 2 teaspoons sugar
- 1 clove garlic, minced

1. Combine all ingredients in small jar with tight-fitting lid; refrigerate until serving time. Shake well before using.

Makes about ¼ cup

11 CATALONIAN STEW

- 2 boneless skinless chicken breasts, cut into bite-size pieces
- 3 ounces pepperoni, diced
- 1 tablespoon vegetable oil
- 2 cans (15 ounces each) tomato sauce
- 3 cups chicken broth
- 1 cup pimiento-stuffed olives, halved
- 2 tablespoons sugar
- 8 ounces uncooked rotini or other shaped pasta
- ⅓ cup chopped parsley
- ⅛ teaspoon crushed saffron (optional)
- 1 cup (4 ounces) SARGENTO® Shredded Mild or Sharp Cheddar Cheese
- 1 cup (4 ounces) SARGENTO® Shredded Monterey Jack Cheese

In Dutch oven, cook chicken and pepperoni in oil over medium heat until chicken is lightly browned, about 5 minutes; drain. Add tomato sauce, chicken broth, olives and sugar. Bring to a boil; reduce heat and simmer, covered, 15 minutes. Return to a boil. Add rotini, parsley and saffron, if desired; cover and cook an additional 15 minutes or until pasta is tender. Combine Cheddar and Monterey Jack cheeses in small bowl. Spoon stew into 6 individual ovenproof serving bowls; sprinkle evenly with cheese. Bake in preheated 350°F oven about 5 minutes or until cheese is melted.

Makes 6 servings

Sesame Pasta Salad

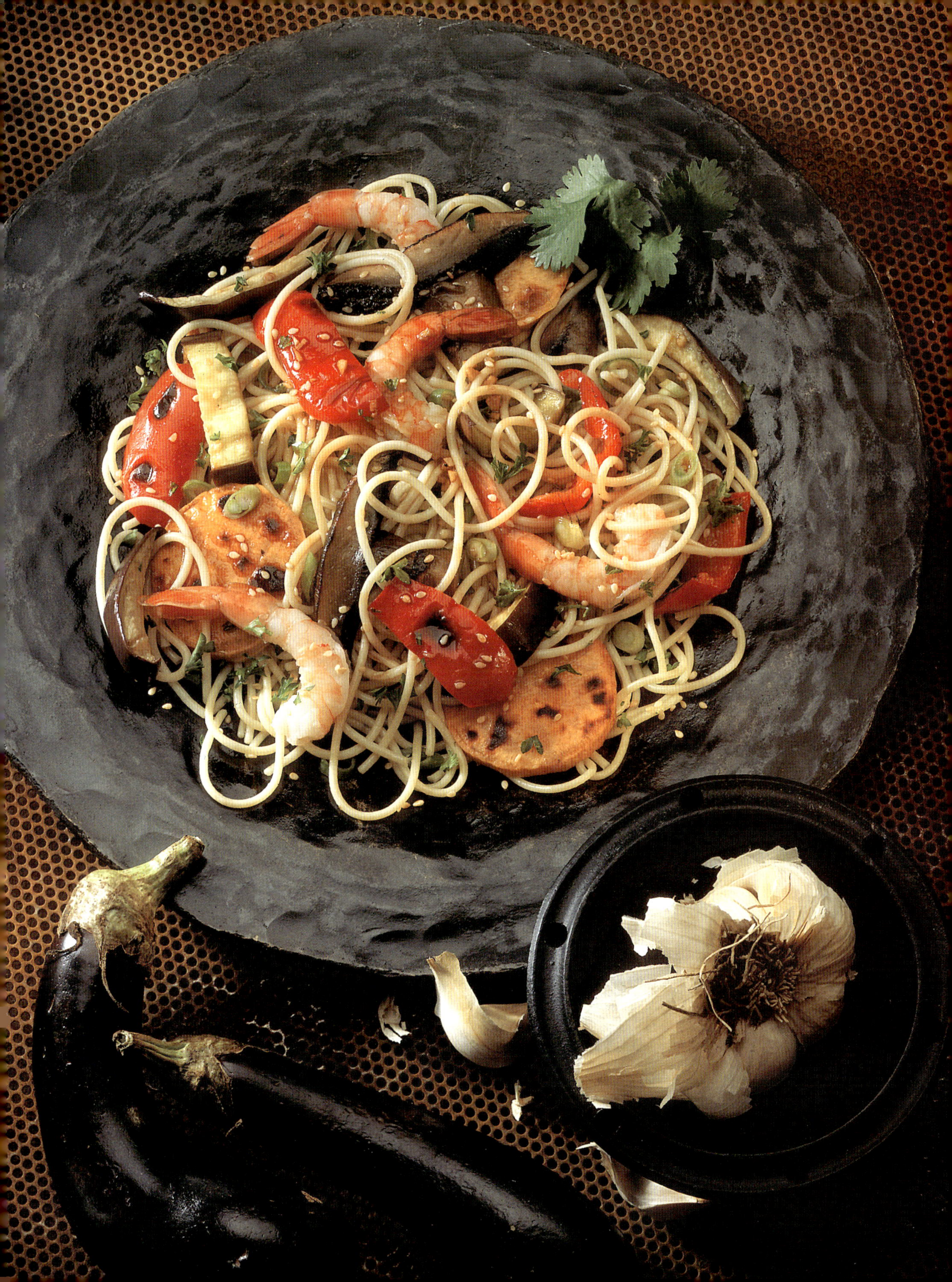

SUPER SALADS & SOUPS

12 SHAKER CHICKEN AND NOODLE SOUP

13 cups chicken broth, divided
¼ cup dry vermouth
¼ cup margarine or butter
1 cup heavy cream
1 package (12 ounces) egg noodles
1 cup thinly sliced celery
1½ cups water
¾ cup all-purpose flour
2 cups diced cooked chicken
   Salt and black pepper to taste
¼ cup finely chopped parsley (optional)

1. Combine 1 cup chicken broth, vermouth and margarine in small saucepan. Bring to a boil over high heat. Continue to boil 15 to 20 minutes or until liquid is reduced to ¼ cup and has a syrupy consistency. Stir in cream. Set aside.

2. Bring remaining broth to a boil in Dutch oven. Add noodles and celery; cook until noodles are just tender.

3. Combine water and flour in medium bowl until smooth. Stir into noodle mixture. Boil 2 minutes, stirring constantly.

4. Stir in reserved cream mixture; add chicken. Season with salt and pepper. Heat just to serving temperature. *Do not boil.* Sprinkle with parsley, if desired. Garnish as desired.
Makes 15 servings

13 COLORFUL GRAPE, PEPPER AND PASTA SALAD

8 ounces dry thin spaghetti, cooked
   Mustard Vinaigrette (recipe follows)
1 cup California seedless grapes
½ cup thinly sliced red or yellow
   bell pepper
2 tablespoons minced celery
2 tablespoons green onion
1 tablespoon chopped fresh tarragon*
   Salt and black pepper to taste
¼ cup walnuts,** quartered

*One-half teaspoon dried tarragon leaves may be substituted.

**Walnuts may be omitted; if omitted, substitute 1 tablespoon walnut oil for 1 tablespoon olive oil in vinaigrette.

Combine cooked spaghetti and 3 tablespoons Mustard Vinaigrette; toss to coat and cool. Add remaining ingredients including vinaigrette; mix well. Serve in lettuce-lined bowl; garnish with fresh tarragon sprigs, if desired.
Makes 4 servings

Mustard Vinaigrette: Combine 3 tablespoons white wine vinegar, 2 tablespoons olive oil, 2 tablespoons Dijon mustard, 1 clove minced garlic, ½ teaspoon sugar and ⅛ teaspoon black pepper; mix well
Makes about ⅓ cup

Favorite recipe from **California Table Grape Commission**

Shaker Chicken and Noodle Soup

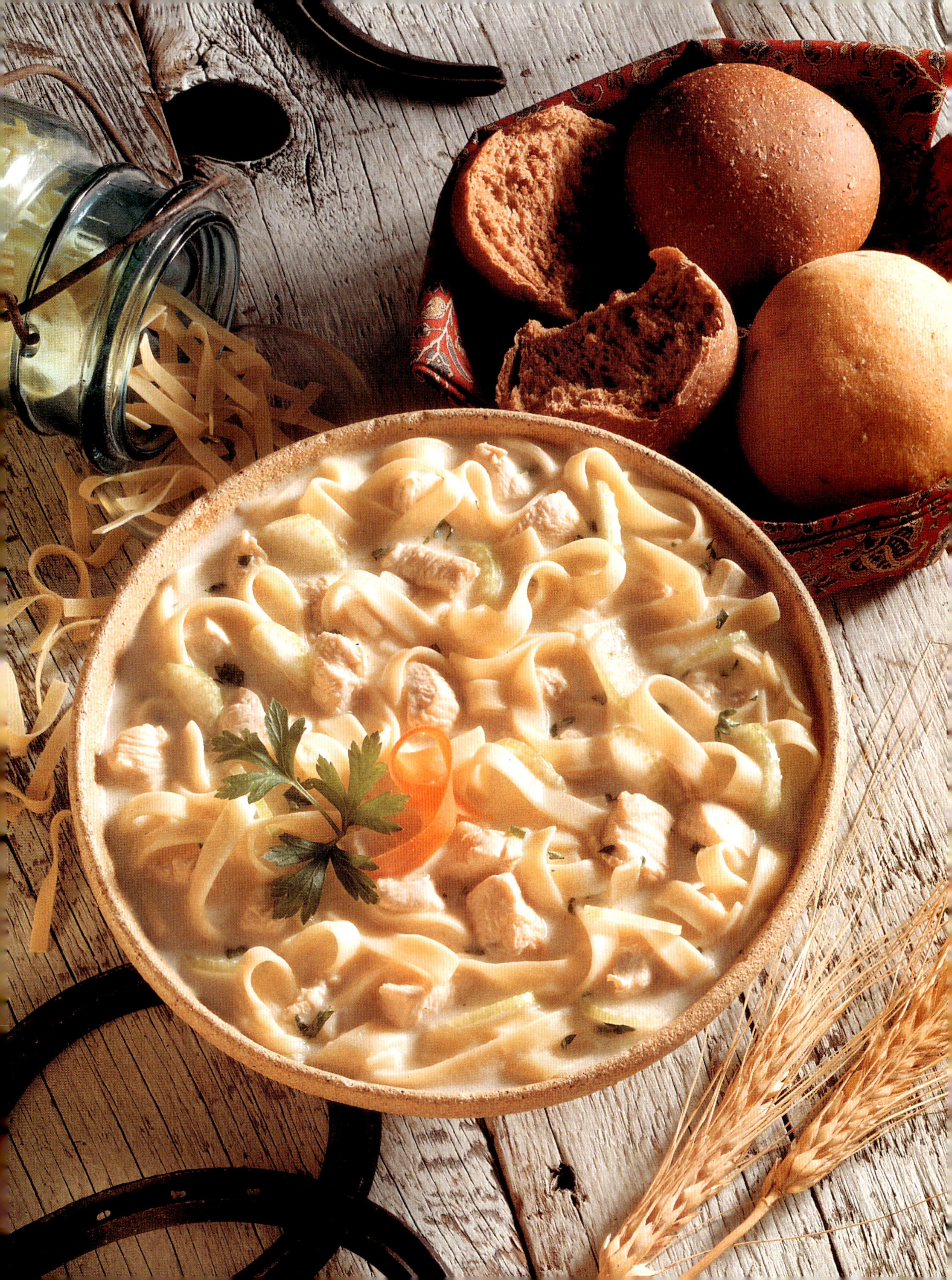

SUPER SALADS & SOUPS

14 SAN MARCOS CHILI PEPPER PENNE SALAD

1 (12-ounce) package PASTA LaBELLA® Chili Pepper Penne Rigate
1 cup large diced avocado
¾ cup julienned red onion
1 cup seeded sliced Anaheim chilies
1 cup large diced tomato
¾ cup peeled seeded sliced cucumber
½ cup light soy sauce
½ cup fresh lime juice
⅓ cup extra-virgin olive oil
⅓ cup red wine vinegar
¼ cup chopped fresh cilantro
¼ teaspoon garlic powder
¼ teaspoon onion powder
¼ teaspoon black pepper
¼ teaspoon salt

Cook pasta according to package directions. When pasta is *al dente*, put in colander and rinse with cold water until cool to touch. Drain pasta well and put in large mixing bowl. Toss pasta with all vegetables and set aside. In separate mixing bowl, whisk together soy sauce, lime juice, oil and vinegar. Blend in spices and mix well. Pour salad dressing over pasta and vegetables. Toss well and serve. *Makes 4 servings*

15 ANGEL HAIR CHICKEN–OLIVE SALAD

4 ounces angel hair pasta
⅓ pound *each* green beans, snow peas and asparagus (or any combination equaling 1 pound)
2 cups shredded cooked chicken
1 cup halved California ripe olives
⅓ cup olive oil
½ cup pine nuts
1 tablespoon minced garlic
1½ teaspoons red pepper flakes
6 tablespoons white wine vinegar
¼ teaspoon salt

Break up pasta coils a bit, then cook according to package directions. Cut beans and snow peas into julienne strips and asparagus diagonally into 1-inch lengths. Drop beans and asparagus into boiling water, cook 1 minute, then drain and run under cold water. *(Snow peas are not cooked.)* Combine pasta, chicken, vegetables and olives in salad bowl.

For dressing, heat olive oil in small skillet, add pine nuts and toast 2 minutes or until light golden. Remove from heat; add garlic, pepper flakes, vinegar and salt (quickly covering skillet to prevent splattering). Pour dressing over salad and toss to coat.
Makes 4 (2-cup) servings

Preparation time: 30 minutes
Cooking time: 10 minutes

Favorite recipe from **California Olive Industry**

SUPER SALADS & SOUPS

16 SPRINGTIME PASTA SALAD

12 ounces spaghetti, linguine or fettuccine, uncooked
8 ounces broccoli florets
8 ounces asparagus, cut into 1-inch pieces
4 scallions or spring onions, cut into 1-inch slices
2 cloves garlic, finely chopped
1 (10-ounce) package frozen peas, thawed and drained
1 green or red bell pepper, coarsely chopped
8 ounces mushrooms, sliced
¼ cup minced fresh parsley

DRESSING
3 tablespoons red wine vinegar
3 tablespoons fresh lemon juice
1 tablespoon Dijon mustard
½ teaspoon dried basil leaves
½ teaspoon dried oregano leaves
½ teaspoon dried thyme leaves
⅛ teaspoon cayenne pepper
Freshly ground black pepper to taste
2 tablespoons vegetable oil

Prepare pasta according to package directions; drain.

In large pot, cook broccoli and asparagus in boiling water until crisp-tender, about 4 minutes. Drain and add to pasta. Add scallions, garlic, peas, bell pepper, mushrooms and parsley to pasta.

In small bowl, whisk together all dressing ingredients except oil. Slowly whisk in oil until dressing is well blended.

Pour dressing over pasta mixture and toss gently until well mixed.

Makes 6 servings

Favorite recipe from **National Pasta Association**

17 CHICKEN AND PASTA SOUP

1 (2½-pound) chicken, cut up
1 (46-fluid ounce) can COLLEGE INN® Chicken Broth
1 (16-ounce) can cut green beans, drained
1 (6-ounce) can tomato paste
1 cup uncooked small shell macaroni
1 teaspoon dried basil leaves

In large saucepan, over medium-high heat, bring chicken and chicken broth to a boil; reduce heat. Cover; simmer 25 minutes or until chicken is tender. Remove chicken; cool slightly. Add remaining ingredients to broth. Heat to a boil; reduce heat. Cover; simmer 20 minutes or until macaroni is cooked. Meanwhile, remove chicken from bones and cut into bite-size pieces. Add to soup; cook 5 minutes more.

Makes 6 servings

SUPER SALADS & SOUPS

18 ZESTY ROMAINE AND PASTA SALAD

- 6 ounces bow tie pasta
- 1 cup broccoli florets
- ¼ cup water
- ¼ cup red wine vinegar
- 2 tablespoons sugar
- 1 tablespoon finely chopped fresh basil
- 1 tablespoon lemon juice
- 1 tablespoon Dijon mustard
- 1 clove garlic, minced
- ½ teaspoon ground black pepper
- 6 cups washed and torn romaine lettuce leaves
- 1 can (15 ounces) kidney beans, drained and rinsed
- 1 cup carrot slices
- 1 small red onion, cut into halves and thinly sliced
- ½ cup grated Parmesan cheese

1. Cook pasta according to package directions, adding broccoli during last 3 minutes of cooking; drain. Rinse with cold water; drain.

2. To make dressing, whisk water, vinegar, sugar, basil, lemon juice, mustard, garlic and pepper in small bowl until well blended.

3. Combine lettuce, pasta mixture, beans, carrots and onion in large bowl. Add dressing; toss to coat. Sprinkle with cheese.

Makes 4 servings

19 DIJON ASPARAGUS CHICKEN SALAD

- 1 cup HELLMANN'S® or BEST FOODS® Real or Light Mayonnaise or Low Fat Mayonnaise Dressing
- 2 tablespoons Dijon mustard
- 2 tablespoons lemon juice
- 1 teaspoon salt
- ½ teaspoon black pepper
- 6 ounces MUELLER'S® Twist Trio®, cooked and drained
- 1 pound skinless boneless chicken breasts, cooked and chopped
- 1 package (10 ounces) frozen asparagus spears, thawed and cut into 2-inch pieces
- 1 red bell pepper, cut into 1-inch pieces

In large bowl, combine mayonnaise, mustard, lemon juice, salt and black pepper; mix well. Add remaining ingredients; mix lightly. Cover; refrigerate.

Makes 6 servings

Zesty Romaine and Pasta Salad

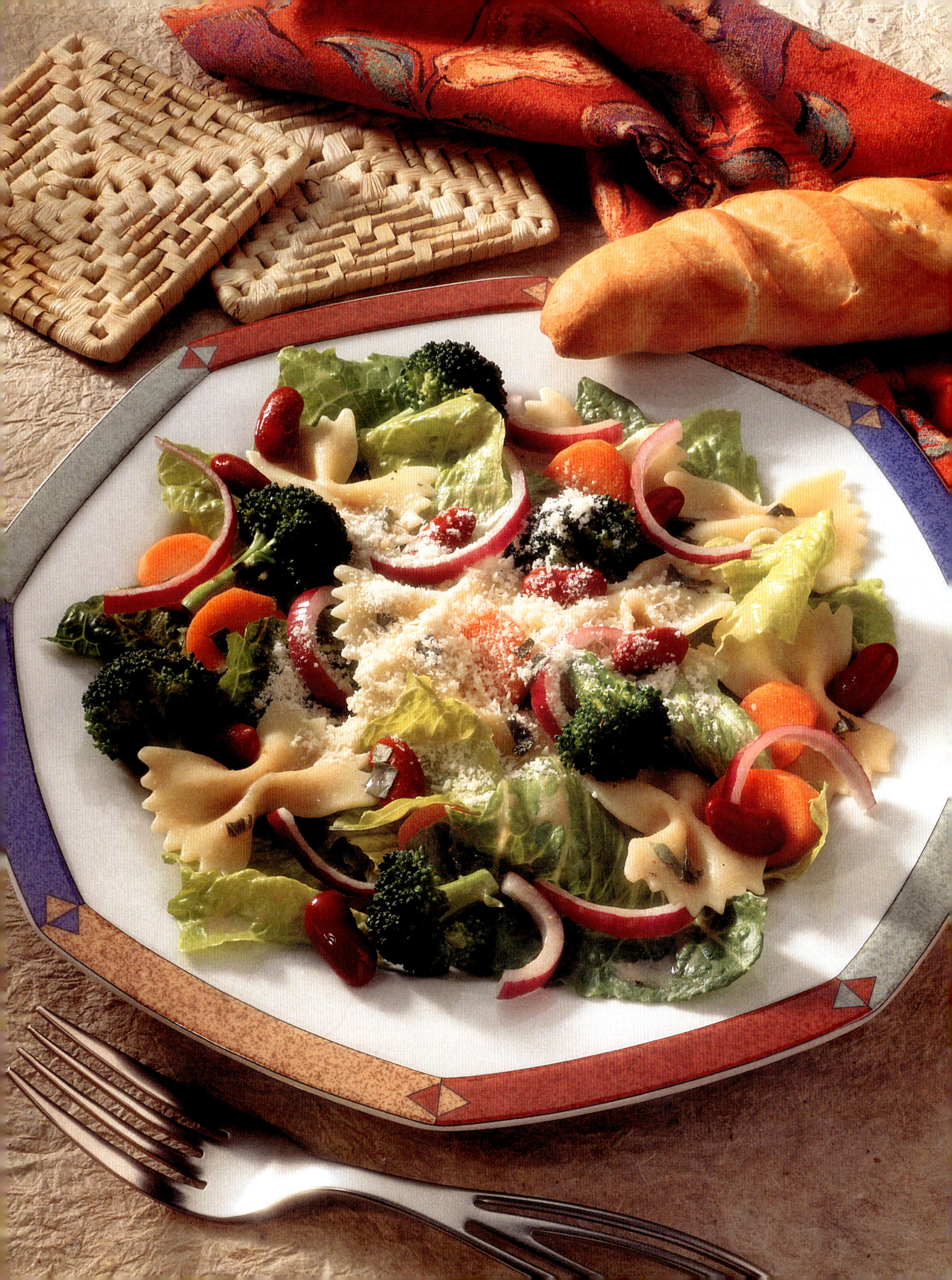

SUPER SALADS & SOUPS

20 PLENTIFUL "P'S" SALAD

4 cups fresh black-eyed peas
1½ cups uncooked rotini pasta
1 medium red bell pepper, chopped
1 medium green bell pepper, chopped
1 medium purple onion, chopped
4 slices provolone cheese, chopped
4 slices salami or pepperoni, chopped
1 jar (4½ ounces) whole mushrooms, drained
1 jar (2 ounces) chopped pimientos, drained
2 tablespoons chopped fresh parsley
2 tablespoons dry Italian salad dressing mix
½ teaspoon salt
¼ teaspoon black pepper
½ cup wine vinegar
¼ cup sugar
¼ cup vegetable oil
Onion slices and fresh herb sprigs for garnish

1. Place peas in large saucepan. Cover with water; bring to a boil over high heat. Reduce heat to low. Simmer, covered, until peas are soft when pierced with fork, 15 to 20 minutes. Drain and set aside.

2. Cook rotini according to package directions until *al dente*. Drain and set aside.

3. Combine peas, pasta, bell peppers, chopped onion, provolone cheese, salami, mushrooms, pimientos and parsley in large bowl; set aside.

4. Combine salad dressing mix, salt and black pepper in small bowl. Add vinegar and sugar; mix well. Whisk in oil.

5. Add oil mixture to pea mixture. Toss lightly until well combined. Cover; refrigerate at least 2 hours before serving. Garnish, if desired. *Makes 12 first-course servings*

NOTE: Other vegetables such as cauliflower, broccoli, carrots or celery can be added.

*Favorite recipe from **Black-Eyed Pea Jamboree***

21 CHICKEN PASTA SALAD SUPREME

3 cups diced cooked chicken
1 package (8 ounces) small shell macaroni, cooked according to package directions, drained
1 medium red pepper, cut in 1½×¼-inch strips
1 package (8 ounces) frozen snow peas, thawed and drained
¼ cup sliced green onions
¾ cup bottled, reduced-calorie oil and vinegar dressing
1 cup cherry tomatoes, halved
Lettuce leaves

In large bowl, place chicken, macaroni, red pepper, snow peas and green onions; toss to mix. Pour dressing over chicken mixture; toss to mix. Cover and chill until ready to serve. Add tomatoes; toss gently. Serve on lettuce-lined plates. *Makes 6 servings*

*Favorite recipe from **Delmarva Poultry Industry, Inc.***

Plentiful "P's" Salad

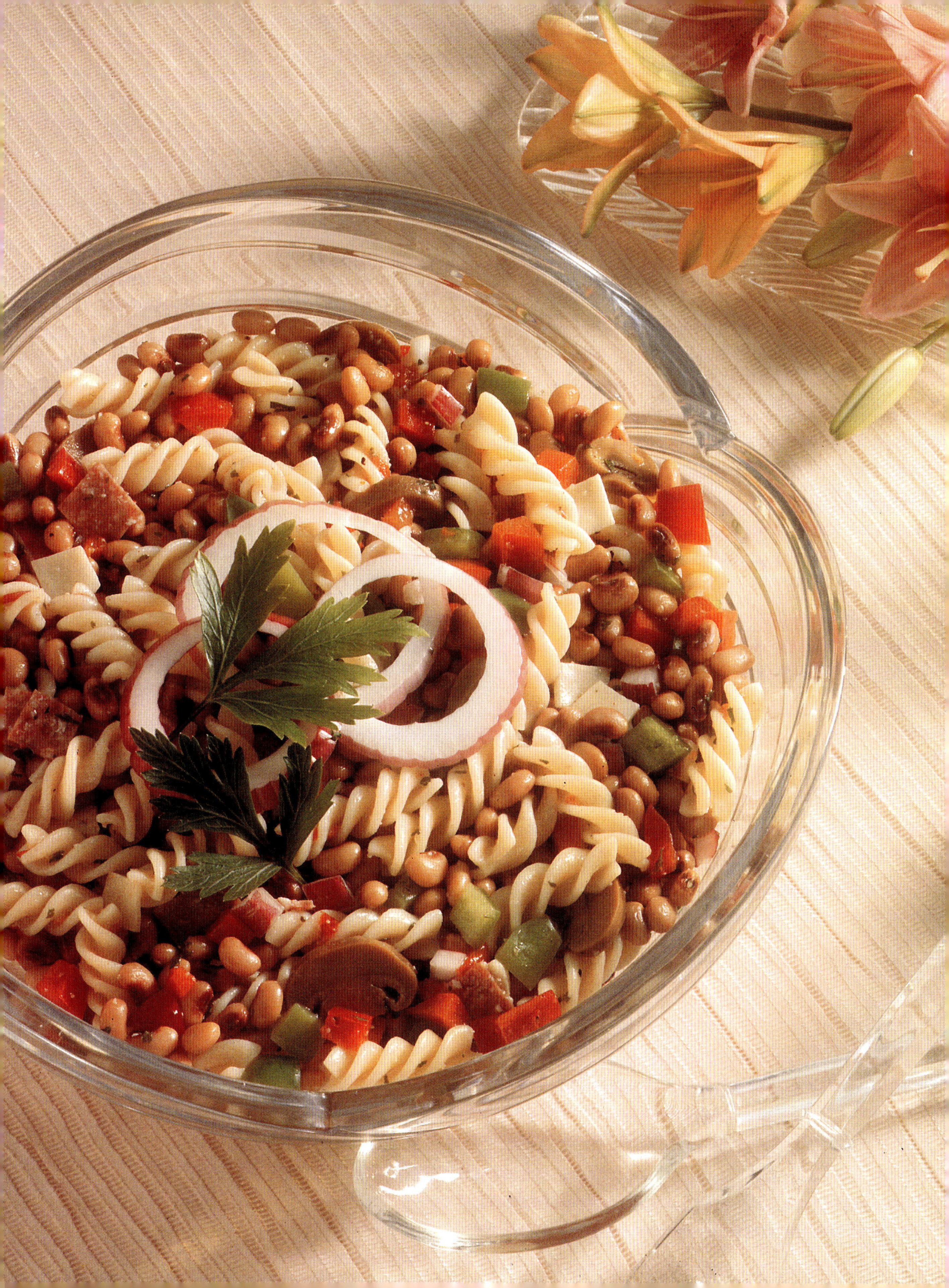

SUPER SALADS & SOUPS

22 SAUSAGE MINESTRONE SOUP

2 tablespoons olive oil
1 large onion, chopped
3 cloves garlic, minced
3 cups water
1 can (14½ ounces) stewed tomatoes, undrained
1 can (10½ ounces) kosher condensed beef or chicken broth
1 teaspoon dried basil leaves
1 teaspoon dried oregano leaves
¼ teaspoon crushed red pepper
1 package (12 ounces) HEBREW NATIONAL® Lean Smoked Turkey Sausage
½ cup small pasta such as ditalini or small bow ties
1 can (16 ounces) cannellini beans, drained

Heat oil in large saucepan over medium heat. Add onion and garlic; cook 8 minutes, stirring occasionally. Add water, tomatoes with liquid, broth, basil, oregano and crushed pepper; bring to a boil.

Meanwhile, cut sausage crosswise into ½-inch slices. Cut each slice into quarters. Stir sausage and pasta into soup; simmer 15 minutes or until pasta is tender. Add beans; cook until heated through.
Makes 6 servings

23 PASTA AND WALNUT FRUIT SALAD

½ (1-pound) package medium pasta shells, uncooked
1 (8-ounce) container nonfat plain yogurt
¼ cup frozen orange juice concentrate, thawed
1 (15-ounce) can juice-pack mandarin oranges, drained
1 cup seedless red grapes, cut into halves
1 cup seedless green grapes, cut into halves
1 apple, cored and chopped
½ cup sliced celery
½ cup walnut halves

Cook shells according to package directions; drain. In small bowl, blend yogurt and orange juice concentrate. In large bowl, combine shells and remaining ingredients. Add yogurt mixture; toss to coat. Cover; chill thoroughly. *Makes 6 to 8 servings*

PASTA SUBSTITUTIONS: mostaccioli, elbow macaroni, rotini, farfalle

Favorite recipe from **Walnut Marketing Board**

Sausage Minestrone Soup

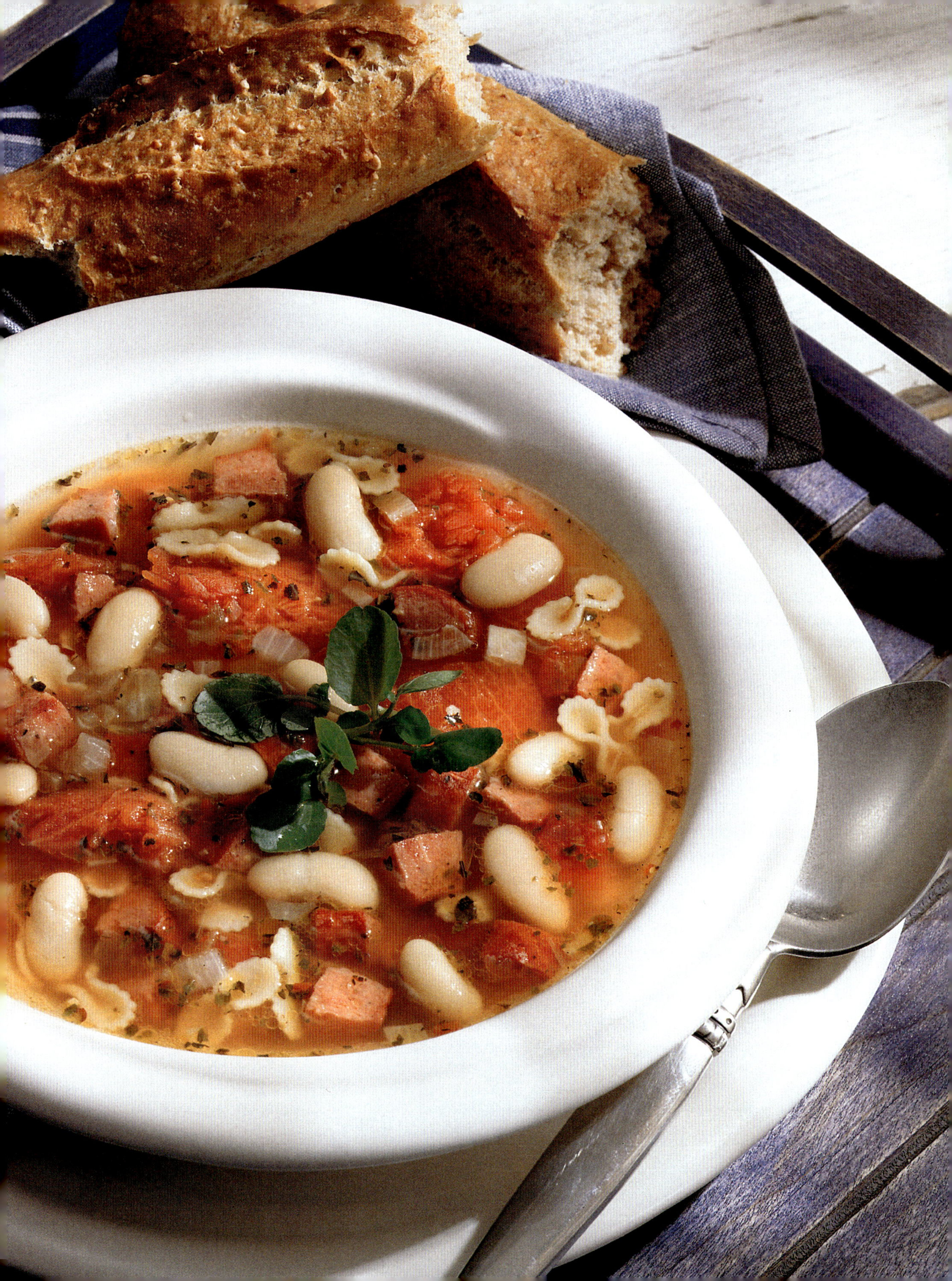

SUPER SALADS & SOUPS

24 PASTA PRIMAVERA SALAD

¾ pound uncooked corkscrew pasta, hot cooked and drained
3 tablespoons olive or vegetable oil
2 medium zucchini, cut into ¼-inch slices
1 cup broccoli flowerets, steamed crisp-tender
1 large red or green bell pepper, cut into small chunks
½ cup cherry tomato halves
⅓ cup sliced radishes
3 green onions, chopped
2 tablespoons drained capers (optional)
1 cup prepared HIDDEN VALLEY RANCH® Original Ranch® Salad Dressing

In large bowl, toss pasta with oil; cool. Add remaining ingredients; toss again. Cover; refrigerate at least 2 hours. Just before serving; add additional salad dressing, if desired. *Makes 4 servings*

25 CENTENNIAL APPLE PASTA SALAD

2 cups dry pasta, cooked according to package directions
2 cups (about ¾ pound) cored and cubed Red Delicious apples
1 cup coarsely chopped walnuts
¼ cup chopped green onions
¼ cup *each* mayonnaise and plain yogurt
1 tablespoon Dijon mustard
   Salt and black pepper to taste

Combine all ingredients; toss to mix well. Refrigerate at least 1 hour.
Makes 4 to 6 servings

Preparation time: about 15 minutes

Favorite recipe from **Washington Apple Commission**

26 CREAMY ITALIAN PASTA SALAD

1 cup HELLMANN'S® or BEST FOODS® Real or Light Mayonnaise or Low Fat Mayonnaise Dressing
2 tablespoons red wine vinegar
1 clove garlic, minced
1 tablespoon chopped fresh basil *or* 1 teaspoon dried basil
1 teaspoon salt
¼ teaspoon freshly ground black pepper
1½ cups twist or spiral pasta, cooked, rinsed with cold water and drained
1 cup quartered cherry tomatoes
½ cup coarsely chopped green bell pepper
½ cup slivered pitted ripe olives

In large bowl, combine mayonnaise, vinegar, garlic, basil, salt and black pepper. Stir in pasta, tomatoes, bell pepper and olives. Cover; chill. *Makes about 6 servings*

Pasta Primavera Salad

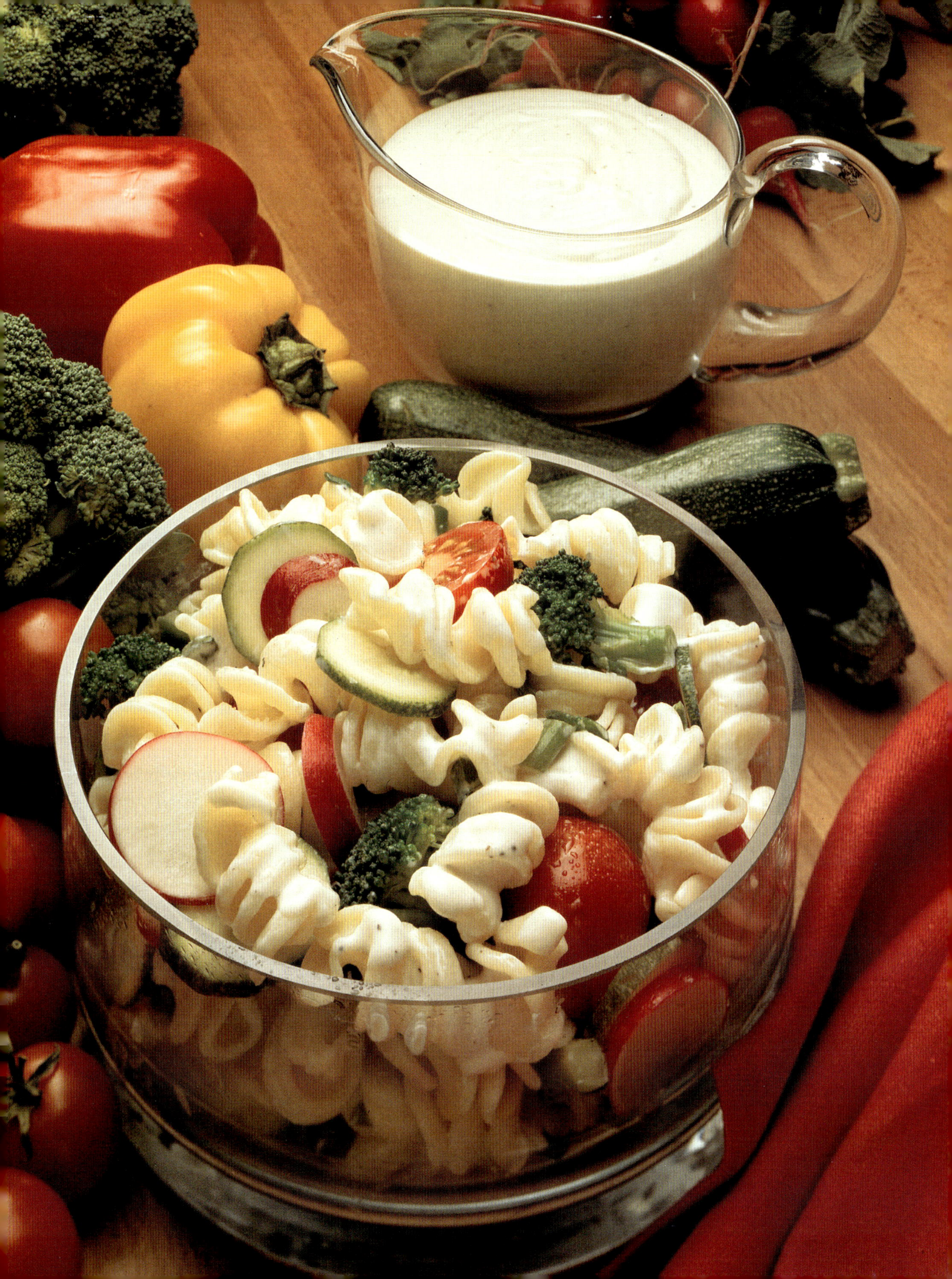

SUPER SALADS & SOUPS

27 ALBACORE SALAD PUTTANESCA WITH GARLIC VINAIGRETTE

2 cups cooked, chilled angel hair pasta
2 cups chopped, peeled plum tomatoes
1 can (4¼ ounces) chopped* ripe olives, drained
1 cup Garlic Vinaigrette Dressing (recipe follows)
1 can (6 ounces) STARKIST® Solid White Tuna, drained and flaked
¼ cup chopped fresh basil leaves

If you prefer, olives may be sliced rather than chopped.

In large bowl, combine chilled pasta, tomatoes, olives and 1 cup Garlic Vinaigrette Dressing. Add tuna and basil leaves; toss. Serve immediately. *Makes 2 servings*

GARLIC VINAIGRETTE DRESSING
⅓ cup red wine vinegar
2 tablespoons lemon juice
1 to 2 cloves garlic, minced or pressed
1 teaspoon ground black pepper
Salt to taste
1 cup olive oil

In small bowl, whisk together vinegar, lemon juice, garlic, pepper and salt. Slowly add oil, whisking continuously, until well blended.

28 PASTA FAZOOL

2 tablespoons olive oil
1 cup chopped onion
½ cup *each* sliced carrot and sliced celery
2 cloves garlic, minced
4 cups chicken broth
1 (15-ounce) can HUNT'S® Tomato Sauce
1 (15-ounce) can white kidney beans, drained
1 (14½-ounce) can HUNT'S® Choice-Cut™ Diced Tomatoes with Italian Style Herbs
1 (8-ounce) can red kidney beans, drained
½ cup uncooked elbow macaroni
2 tablespoons chopped fresh parsley
2 teaspoons fresh basil leaves
½ teaspoon *each* dried oregano leaves and salt
¼ teaspoon black pepper
Fresh grated Parmesan cheese

In Dutch oven, heat oil and sauté onion, carrot, celery and garlic until tender. Stir in remaining ingredients *except* Parmesan cheese. Bring to a boil, reduce heat and simmer 10 to 15 minutes or until macaroni is tender. Sprinkle Parmesan cheese over each serving. *Makes 10 servings*

Albacore Salad Puttanesca with Garlic Vinaigrette

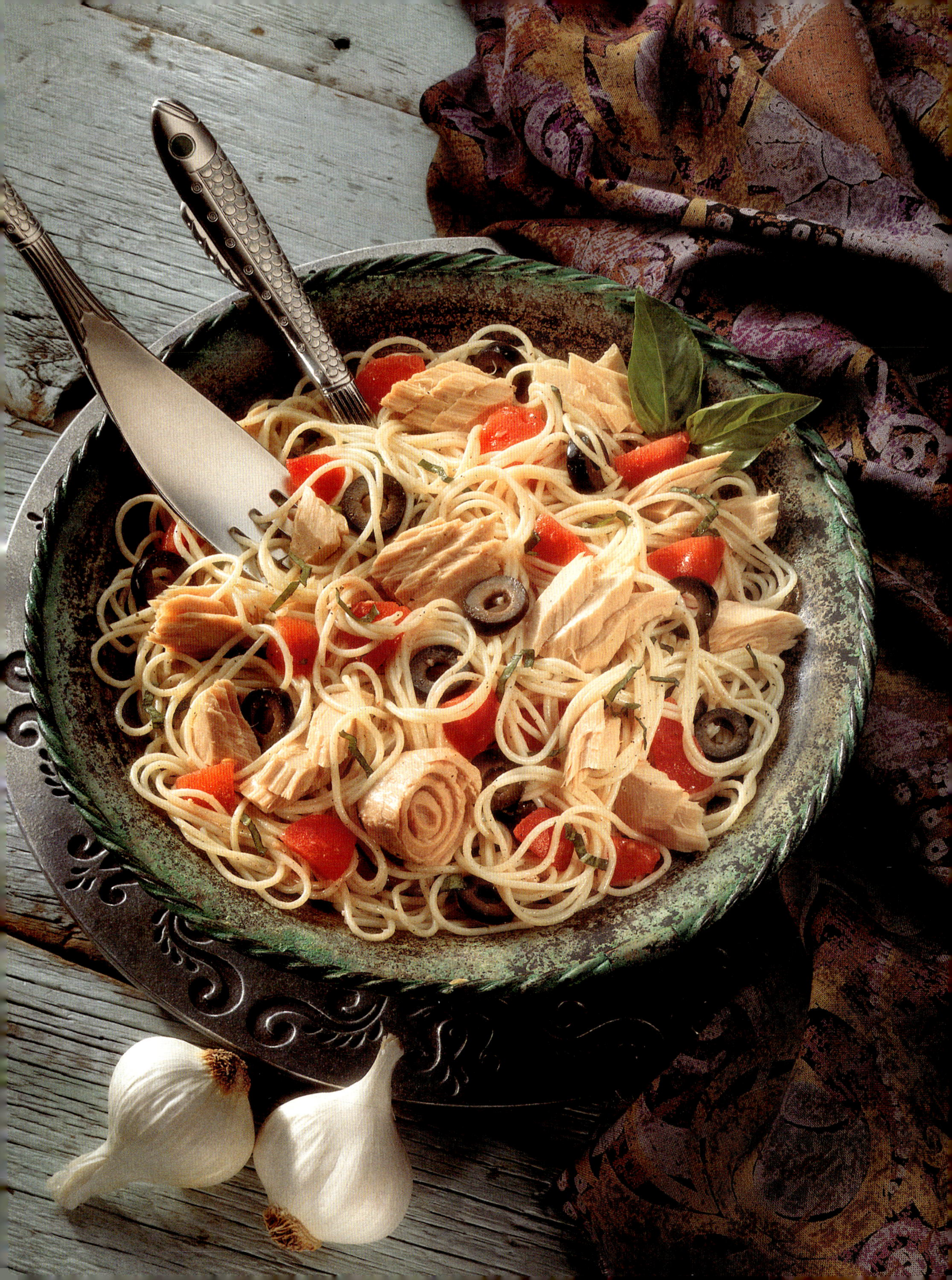

SUPER SALADS & SOUPS

29 ITALIAN PASTA SALAD

- 3 cups (8 ounces) uncooked tri-color rotini, cooked and drained
- 1 cup (4 ounces) KRAFT® 100% Grated Parmesan Cheese
- 1 (8-ounce) bottle KRAFT® House Italian Dressing
- ½ cup *each* chopped red bell pepper and red onion slices
- 2 cups broccoli flowerets
- ½ cup pitted ripe olive slices

• Mix together ingredients in large bowl until well blended. Chill. *Makes 8 cups*

Prep time: 15 minutes

30 SWEET AND SMOKY PASTA SALAD

- 1 can (8 ounces) DOLE® Pineapple Chunks, drained
- 2 cups cooked rotelle pasta
- 1 cup cubed cantaloupe
- ½ cup red or green seedless grapes
- ½ cup cubed baked ham
- 3 to 4 tablespoons honey mustard dressing
- 1 tablespoon minced cilantro

• Combine all ingredients in large bowl. Toss until mixed. *Makes 4 servings*

Prep time: 20 minutes

31 AEGEAN PASTA SALAD

- 1 cup HELLMANN'S® or BEST FOODS® Real or Light Mayonnaise or Low Fat Mayonnaise Dressing
- ⅓ cup milk
- ¼ cup lemon juice
- ¾ cup finely chopped fresh mint leaves
- ½ cup finely chopped fresh parsley
- ½ cup (2 ounces) crumbled feta cheese
- 1 teaspoon salt
- ½ teaspoon black pepper
- 7 ounces MUELLER'S® Twists, cooked, rinsed with cold water and drained
- 2 medium tomatoes, seeded and chopped
- 1 medium cucumber, seeded and chopped
- 1 cup sliced pitted ripe olives
- 3 green onions, sliced

In large bowl, stir mayonnaise, milk, lemon juice, mint, parsley, feta cheese, salt and pepper until well mixed. Add pasta, tomatoes, cucumber, olives and green onions; toss to coat well. Cover; refrigerate. *Makes 8 to 12 servings*

Italian Pasta Salad

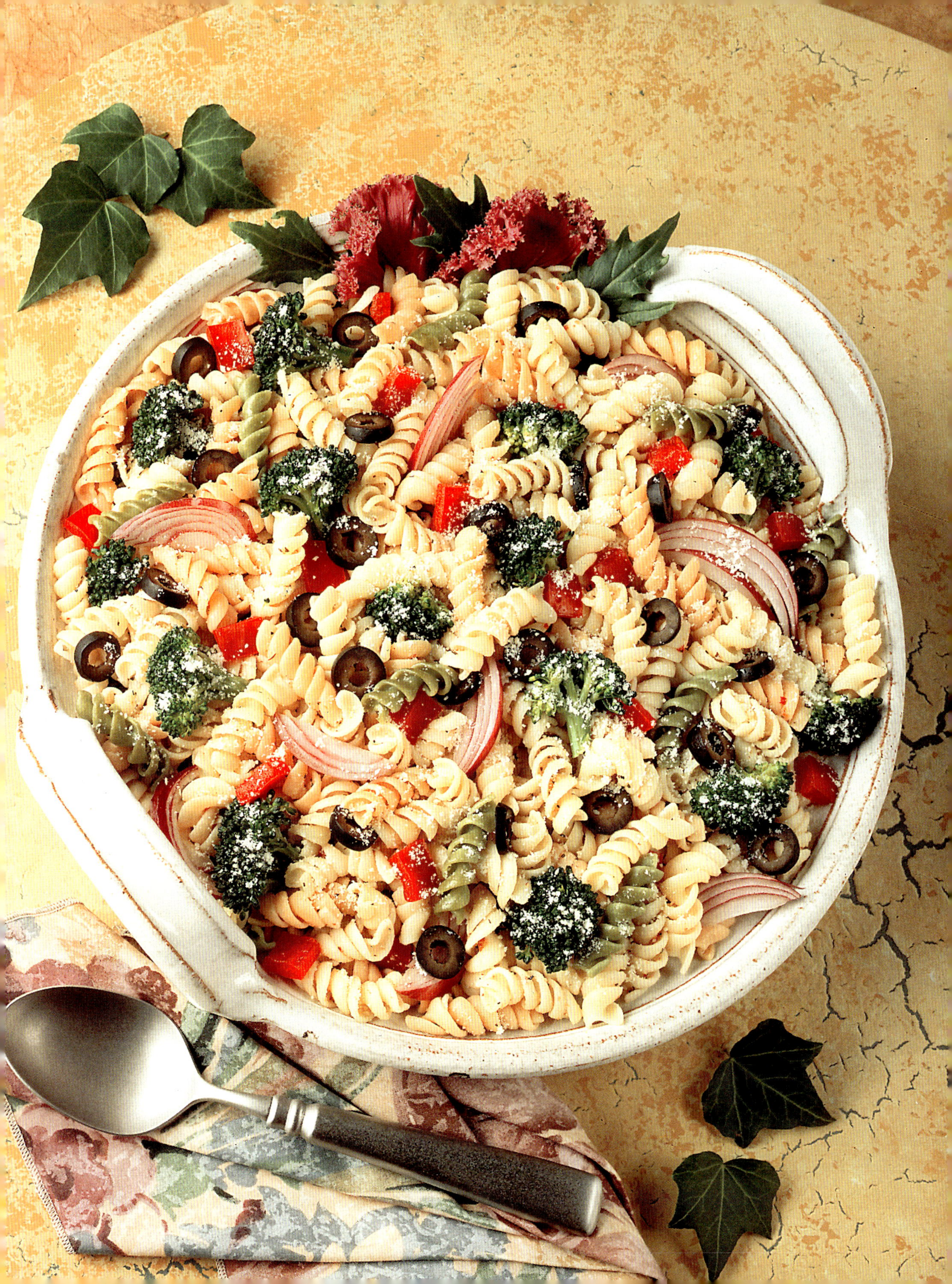

SUPER SALADS & SOUPS

32 BUTTERFLIED SHRIMP AND VERMICELLI SALAD

- ¼ small yellow onion
- 3 tablespoons tarragon vinegar or white wine vinegar
- 2 tablespoons sugar
- ½ teaspoon salt
- ½ teaspoon dry mustard
- ¼ cup extra-virgin olive oil
- ¼ cup vegetable oil
- 1 teaspoon celery seeds
- 1 pound medium shrimp, peeled and deveined
- 8 ounces uncooked vermicelli pasta, broken into 2-inch lengths
- 1 cup finely chopped celery
- 1 cup seedless grapes, cut into halves
- 1 jar (4 ounces) sliced pimientos, drained
- 3 tablespoons mayonnaise
- 2 oranges, peeled and cut into sections *or* 1 cup mandarin orange slices
- 1 head Bibb lettuce
- 5 green onions, sliced for garnish

1. To prepare dressing, place yellow onion and vinegar in food processor; process using on/off pulses until onion is finely chopped. Add sugar, salt and mustard; process until mixture is blended.

2. With motor running, slowly pour olive oil and vegetable oil through feed tube; process until smooth. Add celery seeds; process until mixture is blended. Set aside.

3. Prepare water for cooking pasta according to package directions. When water comes to a boil, add half the shrimp; simmer 1 minute or until shrimp turn pink and opaque. Remove shrimp with slotted spoon; place in large bowl. Repeat with remaining shrimp. Reserve 5 shrimp for garnish.

4. Add pasta to cooking water. Cook according to package directions. Rinse under cold water; drain. Add pasta, celery, grapes and pimientos to shrimp. Toss with mayonnaise and dressing. Gently toss with orange segments. Chill several hours or overnight. Serve on lettuce-lined plates. Garnish with reserved shrimp and green onions. *Makes 5 servings*

33 TORTELLINI SOUP

- 1 tablespoon FLEISCHMANN'S® Margarine
- 2 cloves garlic, minced
- 2 cans (13¾ fluid ounces each) COLLEGE INN® Chicken or Beef Broth
- 1 package (8 ounces) fresh or frozen cheese-filled tortellini, thawed
- 1 can (14½ ounces) stewed tomatoes, cut up, undrained
- 1 package (10 ounces) fresh or frozen spinach, thawed
- Grated Parmesan cheese

In large saucepan, melt margarine over medium-high heat. Add garlic; cook and stir 2 to 3 minutes or until lightly browned. Add broth and tortellini; bring to a boil. Reduce heat to low; simmer 10 minutes, stirring occasionally. Add tomatoes and spinach; simmer an additional 5 minutes. Top individual servings with Parmesan cheese.
Makes 6 servings

Butterflied Shrimp and Vermicelli Salad

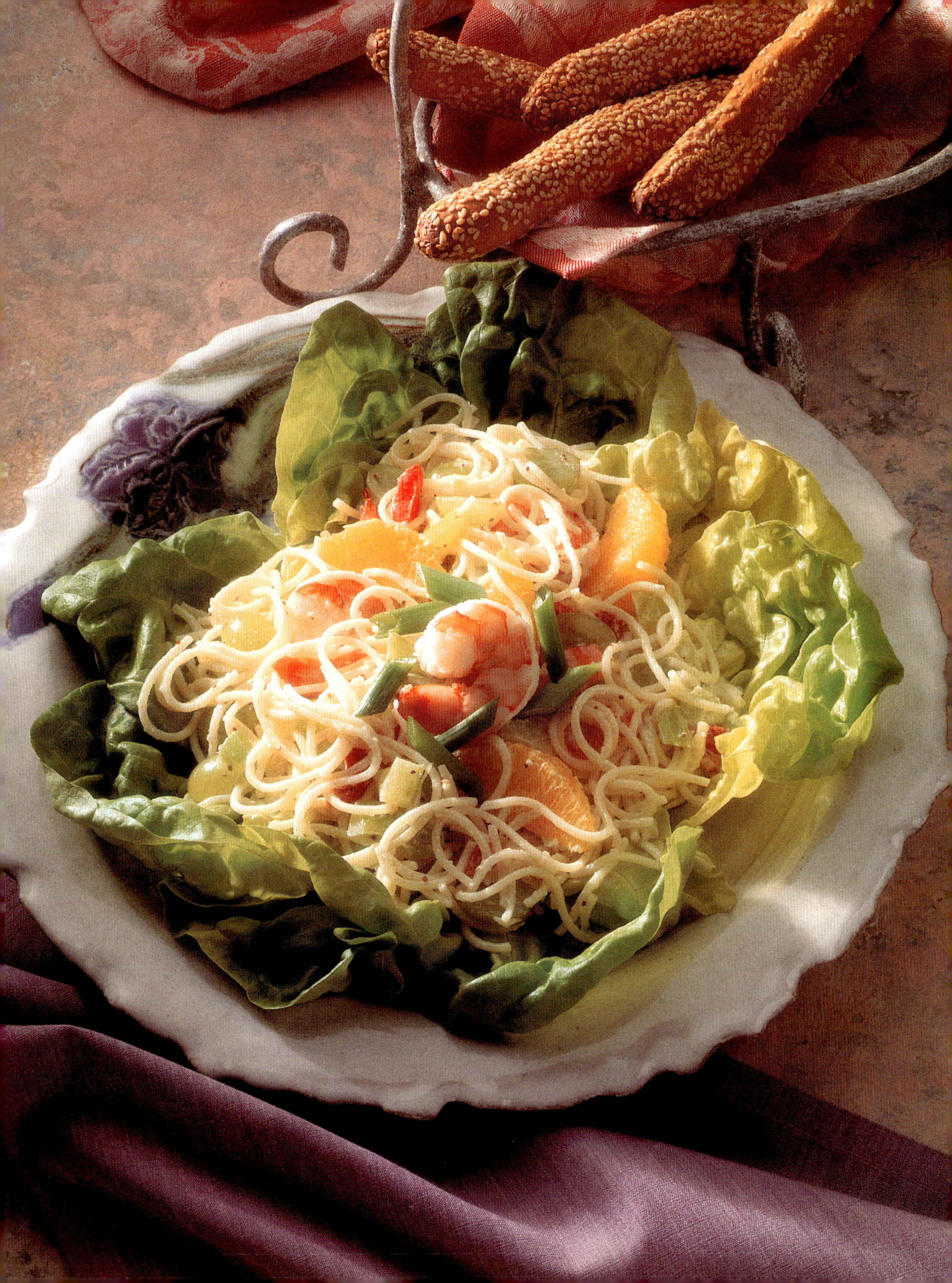

34 MIDSUMMER'S NIGHT SPLIT PEAS & PASTA

SALAD
- 2 pounds rotini (corkscrew) pasta, uncooked
- 2 cups USA green or yellow split peas, washed
- 1 quart cold water
- 1 pound roasted or smoked turkey breast, thinly sliced
- 2 cups shredded carrots
- 1 cup finely chopped red bell pepper
- 1 cup sliced black olives
- ¾ cup sliced green onions
- ½ cup grated Parmesan cheese
- ½ cup chopped fresh parsley

DRESSING
- 1 quart plain nonfat yogurt
- 2 tablespoons minced garlic
- ½ cup tarragon-flavored vinegar
- ⅓ cup olive oil
- 1 tablespoon ground mustard
- 2 teaspoons dried oregano leaves
- 2 teaspoons dried basil leaves
- 1 teaspoon crushed red pepper
- Salt to taste

1. Cook pasta according to package directions. Drain. Rinse under cool running water; drain. Cool.

2. Combine split peas and water in large saucepan; bring to a boil over high heat. Reduce heat to medium-low; cover. Simmer 20 minutes or until peas are tender. Drain; cool.

3. Combine pasta, peas, turkey, carrots, bell pepper, olives, green onions, cheese and parsley in large bowl or serving container.

4. Combine yogurt, garlic, vinegar, oil, ground mustard, oregano, basil, red pepper and salt in small bowl until well blended.

5. Pour dressing over split pea mixture; toss to coat. Cover; refrigerate 2 hours before serving. *Makes 24 servings*

Favorite recipe from **USA Dry Pea & Lentil Council**

35 TURKEY FRUITED BOW TIE SALAD

- ½ pound no-salt turkey breast, cut into ½-inch cubes
- 2 cups bow tie pasta, cooked according to package directions and drained
- 1 can (10½ ounces) mandarin oranges, drained
- 1 medium red apple, chopped
- 1 cup seedless grapes, cut into halves
- ½ cup celery, sliced
- ½ cup low-fat lemon yogurt
- 2 tablespoons frozen orange juice concentrate, thawed
- ¼ teaspoon ground ginger

1. In large bowl, combine turkey, pasta, oranges, apple, grapes and celery.

2. In small bowl, combine yogurt, juice concentrate and ginger. Fold dressing into turkey mixture and toss to coat. Cover and refrigerate until ready to serve.
Makes 4 servings

Favorite recipe from **National Turkey Federation**

SUPER SALADS & SOUPS

36 TASARA STYLE CAVATAPPI PASTA SALAD

1 (16-ounce) package PASTA LaBELLA® Cavatappi
1½ cups bell pepper strips
1 cup julienned red onion
¾ cup broken black olives
1½ cups diced plum tomatoes
⅓ cup minced green onions
6 ounces pepperoni, sliced
2 cups Italian dressing
2 tablespoons grated Parmesan cheese
2 tablespoons grated Romano cheese
Salt and black pepper to taste

Cook pasta according to package directions. When pasta is *al dente*, drain in colander. Rinse pasta with cold water until cool to the touch. Toss pasta in colander to remove any excess water. Put pasta in large mixing bowl and toss with remaining ingredients. Chill and serve. *Makes 4 servings*

37 PARTY PASTA SALAD

8 ounces (3 cups) uncooked bow tie pasta
¾ cup dried tart cherries
½ cup chopped carrot
½ cup chopped cucumber
¼ cup chopped green onions
¼ cup red wine vinegar
3 tablespoons vegetable oil
2 tablespoons lemon juice
2 tablespoons Dijon mustard
1 teaspoon dried basil leaves
½ teaspoon dried oregano leaves
¼ teaspoon dried thyme leaves
Freshly ground black pepper to taste

Cook pasta according to package directions. Drain well. In large bowl, combine pasta, cherries, carrot, cucumber and green onions; mix gently.

In small bowl, combine vinegar, oil, lemon juice, mustard, basil, oregano, thyme and pepper; mix well. Pour over pasta mixture; mix gently. Refrigerate, covered, at least 2 hours or overnight. Mix gently before serving. *Makes 8 servings*

Favorite recipe from **Cherry Marketing Institute, Inc.**

SUPER SALADS & SOUPS

38 QUICK BEEF SOUP

1½ pounds lean ground beef
1 cup chopped onion
2 cloves garlic, finely chopped
1 can (28 ounces) tomatoes, undrained
6 cups water
6 beef bouillon cubes
¼ teaspoon black pepper
½ cup uncooked orzo pasta
1½ cups frozen peas, carrots and corn vegetable blend
French bread (optional)

Cook beef, onion and garlic in large saucepan over medium-high heat until beef is brown, stirring to separate beef; drain fat.

Process tomatoes with juice in blender or food processor until smooth. Add tomatoes, water, bouillon cubes and pepper to beef mixture. Bring to a boil; reduce heat to low. Simmer, uncovered, 20 minutes. Add orzo and vegetables. Simmer an additional 15 minutes. Serve with French bread, if desired.   *Makes 6 servings*

*Favorite recipe from **North Dakota Beef Commission***

39 PASTA CHICKEN BREAST SALAD

8 ounces rotelle pasta
2 (3-ounce) boneless skinless chicken breasts
2 teaspoons lemon pepper
½ head lettuce
5 fresh spinach leaves
½ cup halved red grapes
½ cup halved strawberries*
Fat-free raspberry vinaigrette dressing

Seasonal fruit may be substituted.

Cook pasta according to package directions. Drain and rinse with cold water; set aside. Sprinkle chicken breasts with lemon pepper and broil or grill over medium heat 10 minutes, turning once. While pasta and chicken cook, prepare vegetables and fruit. Tear lettuce and spinach; place on 2 dinner plates. Sprinkle pasta, grapes and strawberries over greens. Slice chicken breasts lengthwise and place on top. Serve with vinaigrette dressing.
Makes 2 servings

*Favorite recipe from **North Dakota Wheat Commission***

Quick Beef Soup

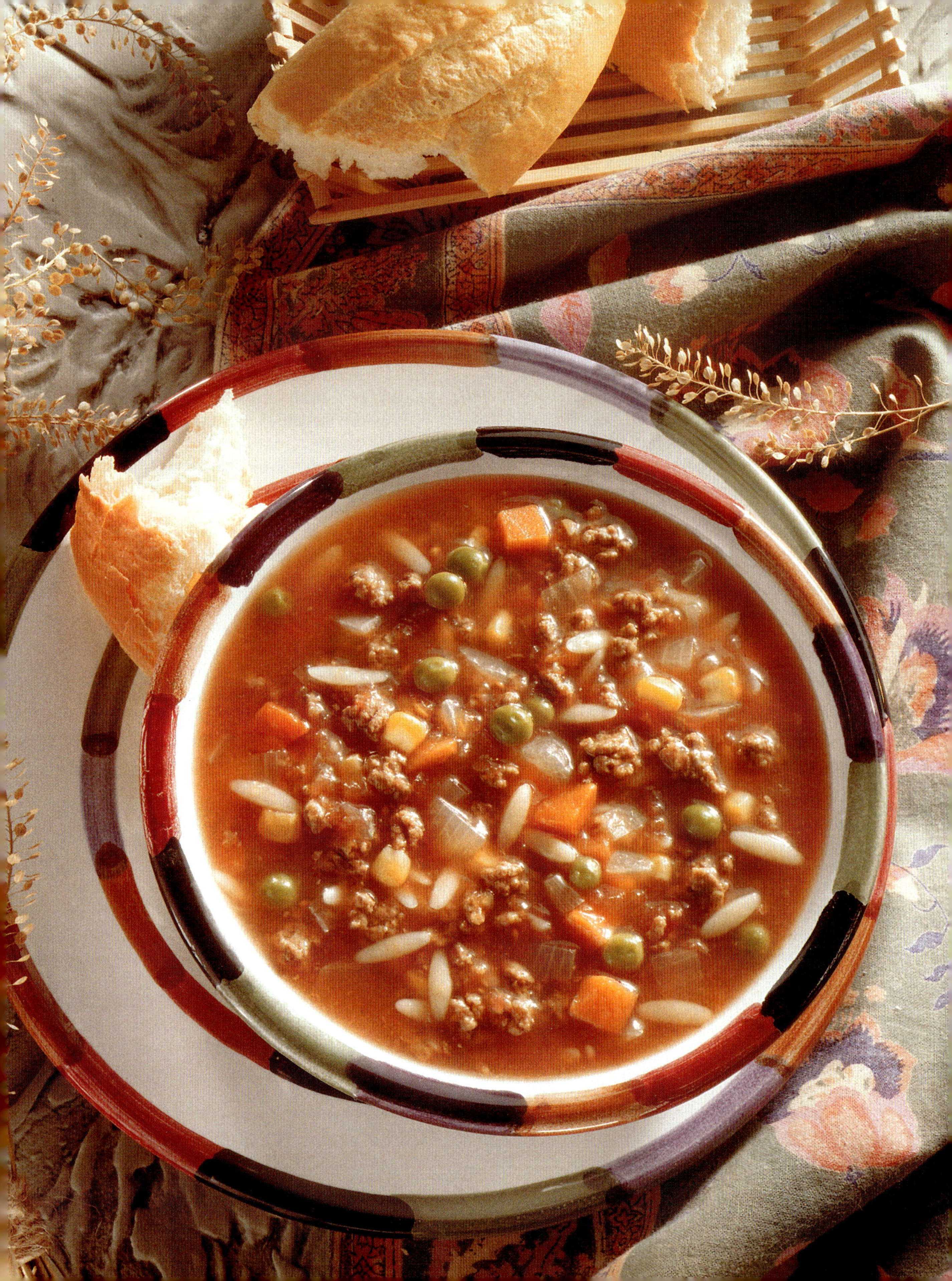

SUPER SALADS & SOUPS

40 SEAFOOD PEA–ISTA SALAD

8 ounces corkscrew pasta
1 cup broccoli florets
½ cup mayonnaise or salad dressing
¼ cup zesty Italian salad dressing
2 tablespoons grated Parmesan cheese
2 cups canned green or yellow black-eyed peas, rinsed
1½ cups (about 8 ounces) chopped imitation crabmeat
½ cup chopped green bell pepper
½ cup chopped tomato
¼ cup sliced green onions

1. Cook pasta according to package directions; drain.

2. Heat 1 quart lightly salted water in 2-quart saucepan over high heat to a boil. Add broccoli. Return to a boil; boil 3 minutes or until crisp-tender. Drain broccoli from saucepan, then immediately plunge into cold water to stop cooking. Drain and cool.

3. Combine mayonnaise, dressing and cheese in large bowl until well blended.

4. Add pasta, broccoli, peas, crabmeat, pepper, tomato and onions; toss gently to coat. Cover; refrigerate at least 2 hours before serving. *Makes 4 to 6 servings*

Favorite recipe from **Black-Eyed Pea Jamboree**

41 MINUTE LAMB MINESTRONE

1½ cups (8 ounces) cooked American Lamb, cut into small cubes*
1 package (16 ounces) seasoned frozen pasta and vegetable mix
4½ cups reduced-sodium beef broth *or* 4½ cups water plus 1 tablespoon beef bouillon granules
1 can (14½ ounces) diced tomatoes or whole tomatoes, cut up
3 tablespoons tomato paste
1 can (8¾ ounces) kidney beans, drained
1 teaspoon Italian seasoning
Pesto (optional)

*To substitute fresh American lamb, spray saucepan with nonstick pan coating and stir-fry briefly. Continue as directed.

In large saucepan, combine pasta/vegetable mix and beef broth. Bring to a boil; reduce heat. Cover and simmer 5 minutes. Stir in tomatoes, tomato paste, kidney beans, Italian seasoning and lamb. Bring to a boil; cook 1 minute to heat through. Serve with dollop of pesto, if desired.
Makes 6 servings

Favorite recipe from **American Lamb Council**

Seafood Pea-Ista Salad

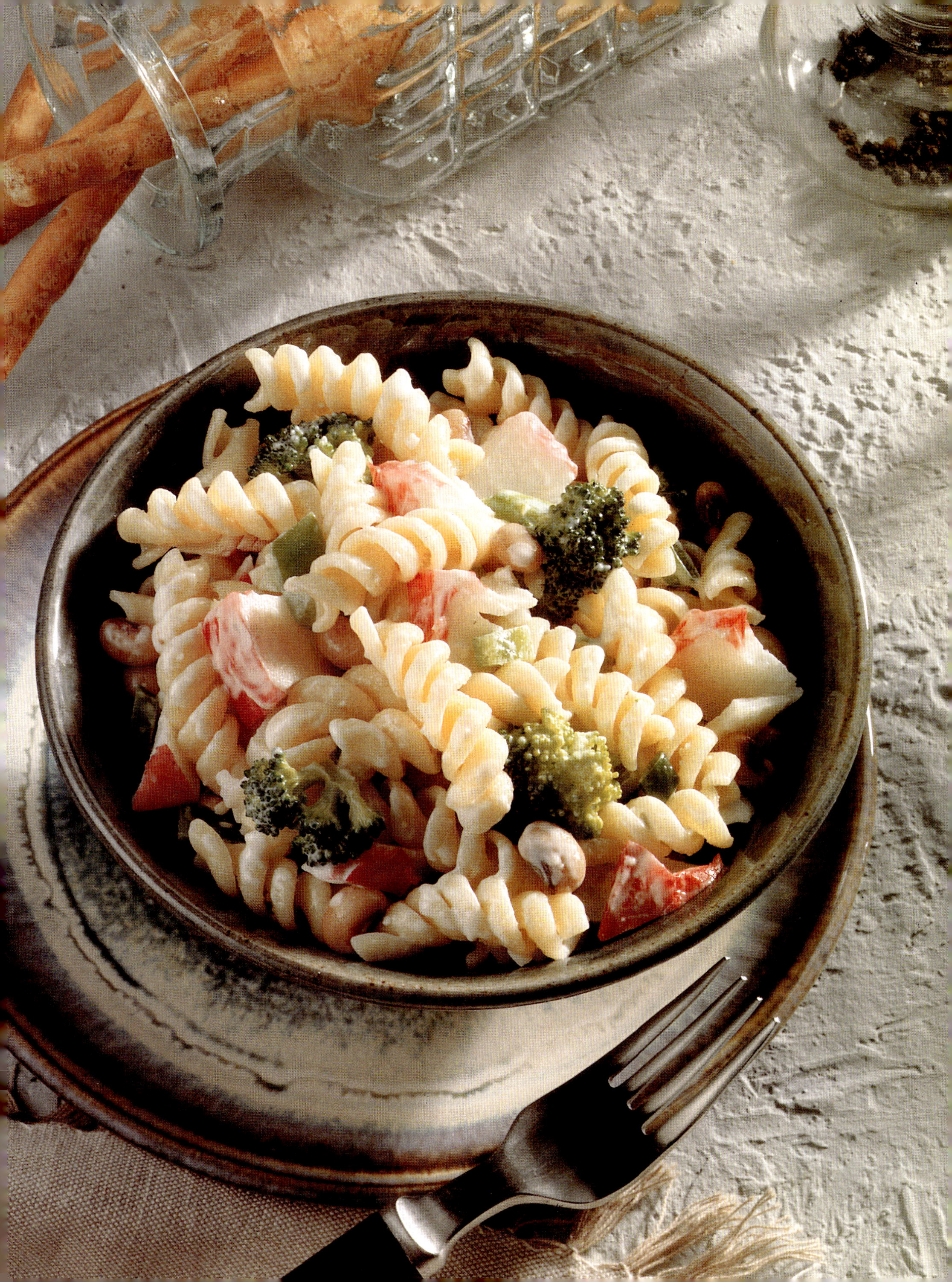

SUPER SALADS & SOUPS

42 SMOKED TURKEY AND PEPPER PASTA SALAD

¾ cup MIRACLE WHIP® Salad Dressing
1 tablespoon Dijon mustard
½ teaspoon dried thyme leaves
8 ounces fettuccine, cooked, drained
1 cup (8 ounces) diced LOUIS RICH® Hickory Smoked Breast of Turkey
¾ cup zucchini slices, cut into halves
½ cup red bell pepper strips
½ cup yellow bell pepper strips
Salt and black pepper

- Mix salad dressing, mustard and thyme in large bowl until well blended. Add pasta, turkey and vegetables; mix lightly. Season with salt and black pepper to taste.

- Cover; refrigerate at least 1 hour before serving. Add additional salad dressing before serving, if desired.   *Makes 6 servings*

43 SEAFOOD ORZO SALAD

1 cup orzo pasta
2 tablespoons olive oil, divided
½ pound medium shrimp, peeled and deveined
½ pound bay scallops
1 clove garlic, minced
2 green onions, sliced
2 tablespoons chopped fresh dill
1 tablespoon lemon juice
1 teaspoon salt
1 teaspoon TABASCO® pepper sauce

Prepare orzo according to package directions. Drain.

Meanwhile, in large skillet, heat 1 tablespoon olive oil over medium-high heat. Add shrimp, scallops and garlic; cook about 5 minutes or until seafood is tender, stirring occasionally.

In large bowl, toss seafood mixture, orzo, green onions, dill, lemon juice, salt, TABASCO sauce and remaining olive oil until well mixed. Serve immediately or refrigerate to serve cold later.
Makes 4 servings

Smoked Turkey and Pepper Pasta Salad

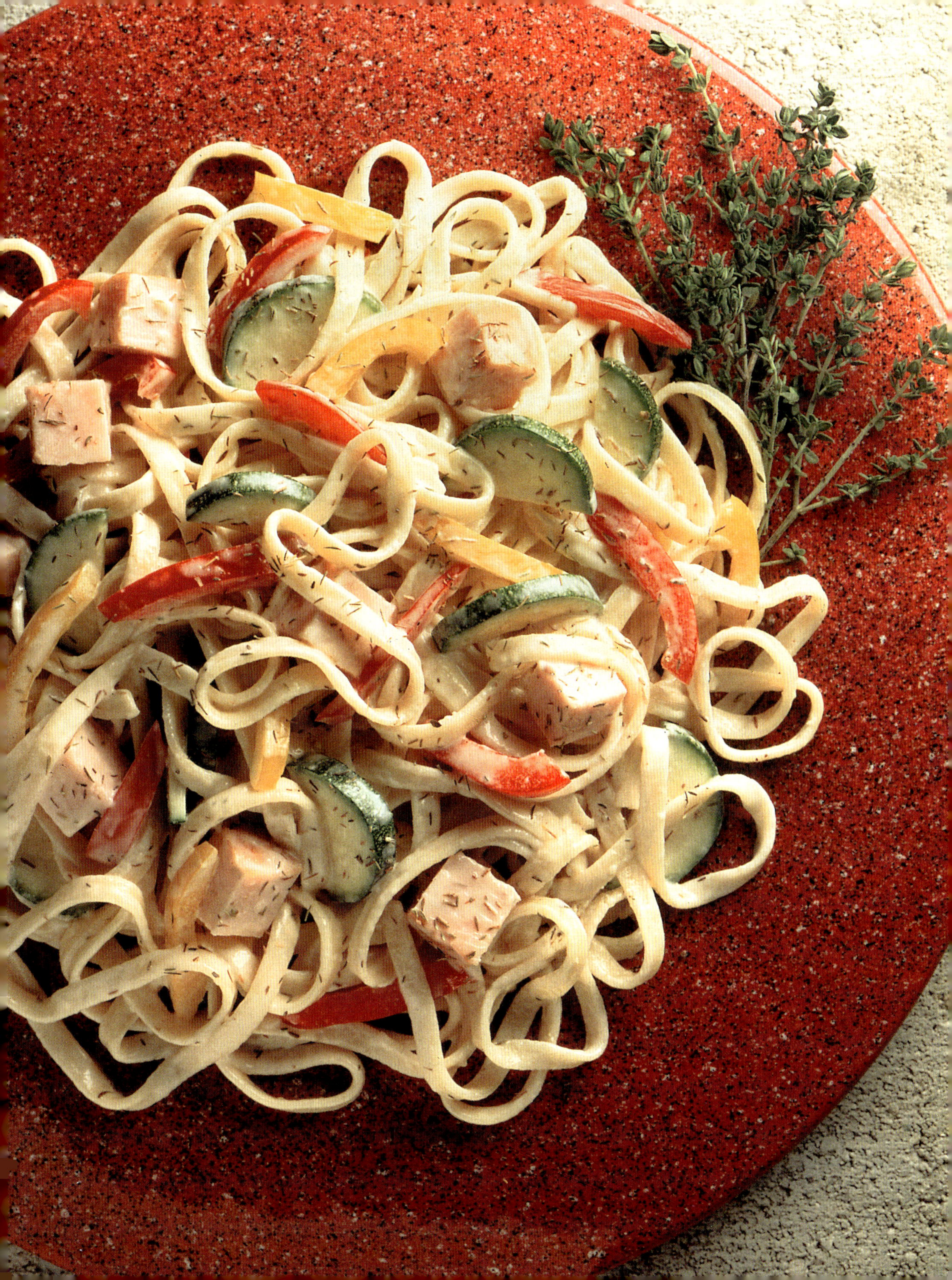

SUPER SALADS & SOUPS

44 TURKEY 'N SPAGHETTI SUMMER SALAD

- 10 ounces uncooked spaghetti
- 1 medium zucchini, thinly sliced
- 2 cups cut-up cooked turkey
- 1 can (8 ounces) cut green beans, drained
- 18 cherry tomatoes, cut into halves
- ⅓ cup sliced pitted ripe olives
- 2 medium green onions, chopped
- ¼ cup grated Parmesan cheese
- 1 teaspoon salt
- ⅔ cup olive oil
- ¼ cup white wine vinegar
- 2 tablespoons water
- 1 (0.6-ounce) packet Italian salad dressing mix

Cook spaghetti according to package directions; drain and rinse with cold water. Meanwhile, in small saucepan, cook zucchini in small amount of boiling water just until tender. Rinse in cold water; drain. In large bowl, combine spaghetti, zucchini, turkey, green beans, tomatoes, olives and onions. Sprinkle with Parmesan cheese and salt. In small jar or cruet, combine oil, vinegar, water and salad dressing mix. Pour over spaghetti mixture; toss lightly to coat. Refrigerate several hours or overnight to blend flavors. *Makes 6 to 8 servings*

Favorite recipe from **California Poultry Industry Federation**

45 PIZZA PASTA SALAD

- 1 pound uncooked rotini, twists or other medium pasta shape
- 3 ounces (about ¾ cup) sliced pepperoni
- ¼ pound (1 cup) sliced provolone cheese
- 12 cherry tomatoes, cut into halves
- ½ cup grated Parmesan cheese
- ½ cup nonfat Italian salad dressing
- 1 teaspoon Italian seasoning
- ½ teaspoon minced garlic
- 2½ (7-inch-round) pita breads
- 1 green bell pepper, cut into rings

Prepare pasta according to package directions; drain and place in large bowl. Cut each pepperoni slice into quarters and slice provolone cheese into matchstick-size pieces; add to pasta. Add cherry tomatoes, Parmesan cheese, Italian dressing, Italian seasoning and garlic; mix well. Quarter pita bread rounds and place around large platter. Place pasta salad in center; garnish with bell pepper rings. *Makes 6 servings*

Favorite recipe from **National Pasta Association**

Turkey 'n Spaghetti Summer Salad

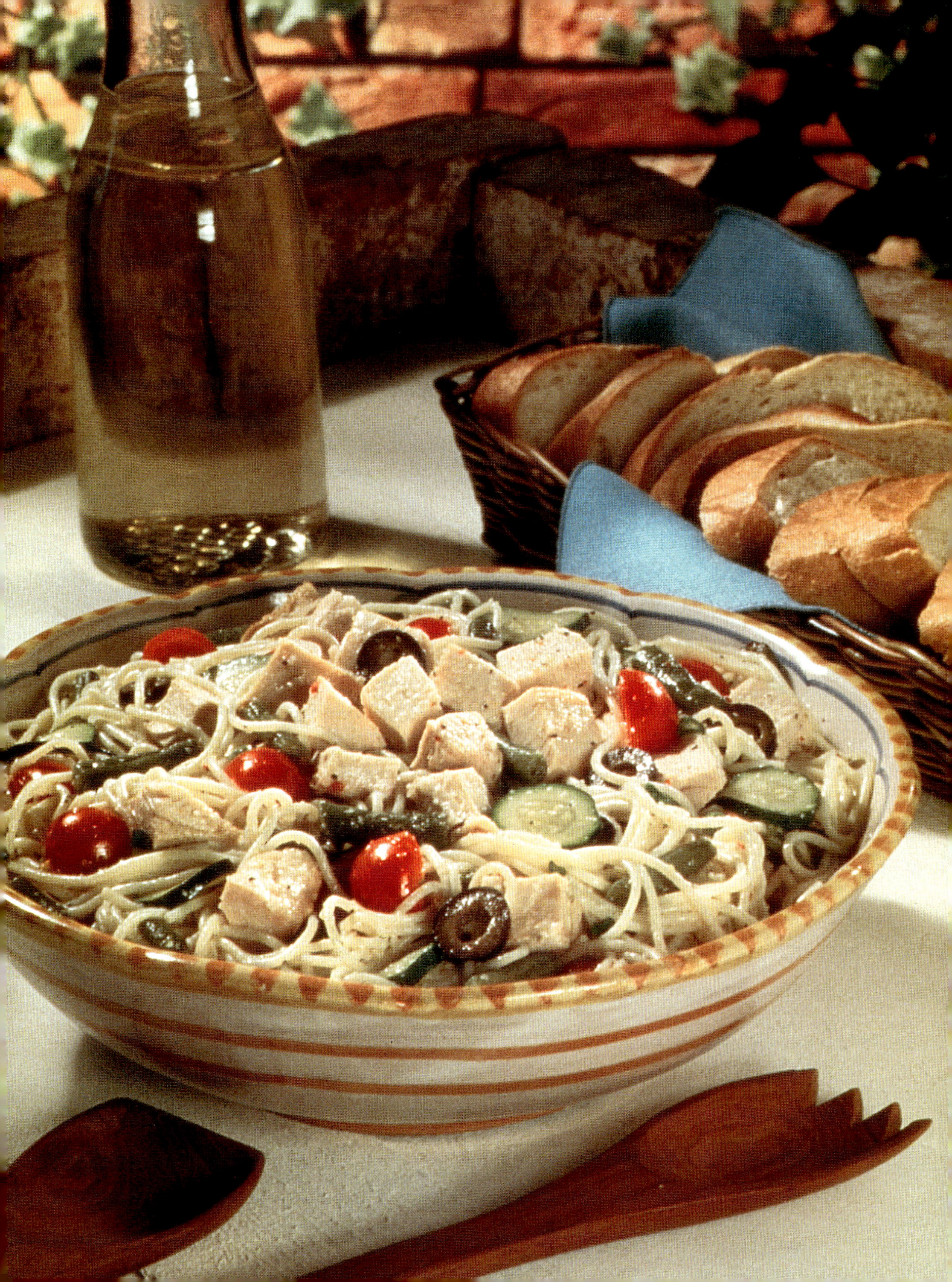

SUPER SALADS & SOUPS

46 CARIBBEAN PASTA SALAD WITH TROPICAL ISLAND DRESSING

1 can black beans, drained and rinsed
½ cup thawed orange juice concentrate
½ teaspoon ground allspice
6 ounces mafalda pasta
1 teaspoon vegetable oil
4 cups washed and torn romaine lettuce leaves
1½ cups fresh pineapple chunks
1 mango, peeled and sliced
1 cup shredded cabbage
⅓ cup chopped onion
⅓ cup chopped red bell pepper
8 ounces piña colada-flavored yogurt
½ cup orange juice
1 teaspoon grated fresh ginger
2 oranges

1. Combine beans, juice concentrate and allspice in medium bowl. Cover and refrigerate 1 hour; drain and discard liquid from beans.

2. Cook pasta according to package directions. Drain. Rinse under cold water until cool; drain again. Return to pan; toss with oil.

3. To assemble salad, divide lettuce, pasta, pineapple, beans, mango, cabbage, onion and bell pepper among 6 plates.

4. To prepare dressing, combine yogurt, orange juice and ginger in small bowl. Remove colored portion of peel of 1 orange using vegetable peeler. Finely chop peel to measure 1 tablespoon; stir into dressing.

5. Remove white portion of peel from orange and completely peel remaining orange. Separate oranges into sections; arrange on salads. Serve with dressing.
Makes 6 servings

47 TURKEY FRANKS AND PASTA SALAD

8 ounces spiral pasta, cooked
½ pound turkey frankfurters, cut into ¼-inch-thick slices
1 cup yellow squash, cut into ⅛-inch slices
1 cup zucchini, cut into ⅛-inch slices
½ cup reduced-calorie Italian salad dressing
⅓ cup green onions, sliced, including green tops
1 tablespoon dried parsley
¾ teaspoon Italian seasoning
1 clove garlic, finely minced
1 cup large cherry tomatoes, cut into quarters

1. In large bowl, combine pasta, frankfurters, squash, zucchini, dressing, onions, parsley, Italian seasoning and garlic. Cover and refrigerate overnight.

2. Before serving, fold in tomatoes.
Makes 8 servings

Favorite recipe from **National Turkey Federation**

Caribbean Pasta Salad with Tropical Island Dressing

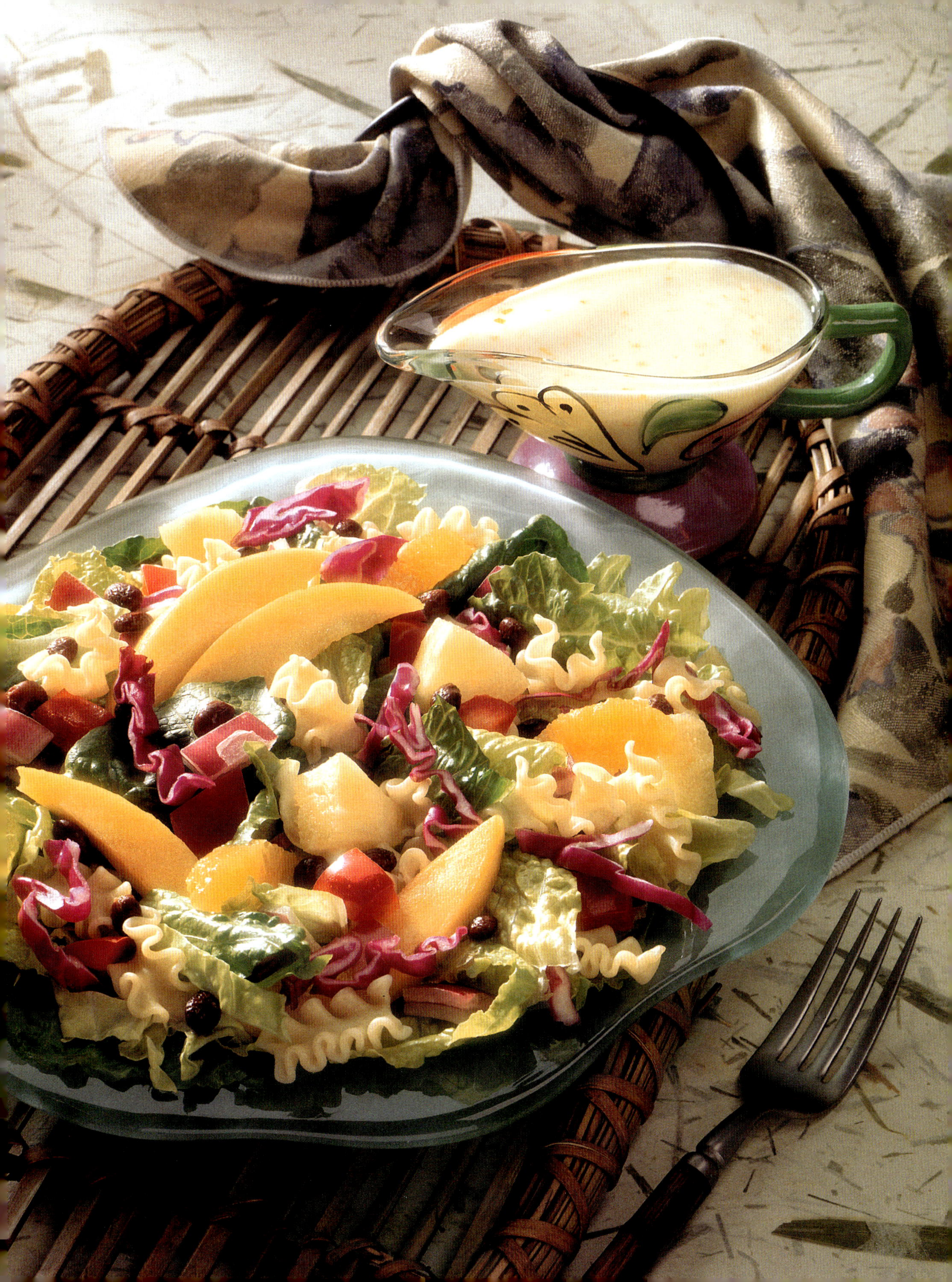

SUPER SALADS & SOUPS

48 CLASSIC MEATBALL SOUP

2 pounds beef bones
3 ribs celery
2 carrots
1 medium onion, cut into halves
1 bay leaf
6 cups cold water
1 egg
4 tablespoons chopped fresh parsley, divided
1 teaspoon salt, divided
½ teaspoon dried marjoram leaves
¼ teaspoon ground black pepper, divided
½ cup soft fresh bread crumbs
¼ cup grated Parmesan cheese
1 pound ground beef
1 can (14½ ounces) whole peeled tomatoes, undrained
½ cup uncooked rotini or small macaroni
Salt and black pepper to taste

1. To make stock, rinse bones. Combine bones, celery, carrots, onion and bay leaf in 6-quart stockpot. Add water. Bring to a boil; reduce heat to low. Cover partially and simmer 1 hour, skimming foam occasionally.

2. Preheat oven to 400°F. Spray 13×9-inch baking pan with nonstick cooking spray. Combine egg, 3 tablespoons parsley, ½ teaspoon salt, marjoram and ⅛ teaspoon pepper in medium bowl; whisk lightly. Stir in bread crumbs and cheese. Add beef; mix well.

3. Place meat mixture on cutting board; pat evenly into 1-inch-thick square. With sharp knife, cut meat into 1-inch squares; shape each square into a ball. Place meatballs in prepared pan; bake 20 to 25 minutes until brown on all sides and cooked through, turning occasionally. Drain on paper towels.

4. Strain stock through sieve into medium bowl. Slice celery and carrots; reserve. Discard bones, onion and bay leaf. To degrease stock, let stand 5 minutes to allow fat to rise. Holding paper towel, quickly pull across surface only, allowing towel to absorb fat. Discard. Repeat with clean paper towels as many times as needed to remove all fat.

5. Return stock to stockpot. Drain tomatoes, reserving juice. Chop tomatoes; add to stock with juice. Bring to a boil; boil 5 minutes. Stir in rotini, remaining ½ teaspoon salt and ⅛ teaspoon pepper. Cook 6 minutes, stirring occasionally. Add reserved vegetables and meatballs. Reduce heat to medium; cook 10 minutes until hot. Stir in remaining 1 tablespoon parsley. Season to taste with salt and black pepper.

Makes 4 to 6 servings

Classic Meatball Soup

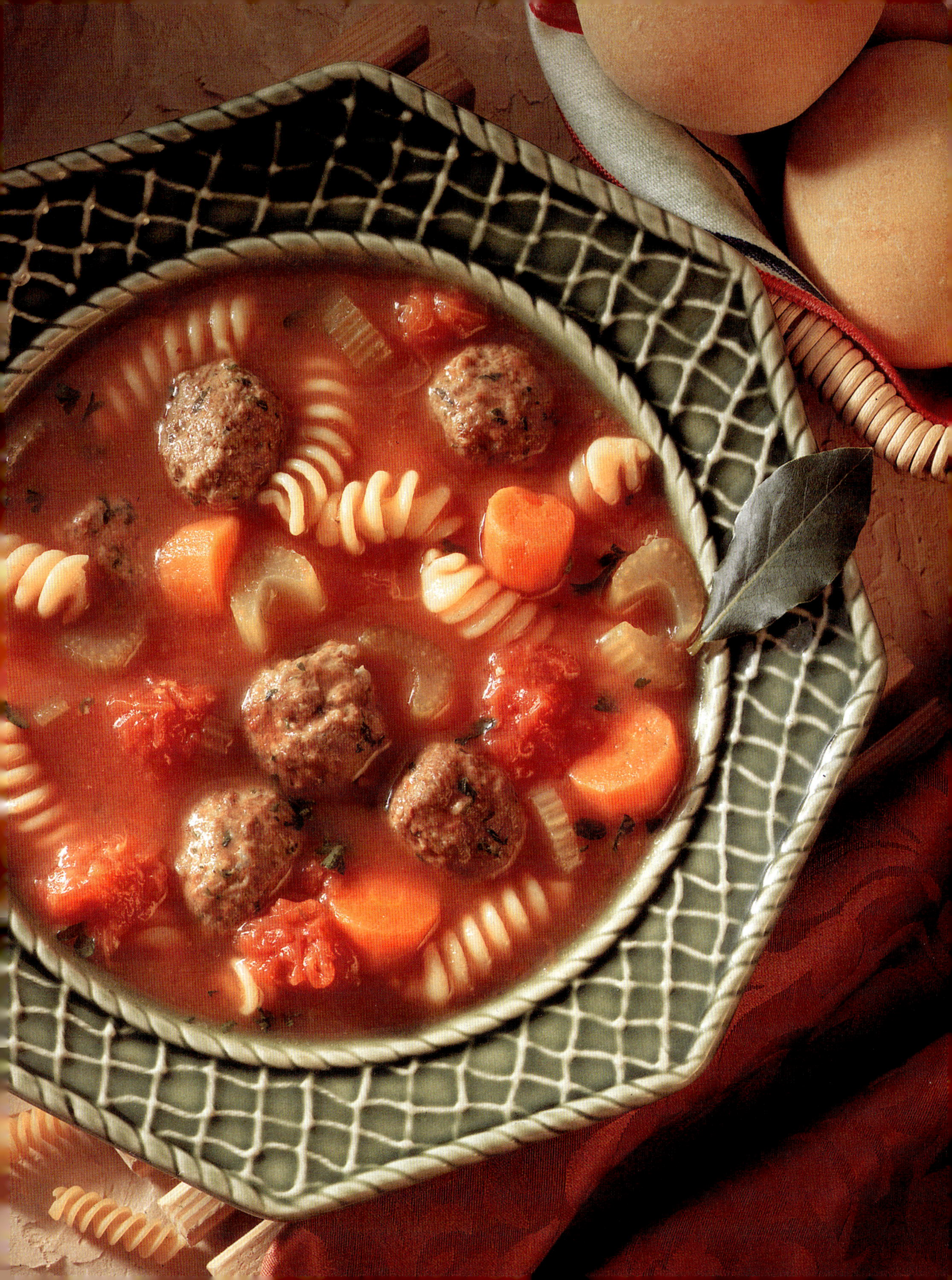

SUPER SALADS & SOUPS

49 SOUTHWEST RUFFLE SALAD

- ⅔ cup HELLMANN'S® or BEST FOODS® Real or Light Mayonnaise or Low Fat Mayonnaise Dressing
- ⅓ cup sour cream
- ¼ cup chopped cilantro
- 2 tablespoons milk
- 2 tablespoons lime juice
- 1 fresh jalapeño pepper, seeded and minced
- 1 teaspoon salt
- 7 ounces MUELLER'S® Pasta Ruffles, cooked, rinsed with cold water and drained
- 2 large tomatoes, seeded and chopped
- 1 yellow bell pepper, chopped
- 1 zucchini, quartered lengthwise and thinly sliced
- 3 green onions, thinly sliced

In large bowl, combine mayonnaise, sour cream, cilantro, milk, lime juice, jalapeño pepper and salt. Add pasta, tomatoes, yellow bell pepper, zucchini and green onions; toss to coat well. Garnish as desired. Cover; refrigerate. *Makes 6 to 8 servings*

50 CHICKPEA & PASTA SOUP

- Nonstick cooking spray
- 1 small onion, chopped
- 2 cloves garlic, minced
- 2 teaspoons dried oregano leaves
- ½ teaspoon dried rosemary
- 2 cans (14½ ounces each) ⅓-less-salt chicken broth
- 1 can (15½ ounces) zucchini and tomatoes
- ½ can (15 ounce size) chickpeas, rinsed well, drained
- 1 package (9 ounces) reduced-fat cheese tortellini
- ¼ teaspoon salt
- ¼ teaspoon black pepper

Spray large saucepan with cooking spray; heat over medium heat until hot. Sauté onion and garlic until tender; stir in oregano and rosemary and cook 1 to 2 minutes.

Add chicken broth, zucchini and tomatoes, and chickpeas. Heat to a boil. Add tortellini; reduce heat and simmer, uncovered, until tortellini are *al dente*, about 5 minutes. Stir in salt and pepper. *Makes 6 servings (about 1½ cups each)*

Favorite recipe from **Canned Food Information Council**

Southwest Ruffle Salad

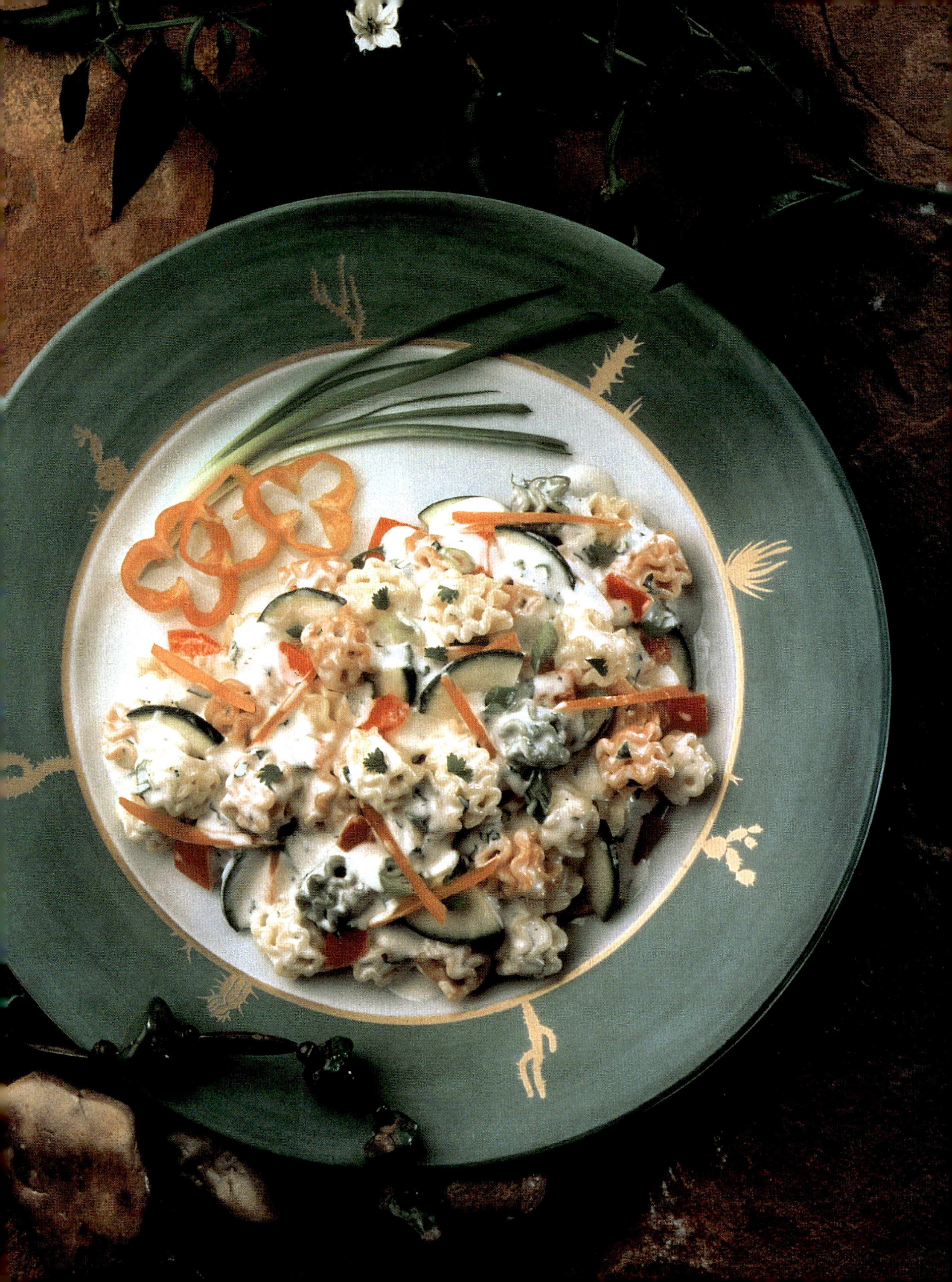

SUPER SALADS & SOUPS

51 ANTIPASTO SALAD

1 cup MIRACLE WHIP® Salad Dressing
½ cup milk
2 (0.6-ounce) packages GOOD SEASONS® Zesty Italian Salad Dressing Mix
5⅓ cups (16 ounces) uncooked mostaccioli, cooked and drained
1 (8-ounce) package cotto salami slices, cut into strips
1 (8-ounce) package CASINO® Natural Low-Moisture Part-Skim Mozzarella Cheese, cubed
¾ cup *each* thin red bell pepper strips and thin zucchini strips
½ cup pitted ripe olives, drained, halved

- Mix together salad dressing, milk, dressing mix and pasta in large shallow bowl.

- Arrange remaining ingredients over pasta mixture; cover and chill.

Makes 18 servings (about 14 cups)

52 HEARTY FETTUCCINE, HAM AND BEAN SOUP

2 tablespoons olive oil
1 cup canned chunky Italian tomato sauce
2 cloves garlic, chopped
1 cup diced cooked ham
4 cups canned nonfat, low-salt chicken broth, divided
1 (15-ounce) can chickpeas, drained, divided
4 ounces fettuccine (broken into thirds), elbows or rotini
Parmesan cheese

Heat oil in large saucepan over medium heat. Add tomato sauce, garlic and ham. Simmer 5 minutes. Add 3 cups broth; stir to blend. Purée remaining broth and 1 cup chickpeas in blender. Add to saucepan; add remaining chickpeas. Bring to a boil; reduce heat and simmer 10 minutes. Add pasta; cook until tender, about 10 minutes. Serve, passing Parmesan cheese separately.

Makes 4 to 6 servings

Favorite recipe from **North Dakota Wheat Commission**

Antipasto Salad

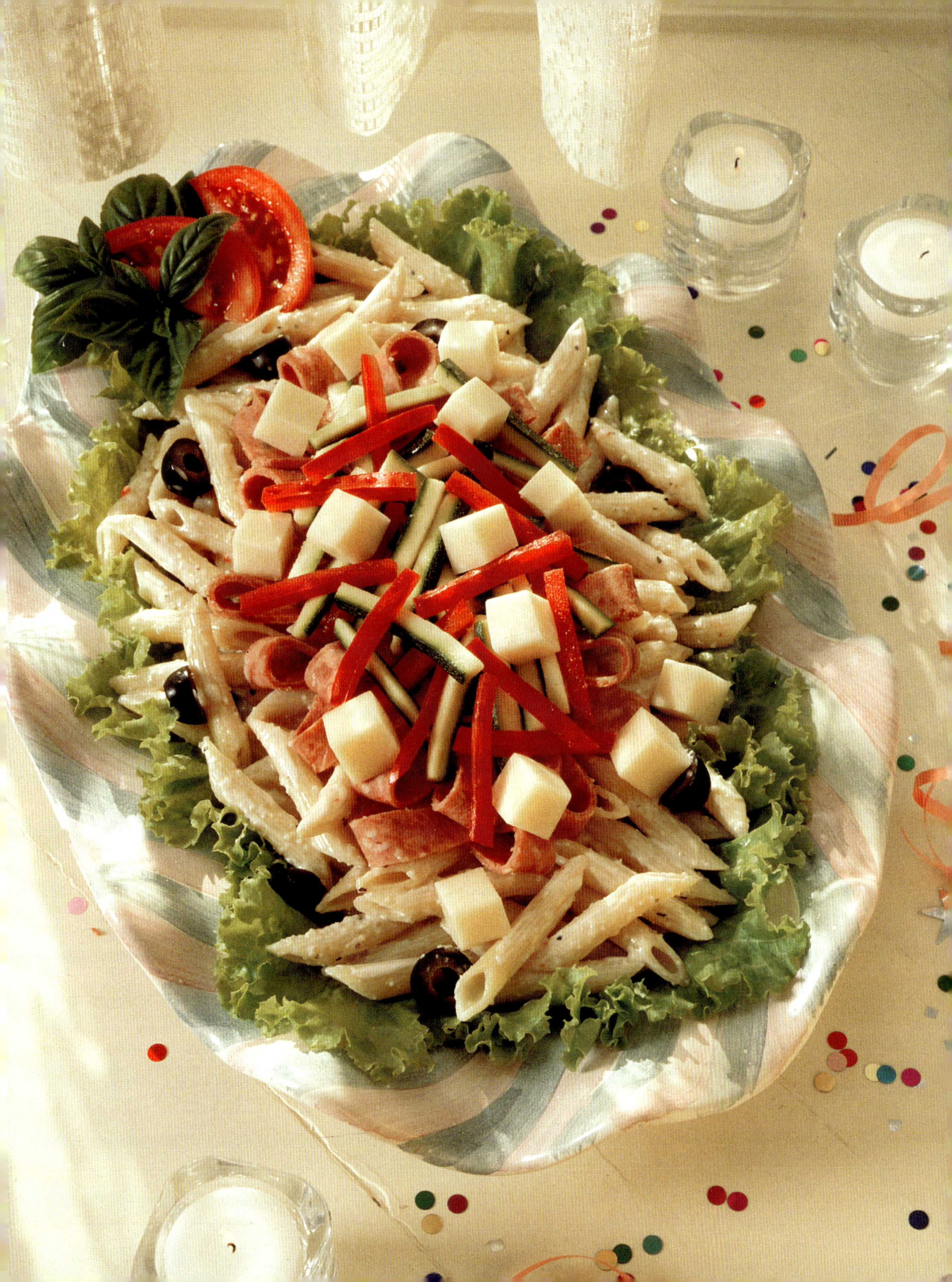

SUPER SALADS & SOUPS

53 COLORFUL TURKEY PASTA SALAD

2½ cups tri-color rotini pasta, cooked and drained
2 cups oven roasted turkey breast meat, cubed
½ cup onion, thinly sliced
¼ cup celery, thinly sliced
¼ cup parsley, chopped
1½ teaspoons fresh tarragon, chopped *or*
    ½ teaspoon dried tarragon leaves
1 tablespoon oil
2 tablespoons tarragon vinegar
1 tablespoon lemon juice
2 tablespoons reduced-calorie mayonnaise

In large bowl, combine pasta, turkey, onion, celery, parsley, tarragon, oil, vinegar, juice and mayonnaise. Mix thoroughly; cover and refrigerate 1 to 2 hours or overnight.

Makes 4 servings

Favorite recipe from **National Turkey Federation**

54 SPICY GRAPE PASTA SALAD

8 ounces angel hair pasta, cooked and drained
Spicy Asian Dressing (recipe follows), divided
2 cups julienned cooked chicken
1½ cups California seedless grapes
1 cup cut asparagus*
1 cup julienned red bell pepper
½ cup diagonally sliced celery
¼ cup sliced green onions with tops
2 tablespoons chopped cilantro or fresh basil leaves

Broccoli florets may be substituted.

Combine hot pasta with ¼ cup Spicy Asian Dressing; cool to room temperature. Add remaining ¼ cup dressing and all remaining ingredients; toss lightly.

Makes 6 to 8 servings

Spicy Asian Dressing: Combine ¼ cup rice vinegar or white wine vinegar, 2 tablespoons vegetable oil, 2 tablespoons soy sauce, ½ teaspoon grated fresh ginger, ¼ teaspoon red pepper flakes, ¼ teaspoon sesame oil and 1 clove garlic; mix well. Let stand at least 30 minutes; remove garlic before serving.

Makes ½ cup

Prep time: About 45 minutes

Favorite recipe from **California Table Grape Commission**

SUPER SALADS & SOUPS

55 CHICKEN NOODLE SOUP

1 (46-fluid ounce) can COLLEGE INN® Chicken Broth
½ pound boneless skinless chicken, cut into bite-size pieces
1½ cups uncooked medium egg noodles
1 cup sliced carrots
½ cup chopped onion
⅓ cup sliced celery
1 teaspoon dill weed
¼ teaspoon ground black pepper

In large saucepan, over medium-high heat, heat chicken broth, chicken, noodles, carrots, onion, celery, dill and pepper to a boil. Reduce heat; simmer 20 minutes or until chicken and noodles are cooked.
Makes 8 servings

56 ORZO SALAD

3 cups cooked orzo pasta
1 can (8½ ounces) peas, drained
½ cup sliced red bell pepper
½ cup sliced green bell pepper
⅓ cup pitted ripe olives
⅓ cup toasted canned slivered almonds
Creamy Vinaigrette (recipe follows)

Combine orzo, peas, peppers, olives and almonds in medium bowl. Make Creamy Vinaigrette; pour over salad and toss.
Makes 8 to 10 servings

VARIATION: Add 1 can (1 pound) cubed ham or 3 cans (4½ ounces each) medium shrimp, drained.

CREAMY VINAIGRETTE
¼ cup reduced-fat mayonnaise
2 tablespoons white wine vinegar
2 tablespoons olive or vegetable oil
2 tablespoons water

Beat ingredients until smooth in small bowl.
Makes about ⅔ cup

*Favorite recipe from **Canned Food Information Council***

SUPER SALADS & SOUPS

57 CAJUN PORK WITH PASTA SALAD

1 boneless pork tenderloin (about 12 ounces), visible fat trimmed
Cajun Spice Rub (recipe follows)
Nonstick cooking spray
8 ounces fresh or thawed frozen sliced okra
½ red bell pepper, sliced
½ yellow bell pepper, sliced
1 teaspoon minced jalapeño pepper*
1 small onion, sliced
¼ cup fat-free reduced-sodium chicken broth
8 ounces farfalle pasta, cooked and kept warm

*Jalapeño peppers can sting and irritate the skin; wear rubber gloves when handling peppers and do not touch eyes.

1. Cut pork into ¼-inch-thick slices; coat with Cajun Spice Rub. Spray medium skillet with cooking spray. Heat over medium heat until hot. Cook and stir pork 2 to 3 minutes on each side until browned. Remove from skillet.

2. Add okra to skillet; cook 3 to 5 minutes or until browned. Add bell peppers, jalapeño pepper, onion and chicken broth; bring to a boil. Reduce heat; simmer, covered, 3 to 5 minutes or until vegetables are crisp-tender. Add pork and cook 2 to 3 minutes. Season to taste with salt and black pepper. Place pasta on platter; spoon pork mixture over top and toss. *Makes 4 main-dish servings*

CAJUN SPICE RUB

2 teaspoons dried oregano leaves
1 teaspoon garlic powder
1 teaspoon dried thyme leaves
½ teaspoon dried mustard
½ teaspoon paprika
¼ teaspoon salt
¼ teaspoon dried cumin
¼ teaspoon ground allspice
¼ teaspoon ground red pepper
¼ teaspoon black pepper

1. Combine ingredients in small bowl.
Makes about 2 tablespoons

58 SUPER SIMPLE CHICKEN SOUP

4 cups water
1 can (14½ ounces) chicken broth
2 teaspoons soy sauce
3 boneless skinless chicken breast halves
1⅓ cups SONOMA Dried Tomato Halves, snipped into quarters
½ cup uncooked elbow macaroni
⅓ cup sliced green onions
½ teaspoon dried thyme leaves
1 package (10 ounces) frozen peas and carrots

In 3-quart saucepan, combine water, chicken broth and soy sauce; bring to a boil. Cut chicken into 1-inch chunks and add to liquid with tomatoes. Simmer 10 minutes. Add macaroni, onions and thyme. Simmer until macaroni is cooked, about 10 minutes, adding peas and carrots after 5 minutes.
Makes 4 to 6 main-dish servings (about 2 quarts)

Cajun Pork with Pasta Salad

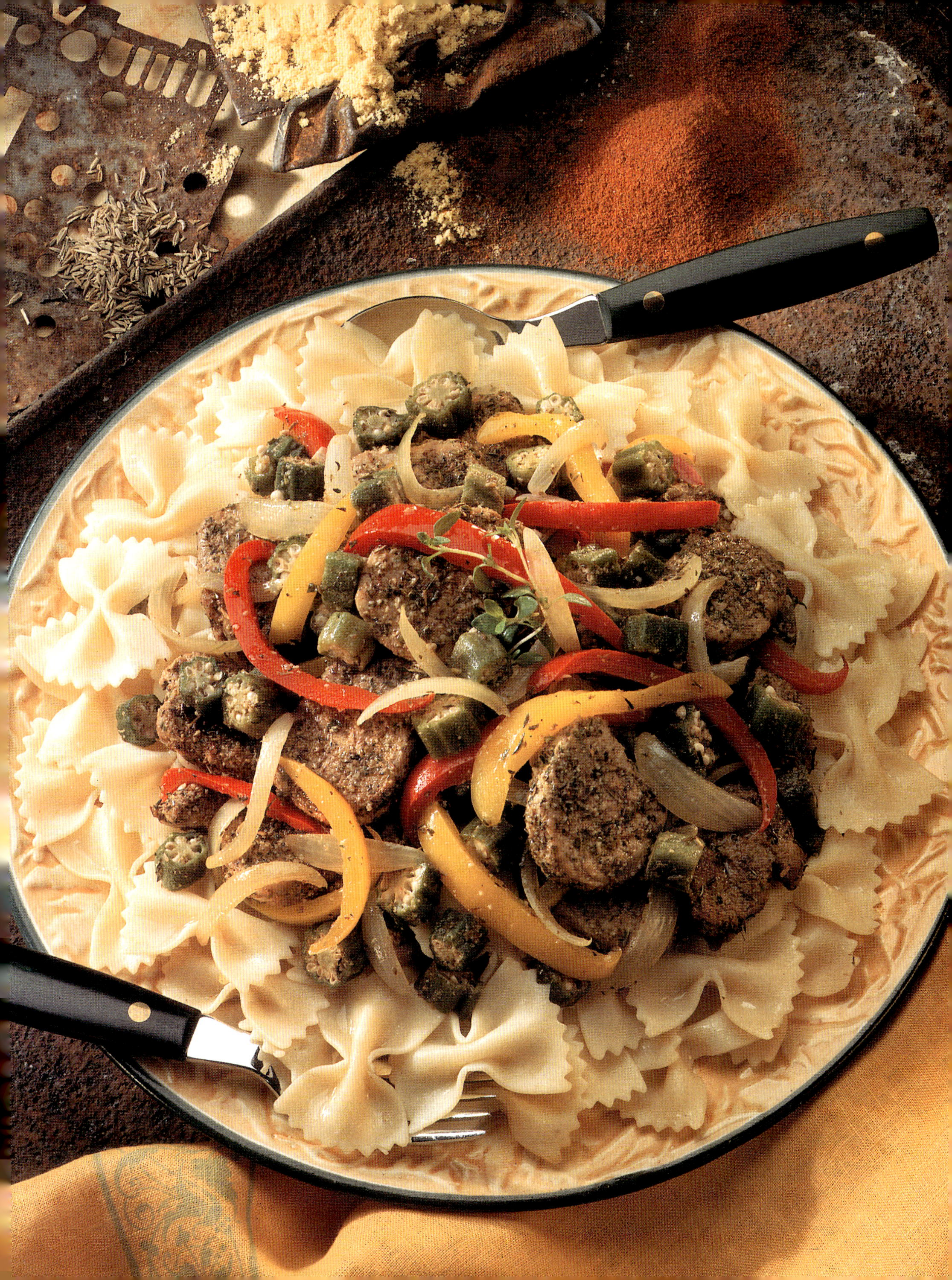

OUT OF THE OVEN

59 LASAGNA SUPREME

- 8 ounces lasagna noodles
- ½ pound ground beef
- ½ pound mild Italian sausage, casing removed
- 1 medium onion, chopped
- 2 cloves garlic, minced
- 1 can (14½ ounces) whole peeled tomatoes, undrained and chopped
- 1 can (6 ounces) tomato paste
- 2 teaspoons dried basil leaves
- 1 teaspoon dried marjoram leaves
- 1 can (4 ounces) sliced mushrooms, drained
- 2 eggs
- 1 pound cream-style cottage cheese
- ¾ cup Parmesan cheese, divided
- 2 tablespoons dried parsley flakes
- ½ teaspoon salt
- ½ teaspoon ground black pepper
- 2 cups (8 ounces) shredded Cheddar cheese
- 3 cups (12 ounces) shredded mozzarella cheese
- Mixed salad (optional)

1. Cook lasagna noodles according to package directions; drain.

2. Cook meats, onion and garlic in large skillet over medium-high heat until meat is brown, stirring to separate meat. Drain drippings.

3. Add tomatoes with juice, tomato paste, basil and marjoram. Reduce heat to low. Cover; simmer 15 minutes, stirring often. Stir in mushrooms; set aside.

4. Preheat oven to 375°F. Beat eggs in large bowl; add cottage cheese, ½ cup Parmesan cheese, parsley, salt and pepper. Mix well.

5. Place half the noodles on bottom of 13×9-inch baking pan. Spread half the cottage cheese mixture over noodles, then half the meat mixture and half the Cheddar cheese and mozzarella cheese. Repeat layers. Sprinkle with remaining ¼ cup Parmesan cheese.

6. Bake lasagna 40 to 45 minutes or until bubbly. Let stand 10 minutes before cutting. Serve with mixed salad, if desired.

Makes 8 to 10 servings

NOTE: Lasagna may be assembled, covered and refrigerated up to 2 days in advance. Bake, uncovered, in preheated 375°F oven 60 minutes or until bubbly.

Lasagna Supreme

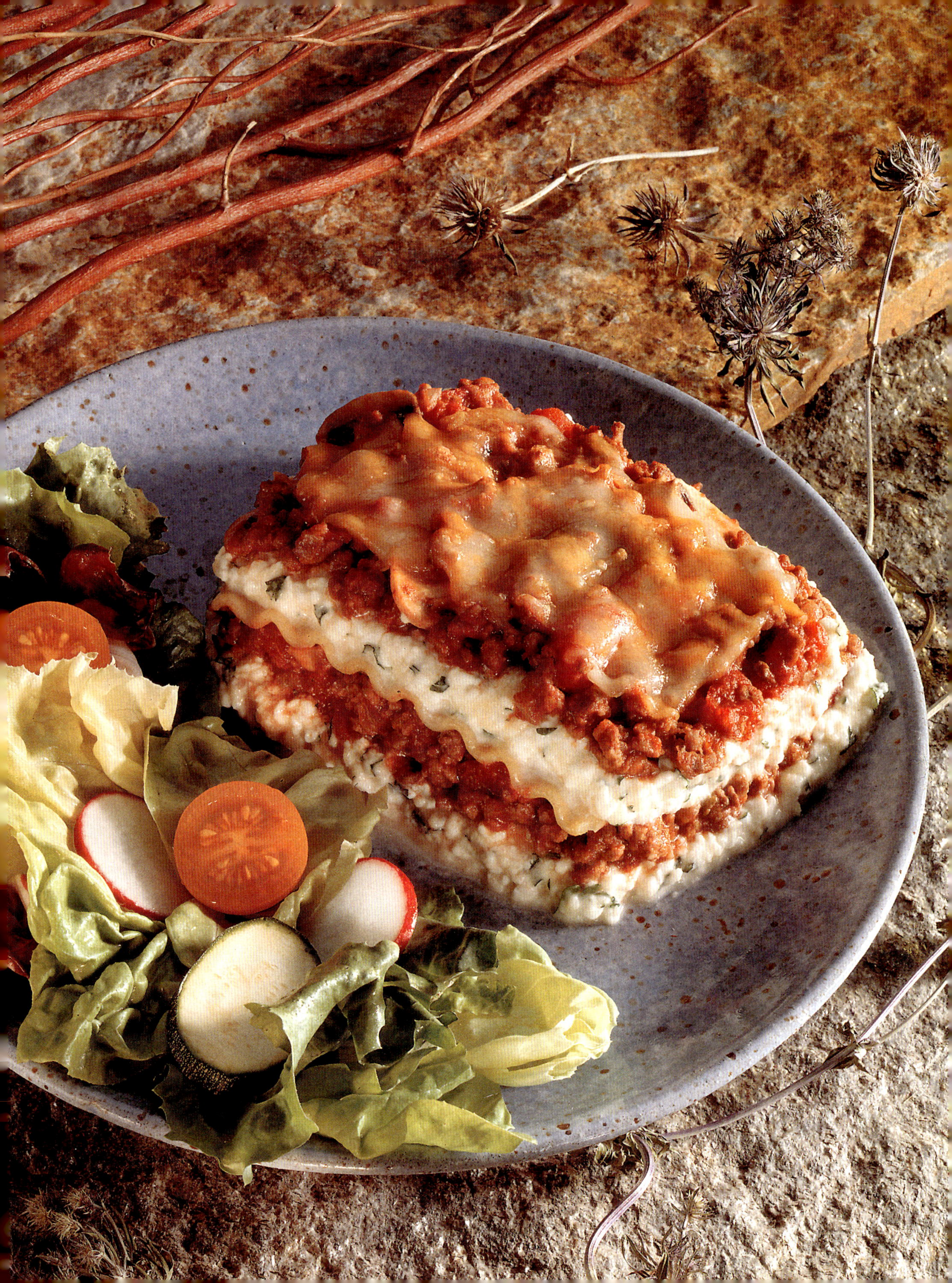

OUT OF THE OVEN

60 ITALIAN THREE-CHEESE MACARONI

2 cups uncooked elbow macaroni
4 tablespoons margarine or butter
3 tablespoons all-purpose flour
1 teaspoon dried Italian seasoning
½ to 1 teaspoon black pepper
½ teaspoon salt
2 cups milk
¾ cup (3 ounces) shredded Cheddar cheese
¼ cup grated Parmesan cheese
1 can (14½ ounces) diced tomatoes, drained
1 cup (4 ounces) shredded mozzarella cheese
½ cup dry bread crumbs
    Fresh chives and oregano sprig (optional)

PREHEAT oven to 350°F. Spray 2-quart round casserole with nonstick cooking spray.

COOK pasta according to package directions until *al dente*. Drain and set aside.

Meanwhile, MELT margarine in medium saucepan over medium heat. Add flour, Italian seasoning, pepper and salt, stirring until smooth. Gradually add milk, stirring constantly until slightly thickened. Add Cheddar and Parmesan cheeses; stir until cheeses melt.

LAYER pasta, tomatoes and cheese sauce in prepared dish. Repeat layers.

COMBINE mozzarella cheese and bread crumbs in small bowl. Sprinkle evenly over casserole. Spray bread crumb mixture several times with cooking spray.

BAKE, covered, 30 minutes or until hot and bubbly. Uncover and bake 5 minutes or until top is golden brown. Garnish with chives and oregano, if desired.

Makes 4 servings

61 CHEESE STUFFED SHELLS WITH BASIL

1 cup (8 ounces) low-fat ricotta cheese
1 (8-ounce) package HEALTHY CHOICE® Fat Free natural shredded Mozzarella Cheese, divided
1 cup chopped fresh basil
2 teaspoons minced fresh garlic
6 ounces (16 shells) jumbo pasta shells, cooked
1 (26-ounce) jar HEALTHY CHOICE® Pasta Sauce

Preheat oven to 350°F. In large bowl, stir together ricotta cheese, 1 cup mozzarella cheese, basil and garlic. Fill each shell with about 2 tablespoons cheese filling. Place in 12×7-inch baking dish sprayed with nonstick cooking spray. Pour sauce over filled shells. Sprinkle with remaining mozzarella cheese. Cover and bake at 350°F, 20 to 25 minutes.

Makes 8 servings

Italian Three-Cheese Macaroni

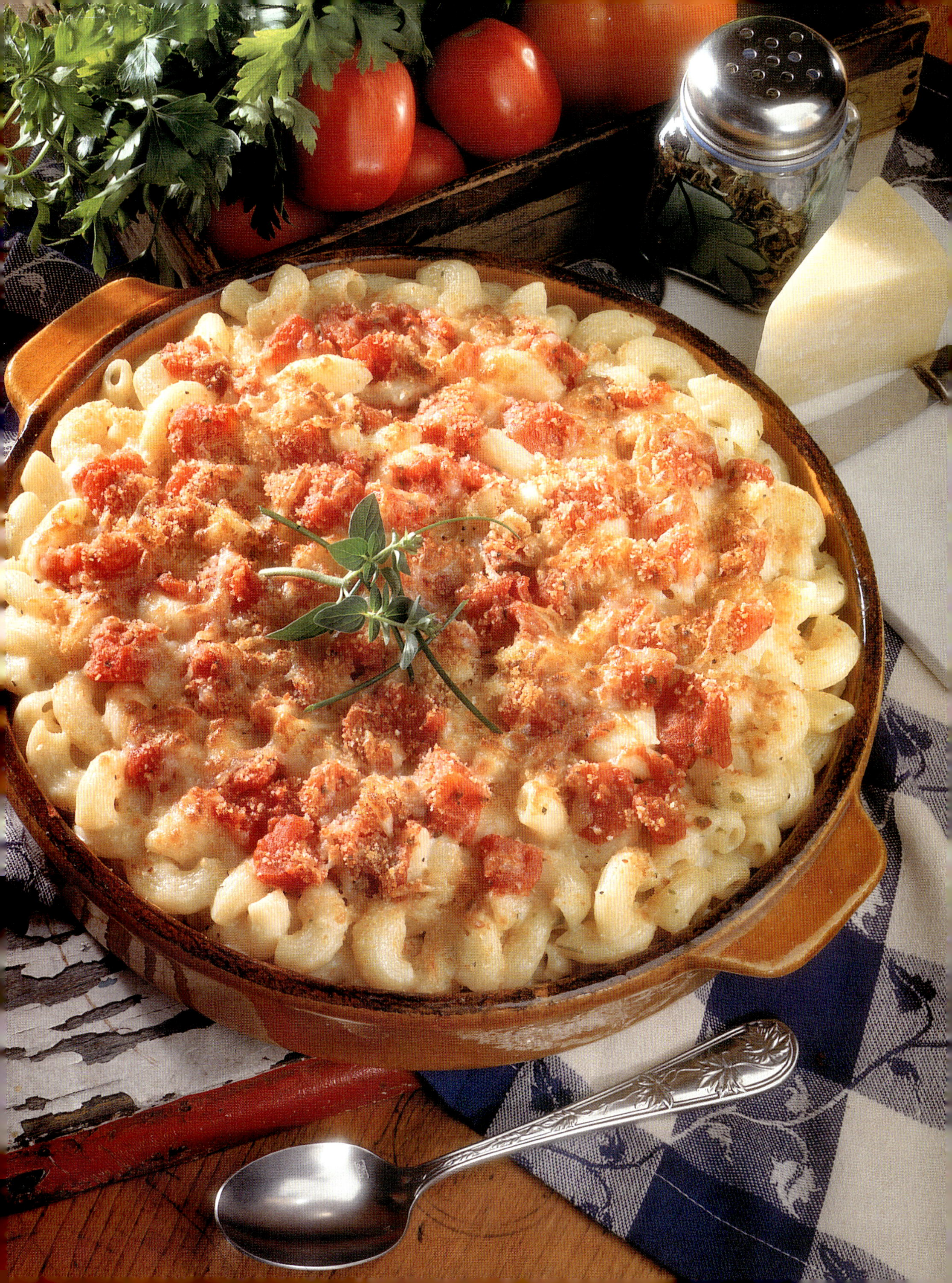

OUT OF THE OVEN

62 LEMONY DILL SALMON AND SHELL CASSEROLE

- 6 ounces uncooked medium shell pasta
- Nonstick cooking spray
- 1½ cups sliced mushrooms
- ⅓ cup sliced green onions
- 1 clove garlic, minced
- 2 cups skim milk
- 3 tablespoons all-purpose flour
- 1 tablespoon grated lemon peel
- ¾ teaspoon dried dill weed
- ¼ teaspoon salt
- ⅛ teaspoon ground black pepper
- 1½ cups frozen green peas
- 1 can (7½ ounces) salmon, drained and flaked

1. Preheat oven to 350°F. Cook pasta according to package directions, omitting salt. Rinse; drain. Set aside.

2. Spray medium nonstick saucepan with cooking spray; heat over medium heat until hot. Add mushrooms, onions and garlic; cook and stir 5 minutes or until vegetables are tender.

3. Combine milk and flour in medium bowl until smooth. Stir in lemon peel, dill weed, salt and pepper. Stir into saucepan; heat over medium-high heat 5 to 8 minutes or until thickened, stirring constantly. Remove saucepan from heat. Stir in pasta, peas and salmon. Pour pasta mixture into 2-quart casserole.

4. Bake, covered, 35 to 40 minutes. Serve immediately. Garnish as desired.

Makes 6 servings

63 WISCONSIN CHEESE PASTA CASSEROLE

- 1 pound spaghetti or fettuccine, broken into 3-inch pieces
- 1 quart prepared spaghetti sauce
- ½ cup plus ⅓ cup (2½ ounces) grated Wisconsin Romano cheese, divided
- 1¾ cups (7 ounces) sliced or shredded Wisconsin Colby cheese
- 1½ cups (6 ounces) shredded Wisconsin Mozzarella cheese

Prepare pasta according to package directions; drain. Toss warm pasta with prepared spaghetti sauce to coat. Add ½ cup Romano cheese to mixture and mix well. Spread half of sauced pasta onto bottom of 13×9×2-inch baking dish. Top with 1 cup Colby cheese. Spread remaining pasta over cheese. Top with remaining ¾ cup Colby cheese. Sprinkle with remaining ⅓ cup Romano cheese and Mozzarella cheese. Bake at 350°F for 35 to 40 minutes or until top is lightly browned and casserole is bubbly. Remove from heat and let stand at least 10 minutes before serving.

Makes 6 to 8 servings

Favorite recipe from **Wisconsin Milk Marketing Board**

Lemony Dill Salmon and Shell Casserole

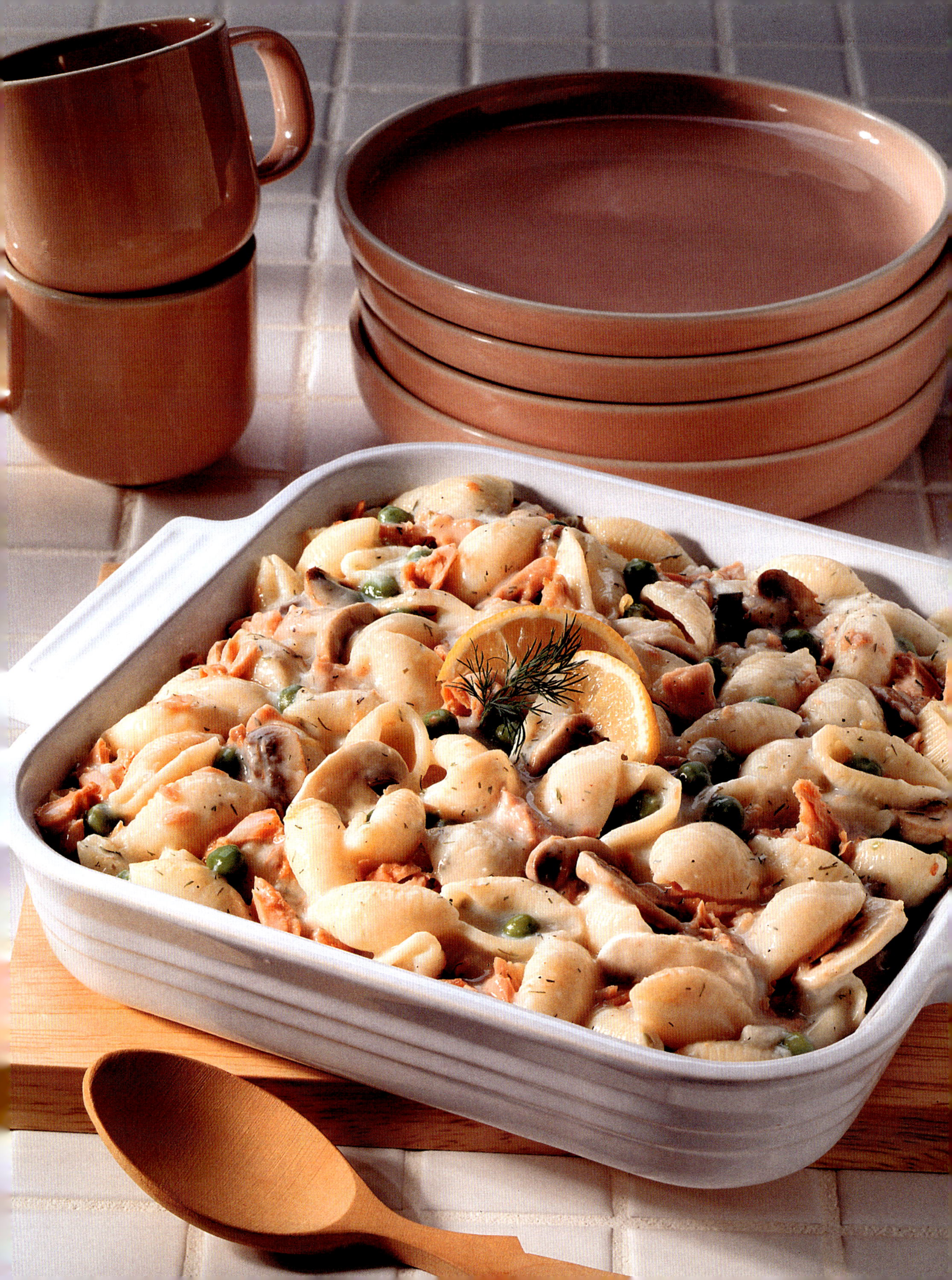

OUT OF THE OVEN

64 APPLE LASAGNA

- 8 lasagna noodles
- 2 cups (8 ounces) shredded Cheddar cheese
- 1 cup ricotta cheese
- 1 egg, lightly beaten
- ¼ cup granulated sugar
- 1 teaspoon almond extract
- 2 cans (20 ounces each) apple pie filling
- 6 tablespoons all-purpose flour
- ⅓ cup plus 6 tablespoons packed brown sugar, divided
- ¼ cup quick-cooking oats
- ½ teaspoon ground cinnamon
- Dash ground nutmeg
- 3 tablespoons margarine
- 1 cup sour cream

1. Cook lasagna noodles according to package directions; drain.

2. Preheat oven to 350°F. Grease 13×9-inch baking pan.

3. Combine Cheddar cheese, ricotta cheese, egg, granulated sugar and almond extract in medium bowl; blend well.

4. Spread 1 can apple pie filling on bottom of prepared pan. Layer half the noodles over filling, then spread cheese mixture over noodles. Top with remaining noodles, then remaining can of apple pie filling.

5. Combine flour, 6 tablespoons brown sugar, oats, cinnamon and nutmeg in small bowl. Cut in margarine with pastry blender or 2 knives until crumbly. Sprinkle over apple pie filling.

6. Bake lasagna 45 minutes. Cool 15 minutes.

7. Meanwhile, prepare garnish by blending sour cream and remaining ⅓ cup brown sugar in small bowl until smooth. Cover; refrigerate.

8. To serve, cut lasagna into squares and garnish with sour cream mixture.

Makes 12 to 15 servings

65 MANICOTTI ALLA PERDUE

- 2 cups finely chopped cooked PERDUE® Chicken or Turkey
- 1 container (15 ounces) ricotta cheese
- 1 egg, lightly beaten
- 1 package (10 ounces) frozen chopped spinach, thawed and well drained
- ¼ cup grated Parmesan cheese
- ½ teaspoon ground nutmeg
- 3 cups marinara or spaghetti sauce, divided
- 1 package (8 ounces) manicotti shells, cooked
- ½ to ¾ cup shredded mozzarella cheese

Preheat oven to 350°F. In medium bowl, combine first 6 ingredients. Into 12×9-inch baking pan, spoon a thin layer of marinara sauce. Fill manicotti shells with chicken or turkey mixture and arrange over sauce. Pour remaining sauce on top; sprinkle with mozzarella. Bake 25 to 30 minutes until hot and bubbly.

Makes 4 to 6 servings

Apple Lasagna

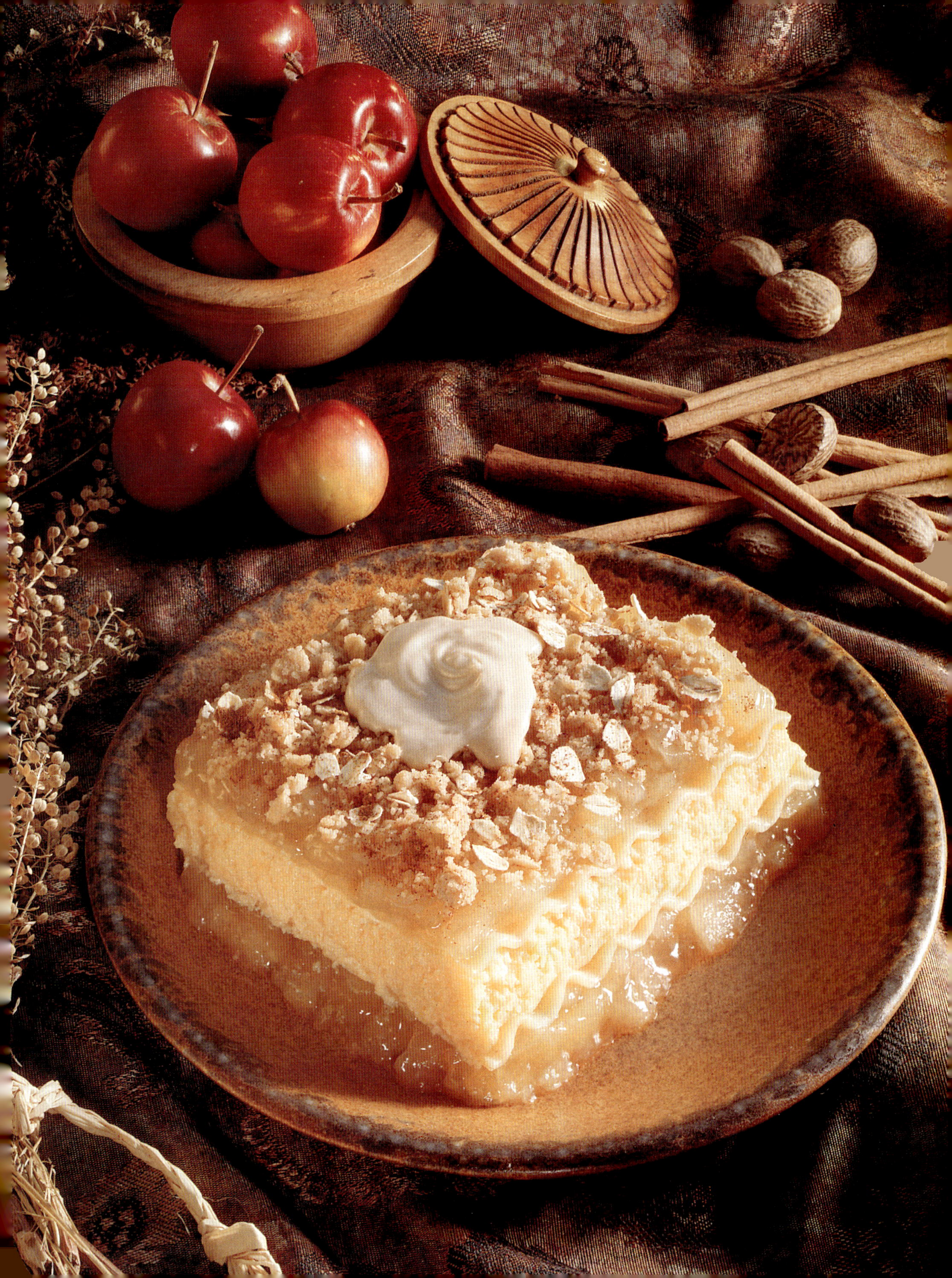

OUT OF THE OVEN

66 CHILI WAGON WHEEL CASSEROLE

- 8 ounces uncooked wagon wheel or other pasta
- 1 pound lean ground sirloin or ground turkey breast
- ¾ cup chopped green bell pepper
- ¾ cup chopped onion
- 1 can (14½ ounces) no-salt-added stewed tomatoes
- 1 can (8 ounces) no-salt-added tomato sauce
- ½ teaspoon ground black pepper
- ¼ teaspoon ground allspice
- ½ cup (2 ounces) shredded reduced-fat Cheddar cheese

1. Preheat oven to 350°F. Cook pasta according to package directions, omitting salt. Drain and rinse; set aside.

2. Spray large nonstick skillet with nonstick cooking spray. Add ground sirloin, bell pepper and onion; cook 5 minutes or until meat is no longer pink, stirring frequently. (Drain mixture if using ground sirloin.)

3. Stir in tomatoes, tomato sauce, black pepper and allspice; cook 2 minutes. Stir in pasta. Spoon mixture into 2½-quart casserole. Sprinkle with cheese.

4. Bake 20 to 25 minutes or until heated through. *Makes 6 servings*

67 PESTO LASAGNA ROLLS

- 2 cups fresh basil leaves
- 2 cloves garlic
- 1 cup (3 ounces) SARGENTO® Fancy Shredded Parmesan Cheese, divided
- ¾ cup olive oil
- 1 container (15 ounces) SARGENTO® Ricotta Cheese*
- 1 cup (4 ounces) SARGENTO® Light Fancy Shredded Mozzarella Cheese
- 1 egg, beaten
- 1 cup diced zucchini
- 16 lasagna noodles, cooked, drained and cooled

*SARGENTO® Part-Skim Ricotta or Lite Ricotta can also be used.

Prepare pesto sauce in covered blender or food processor by processing basil with garlic until chopped. Add ½ cup Parmesan cheese; process until well mixed. With machine running, slowly add oil and continue processing until smooth. Set aside. In medium bowl, combine ricotta and mozzarella cheeses, remaining ½ cup Parmesan cheese and egg; blend well. Fold in zucchini. Spread 2 heaping tablespoons cheese mixture on each lasagna noodle. Roll up each noodle lengthwise and stand vertically in greased 11×7-inch baking dish. Pour pesto sauce over lasagna rolls; cover and bake in preheated 350°F oven 40 minutes or until bubbly and heated through. *Makes 8 servings*

Chili Wagon Wheel Casserole

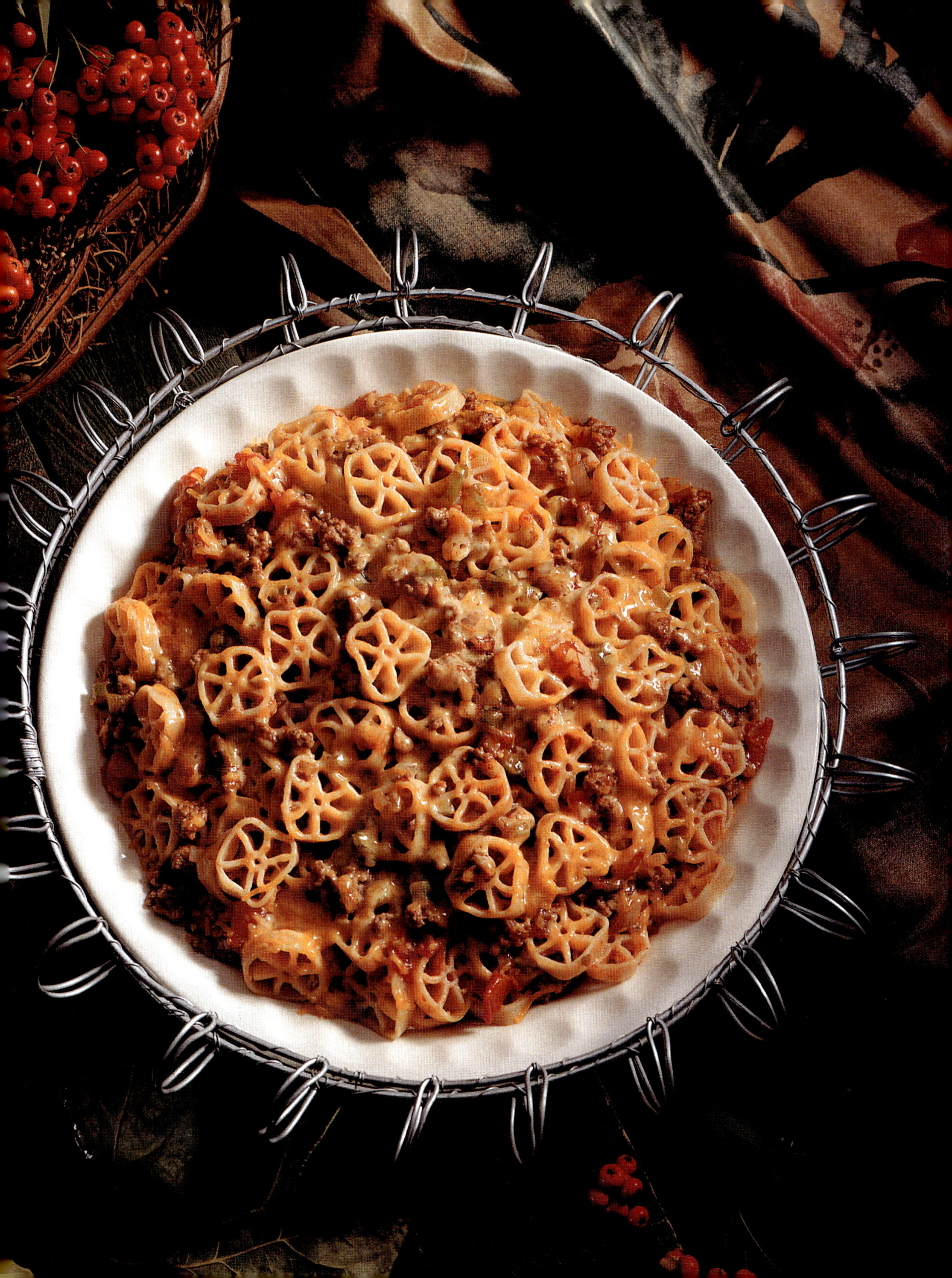

365 Favorite Brand Name Pasta Recipes

OUT OF THE OVEN

68 CHICKEN MARSALA

- 4 cups (6 ounces) uncooked broad egg noodles
- ½ cup Italian-style dry bread crumbs
- 1 teaspoon dried basil leaves
- 1 egg
- 1 teaspoon water
- 4 boneless skinless chicken breast halves
- 3 tablespoons olive oil, divided
- ¾ cup chopped onion
- 8 ounces cremini or button mushrooms, sliced
- 3 cloves garlic, minced
- 3 tablespoons all-purpose flour
- 1 can (14½ ounces) chicken broth
- ½ cup dry marsala wine
- ¾ teaspoon salt
- ¼ teaspoon black pepper
- Chopped fresh parsley (optional)

PREHEAT oven to 375°F. Spray 11×7-inch baking dish with nonstick cooking spray.

COOK noodles according to package directions until *al dente.* Drain and place in prepared dish.

Meanwhile, COMBINE bread crumbs and basil on shallow plate or pie plate. Beat egg with water on another shallow plate or pie plate. Dip chicken in egg mixture, letting excess drip off. Roll in crumb mixture, patting to coat.

HEAT 2 tablespoons oil in large skillet over medium-high heat until hot. Cook chicken 3 minutes per side or until browned. Transfer to clean plate; set aside.

HEAT remaining 1 tablespoon oil in same skillet over medium heat. Add onion; cook and stir 5 minutes. Add mushrooms and garlic; cook and stir 3 minutes. Sprinkle flour over onion mixture; cook and stir 1 minute. Add broth, wine, salt and pepper; bring to a boil over high heat. Cook and stir 5 minutes or until sauce thickens. Reserve ½ cup sauce. Pour remaining sauce over noodles; stir until noodles are well coated. Place chicken on top of noodles. Spoon reserved sauce over chicken.

BAKE, uncovered, 20 minutes or until chicken is no longer pink in centers, juices run clear and sauce is hot and bubbly. Sprinkle with parsley, if desired.

Makes 4 servings

69 ZUCCHINI PASTA BAKE

- 1½ cups uncooked pasta tubes
- ½ pound ground beef
- ½ cup chopped onion
- 1 clove garlic, minced
- Salt and black pepper
- 1 teaspoon dried basil, crushed
- 1 can (14½ ounces) DEL MONTE® FreshCut™ Zucchini with Italian-Style Tomato Sauce
- 1 cup (4 ounces) shredded Monterey Jack cheese

Cook pasta according to package directions; drain. In large skillet, cook beef with onion and garlic; drain. Season with salt and pepper. Stir in basil and zucchini with tomato sauce. Place pasta in 8-inch square baking dish. Top with meat mixture. Bake at 350°F for 15 minutes. Top with cheese. Bake 3 minutes or until cheese is melted.

Makes 4 servings

Prep and Cook time: 33 minutes

Chicken Marsala

64

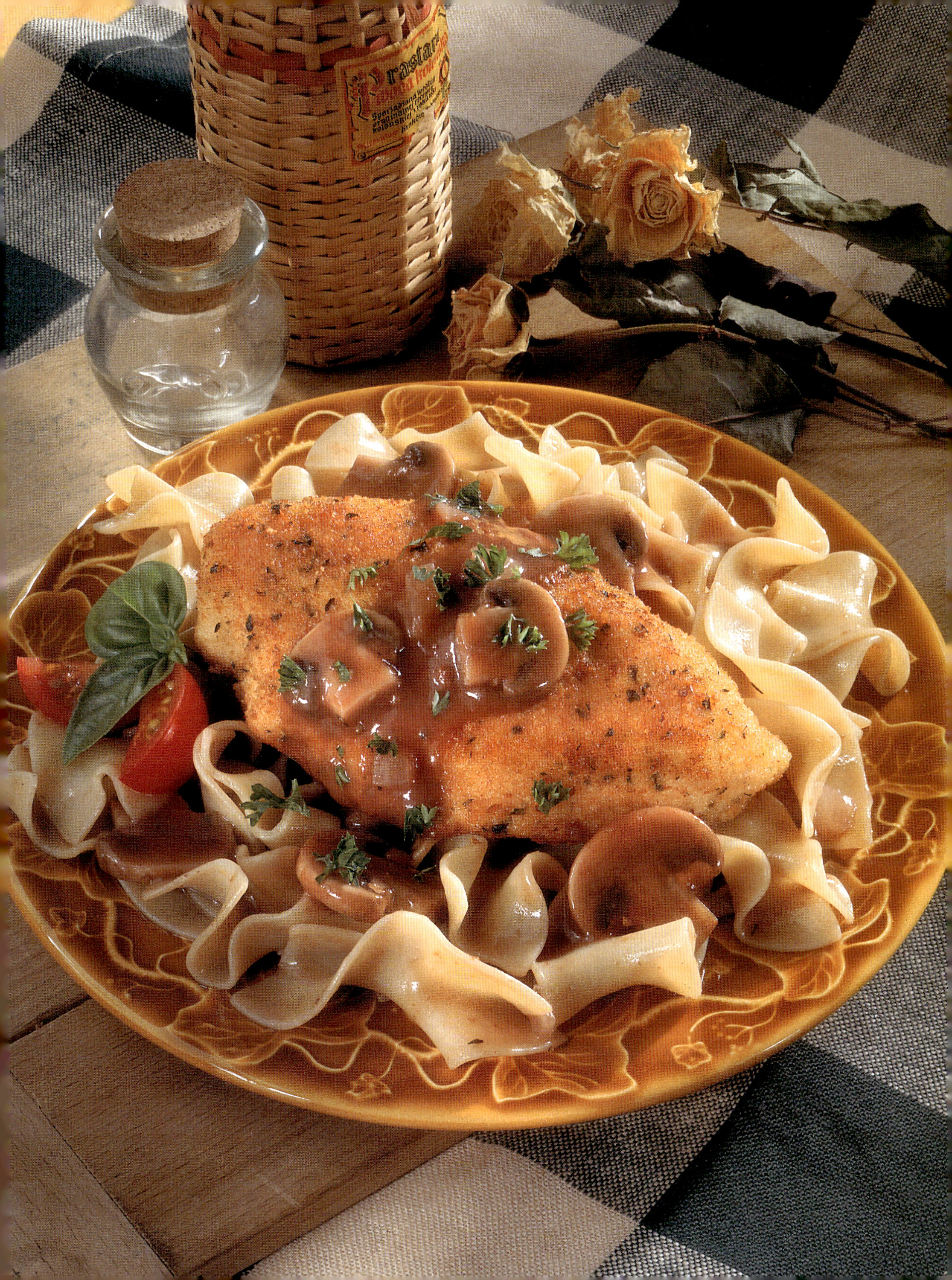

365 Favorite Brand Name Pasta Recipes

OUT OF THE OVEN

70 SPICY MANICOTTI

- 3 cups ricotta cheese
- 1 cup grated Parmesan cheese, divided
- 2 eggs, beaten lightly
- 2½ tablespoons chopped fresh parsley
- 1 teaspoon dried Italian seasoning
- ½ teaspoon garlic powder
- ½ teaspoon salt
- ½ teaspoon black pepper
- 1 pound spicy Italian sausage
- 1 can (28 ounces) crushed tomatoes in purée, undrained
- 1 jar (26 ounces) marinara or spaghetti sauce
- 8 ounces uncooked manicotti shells

PREHEAT oven to 375°F. Spray 13×9-inch baking dish with nonstick cooking spray.

COMBINE ricotta cheese, ¾ cup Parmesan cheese, eggs, parsley, Italian seasoning, garlic powder, salt and pepper in medium bowl; set aside.

CRUMBLE sausage into large skillet; brown over medium-high heat until no longer pink, stirring to separate sausage. Drain sausage on paper towels; drain fat from skillet.

ADD tomatoes with juice and marinara sauce to same skillet; bring to a boil over high heat. Reduce heat to low; simmer, uncovered, 10 minutes. Pour about one third of sauce into prepared dish.

STUFF each uncooked shell with about ½ cup cheese mixture. Place in dish. Top shells with sausage; pour remaining sauce over shells.

COVER tightly with foil and bake 50 minutes to 1 hour or until noodles are cooked. Let stand 5 minutes before serving. Serve with remaining ¼ cup Parmesan cheese.

Makes 8 servings

71 MACARONI ITALIANO

- 1 tablespoon salt
- 8 ounces elbow macaroni
- 2 cups (16 ounces) canned tomatoes, undrained
- ½ teaspoon low-sodium baking soda
- 1 cup (8 ounces) canned tomato sauce
- 1¼ cups low-fat cottage cheese, at room temperature
- ¼ cup grated Parmesan cheese
- 1 (10-ounce) package frozen chopped spinach, thawed and squeezed dry
- 1½ cups frozen peas, thawed
- 1 teaspoon dried basil leaves
- ½ teaspoon black pepper
- ¾ cup chopped toasted* California walnuts
- 2 tablespoons chopped fresh parsley

Toasting is optional.

Bring about 6 quarts of water to a boil with 1 tablespoon salt. Add macaroni and cook, stirring occasionally, for about 8 minutes, or until done.

While macaroni is cooking, place tomatoes with juice into large bowl. Add baking soda; with fork or fingers, break tomatoes into small chunks. Stir in tomato sauce. Add cottage cheese, Parmesan cheese, spinach, peas, basil and pepper; toss to combine and set aside. When macaroni is done, drain well. Add to cheese mixture, toss to mix thoroughly; pour mixture into oiled 2½-quart baking dish.

Preheat oven to 350°F. Cover baking dish with foil and bake casserole for 20 minutes; uncover and bake 10 minutes more. Stir in walnuts and sprinkle with parsley.

Makes 6 servings

Favorite recipe from **Walnut Marketing Board**

Spicy Manicotti

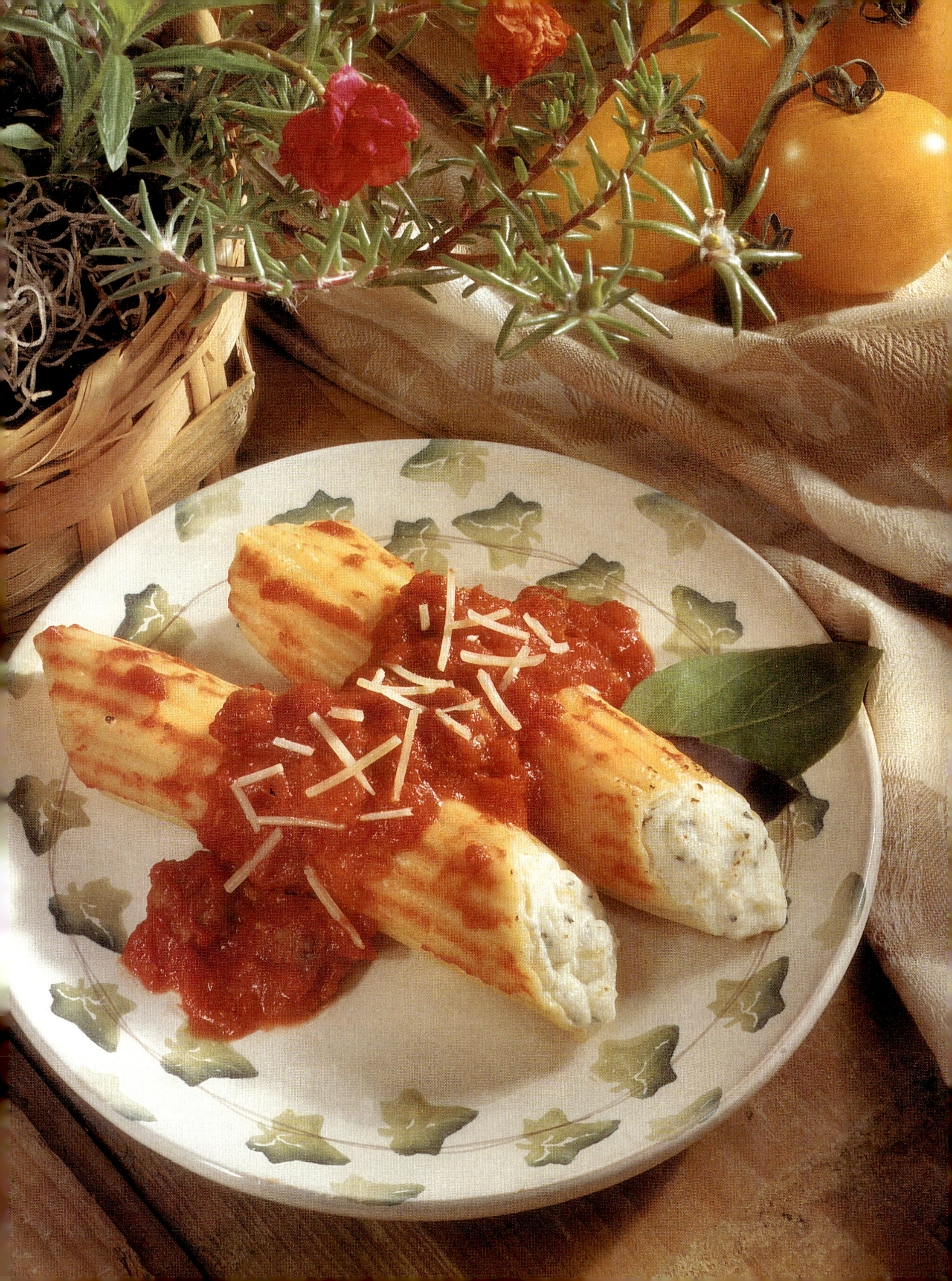

OUT OF THE OVEN

72 SKATE NOODLE CASSEROLE

12 ounces egg noodles
1½ cups low-fat milk
1 can (12 ounces) evaporated skimmed milk
1 cup chopped onion
½ teaspoon salt
¼ teaspoon black pepper
¼ teaspoon hot pepper sauce
1 pound pan-ready skate fillets, cut into 1½-inch squares
¼ cup butter or margarine, divided
2 tablespoons olive oil
1 pound fresh mushrooms, sliced
⅓ cup all-purpose flour
⅓ cup sherry
1 cup fresh bread crumbs or crushed buttery crackers
Finely snipped fresh parsley for garnish

Cook noodles in boiling salted water; drain and set aside while preparing sauce. In 3-quart saucepan, combine milk, evaporated milk, onion, salt, pepper and pepper sauce. Simmer 10 minutes, stirring occasionally. Add skate; simmer 3 more minutes. Remove pan from heat; set aside.

In large skillet, heat 3 tablespoons butter and oil; sauté mushrooms until lightly browned. Stir in flour and remove pan from heat. Using strainer, add milk mixture used to cook skate. Stir thoroughly, return skillet to heat and cook until sauce is thickened. Stir in sherry.

In large bowl, combine mushroom sauce with noodles, skate and onion. Place in large casserole dish or in individual, ovenproof au gratin dishes.

Combine remaining 1 tablespoon butter, softened or melted, with crumbs; sprinkle over casserole. Bake uncovered at 350°F for 20 to 25 minutes or until topping is golden brown and sauce is bubbly. Garnish with parsley and serve.

Makes 6 to 7 servings

Favorite recipe from **Surimi Seafood Education Center**

73 ITALIAN ANTIPASTO BAKE

2 cups rotini or elbow macaroni, cooked in unsalted water and drained
1 bag (16 ounces) frozen vegetable combination (broccoli, water chestnuts, red bell pepper), thawed and drained
2 chicken breast halves, skinned, boned and cut into strips
⅔ cup bottled Italian salad dressing
½ cup drained garbanzo beans (optional)
¼ cup sliced pitted ripe olives (optional)
¼ cup (1 ounce) grated Parmesan cheese
½ teaspoon Italian seasoning
1 cup (4 ounces) shredded mozzarella cheese, divided
1⅓ cups (2.8-ounce can) FRENCH'S® French Fried Onions, divided

Preheat oven to 350°F. In 13×9-inch baking dish, combine hot pasta, vegetables, chicken, salad dressing, garbanzo beans, olives, Parmesan cheese and Italian seasoning. Stir in ½ cup mozzarella cheese and ⅔ cup French Fried Onions. Bake, covered, for 35 minutes or until chicken is done. Top with remaining mozzarella cheese and ⅔ cup onions; bake, uncovered, 5 minutes or until onions are golden brown.

Makes 4 to 6 servings

OUT OF THE OVEN

MICROWAVE DIRECTIONS: In 12×8-inch microwave-safe dish, combine ingredients, except chicken strips, as above. Arrange uncooked chicken strips around edges of dish. Cook, covered, at HIGH 6 minutes. Stir center of casserole; rearrange chicken and rotate dish. Cook, covered, 5 to 6 minutes or until chicken is done. Stir casserole to combine chicken and pasta mixture. Top with remaining mozzarella cheese and onions; cook, uncovered, 1 minute or until cheese melts. Let stand 5 minutes.

74 SEAFOOD LASAGNA WITH SPAGHETTI SQUASH AND BROCCOLI

- 1 tablespoon olive oil
- 1 cup minced shallots
- 16 small mushrooms, cut into halves
- 1 tablespoon minced garlic (2 to 4 cloves)
- 1 teaspoon dried thyme leaves
- 3 tablespoons all-purpose flour
- 2 cups dry white wine or chicken broth
- 1 cup bottled clam juice
- ¼ teaspoon freshly ground nutmeg
- Ground black pepper to taste
- 1½ pounds cooked seafood mixture of firm-textured fish (such as salmon) and scallops, cut into bite-size pieces, divided
- 6 lasagna noodles, cooked and drained
- 4 ounces (1½ to 2 cups) stuffing mix
- 1 (10-ounce) package frozen chopped broccoli, thawed
- 1 pound JARLSBERG LITE Cheese, shredded
- 3 cups cooked spaghetti squash

Heat oil in large skillet over medium-high heat. Sauté shallots, mushrooms, garlic and thyme in oil 4 minutes or until shallots begin to brown. Add flour; cook, stirring constantly, 2 to 3 minutes. Add wine, clam juice, nutmeg and pepper. Boil 3 minutes to thicken and reduce liquid. Add fish pieces and simmer 3 minutes. Add scallops; remove skillet from heat and set aside.

Arrange 3 lasagna noodles on bottom of 3½-quart, rectangular baking dish. Evenly sprinkle with stuffing mix. Reserve 1 cup sauce mixture; spoon remaining sauce mixture over stuffing mix. Cover evenly with broccoli, ⅔ of cheese and 2 cups spaghetti squash. Cover with remaining lasagna noodles, cheese, reserved sauce mixture and remaining spaghetti squash. Press down firmly.* Cover tightly with tented foil and bake at 350°F, 45 to 50 minutes or until heated through.

Makes 10 to 12 servings

*Recipe can be made ahead up to this point and refrigerated. Bring to room temperature before baking.

TIP: To cook spaghetti squash, pierce in several places and place on baking sheet in 350°F oven for 1 hour or until tender when pierced with knife. When squash is cool, cut in half, scoop out seeds and remove strands with two forks. Squash may be prepared ahead and refrigerated until needed.

Favorite recipe from **Norseland, Inc.**

OUT OF THE OVEN

75 LAMB AND SPINACH MANICOTTI

SAUCE
- 1½ pounds ground American lamb
- 1 small onion, chopped
- 1 (16-ounce) jar prepared tomato sauce
- ½ teaspoon salt
- ¼ teaspoon black pepper

STUFFING
- 1 tablespoon butter or margarine
- 1 large onion, finely chopped
- 2 cloves garlic, minced
- 2 (10-ounce) packages frozen chopped spinach, thawed and drained
- 2 eggs, lightly beaten
- ½ teaspoon salt
- 1 teaspoon dried oregano leaves
- ½ teaspoon chopped fresh basil leaves
- 1 cup ricotta cheese

- 1 (5-ounce) package manicotti pasta, cooked and cooled
- 1 cup shredded Monterey Jack cheese
- ½ cup grated Parmesan cheese

To make sauce, brown lamb and onion in medium saucepan. Drain well. Add tomato sauce, salt and pepper. Simmer 15 to 20 minutes.

To make stuffing, melt butter in skillet. Add onion and garlic; cook, stirring constantly, until onion is transparent. Add spinach; cook until moisture has evaporated. Remove from heat.

Add eggs, salt, oregano, basil and ricotta. Stuff pasta. Pour thin layer of sauce into a large baking dish. Arrange stuffed manicotti on sauce. Top with remaining sauce. Cover with Monterey Jack and Parmesan cheeses.

Bake, uncovered, at 350°F for 25 to 30 minutes, or until bubbly and heated throughout. *Makes 8 servings*

Favorite recipe from **American Lamb Council**

76 ARTICHOKE–OLIVE CHICKEN BAKE

- 1½ cups uncooked rotini
- 1 tablespoon olive oil
- 1 medium onion, chopped
- ½ green bell pepper, chopped
- 2 cups shredded cooked chicken
- 1 can (14½ ounces) diced tomatoes with Italian-style herbs, undrained
- 1 can (14 ounces) artichoke hearts, drained and quartered
- 1 can (6 ounces) sliced black olives, drained
- 1 teaspoon dried Italian seasoning
- 2 cups (8 ounces) shredded mozzarella cheese
- Fresh basil sprig (optional)

PREHEAT oven to 350°F. Spray 13×9-inch baking dish with nonstick cooking spray.

COOK pasta according to package directions until *al dente.* Drain and set aside.

Meanwhile, HEAT oil in large deep skillet over medium heat until hot. Add onion and pepper; cook and stir 1 minute. Add chicken, tomatoes with juice, pasta, artichokes, olives and Italian seasoning; mix until combined.

PLACE half of chicken mixture in prepared dish; sprinkle with half of cheese. Top with remaining chicken mixture and cheese.

BAKE, covered, 35 minutes or until hot and bubbly. Garnish with basil, if desired.

Makes 8 servings

Artichoke-Olive Chicken Bake

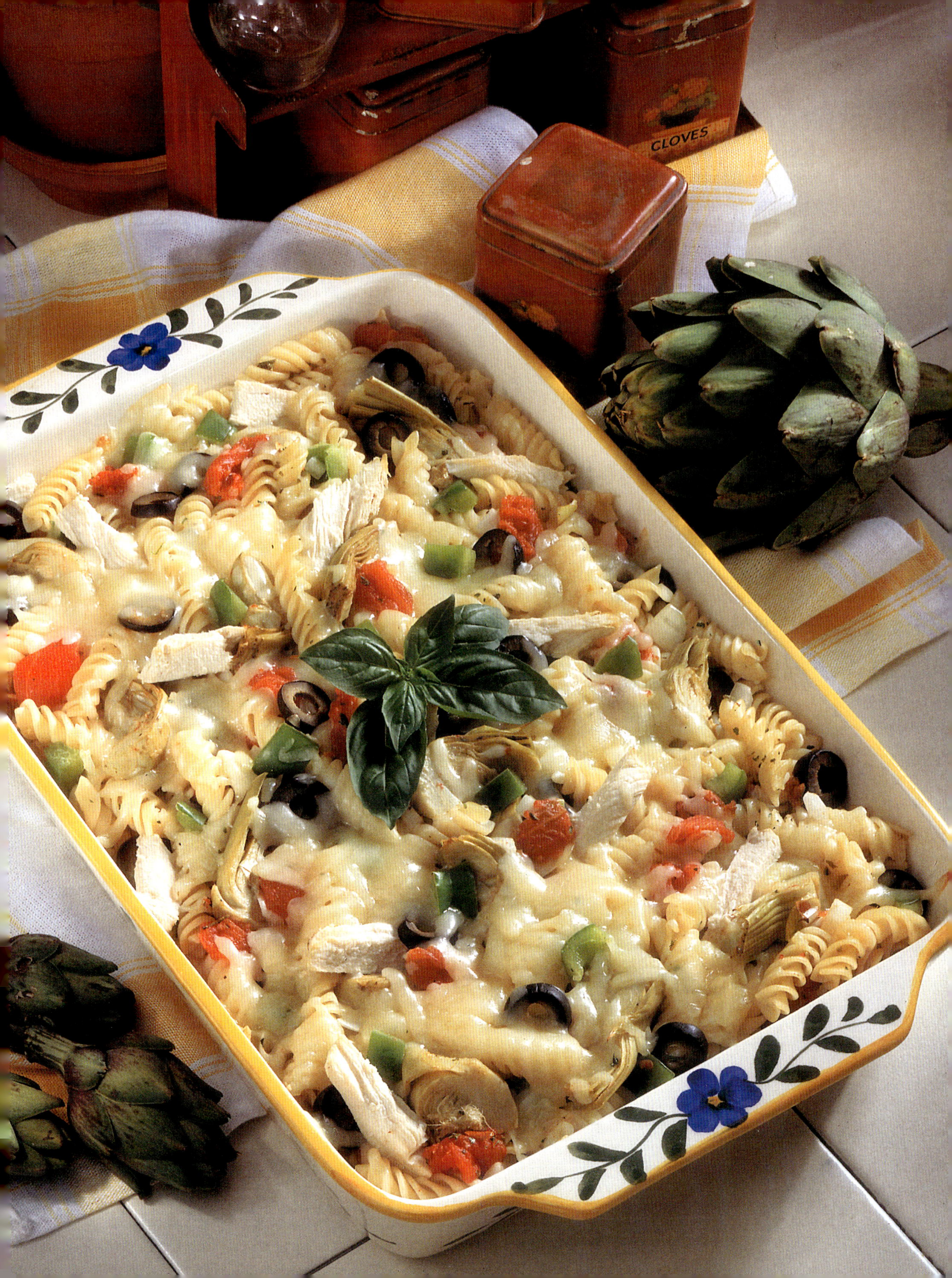
CLOVES

77 SEAFOOD LASAGNA

- 1 package (16 ounces) lasagna noodles
- ½ pound flounder fillets
- ½ pound bay scallops
- 2 tablespoons margarine or butter
- 1 large onion, finely chopped
- 1 package (8 ounces) cream cheese, cut into ½-inch pieces, at room temperature
- 1½ cups cream-style cottage cheese
- 2 teaspoons dried basil leaves
- ½ teaspoon salt
- ⅛ teaspoon black pepper
- 1 egg, lightly beaten
- 2 cans (10¾ ounces each) cream of mushroom soup
- ⅓ cup milk
- 1 clove garlic, minced
- ½ pound medium raw shrimp, peeled and deveined
- ½ cup dry white wine
- 1 cup (4 ounces) shredded mozzarella cheese
- 2 tablespoons grated Parmesan cheese

1. Cook lasagna noodles according to package directions; drain.

2. Rinse flounder and scallops. Pat dry with paper towels. Cut flounder into ½-inch cubes.

3. Melt margarine in large skillet over medium heat. Cook onion in hot margarine until tender, stirring frequently. Stir in cream cheese, cottage cheese, basil, salt and pepper; mix well. Stir in egg; set aside.

4. Combine soup, milk and garlic in large bowl until well blended. Stir in flounder, scallops, shrimp and wine.

5. Preheat oven to 350°F. Grease 13×9-inch baking pan.

6. Place layer of noodles in prepared pan, overlapping the noodles. Spread half the cheese mixture over noodles. Place a layer of noodles over cheese mixture and top with half the seafood mixture. Repeat layers. Sprinkle with mozzarella and Parmesan cheeses.

7. Bake 45 minutes or until bubbly. Let stand 10 minutes before cutting.

Makes 8 to 10 servings

Seafood Lasagna

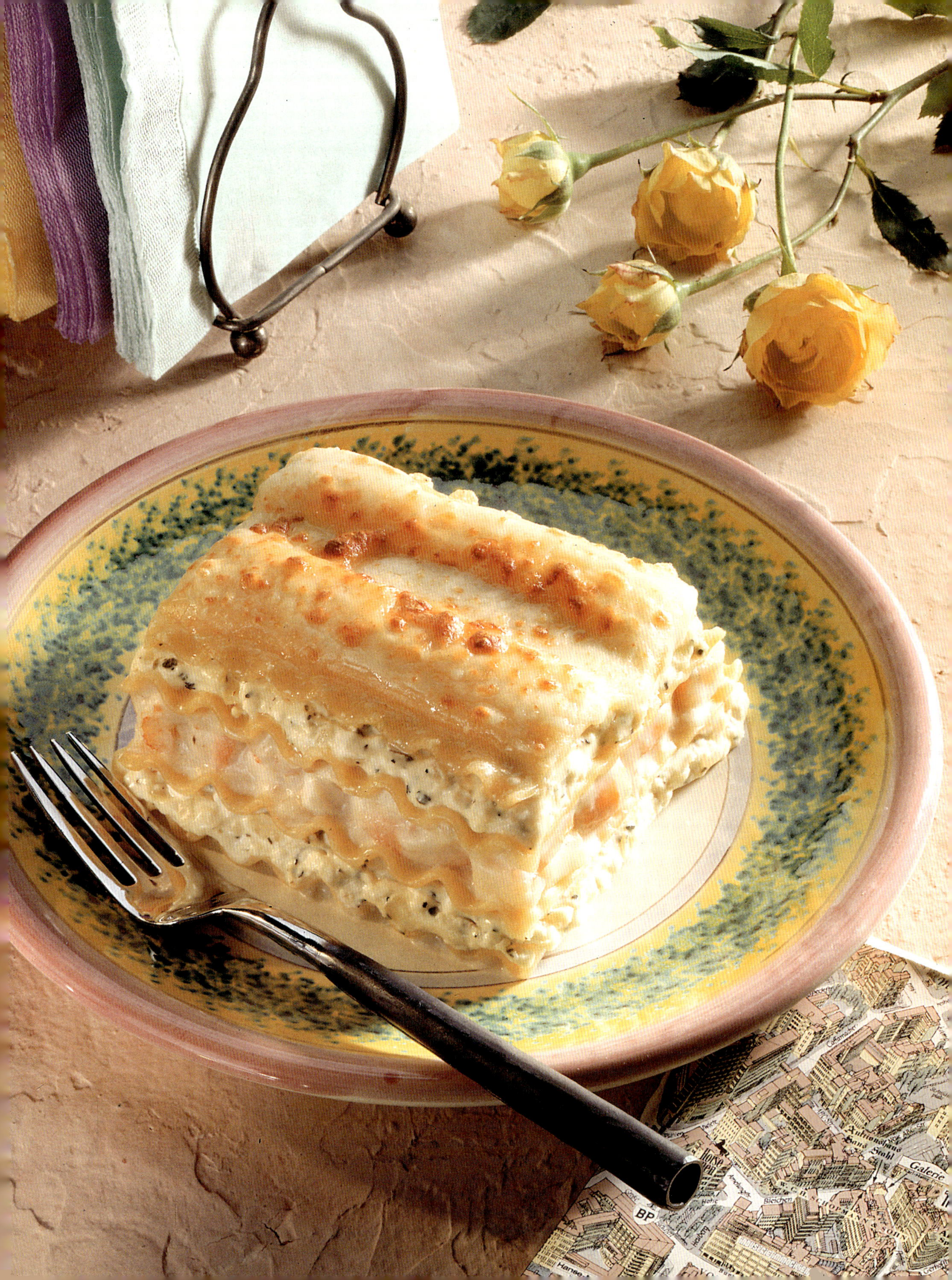
Galerie
BP

365 Favorite Brand Name Pasta Recipes

OUT OF THE OVEN

78 MANICOTTI FLORENTINE

- 1 package (10 ounces) frozen chopped spinach
- ½ cup chopped onion
- 1 clove garlic, minced
- ½ cup QUAKER® Oat Bran hot cereal, uncooked
- ½ cup low-fat cottage cheese
- 2 teaspoons dried basil leaves, crumbled, divided
- ½ teaspoon dried oregano leaves, crumbled
- 8 manicotti noodles, uncooked
- 2 cans (8 ounces each) low-sodium tomato sauce, divided
- ¼ cup (1 ounce) shredded part-skim mozzarella cheese

Heat oven to 375°F. Cook spinach according to package directions with onion and garlic. Cool slightly; drain. Stir in oat bran, cottage cheese, 1 teaspoon basil and oregano; set aside. Cook manicotti in boiling water 4 minutes; drain.

Spread 1½ cans tomato sauce on bottom of 11×7-inch baking dish. Stuff each manicotti with about 3 tablespoons spinach mixture; arrange in baking dish. Pour remaining ½ can sauce over manicotti. Sprinkle with remaining 1 teaspoon basil. Top with mozzarella cheese. Cover; bake 25 to 30 minutes or until bubbly.

Makes 4 servings

MICROWAVE DIRECTIONS: Prepare as directed; place in 11×7-inch microwavable dish. Do not top manicotti with cheese. Cover with plastic wrap; vent. Microwave at HIGH 4 minutes. Remove plastic wrap; top with mozzarella cheese. Microwave at HIGH 2 to 3 minutes or until cheese is melted.

79 SPINACH–CHEESE PASTA CASSEROLE

- 8 ounces uncooked pasta shells
- 2 eggs
- 1 cup ricotta cheese
- 1 jar (26 ounces) marinara sauce
- 1 teaspoon salt
- 1 package (10 ounces) frozen chopped spinach, thawed and squeezed dry
- 1 cup (4 ounces) shredded mozzarella cheese
- ¼ cup grated Parmesan cheese

PREHEAT oven to 350°F. Spray 1½-quart round casserole with nonstick cooking spray.

COOK pasta according to package directions until *al dente*. Drain.

Meanwhile, WHISK eggs in large bowl until blended. Add ricotta cheese; stir until combined. Stir pasta, marinara sauce and salt in large bowl until pasta is well coated. Pour pasta mixture into prepared dish. Top with ricotta mixture and spinach. Sprinkle mozzarella and Parmesan cheeses evenly over casserole.

BAKE, covered, 30 minutes. Uncover and bake 15 minutes or until hot and bubbly.

Makes 6 to 8 servings

Spinach-Cheese Pasta Casserole

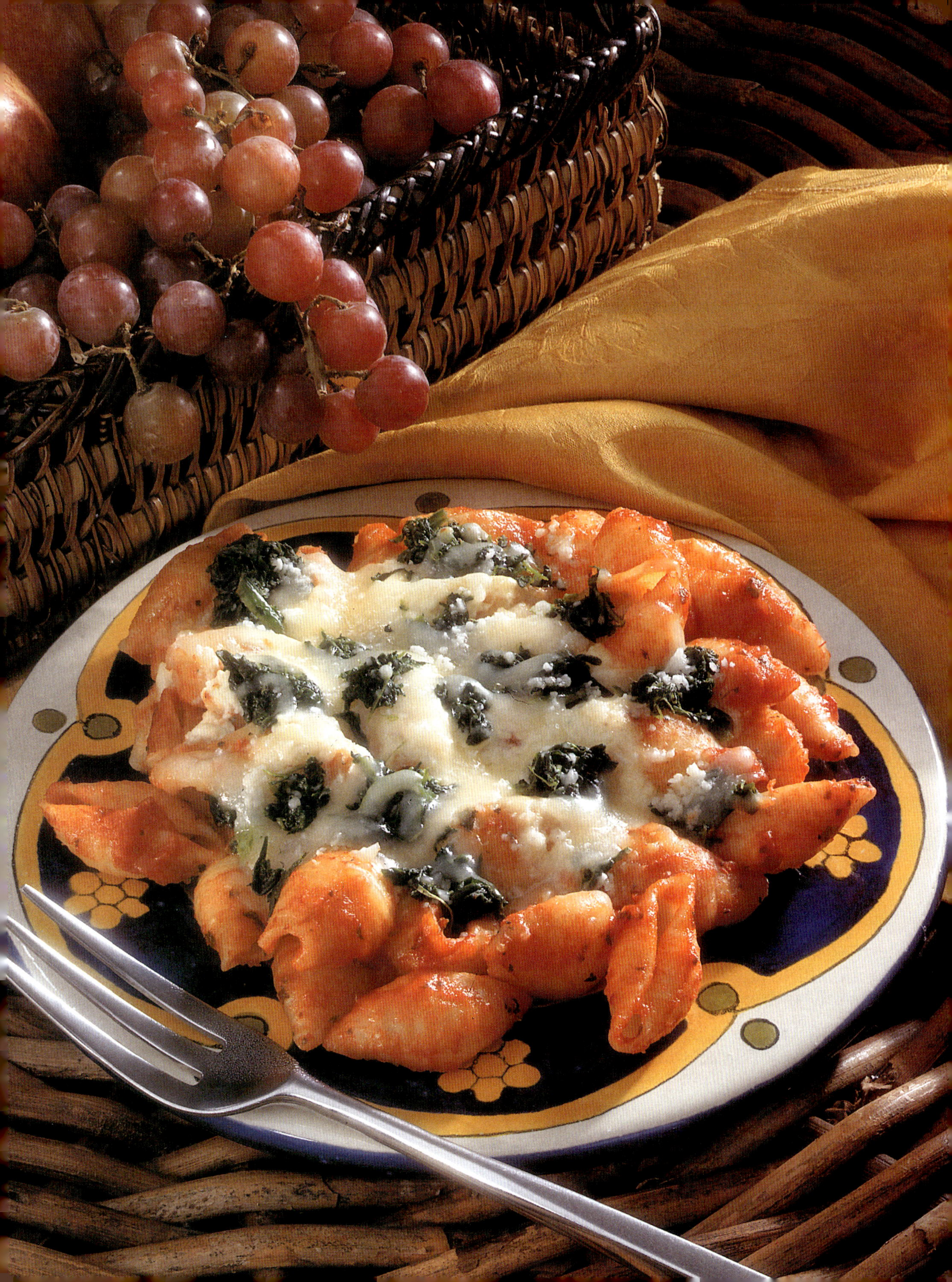

OUT OF THE OVEN

80 PASTA WITH SALMON AND DILL

- 6 ounces uncooked mafalda pasta
- 1 tablespoon olive oil
- 2 ribs celery, sliced
- 1 small red onion, chopped
- 1 can (10¾ ounces) condensed cream of celery soup, undiluted
- ¼ cup reduced-fat mayonnaise
- ¼ cup dry white wine
- 3 tablespoons chopped fresh parsley
- 1 teaspoon dried dill weed
- 1 can (7½ ounces) pink salmon, drained
- ½ cup dry bread crumbs
- 1 tablespoon margarine or butter, melted
  Fresh dill sprigs and red onion slices (optional)

PREHEAT oven to 350°F. Spray 1-quart square baking dish with nonstick cooking spray.

COOK pasta according to package directions until *al dente*. Drain and set aside.

Meanwhile, HEAT oil in medium skillet over medium-high heat until hot. Add celery and chopped onion; cook and stir 2 minutes or until vegetables are tender. Set aside.

COMBINE soup, mayonnaise, wine, parsley and dill in large bowl. Stir in pasta, vegetables and salmon until pasta is well coated. Pour salmon mixture into prepared dish.

COMBINE bread crumbs and margarine in small bowl; sprinkle evenly over casserole.

BAKE, uncovered, 25 minutes or until hot and bubbly. Garnish with dill and red onion slices, if desired. *Makes 4 servings*

81 TWISTY BEEF BAKE

- 1 pound ground beef
- 2 cups rotini or elbow macaroni, cooked in unsalted water and drained
- 1⅓ cups (2.8-ounce can) FRENCH'S® French Fried Onions, divided
- 1 cup (4 ounces) shredded Cheddar cheese, divided
- 1 can (10¾ ounces) condensed cream of mushroom soup, undiluted
- 1 can (14½ ounces) whole tomatoes, undrained and chopped
- ¼ cup chopped green bell pepper
- ¼ teaspoon seasoned salt

Preheat oven to 375°F. In large skillet, brown ground beef; drain. Stir in hot macaroni, ⅔ cup French Fried Onions, ½ cup cheese, soup, tomatoes, bell pepper and seasoned salt. Mix well. Pour into 2-quart casserole. Bake, covered, 30 minutes or until heated through. Top with remaining cheese and ⅔ cup onions; bake, uncovered, 3 minutes or until onions are golden brown.
Makes 4 to 6 servings

MICROWAVE DIRECTIONS: Crumble ground beef into 2-quart microwave-safe casserole. Cook, covered, at HIGH 4 to 6 minutes or until beef is cooked. Stir beef halfway through cooking time. Drain well. Add remaining ingredients as above. Cook, covered, 10 to 14 minutes or until heated through. Stir beef mixture halfway through cooking time. Top with remaining cheese and onions; cook, uncovered, 1 minute or until cheese melts. Let stand 5 minutes.

Pasta with Salmon and Dill

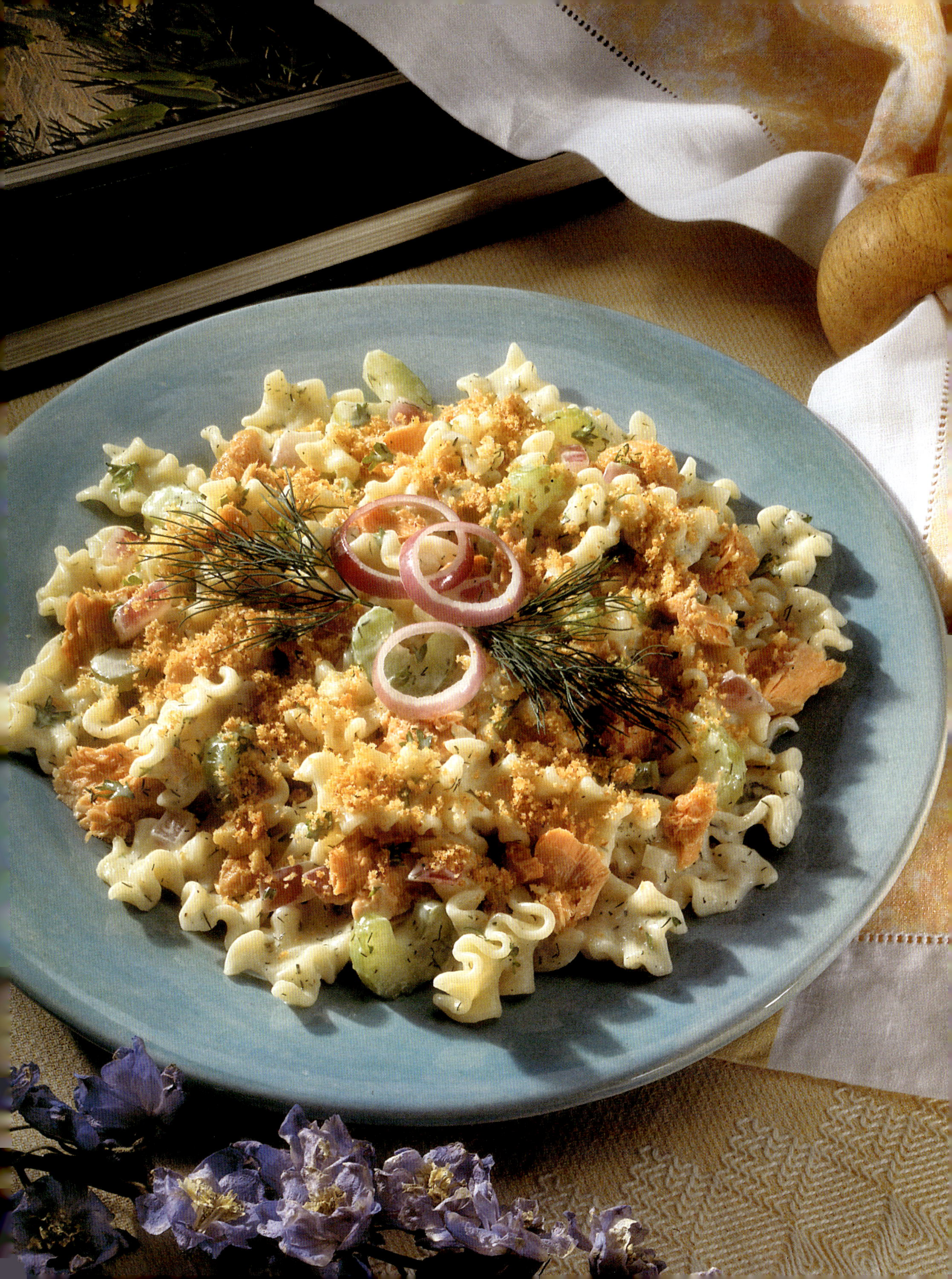

OUT OF THE OVEN

82 CHEESY PASTA SWIRLS

- 4 ounces fettuccine, cooked in unsalted water and drained
- 1 bag (16 ounces) frozen vegetable combination (peas, carrots, cauliflower), thawed and drained
- 1 cup (4 ounces) shredded mozzarella cheese
- ½ cup (2 ounces) cubed provolone cheese
- 1⅓ cups (2.8-ounce can) FRENCH'S® French Fried Onions, divided
- 1 can (10¾ ounces) condensed cream of mushroom soup
- ¾ cup milk
- ½ teaspoon garlic salt
- ⅓ cup (about 1½ ounces) grated Parmesan cheese

Preheat oven to 350°F. In 12×8-inch baking dish, combine vegetables, mozzarella, provolone and ⅔ cup French Fried Onions. Twirl a few strands of hot fettuccine around long-tined fork to form a pasta swirl. Remove pasta swirl from fork; stand upright on top of vegetable mixture. Repeat process to form 5 more swirls. In medium bowl, stir together soup, milk and garlic salt; pour over pasta swirls and vegetable mixture. Bake, loosely covered, for 30 minutes or until vegetables are done. Top pasta swirls with Parmesan cheese; sprinkle remaining ⅔ cup onions around swirls. Bake, uncovered, 5 minutes or until onions are golden brown.
Makes 6 servings

MICROWAVE DIRECTIONS: In 12×8-inch microwave-safe dish, prepare vegetable mixture as above. Form pasta swirls and place on vegetables as above. Prepare soup mixture as above; pour over pasta and vegetables. Cook, loosely covered, at HIGH 14 to 16 minutes or until vegetables are done. Rotate dish halfway through cooking time. Top pasta swirls with Parmesan cheese and remaining onions as above; cook, uncovered, 1 minute. Let stand 5 minutes.

83 SPAM™ LASAGNA

- 6 uncooked lasagna noodles, divided
- 2½ cups chunky spaghetti sauce
- 2 teaspoons dried basil leaves
- 1 (12-ounce) can SPAM® Luncheon Meat, thinly sliced, divided
- 2 cups (8 ounces) shredded mozzarella cheese, divided
- ⅓ cup grated Parmesan cheese

Heat oven to 350°F. Cook lasagna noodles according to package directions. In large bowl, combine spaghetti sauce and basil. In 9-inch square baking pan, spread ½ cup spaghetti sauce. Top with 3 lasagna noodles, cutting and overlapping noodles to fit, ½ of the SPAM® and ½ of the mozzarella cheese. Spread 1½ cups spaghetti sauce over mozzarella cheese. Repeat layers, ending with spaghetti sauce. Top with Parmesan cheese. Bake 45 to 50 minutes or until thoroughly heated. *Makes 6 servings*

SPAM™ Lasagna

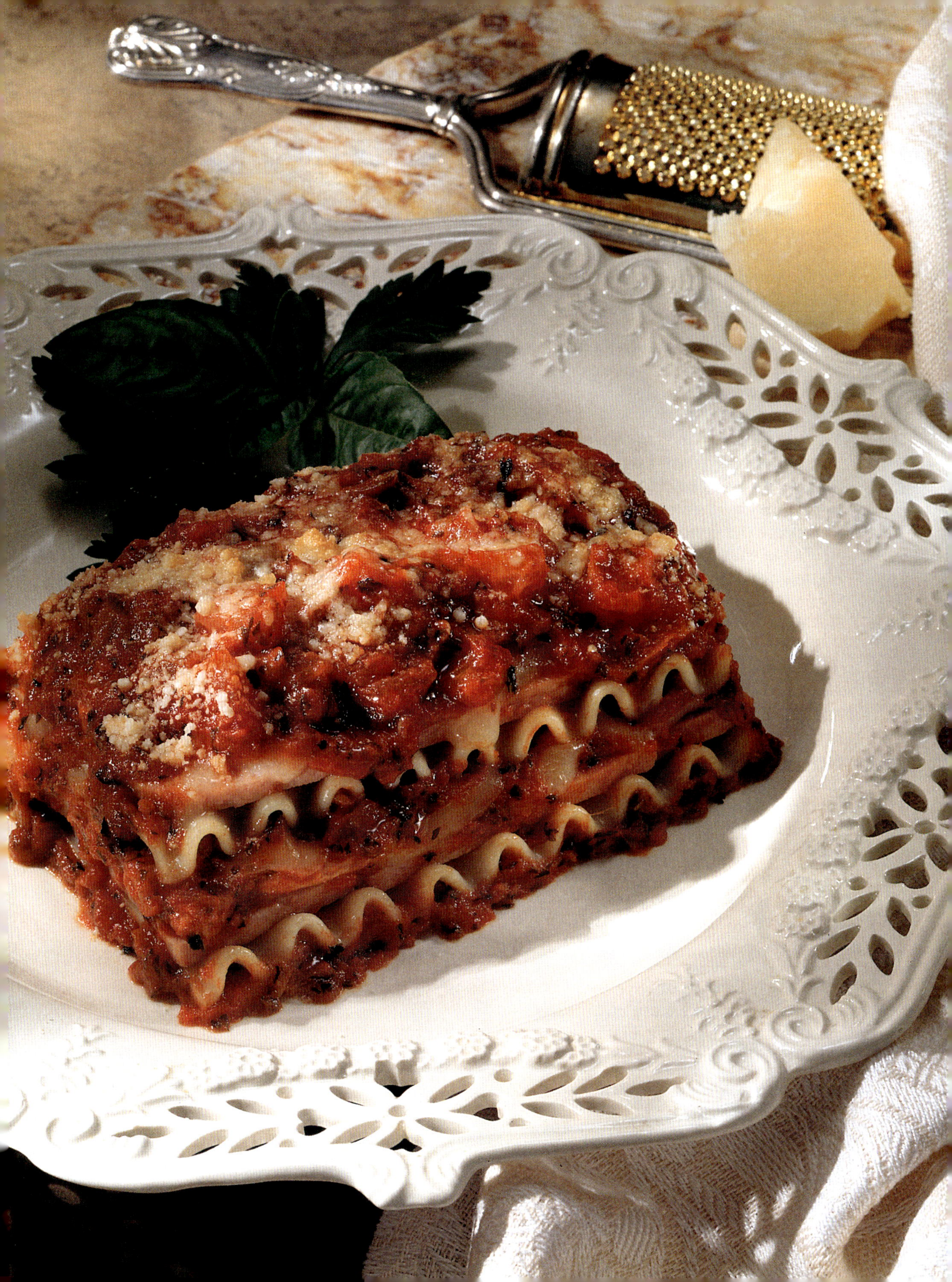

OUT OF THE OVEN

84 TURKEY STUFFED PASTA ITALIANO

- 1 pound ground California turkey
- 1 cup minced onion
- 1 cup grated peeled eggplant
- 2 cloves garlic, minced
- Salt and black pepper
- 1 can (28 ounces) tomatoes, undrained
- 1 can (8 ounces) tomato sauce
- 1 cup red wine or water
- 1 teaspoon garlic salt
- 1 teaspoon dried oregano leaves
- 1 teaspoon dried basil leaves
- ½ teaspoon dried tarragon leaves
- ½ teaspoon crushed red pepper
- 1 package (12 ounces) uncooked jumbo pasta shells
- ½ cup grated Parmesan cheese
- ¾ cup (3 ounces) shredded mozzarella cheese

In large nonstick skillet, brown turkey, onion, eggplant and garlic until turkey is no longer pink; drain. Season with salt and pepper; reserve. In small saucepan, simmer tomatoes with juice, tomato sauce, wine and seasonings 15 minutes. Cook pasta shells until done, but still firm; drain. In large bowl, combine turkey mixture and Parmesan cheese with half the tomato sauce mixture. Stuff shells; place in 13×9-inch pan. Spoon remaining sauce mixture over shells; top with mozzarella cheese. Bake at 350°F for 30 minutes. *Makes 8 to 10 servings*

NOTE: Shells can be stuffed ahead of time and refrigerated. Add sauce and mozzarella cheese just before baking. Increase cooking time by 8 to 10 minutes.

Favorite recipe from **California Poultry Industry Federation**

85 LASAGNE ROLLS

- 1 tablespoon olive oil
- 4 ounces cremini or white mushrooms, chopped
- ½ cup chopped onion
- 2 cloves garlic, minced
- 1 package (about 1¼ pounds) PERDUE® Fresh Ground Chicken, Ground Turkey or Ground Turkey Breast Meat
- 2 tablespoons butter or margarine
- ¼ cup all-purpose flour
- 1¼ cups milk
- Salt and ground black pepper to taste
- Dash ground nutmeg
- 16 curly lasagne noodles, cooked *al dente*
- 2 packages (10 ounces each) frozen chopped spinach, thawed and well drained
- ¼ cup shredded mozzarella cheese
- 2 cups marinara sauce

Preheat oven to 350°F. Grease large, shallow baking dish. In large skillet, over medium-high heat, heat 1 tablespoon oil. Add mushrooms, onion and garlic; sauté 2 to 3 minutes. Add chicken; sauté 5 minutes or until cooked through. With slotted spoon, remove chicken mixture from skillet.

Add butter to remaining liquid in skillet; melt over medium-high heat. Add flour and whisk to blend; cook 2 to 3 minutes, whisking often. Whisk in milk until thickened (sauce will be very thick). Return chicken mixture to skillet and stir well. Season with salt, pepper and nutmeg.

OUT OF THE OVEN

Lay lasagne noodles on work surface. Divide spinach among noodles and spread out in a thin layer. Divide chicken mixture among noodles and spread out in a thin layer on top of spinach. Sprinkle noodles with mozzarella. Roll noodles up, jelly-roll style, enclosing filling; place in prepared baking dish, curly side down. Spoon marinara sauce over and around rolls. Bake, loosely covered, 20 to 30 minutes until hot and bubbly.

Makes 8 servings

86 TUNA & ZUCCHINI–STUFFED MANICOTTI

- 1 cup diced zucchini
- ½ cup chopped onion
- 1 clove garlic, minced
- 1 tablespoon vegetable oil
- 1 can (6 ounces) STARKIST® Tuna, drained and flaked
- 1 cup low-fat ricotta cheese
- ½ cup shredded mozzarella cheese
- ¼ cup grated Parmesan or Romano cheese
- 1 extra-large egg, lightly beaten
- 2 teaspoons dried basil, crushed
- 8 manicotti shells, cooked and drained

MARINARA SAUCE
- 1½ cups chopped fresh tomatoes
- 1¼ cups tomato sauce
- 2 tablespoons minced parsley
- 1 teaspoon dried basil, crushed
- 1 teaspoon dried oregano or marjoram, crushed
- Salt and pepper to taste

In a medium skillet, sauté zucchini, onion and garlic in oil for 3 minutes; remove from heat. Stir in tuna. In a medium bowl, stir together ricotta, mozzarella, Parmesan, egg and basil until blended. Stir cheese mixture into tuna mixture; set aside.

Preheat oven to 350°F. Place drained manicotti shells in a bowl of cold water. Set aside. For Marinara Sauce, in a medium saucepan, stir together tomatoes, tomato sauce and herbs. Heat to a boil; remove from heat. Season to taste with salt and pepper. Transfer mixture to blender container or food processor bowl. Cover and process in 2 batches until nearly smooth. Spray a 13×9×2-inch baking dish with aerosol shortening.

Spread ½ cup of the Marinara Sauce over bottom of baking dish. Blot manicotti shells carefully with paper towels. Generously pipe filling into shells. In baking dish, arrange manicotti in a row. Pour remaining sauce over manicotti; cover with foil. Bake for 30 minutes; uncover and bake for 5 to 10 minutes more, or until sauce is bubbly. Let stand for 5 minutes before serving.

Makes 4 servings

Preparation time: 30 minutes

OUT OF THE OVEN

87 REUBEN NOODLE BAKE

- 8 ounces uncooked egg noodles
- 5 ounces thinly sliced deli-style corned beef
- 1 can (14½ ounces) sauerkraut with caraway seeds, drained
- 2 cups (8 ounces) shredded Swiss cheese
- ½ cup Thousand Island dressing
- ½ cup milk
- 1 tablespoon prepared mustard
- 2 slices pumpernickel bread
- 1 tablespoon margarine or butter, melted
- Red onion slices (optional)

PREHEAT oven to 350°F. Spray 13×9-inch baking dish with nonstick cooking spray.

COOK noodles according to package directions until *al dente*. Drain.

Meanwhile, CUT corned beef into bite-size pieces. Combine noodles, corned beef, sauerkraut and cheese in large bowl. Pour into prepared dish.

COMBINE dressing, milk and mustard in small bowl. Spoon dressing mixture evenly over noodle mixture.

TEAR bread into large pieces. Process in food processor or blender until crumbs form. Combine bread crumbs and margarine in small bowl; sprinkle evenly over casserole.

BAKE, uncovered, 25 to 30 minutes or until heated through. Garnish with red onion, if desired. *Makes 6 servings*

SERVING SUGGESTION: Serve with a mixed green salad.

88 TOMATO PESTO LASAGNA

- 8 ounces uncooked lasagna noodles
- 1 pound sausage or ground beef
- 1 can (14½ ounces) DEL MONTE® Chunky Pasta Recipe Stewed Tomatoes, undrained
- 1 can (6 ounces) DEL MONTE® Tomato Paste
- ¾ cup water
- 8 ounces ricotta cheese
- 1 package (4 ounces) frozen pesto, thawed
- 8 ounces (2 cups) shredded mozzarella cheese

Cook noodles according to package directions; rinse, drain and separate noodles. Brown meat in 10-inch skillet; drain. Stir in tomatoes with juice, tomato paste and water; mix well. In 2-quart or 9-inch square baking dish, layer ⅓ meat sauce, half each of noodles, ricotta cheese, pesto and mozzarella cheese; repeat layers ending with meat sauce. Bake at 350°F for 30 minutes or until heated through. *Makes 6 servings*

Prep time: 20 minutes
Bake time: 30 minutes

MICROWAVE DIRECTIONS: Prepare lasagna noodles as directed above. In 9-inch square microwavable dish, assemble lasagna as directed above. Cover with plastic wrap; cook at HIGH 10 minutes, rotating dish after 5 minutes.

Reuben Noodle Bake

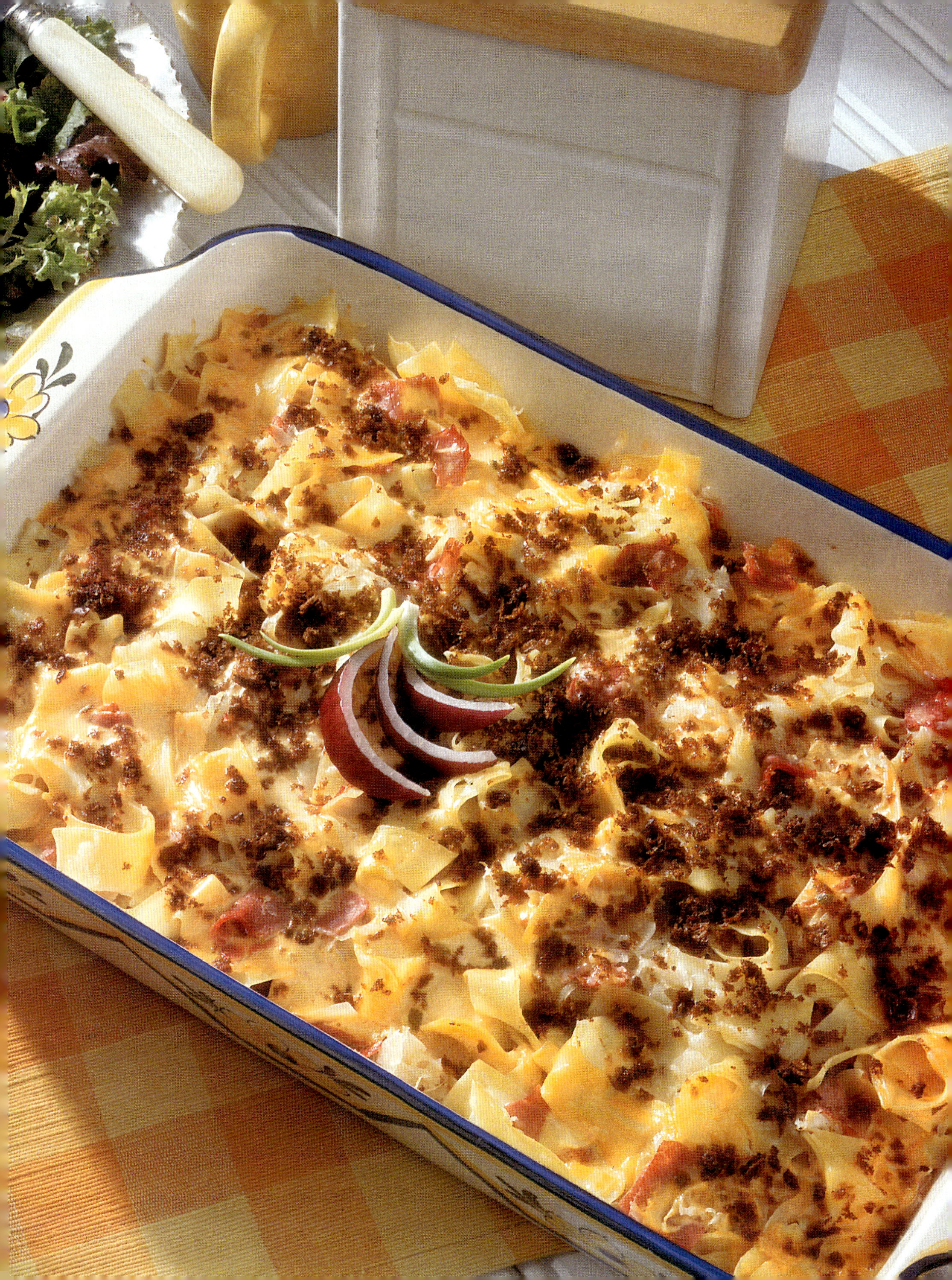

OUT OF THE OVEN

89 CHILLED SEAFOOD LASAGNA WITH HERBED CHEESE

- 8 (2-inch-wide) uncooked lasagna noodles
- 2 cups ricotta cheese
- 1½ cups mascarpone cheese
- 2 tablespoons lemon juice
- 1 tablespoon minced fresh basil leaves
- 1 tablespoon minced fresh dill
- 1 tablespoon minced fresh tarragon leaves
- ¼ teaspoon white pepper
- 1 pound lox, divided
- 4 ounces Whitefish caviar, gently rinsed
- Lox and fresh tarragon sprigs for garnish

1. Cook lasagna noodles according to package directions until *al dente*. Drain and set aside.

2. Process ricotta cheese, mascarpone cheese, lemon juice, basil, dill, tarragon leaves and pepper in food processor or blender until well combined.

3. Line terrine mold* with plastic wrap, allowing wrap to extend 5 inches over sides of mold.

4. Place 1 noodle on bottom of mold. Spread ½ cup cheese mixture over noodle. Cover cheese mixture with 2 ounces lox; spread 2 rounded teaspoons caviar over lox. Repeat layers with remaining ingredients, ending with noodle. Set aside remaining 2 ounces lox for garnish.

5. Cover; refrigerate several hours or until firm. Carefully lift lasagna from mold and remove plastic wrap.

6. Garnish with remaining strips of lox rolled to look like roses and fresh tarragon sprigs, if desired. Slice with warm knife.

Makes 24 first-course servings

*Can be prepared without terrine mold. Layer lasagna on plastic wrap. Cover and wrap with foil.

90 SWISSED HAM AND NOODLES CASSEROLE

- 2 tablespoons butter
- ½ cup chopped onion
- ½ cup chopped green bell pepper
- 1 can (10½ ounces) condensed cream of mushroom soup, undiluted
- 1 cup dairy sour cream
- 1 package (8 ounces) medium noodles, cooked and drained
- 2 cups (8 ounces) shredded Wisconsin Swiss cheese
- 2 cups (about ¾ pound) cubed cooked ham

In 1-quart saucepan, melt butter; sauté onion and bell pepper. Remove from heat; stir in soup and sour cream. In buttered 2-quart casserole, layer ⅓ of the noodles, ⅓ of the Swiss cheese, ⅓ of the ham and ½ soup mixture. Repeat layers, ending with final ⅓ layer of noodles, cheese and ham. Bake in preheated 350°F oven 30 to 45 minutes or until heated through.

Makes 6 to 8 servings

Favorite recipe from **Wisconsin Milk Marketing Board**

Chilled Seafood Lasagna with Herbed Cheese

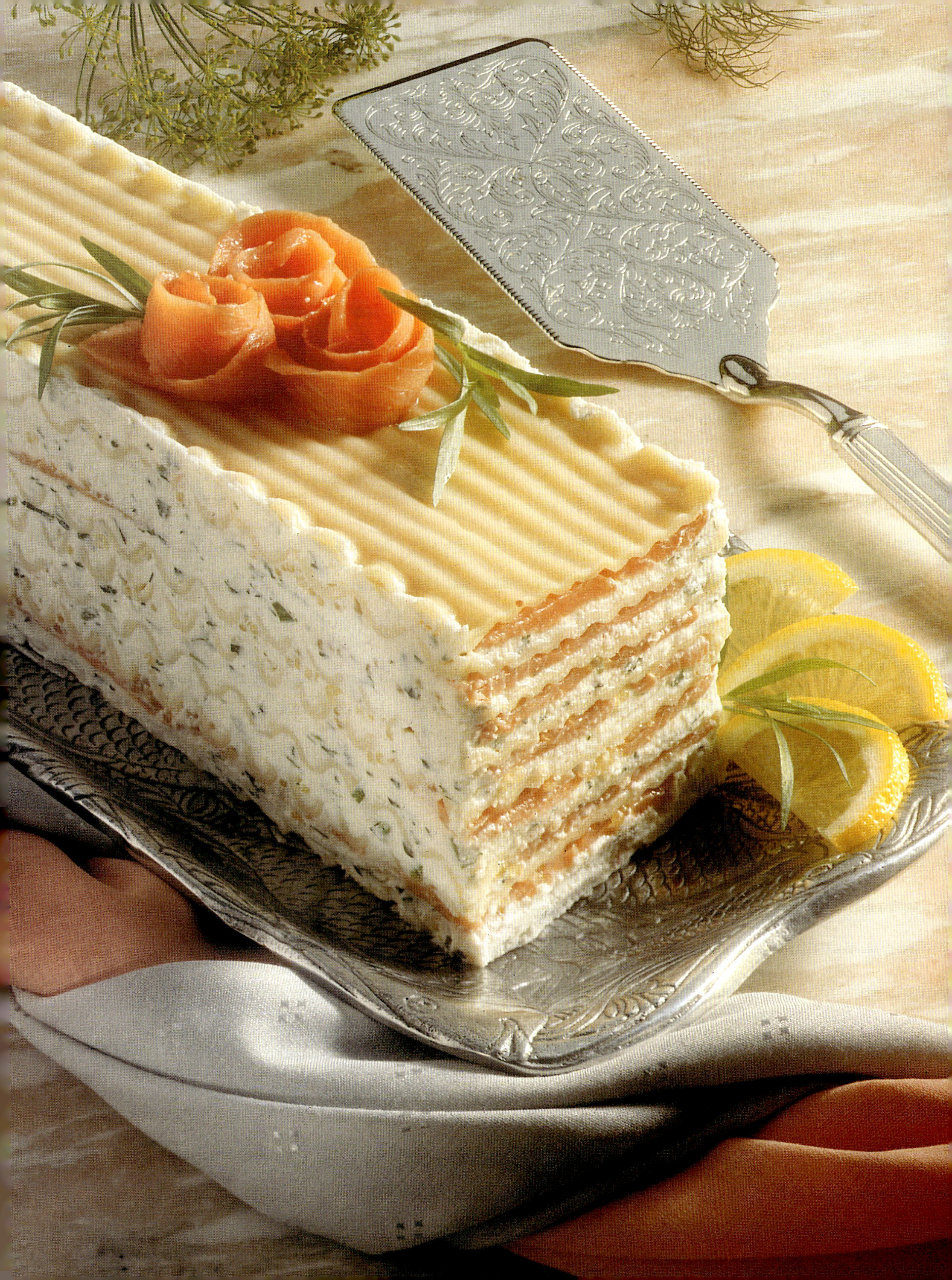

91 FAJITA STUFFED SHELLS

- ¼ cup fresh lime juice
- 1 clove garlic, minced
- ½ teaspoon dried oregano leaves
- ¼ teaspoon ground cumin
- 1 (6-ounce) boneless lean round or flank steak
- 1 medium green bell pepper, cut into halves
- 1 medium onion, cut into halves
- 12 uncooked jumbo pasta shells (about 6 ounces)
- ½ cup reduced-fat sour cream
- 2 tablespoons shredded reduced-fat Cheddar cheese
- 1 tablespoon minced fresh cilantro
- ⅔ cup chunky salsa
- 2 cups shredded leaf lettuce

1. Combine lime juice, garlic, oregano and cumin in shallow nonmetallic dish. Add steak, bell pepper and onion. Cover and refrigerate 8 hours or overnight.

2. Preheat oven to 350°F. Cook pasta shells according to package directions, omitting salt. Drain and rinse well under cold water; set aside.

3. Grill steak and vegetables over medium-hot coals 3 to 4 minutes per side or until desired doneness; cool slightly. Cut steak into thin slices. Chop vegetables. Place steak slices and vegetables in medium bowl. Stir in sour cream, Cheddar cheese and cilantro. Stuff shells evenly with meat mixture, mounding slightly.

4. Arrange shells in 8-inch baking dish. Pour salsa over filled shells. Cover with foil and bake 15 minutes or until heated through. Divide lettuce evenly among 4 plates; arrange 3 shells on each plate.

Makes 4 servings

92 CHILE CHEESE MACARONI

- 8 ounces uncooked elbow macaroni, cooked and drained
- 2 cups (8 ounces) shredded processed American cheese
- 2 (4-ounce) cans *or* 1 (7-ounce) can ORTEGA® Diced Green Chiles, undrained
- ¼ cup milk
- ⅛ teaspoon ground black pepper
- ¼ cup chopped parsley (optional)

In large bowl, combine macaroni, cheese, chiles, milk and pepper. Spoon into greased 1½-quart casserole; cover. Bake at 350°F for 45 minutes or until hot. Garnish with parsley, if desired. *Makes 4 (1-cup) servings*

Fajita Stuffed Shells

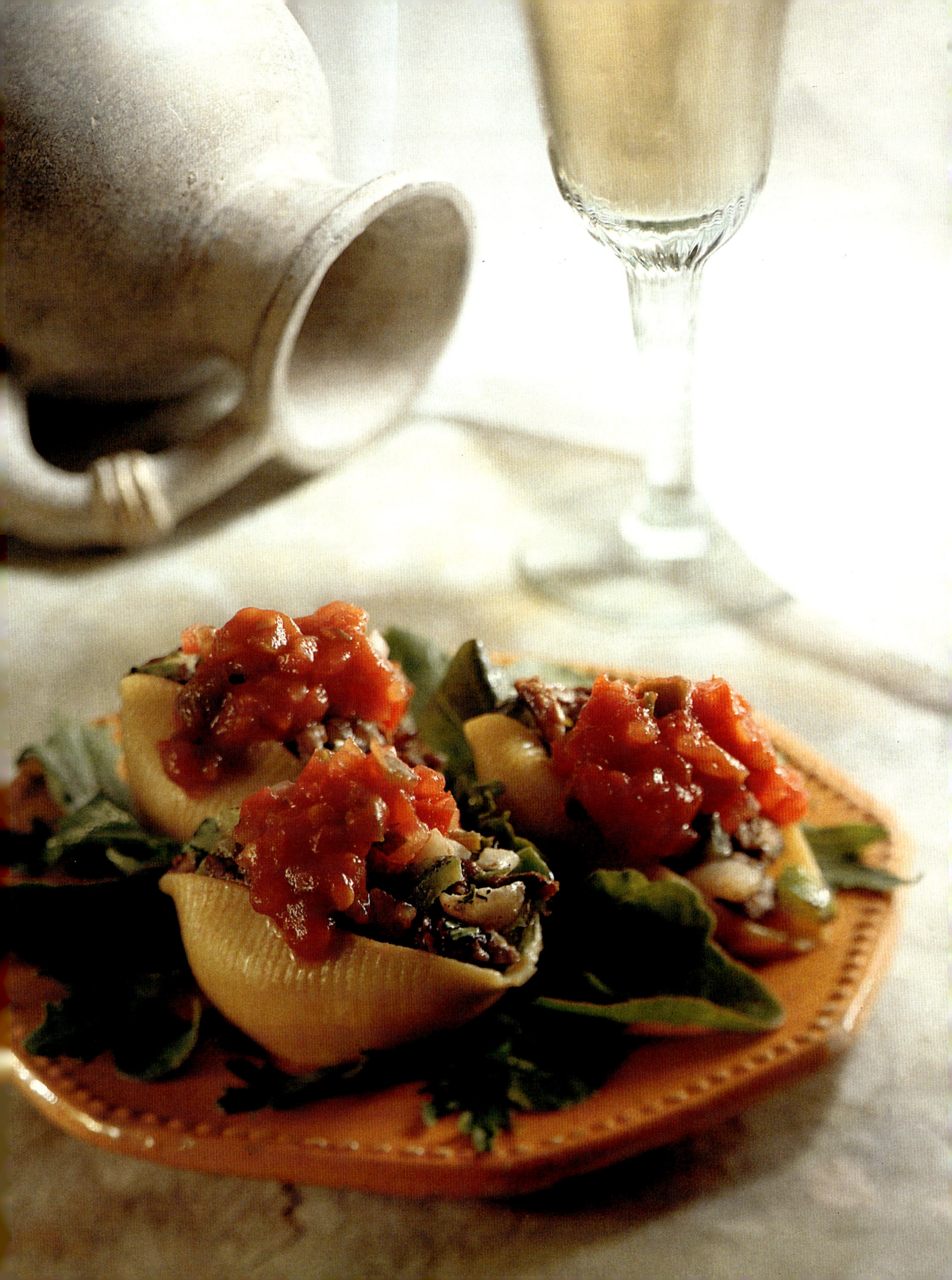

365 Favorite Brand Name Pasta Recipes

OUT OF THE OVEN

93 DOUBLE SPINACH BAKE

- 8 ounces uncooked spinach fettuccine noodles
- 1 cup fresh mushroom slices
- 1 green onion with top, finely chopped
- 1 clove garlic, minced
- 4 to 5 cups fresh spinach, coarsely chopped *or* 1 package (10 ounces) frozen spinach, thawed and drained
- 1 tablespoon water
- 1 container (15 ounces) nonfat ricotta cheese
- ¼ cup skim milk
- 1 egg
- ½ teaspoon ground nutmeg
- ½ teaspoon ground black pepper
- ¼ cup (1 ounce) shredded reduced-fat Swiss cheese

1. Preheat oven to 350°F. Cook pasta according to package directions, omitting salt. Drain; set aside.

2. Spray medium skillet with nonstick cooking spray. Add mushrooms, green onion and garlic. Cook and stir over medium heat until mushrooms are softened. Add spinach and water. Cover; cook until spinach is wilted, about 3 minutes.

3. Combine ricotta cheese, milk, egg, nutmeg and pepper in large bowl. Gently stir in noodles and vegetables; toss to coat evenly.

4. Lightly coat shallow 1½-quart casserole with nonstick cooking spray. Spread noodle mixture in casserole. Sprinkle with Swiss cheese.

5. Bake 25 to 30 minutes or until knife inserted halfway into center comes out clean. *Makes 6 (1-cup) servings*

94 TURTLE SHELLS

- 24 jumbo shells, uncooked
- 1 (10-ounce) package frozen chopped spinach, thawed
- 8 ounces shredded part-skim mozzarella cheese (about 1¾ cup)
- 1½ cups low-fat, part-skim ricotta cheese
- 3 medium carrots, peeled and grated (about ⅔ cup)
- 3 egg whites
- ¼ teaspoon freshly ground black pepper
  Large pinch ground nutmeg
- 2 cups canned low-sodium tomato sauce
- ¼ cup Parmesan cheese (optional)

Cook pasta according to package directions; drain and rinse under cold water until completely cool. Drain thoroughly.

Preheat oven to 350°F. Squeeze as much water as possible from thawed spinach. In large bowl, stir together spinach, mozzarella, ricotta, carrots, egg whites, pepper and nutmeg until thoroughly blended.

Line bottom of 11×7-inch baking dish with ½ cup tomato sauce. Divide ricotta mixture among pasta shells, pressing filling into shells with spoon to completely fill each shell. Arrange shells side by side in baking dish. Coat shells with even layer of remaining tomato sauce. Sprinkle with Parmesan cheese, if desired.

Bake until centers of shells are heated through and sauce is bubbling, about 40 minutes. Let stand 10 minutes before serving. *Makes 6 servings*

Favorite recipe from **National Pasta Association**

Double Spinach Bake

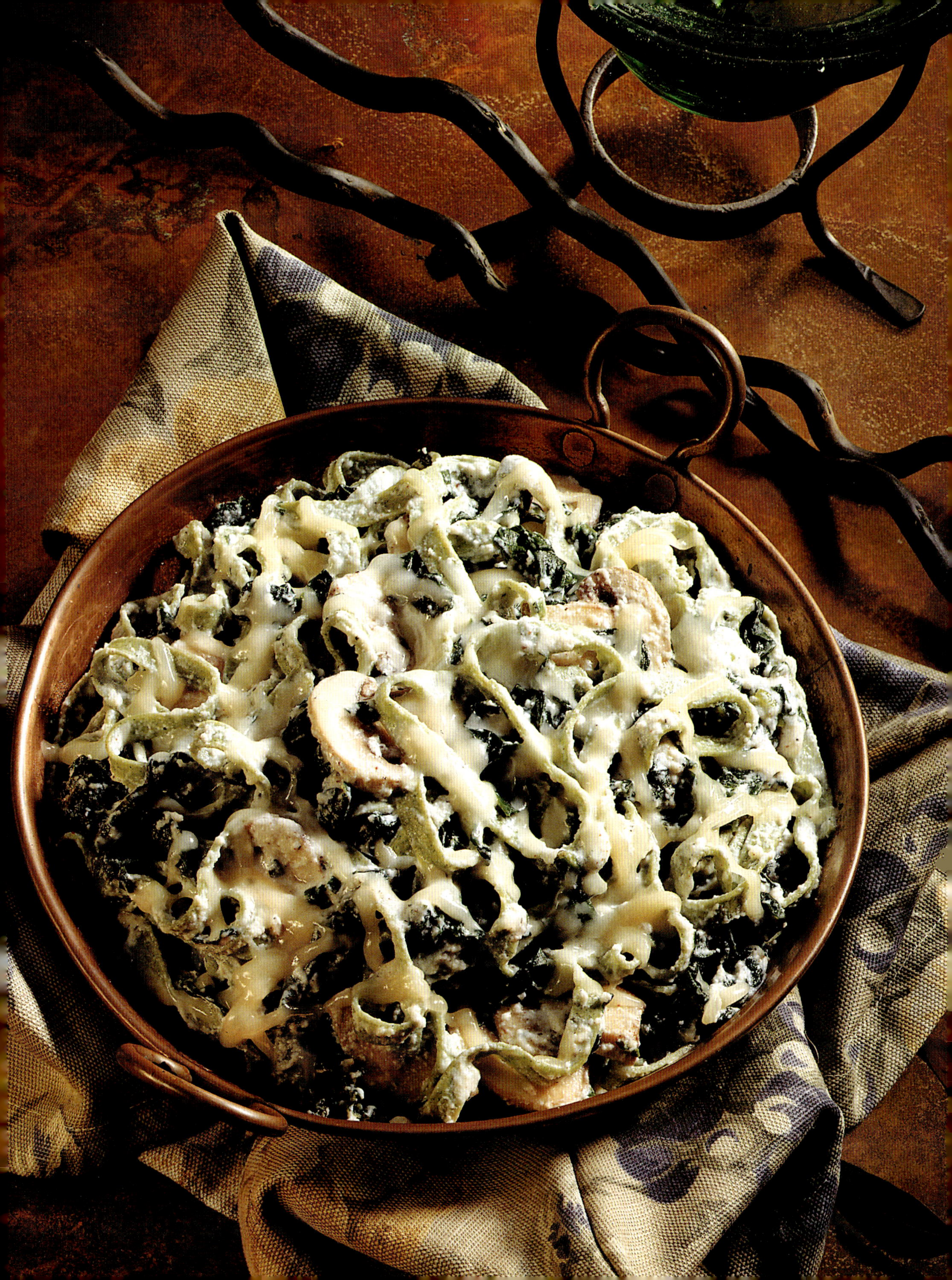

OUT OF THE OVEN

95 SPETZQUE

9 lasagna noodles
2 pounds ground beef
1 can (4½ ounces) chopped black olives, drained
1 can (4 ounces) mushroom stems and pieces, drained
1 small onion, finely chopped
1 jar (16 ounces) spaghetti sauce
Dash black pepper
Dash dried oregano leaves
Dash Italian seasoning
1¼ cups frozen corn, thawed
1¼ cups frozen peas, thawed
2 cups (8 ounces) shredded mozzarella cheese

1. Cook lasagna noodles according to package directions; drain.

2. Cook beef in large skillet over medium-high heat until meat is brown, stirring to separate meat; drain drippings.

3. Add olives, mushrooms and onion. Cook, stirring occasionally, until vegetables are tender. Add spaghetti sauce, pepper, oregano and Italian seasoning. Heat through, stirring occasionally; set aside.

4. Preheat oven to 350°F.

5. Place 3 noodles on bottom of 13×9-inch baking pan. Spread half the beef mixture over noodles, then half the corn and peas. Repeat layers ending with noodles.

6. Bake lasagna 25 minutes. Sprinkle with cheese; bake 5 minutes more or until bubbly. Let stand 10 minutes before cutting. Garnish as desired. *Makes 6 servings*

96 SEAFOOD LASAGNA

4 ounces lasagna noodles
1 jar (28 ounces) spaghetti sauce or favorite homemade recipe
1 package (6 ounces) frozen cooked salad shrimp, thawed and drained
4 ounces Surimi Seafood, thawed and thinly sliced
½ cup low-fat ricotta cheese
¼ cup freshly grated Parmesan cheese
1 tablespoon minced fresh parsley
⅛ teaspoon black pepper
⅔ cup shredded low-fat mozzarella cheese

Preheat oven to 375°F. Prepare lasagna according to package directions. Empty spaghetti sauce into saucepan and simmer 10 minutes until thickened and reduced to about 3 cups; stir in shrimp and Surimi Seafood. Combine ricotta cheese, Parmesan cheese, parsley and pepper in small bowl.

To assemble lasagna, place half of noodles in 8×8-inch casserole. Top with half of seafood sauce and drop half of ricotta mixture by small teaspoonfuls on top. Sprinkle with half of mozzarella cheese. Repeat layers. Bake for 35 minutes or until bubbly. Let stand 10 minutes before cutting.
Makes 6 servings

Favorite recipe from **National Fisheries Institute**

Spetzque

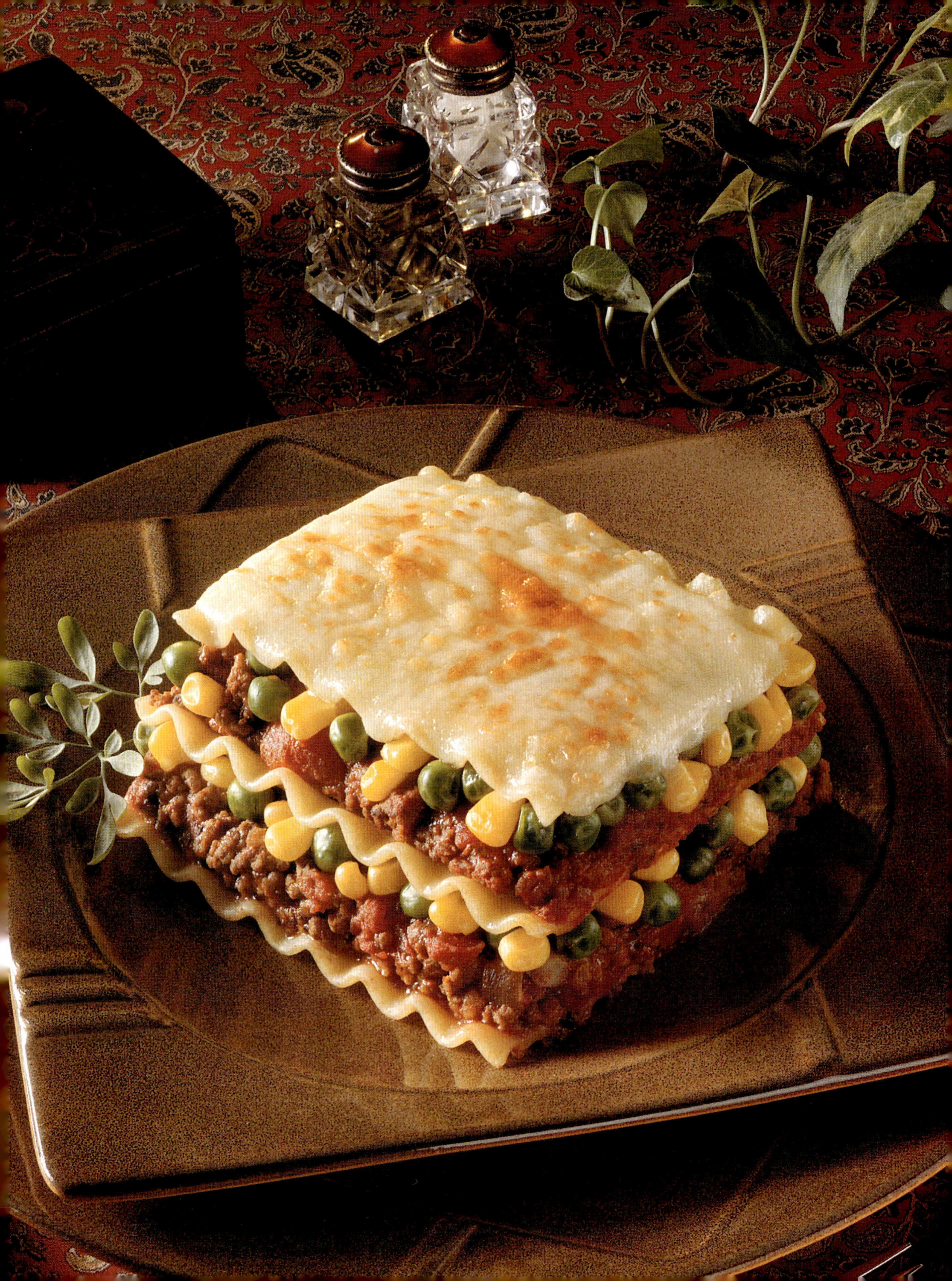

97 CANNELLONI WITH TOMATO–EGGPLANT SAUCE

- 10 ounces fresh spinach
- 1 cup nonfat ricotta cheese
- 4 egg whites, beaten
- ¼ cup (1 ounce) grated Parmesan cheese
- 2 tablespoons finely chopped fresh parsley
- ½ teaspoon salt (optional)
- 8 manicotti shells, cooked
- Tomato-Eggplant Sauce (recipe follows)
- 1 cup (4 ounces) shredded reduced-fat mozzarella cheese

1. Preheat oven to 350°F. Wash spinach; do not pat dry. In small skillet, cook spinach, covered, over medium-high heat 3 to 5 minutes or until spinach is wilted. Cool slightly and drain; chop finely.

2. Combine spinach, ricotta cheese, egg whites, Parmesan cheese, parsley and salt, if desired, in large bowl; mix well. Spoon mixture into manicotti shells; arrange in 13×9-inch baking pan. Spoon Tomato-Eggplant Sauce over manicotti; sprinkle with mozzarella cheese. Bake, uncovered, 25 to 30 minutes or until hot.

Makes 4 servings

TOMATO–EGGPLANT SAUCE
- Olive oil-flavored nonstick cooking spray
- 1 small eggplant, coarsely chopped
- ½ cup chopped onion
- 2 cloves garlic, minced
- ½ teaspoon dried tarragon leaves
- ¼ teaspoon dried thyme leaves
- 1 can (16 ounces) no-salt-added whole tomatoes, undrained and coarsely chopped

1. Spray skillet with cooking spray; heat over medium heat until hot. Add eggplant, onion, garlic, tarragon and thyme; cook and stir about 5 minutes or until vegetables are tender. Add tomatoes. Reduce heat and simmer, uncovered, 3 to 4 minutes.

Makes about 2½ cups

98 BAKED CHEESEY ROTINI

- ¾ pound lean ground beef
- ½ cup chopped onion
- 2 cups cooked rotini, drained
- 1 (15-ounce) can HUNT'S® Ready Tomato Sauces Chunky Italian
- ¼ cup chopped green bell pepper
- ¾ teaspoon garlic salt
- ¼ teaspoon black pepper
- 1½ cups cubed processed American cheese

Preheat oven to 350°F. In large skillet, brown beef with onion; drain. Stir in rotini, tomato sauce, bell pepper, garlic salt and black pepper. Pour beef mixture into 1½-quart casserole. Top with cheese. Bake, covered, 20 minutes or until sauce is bubbly.

Makes 6 servings

Cannelloni with Tomato-Eggplant Sauce

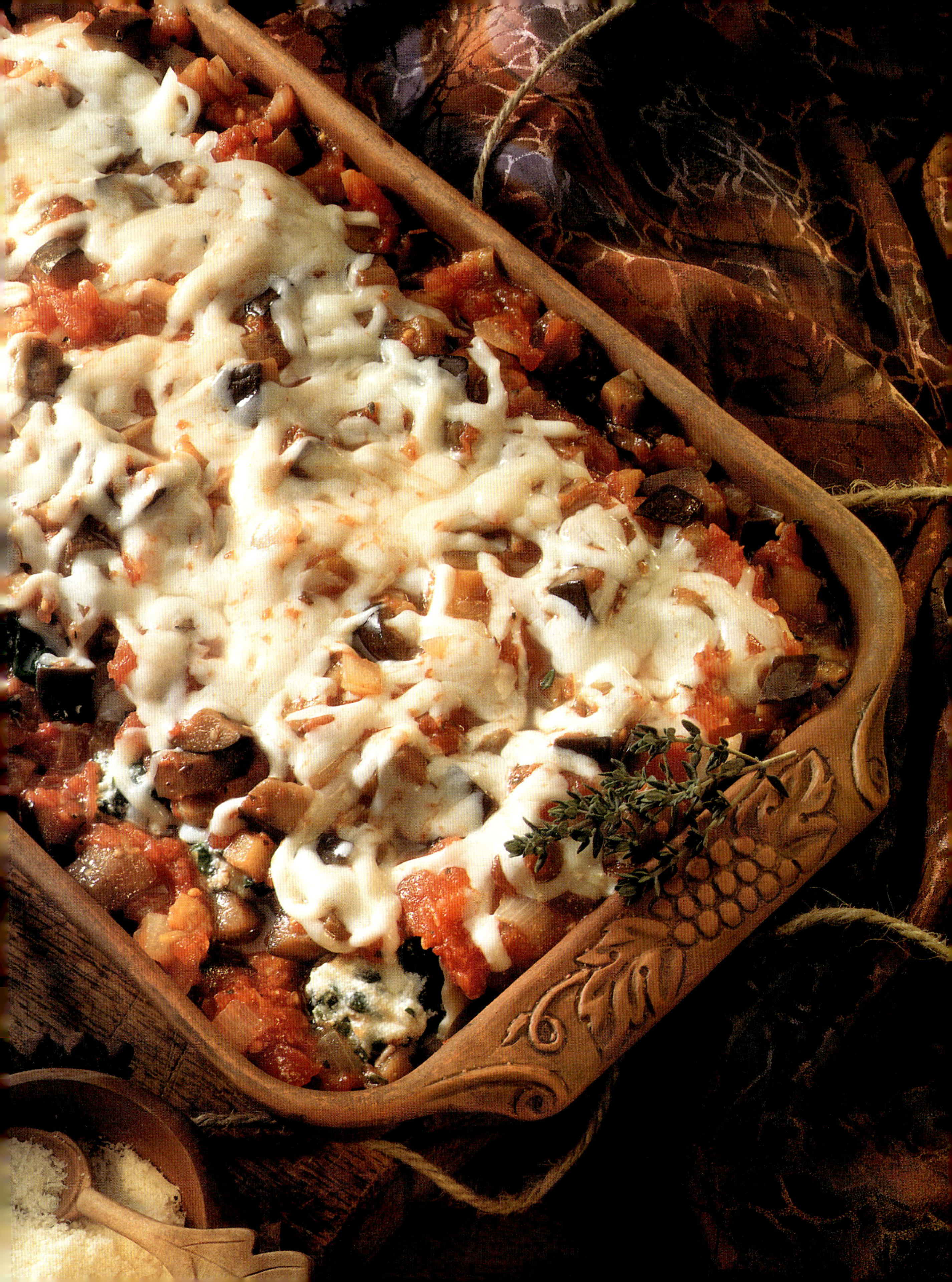

OUT OF THE OVEN

99 PIZZA CHICKEN BAKE

3½ cups uncooked bow tie pasta
1 tablespoon vegetable oil
1 cup sliced mushrooms
1 jar (26 ounces) herb-flavored spaghetti sauce
1 teaspoon pizza seasoning blend
3 boneless skinless chicken breast halves (about ¾ pound), cut into quarters
1 cup (4 ounces) shredded mozzarella cheese

PREHEAT oven to 350°F. Spray 2-quart round casserole with nonstick cooking spray.

COOK pasta according to package directions until *al dente*. Drain and place in prepared dish.

Meanwhile, HEAT oil in large skillet over medium-high heat until hot. Add mushrooms; cook and stir 2 minutes. Remove from heat. Stir in spaghetti sauce and pizza seasoning.

POUR half of spaghetti sauce mixture into casserole; stir until pasta is well coated. Arrange chicken on top of pasta. Pour remaining spaghetti sauce mixture evenly over chicken.

BAKE, covered, 50 minutes or until chicken is no longer pink in centers. Remove from oven; sprinkle with cheese. Cover and let stand 5 minutes before serving.

Makes 4 servings

100 ITALIAN DELIGHT

½ pound Italian sausage, casing removed and sausage crumbled
½ pound ground turkey
1 cup chopped onion
1 teaspoon fresh minced garlic
1 (15-ounce) can HUNT'S® Tomato Sauce
1 (7½-ounce) can HUNT'S® Whole Peeled Tomatoes, undrained and crushed
1 (6-ounce) can sliced mushrooms, drained
1 (2¼-ounce) can sliced black olives, drained
¼ cup chopped fresh parsley
1 teaspoon *each* dried basil and oregano leaves
¼ teaspoon black pepper
¼ cup grated Parmesan cheese
½ (12-ounce) package wide egg noodles, cooked and drained
1 cup shredded mozzarella cheese

In large Dutch oven, brown sausage and turkey with onion and garlic until meat is no longer pink; drain. Add remaining ingredients except Parmesan cheese, noodles and mozzarella cheese; simmer 5 minutes. Stir in Parmesan cheese and noodles; blend well. Pour noodle mixture into greased 13×9×2-inch baking dish. Bake, covered, at 350°F for 20 minutes. Sprinkle mozzarella cheese over noodle mixture and bake, uncovered, for an additional 5 to 7 minutes.

Makes 6 to 8 servings

Pizza Chicken Bake

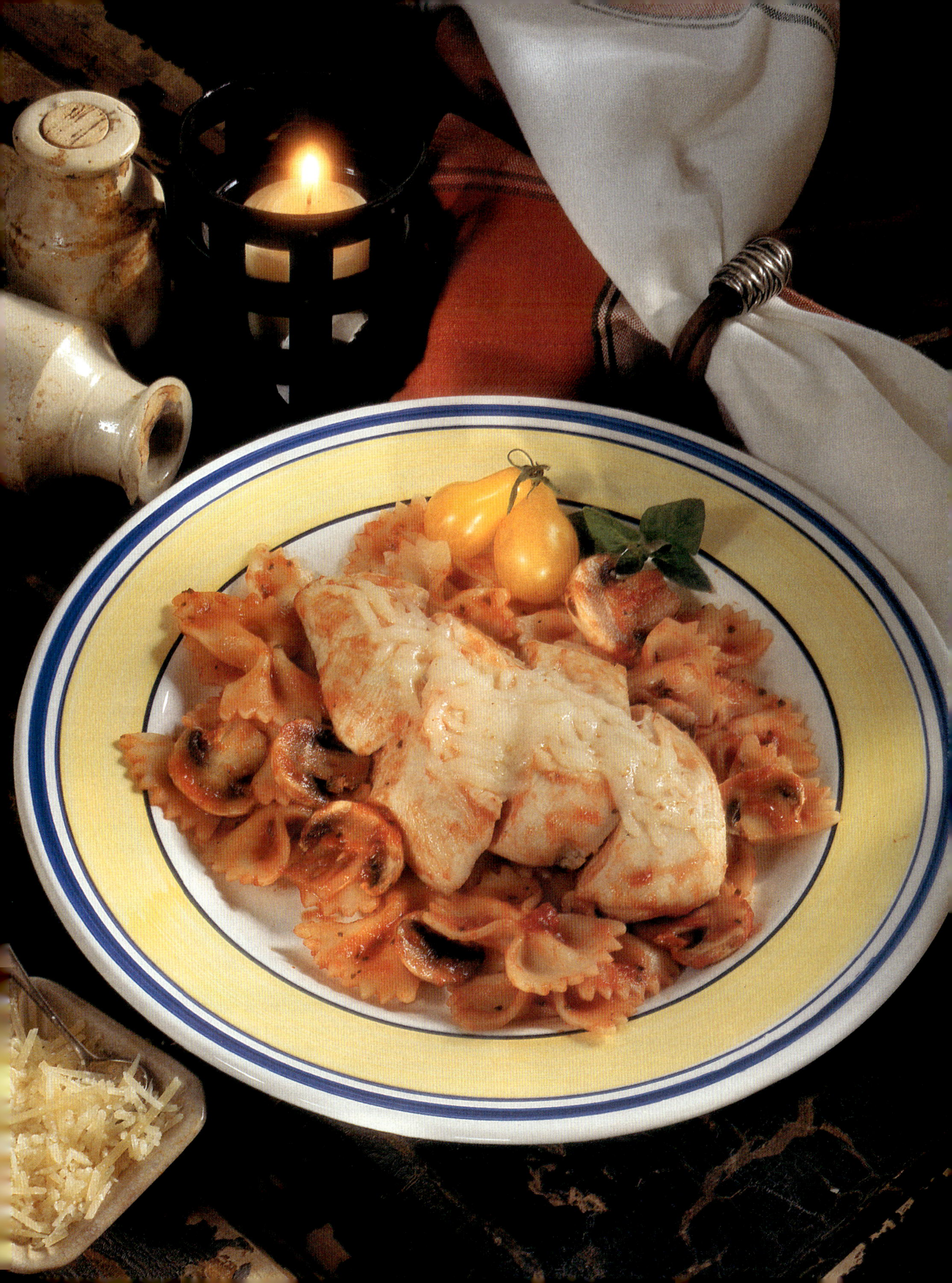

OUT OF THE OVEN

101 THREE CHEESE VEGETABLE LASAGNA

- 1 large onion, chopped
- 3 cloves garlic, minced
- 1 teaspoon olive oil
- 1 can (28 ounces) no-salt-added tomato purée
- 1 can (14½ ounces) no-salt-added tomatoes, undrained and chopped
- 2 cups (6 ounces) sliced fresh mushrooms
- 1 zucchini, diced
- 1 large green bell pepper, chopped
- 2 teaspoons dried basil, crushed
- 1 teaspoon *each* salt and sugar (optional)
- ½ teaspoon *each* red pepper flakes and dried oregano, crushed
- 2 cups (15 ounces) SARGENTO® Light Ricotta Cheese
- 1 package (10 ounces) frozen chopped spinach, thawed and squeezed dry
- 2 egg whites
- 2 tablespoons (½ ounce) SARGENTO® Fancy Shredded Parmesan Cheese
- ½ pound lasagna noodles, cooked according to package directions, without oil or salt
- ¾ cup (3 ounces) *each* SARGENTO® Light Fancy Shredded Mozzarella and Mild Cheddar Cheese, divided

Spray large skillet with nonstick vegetable spray. Add onion, garlic and olive oil; cook over medium heat until tender, stirring occasionally. Add tomato purée, tomatoes, tomato liquid, mushrooms, zucchini, bell pepper, basil, salt, sugar, pepper flakes and oregano. Heat to a boil. Reduce heat; cover and simmer 10 minutes or until vegetables are crisp-tender.

Combine Ricotta cheese, spinach, egg whites and Parmesan cheese; mix well. Spread 1 cup sauce on bottom of 13×9-inch baking dish. Layer 3 lasagna noodles over sauce. Top with half of Ricotta cheese mixture and 2 cups of remaining sauce. Repeat layering with 3 more lasagna noodles, remaining Ricotta mixture and 2 cups sauce. Combine Mozzarella and Cheddar cheeses. Sprinkle ¾ cup cheese mixture over sauce. Top with remaining lasagna noodles and sauce. Cover with foil; bake at 375°F 30 minutes. Uncover; bake 15 minutes more. Sprinkle with remaining ¾ cup cheese mixture. Let stand 10 minutes before serving. *Makes 10 servings*

102 ITALIAN LASAGNA ROLLS

- 8 ounces lasagna noodles (about 12 noodles)
- 2 (10-ounce) packages frozen spinach, thawed and well drained
- 16 ounces nonfat cottage cheese
- 2½ cups shredded mozzarella cheese, divided
- 1½ cups grated Parmesan cheese, divided
- 8 ounces nonfat cream cheese, softened
- ½ teaspoon dried basil leaves
- ¼ teaspoon salt
- ¼ teaspoon black pepper
- ¼ teaspoon dried oregano leaves
  Light Tomato Sauce (recipe follows)

Cook lasagna noodles according to package directions; drain and cool slightly.

Combine spinach, cottage cheese, 2 cups mozzarella cheese, 1 cup Parmesan cheese, cream cheese, basil, salt, pepper and oregano in large bowl; stir well.

OUT OF THE OVEN

Spread scant ½ cup spinach mixture on each lasagna noodle; starting at narrow end, roll up jelly-roll style. Place lasagna rolls, seam side down, in 13×9×2-inch baking dish. Pour Light Tomato Sauce evenly over rolls; sprinkle with remaining ½ cup mozzarella cheese and ½ cup Parmesan cheese.

Bake at 350°F 50 to 60 minutes, covering baking dish with foil for first 30 minutes. (To prevent mozzarella cheese from sticking, coat foil with cooking spray.)

Makes 5 to 6 servings

LIGHT TOMATO SAUCE
- 1 large onion, chopped
- ¼ cup finely chopped green bell pepper
- 3 cloves garlic, minced
- 3 tablespoons low-fat margarine
- 2 (28-ounce) cans crushed tomatoes in tomato purée
- 1 (15-ounce) can tomato sauce
- 2 tablespoons sugar
- 2 teaspoons dried basil leaves
- 2 teaspoons dried Italian seasoning
- ¼ teaspoon salt
- ¼ teaspoon black pepper

Sauté onion, bell pepper and garlic in margarine in large skillet until tender. Add remaining ingredients; simmer 30 minutes.

Favorite recipe from **North Dakota Wheat Commission**

103 MANICOTTI PARMIGIANA

- 1 can (32 ounces) tomatoes, chopped
- 1 can (8 ounces) tomato sauce
- 1 package (1½ ounces) LAWRY'S® Original Style Spaghetti Sauce Spices & Seasonings
- 2 tablespoons LAWRY'S® Garlic Spread Concentrate
- 1½ teaspoons LAWRY'S® Seasoned Salt
- 8 manicotti shells
- 1 pound ground beef
- ¼ cup chopped green bell pepper
- ½ pound (about 2 cups) shredded mozzarella cheese
- Grated Parmesan cheese
- Finely chopped parsley

In large saucepan, combine tomatoes, tomato sauce, Spaghetti Sauce Spices & Seasonings, Garlic Spread Concentrate and Seasoned Salt. Bring to a boil. Reduce heat; simmer, covered, 20 minutes, stirring occasionally.

Meanwhile, cook manicotti shells according to package directions; drain. In medium skillet, brown ground beef and bell pepper until beef is crumbly; drain fat. Remove from heat; stir in mozzarella cheese. Stuff manicotti shells with beef mixture. Pour ¾ of spaghetti sauce on bottom of 12×8×2-inch baking dish. Place stuffed manicotti shells on sauce; top with remaining sauce. Sprinkle with Parmesan cheese. Bake, uncovered, in 375°F oven 30 minutes. Garnish with chopped parsley.

Makes 4 to 8 servings

PRESENTATION: This recipe is easily doubled for a party.

OUT OF THE OVEN

104 CREAMY "CRAB" FETTUCCINE

- 1 pound imitation crabmeat sticks
- 6 ounces uncooked fettuccine
- 3 tablespoons margarine or butter, divided
- 1 small onion, chopped
- 2 ribs celery, chopped
- ½ medium red bell pepper, chopped
- 2 cloves garlic, minced
- 1 cup reduced-fat sour cream
- 1 cup reduced-fat mayonnaise
- 1 cup (4 ounces) shredded sharp Cheddar cheese
- 2 tablespoons chopped fresh parsley
- ¼ teaspoon salt
- ⅛ teaspoon black pepper
- ½ cup cornflake crumbs
- Fresh chives (optional)

PREHEAT oven to 350°F. Spray 2-quart square baking dish with nonstick cooking spray.

CUT crabmeat into bite-size pieces; set aside.

COOK pasta according to package directions until *al dente*. Drain and set aside.

Meanwhile, MELT 1 tablespoon margarine in large skillet over medium-high heat. Add onion, celery, bell pepper and garlic; cook and stir 2 minutes or until vegetables are tender. Set aside.

COMBINE sour cream, mayonnaise, cheese, parsley, salt and black pepper in large bowl. Add crabmeat, pasta and vegetable mixture, stirring gently to combine. Pour into prepared dish.

MELT remaining 2 tablespoons margarine. Combine cornflake crumbs and margarine in small bowl; sprinkle evenly over casserole.

BAKE, uncovered, 30 minutes or until hot and bubbly. Garnish with chives, if desired.

Makes 6 servings

105 EASY MACARONI AND CHEESE

- 1 (46-fluid ounce) can COLLEGE INN® Chicken or Beef Broth
- 1 (12-ounce) package uncooked spiral macaroni
- ½ cup FLEISCHMANN'S® Margarine, divided
- ¼ cup all-purpose flour
- 2 cups (8 ounces) shredded Cheddar cheese
- 30 RITZ® Crackers, coarsely crushed

In large heavy saucepan, heat broth to a boil; add macaroni and cook according to package directions, omitting salt. Drain, reserving 2 cups broth (if necessary, add water). Set aside.

In medium saucepan, over medium-high heat, melt ¼ cup margarine. Blend in flour. Gradually add reserved broth, stirring constantly until mixture thickens and boils. Cook and stir 2 minutes. Stir in cheese until melted. Combine cheese sauce and macaroni in 2-quart casserole. Melt remaining ¼ cup margarine; stir in cracker crumbs. Sprinkle over macaroni mixture. Bake at 400°F for 30 minutes or until hot.

Makes 6 to 8 servings

Creamy "Crab" Fettuccine

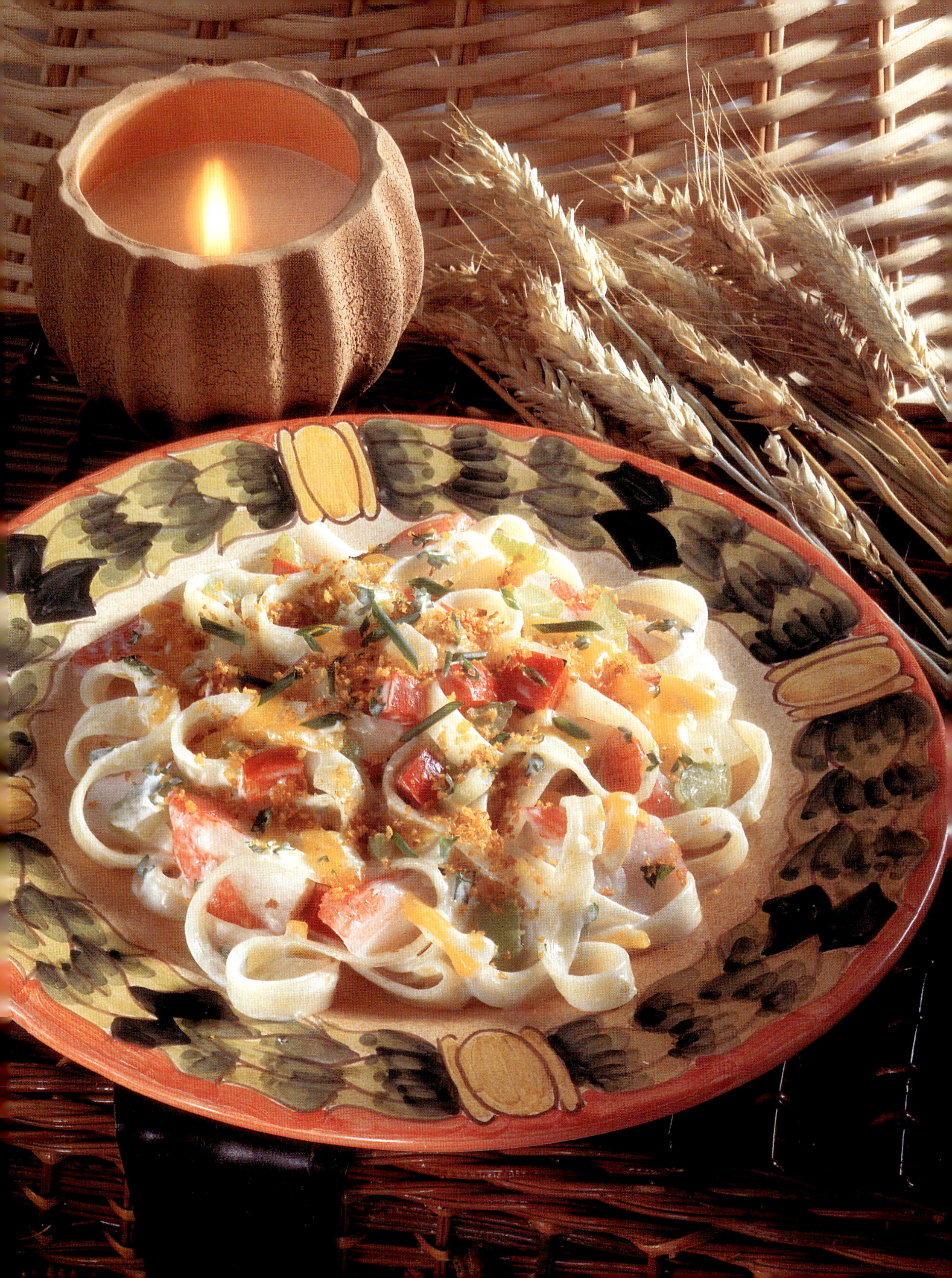

106 SPINACH STUFFED MANICOTTI

- 1 package (10 ounces) frozen spinach
- 8 manicotti shells
- 1½ teaspoons olive oil
- 1 teaspoon dried rosemary
- 1 teaspoon dried sage leaves
- 1 teaspoon dried oregano leaves
- 1 teaspoon dried thyme leaves
- 1 teaspoon chopped garlic
- 1½ cups fresh or canned tomatoes, chopped
- 4 ounces ricotta cheese
- 1 slice whole wheat bread, torn into coarse crumbs
- 2 egg whites, lightly beaten
- Yellow pepper rings and sage sprig for garnish

1. Cook spinach according to package directions. Place in colander to drain. Let stand until cool enough to handle. Squeeze spinach with hands to remove excess moisture. Set aside.

2. Cook pasta; drain. Rinse under warm running water; drain.

3. Preheat oven to 350°F. Heat oil in small saucepan over medium heat. Cook and stir rosemary, sage, oregano, thyme and garlic in hot oil about 1 minute. *Do not let herbs turn brown.* Add tomatoes; reduce heat to low. Simmer, uncovered, 10 minutes, stirring occasionally.

4. Combine spinach, cheese and crumbs in bowl. Fold in egg whites. Fill shells with spinach mixture.

5. Place ⅓ of tomato mixture on bottom of 13×9-inch baking pan. Arrange manicotti in pan. Pour remaining tomato mixture over top. Cover with foil.

6. Bake 30 minutes or until bubbly. Garnish, if desired. *Makes 4 servings*

107 TURKEY NOODLE DANDY (AN ALL-AMERICAN FAVORITE)

- 1 package (8 ounces) medium noodles
- 1 pound fresh ground California turkey
- 3 tablespoons butter or margarine, divided
- 2 cans (8 ounces each) tomato sauce
- 1 cup cottage cheese
- 1 package (8 ounces) cream cheese, softened
- ¼ cup sour cream
- ⅓ cup chopped green onions

Cook noodles according to package directions; drain. Meanwhile, sauté ground turkey in 1 tablespoon butter, stirring, until no longer pink. Stir in tomato sauce. Set aside. In medium bowl, combine remaining ingredients except butter. In 2-quart casserole, spread half the noodles; cover with cheese mixture, then with remaining noodles. Melt remaining 2 tablespoons butter and spoon over all; top with turkey-tomato mixture. Refrigerate. To serve, bake, uncovered, in 375°F oven until hot, about 40 to 45 minutes. Or, immediately after mixing, bake in 375°F oven 30 minutes.
Makes 6 servings

Favorite recipe from **California Poultry Industry Federation**

Spinach Stuffed Manicotti

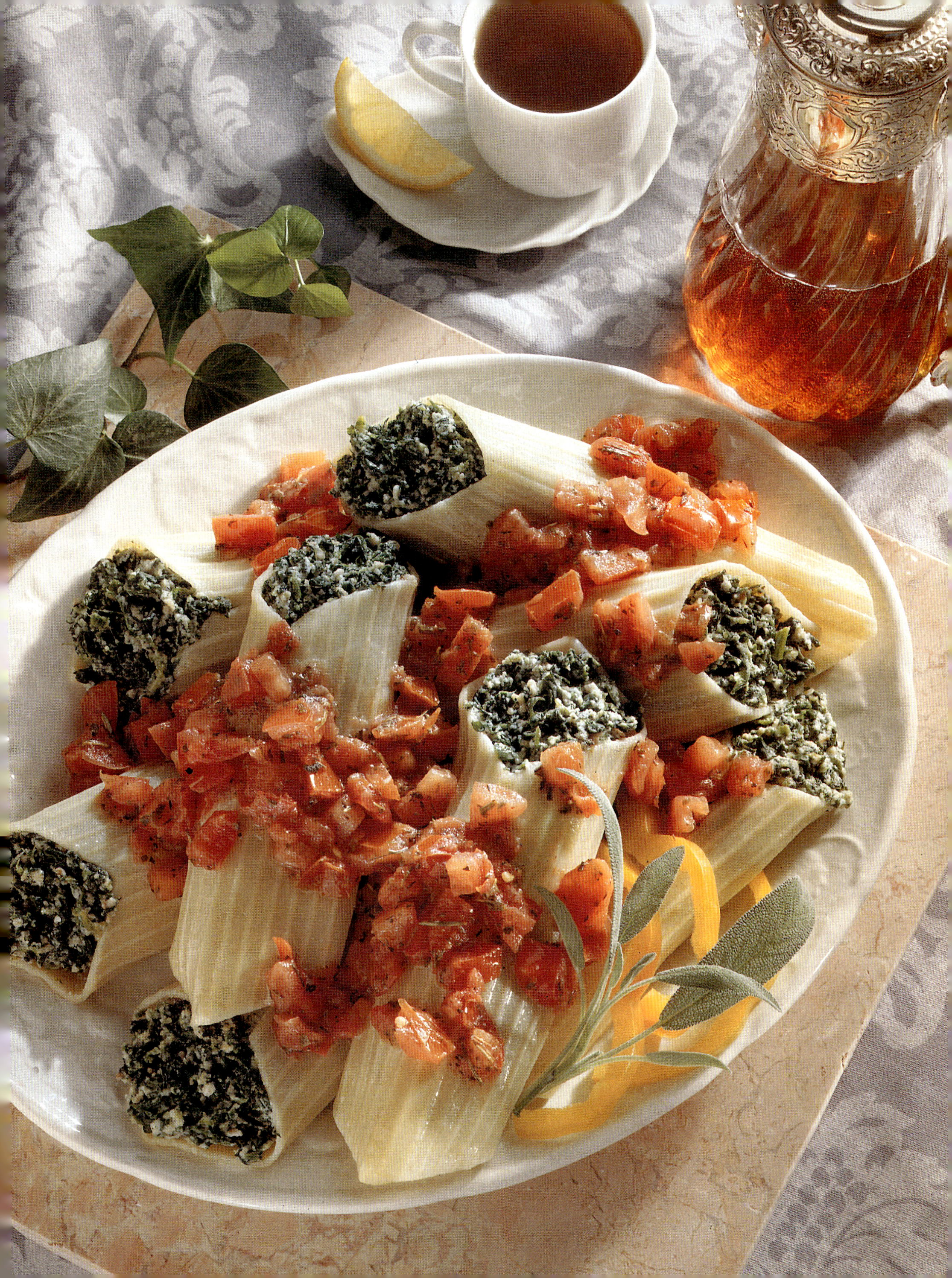

OUT OF THE OVEN

108 TUNA NOODLE CASSEROLE

7 ounces uncooked elbow macaroni
2 tablespoons margarine or butter
¾ cup chopped onion
½ cup thinly sliced celery
½ cup finely chopped red bell pepper
2 tablespoons all-purpose flour
1 teaspoon salt
⅛ teaspoon ground white pepper
1½ cups milk
1 can (6 ounces) albacore tuna in water, drained
½ cup grated Parmesan cheese, divided
Fresh dill sprigs (optional)

PREHEAT oven to 375°F. Spray 8-inch square baking dish with nonstick cooking spray.

COOK pasta according to package directions until *al dente*. Drain and set aside.

Meanwhile, MELT margarine in large deep skillet over medium heat. Add onion; cook and stir 3 minutes. Add celery and bell pepper; cook and stir 3 minutes. Sprinkle flour, salt and white pepper over vegetables; cook and stir 1 minute. Gradually stir in milk; cook and stir until thickened. Remove from heat.

ADD pasta, tuna and ¼ cup cheese to skillet; stir until pasta is well coated. Pour tuna mixture into prepared dish; sprinkle evenly with remaining ¼ cup cheese.

BAKE, uncovered, 20 to 25 minutes or until hot and bubbly. Garnish with dill, if desired.

Makes 4 servings

109 SHELLS FLORENTINE

1 cup coarsely chopped mushrooms (about 4 ounces)
½ cup chopped onion
1 clove garlic, minced
1 teaspoon Italian seasoning
¼ teaspoon ground black pepper
2 tablespoons FLEISCHMANN'S® Margarine
1 (16-ounce) container low-sodium, low-fat cottage cheese (1% milk fat)
1 (10-ounce) package frozen chopped spinach, thawed and well drained
6 tablespoons EGG BEATERS® Healthy Real Egg Product
24 jumbo macaroni shells, cooked in unsalted water and drained
1 (15¼-ounce) jar spaghetti sauce, divided

In large skillet, over medium-high heat, cook and stir mushrooms, onion, garlic, Italian seasoning and pepper in margarine until vegetables are tender, about 4 minutes. Remove from heat; stir in cottage cheese, spinach and egg product. Spoon mixture into shells.

Spread ½ cup spaghetti sauce on bottom of 13×9×2-inch baking dish; arrange shells over sauce. Top with remaining sauce; cover. Bake at 350°F for 35 minutes or until hot.

Makes 8 servings

Prep time: 30 minutes
Bake time: 35 minutes

Tuna Noodle Casserole

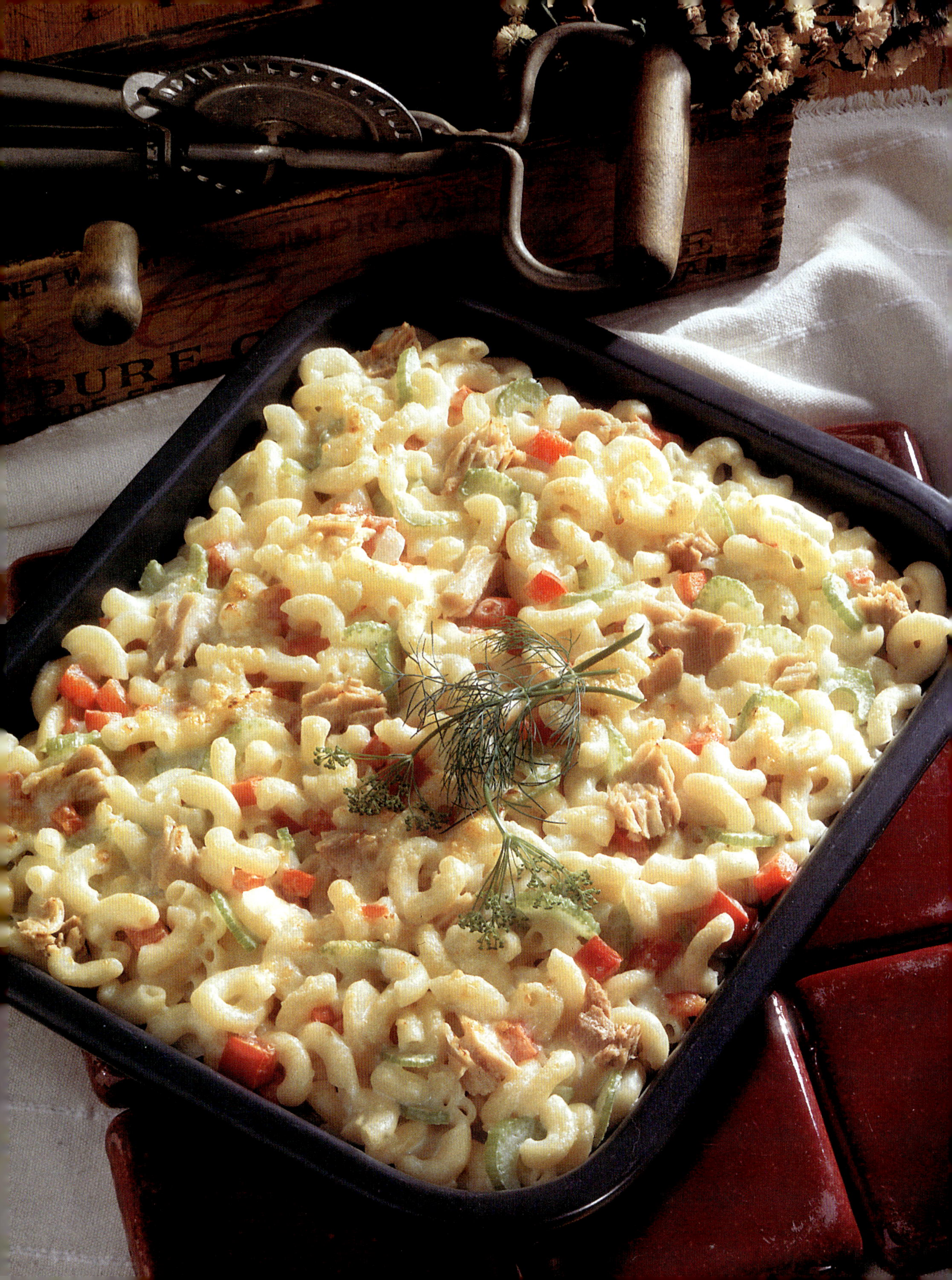

OUT OF THE OVEN

110 EASY CHEESY LASAGNA

- 2 tablespoons olive oil
- 3 small zucchini, cut into quarters and thinly sliced crosswise
- 1 package (8 ounces) mushrooms, thinly sliced
- 1 medium onion, chopped
- 5 cloves garlic, minced
- 2 containers (15 ounces each) reduced-fat ricotta cheese
- ¼ cup grated Parmesan cheese
- 2 eggs
- ½ teaspoon dried Italian seasoning
- ¼ teaspoon garlic salt
- ⅛ teaspoon black pepper
- 1 can (28 ounces) crushed tomatoes in purée, undrained
- 1 jar (26 ounces) spaghetti sauce
- 1 package (16 ounces) lasagna noodles, uncooked
- 4 cups (16 ounces) shredded mozzarella cheese

PREHEAT oven to 375°F. Spray 13×9-inch baking dish or lasagna pan with nonstick cooking spray.

HEAT oil in large skillet over medium heat until hot. Add zucchini, mushrooms, onion and garlic; cook and stir 5 minutes.

COMBINE ricotta cheese, Parmesan cheese, eggs, Italian seasoning, garlic salt and pepper in medium bowl. Combine tomatoes and spaghetti sauce in another medium bowl.

SPREAD about ¾ cup tomato mixture in prepared dish. Place layer of uncooked noodles over tomato mixture, overlapping noodles. Spread half of vegetable mixture over noodles; top with half of ricotta cheese mixture. Sprinkle 1 cup mozzarella cheese over ricotta cheese mixture. Top with second layer of noodles. Spread about 1 cup tomato mixture over noodles. Top with remaining vegetable and ricotta cheese mixtures. Sprinkle with 1 cup mozzarella cheese. Top with third layer of noodles. Spread remaining tomato mixture over noodles. Sprinkle remaining 2 cups mozzarella cheese evenly over top.

COVER tightly with foil and bake 1 hour or until noodles in center are soft. Uncover; bake 5 minutes or until cheese is melted and lightly browned. Cover and let stand 15 minutes before serving.

Makes 6 servings

Easy Cheesy Lasagna

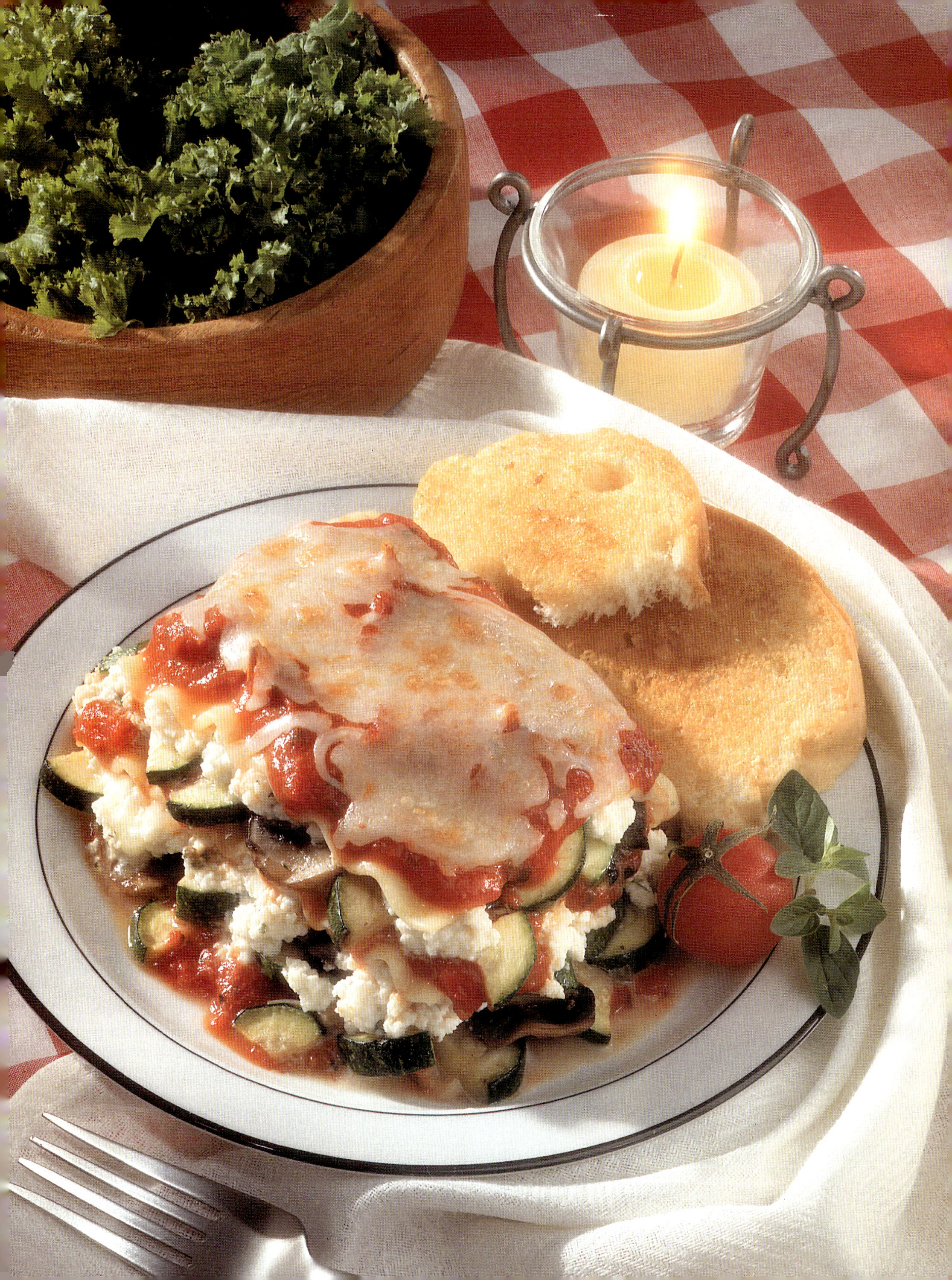

FROM THE BUTCHER SHOP

111 CREAMY CHICKEN AND RED PEPPER PASTA

   3 tablespoons vegetable oil, divided
  ¼ cup pine nuts or coarsely chopped walnuts
1½ pounds boneless, skinless chicken thighs
     Salt and black pepper
   1 pound uncooked fettuccine
  ¼ cup margarine or butter
   3 cloves garlic, minced
   2 tablespoons all-purpose flour
1½ cups half-and-half
  ½ cup chicken broth
  ½ cup prepared roasted red peppers, drained and sliced
  ¼ cup sliced pitted black olives
  ⅓ cup grated Romano cheese

1. Heat 1 tablespoon oil in small skillet over medium-low heat. Add pine nuts; cook and stir 30 to 45 seconds until light brown, shaking pan constantly. Remove with slotted spoon; drain on paper towels.

2. Sprinkle chicken with salt and black pepper. Heat remaining 2 tablespoons oil in large skillet over medium-high heat. Add chicken and cook 12 to 15 minutes until browned on both sides and no longer pink in center. Remove chicken from skillet. Refrigerate until cool enough to handle. Cut into bite-size pieces.

3. Cook pasta according to package directions. Rinse under warm running water; drain.

4. Melt margarine in medium saucepan over medium heat. Add garlic; cook and stir until golden. Stir in flour until smooth. Cook 1 minute. Gradually stir in half-and-half and chicken broth. Bring to a boil over medium heat; continue boiling 3 to 4 minutes or until slightly thickened and reduced.

5. Place fettuccine in large bowl. Add chicken, pine nuts, red peppers and olives. Toss gently to coat. Pour sauce over fettuccine; toss gently. Add cheese and salt and black pepper to taste; toss. Garnish as desired. *Makes 4 main-dish servings*

Creamy Chicken and Red Pepper Pasta

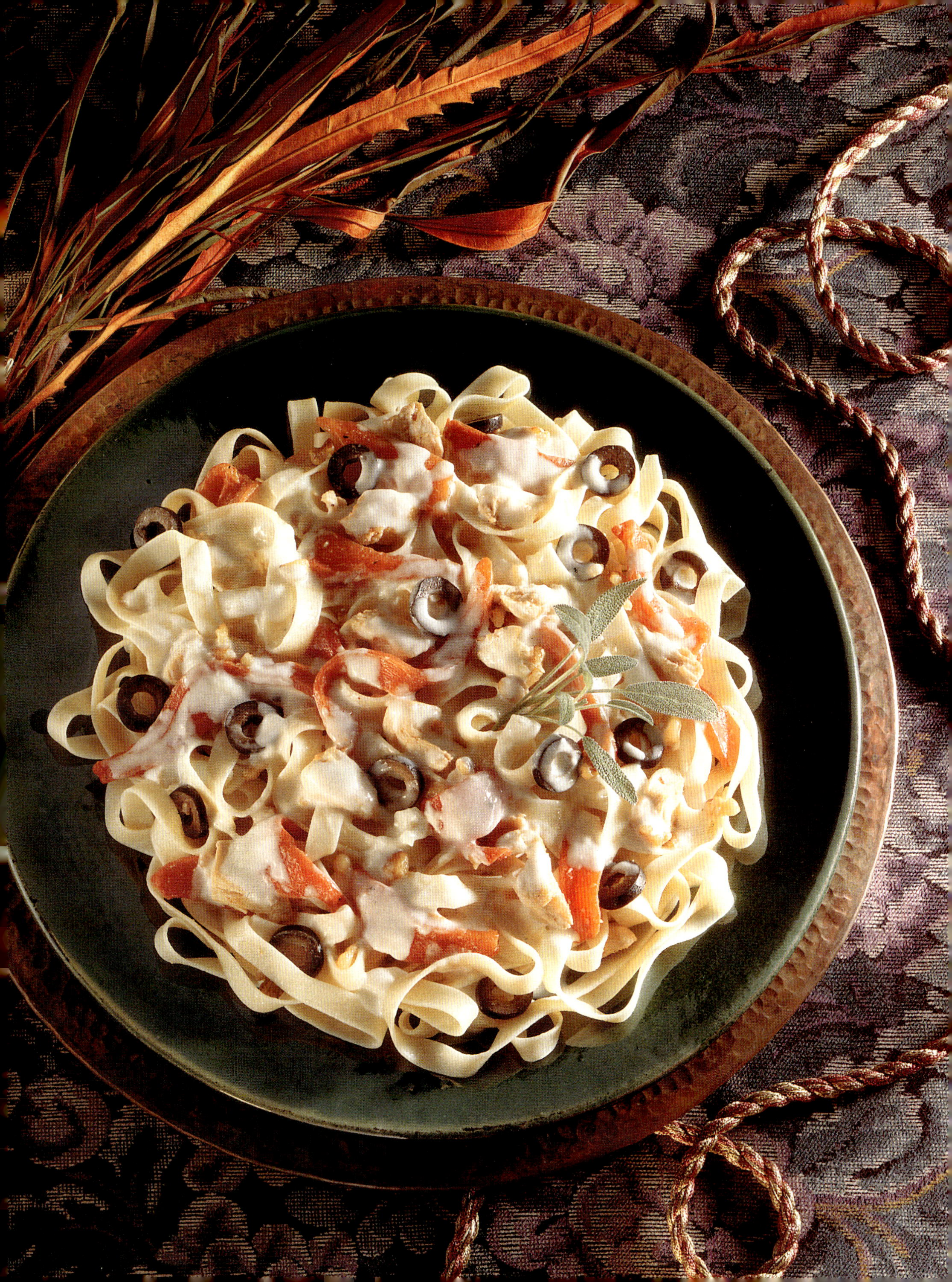

FROM THE BUTCHER SHOP

112 MAFALDA AND MEATBALLS

- 1 teaspoon olive oil
- 2 cloves garlic, minced, divided
- 2 cans (14½ ounces each) no-salt-added stewed tomatoes, undrained
- ½ teaspoon dried basil leaves
- 8 ounces lean ground beef
- 8 ounces ground turkey
- ⅓ cup dry French bread crumbs
- 3 tablespoons fat-free reduced-sodium chicken broth
- 3 tablespoons cholesterol-free egg substitute
- 1 teaspoon fennel seeds
- ¼ teaspoon salt
- ⅛ teaspoon black pepper
- 8 ounces uncooked mafalda or spaghetti noodles

1. Heat oil in large nonstick saucepan over medium-high heat. Add half of garlic; cook 1 minute. Add tomatoes and basil; bring to a boil. Reduce heat. Simmer, uncovered, 20 to 25 minutes or until sauce thickens, stirring occasionally.

2. Meanwhile, combine beef, turkey, bread crumbs, chicken broth, egg substitute, fennel seeds, remaining half of garlic, salt and pepper in large bowl; mix well. With wet hands, shape meat mixture into 12 (1-inch) balls.

3. Preheat broiler. Spray broiler pan with nonstick cooking spray. Arrange meatballs on broiler pan. Broil, 4 inches from heat, 10 minutes or until no longer pink in centers. Remove and add to tomato mixture. Cover; cook 5 to 10 minutes or until heated through.

4. Cook noodles according to package directions, omitting salt. Drain. Arrange noodles on serving platter. Pour meatballs and sauce over pasta. Serve with grated Parmesan cheese, if desired.

Makes 4 servings

113 PESTO CHICKEN PASTA

- 2 boneless skinless chicken breast halves, cut into strips
- 1 red bell pepper, cut into strips
- 1 tablespoon oil
- 1 package (9 ounces) DiGIORNO® Mozzarella Garlic Tortelloni, cooked, drained
- 1 package (7 ounces) DiGIORNO® Pesto Sauce

COOK and stir chicken and pepper in oil until chicken is cooked through.

TOSS with tortelloni and sauce.

Makes 4 servings

Prep time: 10 minutes
Cook time: 10 minutes

Mafalda and Meatballs

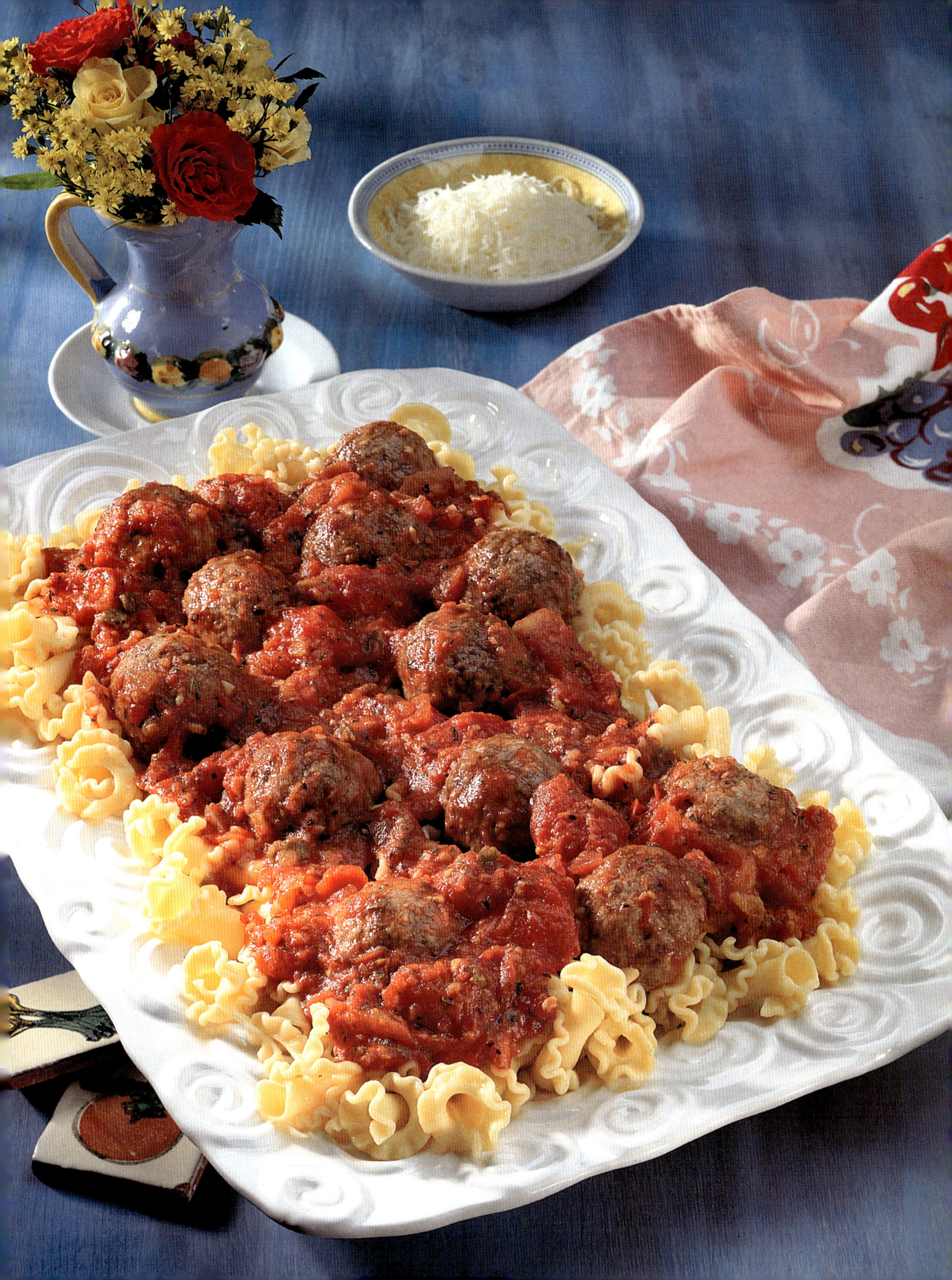

FROM THE BUTCHER SHOP

114 SPAM™ CONFETTI PASTA

    Nonstick cooking spray
2 cups frozen whole kernel corn, thawed
1 (12-ounce) can SPAM® Luncheon Meat, cut into 2-inch strips
1 red bell pepper, chopped
1 green bell pepper, chopped
¾ cup chopped red onion
1½ cups whipping cream
2 tablespoons chili powder
¼ teaspoon black pepper
12 ounces angel hair pasta, cooked and drained
2 tomatoes, peeled and chopped
¼ cup minced fresh cilantro

In large skillet coated with cooking spray, sauté corn, SPAM®, bell peppers and onion over medium heat 5 minutes or until tender. Transfer mixture to bowl; keep warm. To same skillet, add cream, chili powder and black pepper. Bring to a boil; boil 5 minutes or until cream has thickened slightly, stirring occasionally. Pour over pasta and toss well. Spoon SPAM™ mixture over pasta. To serve, sprinkle with tomatoes and cilantro.

Makes 6 servings

115 PASTA WITH CHICKEN AND PEPPERS

5 tablespoons FILIPPO BERIO® Extra Virgin Olive Oil, divided
1 large boneless chicken breast, skinned and cut into julienne strips (1 pound)
1 medium onion, chopped
1 medium red bell pepper, cut into julienne strips
1 medium green bell pepper, cut into julienne strips
1 clove garlic, minced
⅛ teaspoon ground red pepper
2 large tomatoes, chopped
¾ pound uncooked pasta tubes, such as penne

1. Heat 2 tablespoons olive oil over medium heat in large skillet. Cook and stir chicken until tender. Remove chicken; set aside.

2. Add 2 tablespoons olive oil to skillet; cook and stir onion and bell peppers until tender.

3. Return chicken to pan; add garlic and ground red pepper. Cook 3 minutes, stirring constantly.

4. Add tomatoes; simmer 10 minutes.

5. While chicken mixture is simmering, cook pasta according to package directions; *do not overcook.* Drain and toss with remaining 1 tablespoon olive oil in large bowl. Serve with sauce.

Makes 4 servings

Prep time: 15 minutes
Cook time: 25 minutes

SPAM™ Confetti Pasta

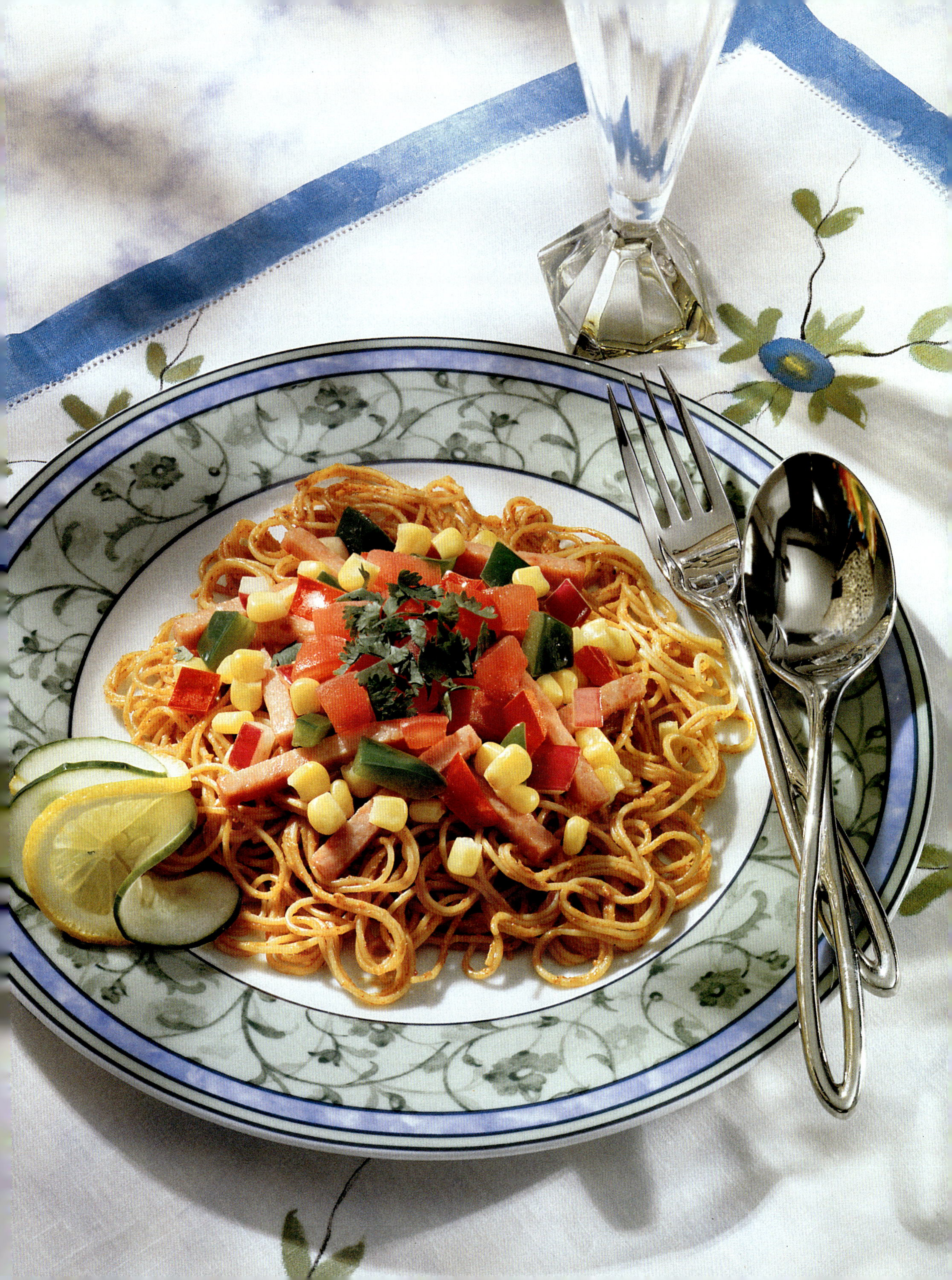

FROM THE BUTCHER SHOP

116 SPICY HAM & CHEESE PASTA

- ½ (16-ounce) package corkscrew pasta
- 2 tablespoons olive oil
- 1 large red bell pepper, cut into julienne strips
- 1 small red onion, diced
- 1 large clove garlic, crushed
- 8 ounces cooked ham, cut into ½-inch cubes
- 1 cup ricotta cheese
- 3 tablespoons chopped fresh parsley
- 1 teaspoon TABASCO® pepper sauce
- ¾ teaspoon salt

Prepare pasta according to package directions; drain. Meanwhile, heat olive oil in medium skillet over medium heat. Add and cook bell pepper, onion and garlic until crisp-tender, about 5 minutes. Add ham; cook 3 minutes longer, stirring occasionally.

In large bowl, toss cooked pasta with ham mixture, ricotta cheese, parsley, TABASCO sauce and salt; mix well.

Makes 4 servings

Spicy Ham & Cheese Pasta

FROM THE BUTCHER SHOP

117 SAUSAGE & FETA STRATA

8 ounces medium pasta shells, cooked and drained
1 pound Italian sausage
2 tablespoons vegetable oil
1 cup sliced green onions with tops
3 cloves garlic, minced
1 cup water
1 can (6 ounces) CONTADINA® Tomato Paste
2/3 cup dry red wine
3/4 teaspoon fennel seed
1/2 teaspoon dried rosemary, crushed
2 cups (8 ounces) crumbled feta cheese or ricotta cheese
2 cups sliced zucchini (about 2 medium zucchini)

Brown sausage in oil in 10-inch skillet over medium heat; drain on paper towels, reserving drippings in skillet. Add onions and garlic to reserved drippings. Cook and stir 3 minutes. Stir in water, tomato paste, wine, fennel and rosemary. Bring to a boil. Reduce heat to low; simmer 6 minutes, stirring occasionally. Spoon 1/2 of pasta into greased 2-quart baking dish; top with layers of 1/2 each of sauce and cheese. Place zucchini over cheese. Repeat layers of pasta, sauce and cheese. Arrange sausage on top to resemble pinwheel. Bake at 350°F, 35 to 40 minutes or until hot and bubbly.

Makes 8 servings

118 VEAL 'N' SPAGHETTI CASSEROLE

CASSEROLE
1 1/2 pounds boneless veal shoulder, cut into 1-inch cubes
3/4 cup chopped onion
1 teaspoon salt
1/2 teaspoon black pepper
2 cups water
1 package (7 ounces) uncooked thin spaghetti, hot cooked and drained
1 can (6 ounces) sliced mushrooms, undrained
1 cup sour cream

TOPPING
3 tablespoons CRISCO® all-vegetable shortening
1 cup fresh bread crumbs
1/2 cup grated Parmesan cheese
1/2 cup snipped parsley

Place veal, onion, salt, pepper and water in Dutch oven. Bring to a boil. Reduce heat to low; simmer, covered, until meat is tender (about 30 minutes).

Preheat oven to 350°F. Mix cooked spaghetti, undrained mushrooms and sour cream into veal mixture. Turn into greased 2 1/2-quart casserole.

For Topping, melt shortening in small skillet; stir in bread crumbs. Remove from heat; stir in cheese and parsley. Sprinkle over veal mixture.

Bake, uncovered, 35 to 40 minutes or until mixture is bubbly and crumb topping is golden brown.

Makes 8 servings

FROM THE BUTCHER SHOP

119 THIN-SLICED PANZANELLA

- 3 tablespoons extra-virgin olive oil
- 1 clove garlic, pressed or minced
- 1 package (about 1 pound) PERDUE® FIT 'N EASY® Fresh Skinless and Boneless Thin-Sliced Chicken Breast
- 1 teaspoon dried Italian herb seasoning
  Salt and ground black pepper to taste
- 6 ripe Italian plum tomatoes, cut into halves
- 10 to 12 fresh basil leaves, divided
- 1 tablespoon balsamic vinegar
- 8 ounces uncooked fettuccine
- 2 tablespoons grated Romano cheese
- 1 large bunch arugula, well rinsed

In small bowl, combine oil and garlic. Remove 2 teaspoons oil mixture and use to rub chicken. Sprinkle chicken with Italian seasoning, salt and pepper; refrigerate until ready to cook.

Prepare outdoor grill for cooking or preheat broiler. In food processor, combine 1 tablespoon reserved oil mixture, tomatoes, *half* the basil and vinegar. Pulse on and off to chop tomatoes. Season sauce with salt and pepper and set aside.

Cook pasta according to package directions. Drain and toss with remaining oil mixture, cheese and salt and pepper.

Grill or broil chicken 3 to 6 inches from heat source 1½ to 2 minutes on each side until cooked through. To serve, spoon warm pasta over arugula; top with chicken and tomato sauce and garnish with remaining basil leaves. *Makes 4 servings*

120 ROTINI WITH CAULIFLOWER AND PROSCIUTTO

- 8 ounces uncooked rotini pasta
- 1 head cauliflower, separated into florets
- ¼ cup FILIPPO BERIO® Extra Virgin Olive Oil
- 1 onion, thinly sliced
  Salt and freshly ground black pepper to taste
- ¼ pound thinly sliced prosciutto (preferably imported), cut into bite-size pieces

Cook pasta according to package directions until *al dente* (tender but still firm). Drain. In large saucepan, cook cauliflower florets in boiling salted water 3 to 5 minutes or until tender. Add to colander with pasta. Drain; transfer to large bowl. In medium saucepan, heat olive oil over medium heat until hot. Add onion; cook and stir 5 to 7 minutes or until tender. Add onion with olive oil to pasta mixture; toss until lightly coated. Season to taste with salt and pepper. Top with prosciutto. *Makes 4 servings*

Thin-Sliced Panzanella

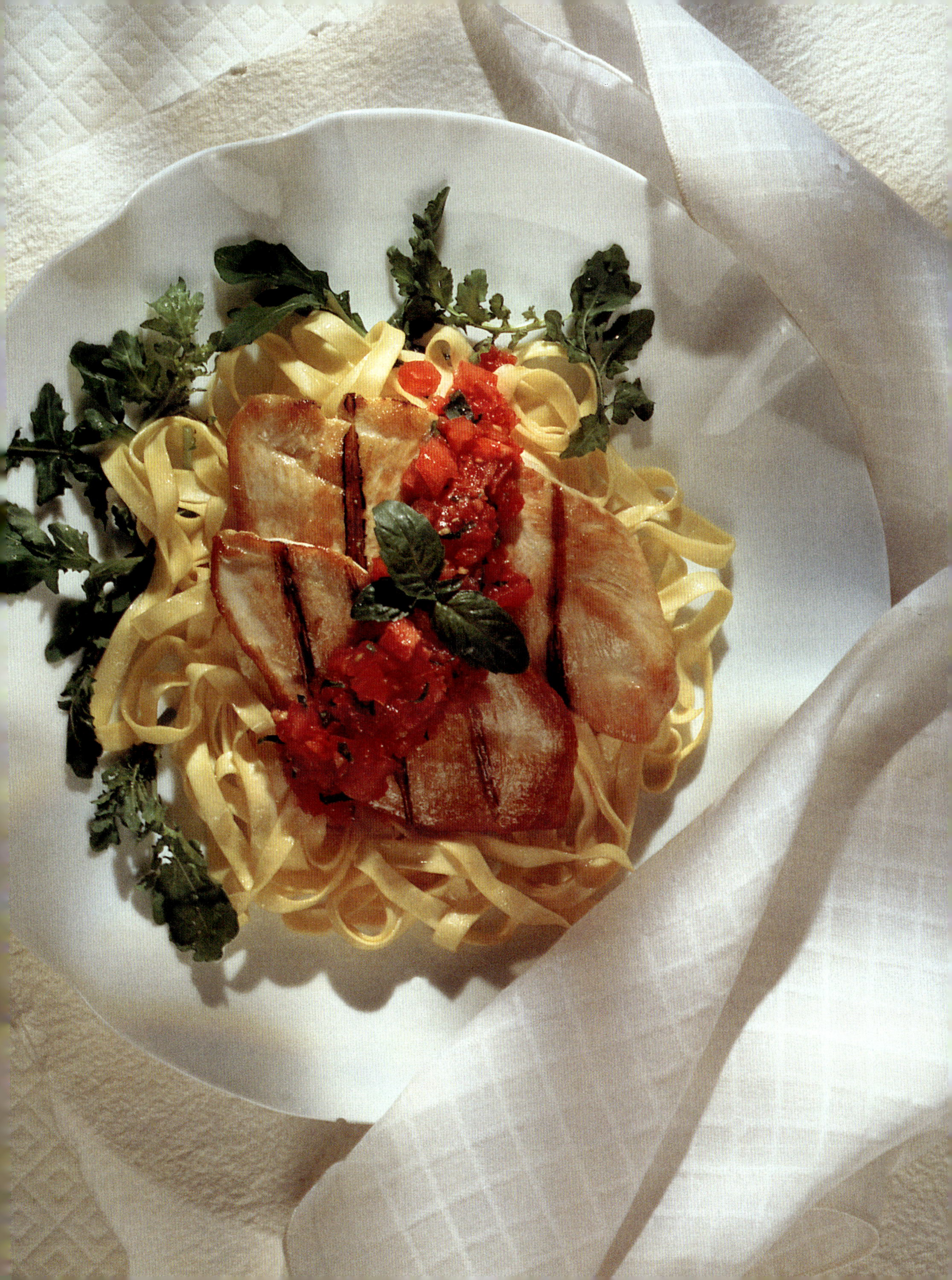

FROM THE BUTCHER SHOP

121 CHICKEN RAGOUT WITH ORZO

- ¾ cup (4 ounces) orzo, cooked and drained
- 1 tablespoon olive oil
- ⅔ cup chopped onion
- 1 can (4 ounces) mushrooms, drained
- ⅓ cup celery slices
- ⅓ cup finely chopped carrot
- ¼ pound Italian sausage, casing removed, crumbled
- 4 OSCAR MAYER® Bacon Slices, chopped
- 1½ pounds boneless, skinless chicken breasts, cut into ½-inch pieces
- 1 bay leaf
- 1 large clove garlic, minced
- ¾ cup dry Marsala wine
- 1 can (14½ ounces) tomatoes, cut up, undrained
- 1 cup chicken broth
- ⅛ teaspoon ground cloves
- 1 container (8 ounces) PHILADELPHIA BRAND® Soft Cream Cheese with Olives & Pimento

• Heat oil in Dutch oven over medium-high heat. Add onion, mushrooms, celery, carrot, sausage and bacon; cook and stir until vegetables are tender and sausage is browned, about 5 minutes.

• Add chicken, bay leaf and garlic; cook, stirring occasionally, 4 minutes.

• Add wine. Bring to a boil; reduce heat to low. Simmer 10 to 15 minutes or until only slight amount of liquid remains.

• Stir in tomatoes, broth and cloves. Bring to a boil over medium-high heat; reduce heat to low. Simmer 20 minutes or until slightly thickened, stirring occasionally. Remove from heat.

• Stir in cream cheese and orzo.

Makes 6 servings

Prep time: 30 minutes
Cook time: 40 minutes

122 COUNTRY STYLE CRACKED BLACK PEPPER FETTUCCINE

- 1 package (12 ounces) PASTA LaBELLA® Cracked Black Pepper Fettuccine
- 3 tablespoons sweet cream butter
- 2 tablespoons olive oil
- ½ tablespoon sliced fresh garlic
- 1 cup julienned ham
- ¾ cup broccoli florets
- ¾ cup diced tomato
- Salt and black pepper to taste
- ¼ cup grated Romano cheese

Cook pasta according to package directions. Meanwhile, heat butter and olive oil in large skillet. Sauté garlic, ham, broccoli and tomato 5 minutes. Immediately add hot pasta, salt and pepper; toss well. Sprinkle with cheese and serve.

Makes 4 main-dish servings

FROM THE BUTCHER SHOP

123 QUICK TURKEY TORTELLONI

- 1 package (10 ounces) DiGIORNO® Alfredo or Four Cheese Sauce
- 1 package (10 ounces) frozen chopped broccoli, thawed, drained *or* 2 cups broccoli flowerets, cooked tender-crisp, drained
- ½ pound cooked turkey, cut into strips (about 1½ cups)
- 1 jar (2½ ounces) sliced mushrooms, drained (optional)
- 1 package (9 ounces) DiGIORNO® Mushroom or Mozzarella Garlic Tortelloni, cooked, drained
- Toasted sliced almonds (optional)

HEAT sauce, broccoli, turkey and mushrooms in saucepan on medium heat.

SPOON over hot tortelloni. Sprinkle with almonds, if desired.

Makes 3 to 4 servings

Prep time: 5 minutes
Cook time: 10 minutes

124 SPEEDY STROGANOFF

- 1 pound beef sirloin, cut into narrow strips
- 1 tablespoon CRISCO® all-vegetable shortening
- 1 medium onion, sliced
- 1 clove garlic, minced
- 1 can (10¾ ounces) condensed cream of mushroom soup
- 1 cup sour cream
- 1 can (4 ounces) sliced mushrooms, undrained
- 2 tablespoons ketchup
- 2 teaspoons Worcestershire sauce
- Poppy Noodles (recipe follows)

In large skillet, brown beef strips in hot shortening. Add onion and garlic; cook until onion is crisp-tender. Combine soup, sour cream, mushrooms with liquid, ketchup and Worcestershire; pour over beef mixture. Cook and stir over low heat until hot. Serve over Poppy Noodles. *Makes 4 servings*

POPPY NOODLES Toss 4 cups hot cooked noodles with 1 tablespoon butter and 1 teaspoon poppy seeds.

FROM THE BUTCHER SHOP

125 PASTA PAPRIKASH

Nonstick cooking spray
12 ounces beef round steak, cut into 1-inch cubes
4 tablespoons all-purpose flour, divided
2 cans (about 14 ounces each) beef broth, divided
2 green bell peppers, sliced
1 onion, sliced
2 cloves garlic, minced
2 tablespoons sweet Hungarian paprika
¼ teaspoon black pepper
⅛ teaspoon ground red pepper
1 can (6 ounces) reduced-sodium tomato paste
1 cup reduced-fat sour cream
Salt to taste (optional)
8 ounces fettuccine, cooked and kept warm

1. Spray large skillet with cooking spray. Heat over medium heat until hot. Coat beef with 2 tablespoons flour; cook 5 to 8 minutes or until browned. Add 1 cup beef broth and bring to a boil. Reduce heat and simmer, covered, 15 to 20 minutes or until beef is tender. Remove beef from skillet.

2. Add bell peppers, onion and garlic to skillet; cook and stir about 5 minutes or until tender. Stir in remaining 2 tablespoons flour, paprika, black pepper and red pepper; cook, stirring constantly, 1 minute. Stir in tomato paste and ½ cup remaining broth. Add beef and remaining broth and bring to a boil. Reduce heat and simmer, uncovered, 5 to 7 minutes or until sauce is thickened.

3. Stir in sour cream; cook over low heat 1 to 2 minutes, stirring frequently. Season to taste with salt, if desired. Serve over fettuccine. *Makes 4 servings*

126 SCALLOPED CHICKEN & PASTA

¼ cup margarine or butter, divided
1 package (6.2 ounces) PASTA RONI™ White Cheddar Sauce with Shells
2 cups frozen mixed vegetables
⅔ cup milk
2 cups chopped cooked chicken or ham
¼ cup dry bread crumbs

1. Preheat oven to 450°F.

2. In 3-quart saucepan, combine 2¼ cups water and 2 tablespoons margarine. Bring just to a boil. Stir in pasta and frozen vegetables. Reduce heat to medium.

3. Boil, uncovered, stirring frequently, 12 to 14 minutes or until most of water is absorbed. Add contents of seasoning packet, milk and chicken. Continue cooking 3 minutes.

4. Meanwhile, melt remaining 2 tablespoons margarine in small saucepan; stir in bread crumbs.

5. Transfer pasta mixture to 8- or 9-inch square glass baking dish. Sprinkle with bread crumbs. Bake 10 minutes or until bread crumbs are browned and edges are bubbly. *Makes 4 servings*

Pasta Paprikash

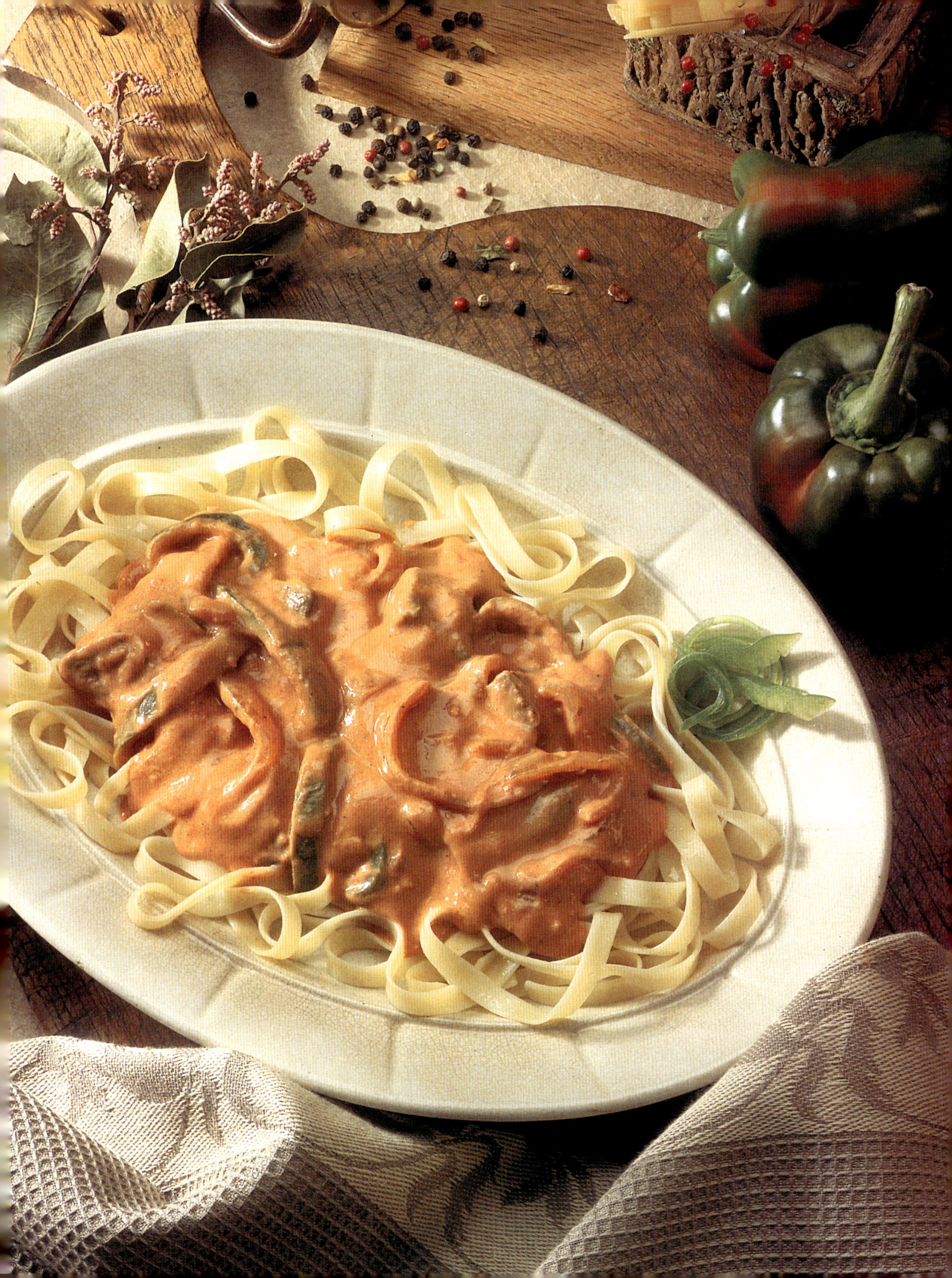

FROM THE BUTCHER SHOP

127 CREAMY HERBED CHICKEN

- 1 package (9 ounces) fresh bow tie pasta or fusilli*
- 1 tablespoon vegetable oil
- 2 boneless skinless chicken breasts, cut into halves, then cut into ½-inch strips
- 1 small red onion, cut into slices
- 1 package (10 ounces) frozen green peas, thawed and drained
- 1 yellow or red bell pepper, cut into strips
- ½ cup chicken broth
- 1 container (8 ounces) soft cream cheese with garlic and herbs
- Salt and black pepper to taste

Substitute dried bow tie pasta or fusilli for fresh pasta. Cooking time will be longer; follow package directions.

Cook pasta in lightly salted boiling water according to package directions, about 5 minutes; drain.

Meanwhile, heat oil in large skillet or wok over medium-high heat. Add chicken and onion; cook and stir 3 minutes or until chicken is no longer pink in center. Add peas and bell pepper; cook and stir 4 minutes. Reduce heat to medium.

Stir in broth and cream cheese. Cook, stirring constantly, until cream cheese is melted. Combine pasta and chicken mixture in serving bowl; mix lightly. Season with salt and black pepper to taste. Garnish as desired.
Makes 4 servings

SERVING SUGGESTION: Serve with tomatoes vinaigrette and crusty country bread.

128 SAVORY SAUSAGE & SPINACH PENNE

- 8 ounces penne pasta
- 2 tablespoons olive oil
- 3 cloves garlic, minced
- 1 pound sweet sausage, casing removed
- 1 pound fresh leaf spinach
- 1 cup crushed tomatoes
- ½ cup chicken broth
- ½ cup dry white wine
- ¾ cup oil-packed sun-dried tomatoes, chopped *or* ¼ cup dried sun-dried tomatoes, chopped
- 1 tablespoon fresh chopped basil *or* 1 teaspoon dried basil leaves
- 2 teaspoons TABASCO® pepper sauce
- Salt and black pepper to taste
- Parmesan cheese to taste

In medium saucepan, cook pasta and set aside. In large skillet over medium-high heat, add oil and garlic; sauté until garlic is lightly browned. Add crumbled sausage; sauté 4 minutes, then push to the sides of the pan. Add spinach; sauté until wilted, about 3 minutes. Add crushed tomatoes, chicken broth, white wine, sun-dried tomatoes, basil and TABASCO sauce; cook 5 minutes. Remove from heat; add cooked pasta and toss lightly. Add salt and pepper to taste. Sprinkle with Parmesan cheese and serve warm.
Makes 6 to 8 servings

Preparation time: 10 minutes
Cooking time: 15 minutes

Creamy Herbed Chicken

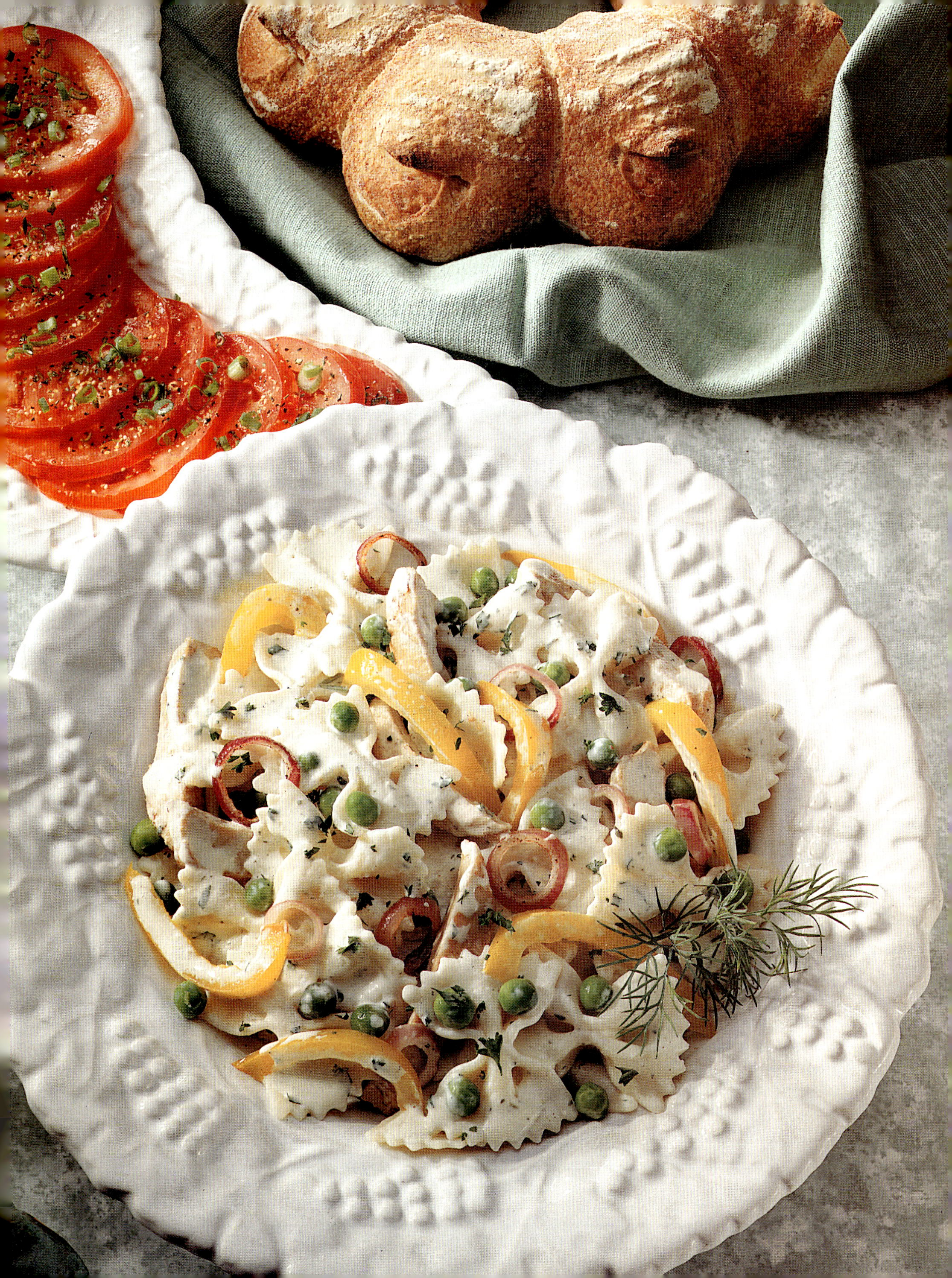

FROM THE BUTCHER SHOP

129 JERK CHICKEN AND PASTA

    Jerk Sauce (recipe follows)
12 ounces boneless skinless chicken breasts
    Nonstick cooking spray
1 cup fat-free reduced-sodium chicken broth
1 green bell pepper, sliced
2 green onions, sliced
8 ounces fettuccine, cooked and kept warm
    Grated Parmesan cheese (optional)

1. Spread Jerk Sauce on both sides of chicken. Place in glass dish; refrigerate, covered, 15 to 30 minutes.

2. Spray skillet with cooking spray. Heat over medium heat until hot. Add chicken; cook 5 to 10 minutes until no longer pink in center. Add chicken broth, bell pepper and onions; bring to a boil. Reduce heat; simmer, uncovered, 5 to 7 minutes or until vegetables are crisp-tender and broth is reduced to thin sauce consistency. Remove chicken from skillet; cut into slices. Toss pasta, chicken and vegetable mixture in bowl. Sprinkle with Parmesan cheese, if desired.

Makes 4 servings

JERK SAUCE
  2 tablespoons lime juice
  ¼ cup loosely packed fresh cilantro
  2 tablespoons coarsely chopped fresh ginger
  3 cloves garlic
  2 tablespoons black pepper
  1 tablespoon ground allspice
  ½ teaspoon curry powder
  ¼ teaspoon ground cloves
  ⅛ teaspoon ground red pepper

1. Combine all ingredients in food processor or blender; process until thick paste consistency.

130 MEXICAN EYE–OPENER WITH CHILI PEPPER PASTA

1 cup cooked PASTA LaBELLA® Chili Pepper Linguine
3 eggs
1 tablespoon water
1 tablespoon olive oil
2½ ounces chorizo sausage
1 ounce diced onion
1 ounce diced bell pepper
1½ ounces shredded Cheddar cheese

In small bowl, lightly beat eggs and water; set aside. Heat olive oil in nonstick skillet. Sauté chorizo, onion and bell pepper 1 to 2 minutes. Add chili pepper pasta; cook until pasta begins to crackle. Add egg mixture and cook in normal omelet fashion. When pasta is flipped over, sprinkle with Cheddar cheese. Melt and serve.

Makes 1 serving

TIP: Can be served with salsa and sour cream.

Jerk Chicken and Pasta

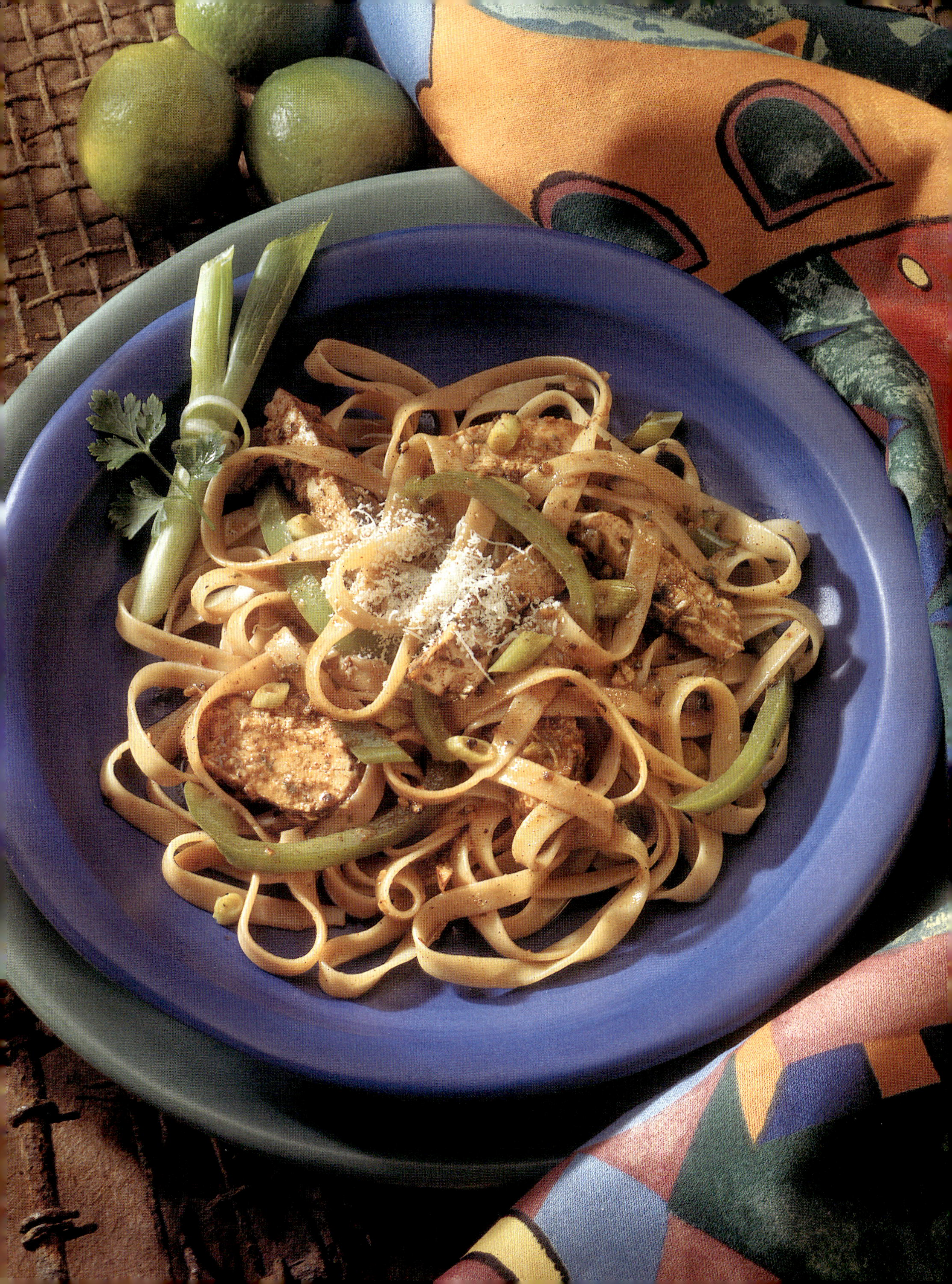

FROM THE BUTCHER SHOP

131 CHICKEN STROGANOFF

2 pounds boneless chicken breasts, skinned and cut into thin strips
½ cup all-purpose flour
1½ teaspoons salt
⅛ teaspoon black pepper
⅓ cup plus 3 tablespoons CRISCO® all-vegetable shortening, divided
½ cup finely chopped onion
2 cups chicken broth
½ pound fresh mushrooms, cleaned and sliced
¾ cup sour cream
3 tablespoons tomato paste
1 teaspoon Worcestershire sauce
Buttered noodles

Coat chicken strips evenly with mixture of flour, salt and pepper.

Melt ⅓ cup shortening in large heavy skillet. Add chicken strips and onion; cook and stir until chicken is evenly browned on all sides. Add broth; cover. Simmer about 20 minutes or until meat is tender. Remove from heat.

Melt 3 tablespoons shortening in small skillet over medium heat. Add mushrooms; cook and stir until lightly browned and tender. Add to chicken mixture.

Combine sour cream, tomato paste and Worcestershire sauce; add in small amounts to chicken mixture, stirring until well combined.

Return to heat. Cook and stir over low heat until hot. Serve with buttered noodles.

Makes 8 servings

132 ITALIAN SAUSAGE WITH KRAUT AND FETTUCCINE

7 ounces fettuccine, cooked and drained
4 slices bacon
1 large onion, chopped
1 small red bell pepper, sliced into strips
1 cup thinly sliced mushrooms
1 tablespoon packed brown sugar
¼ cup red wine
1 can (14 ounces) FRANK'S or SNOWFLOSS Kraut, drained
1 package (12 ounces) precooked link Italian sausage, thickly sliced
2 tablespoons dried parsley flakes
4 tablespoons butter

In large skillet over medium heat, cook bacon until crisp; remove bacon from skillet, reserving drippings in skillet. Drain bacon on paper towels; crumble and set aside. Add onion, pepper and mushrooms to reserved drippings in skillet; cook and stir until tender. Stir in brown sugar, wine and kraut. Add sausage and parsley; cover. Reduce heat to low; simmer 8 minutes or until thoroughly heated, stirring occasionally. Add butter to hot pasta; toss to coat. Add bacon and kraut mixture; mix lightly.

Makes 4 to 6 servings

FROM THE BUTCHER SHOP

133 COUNTRY NOODLES AND HAM

- 1 package (1 pound) PASTA L<small>A</small>BELLA® Medium or Extra Wide Egg Noodles
- ¼ cup olive oil
- ½ cup diced yellow onion
- 12 ounces ham, diced large
- 1 cup sliced mushrooms
- 1 cup frozen peas, thawed
- 1 tablespoon chopped garlic
- 2 cups chicken broth
- Salt and black pepper to taste
- 3 tablespoons sweet cream butter
- ⅓ cup grated Parmesan cheese

Cook pasta according to package directions. Meanwhile, heat olive oil in large pot over high heat. Sauté onion and ham 3 minutes. Add mushrooms, peas and garlic; cook 6 minutes. Add chicken broth, salt, pepper and butter. Simmer 3 minutes. Spoon ham mixture over noodles. Sprinkle with Parmesan cheese and serve.

Makes 3 main-dish servings

134 HARVEST DRUMS

- 1 package (about 1¼ pounds) PERDUE® Fresh Skinless Chicken Drumsticks
- ½ teaspoon dried Italian herb seasoning
- Salt and ground black pepper to taste
- 3 slices bacon, diced
- 2 cans (14½ ounces each) pasta-ready tomatoes with cheeses
- 1 small onion, chopped
- 1 clove garlic, minced
- ¼ cup red wine
- 1 small zucchini, scrubbed and julienned
- 1 package (12 ounces) angel hair pasta, cooked and drained

Sprinkle chicken with Italian seasoning and salt and pepper to taste. In large nonstick skillet over medium-low heat, cook bacon about 5 minutes, until crisp. Remove from skillet; drain and crumble. Increase heat to medium-high. Add chicken to bacon drippings (or replace drippings with 1½ tablespoons olive oil); cook 4 to 5 minutes on all sides or until brown, turning often.

In large slow cooker, combine tomatoes, bacon, onion, garlic and wine. Add chicken; cook on high 1½ to 1¾ hours, or until fork-tender. Add zucchini during last 5 minutes of cooking. Serve chicken and vegetables over angel hair pasta.

Makes 3 to 4 servings

FROM THE BUTCHER SHOP

135 BOW TIE PASTA WITH CHICKEN AND ROAST GARLIC

- 1 head garlic
- 3 tablespoons plus 1 teaspoon olive oil, divided
- 1½ pounds assorted wild mushrooms (such as shiitake, portobello or cremini), sliced
- 1 can (14½ ounces) diced tomatoes, undrained
- ¾ cup chopped green onions
- 1½ cups chicken broth
- 1½ pounds cooked skinless, boneless chicken breasts, diced
- ¼ cup chopped fresh cilantro
- 2 teaspoons salt
- 1 teaspoon black pepper
- 1 pound bow tie pasta, cooked and drained

1. Preheat oven to 325°F. Cut off ¼ inch of garlic top. Rub 1 teaspoon olive oil on garlic head. Wrap garlic in aluminum foil, cook 45 minutes; let cool. Squeeze garlic pulp into small bowl; set aside.

2. Heat remaining 3 tablespoons olive oil in large skillet over high heat until hot. Add mushrooms; cook and stir 3 minutes. Add tomatoes and green onions; cook and stir 2 minutes. Add broth, scraping bottom of skillet clean. Simmer 5 minutes or until broth reduces to 1 cup. Add garlic, chicken, cilantro, salt and pepper; cook 2 minutes.

3. Combine sauce with pasta in large bowl; stir gently. *Makes 6 servings*

136 RIGATONI

- 2 pounds BOB EVANS FARMS® Italian Dinner Link Sausage
- 2 medium onions, sliced
- 3 green bell peppers, sliced
- 3 red bell peppers, sliced
- 3 cloves garlic, minced
- 1 tablespoon sugar
- 1 teaspoon dried oregano leaves
- 1 teaspoon dried basil leaves
- 1 teaspoon dried thyme leaves
- Salt and black pepper to taste
- 1 (1-quart) can crushed Italian plum tomatoes, undrained
- 1 pound rigatoni pasta, cooked according to package directions and drained
- Chopped fresh parsley (optional)

Cut sausage into 1-inch pieces. Cook in large saucepan over medium-high heat until well browned. Remove sausage to paper towels; set aside. Drain off all but ¼ cup drippings. Add all remaining ingredients to drippings except tomatoes, pasta and parsley. Cook and stir until vegetables are tender. Stir in reserved sausage and tomatoes with juice. Bring to a boil. Reduce heat to low; simmer 15 minutes. Serve over hot pasta. Garnish with chopped parsley, if desired. Refrigerate leftovers. *Makes 8 to 10 servings*

Bow Tie Pasta with Chicken and Roast Garlic

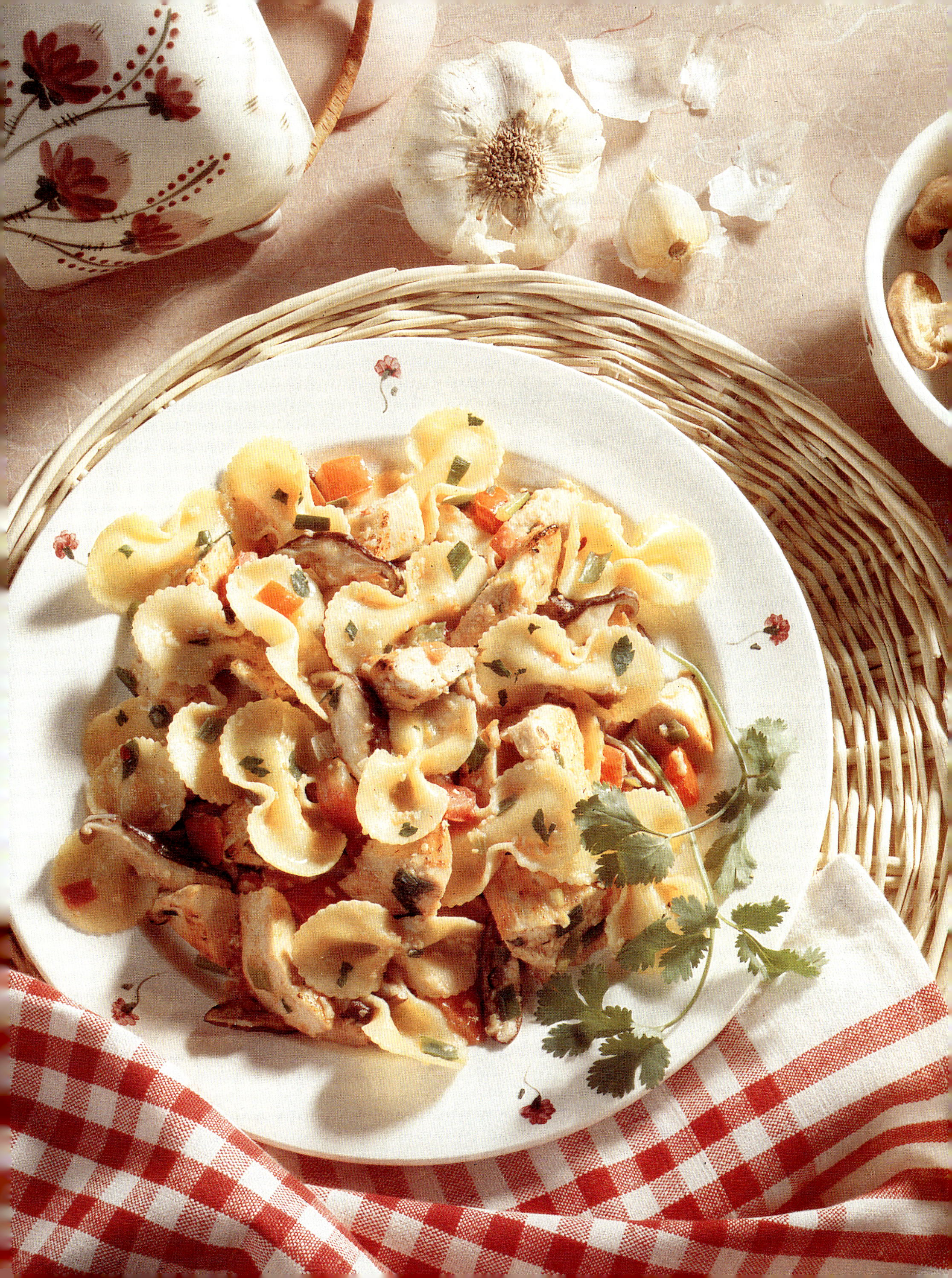

FROM THE BUTCHER SHOP

137 MANY PEPPERED FILLETS

- 1 package (about ¾ pound) PERDUE® FIT 'N EASY® Fresh Skinless and Boneless Turkey Breast Fillets
- 1 tablespoon olive oil
  Salt and ground black pepper to taste
- 2 cups sliced bell peppers
- 1 cup sliced onion
- 2 cups hot, cooked couscous or brown rice
- 1 tablespoon minced fresh parsley (optional)

Prepare outdoor grill for cooking or preheat broiler. Rub fillets with oil and lightly season with salt and black pepper. Grill fillets 5 to 6 inches from heat source 3 minutes. Turn fillets over and cover with bell peppers and onion. Grill 5 to 6 minutes longer until turkey is cooked through. Serve with couscous tossed with parsley, if desired.

Makes 4 servings

Many Peppered Fillets

FROM THE BUTCHER SHOP

138 TURKEY ORZO ITALIANO

- ¼ pound mushrooms, sliced
- ½ cup green onions, sliced
- 2 tablespoons margarine
- 2 cups turkey broth or reduced-sodium chicken bouillon
- 1 cup uncooked orzo pasta
- ½ teaspoon Italian seasoning
- ½ teaspoon salt
- ⅛ teaspoon white pepper
- 2 cups cubed cooked turkey

1. In large skillet, over medium-high heat, sauté mushrooms and onions in margarine 1 minute. Add turkey broth and bring to a boil.

2. Stir in orzo, Italian seasoning, salt and pepper; bring to a boil. Reduce heat and simmer, covered, 15 minutes or until orzo is tender and liquid has been absorbed. Stir in turkey and heat through.

Makes 4 servings

Favorite recipe from **National Turkey Federation**

139 ROTINI AND TURKEY MOZZARELLA

- 2 tablespoons olive or vegetable oil
- 1½ cups thinly sliced zucchini
- 1 cup chopped onion
- 2 cloves garlic, minced
- 3½ cups (28-ounce can) CONTADINA® Crushed Tomatoes
- 2 cups cubed cooked turkey, chicken, ham or smoked turkey
- ¾ cup whole kernel corn
- 2 teaspoons Italian herb seasoning
- ½ teaspoon salt
- ¼ teaspoon ground black pepper
- 8 ounces dry rotini, cooked, drained
- 1½ cups (6 ounces) shredded mozzarella cheese
- ⅔ cup (about 3 ounces) grated Parmesan cheese
- 3 tablespoons chopped fresh parsley *or* 1 teaspoon dried parsley flakes

In large skillet, heat oil. Add zucchini, onion and garlic; sauté 3 to 5 minutes or until vegetables are tender. Stir in crushed tomatoes, turkey, corn, Italian seasoning, salt and pepper. Bring to a boil. Reduce heat to low; simmer, uncovered, 5 minutes or until heated through. Remove from heat; stir in pasta. Spoon half of pasta mixture into greased 13×9-inch baking dish; top with half of mozzarella and Parmesan cheeses. Repeat layers. Bake in preheated 350°F oven 20 to 25 minutes or until heated through. Let stand 5 minutes. Sprinkle with parsley just before serving.

Makes 8 servings

FROM THE BUTCHER SHOP

140 SPAM™ FETTUCCINI PRIMAVERA

1 tablespoon butter or margarine
2 tablespoons all-purpose flour
1½ cups skim milk
½ cup low-sodium chicken broth
1½ teaspoons dried basil leaves
12 ounces uncooked fettuccini
1 (12-ounce) can SPAM® Lite Luncheon Meat, cut into julienne strips
1 (16-ounce) package frozen broccoli, carrot and cauliflower combination, cooked and drained
⅔ cup grated Parmesan cheese

In small saucepan, melt butter. Stir in flour. Cook and stir 1 minute. Stir in milk, chicken broth and basil. Bring to a boil, stirring constantly, until thickened; keep warm. In 5-quart saucepan, cook fettuccini according to package directions; drain and return to saucepan. Stir in SPAM®, vegetables and sauce. Cook and stir over medium-high heat until thoroughly heated. Stir in Parmesan cheese.   *Makes 6 to 8 servings*

141 CACCIATORE PINEAPPLE CHICKEN

1 can (20 ounces) DOLE® Pineapple Chunks
4 boneless, skinless chicken breast halves
1 teaspoon garlic powder
1 teaspoon vegetable or olive oil
1 medium onion, thinly sliced
1 tablespoon dried oregano leaves
1 can (14½ ounces) stewed tomatoes
¼ cup small pitted ripe olives (optional)
2 teaspoons cornstarch
1½ teaspoons instant chicken bouillon granules
8 ounces twistee noodles, cooked
Chopped parsley (optional)

- DRAIN pineapple; reserve juice.

- SPRINKLE chicken with garlic powder. In nonstick skillet, brown chicken in oil. Add onion and oregano. Cook until onion is tender.

- ADD tomatoes, pineapple and olives to skillet. Cover; cook 3 more minutes.

- STIR cornstarch and bouillon into reserved juice. Add to skillet. Cook, stirring, until sauce boils and thickens. Cover; cook 5 more minutes.

- SPOON chicken and sauce over noodles. Sprinkle with parsley, if desired.
Makes 4 servings

Prep time: 10 minutes
Cook time: 15 minutes

SPAM™ Fettuccini Primavera

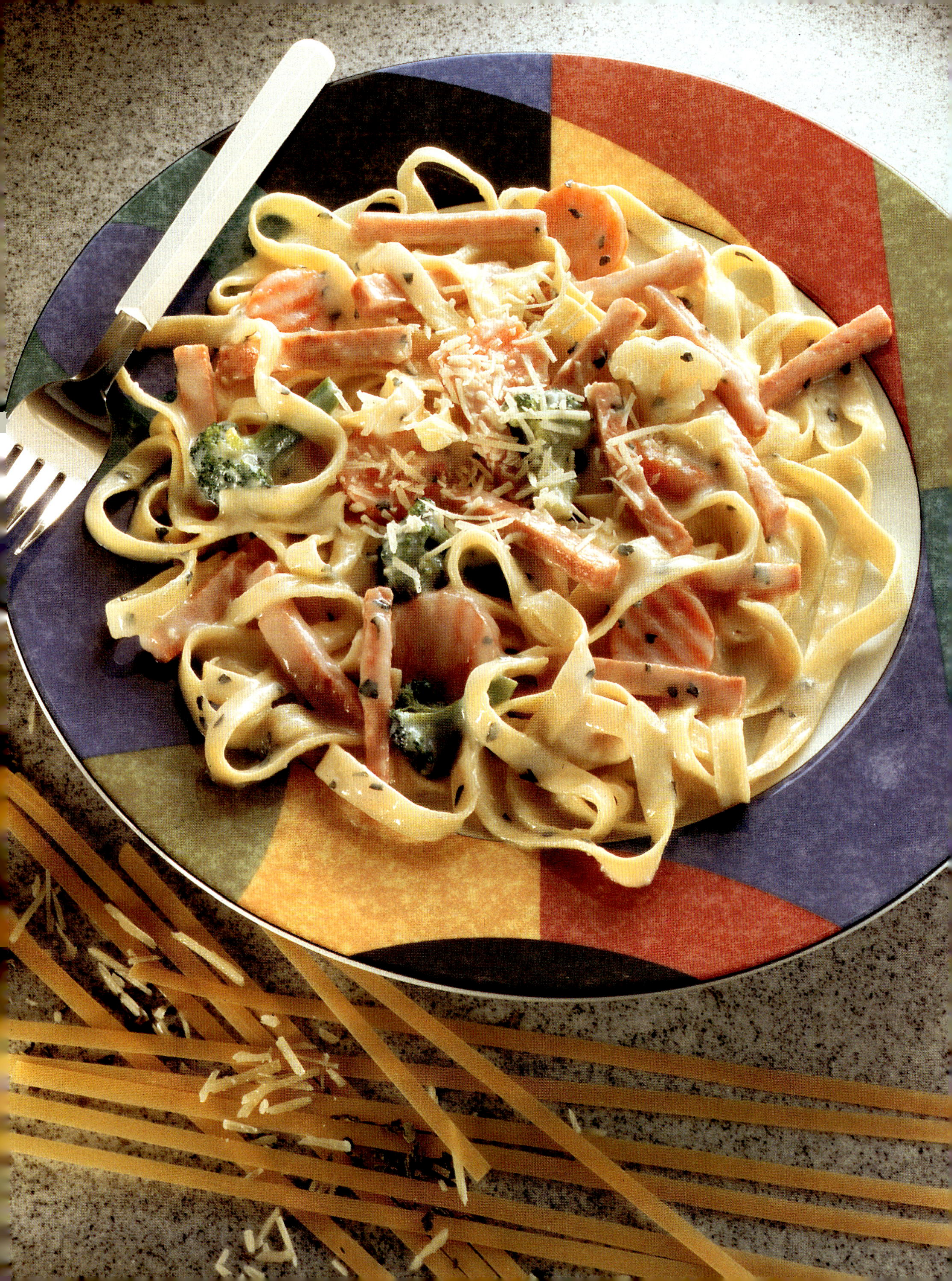

FROM THE BUTCHER SHOP

142 DELICIOUS CHICKEN PASTA

- 2 whole skinless boneless chicken breasts (about 12 ounces)
- 3 teaspoons CHEF PAUL PRUDHOMME'S® Meat Magic®, divided
- 1 cup chopped white onion
- ½ cup chopped celery
- ½ cup chopped green bell pepper
- 2 cups defatted chicken stock, divided
- 2 tablespoons all-purpose flour
- 3 cups thinly sliced fresh mushrooms
- 1 teaspoon minced garlic
- ½ cup chopped green onions
- 6 ounces pasta (fettuccine, angel hair or your favorite), cooked according to package directions

Cut chicken into thin strips; place in small bowl and combine thoroughly with 2 teaspoons Meat Magic®.

Place skillet over high heat and add white onion, celery, bell pepper and remaining 1 teaspoon Meat Magic®. Cook over high heat, shaking pan and stirring occasionally (don't scrape), 5 minutes. Add ½ cup chicken stock, scraping up browned coating on bottom of pan; cook another 4 minutes. Stir in chicken mixture and cook 4 minutes. Add flour and stir well, cooking another 2 minutes. Add mushrooms and garlic, folding carefully so mushrooms don't break.

Add ½ cup chicken stock and scrape bottom of pan. Cook 4 minutes and add another ½ cup stock, stirring and scraping. Continue cooking 5 minutes more; add green onions and remaining ½ cup stock. Stir and scrape well. Cook 5 more minutes or until chicken is tender; remove from heat. Serve with pasta.

Makes 6 servings

143 PENNE WITH EGGPLANT AND TURKEY SAUSAGE

- 1 pound Italian turkey sausage, cut into 1-inch rings
- 1 medium eggplant, cut into ½-inch cubes
- 3 cups prepared chunky vegetable spaghetti sauce
- 12 ounces penne pasta, cooked according to package directions
- 4 ounces Asiago cheese, shredded

1. In large nonstick skillet over medium heat, sauté turkey sausage and eggplant 12 to 15 minutes or until sausage is no longer pink and eggplant is soft and lightly browned. Add spaghetti sauce to turkey mixture and simmer 3 minutes or until heated throughout.

2. To serve, spoon sauce over penne and top with cheese.

Makes 8 servings

Favorite recipe from **National Turkey Federation**

FROM THE BUTCHER SHOP

144 PASTA PRIMAVERA WITH ITALIAN SAUSAGE

8 ounces mild Italian sausage, casing removed, sliced
1 small onion, diced (about ½ cup)
1 large clove garlic, minced
1 medium zucchini, sliced (about 1 cup)
1¾ cups (14½-ounce can) CONTADINA® Pasta Ready Chunky Tomatoes Primavera, undrained
½ cup sliced pitted ripe olives, drained
¼ cup dry red wine or beef broth
8 ounces dry pasta, cooked, drained, kept warm
Chopped fresh basil (optional)
Grated Parmesan cheese (optional)

In large skillet, cook sausage until no longer pink. Remove sausage from skillet, reserving drippings in skillet. Add onion and garlic to skillet; sauté 1 minute. Add zucchini; sauté 2 minutes. Reduce heat to medium. Add tomatoes and juice, olives, wine and sausage; simmer, uncovered, 5 to 7 minutes or until heated through. Serve over pasta. Sprinkle with basil and Parmesan cheese, if desired.
Makes 4 servings

145 CREAMY ORZO WITH PROSCIUTTO

1 package (1 pound) orzo, cooked and drained
2 tablespoons butter or margarine
2 cloves garlic, minced
1 package (8 ounces) PHILADELPHIA BRAND® Cream Cheese, cubed
½ cup chicken broth
Dash turmeric
1 package (10 ounces) frozen peas, thawed and drained
3 ounces thinly sliced prosciutto, cut into julienne strips
Salt and pepper

• Melt butter in large saucepan over low heat. Add garlic; cook and stir until tender. Add cream cheese, broth and turmeric; stir until cream cheese is melted.

• Stir in orzo, peas and prosciutto; heat thoroughly, stirring occasionally. Season with salt and pepper to taste. Serve with grated Parmesan cheese, if desired.
Makes 8 to 10 side-dish servings

Prep time: 25 minutes

TIP: Recipe can be doubled for a main-dish meal.

FROM THE BUTCHER SHOP

146 TURKEY PESTO MEATBALLS WITH ZUCCHINI AND PASTA

1½ cups fresh basil leaves, packed
1½ pounds California-grown ground turkey
¾ cup freshly grated Parmesan cheese
1 cup soft white bread crumbs
3 large cloves fresh garlic, minced
1 egg, lightly beaten
½ teaspoon salt
½ teaspoon black pepper
2 tablespoons olive oil
1¼ cups chicken or turkey broth
1 to 1½ pounds fine egg noodles
3 cups thinly sliced zucchini
8 basil sprigs for garnish
Additional Parmesan cheese for topping

Place basil leaves in food processor or blender and chop finely. Transfer to large bowl with turkey, Parmesan cheese, bread crumbs, garlic, egg, salt and pepper. Mix ingredients with fork (do not mix with your hands or the meat will become tough). Shape into small balls with your hands. Heat 1 tablespoon olive oil in large nonstick skillet; brown half the meatballs on all sides. Remove from pan with slotted spoon and repeat with remaining oil and meatballs. Return first batch of meatballs to skillet; pour in broth and bring to a boil. Reduce heat and simmer 12 minutes. After 8 minutes, place noodles in boiling water and cook according to package directions. At same time, add zucchini to meatballs and cook until crisp-tender; *do not overcook.* Serve meatballs and zucchini over cooked pasta in warmed shallow bowls. Garnish with sprig of basil and pass additional Parmesan cheese at table.

Makes 8 servings

Favorite recipe from **California Poultry Industry Federation**

147 QUICK CHICKEN MARINARA

1 tablespoon olive oil
2 boneless skinless chicken breast halves (about ¾ pound), cut into strips
1 yellow or green bell pepper, cut into strips
1 package (15 ounces) DiGIORNO® Marinara Sauce
1 package (9 ounces) DiGIORNO® Spinach Fettuccine, cooked, drained

HEAT oil in skillet over medium-high heat. Add chicken and pepper; cook and stir 3 minutes.

STIR in sauce. Cook over medium heat 3 to 5 minutes or until chicken is cooked through. Serve over hot fettuccine. Top with DiGIORNO® Shredded Parmesan Cheese, if desired.

Makes 4 servings

Prep time: 10 minutes
Cook time: 8 minutes

Turkey Pesto Meatballs with Zucchini and Pasta

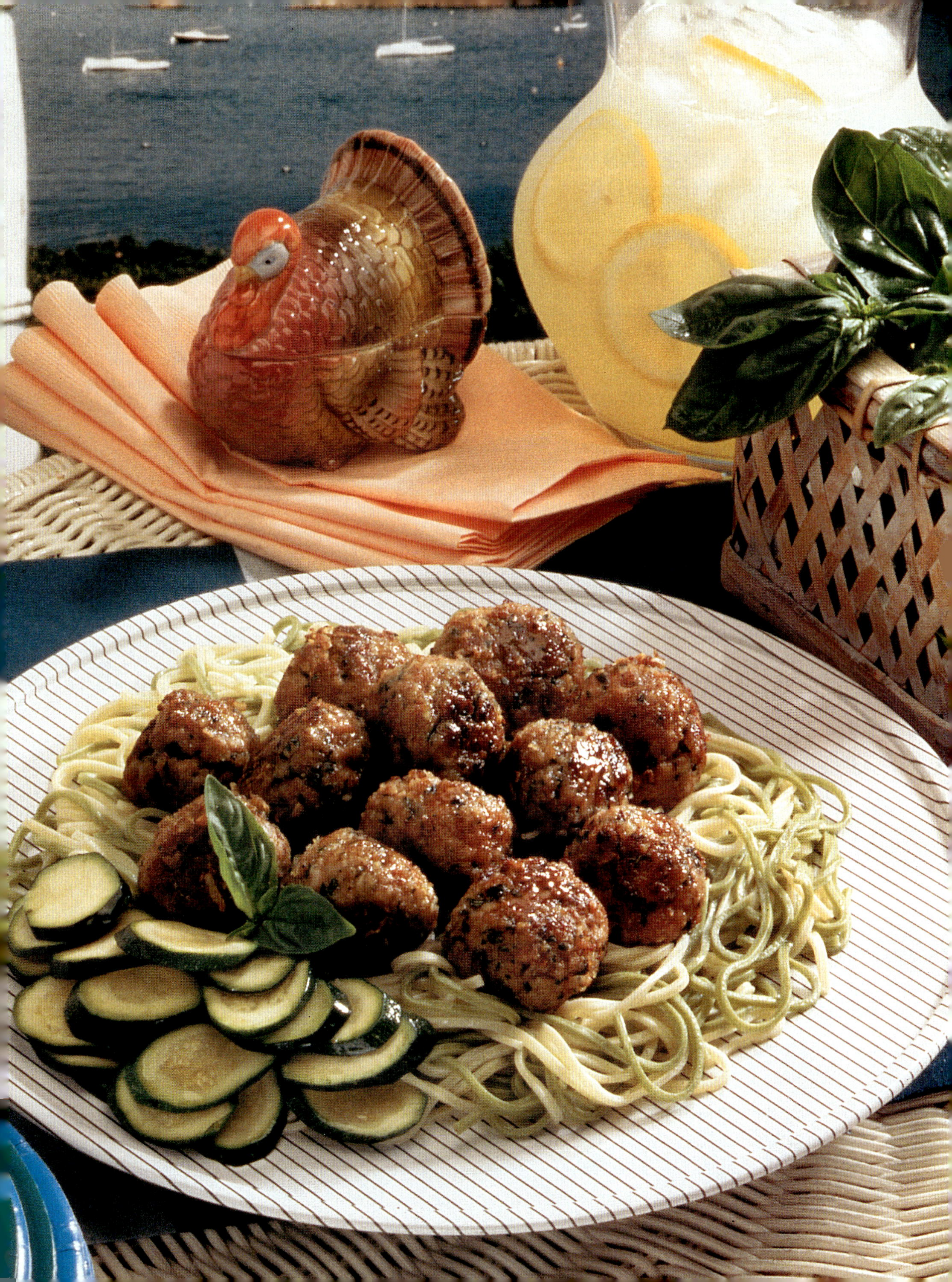

FROM THE BUTCHER SHOP

148 NEW ORLEANS SAUSAGE AND NOODLES

- 1 package (4½ or 5¼ ounces) Alfredo noodles and sauce mix
- ¼ teaspoon ground red pepper
- 1 package (9 ounces) frozen artichoke hearts, thawed
- 1 tablespoon olive oil
- 1 package (14 ounces) LOUIS RICH® Turkey Smoked Sausage, cut diagonally into ¼-inch slices
- 1 clove garlic, minced
- 1 tomato, chopped

• Prepare Alfredo noodle mix according to package directions, stirring in red pepper and artichoke hearts during last 3 minutes of cooking time.

• Meanwhile, heat oil in large skillet over medium heat. Add sausage and garlic; cook and stir 5 minutes or until sausage is lightly browned.

• Stir tomato into sausage mixture; cook an additional 2 minutes. Serve over hot noodle mixture.   *Makes 4 to 6 servings*

New Orleans Sausage and Noodles

FROM THE BUTCHER SHOP

149 HE-MAN STEW

- 1 package (about 3½ pounds) PERDUE® Fresh Skinless Pick of the Chicken
- Salt and ground black pepper to taste
- 2 tablespoons olive oil
- 1 can (12 ounces) lite beer
- 1 can (28 ounces) whole plum tomatoes, drained and chopped
- 1 onion, sliced into rings
- ¼ cup spicy brown mustard
- 4 cups cooked elbow macaroni

Season chicken with salt and pepper to taste. In large nonstick skillet over medium-high heat, heat oil. Add chicken; cook 5 to 6 minutes on each side for larger pieces, 3 to 4 minutes on each side for smaller pieces, or until brown, turning often. In large slow cooker, combine beer, tomatoes, onion and mustard. Add chicken. Cook on high 1½ to 2 hours, or until chicken is fork-tender. Serve over macaroni.

Makes 3 to 4 servings

150 LAMB AND SPAGHETTI PRIMAVERA

- ½ pound lean ground American lamb
- 2 tablespoons grated Parmesan cheese
- ¼ teaspoon garlic powder
- 2 cups meatless spaghetti sauce
- 1 small zucchini, cut into halves lengthwise and sliced (1½ cups)
- 1½ cups sliced fresh mushrooms
- 8 ounces spaghetti or linguine
- ½ cup (2 ounces) Asiago cheese, shredded*

*Grated fresh Parmesan cheese may be substituted.

In small bowl, combine ground lamb, Parmesan cheese and garlic powder; mix well. Form into 24 (¾-inch) balls. Meanwhile, heat spaghetti sauce in large saucepan. Add meatballs to sauce; bring to a boil. Reduce heat; cover and simmer 5 minutes. Stir in zucchini and mushrooms; cook 6 to 8 minutes or until vegetables are tender.

Meanwhile, cook pasta according to package directions; drain. Serve meatball mixture over pasta; top with Asiago cheese.

Makes 4 servings

Favorite recipe from **American Lamb Council**

FROM THE BUTCHER SHOP

151 FIESTA CHICKEN BREASTS

- 12 ounces uncooked spinach fettuccine or linguine
- 3 tablespoons butter or margarine
- 3 whole chicken breasts, split, boned and skinned
- 1 jar (7 ounces) roasted red peppers, drained and sliced into ½-inch strips (1 cup)
- ¼ cup sliced green onions
- ¼ cup all-purpose flour
- 1 cup chicken broth
- 1 cup milk
- ¼ cup dry white wine
- 1½ cups (6 ounces) SARGENTO® Shredded Monterey Jack or Mild Cheddar Cheese
- ¼ cup coarsely chopped fresh cilantro

Cook fettuccine according to package directions. Drain well and transfer to serving platter; keep warm. Meanwhile, melt butter in large skillet over medium heat. Add chicken; cook until golden brown and cooked through, about 5 minutes per side. Place chicken over fettuccine. Top with red pepper strips; keep warm. Add green onions to drippings in skillet; cook 1 minute. Add flour; cook 1 minute, stirring constantly. Add broth, milk and wine; bring to a boil and cook until thickened, stirring constantly. Add Monterey Jack cheese; stir until melted. Pour evenly over chicken, peppers and fettuccine; sprinkle with cilantro.

Makes 6 servings

152 HEARTY ITALIAN MEDLEY

- 1 DOLE® Fresh Pineapple
- 1 pound hot Italian sausage, cut into bite-size pieces
- 1 onion, chopped
- 3 zucchini, chunked
- 1 eggplant, chunked
- 1 DOLE® Green Bell Pepper, seeded, chunked
- ¼ cup water
- 2 cups prepared marinara sauce
- 1 tomato, chunked
- 4 cups hot cooked noodles

• TWIST crown from pineapple. Cut pineapple into quarters. Cut fruit from shells. Trim off core and cut fruit into bite-size pieces.

• BROWN sausage and onion in large skillet or Dutch oven. Add zucchini, eggplant, bell pepper and water. Cover; simmer 10 minutes until tender.

• STIR in marinara sauce, tomato and pineapple. Simmer 5 minutes. Serve over hot cooked noodles. *Makes 8 servings*

Prep time: 10 minutes
Cook time: 17 minutes

Fiesta Chicken Breasts

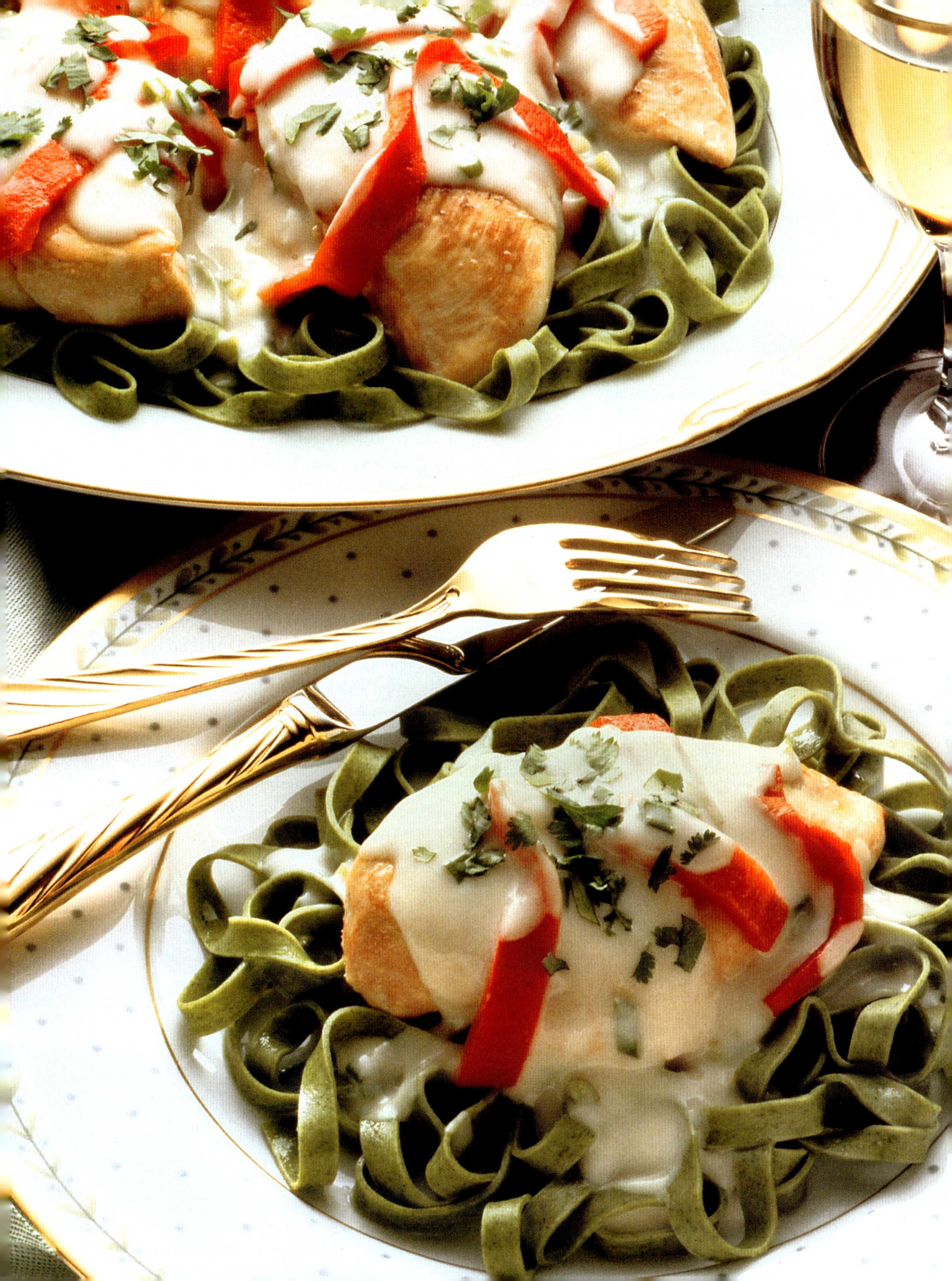

FROM THE BUTCHER SHOP

153 CHICKEN AND PASTA IN CREAM SAUCE

- 5 ounces thin spaghetti, cooked, drained, kept warm
- 6 tablespoons unsalted butter
- 1 tablespoon CHEF PAUL PRUDHOMME'S® Poultry Magic®
- 1/2 pound diced boneless, skinless chicken breasts
- 1/4 cup finely chopped green onions with tops
- 2 cups heavy cream or half-and-half

Melt butter in large skillet over medium heat. Add Poultry Magic® and chicken; cook 1 minute. Add onions; cook and stir 1 to 2 minutes. Gradually add cream, stirring until well blended. Bring to a boil. Reduce heat to low; simmer, uncovered, 2 to 3 minutes or until sauce starts to thicken, stirring frequently. Add pasta; toss to coat. Heat thoroughly, stirring occasionally. Serve immediately.

Makes 2 main-dish servings

154 PASTA WITH SAUSAGE AND MUSTARD SAUCE

- 1 cup BLUE DIAMOND® Blanched Slivered Almonds
- 5 tablespoons olive oil, divided
- 2 red or green bell peppers, diced
- 1 pound Italian sausage, casing removed
- 3 cloves garlic, finely chopped
- 2 tablespoons chopped fresh basil *or* 1 teaspoon dried basil leaves
- 3/4 cup dry white wine
- 3/4 cup heavy cream
- 1 1/2 tablespoons Dijon mustard
- 1/4 teaspoon black pepper
- 1 pound fresh pasta *or* 8 ounces dried pasta, cooked

Sauté almonds in 1 tablespoon oil in medium saucepan until golden; reserve. Add remaining 4 tablespoons oil to pan. Sauté bell peppers and sausage until bell peppers are just tender and sausage is browned and crumbly, about 3 minutes. Stir in garlic, basil, wine and cream. Cook over high heat until liquid thickens and coats the back of a spoon, about 3 minutes. Stir in mustard and black pepper. Add almonds. Toss with hot, cooked pasta.

Makes 4 to 6 servings

FROM THE BUTCHER SHOP

155 TURKEY AND BOW TIE PASTA

¼ cup plus 1 tablespoon all-purpose flour
2 cups skim milk
1 cup white wine
1 teaspoon Italian seasoning
Dash black pepper
1 pound turkey kielbasa or smoked turkey sausage, cut into ½-inch slices
1 package (10 ounces) frozen mixed vegetables, thawed and drained
6 ounces bow tie pasta, cooked according to package directions and drained
Poppy seeds

1. In medium saucepan, combine flour and milk. Add wine, Italian seasoning and pepper, stirring until smooth. Over medium heat, cook mixture until thick and bubbly, stirring constantly. Fold in turkey kielbasa, vegetables and pasta; reduce heat to medium-low and cook 5 to 8 minutes or until heated throughout.

2. To serve, top pasta mixture with poppy seeds. *Makes 6 servings*

Favorite recipe from **National Turkey Federation**

156 PEPPER CHICKEN

¼ cup all-purpose flour
2 teaspoons garlic salt
1½ to 2 teaspoons black pepper
8 boneless chicken breasts
¼ cup WESSON® Oil
1 small onion, chopped
1 cup thinly sliced celery
3 medium cloves garlic, minced
1 (15-ounce) can HUNT'S® Tomato Sauce
1 (6-ounce) can HUNT'S® Tomato Paste
1 cup chicken broth
1 (7-ounce) can ROSARITA® Whole Green Chiles, cut into strips
2 tablespoons wine
1 tablespoon chopped fresh basil
1 teaspoon sugar (optional)
Hot cooked pasta or rice

In food storage bag, combine flour, garlic salt and black pepper. Place chicken in bag and shake to coat with flour mixture. In large skillet, heat oil; sauté chicken on both sides until browned. Remove and set aside. Add onion, celery and garlic; sauté until tender. Stir in tomato sauce, tomato paste and chicken broth; mix well. Stir in remaining ingredients except pasta. Place chicken on top of sauce, cover and simmer 30 minutes. Serve over cooked pasta.
Makes 8 servings

FROM THE BUTCHER SHOP

157 SAUSAGE & PASTA PRIMAVERA

- 4 ounces uncooked spaghetti
- 12 ounces fully cooked beef knockwurst or beef polish sausage links, cut diagonally into 1/2-inch-thick slices
- 1/2 pound fresh asparagus,* trimmed, cut diagonally into 1-inch pieces
- 1 medium onion, cut lengthwise into thin wedges
- 1/4 cup water
- 1 clove garlic, minced
- 2 medium tomatoes, coarsely chopped
- 2 tablespoons finely chopped fresh basil *or* 1 1/2 teaspoons dried basil leaves
- 2 tablespoons grated Parmesan cheese (optional)

*Or, substitute 1 package (10 ounces) frozen cut asparagus for fresh asparagus. Use as directed.

1. Cook spaghetti according to package directions. Drain; keep warm.

2. Meanwhile, combine beef knockwurst, asparagus, onion, water and garlic in large skillet. Cook over medium-high heat 5 to 7 minutes or until asparagus is crisp-tender, stirring occasionally. Add spaghetti, tomatoes and basil; toss lightly. Cook 2 minutes or until heated through.

3. Sprinkle with cheese, if desired.

Makes 4 (2-cup) servings

Favorite recipe from **National Cattlemen's Beef Association**

158 BURGUNDY BEEF PASTA

- 8 ounces uncooked linguine
- 1 pound top sirloin, very thinly sliced crosswise
- 2 cloves garlic, minced
- 1/2 teaspoon dried thyme leaves
- 2 teaspoons vegetable oil
- 1/4 pound fresh mushrooms, sliced
- 1 can (14 1/2 ounces) DEL MONTE® Stewed Tomatoes (No Salt Added)
- 1 can (8 ounces) DEL MONTE® Tomato Sauce (No Salt Added)
- 3/4 cup dry red wine
- Chopped parsley (optional)

Cook pasta according to package directions; drain.

In large skillet, cook sirloin, garlic and thyme in oil over medium-high heat 3 minutes. Add mushrooms; cook 1 minute. Add tomatoes, tomato sauce and wine. Cook, uncovered, over medium heat 15 minutes, stirring occasionally. Serve over pasta. Garnish with chopped parsley, if desired. *Makes 4 servings*

Prep time: 10 minutes
Cook time: 20 minutes

HINT: Cook pasta ahead; rinse and drain. Cover and refrigerate. Just before serving, heat in microwave or dip in boiling water.

Sausage & Pasta Primavera

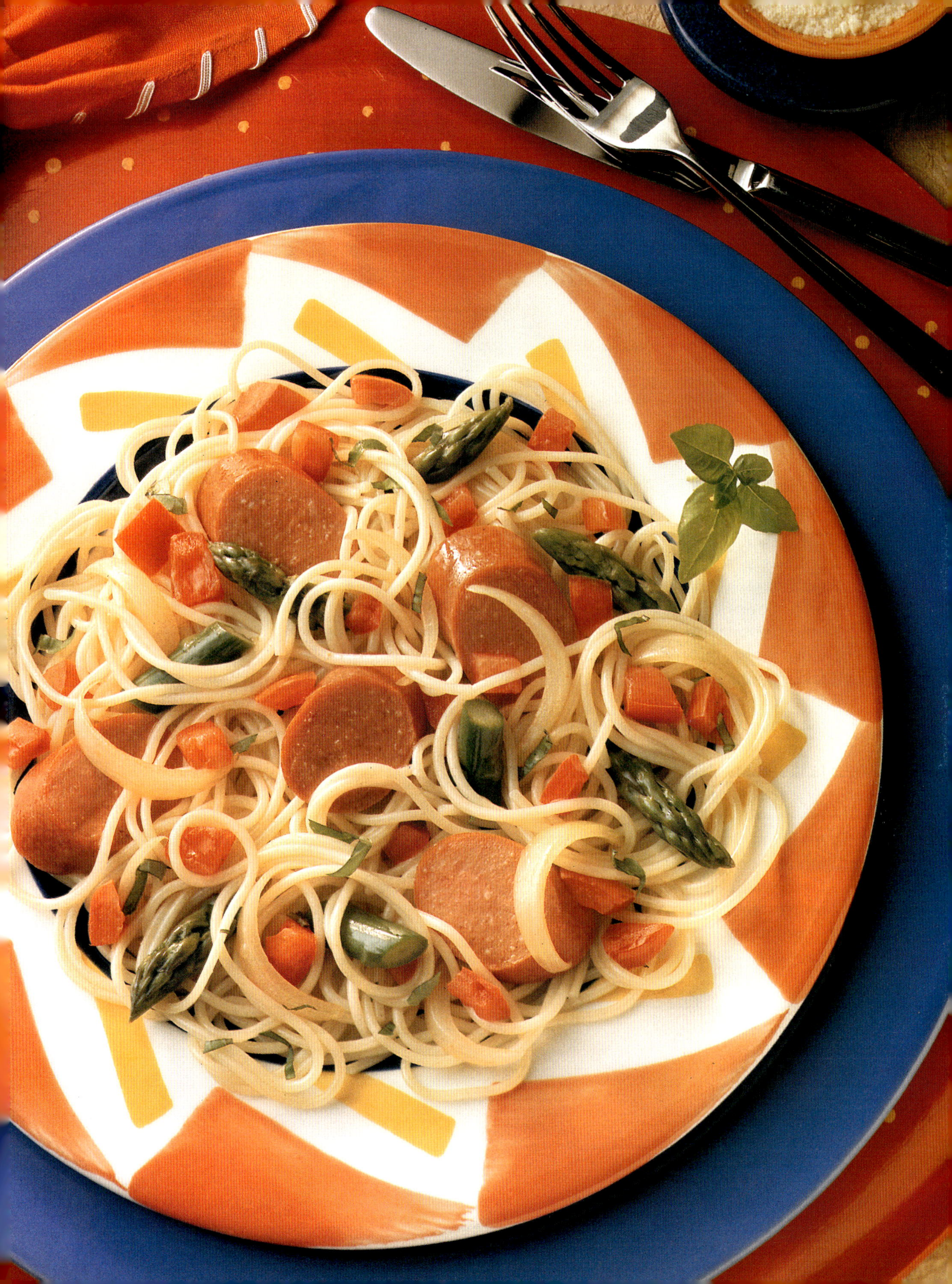

CATCH OF THE DAY

159 SCALLOPS WITH VERMICELLI

- 1 pound bay scallops
- 2 tablespoons fresh lemon juice
- 2 tablespoons chopped fresh parsley
- 1 onion, chopped
- 1 clove garlic, minced
- 2 tablespoons olive oil
- 2 tablespoons butter, divided
- 1½ cups canned Italian tomatoes, undrained and chopped
- 2 tablespoons chopped fresh basil *or* ½ teaspoon dried basil leaves
- ¼ teaspoon dried oregano leaves
- ¼ teaspoon dried thyme leaves
- 2 tablespoons heavy cream
- Dash ground nutmeg
- 12 ounces uncooked vermicelli, hot cooked and drained

Rinse scallops. Combine scallops, juice and parsley in glass dish. Cover; marinate in refrigerator while preparing sauce.

Cook and stir onion and garlic in oil and 1 tablespoon butter in large skillet over medium-high heat until onion is tender. Add tomatoes with juice, basil, oregano and thyme. Reduce heat to low. Cover; simmer 30 minutes, stirring occasionally.

Drain scallops; cook and stir in remaining 1 tablespoon butter in another large skillet over medium heat until scallops are opaque, about 2 minutes. Add cream, nutmeg and tomato sauce mixture.

Pour sauce over vermicelli in large bowl; toss gently to coat. Garnish as desired.

Makes 4 servings

Favorite recipe from **New Jersey Department of Agriculture**

Scallops with Vermicelli

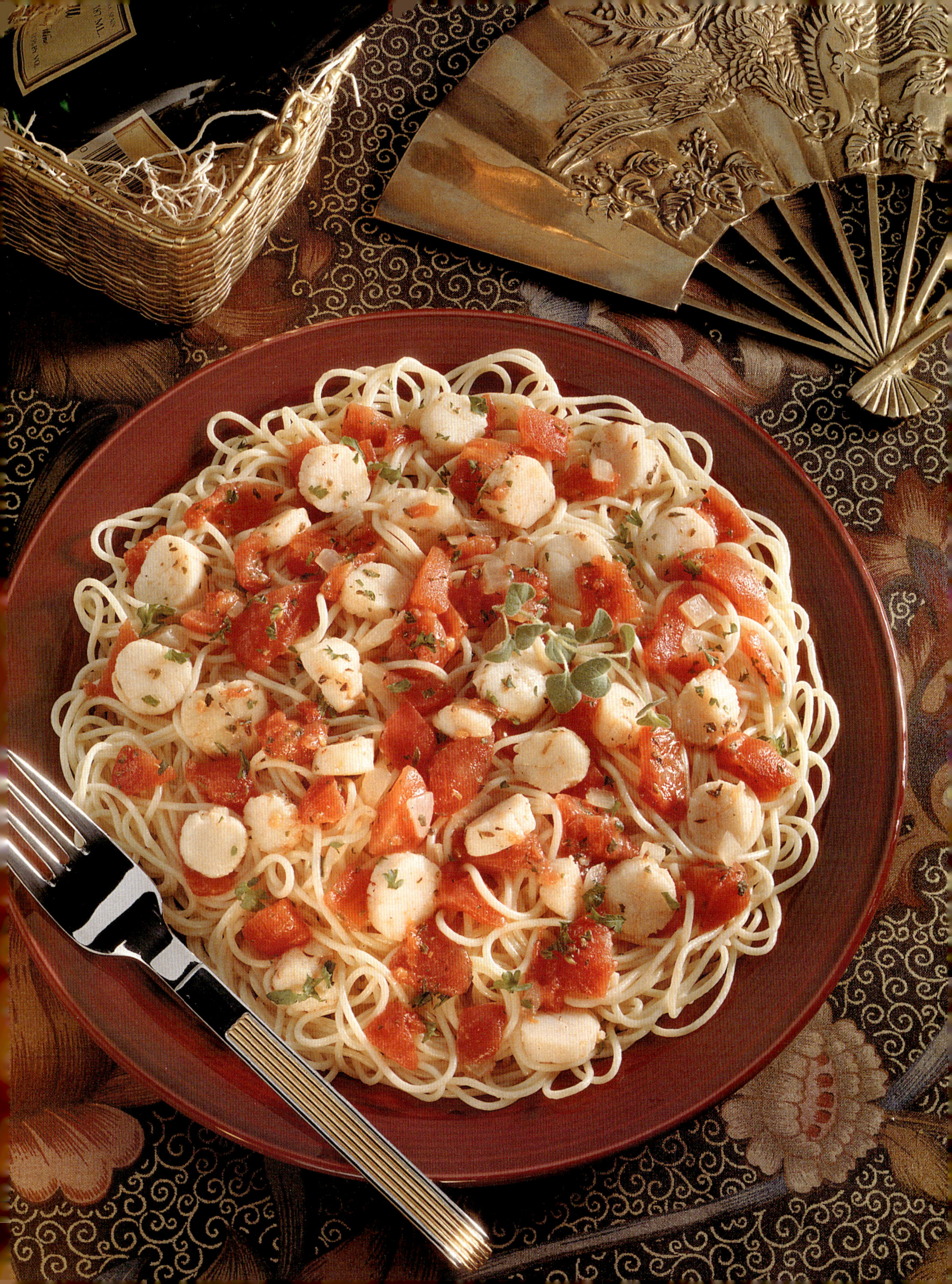

CATCH OF THE DAY

160 ORZO RISOTTO WITH SHRIMP AND VEGETABLES

    Nonstick cooking spray
    1 zucchini, cut into halves, then sliced
    2 teaspoons grated lemon peel
    1 cup sliced mushrooms
    ½ cup chopped onion
    2 cloves garlic, minced
    ¾ teaspoon dried sage leaves
    ¼ to ½ teaspoon dried thyme leaves
1¼ cups uncooked orzo pasta
    2 cans (about 14 ounces each) fat-free reduced-sodium chicken broth
    8 ounces shrimp, peeled and deveined
    ¾ cup frozen peas, thawed
    ¼ cup grated Parmesan cheese
    Salt and black pepper to taste (optional)

1. Spray large saucepan with cooking spray. Heat over medium heat until hot. Add zucchini and lemon peel; cook and stir 2 to 3 minutes or until zucchini is tender. Remove from saucepan; set aside.

2. Add mushrooms, onion, garlic, sage and thyme to same saucepan; cook and stir 2 to 3 minutes or until onion is tender. Stir in orzo; cook and stir until browned.

3. Meanwhile, bring chicken broth to a boil in medium saucepan. Add broth to orzo mixture, ½ cup at a time, stirring constantly until broth is absorbed before adding next ½ cup. Continue cooking 10 to 15 minutes or until orzo is tender.

4. Stir shrimp and peas into orzo mixture during last half of cooking time; stir in zucchini mixture during last 2 to 3 minutes of cooking time. Stir in cheese; season to taste with salt and pepper, if desired.

Makes 4 servings

161 CREAMY SEAFOOD PASTA

1 cup HOLLAND HOUSE® Vermouth Cooking Wine
1 cup water
½ pound fresh or frozen scallops, thawed
½ pound fresh or frozen uncooked shrimp, peeled, deveined
1 cup whipping cream
1 clove garlic, minced
2 teaspoons cornstarch
1 tablespoon lemon juice
2 tablespoons freshly grated Parmesan cheese
2 tablespoons margarine or butter
2 cups shredded zucchini (2 medium)
8 ounces spinach fettuccine, cooked, drained

Bring cooking wine and water to a boil in large saucepan. Add scallops and shrimp; cook 2 to 3 minutes or until shrimp turn pink. Drain, reserving 1 cup liquid. Set seafood mixture aside; keep warm. Return reserved liquid to saucepan; stir in whipping cream and garlic. Bring to a boil; reduce heat. Simmer over medium heat until sauce is reduced by half, about 15 minutes, stirring occasionally. In small dish, combine cornstarch and lemon juice; mix well. Stir into sauce. Cook over medium heat until mixture boils and thickens, about 10 minutes. Stir in cheese. Melt margarine in small saucepan over high heat. Add zucchini; cook 1 minute or until softened. Stir zucchini and seafood into sauce. Serve over cooked fettuccine.

Makes 6 servings

Orzo Risotto with Shrimp and Vegetables

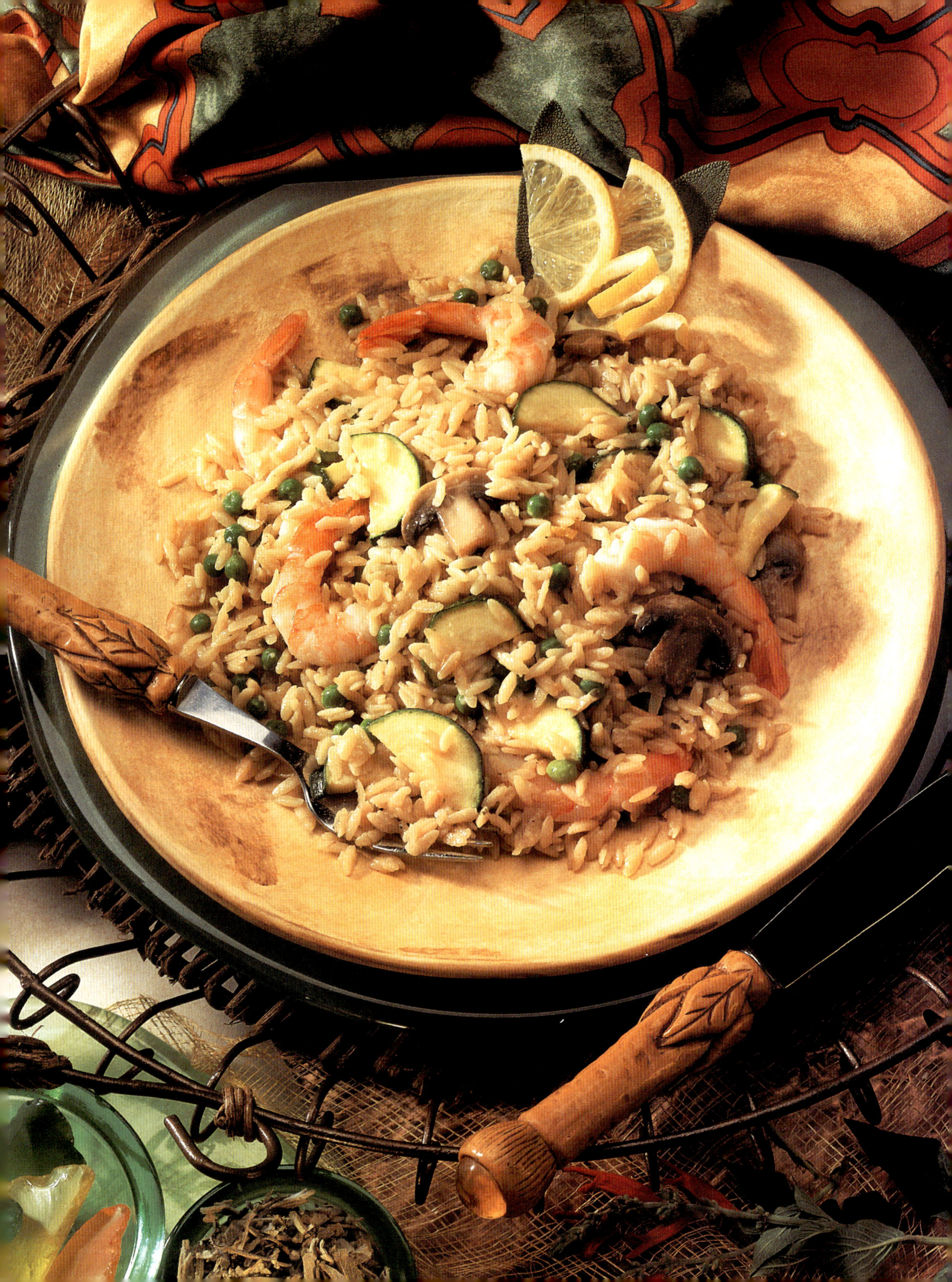

CATCH OF THE DAY

162 DEEP FRIED STUFFED SHELLS

16 uncooked jumbo pasta shells
2 eggs, divided
1 can (6 ounces) tuna, drained and flaked *or* 1 can (6 ounces) crabmeat, drained, flaked and cartilage removed
1 cup (4 ounces) shredded Cheddar or Swiss cheese
1 medium tomato, peeled, seeded and chopped
2 tablespoons sliced green onions
½ teaspoon dried basil leaves
⅛ teaspoon black pepper
1 tablespoon water
1 cup dry bread crumbs
Vegetable oil for frying
Tartar sauce for serving
Crisp salad greens, carrot curls and dill sprigs for garnish

1. Cook shells according to package directions until *al dente*; drain. Rinse under cold running water; drain again. Invert shells onto paper-towel-lined plate to cool.

2. Lightly beat 1 egg in large bowl. Add tuna, cheese, tomato, green onions, basil and pepper; mix well.

3. Using large spoon, stuff cooled shells with tuna mixture.

4. Beat remaining 1 egg with water in small bowl. Place bread crumbs in large, shallow dish. Dip each stuffed shell in egg mixture and roll in bread crumbs.

5. Heat 2 inches oil in large, heavy saucepan over medium-high heat until oil reaches 365°F; adjust heat to maintain temperature. Fry shells, a few at a time, in hot oil 1½ to 2 minutes until golden brown, turning once. Remove with slotted spoon; drain on paper towels.

6. Serve with tartar sauce. Garnish, if desired. *Makes 8 servings*

163 ELAINE'S TUNA TETRAZZINI

8 ounces fresh mushrooms, sliced
1 cup chopped onion
2 tablespoons vegetable oil
3 tablespoons all-purpose flour
1 cup chicken broth
½ cup low-fat milk
½ teaspoon paprika
½ teaspoon salt
¼ teaspoon pepper
1 can (6 ounces) STARKIST® Tuna, drained and broken into chunks
¼ cup grated Parmesan or Romano cheese
2 tablespoons minced parsley
8 ounces thin spaghetti or linguine, broken into halves, hot cooked

In large skillet, sauté mushrooms and onion in oil for 3 minutes, or until limp. Sprinkle flour over vegetables; stir until blended. Add chicken broth and milk all at once; cook and stir until mixture thickens and bubbles. Stir in paprika, salt and pepper; cook 2 minutes more. Stir in tuna, cheese and parsley; cook 1 to 2 minutes, or until heated through. Spoon over pasta. *Makes 4 servings*

Preparation time: 20 minutes

Deep Fried Stuffed Shells

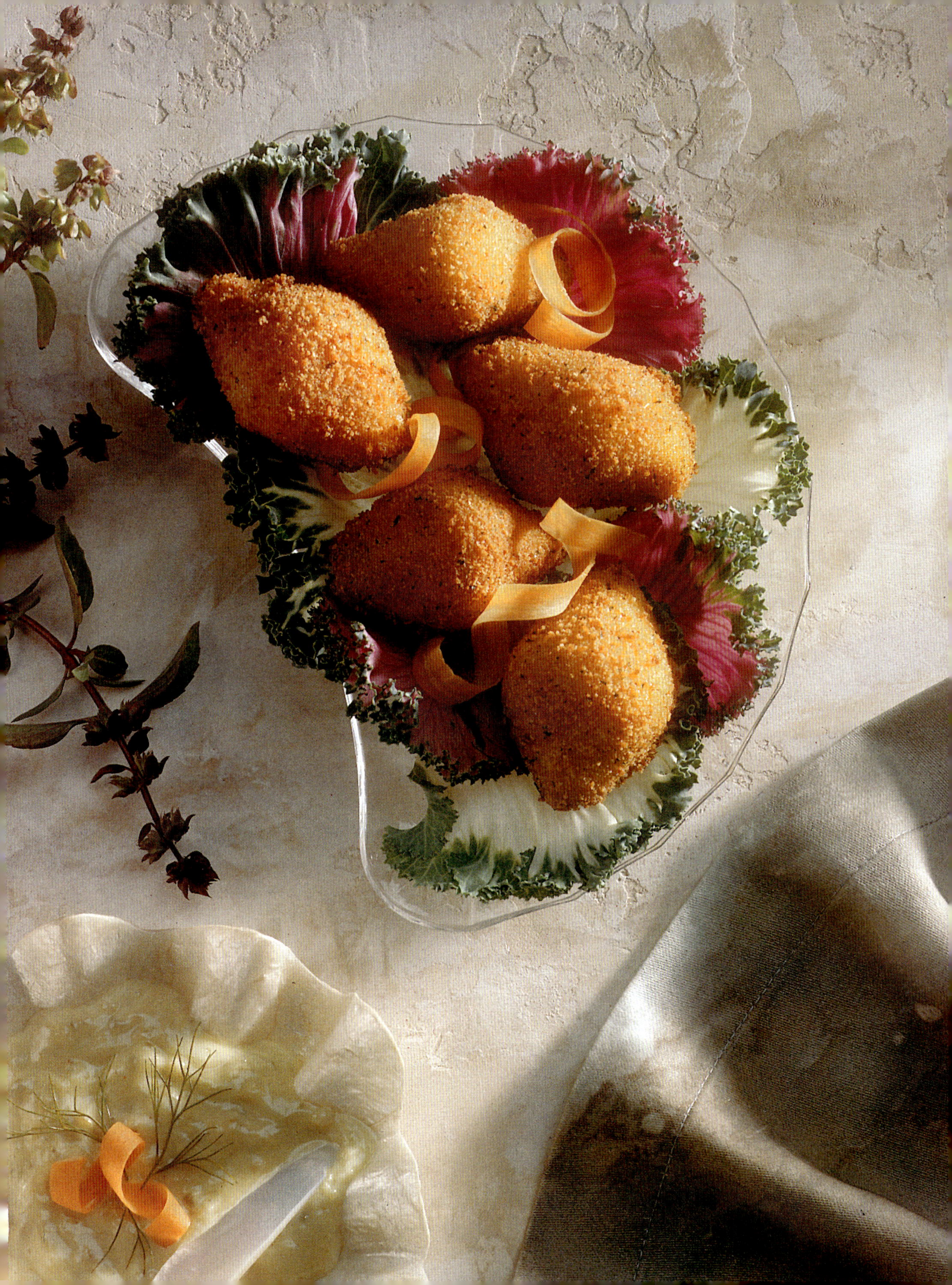

CATCH OF THE DAY

164 BOW TIES ALLE PORTOFINO

- 1 pound bow tie, radiatore or other medium pasta, uncooked
- 1 pound small frozen shrimp, thawed *or* 1 pound medium fresh shrimp, shelled, deveined
- 12 sun-dried tomatoes, rehydrated, drained, cut into thin strips
- 8 fresh plum tomatoes, chopped
- 2 bunches arugula, washed, torn into bite-size pieces
- 6 sprigs fresh Italian parsley, coarsely chopped
- ½ small bunch fresh basil, leaves picked, coarsely chopped
- ¼ cup olive or vegetable oil
- Juice of 1 lemon
- Salt and freshly ground black pepper to taste

Cook pasta according to package directions. While pasta is cooking, steam shrimp until opaque. Place shrimp in large mixing bowl. Add sun-dried tomatoes, plum tomatoes, arugula, parsley and basil; toss gently.

When pasta is done, drain well; immediately add to shrimp mixture. Add oil, lemon juice, salt and pepper; toss well. Serve immediately. *Makes 6 servings*

Favorite recipe from **National Pasta Association**

165 SEASIDE SQUASH SPAGHETTI

- 8 ounces spaghetti or linguine
- 2 teaspoons olive oil, divided
- 2 cloves garlic, crushed, divided
- 1 medium onion, cut into halves then sliced
- 1 medium yellow squash, sliced
- 1 medium zucchini, sliced
- 1 medium tomato, sliced
- 1 teaspoon garlic salt
- ½ teaspoon paprika
- Black pepper to taste
- 1 teaspoon dried basil *or* 2 teaspoons fresh basil leaves
- ½ cup fat-free ranch dressing
- 16 medium, cooked frozen shrimp, thawed

Cook spaghetti according to package directions, drain and toss with 1 teaspoon oil and 1 clove crushed garlic. Keep warm.

In large skillet, heat remaining 1 teaspoon oil; sauté onion and remaining garlic until sizzling. Add yellow squash, zucchini, tomato, garlic salt, paprika, pepper and basil. Cover and simmer.

Add dressing and shrimp, stirring contents until mixed. Cook mixture 1 minute or until bubbly. Serve over warm pasta. Garnish with fresh basil. *Makes 6 servings*

Favorite recipe from **North Dakota Wheat Commission**

Bow Ties Alle Portofino

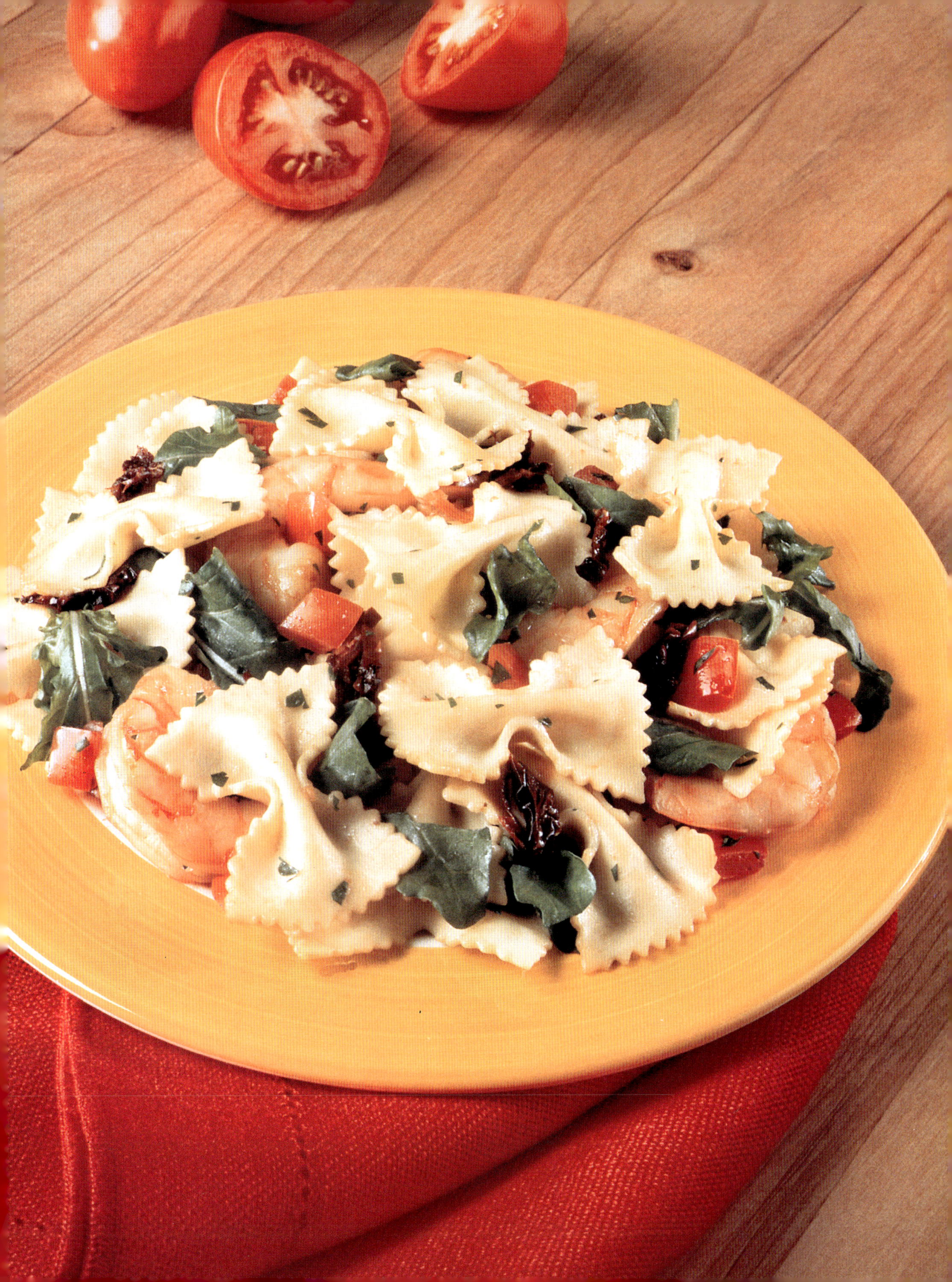

CATCH OF THE DAY

166 SPICY TUNA AND LINGUINE WITH GARLIC AND PINE NUTS

- 2 tablespoons olive oil
- 4 cloves garlic, minced
- 2 cups sliced mushrooms
- ½ cup chopped onion
- ½ teaspoon crushed red pepper
- 2½ cups chopped plum tomatoes
- 1 can (14½ ounces) chicken broth plus water to equal 2 cups
- ½ teaspoon salt
- ¼ teaspoon coarsely ground black pepper
- 1 package (9 ounces) uncooked fresh linguine
- 1 can (12 ounces) STARKIST® Solid White Tuna, drained and chunked
- ⅓ cup chopped fresh cilantro
- ⅓ cup toasted pine nuts or almonds

In 12-inch skillet, heat olive oil over medium-high heat; sauté garlic, mushrooms, onion and red pepper until golden brown. Add tomatoes, chicken broth mixture, salt and black pepper; bring to a boil.

Separate uncooked linguine into strands; place in skillet and spoon sauce over. Reduce heat to simmer; cook, covered, 4 more minutes or until cooked through. Toss gently; add tuna and cilantro and toss again. Sprinkle with pine nuts.

Makes 4 to 6 servings

167 SHRIMP CREOLE PRONTO

- 2 tablespoons vegetable oil
- 1 cup chopped onion
- 1 cup chopped celery
- 1 green bell pepper, chopped
- 2 cloves garlic, minced
- 2 cups chopped, peeled tomatoes
- 1 (8-ounce) can tomato sauce
- ½ cup HOLLAND HOUSE® Marsala Cooking Wine
- ¼ to ½ teaspoon hot pepper sauce
- ¼ teaspoon freshly ground black pepper
- 1 pound fresh or frozen uncooked shrimp, peeled, deveined
- 1 (10-ounce) package egg noodles, cooked, drained or hot cooked rice

Heat oil in large saucepan over medium-high heat. Add onion, celery, bell pepper and garlic; cook 2 to 3 minutes. Add tomatoes; cook 2 to 3 minutes, stirring occasionally. Add remaining ingredients except noodles; cook 2 to 3 minutes or until shrimp turn pink. Serve over noodles.

Makes 4 servings

CATCH OF THE DAY

168 HOMBRE SHRIMP AND FETTUCCINE WITH SALSA PESTO

   1 cup NEWMAN'S OWN® Salsa (medium or hot)
   2 tablespoons fresh lemon juice
   2 cloves garlic, minced
   ½ teaspoon salt
  20 large shrimp, peeled, deveined and tails left intact
   1 pound fettuccine, cooked *al dente* and drained
   Lemon wedges and parsley sprigs

SALSA PESTO
   ¾ cup NEWMAN'S OWN® Salsa (medium or hot), divided
   2 cloves garlic, minced
   1¼ cups firmly packed, rinsed, stemmed and drained spinach leaves
   ½ cup fresh cilantro*
   ½ cup grated Parmesan cheese
   ¾ cup toasted pine nuts, divided
   ⅓ cup olive oil

Basil can be substituted for cilantro, if preferred.

Combine 1 cup Newman's Own® Salsa, lemon juice, garlic and salt in glass mixing bowl.

Rinse shrimp and pat dry. Thread onto 4 soaked wooden skewers; grill or broil 5 to 8 minutes or until shrimp is cooked through, turning and basting occasionally with sauce. Keep shrimp and remaining sauce warm.

For pesto, place ¼ cup Newman's Own® Salsa, garlic, spinach, cilantro, Parmesan cheese, ½ cup pine nuts and oil in blender. Cover; purée until thick and smooth. Transfer pesto to large mixing bowl; stir in remaining salsa. Add warm fettuccine; toss to coat.

Evenly divide fettuccine mixture among 4 individual serving plates. Sprinkle reserved pine nuts over each portion. Top each with a warm shrimp skewer. Serve with warm sauce. Sprinkle with Parmesan cheese; garnish with lemon wedges and parsley sprigs.

Makes 4 servings

169 SPICY PASTA DEL MAR

   1 medium onion, diced
   1 teaspoon olive oil
   1 (10-ounce) can baby clams, drained
   2 teaspoons minced garlic
   1 (26-ounce) jar HEALTHY CHOICE® Traditional Pasta Sauce
   1 teaspoon dried basil leaves
   ½ teaspoon dried thyme leaves
   ⅛ teaspoon black pepper
   ⅛ teaspoon cayenne pepper
   ½ pound raw medium shrimp, peeled and deveined
   ½ pound linguini, cooked and drained

In large saucepan, sauté onion in hot oil until tender. Add clams and garlic; cook and stir 1 minute longer. Stir in pasta sauce, basil, thyme, black pepper and cayenne pepper. Heat, stirring occasionally, until mixture comes to a boil. Add shrimp; reduce heat to medium. Cook until shrimp are pink and cooked through. Serve sauce over linguini.

Makes 6 servings

CATCH OF THE DAY

170 CRABMEAT WITH HERBS AND PASTA

- 1 small onion, minced
- 1 carrot, shredded
- 1 clove garlic, minced
- 1/3 cup olive oil
- 3 tablespoons butter or margarine
- 6 ounces canned crabmeat, drained and flaked
- 1/4 cup chopped fresh basil *or* 1 teaspoon dried basil leaves
- 2 tablespoons chopped fresh parsley
- 1 tablespoon lemon juice
- 1/2 cup chopped pine nuts (optional)
- 1/2 teaspoon salt
- 1/2 package (8 ounces) uncooked vermicelli, hot cooked and drained

In large skillet over medium-high heat, cook and stir onion, carrot and garlic in hot oil and butter until vegetables are tender, but not brown. Reduce heat to medium. Stir in crabmeat, basil, parsley and lemon juice. Cook 4 minutes, stirring constantly. Stir in pine nuts and salt. Pour sauce over vermicelli in large bowl; toss gently to coat. Garnish as desired. *Makes 4 servings*

Favorite recipe from **New Jersey Department of Agriculture**

171 LOW–FAT SEAFOOD FETTUCCINE

- 8 ounces fettuccine
- Vegetable cooking spray
- 2 cups sliced fresh mushrooms
- 3/4 cup chopped onion
- 1/2 cup chopped green bell pepper
- 1 cup evaporated skimmed milk
- 1 (10 3/4-ounce) can low-fat, low-sodium cream of mushroom soup
- 1/4 teaspoon garlic salt
- 1/2 teaspoon dried parsley flakes
- 1 pound frozen medium shrimp, cooked
- 1 pound imitation crabmeat, chopped
- Dry bread crumbs (optional)

Cook pasta according to package directions.

Spray electric skillet with cooking spray and heat to 300°F. Sauté mushrooms, onion and bell pepper until tender, about 6 minutes.

Add milk, soup, garlic salt, parsley flakes, shrimp and crabmeat. Reduce skillet temperature to simmer. Cook and stir until thoroughly heated, about 10 to 15 minutes. Serve over hot pasta. Garnish with bread crumbs, if desired. *Makes 5 servings*

Favorite recipe from **North Dakota Wheat Commission**

Crabmeat with Herbs and Pasta

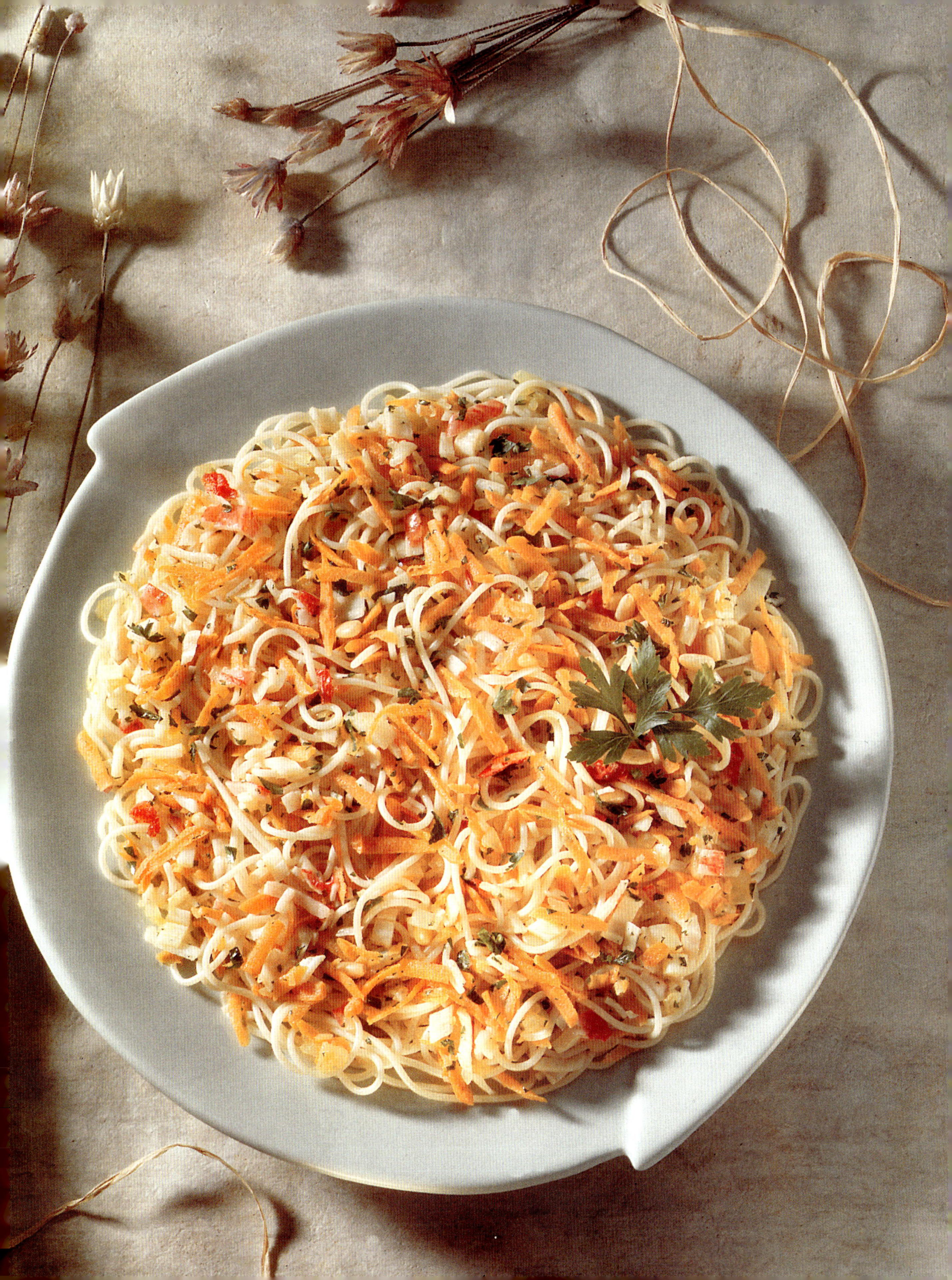

CATCH OF THE DAY

172 SHRIMP RAVIOLI WITH CURRY SAUCE

    Nonstick cooking spray
- ½ cup finely chopped mushrooms
- 4 green onions, thinly sliced
- 2 tablespoons minced fresh ginger
- 3 cloves garlic, minced
- 8 ounces shrimp, finely chopped
- 32 wonton wrappers
    Curry Sauce (recipe follows)
- 2 tablespoons finely chopped fresh cilantro

1. Spray medium skillet with cooking spray; heat over medium heat until hot. Add mushrooms, green onions, ginger and garlic; cook and stir 2 to 3 minutes. Add shrimp; cook 3 to 5 minutes or until shrimp turn pink and opaque. Season to taste. Place rounded tablespoonful shrimp mixture in center of 1 wonton wrapper; brush edges with water. Top with another wonton wrapper; seal edges. Repeat with remaining shrimp mixture and wonton wrappers.

2. Bring 2 quarts water to a boil in saucepan; add 4 to 6 ravioli. Cook 3 to 4 minutes or until ravioli are tender. Remove and repeat with remaining ravioli. Serve with warm Curry Sauce. Sprinkle with cilantro. Garnish as desired. *Makes 4 servings*

CURRY SAUCE

    Nonstick cooking spray
- ¼ cup finely chopped onion
- 1 clove garlic, minced
- 1½ tablespoons all-purpose flour
- 1½ teaspoons curry powder
- ⅛ teaspoon ground cumin
- 1 cup fat-free reduced-sodium chicken broth

1. Spray small saucepan with cooking spray; heat over medium heat until hot. Add onion and garlic; cook and stir 2 to 3 minutes. Stir in flour, curry powder and cumin; cook and stir 1 to 2 minutes. Add chicken broth. Cook and stir 1 minute or until thickened. Season to taste. *Makes 4 servings*

173 CRAB BASIL FETTUCCINE

- 3 tablespoons margarine or butter
- 3 tablespoons olive oil
- 2 tomatoes, peeled, seeded, chopped
- 1 clove garlic, minced
- ⅓ cup whipping cream
- ½ cup HOLLAND HOUSE® White Cooking Wine
- ½ cup chopped fresh basil
- ½ cup cooked fresh or frozen crabmeat
- ¼ cup freshly grated Parmesan cheese, divided
- ¼ cup chopped fresh parsley, divided
- 1 pound fettuccine, cooked, drained

Melt margarine and oil in medium saucepan over medium heat. Add tomatoes and garlic; simmer until tomatoes are softened. Add whipping cream and cooking wine; simmer 10 minutes. Stir in basil and crabmeat; simmer 3 minutes. Add 2 tablespoons cheese and 2 tablespoons parsley. Serve over cooked fettuccine. Sprinkle with remaining cheese and parsley. *Makes 6 servings*

Shrimp Ravioli with Curry Sauce

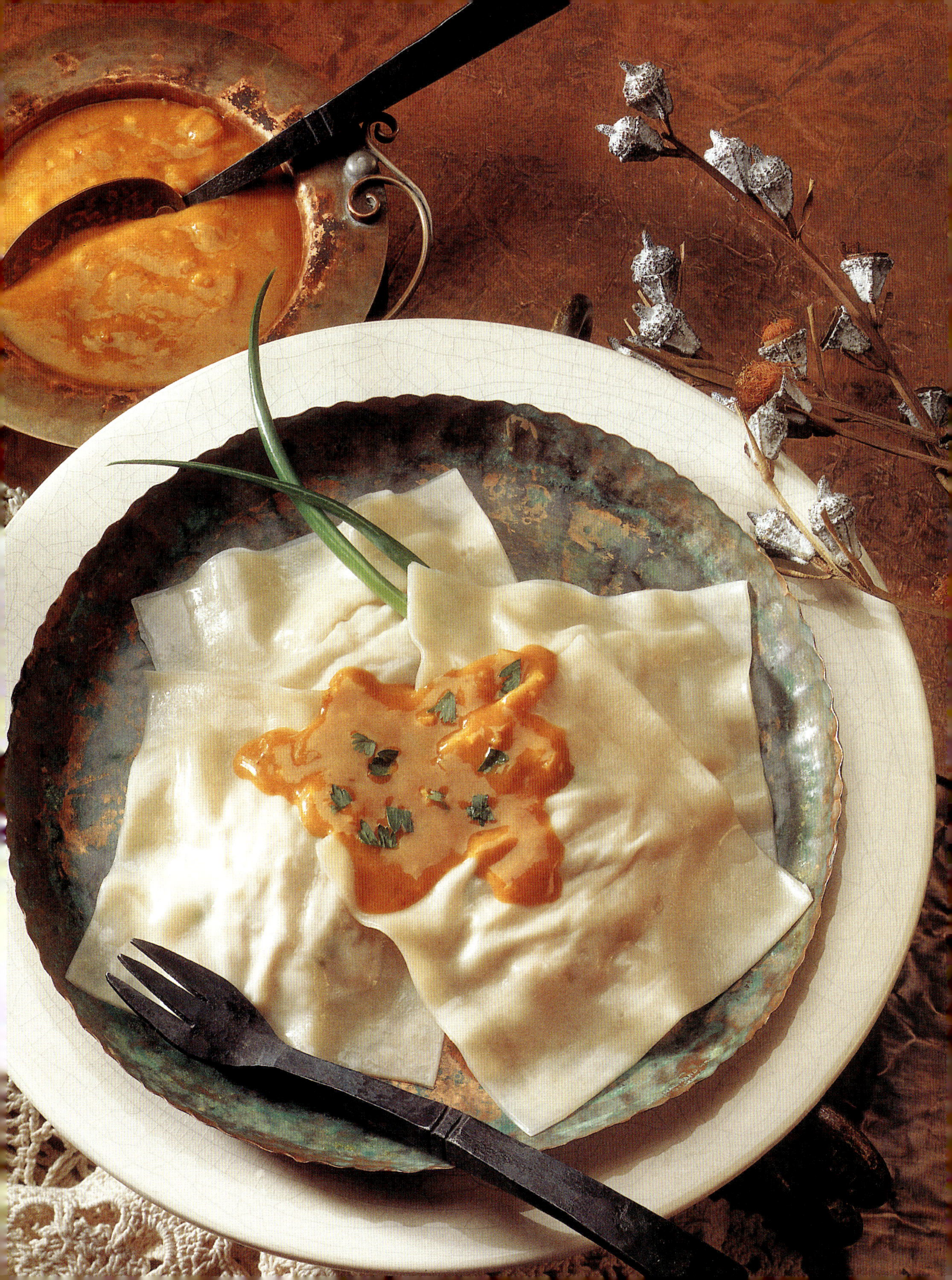

CATCH OF THE DAY

174 SHRIMP WITH PASTA

- 1 package fresh angel hair pasta
- 2 tablespoons extra-virgin olive oil
- 2 tablespoons chopped onion
- 1 teaspoon chopped garlic
- 12 medium shrimp, peeled and deveined
- ½ cup dry white wine
- 1 cup fish stock or bottled clam juice
- 2 teaspoons chopped Italian parsley
- 1 teaspoon chopped fresh basil leaves
- 2 tablespoons lemon juice
- ¼ teaspoon TABASCO® pepper sauce
- 1 teaspoon Worcestershire sauce
- ½ teaspoon salt

Boil large pot of water and cook pasta according to package instructions. While water is heating, heat olive oil in medium skillet until very hot. Sauté onion and garlic until lightly browned. Add shrimp and sauté until pink; remove and keep warm.

Add white wine and fish stock to skillet. Bring to a boil and add remaining ingredients. Return shrimp to skillet and simmer about 30 seconds on each side. Remove shrimp and arrange over cooked pasta; pour sauce over all.

Makes 2 servings

175 SEAFARERS' SUPPER

- 1 tablespoon olive or vegetable oil
- 1 cup chopped green bell pepper
- ½ cup chopped onion
- 2 cloves garlic, minced
- 1¾ cups (14½-ounce can) CONTADINA® Italian-Style Stewed Tomatoes, undrained
- 1 cup chicken broth
- ⅔ cup (6-ounce can) CONTADINA® Italian Paste
- ¼ teaspoon salt
- ¼ teaspoon ground black pepper
- 1 pound orange roughy, cut into 1-inch pieces
- 12 ounces dry linguine, cooked, drained, kept warm
- Chopped fresh Italian parsley (optional)

In large skillet, heat oil. Add bell pepper, onion and garlic; sauté 3 minutes or until vegetables are crisp-tender. Stir in tomatoes and juice, chicken broth, tomato paste, salt and black pepper. Bring to a boil. Reduce heat to low; simmer, uncovered, 5 minutes. Add orange roughy; simmer 5 minutes or until fish flakes easily when tested with fork. Spoon over pasta. Sprinkle with parsley, if desired.

Makes 4 to 6 servings

CATCH OF THE DAY

176 SEAFOOD SUPREME PASTA PIE

6 ounces fine egg noodles, cooked and drained
2 eggs, lightly beaten
½ cup dairy sour cream
½ cup milk
¼ cup (1 ounce) grated Parmesan cheese
1 teaspoon dried tarragon leaves

SEAFOOD SAUCE
4 tablespoons (½ stick) butter
4 ounces fresh mushrooms, sliced
¼ cup chopped green onions with tops
1 large clove garlic, minced
8 ounces small shrimp, shelled and cleaned
8 ounces bay scallops
1 can (6 ounces) crabmeat, drained
3 tablespoons all-purpose flour
½ teaspoon seasoned salt
¼ teaspoon black pepper
1½ cups half-and-half
1 cup (4 ounces) finely shredded Swiss cheese, divided
1 cup dry white wine

Preheat oven to 350°F. In medium bowl, blend together eggs, sour cream, milk, Parmesan cheese and tarragon. Stir in noodles; spoon into buttered 9-inch pie plate. Cover with foil. Bake 35 to 45 minutes or until knife inserted near center comes out clean.

Meanwhile, melt butter in large skillet over medium heat. Add mushrooms, onions and garlic; cook and stir 2 minutes. Add seafood; cook and stir 3 minutes. Add flour, salt and pepper. Gradually stir in half-and-half and ½ cup Swiss cheese. Cook, stirring constantly, until mixture thickens. Stir in wine. To serve, cut pasta pie into wedges; serve with Seafood Sauce. Sprinkle individual servings with remaining ½ cup Swiss cheese.   *Makes 6 to 8 servings*

Favorite recipe from **Southeast United Dairy Industry Association, Inc.**

177 PASTA PUTTANESCA WITH SARDINES

1 jar (26 ounces) marinara sauce
¼ cup kalamata olives, pitted
1 tablespoon capers
1 can sardines packed in oil, drained
   Freshly ground black pepper to taste (optional)
12 ounces fusilli or rigatoni pasta

Place marinara sauce in medium saucepan and simmer over medium-high heat. Coarsely chop olives with capers. Stir into heated sauce with drained sardines, breaking sardines up with a spoon. Add black pepper, if desired.

Meanwhile, cook pasta *al dente* according to package directions; drain and transfer to large bowl. Pour sauce over pasta and toss.
   Makes 4 servings

Favorite recipe from **North Atlantic Sardine Council**

CATCH OF THE DAY

178 SKILLET SHRIMP WITH ROTELLE

3 tablespoons FILIPPO BERIO® Olive Oil
1 medium onion, chopped
2 cloves garlic, minced
2 cups uncooked rotelle or other curly pasta
3 cups chicken broth
1 cup asparagus tips
¾ pound raw medium shrimp, shelled and deveined
¾ cup halved cherry tomatoes
¼ cup pitted ripe olives
1 teaspoon dried oregano leaves
1 teaspoon dried basil leaves
  Salt and freshly ground black pepper to taste

In large skillet, heat olive oil over medium heat until hot. Add onion and garlic; cook and stir 4 to 6 minutes or until onion is softened, but not brown. Add pasta; stir to coat pasta with oil. Increase heat to high; pour in chicken broth. Bring to a boil. Reduce heat to medium-high; cook, stirring occasionally, 12 to 14 minutes or until pasta is *al dente* (tender but still firm). Add asparagus. Cook, stirring frequently, 2 to 3 minutes or until asparagus is tender-crisp. Add shrimp, tomatoes, olives, oregano and basil. Cook, stirring frequently, 3 minutes or until liquid is almost completely absorbed and shrimp are opaque *(do not overcook shrimp)*. Season to taste with salt and pepper.   *Makes 4 to 6 servings*

179 SCALLOPS WITH LINGUINE AND SPINACH

2 to 3 tablespoons olive oil
1½ cups finely chopped onion
1 cup slivered red bell pepper
2 tablespoons minced garlic
⅛ to ¼ teaspoon ground red pepper
⅓ cup fresh lemon juice
1 tablespoon packed brown sugar
1 tablespoon minced lemon peel
1 teaspoon salt
1 teaspoon black pepper
¾ pound uncooked linguine
1 (10-ounce) package frozen, chopped spinach, thawed and drained
1½ pounds cooked scallops
⅓ cup feta cheese, coarsely crumbled

Heat oil in large heavy skillet over medium-low heat until hot. Add onion, bell pepper, garlic and ground red pepper; cook uncovered until tender, about 10 minutes. Add lemon juice, brown sugar, lemon peel, salt and black pepper; cook 1 minute.

While preparing onion mixture, cook pasta until tender, 8 to 10 minutes. About one minute before pasta is done, add spinach. Drain pasta and spinach and place in large, warm serving bowl. Add onion mixture and toss to coat. Taste and adjust seasonings. Add cooked and warmed scallops to pasta and sprinkle with feta cheese.

Makes 4 servings

Favorite recipe from **National Fisheries Institute**

Skillet Shrimp with Rotelle

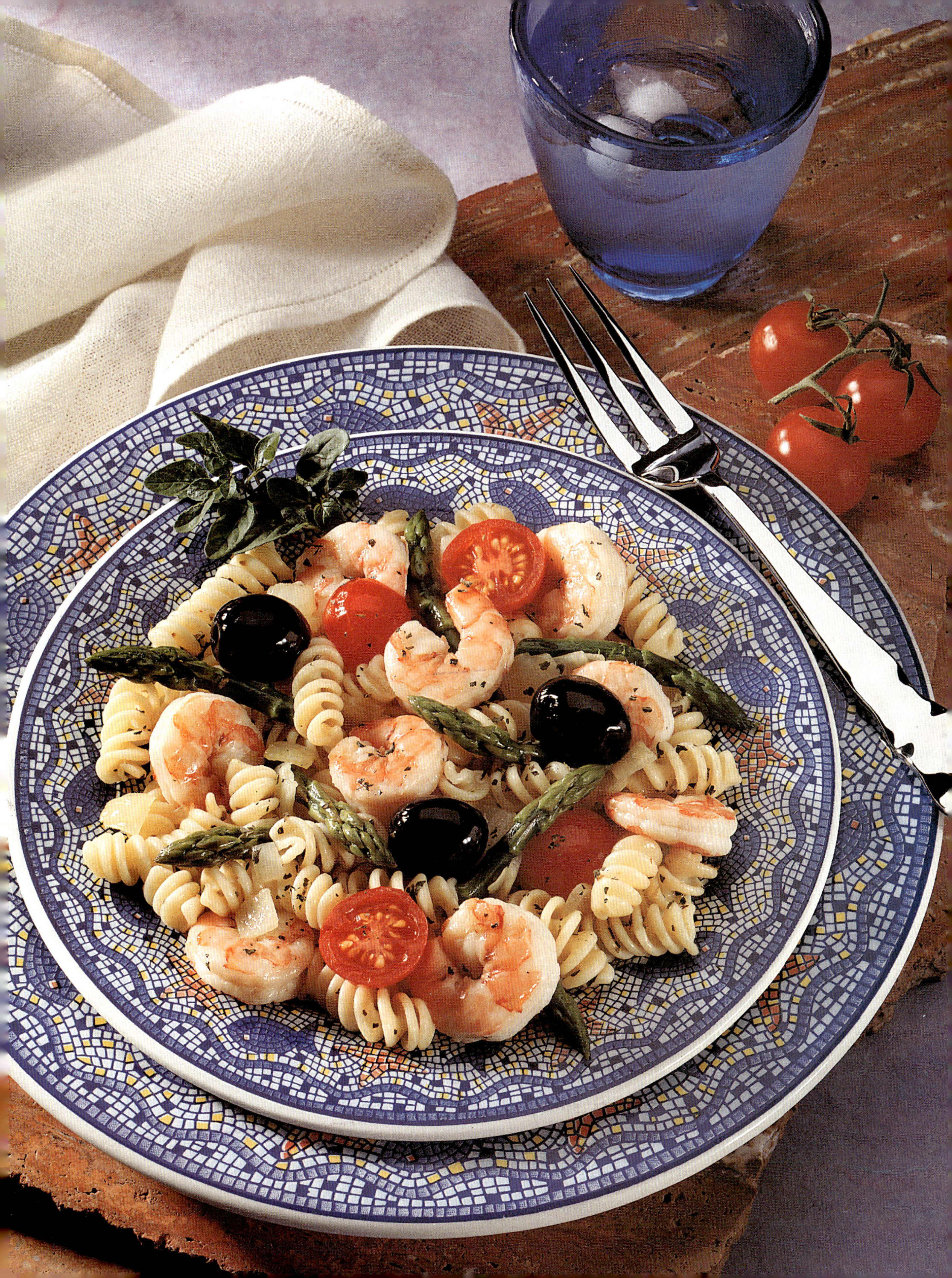

CATCH OF THE DAY

180 SPAGHETTI WITH SEAFOOD MARINARA SAUCE

- 8 fresh oysters
- 2 tablespoons olive oil
- 1/3 cup chopped onion
- 1 clove garlic, minced
- 1/2 cup dry white wine
- 10 ounces uncooked dry spaghetti
- 6 flat anchovy fillets, minced
- 5 large ripe fresh tomatoes, seeded and chopped
- 1 tablespoon tomato paste
- 3/4 teaspoon dried basil leaves
- 3/4 teaspoon salt
- 1/2 teaspoon dried oregano leaves
- 1/8 teaspoon black pepper
- 1 pound fresh medium shrimp, shelled and deveined
- 1/2 pound fresh scallops, cut into 3/4-inch pieces
- 3 tablespoons chopped fresh parsley
- Fresh basil leaves for garnish

1. Scrub oysters thoroughly with stiff brush under cold running water. Place on tray and refrigerate 1 hour to help oysters relax.

2. Shuck oysters, reserving oyster. Strain oyster liquor through triple thickness of dampened cheesecloth into small bowl; set aside oyster liquor.

3. Heat oil in 3-quart saucepan over medium-high heat. Add onion; cook and stir 4 minutes or until soft. Add garlic; cook 30 seconds. Add wine; cook 4 to 5 minutes until wine has evaporated. Remove from heat; cover and set aside.

4. Cook spaghetti in large pot of boiling salted water 8 to 10 minutes just until *al dente*; drain well.

5. Stir reserved oyster liquor and anchovies into reserved onion mixture in saucepan; add tomatoes, tomato paste, basil, salt, oregano and pepper. Mix well. Bring to a boil over high heat; reduce heat to medium. Cook, uncovered, 20 minutes or until sauce thickens, stirring occasionally.

6. Stir in shrimp, scallops and oysters. Cover and cook 2 to 3 minutes until shrimp turn opaque and are cooked through, stirring occasionally. Stir in parsley.

7. Combine hot spaghetti with seafood sauce in large serving bowl; toss until well coated. Garnish, if desired. Serve immediately. *Makes 4 to 5 servings*

181 LINGUINE WITH WHITE CLAM SAUCE

- 8 ounces linguine or spaghetti
- 2 tablespoons butter
- 1 tablespoon flour
- 1 (10-ounce) can clam juice
- 1 tablespoon dried parsley leaves
- 1 teaspoon dried thyme leaves
- 2 (6½-ounce) cans minced clams

Prepare pasta according to package directions; drain.

Melt butter in small saucepan; add flour and mix. Add clam juice and stir until smooth. Add parsley and thyme and cook over low heat 5 minutes. Add clams to mixture and cook 5 minutes more. Serve over pasta.
Makes 4 servings

Favorite recipe from **National Pasta Association**

Spaghetti with Seafood Marinara Sauce

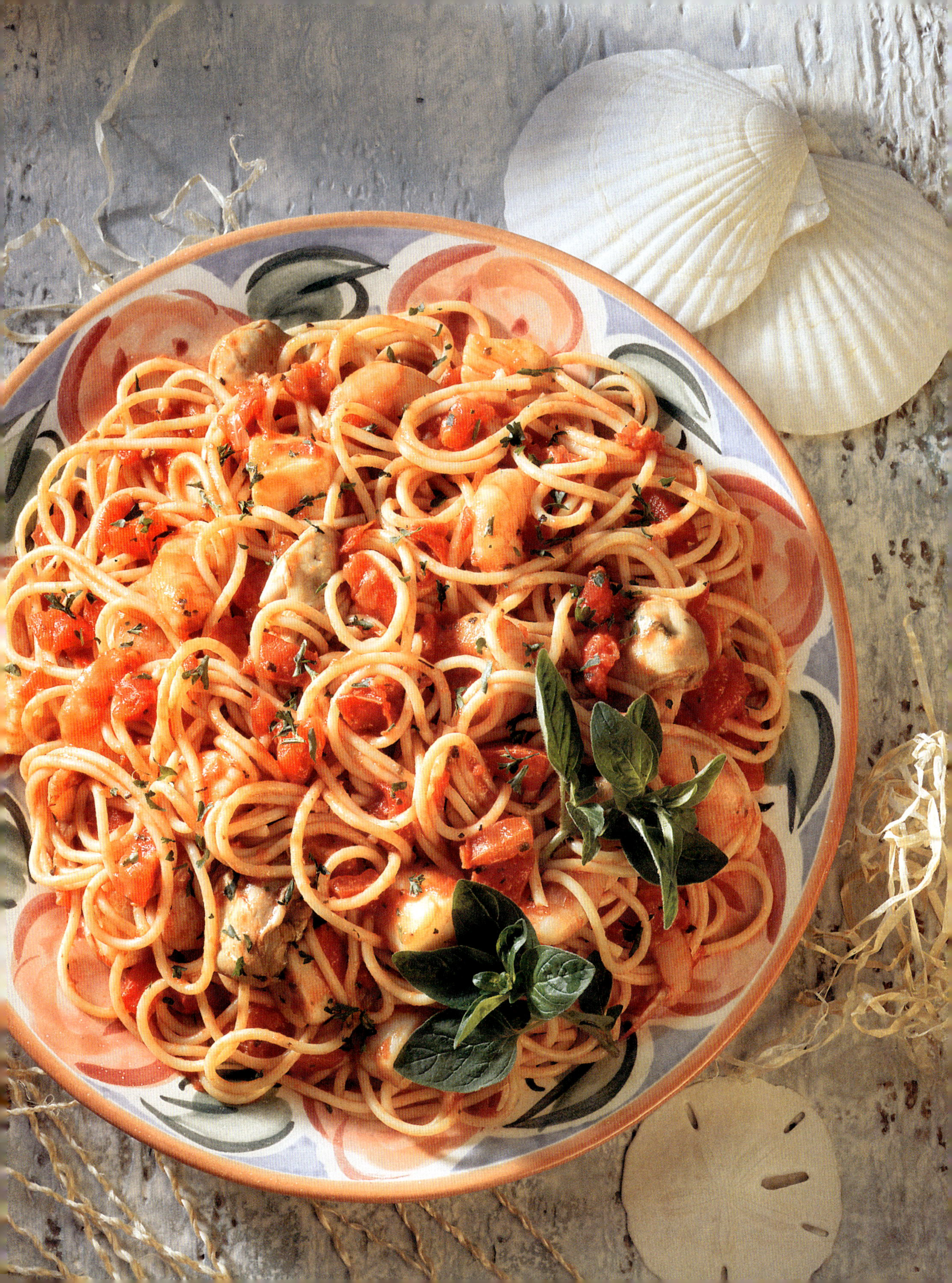

CATCH OF THE DAY

182 FETTUCCINE À LA TUNA

½ cup broccoli florets
½ cup chopped red bell pepper
1 tablespoon sliced green onion
1 clove garlic, minced
1 tablespoon butter or margarine
¼ cup low-fat milk
¼ cup low-fat ricotta cheese
  Salt and pepper to taste
1 can (3 ounces) STARKIST® Tuna, drained and broken into small chunks
2 ounces fettuccine or linguine, cooked and drained
1 tablespoon grated Parmesan or Romano cheese (optional)

In small saucepan, steam broccoli and bell pepper over simmering water 5 minutes. Drain liquid from vegetables and remove steamer. In same pan, sauté onion and garlic in butter 2 minutes. Add milk and ricotta cheese, stirring well with wire whisk. Season to taste with salt and pepper. Add tuna and vegetables; cook over low heat 2 minutes. Toss fettuccine with tuna mixture. Spoon onto plate; sprinkle with Parmesan cheese, if desired. *Makes 1 serving*

Preparation time: 15 minutes

183 PENNE PASTA WITH SHRIMP & ROASTED RED PEPPER SAUCE

12 ounces uncooked penne pasta
1 cup low-sodium chicken or vegetable broth, defatted
1 cup GUILTLESS GOURMET® Roasted Red Pepper Salsa
1 cup chopped fresh or low-sodium canned tomatoes, drained
12 ounces medium raw shrimp, peeled and deveined
  Fresh Italian parsley sprigs (optional)

Cook pasta according to package directions; drain and keep warm.

Meanwhile, combine broth, salsa and tomatoes in 1-quart saucepan. Bring to a boil over medium-high heat. Reduce heat to medium; simmer about 5 minutes or until hot. Allow to cool slightly.

Pour broth mixture into food processor or blender; process until smooth. Return to saucepan; bring back to a simmer. Add shrimp; simmer 2 minutes or just until shrimp turn pink and opaque. *Do not overcook.* To serve, divide pasta among 4 warm serving plates. Cover each serving with sauce, dividing shrimp equally among servings. Garnish with parsley, if desired.
Makes 4 servings

Fettuccine à la Tuna

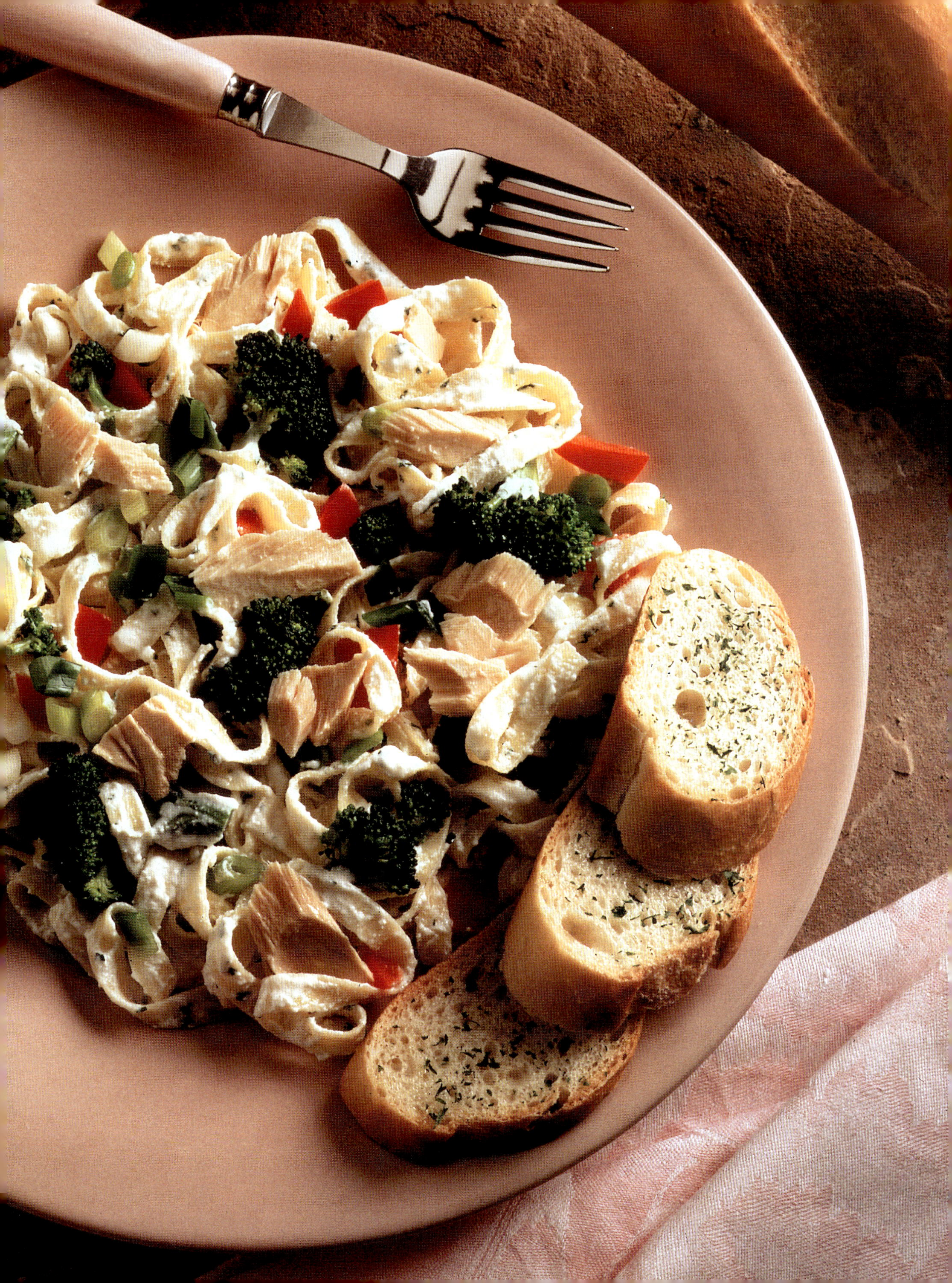

CATCH OF THE DAY

184 PASTA VERDE DE MAR

1 pound cod fillets
1 can (about 14 ounces) chicken broth
8 ounces spinach linguini or fettuccine
3 tablespoons olive oil, divided
2 cloves garlic, crushed
6 green onions, bias sliced into ½-inch pieces
1 yellow bell pepper, cut into ¼-inch strips
½ cup fresh basil, chopped *or* 1 tablespoon dried basil leaves
¼ teaspoon red pepper flakes
8 cherry tomatoes, cut into quarters
¼ cup chopped fresh parsley
1 (8-ounce) jar sun-dried tomatoes (optional)

Place cod fillets in 10-inch skillet with chicken broth. (If desired, add 1 slice lemon, 1 bay leaf and a few peppercorns to liquid.) Bring liquid to a boil, cover and immediately reduce heat. Simmer 8 to 10 minutes or until fish becomes opaque. As fish simmers, cook pasta according to package directions, drain, toss with 1 tablespoon olive oil and keep warm.

Remove cooked fish from skillet; keep warm. Pour off cooking liquid, reserving ½ cup. Preheat dry skillet over high heat; add remaining olive oil. Add garlic, green onions, bell pepper, basil and red pepper flakes; stir-fry 3 to 5 minutes or until vegetables are crisp-tender. Remove pan from heat; add cherry tomatoes, parsley and sun-dried tomatoes, if desired, and mix well.

Use fork to break fish into 2-inch pieces; add fish and reserved cooking liquid to vegetables. Add pasta to skillet and toss gently with two forks to combine. Serve immediately. *Makes 4 servings*

Favorite recipe from **National Fisheries Institute**

185 SALMON TORTELLINI

1 package (7 ounces) cheese-filled tortellini, cooked and drained
1 container (8 ounces) PHILADELPHIA BRAND® Soft Cream Cheese with Smoked Salmon
½ cup finely chopped cucumber
1 teaspoon dried dill weed *or* 2 teaspoons fresh dill

• Lightly toss hot tortellini with remaining ingredients. Serve immediately.
Makes 6 to 8 servings

Prep time: 25 minutes

Salmon Tortellini

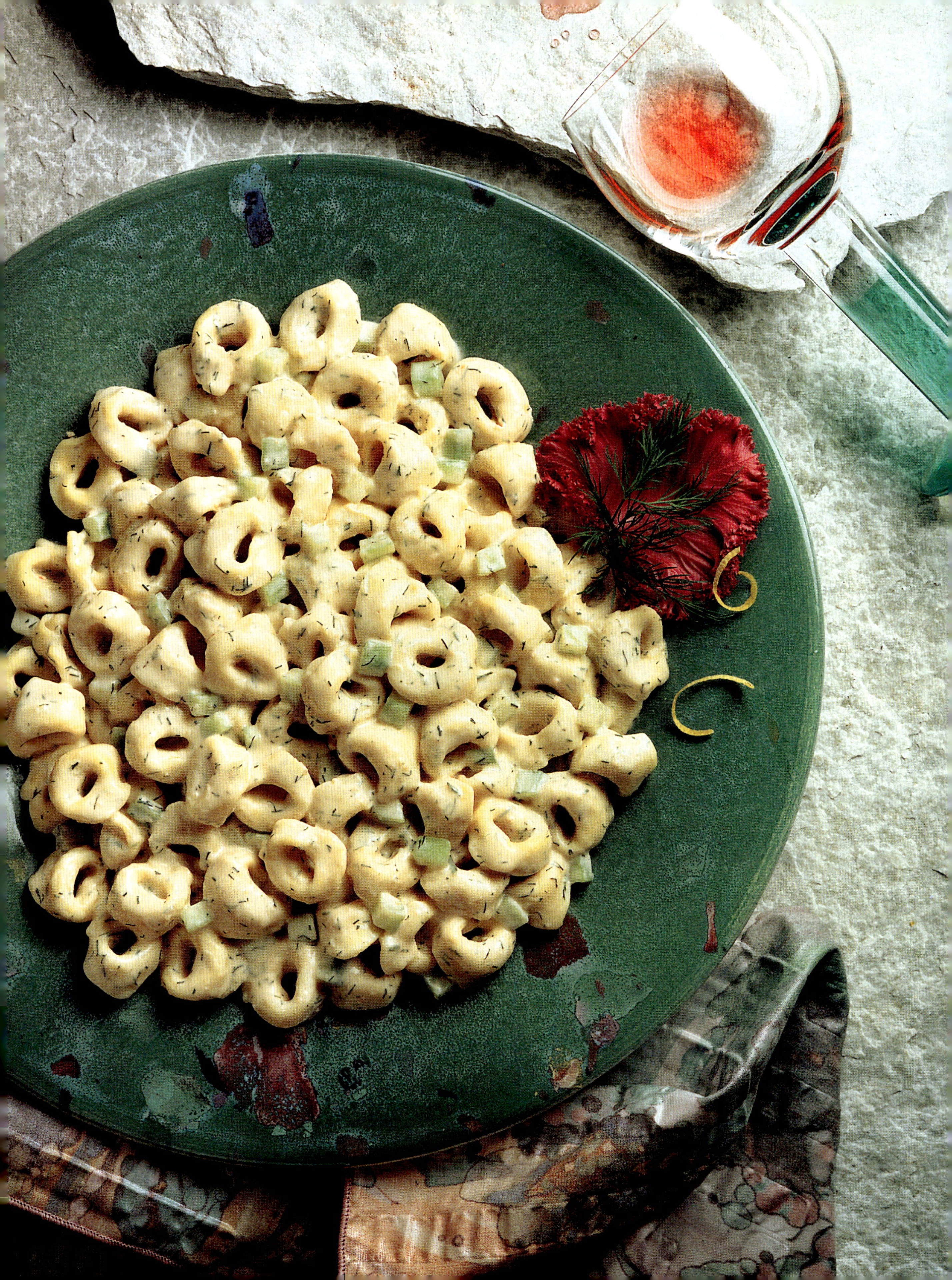

CATCH OF THE DAY

186 SALMON, FETTUCCINE & CABBAGE

- 1 (9-ounce) package fresh fettuccine
- ¼ cup plus 2 tablespoons seasoned rice vinegar
- 2 tablespoons vegetable oil
- ½ small head of cabbage, shredded (about 7 cups)
- ½ teaspoon fennel seeds
- 1 (15½-ounce) can salmon, drained, flaked, bones removed
- Salt and black pepper to taste

1. Cook fettuccine in lightly salted boiling water according to package directions (about 5 minutes); drain.

2. Heat vinegar and oil in large skillet over medium-high heat. Add cabbage; cook 3 minutes or until crisp-tender, stirring occasionally.

3. Stir in fennel seeds. Add fettuccine; toss lightly to coat. Add salmon; mix lightly.

4. Heat thoroughly, stirring occasionally. Season with salt and pepper to taste. Garnish as desired. *Makes 4 servings*

187 PRIMAVERA SAUCE WITH ARTICHOKE AND SHRIMP

- 2 tablespoons olive oil
- 1 cup diced carrots (2 small)
- 1 cup diced celery (2 ribs)
- 1 small onion, diced
- 3 cloves garlic, finely chopped
- 3½ cups (28-ounce can) CONTADINA® Seasoned Crushed Tomatoes with Italian Herbs
- ½ teaspoon salt
- ¼ teaspoon ground black pepper
- 8 ounces medium raw shrimp, peeled and deveined
- 1 cup sliced artichoke hearts, drained
- Fresh chopped basil (optional)

HEAT oil in large skillet over high heat. Add carrots, celery, onion and garlic. Cook 4 to 5 minutes or until carrots are crisp-tender.

ADD crushed tomatoes, salt and pepper. Bring to a boil. Add shrimp and artichoke hearts. Cook 2 to 3 minutes or until shrimp turn pink. Reduce heat to low; simmer 2 minutes to blend flavors.

SPRINKLE with basil, if desired. Serve over hot cooked pasta or rice.

Makes 6 servings

CATCH OF THE DAY

188 SMOKED SALMON AND OLIVE PASTA

- 2 cups heavy cream
- 3 medium cloves garlic
- ¼ teaspoon black pepper
- 1 teaspoon finely chopped lemon peel
- 1 cup pitted California ripe olives, chopped
- ½ cup dry white wine
- 12 ounces fusilli or other corkscrew-type pasta
- 6 ounces smoked salmon, thinly sliced and cut into short strips
- Salt to taste

Combine cream and garlic in large skillet over medium heat; heat thoroughly, stirring frequently. Stir in pepper, lemon peel, olives and wine; bring to a boil. Reduce heat to low; simmer 10 minutes, stirring occasionally. Meanwhile, cook pasta according to package directions; drain. Remove garlic from sauce; discard garlic. Add pasta and salmon to sauce; toss lightly to coat. Season with salt to taste. Top with freshly ground black pepper and chopped fresh parsley, if desired. Serve immediately.

Makes 4 servings

Favorite recipe from ***California Olive Industry***

189 PICK OF THE CROP SARDINE PASTA

- 6 tablespoons olive oil
- 1 onion, chopped
- 2 cloves garlic, minced
- 1 *each* red and yellow bell pepper, sliced into strips
- 4 cups blanched and cooled vegetable pieces
- 1 cup halved cherry tomatoes
- ½ cup fresh lemon juice
- 2 tablespoons chopped fresh thyme *or* 2 teaspoons dried thyme leaves
- 8 ounces dry fettuccine, cooked according to package directions and drained
- Salt and black pepper to taste
- 2 cans (3¾ ounces each) water- or oil-packed sardines, drained
- Parmesan cheese, grated

In large skillet, heat oil over medium heat. Add onion and garlic; sauté until onion is limp, stirring occasionally. Add bell peppers; cook 1 minute. Mix in blanched vegetables, cherry tomatoes, lemon juice, thyme and pasta; cook and toss just until heated through. Season with salt and pepper. Transfer to serving platter; top with sardines and sprinkle with cheese. Serve hot.

Makes 4 servings

Favorite recipe from ***North Atlantic Sardine Council***

CATCH OF THE DAY

190 WINTER PESTO PASTA WITH SHRIMP

- 12 ounces fettuccine, uncooked
- 1 cup chopped fresh kale, washed, stems removed
- ½ cup fresh basil
- ¼ cup grated Parmesan cheese
- 2 cloves garlic, cut into halves
- ⅛ teaspoon salt
- 1 cup plain nonfat yogurt
- 1 teaspoon vegetable oil
- 1 pound medium shrimp, peeled, deveined
- 1 medium red bell pepper, cut into bite-size pieces

Cook pasta according to package directions. While pasta is cooking, purée kale, basil, Parmesan cheese, garlic and salt in food processor or blender until smooth. Stir in yogurt.

Heat oil in large skillet over medium-low heat. Sauté shrimp and bell pepper 4 minutes or until shrimp are opaque.

When pasta is done, drain and transfer to serving bowl. Add kale mixture; toss well. Add shrimp and bell pepper; toss gently. Serve immediately. *Makes 4 servings*

Favorite recipe from **National Pasta Association**

191 GREEN AND GOLD FETTUCCINE WITH SALMON

- 2 cans (6½ ounces each) salmon,* drained
- 2 tablespoons olive oil
- 2 cloves garlic, minced
- ¼ cup minced parsley
- 2 teaspoons minced fresh oregano *or* ½ teaspoon dried oregano leaves
- 2 teaspoons minced fresh basil *or* ½ teaspoon dried basil leaves
- ¼ teaspoon coarsely ground black pepper
- 4 ounces *each* uncooked plain and spinach fettuccine, hot cooked and drained
- 2 teaspoons lemon juice
- Blanched matchstick carrots, asparagus spears or broccoli florets (optional)
- Grated Parmesan cheese

*Canned tuna may be substituted for the salmon.

Place salmon in medium bowl. With fork, break into large chunks and debone; remove skin, if desired. Heat oil in large skillet over medium-high heat until hot. Cook and stir garlic until golden. Add parsley, oregano, basil and pepper; cook and stir 30 seconds. Pour half of herb sauce over fettuccine; toss gently to coat. Arrange on large, heated platter; keep warm.

Add salmon and lemon juice to remaining sauce. Heat, stirring gently, just until salmon is hot. Spoon over hot fettuccine. Garnish with vegetables, if desired. Serve with Parmesan cheese. *Makes 6 servings*

Favorite recipe from **National Fisheries Institute**

Winter Pesto Pasta with Shrimp

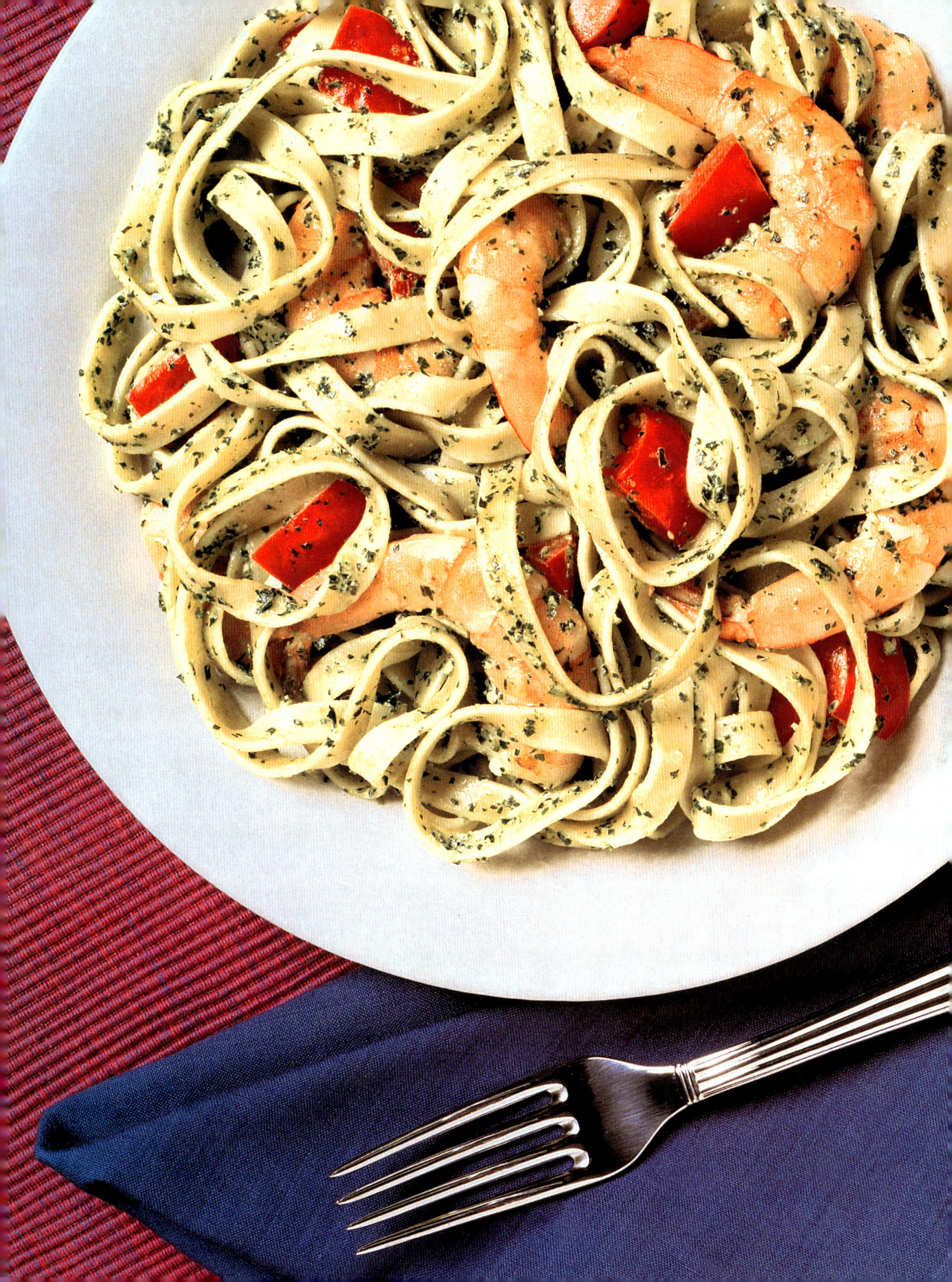

CATCH OF THE DAY

192 JUMBO SHELLS SEAFOOD FANCIES

- 1 package (16 ounces) uncooked jumbo pasta shells
- 1 can (7½ ounces) crabmeat
- 1 cup (4 ounces) grated Swiss cheese
- 1 can (2½ ounces) tiny shrimp, drained
- ½ cup salad dressing or mayonnaise
- 2 tablespoons thinly sliced celery
- 1 tablespoon finely chopped onion
- 1 tablespoon finely chopped pimiento
- Celery leaves (optional)

1. Cook shells according to package directions until *al dente;* drain. Rinse under cold running water; drain again.

2. Invert shells onto paper-towel-lined plate to drain and cool.

3. Drain and discard liquid from crabmeat. Place crabmeat in large bowl; flake with fork into small pieces. Remove any bits of shell or cartilage.

4. Add cheese, shrimp, salad dressing, celery, onion and pimiento to crabmeat. If mixture seems too dry, add more salad dressing.

5. Using large spoon, stuff cooled shells with seafood mixture. Cover; refrigerate until chilled. Garnish with celery leaves, if desired. *Makes 8 appetizer servings*

193 CAJUN SHRIMP FETTUCCINE

- 4 to 6 ounces uncooked fettuccine
- ½ pound medium shrimp, shelled and deveined
- 2 slices bacon, diced
- 2 cloves garlic, minced
- ⅛ to ¼ teaspoon ground red pepper, or to taste
- 1 can (14½ ounces) DEL MONTE® Original Recipe Stewed Tomatoes, undrained
- 1 can (8 ounces) DEL MONTE® Tomato Sauce
- Pinch *each* ground cinnamon and ground cloves
- 1 green bell pepper, cut into thin strips

Cook pasta according to package directions; drain. Cut shrimp in half lengthwise. In large skillet, cook bacon until crisp; drain. Stir in garlic and ground red pepper; cook and stir 1 minute. Add stewed tomatoes with juice, tomato sauce, cinnamon and cloves. Cook, uncovered, over medium heat 10 minutes, stirring occasionally. Add shrimp and bell pepper; cook 2 to 3 minutes or until shrimp are pink. Just before serving, spoon sauce over hot fettuccine. *Makes 4 servings*

Prep time: 10 minutes
Cook time: 20 minutes

HINT: After deveining shrimp, rinse thoroughly under cold water; drain.

Jumbo Shells Seafood Fancies

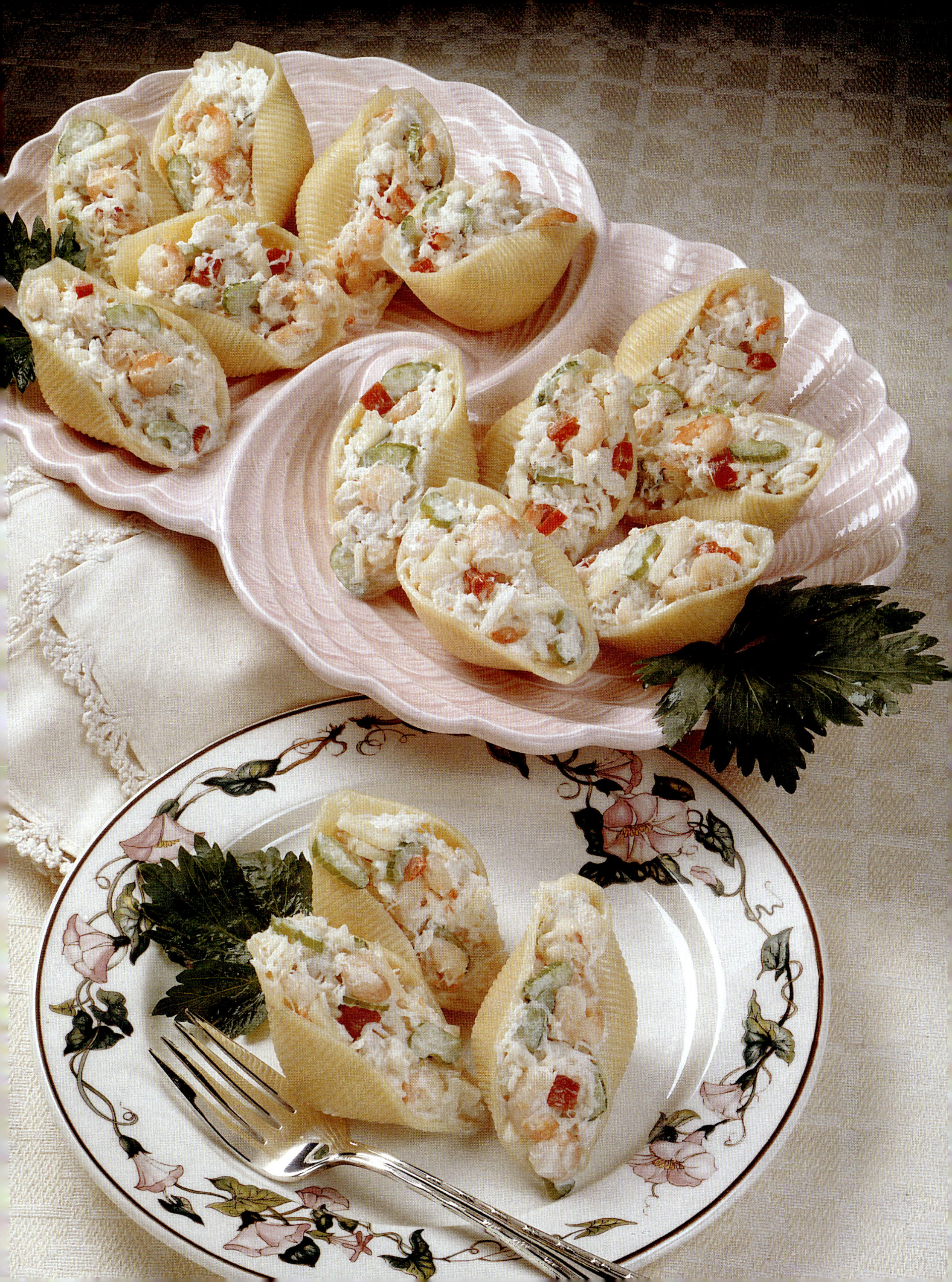

CATCH OF THE DAY

194 GOLDEN APPLE–SALMON PASTA

- 8 ounces salmon, thawed if necessary, cut into ¾-inch chunks*
- 2 tablespoons butter or margarine, divided
- 1 cup sliced mushrooms
- ¾ cup diagonally sliced asparagus**
- ¼ cup chopped onion
- ¼ teaspoon dried oregano leaves
- ⅛ teaspoon salt
- ⅛ teaspoon black pepper
- ⅓ cup half-and-half
- 1 Golden Delicious apple, cored and diced
- 4 ounces fettuccine or spaghetti, cooked and drained
- Grated Parmesan cheese

*Eight ounces tiny pink shrimp can be substituted for salmon.

**One-half cup thawed frozen peas can be substituted for asparagus. Add peas with apple.

Sauté salmon in 1 tablespoon butter 5 minutes or until barely cooked; remove from skillet. Sauté mushrooms, asparagus and onion in remaining 1 tablespoon butter 2 minutes. Add oregano, salt, pepper and half-and-half; cook and stir over high heat 1 minute. Add apple and salmon; cook and stir 30 seconds or until vegetables are tender and salmon flakes easily when tested with fork. Serve over hot fettuccine. Sprinkle with Parmesan cheese.

Makes 2 or 3 servings

NOTE: Recipe may be doubled.

*Favorite recipe from **Washington Apple Commission***

195 SHRIMP PASTA MEDLEY

- ¼ cup (½ stick) butter or margarine
- 1 clove garlic, minced
- 12 ounces medium shrimp, cleaned
- 1 cup half-and-half
- 1 cup pea pods, cut in half diagonally
- 1 red bell pepper, cut into strips
- ¼ cup dry white wine
- ¼ teaspoon crushed red pepper
- 8 ounces linguine, cooked, drained
- 1 wedge (4 ounces) KRAFT® Natural Parmesan Cheese, shredded, divided

• Melt butter in large skillet on medium heat. Add garlic; cook and stir until lightly browned.

• Stir in shrimp, half-and-half, pea pods, bell pepper, wine and crushed red pepper. Simmer 3 to 5 minutes or until shrimp turn pink.

• Pour sauce mixture over hot linguine. Sprinkle with ¾ cup of the cheese; toss to coat. Serve with remaining ¼ cup cheese.

Makes 4 servings

PREP TIME: 10 minutes
COOKING TIME: 10 minutes

VARIATION: Substitute 1½ cups chopped cooked chicken for shrimp.

Golden Apple-Salmon Pasta

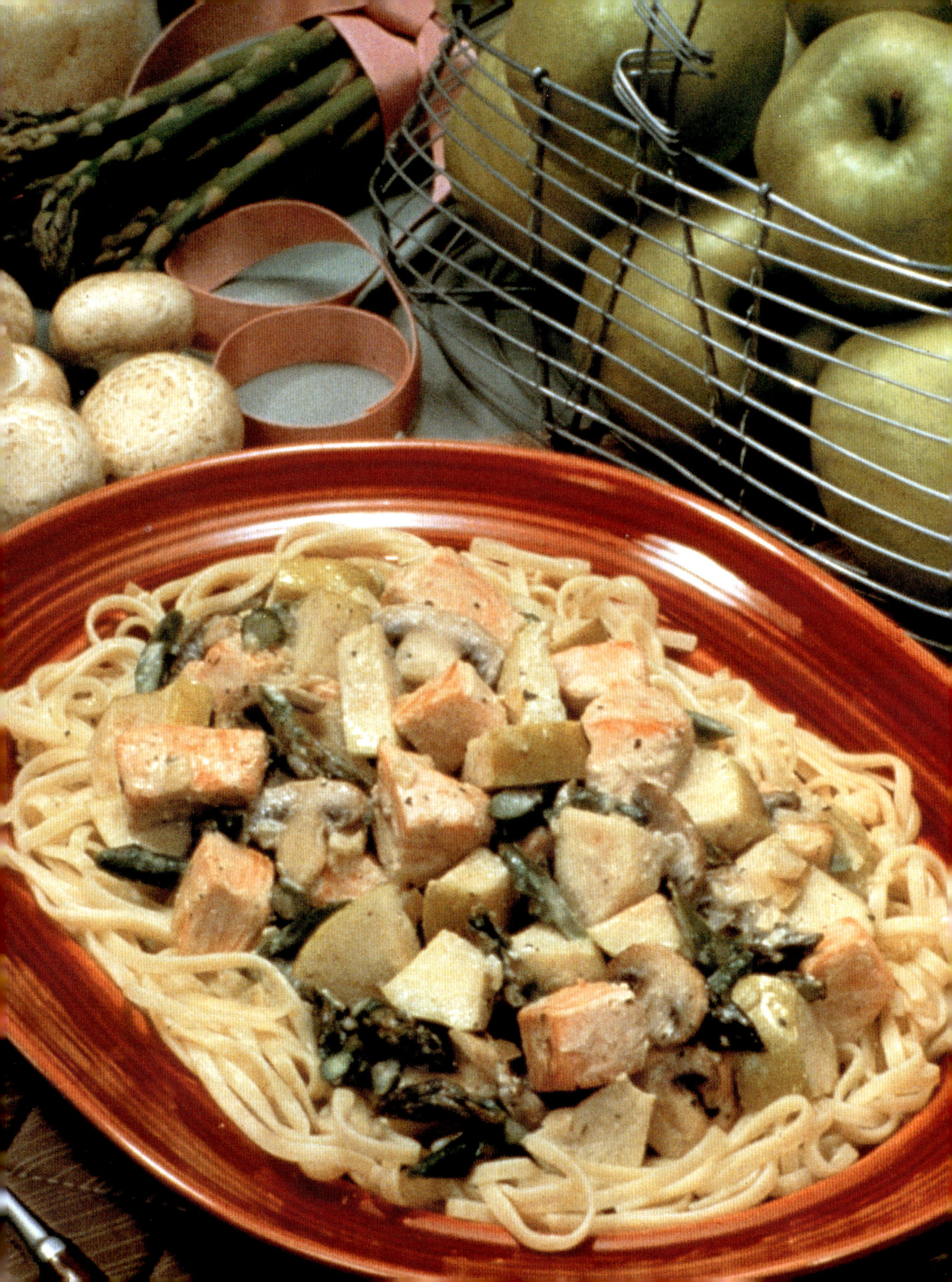

CATCH OF THE DAY

196 UP-TO-THE-MINUTE LINGUINE WITH CLAM SAUCE

2 tablespoons olive oil
1 medium onion, chopped
2 cloves garlic, finely chopped
2 tablespoons all-purpose flour
4 tablespoons chopped parsley, divided
1 teaspoon grated lemon peel
½ to 1 teaspoon Italian seasoning*
¼ teaspoon salt
2 cans (6½ ounces each) minced clams, undrained
1 cup water
1 tablespoon fresh lemon juice
9 ounces linguine
Grated Parmesan cheese (optional)

Equal parts of dried basil and oregano can be substituted for Italian seasoning.

Heat oil in large skillet over medium heat. Add onion and garlic. Cook and stir until onion is soft, but not brown. Stir in flour, 2 tablespoons parsley, lemon peel, Italian seasoning and salt until well blended. Add clams and their juice, water and lemon juice. Bring to a boil. Reduce heat to low and simmer, uncovered, about 5 minutes, stirring occasionally, until slightly thickened.

Cook linguine according to package directions until *al dente*. Drain and rinse. In large bowl, toss linguine with clam sauce. Divide into individual serving bowls. Sprinkle with remaining 2 tablespoons parsley. Serve with grated Parmesan cheese, if desired.   *Makes 4 servings*

Favorite recipe from **Canned Food Information Council**

197 TUNA LINGUINE

1 (6½-ounce) can white albacore tuna, packed in water
6 tablespoons FILIPPO BERIO® Extra Virgin Olive Oil
Juice of 1 lemon
½ cup chopped fresh parsley
¼ teaspoon black pepper
¼ teaspoon salt (optional)
¾ pound uncooked linguine (or any other pasta)

1. Drain tuna. In small bowl, break tuna into chunks; add oil. Stir in lemon juice, parsley, pepper and salt, if desired, until combined.

2. Cook pasta according to package directions; do not overcook. Drain.

3. Spoon tuna sauce over pasta in large bowl; toss gently to coat. Serve.
Makes 4 servings

CATCH OF THE DAY

198 SALMON PASTA WITH PEPPERED CREAM SAUCE

1 (12-ounce) package PASTA LaBELLA® Smoked Salmon Farfalle
2 cups heavy whipping cream
1 (4-ounce) smoked, peppered salmon fillet, skinned and diced
7 tablespoons sweet cream butter
¼ cup minced scallions
   Salt and black pepper to taste
½ cup grated Parmesan cheese

Cook pasta according to package directions. Before draining pasta, reserve ¼ cup cooking liquid.* Meanwhile, heat cream in large nonstick skillet over medium-high heat. When cream begins to thicken, add salmon, butter, scallions, salt and pepper. When sauce has cooked to a medium-thin consistency, add Parmesan cheese and pasta. Mix together well and serve.

Makes 3 main-dish servings

*If sauce becomes too thick, use reserved liquid to thin out the sauce.

199 SHRIMP MARINARA WITH PASTA

8 ounces medium shrimp, peeled, deveined, thawed
¼ cup chopped onion
2 tablespoons chopped green bell pepper
1 clove garlic, crushed
2 tablespoons vegetable oil
1 can (8 ounces) tomato sauce
½ can (3 ounces) tomato paste
½ cup water
1 teaspoon sugar
½ teaspoon dried basil leaves
½ teaspoon dried oregano leaves
⅛ teaspoon black pepper
   Cooked pasta

In large skillet, cook onion, bell pepper and garlic in hot oil until tender. Add tomato sauce, tomato paste, water and seasonings. Cover and simmer 15 minutes, stirring occasionally. Add shrimp. Cover and simmer about 3 minutes or until shrimp are tender. Serve over pasta.

Makes 2 servings

Favorite recipe from **National Fisheries Institute**

CATCH OF THE DAY

200 TORTELLINI WITH THREE-CHEESE TUNA SAUCE

1 pound cheese-filled tortellini, spinach and egg
2 green onions, thinly sliced
1 clove garlic, minced
1 tablespoon butter or margarine
1 cup low-fat ricotta cheese
½ cup low-fat milk
1 can (6 ounces) STARKIST® Tuna, drained and broken into chunks
½ cup shredded low-fat mozzarella cheese
¼ cup grated Parmesan or Romano cheese
2 tablespoons chopped fresh basil *or* 2 teaspoons dried basil, crushed
1 teaspoon grated lemon peel
Fresh tomato wedges for garnish (optional)

Cook tortellini in boiling salted water according to package directions. When tortellini is nearly done, in another saucepan sauté onions and garlic in butter for 2 minutes. Whisk in ricotta cheese and milk. Add tuna, cheeses, basil and lemon peel. Cook over medium-low heat until mixture is heated and cheeses are melted.

Drain pasta; add to sauce. Toss well to coat; garnish with tomato wedges, if desired. Serve immediately.

Makes 4 to 5 servings

Preparation time: 25 minutes

201 SHRIMP FETTUCCINE PRIMAVERA

8 ounces uncooked fettuccine or spinach fettuccine
6 ounces medium shrimp, shelled and deveined
1 package (9 ounces) DOLE® Garden Style Vegetables
¾ cup nonfat or low-fat plain yogurt
¼ cup fat-free or reduced-fat mayonnaise
1 teaspoon dried basil leaves
½ teaspoon dried dill weed
2 tablespoons grated Parmesan cheese

• Prepare fettuccine according to package directions, adding shrimp and vegetables during last 2 minutes of cooking time, cooking until shrimp are pink and vegetables are crisp-tender. Drain.

• Combine yogurt, mayonnaise, basil and dill in large serving bowl. Add drained fettuccine mixture; toss well to coat evenly. Sprinkle with cheese. Serve immediately.

Makes 4 servings

PREP: 10 minutes
COOK: 15 minutes

TIP: If a thinner sauce consistency is desired, add 1 to 2 tablespoons low-fat milk.

Tortellini with Three-Cheese Tuna Sauce

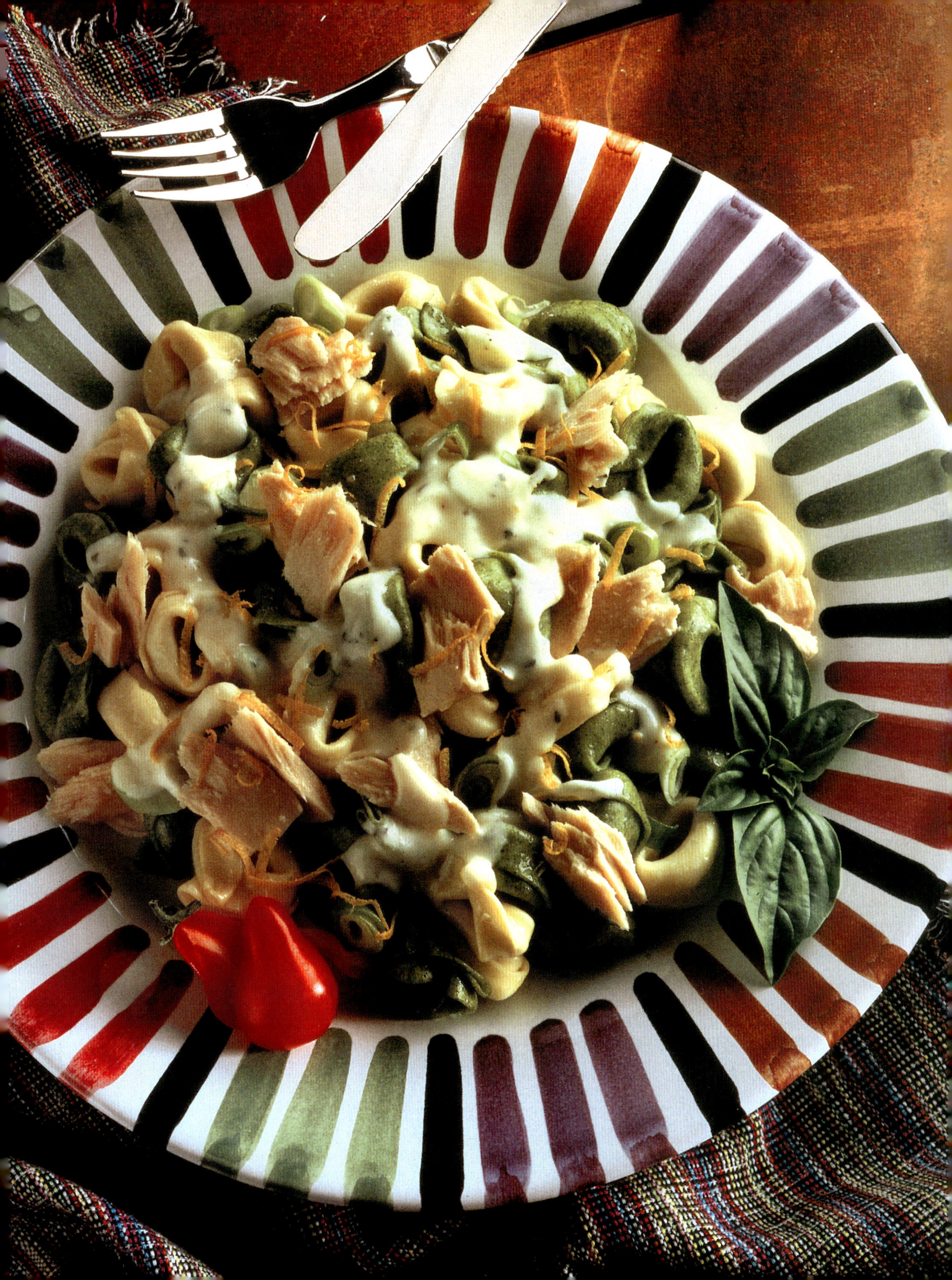

FRESH FROM THE GARDEN

202 ROTINI WITH SUMMER VEGETABLES

- 12 ounces rotini pasta
- 3 cups broccoli florets
- 3 cups sliced carrots
- 3 red bell peppers, cut into 1-inch squares
- ¼ cup water
- ¼ teaspoon plus ⅛ teaspoon red pepper flakes, divided
- 3 cups sliced mushrooms
- 2 cups (8 ounces) shredded part-skim mozzarella cheese
- ¼ cup shredded Asiago cheese
- 3 tablespoons olive oil
- 3 cloves garlic, minced
- 4 cups coarsely chopped, seeded, peeled plum tomatoes
- ⅓ cup chopped fresh basil
- ¼ cup Chardonnay or other dry white wine

1. Cook pasta according to package directions; drain. Place in large bowl.

2. Meanwhile, combine broccoli, carrots, bell peppers, water and ¼ teaspoon red pepper flakes in large microwavable baking dish. Cover loosely and microwave at HIGH 5 minutes or until hot. Stir in mushrooms. Cover and microwave 3 minutes. Allow to stand, covered, 5 minutes.

3. Add vegetables to pasta; toss to combine. Divide mixture between 2 microwavable baking dishes. Sprinkle each with cheeses.

4. To prepare sauce, heat olive oil in medium saucepan over medium-low heat until hot. Add garlic and remaining ⅛ teaspoon red pepper flakes. Cook and stir 1 minute. Add tomatoes. Heat 5 minutes. Stir in basil and wine. Simmer 5 minutes.

5. Meanwhile, to heat pasta mixture, microwave each baking dish at MEDIUM-HIGH (80%) 4 to 5 minutes or until heated through. Serve with sauce.

Makes 10 servings

Rotini with Summer Vegetables

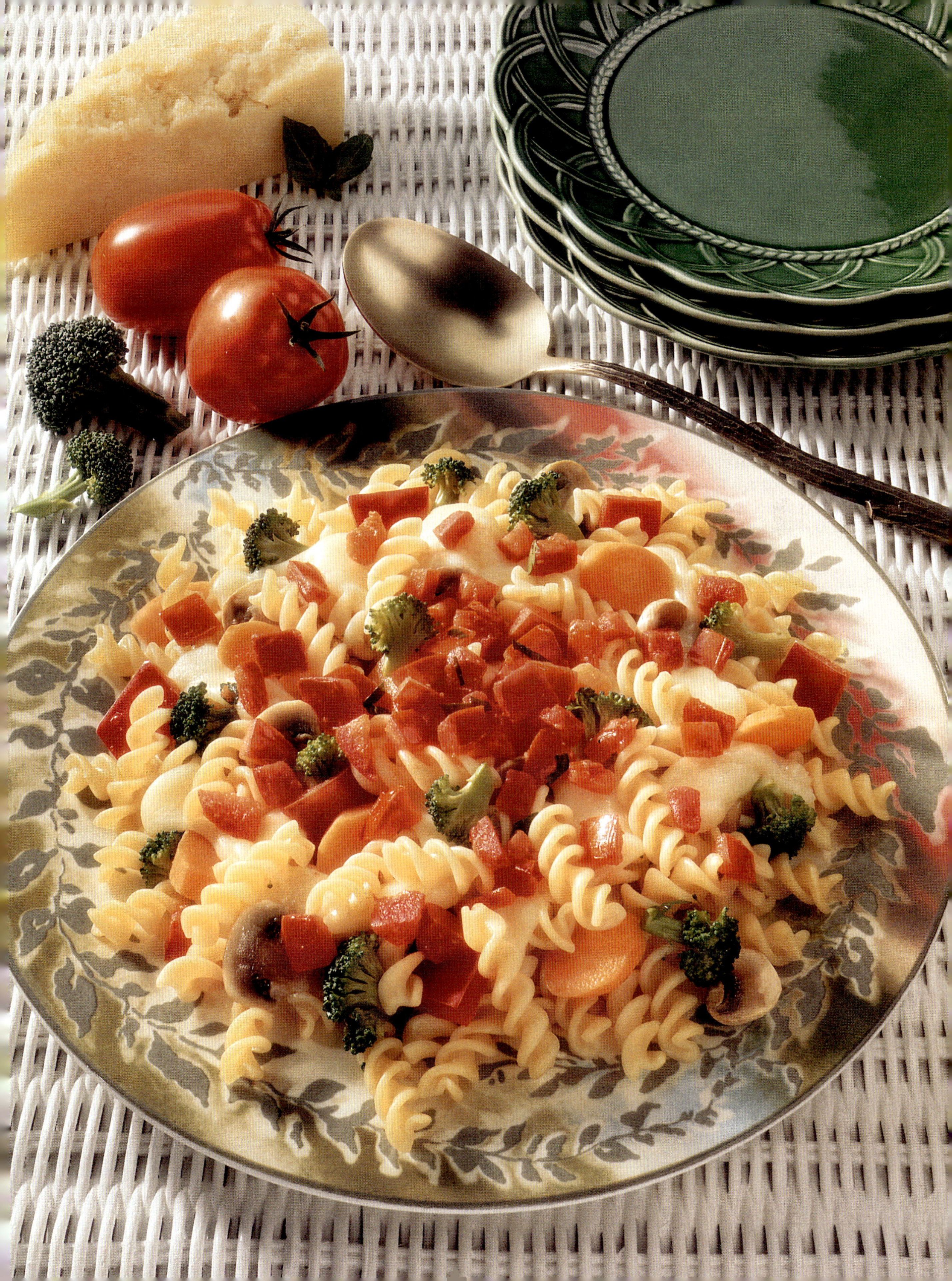

FRESH FROM THE GARDEN

203 TORTELLINI PRIMAVERA

- 1 cup sliced mushrooms
- ½ cup chopped onion
- 1 clove garlic, minced
- 2 tablespoons butter or margarine
- 1 package (10 ounces) frozen chopped spinach, thawed, well drained
- 1 container (8 ounces) PHILADELPHIA BRAND® Soft Cream Cheese
- 1 medium tomato, chopped
- ¼ cup milk
- ¼ cup (1 ounce) KRAFT® 100% Grated Parmesan Cheese
- 1 teaspoon Italian seasoning
- ¼ teaspoon salt
- ¼ teaspoon pepper
- 8 to 9 ounces fresh or frozen cheese-filled tortellini, cooked and drained

Cook and stir mushrooms, onion and garlic in butter in large skillet. Add remaining ingredients except tortellini; mix well. Cook until mixture just begins to boil, stirring occasionally. Stir in tortellini; cook until thoroughly heated. *Makes 4 servings*

Prep time: 10 minutes
Cook time: 10 minutes

204 EASY CHEESE & TOMATO MACARONI

- 2 packages (7 ounces each) macaroni and cheese dinner
- 1 tablespoon olive or vegetable oil
- 1 cup finely chopped onion
- 1 cup thinly sliced celery
- 3½ cups (28-ounce can) CONTADINA® Crushed Tomatoes
- Grated Parmesan cheese (optional)
- Sliced green onion or celery leaves (optional)

Cook macaroni (from macaroni and cheese dinners) according to package directions; drain. In large skillet, heat oil. Add chopped onion and celery; sauté 3 minutes or until vegetables are tender. In small bowl, combine tomatoes and cheese mix from dinner. Stir into vegetable mixture. Simmer 3 to 4 minutes or until mixture is thickened and heated through. Add macaroni to skillet; stir until well coated with sauce. Heat thoroughly, stirring occasionally. Sprinkle with Parmesan cheese and sliced green onion, if desired. *Makes 6 to 8 servings*

Tortellini Primavera

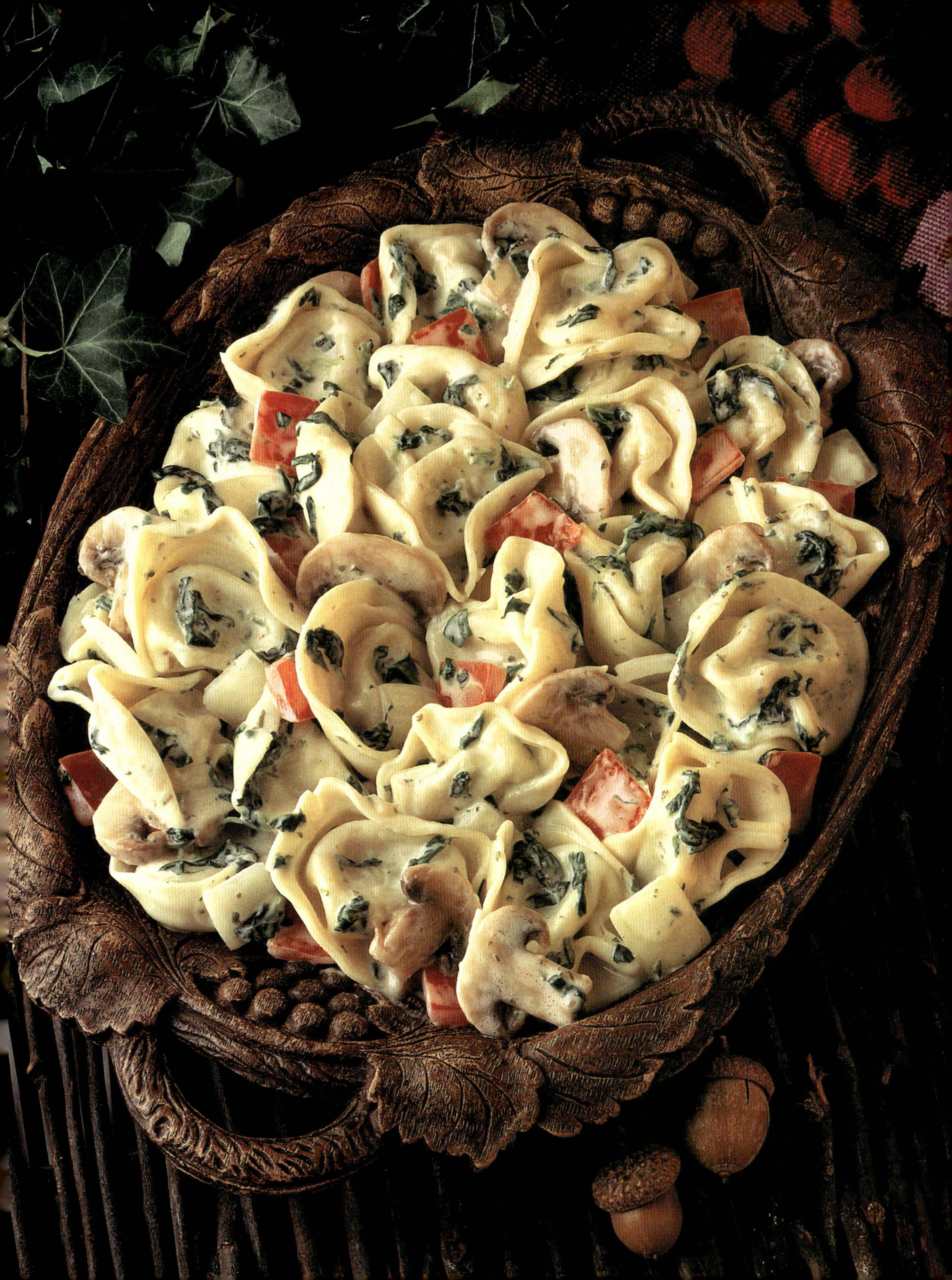

FRESH FROM THE GARDEN

205 PESTO PASTA

- 1 cup packed fresh basil leaves
- 1 (3-ounce) package KRAFT® 100% Shredded Parmesan Cheese *or* KRAFT® 100% Parmesan Cheese wedge, shredded, divided
- ⅓ cup olive oil
- ¼ cup pine nuts
- 1 clove garlic, minced
- 8 ounces uncooked radiatore pasta, hot cooked and drained
- 1 cup pitted ripe olive halves
- 1 cup chopped seeded tomatoes

- Place basil, ½ cup cheese, oil, pine nuts and garlic in food processor container with steel blade attached; process until smooth.

- Toss together basil mixture, pasta, olives and tomatoes in large bowl. Sprinkle with remaining ¼ cup cheese.

Makes 4 servings

Prep/Cook time: 20 minutes

VARIATION: Substitute 8 ounces of your favorite pasta for the radiatore pasta.

206 SONOMA FETTUCCINE ALFREDO

- ½ pound dried fettuccine
- 1 jar (8 ounces) SONOMA Marinated Dried Tomatoes, undrained
- 1½ cups whipping cream, divided
- 1 cup (3 ounces) grated fresh Parmesan cheese
- Salt and black pepper to taste
- 3 tablespoons chopped chives
- ½ teaspoon ground nutmeg

Cook pasta in large pot of boiling salted water 5 to 8 minutes until just tender; drain well. Meanwhile, drain tomato marinating oil into large skillet; snip tomatoes in half and reserve. Add ½ cup cream to skillet. Cook over high heat, stirring constantly, about 3 minutes until slightly thickened. Reduce heat to medium; add cooked pasta and mix gently. Add ½ cup cheese, ½ cup remaining cream and reserved tomatoes. Lift and mix pasta gently. Repeat with remaining cheese and cream; mix again. Season with salt and pepper. Transfer to warmed individual pasta bowls or large platter. Sprinkle with chives and nutmeg. Serve immediately.

Makes 4 servings

Pesto Pasta

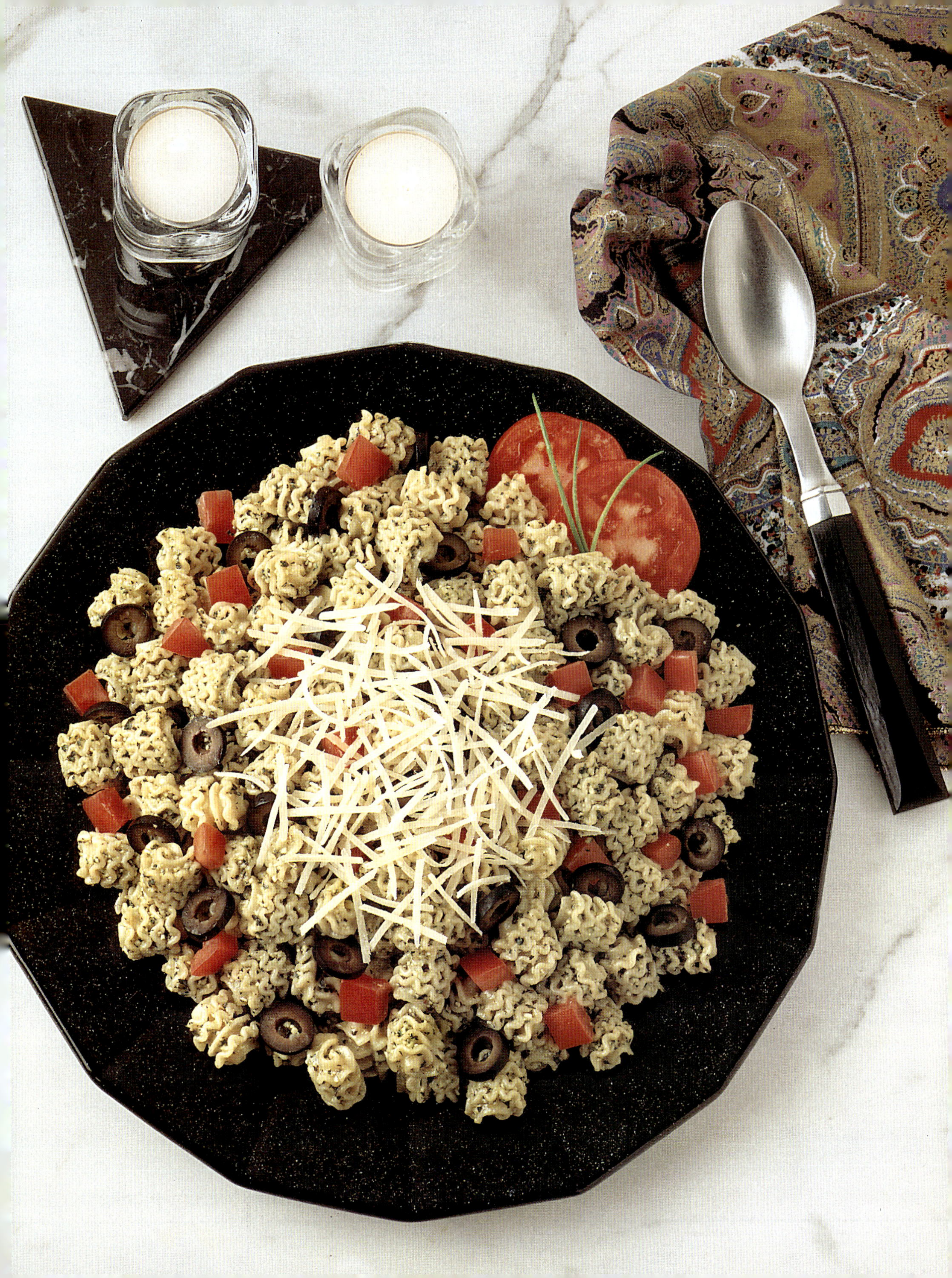

FRESH FROM THE GARDEN

207 LUSCIOUS VEGETARIAN LASAGNA

- 8 ounces lasagna noodles
- 1 can (14½ ounces) whole peeled tomatoes, undrained and coarsely chopped
- 1 can (12 ounces) tomato sauce
- 1 teaspoon dried oregano leaves
- 1 teaspoon dried basil leaves
  Dash black pepper
- 2 tablespoons olive oil
- 1 large onion, chopped
- 1½ teaspoons minced garlic
- 2 small zucchini, diced
- 1 large carrot, diced
- 1 green bell pepper, diced
- 8 ounces mushrooms, sliced
- 1 cup (4 ounces) shredded mozzarella cheese
- 2 cups 1% milk-fat cottage cheese
- 1 cup grated Parmesan or Romano cheese
  Parsley sprigs for garnish

1. Cook lasagna according to package directions; drain.

2. Place tomatoes with juice, tomato sauce, oregano, basil and black pepper in medium saucepan. Bring to a boil over high heat. Reduce heat to low. Simmer, uncovered, 6 to 10 minutes.

3. Heat oil in large skillet over medium-high heat. Cook and stir onion and garlic until onion is golden. Add zucchini, carrot, bell pepper and mushrooms. Cook and stir 5 to 10 minutes or until vegetables are tender. Stir vegetables into tomato mixture; bring to a boil. Reduce heat to low. Simmer, uncovered, 15 minutes.

4. Preheat oven to 350°F. Combine mozzarella, cottage and Parmesan cheeses in large bowl; blend well.

5. Spoon about 1 cup sauce on bottom of 12×8-inch baking pan. Place a layer of noodles over sauce, then half of the cheese mixture and half of the remaining sauce. Repeat layers of noodles, cheese mixture and sauce.

6. Bake lasagna 30 to 45 minutes or until bubbly. Let stand 10 minutes. Garnish with parsley. *Makes 6 to 8 servings*

VARIATION: Other vegetables may be added or substituted for the ones listed above.

208 PEPPERY PASTA TOSS

- 1 cup FLEISCHMANN'S® Margarine
- 1 tablespoon dry sherry
- 2 cloves garlic, minced
- ½ teaspoon dried oregano leaves
- ½ teaspoon dried basil leaves
- ¼ teaspoon coarsely ground black pepper
- ¼ teaspoon red pepper flakes
- 1 pound cooked pasta

In small saucepan, melt margarine. Add sherry, garlic, oregano, basil, black pepper and red pepper. Bring mixture to a boil. Reduce heat to low; simmer 10 minutes. Serve over cooked pasta.

Makes 8 servings

Luscious Vegetarian Lasagna

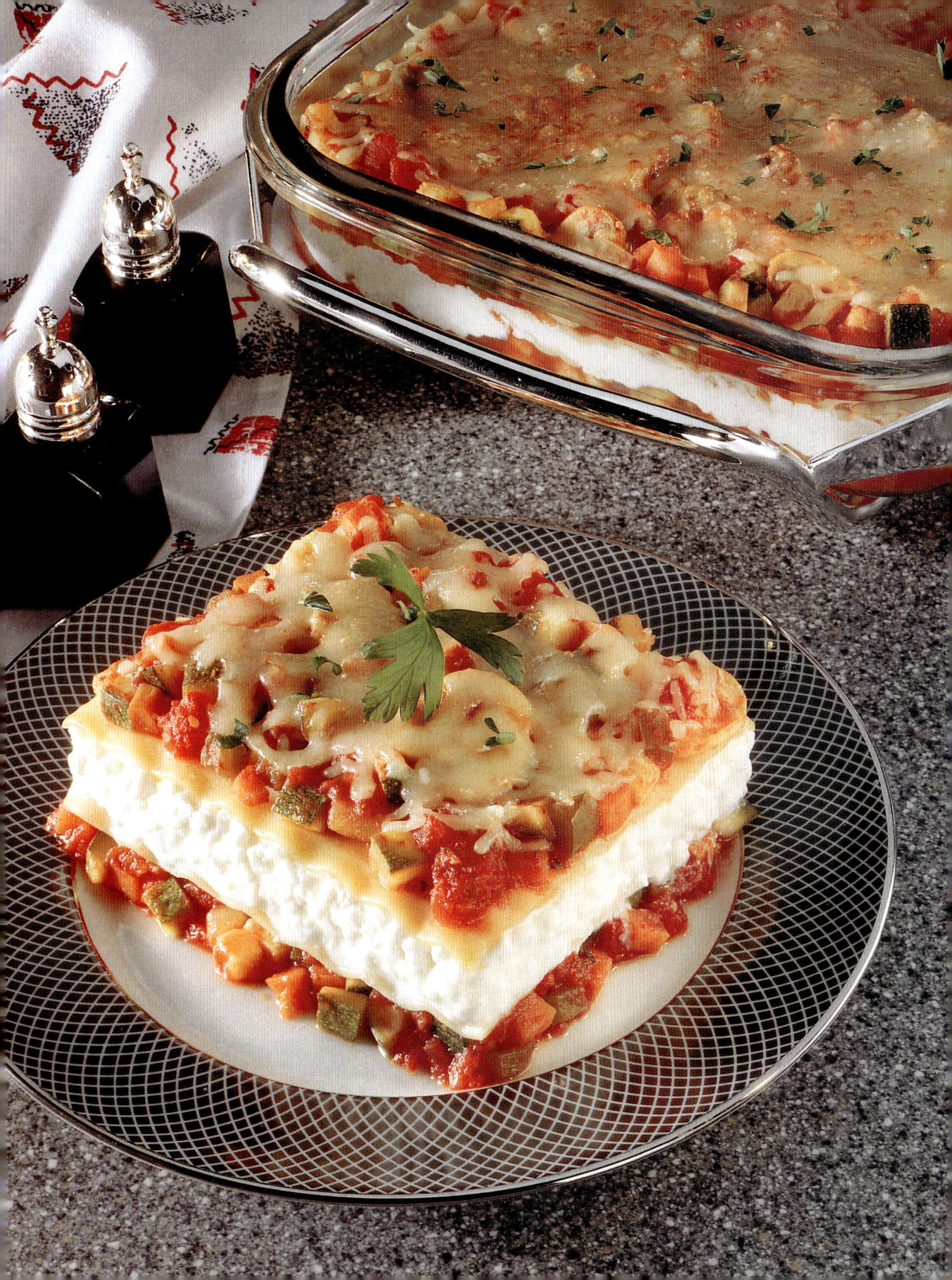

FRESH FROM THE GARDEN

209 PENNE WITH ARTICHOKES

- 1 package (10 ounces) frozen artichoke hearts
- 1¼ cups water
- 2 tablespoons lemon juice
- 5 cloves garlic
- 2 tablespoons olive oil, divided
- 2 ounces oil-packed sun-dried tomatoes, drained
- 2 small dried hot red chilies, crushed
- 2 tablespoons chopped fresh parsley
- ¼ teaspoon salt
- ¼ teaspoon black pepper
- ¾ cup fresh bread crumbs
- 1 tablespoon chopped garlic
- 12 ounces uncooked penne, hot cooked, drained
- 1 tablespoon grated Romano cheese

In medium saucepan over medium heat, cook artichoke hearts in water and lemon juice until tender. Cool artichoke hearts; cut into quarters. Reserve artichoke cooking liquid.

In large skillet over medium-high heat, cook and stir 5 whole cloves garlic in 1½ tablespoons oil until golden. Reduce heat to low. Add artichoke hearts and tomatoes; simmer 1 minute. Stir in reserved artichoke cooking liquid, chilies, parsley, salt and pepper. Simmer 5 minutes. Remove and discard whole cloves garlic.

Meanwhile, in small saucepan over medium heat, cook and stir bread crumbs and 1 tablespoon chopped garlic in remaining ½ tablespoon oil. Pour artichoke sauce over penne in large bowl; toss gently to coat. Sprinkle with bread crumb mixture and cheese.   *Makes 4 to 6 servings*

Favorite recipe from **National Pasta Association**

210 PESTO LINGUINE TOSSED WITH OLIVE OIL AND BROCCOLI

- 1 (12-ounce) package PASTA LaBELLA® Pesto Linguine
- ¼ cup extra-virgin olive oil
- ½ cup julienned yellow onion
- ½ cup diced red bell pepper
- 1½ cups broccoli florets
- Salt and black pepper to taste
- 1 cup pasta cooking broth*
- ¼ cup grated Parmesan cheese

*Before draining pasta, reserve 1 cup cooking liquid for recipe.

Cook pasta *al dente* according to package directions. Meanwhile, heat olive oil in large skillet. Sauté onion and bell pepper 1 minute. Add broccoli; sauté 4 minutes. Season with salt and pepper; add pasta broth. Simmer vegetables 2 minutes. Add hot linguine to vegetable mixture; mix well. Sprinkle with Parmesan cheese and serve.
Makes 4 servings

Penne with Artichokes

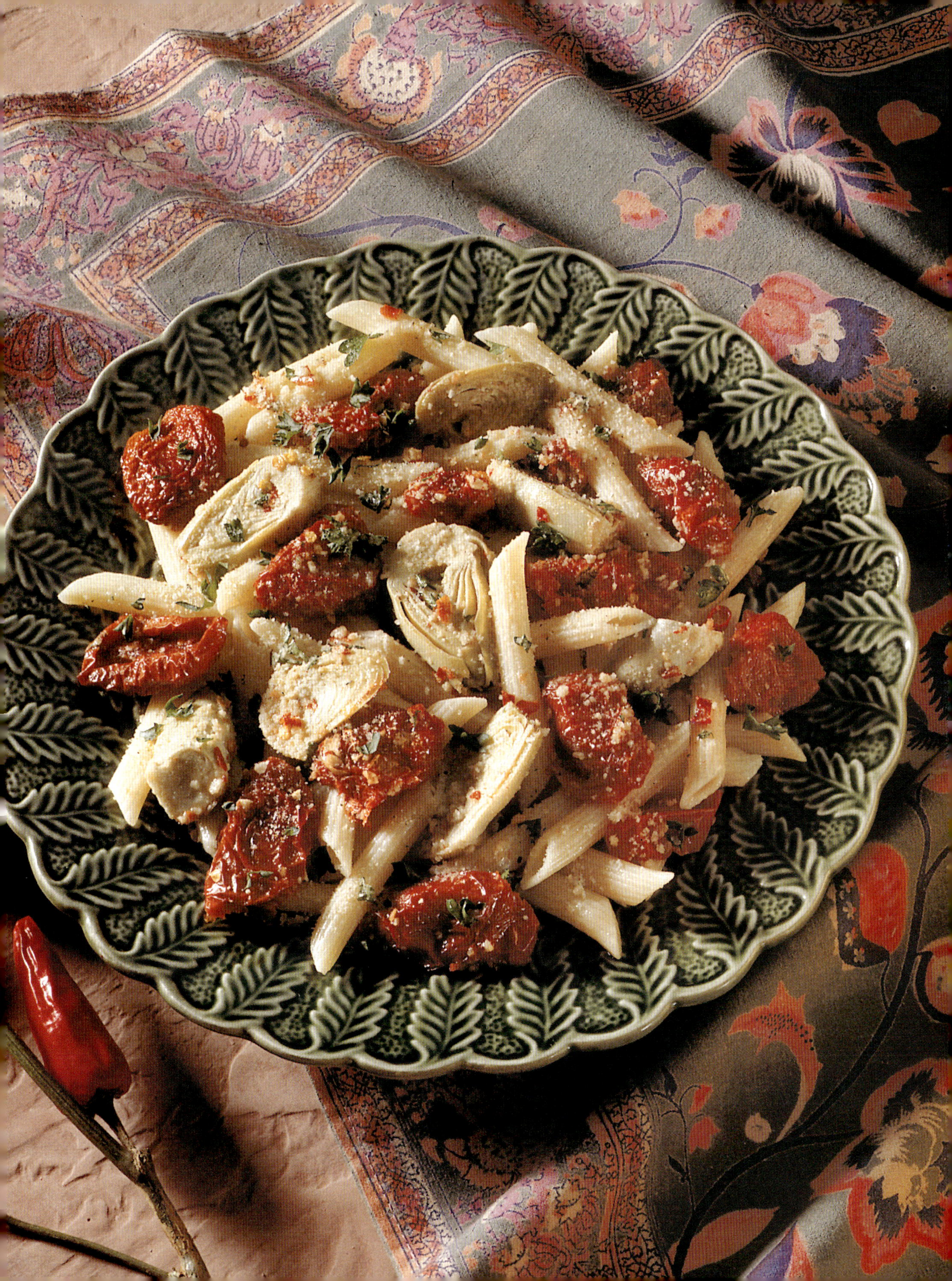

FRESH FROM THE GARDEN

211 FETTUCCINE WITH SUN-DRIED TOMATO CREAM

⅔ cup sun-dried tomatoes
3 to 4 garlic cloves
1 (8-ounce) container PHILADELPHIA BRAND® Soft Cream Cheese
½ teaspoon dried oregano leaves, crushed
¼ cup butter or margarine
¼ cup BREAKSTONE'S® sour cream
1 pound fettuccine, cooked, drained, kept warm
¼ cup olive oil
Salt and pepper
2 tablespoons chopped fresh parsley

- Cover tomatoes with boiling water; let stand 10 minutes. Drain.

- Place tomatoes and garlic in food processor or blender container; process until coarsely chopped. Add cream cheese and oregano; process until well blended.

- Melt butter in medium saucepan; stir in cream cheese mixture and sour cream. Cook until thoroughly heated.

- Toss warm fettuccine with oil.

- Add cream cheese mixture. Season to taste with salt and pepper. Sprinkle with chopped parsley. Serve immediately.

Makes 8 to 10 servings

Prep time: 30 minutes

212 GARDEN LINGUINE

8 ounces linguine or rotini
3 tablespoons olive oil
1 tablespoon butter
1 cup sliced mushrooms
½ cup sliced onions
2 cups snow peas, cut into halves
2 cups diced zucchini
½ red bell pepper, cut into strips (optional)
1 teaspoon dried basil leaves *or* 3 tablespoons fresh basil
½ teaspoon garlic powder
1 teaspoon salt
½ teaspoon black pepper
½ cup Parmesan cheese

Cook linguine as directed on package; drain. Heat oil and butter in saucepan; sauté mushrooms, onions, snow peas, zucchini and bell pepper, if desired, until crisp-tender. Add seasonings to vegetable mixture. Toss with linguine. Sprinkle Parmesan cheese over top.

Makes 4 servings

Favorite recipe from **North Dakota Wheat Commission**

Fettuccine with Sun-Dried Tomato Cream

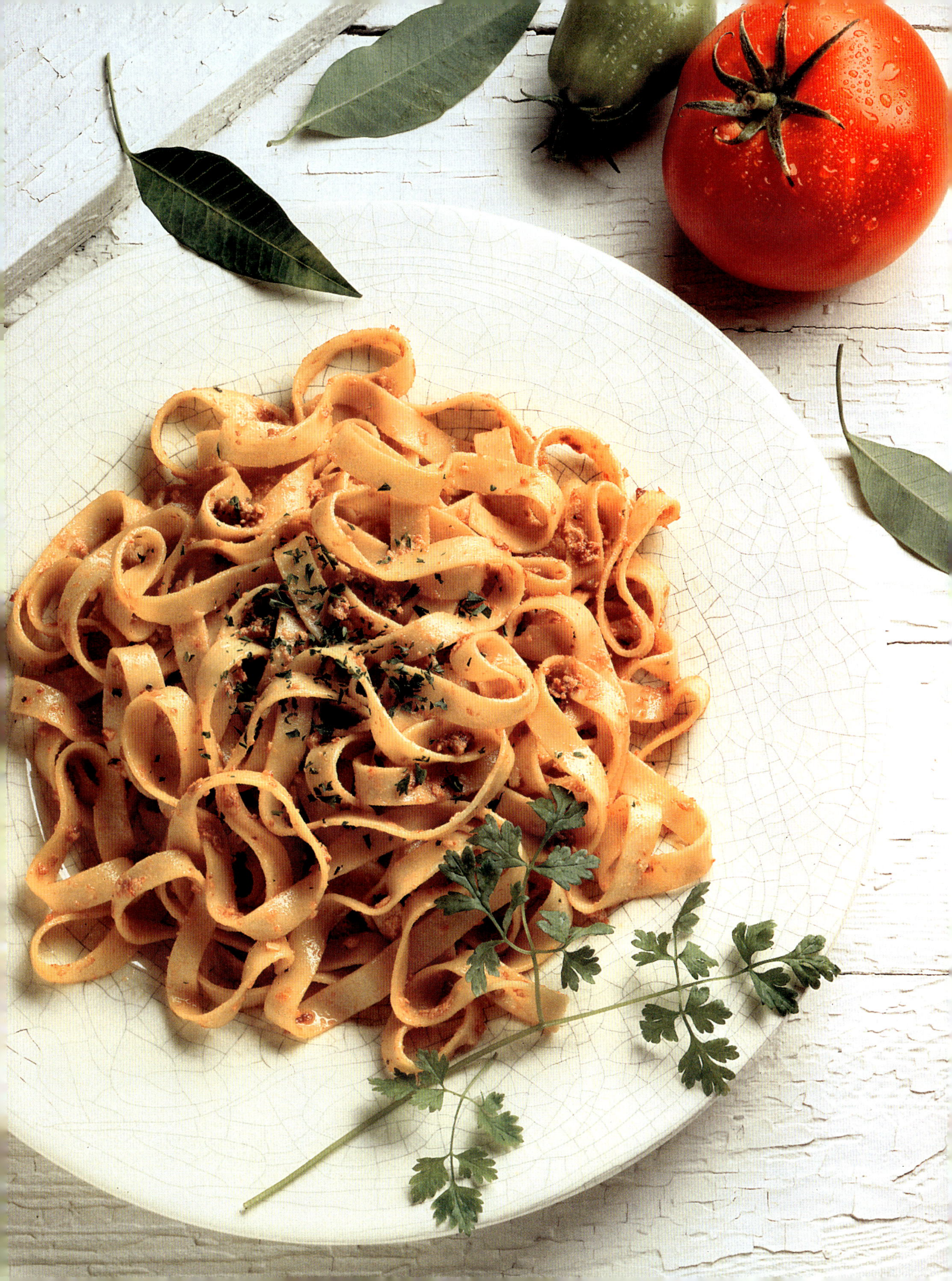

FRESH FROM THE GARDEN

213 FETTUCCINE WITH PESTO

12 ounces uncooked fettuccine
3 cups (1 ounce) loosely packed fresh basil leaves
2/3 cup grated Romano or Parmesan cheese
1/2 cup chopped California walnuts
1/2 cup olive oil
2 cloves garlic, peeled
1/4 teaspoon salt
1/4 teaspoon black pepper

Cook pasta according to package directions; drain. Meanwhile, place basil, cheese, walnuts, oil, garlic, salt and pepper in food processor or blender; process until well blended. (Sauce will thin out over hot pasta.) Place hot pasta in large bowl; add sauce. Toss until well coated. Serve immediately. *Makes 4 to 6 servings*

Favorite recipe from **Walnut Marketing Board**

214 PASTA WITH SUNFLOWER KERNELS

1/2 cup sunflower oil
3 parsley sprigs, chopped
3 cloves garlic, minced
1 teaspoon grated lemon peel
1/2 teaspoon salt
1/2 teaspoon black pepper
8 ounces tomato, spinach or plain spaghetti, cooked, drained
2/3 cup grated Parmesan cheese
1/2 cup roasted sunflower kernels

Heat sunflower oil in small skillet over medium-high heat. Add parsley, garlic and lemon peel; cook and stir 1 minute. Add salt and pepper. Pour over hot pasta. Add Parmesan cheese and sunflower kernels; toss lightly. *Makes 4 servings*

Favorite recipe from **National Sunflower Association**

215 DITALINI WITH ZUCCHINI

8 ounces uncooked ditalini pasta
1/4 cup FILIPPO BERIO® Olive Oil
1 pound zucchini, trimmed and cut into thin rounds
1 onion, thinly sliced
1 tomato
1 tablespoon minced fresh parsley
Salt and freshly ground black pepper to taste

Cook pasta according to package directions until *al dente* (tender but still firm). Drain. In medium skillet, heat olive oil over medium heat until hot. Add zucchini and onion; cook and stir 10 minutes or until zucchini is tender-crisp. Place tomato in small saucepan of boiling water; boil 1 minute. Place in bowl of ice water for 10 seconds. Remove skin with paring knife; chop tomato. In large bowl, combine zucchini mixture, tomato and parsley. Toss with pasta. Season to taste with salt and pepper. *Makes 3 to 4 servings*

FRESH FROM THE GARDEN

216 WINTER PRIMAVERA

1 pound PASTA L<small>A</small>BELLA® Angel Hair
⅓ cup extra-virgin olive oil
1 cup julienned yellow onions
¼ cup thinly sliced fresh garlic
1 cup julienned yellow squash
1 cup julienned zucchini
1 cup julienned carrots
1½ cups finely diced ripe tomatoes
2 teaspoons dried basil leaves *or* ¼ cup fresh basil, chopped
1 teaspoon dried oregano leaves
Salt and black pepper to taste
3 cups tomato juice
½ cup grated Parmesan cheese

Cook pasta according to package directions. Meanwhile, heat olive oil in large pot. Sauté onions and garlic 3 minutes. Add squash, zucchini and carrots; cook 4 minutes. Add tomatoes, basil, oregano, salt and pepper; cook 5 minutes. Add tomato juice; simmer 5 additional minutes. Mix hot pasta with hot primavera sauce. Sprinkle with Parmesan cheese and serve.   *Makes 4 servings*

217 SUMMER SPAGHETTI

1 pound firm ripe fresh plum tomatoes, coarsely chopped
1 medium onion, chopped
6 pitted green olives, chopped
2 medium cloves garlic, minced
⅓ cup chopped fresh parsley
2 tablespoons finely shredded fresh basil *or* ¾ teaspoon dried basil leaves
2 teaspoons drained capers
½ teaspoon paprika
¼ teaspoon dried oregano leaves
1 tablespoon red wine vinegar
½ cup olive oil
1 pound uncooked spaghetti

1. In medium bowl, combine tomatoes, onion, olives, garlic, parsley, basil, capers, paprika and oregano; toss well. Drizzle vinegar over tomato mixture. Pour oil over tomato mixture. Stir until thoroughly mixed. Refrigerate, covered, at least 6 hours or overnight.

2. Just before serving, cook spaghetti according to package directions; drain well. Immediately toss hot pasta with cold marinated tomato sauce. Serve at once.
Makes 4 to 6 servings

FRESH FROM THE GARDEN

218 ROASTED VEGETABLES PROVENÇAL

- 8 ounces medium or large mushrooms, halved
- 1 large zucchini, cut into 1-inch pieces, halved
- 1 large yellow squash or additional zucchini, cut into 1-inch pieces, quartered
- 1 large red or green bell pepper, cut into 1-inch pieces
- 1 small red onion, cut into ¼-inch slices, separated into rings
- 3 tablespoons olive oil
- 2 cloves garlic, minced
- 1 teaspoon dried basil leaves
- 1 teaspoon dried thyme leaves
- ½ teaspoon salt (optional)
- ¼ teaspoon freshly ground black pepper
- 4 large plum tomatoes, quartered
- ⅔ cup milk
- 2 tablespoons margarine or butter
- 1 package (5.1 ounces) PASTA RONI® Angel Hair Pasta with Parmesan Cheese

1. Preheat oven to 425°F. In 15×10-inch jelly-roll pan, combine mushrooms, zucchini, squash, bell pepper and onion. In small bowl, combine oil, garlic, basil, thyme, salt and black pepper. Add to vegetable mixture; toss to coat. Bake 15 minutes; stir in tomatoes. Continue baking 5 to 10 minutes or until vegetables are tender.

2. While vegetables are roasting, combine 1⅓ cups water, milk and margarine in medium saucepan; bring just to a boil. Gradually add pasta while stirring. Stir in contents of seasoning packet. Reduce heat to medium.

3. Boil, uncovered, stirring frequently, 4 minutes. Sauce will be very thin, but will thicken upon standing. Remove from heat.

4. Let stand 3 minutes or until desired consistency. Stir before serving. Serve pasta topped with vegetables.

Makes 4 servings

219 PASTA WITH BELGIOIOSO® GORGONZOLA SAUCE

- 1½ cups whipping cream
- 1½ cups (12 ounces) creamy BELGIOIOSO® Gorgonzola cheese
- 1 pound fettuccine, cooked and drained
  Fresh grated BELGIOIOSO® Parmesan cheese
  Fresh cracked black pepper
  Chopped fresh basil

In medium saucepan, bring cream to a boil over medium heat. Simmer about 5 minutes. Reduce heat to low and stir in Gorgonzola cheese until melted.

Place cooked pasta into large warm bowl, pour sauce over and toss. Sprinkle with Parmesan cheese, pepper and basil.

Makes 6 servings

Roasted Vegetables Provençal

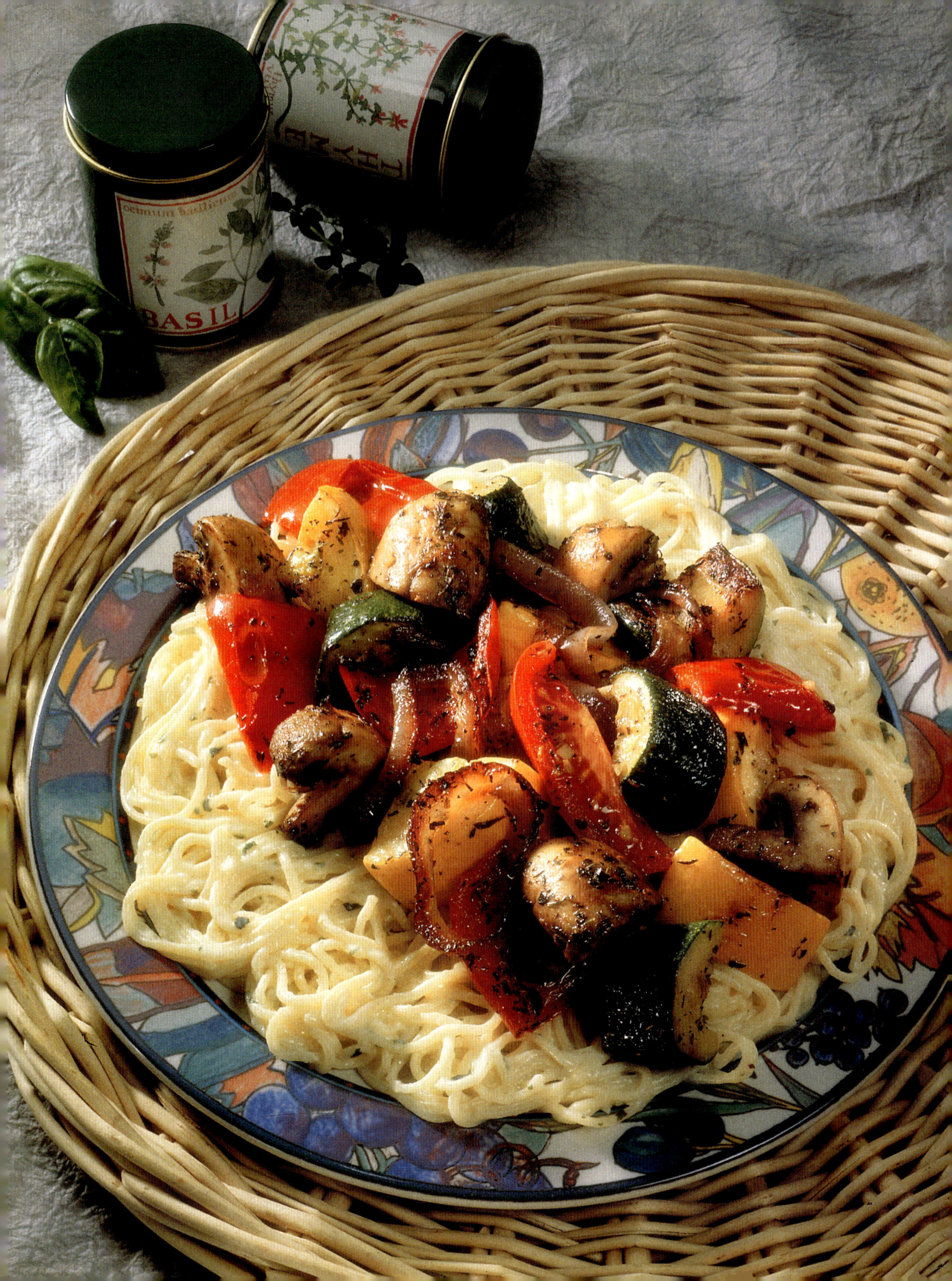
BASIL

FRESH FROM THE GARDEN

220 PASTA WITH ROASTED PEPPERS AND BROCCOLI

1 pound mostaccioli, ziti or other medium pasta, uncooked
2 tablespoons vegetable oil
½ teaspoon red pepper flakes
1 pound (6 cups) broccoli florets
2 jars (6 ounces each) roasted peppers or whole pimientos, drained and diced
Salt and black pepper to taste
¼ cup grated Parmesan cheese

Cook pasta according to package directions; drain well.

Heat oil and red pepper flakes in large skillet over medium heat 2 minutes. Add broccoli; sauté 2 to 3 minutes. Add ½ cup water; cover. Cook broccoli about 3 minutes or until crisp-tender.

Toss pasta with diced peppers. Season to taste with salt and black pepper. Pour broccoli mixture over pasta; sprinkle with Parmesan cheese just before serving.

Makes 6 servings

Favorite recipe from **National Pasta Association**

221 FETTUCCINE WITH FRESH HERB AND PARMESAN SAUCE

8 ounces uncooked fettuccine noodles
3 tablespoons grated Parmesan or pecorino cheese
3 tablespoons FILIPPO BERIO® Extra Virgin Olive Oil
2 tablespoons chopped fresh herbs (basil, oregano or chives)*
1 egg yolk (see note)
½ clove garlic, crushed
Salt and freshly ground pepper to taste

Omit herbs if fresh are unavailable. Do not substitute dried herbs.

Cook pasta according to package directions until *al dente* (tender but still firm). Drain. Meanwhile, in small bowl, combine cheese, olive oil, herbs, egg yolk and garlic.

Return pasta to saucepan; place over very low heat. Pour olive oil mixture over pasta; toss until lightly coated. (Do not overheat mixture—sauce will coat pasta quickly.) Season to taste with salt and pepper.

Makes 2 servings

NOTE: Use Grade A clean, uncracked egg.

Pasta with Roasted Peppers and Broccoli

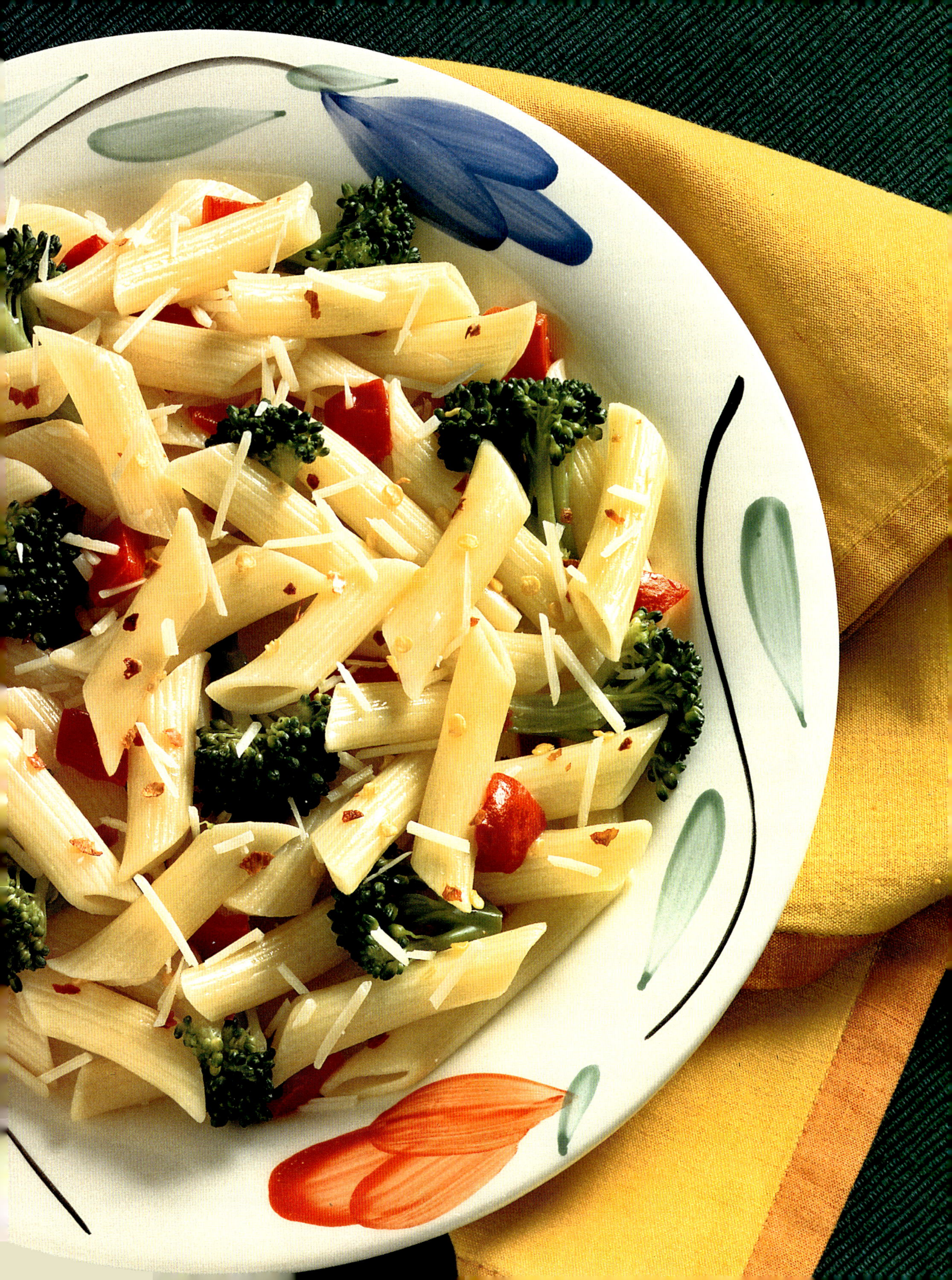

FRESH FROM THE GARDEN

222 EGG NOODLES AND VEGETABLES WITH PESTO

  1 package (16 ounces) enriched fine egg noodles
  5 tablespoons olive oil, divided
10 cloves garlic
  3 cups fresh basil leaves, lightly packed
  3 cups fresh spinach, lightly packed
  ½ cup nonfat Italian salad dressing
  4 cups broccoli florets
  4 cups cauliflower florets
  2 large onions, cut into strips
  2 cups sliced mushrooms
  ½ teaspoon red pepper flakes
  2 pints cherry tomatoes, cut into halves
  ½ cup shredded Asiago cheese

1. Cook noodles according to package directions. Drain; place in large bowl. Toss with 1 tablespoon oil.

2. To make pesto, place garlic in food processor; process briefly until chopped. Add basil; process using on/off pulsing action until finely chopped. Transfer to medium bowl. Process spinach until finely chopped. Add 3 tablespoons oil and salad dressing; process briefly to blend. Add to basil mixture in bowl.

3. Heat remaining 1 tablespoon oil in large nonstick skillet or wok over medium heat until hot. Add broccoli, cauliflower and onions. Cover and cook 5 minutes, stirring occasionally. Add mushrooms and red pepper flakes; cook, uncovered, 5 minutes or until vegetables are crisp-tender. Add vegetable mixture, tomatoes and pesto to noodles; toss until well blended. Serve with cheese. Garnish with fresh basil.

Makes 8 servings

223 FOUR-PEPPER PENNE

  1 medium onion, sliced
  1 small red bell pepper, thinly sliced
  1 small green bell pepper, thinly sliced
  1 small yellow bell pepper, thinly sliced
1½ teaspoons minced garlic
  1 tablespoon vegetable oil
  1 (26-ounce) jar HEALTHY CHOICE® Traditional Pasta Sauce
  1 teaspoon dried basil leaves
  ½ teaspoon dried savory
  ¼ teaspoon black pepper
  ½ pound penne, cooked and drained

In Dutch oven or large nonstick saucepan, cook and stir onion, bell peppers and garlic in hot oil until vegetables are tender-crisp. Add pasta sauce, basil, savory and black pepper. Heat through over medium heat. Serve over penne. *Makes 6 servings*

Egg Noodles and Vegetables with Pesto

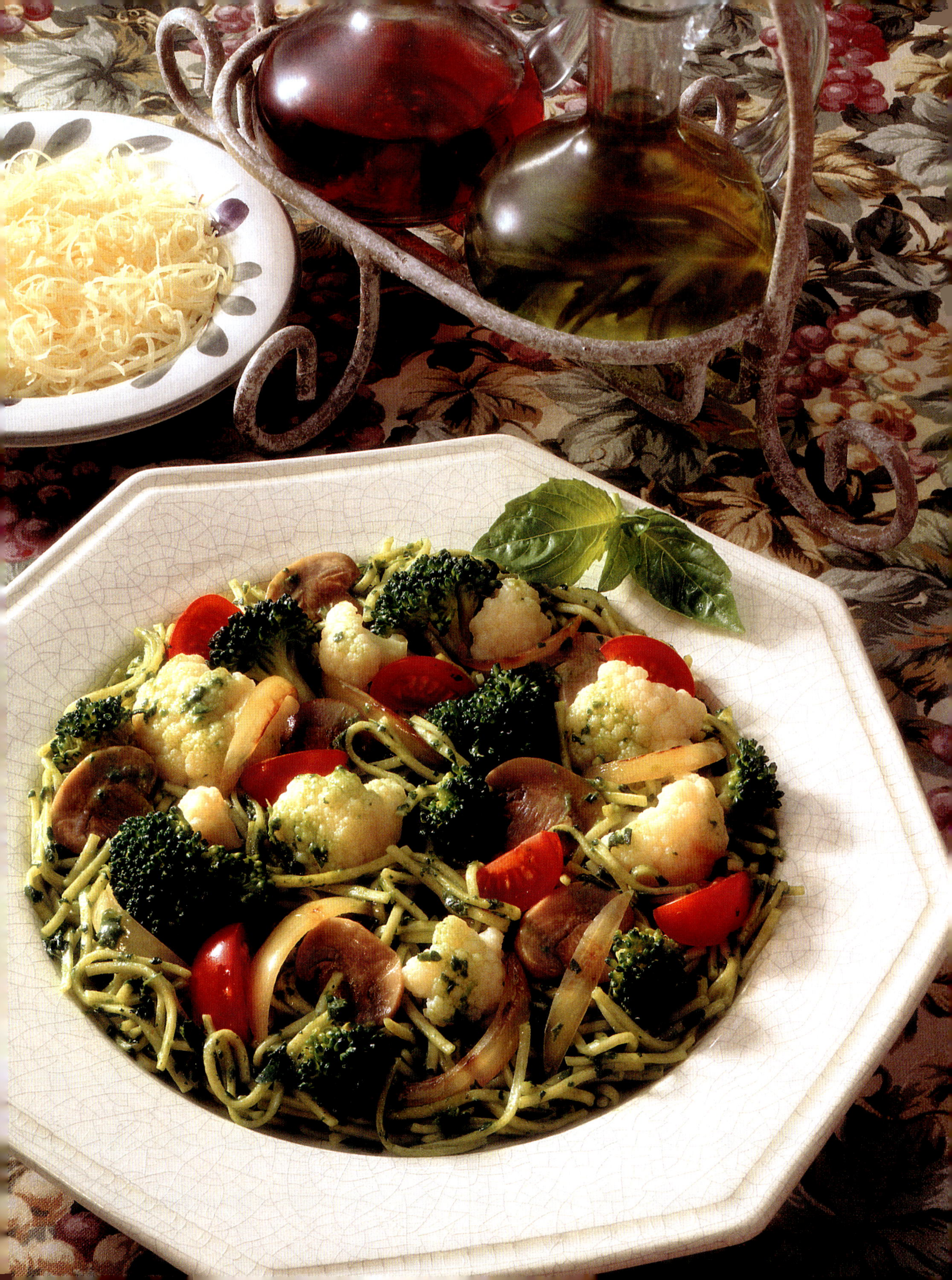

FRESH FROM THE GARDEN

224 COLORFUL PEPPER FUSILLI

- 2 tablespoons olive oil
- 1 onion, chopped
- 1 yellow bell pepper, diced
- 1 red bell pepper, diced
- 1 green bell pepper, diced
- 8 ounces mushrooms, sliced
- 4 green onions, chopped
- 4 cloves garlic, minced
- ¼ teaspoon red pepper flakes
- 2 cans (14½ ounces each) diced tomatoes, undrained
- ½ cup chopped fresh basil *or* 2 teaspoons dried basil leaves
- 1 teaspoon salt
- ½ teaspoon black pepper
- 1 pound fusilli, cooked and drained
- 2 tablespoons chopped fresh parsley

1. Heat olive oil in large skillet over medium-high heat until hot. Add onion and bell peppers; cook and stir 3 minutes. Add mushrooms; cook and stir 2 minutes. Add green onions, garlic and red pepper flakes; cook and stir 2 minutes. Add tomatoes and juice; cook and stir 5 minutes. Add basil, salt and black pepper; stir well.

2. Combine sauce with fusilli in large bowl; stir gently. Sprinkle parsley over top.

Makes 6 servings

225 EASY PASTA PRIMAVERA

- 1 eggplant, peeled and cut into small sticks
- ½ pound fresh mushrooms, sliced
- 2 medium carrots, peeled and sliced diagonally
- 3 to 5 cloves fresh garlic, minced
- 3 tablespoons olive oil
- 2 medium zucchini, shredded
- 1 teaspoon dried oregano leaves
- 1 teaspoon dried basil leaves
- 1 large tomato, cut into wedges
- 2 tablespoons water
- 12 ounces uncooked spaghetti or other thin pasta, hot cooked and drained
- Grated Romano cheese

In large skillet, stir-fry eggplant, mushrooms, carrots and garlic in oil over high heat 2 minutes. Stir in zucchini, oregano and basil; stir-fry 1 minute more. Add tomato wedges and water; cover and steam 2 minutes. Serve over hot pasta; top with grated Romano cheese.

Makes 4 to 6 servings

Favorite recipe from **Christopher Ranch Garlic**

Colorful Pepper Fusilli

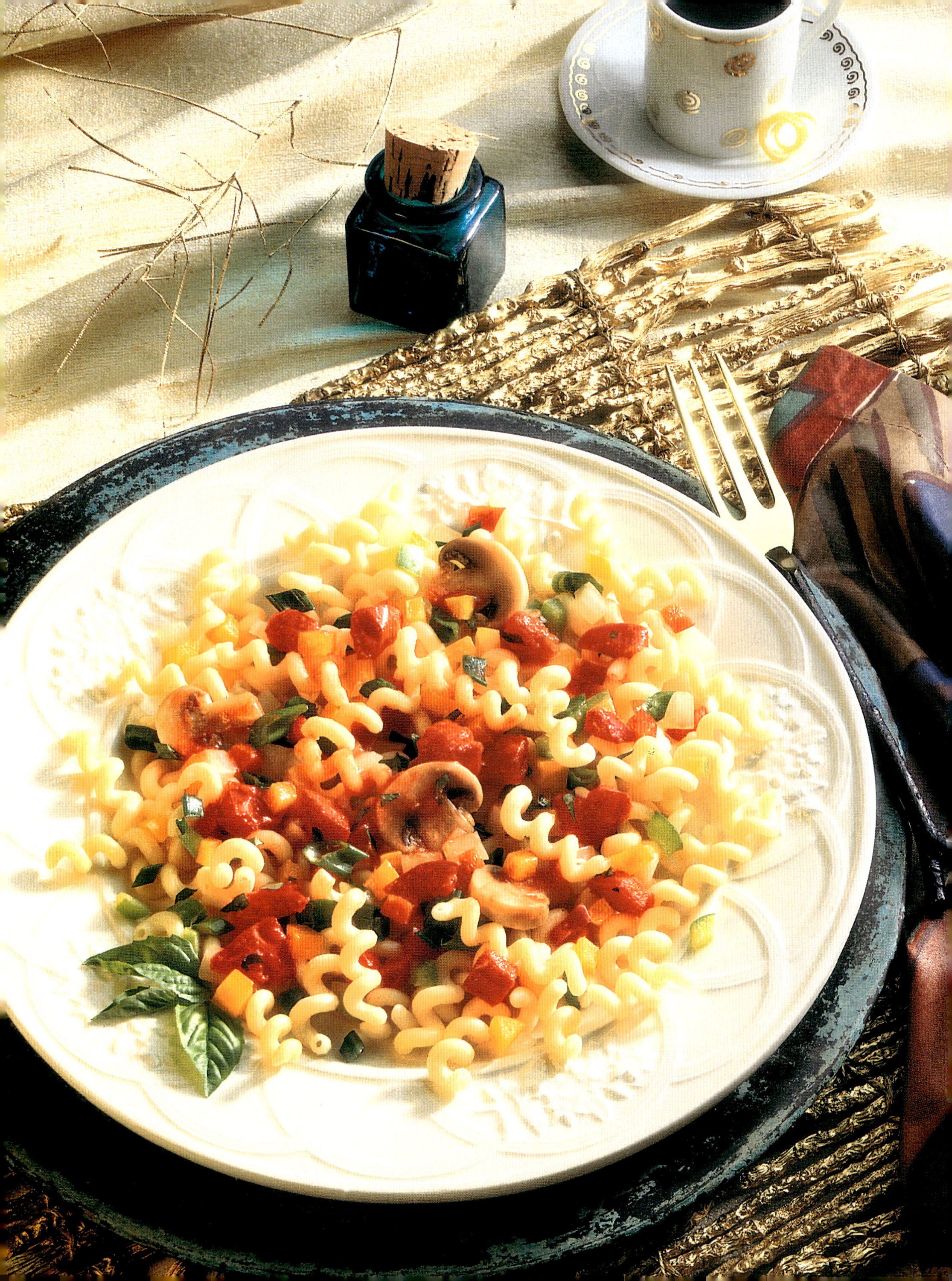

FRESH FROM THE GARDEN

226 VEGGIE LASAGNE

Herbed Tomato Sauce (recipe follows)
1 package (15 ounces) no-fat or reduced-fat ricotta cheese
2 cups shredded part-skim mozzarella cheese
2 tablespoons grated Parmesan cheese
2 teaspoons dried basil leaves
½ teaspoon black pepper
1 can (15 ounces) spinach, drained
1 can (8 ounces) no-salt-added sliced carrots, drained
1 can (7 ounces) 50%-less-salt whole kernel corn, drained
1 can (4 ounces) sliced mushrooms, drained
2 packages (9 ounces each) refrigerated lasagne noodles

Prepare Herbed Tomato Sauce. In medium bowl, combine cheeses, basil and pepper. In medium bowl, combine vegetables. Spread 1 cup Herbed Tomato Sauce on bottom of 13×9×2-inch baking pan; top with ¼ of the uncooked noodles. Spoon ⅓ of the cheese mixture over noodles and spread lightly with spatula; spoon ⅓ of the vegetable mixture over cheese. Repeat layers 2 times, ending with noodles and 1 cup sauce on top. Bake, covered, in preheated 350°F oven 1 hour. Cut into squares. *Makes 12 servings*

HERBED TOMATO SAUCE
1 cup chopped onions
2 large cloves garlic, minced
1 tablespoon olive or vegetable oil
1½ teaspoons Italian herb seasoning
2 cans (16 ounces each) no-salt-added whole tomatoes, undrained, coarsely chopped
1 can (8 ounces) no-salt-added tomato sauce
1 to 2 teaspoons red wine vinegar
1 to 2 teaspoons lemon juice
½ teaspoon salt
½ teaspoon black pepper

Sauté onions and garlic in oil in large saucepan until tender; stir in herb seasoning and cook 1 minute. Add tomatoes and tomato sauce; heat to boiling. Reduce heat and simmer, uncovered, until sauce is reduced to 4 cups, about 15 minutes. Stir in vinegar and lemon juice to taste; stir in salt and pepper. *Makes 4 cups*

Favorite recipe from ***Canned Food Information Council***

FRESH FROM THE GARDEN

227 LINGUINE WITH FRESH TOMATO BASIL SAUCE

- 1 cup chopped onion
- 3 cloves garlic, minced
- 1/4 teaspoon ground black pepper
- 2 tablespoons FLEISCHMANN'S® Margarine
- 2 cups sliced mushrooms
- 3 large tomatoes, peeled, seeded and chopped
- 1 tablespoon dried basil leaves, crushed *or* 1/4 cup chopped fresh basil leaves
- 1 teaspoon sugar
- 12 ounces uncooked linguine, cooked according to package directions in unsalted water and drained

In large skillet, over medium-high heat, cook and stir onion, garlic and pepper in margarine until onion is tender, about 3 minutes. Add mushrooms; cook 5 minutes. Add tomatoes, basil and sugar; heat to a boil. Reduce heat to low; simmer, uncovered, 15 to 20 minutes. Serve over linguine.

Makes 6 servings

228 PASTA WITH SPINACH–CHEESE SAUCE

- 1/4 cup FILIPPO BERIO® Extra Virgin Olive Oil, divided
- 1 medium onion, chopped
- 1 clove garlic, chopped
- 3 cups chopped fresh spinach, washed and well drained
- 1 cup low-fat ricotta or cottage cheese
- 1/2 cup chopped fresh parsley
- 1 teaspoon dried basil leaves
- 1 teaspoon lemon juice
- 1/4 teaspoon black pepper
- 1/4 teaspoon ground nutmeg
- 3/4 pound uncooked spaghetti

1. Heat 3 tablespoons olive oil in large skillet over medium heat. Cook and stir onion and garlic until onion is tender.

2. Add spinach to skillet; cook 3 to 5 minutes or until spinach wilts.

3. Place spinach mixture, cheese, parsley, basil, lemon juice, pepper and nutmeg in covered blender container. Blend until smooth. Leave in blender, covered, to keep sauce warm.

4. Cook pasta according to package directions. Do not overcook. Drain pasta, reserving 1/4 cup water. In large bowl, toss pasta with remaining 1 tablespoon olive oil.

5. Add reserved 1/4 cup water to sauce in blender. Blend; serve over pasta.

Makes 4 servings

FRESH FROM THE GARDEN

229 LEMON–TOSSED LINGUINE

8 ounces uncooked linguine
3 tablespoons fresh lemon juice
2 teaspoons reduced-calorie margarine
2 tablespoons minced chives
1/3 cup skim milk
1 teaspoon cornstarch
1 tablespoon minced fresh dill *or*
    1 teaspoon dried dill weed
1 tablespoon minced fresh parsley *or*
    1 teaspoon dried parsley flakes
2 teaspoons grated lemon peel
1/4 teaspoon ground white pepper
3 tablespoons grated Romano or Parmesan cheese

Cook linguine according to package directions, omitting salt. Drain well. Place in medium bowl; sprinkle lemon juice over linguine.

Meanwhile, melt margarine in small saucepan over medium heat. Add chives; cook until chives are soft. Combine milk and cornstarch in small bowl; stir into saucepan. Cook and stir until thickened. Stir in dill, parsley, lemon peel and pepper.

Pour milk mixture over pasta. Sprinkle with cheese; toss to coat evenly. Garnish with lemon slices and dill sprigs, if desired. Serve immediately. *Makes 6 (1/2-cup) servings*

230 FAST–TRACK FETTUCCINE

1 cup SONOMA Dried Tomato Halves, snipped into strips
1 tablespoon olive oil
4 cloves garlic, chopped
1 can (2 1/4 ounces) sliced ripe olives, drained
3 tablespoons chopped fresh basil *or*
    1 tablespoon dried basil leaves
12 ounces dry fettuccine, cooked and drained
2 cups (8 ounces) grated mozzarella or crumbled feta cheese

In small bowl, cover tomatoes with boiling water; set aside 10 minutes. Meanwhile, heat oil in large skillet. Add garlic and sauté 2 minutes. Drain tomatoes. Add tomatoes, olives and basil to skillet; cook and toss 2 minutes. Add hot fettuccine and cheese. Toss just until heated through and thoroughly blended. Serve immediately.
Makes 4 to 6 servings

Lemon-Tossed Linguine

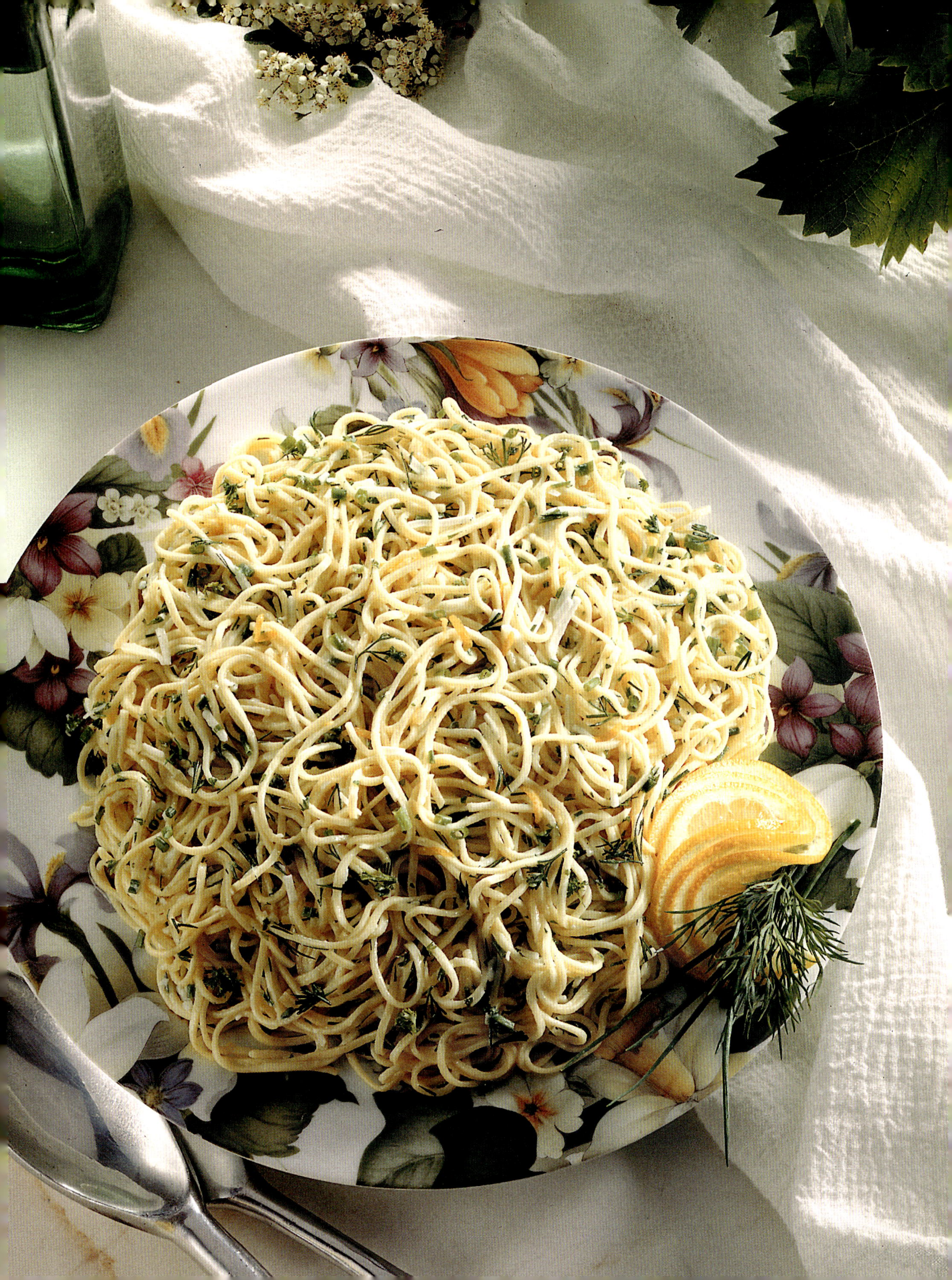

FRESH FROM THE GARDEN

231 PASTA FROM THE GARDEN

1 tablespoon olive oil
¾ cup thinly sliced zucchini
2 tablespoons chopped green onions
3 cloves garlic, minced
1 can (14½ ounces) diced tomatoes, undrained
1 cup vegetable broth
3 tablespoons chopped fresh basil *or* 2 teaspoons dried basil leaves
3 tablespoons grated Romano cheese
1 pound penne, cooked and drained

1. Heat olive oil in large skillet over medium-high heat until hot. Add zucchini; cook and stir 1 minute. Add onions and garlic; cook and stir 1 minute. Add tomatoes and juice; cook and stir 5 minutes. Add vegetable broth, scraping bottom of skillet clean. Simmer 5 minutes or until broth reduces to ½ cup. Add basil and cheese; stir well.

2. Combine sauce with penne in large bowl; stir gently. *Makes 6 servings*

232 STRAW AND HAY FETTUCCINE

6 ounces plain fettuccine, uncooked
6 ounces spinach fettuccine, uncooked
8 ounces fresh mushrooms, sliced
2 teaspoons margarine
2 cups fresh or frozen peas
4 tablespoons low-fat ricotta cheese
4 tablespoons skim milk
2 tablespoons grated Parmesan cheese

Cook pasta according to package directions; drain and transfer to serving bowl. Sauté mushrooms in margarine in large skillet over low heat 5 minutes. Add peas. Cover; cook until tender. Remove from heat; set aside. In small bowl, combine ricotta cheese, milk and Parmesan cheese. Add cheese mixture to mushrooms and peas. Toss with pasta and serve. *Makes 8 servings*

Favorite recipe from **National Pasta Association**

233 FUSILLI WITH BROCCOLI RABE

8 ounces uncooked fusilli pasta
1 pound broccoli rabe, trimmed and cut into 1-inch pieces
⅓ cup FILIPPO BERIO® Extra Virgin Olive Oil
1 clove garlic, minced
Salt and freshly ground black pepper to taste
Grated pecorino cheese

Cook pasta according to package directions until *al dente* (tender but still firm). Drain. In large saucepan, cook broccoli rabe in boiling salted water 3 minutes or until tender. Add to colander with pasta. Drain; transfer to large bowl. In small saucepan, heat olive oil over medium heat until hot. Add garlic; cook and stir 30 seconds to 1 minute or until golden. Add to pasta mixture; toss until well coated. Season to taste with salt and pepper. Top with cheese. *Makes 3 to 4 servings*

Pasta from the Garden

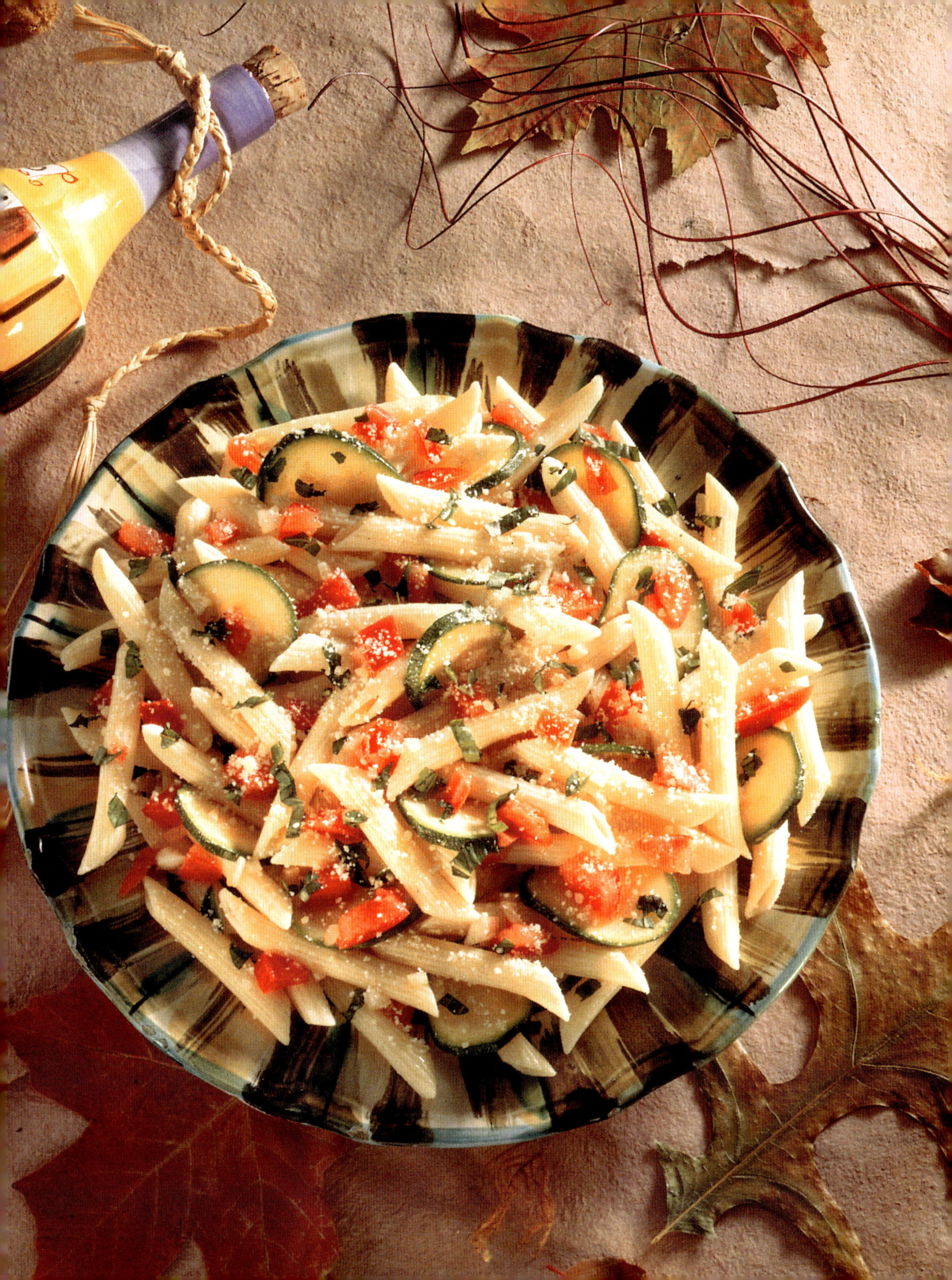

FRESH FROM THE GARDEN

234 SAUCY MEDITERRANEAN FRITTATA

Tomato Sauce (recipe follows)
1 tablespoon olive oil
1 small onion, chopped
1 medium tomato, seeded and diced
1 tablespoon finely chopped fresh basil *or* 1 teaspoon dried basil leaves
¼ teaspoon dried oregano leaves
⅓ cup cooked orzo
⅓ cup chopped pitted black olives
8 eggs
½ teaspoon salt
⅛ teaspoon black pepper
2 tablespoons butter
½ cup (2 ounces) shredded mozzarella cheese

1. Prepare Tomato Sauce.

2. Heat oil in ovenproof 10-inch skillet over medium-high heat. Cook and stir onion until tender. Add tomato, basil and oregano; cook and stir 3 minutes. Stir in orzo and olives; remove from skillet and set aside.

3. Beat eggs, salt and pepper in medium bowl with electric mixer at low speed. Stir in tomato mixture; set aside.

4. Melt butter in same skillet over medium heat. Add egg mixture; top with cheese. Reduce heat to low. Cook 8 to 10 minutes or until bottom and most of middle is set.

5. Place skillet on rack 4 inches from broiler. Broil 1 to 2 minutes or until top is browned. Cut into wedges; serve with Tomato Sauce. Garnish as desired.

Makes 4 to 6 servings

TOMATO SAUCE
1 can (8 ounces) tomato sauce
1 teaspoon minced dried onion
¼ teaspoon dried basil leaves
¼ teaspoon dried oregano leaves
⅛ teaspoon minced dried garlic
⅛ teaspoon black pepper

Combine all ingredients in small saucepan. Bring to a boil over high heat. Reduce heat to low. Simmer, uncovered, over medium-low heat 5 minutes, stirring often. Set aside; keep warm. *Makes about 1 cup*

235 RAVIOLI WITH ROASTED RED PEPPER ALFREDO SAUCE

1 package (10 ounces) DiGIORNO® Alfredo Sauce
1 jar (7 ounces) roasted red peppers, drained, sliced
½ cup toasted chopped walnuts
1 package (9 ounces) DiGIORNO® Four Cheese Ravioli, cooked, drained

HEAT sauce, peppers and walnuts.

TOSS with ravioli. Sprinkle with additional toasted chopped walnuts and chopped fresh parsley. *Makes 4 servings*

Prep time: 10 minutes
Cook time: 10 minutes

Saucy Mediterranean Frittata

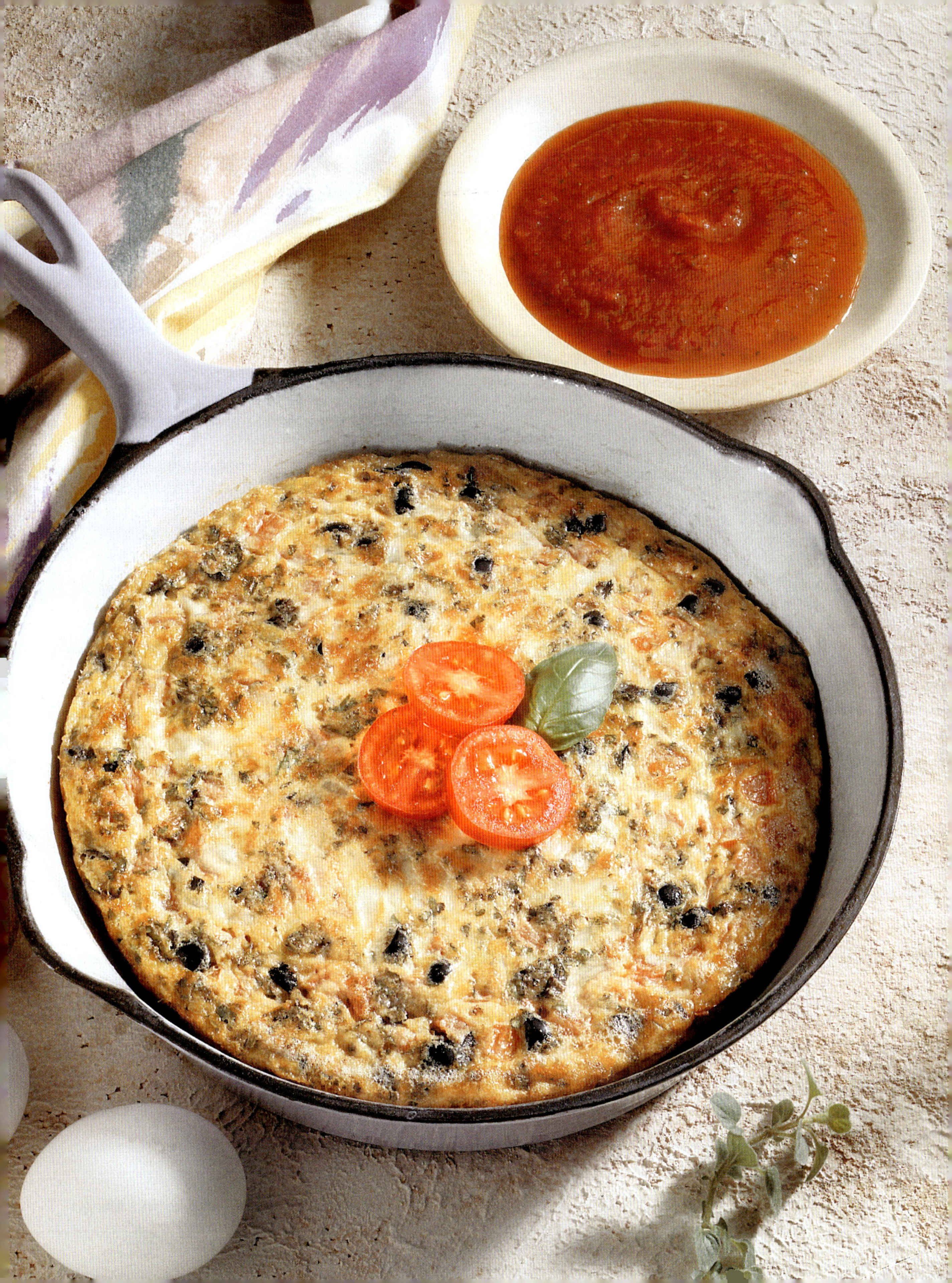

FRESH FROM THE GARDEN

236 LINGUINE WITH ASPARAGUS AND ASIAGO

- 1 pound fresh asparagus, cut into 1-inch pieces
- 16 ounces uncooked linguine, broken in half
- 1 tablespoon margarine or butter
- 1 cup (4 ounces) shredded Asiago or grated Parmesan cheese
- ½ cup sour cream
- ½ cup pitted black olive slices
- Salt and black pepper to taste

1. Place 3 quarts water in Dutch oven; cover and bring to a boil over high heat.

2. Drop asparagus into boiling water; boil 1 to 2 minutes or until crisp-tender. Remove with slotted spoon; rinse under cold water. Drain.

3. Add linguine to boiling water; cook according to package directions until *al dente*. Drain.

4. Combine linguine and margarine in large bowl; toss gently until margarine is melted. Add asparagus, cheese, sour cream and olives; toss gently until linguine is coated and cheese is melted. Season to taste with salt and pepper. Serve immediately.

Makes 4 servings

Prep and cook time: 30 minutes

237 RIGATONI WITH BROCCOLI

- 8 ounces uncooked rigatoni pasta
- 1 bunch fresh broccoli, trimmed and separated into florets with 1-inch stems
- 1 tablespoon FILIPPO BERIO® Extra Virgin Olive Oil
- 1 clove garlic, minced
- Crushed red pepper
- Grated Parmesan cheese

Cook pasta according to package directions until *al dente* (tender but still firm). Add broccoli during last 5 minutes of cooking time; cook until broccoli is tender-crisp. Drain pasta and broccoli; transfer to large bowl. Meanwhile, in small skillet, heat olive oil over medium heat until hot. Add garlic; cook and stir 1 to 2 minutes or until golden. Pour oil mixture over hot pasta mixture; toss until lightly coated. Season to taste with pepper. Top with cheese.

Makes 3 to 4 servings

Linguine with Asparagus and Asiago

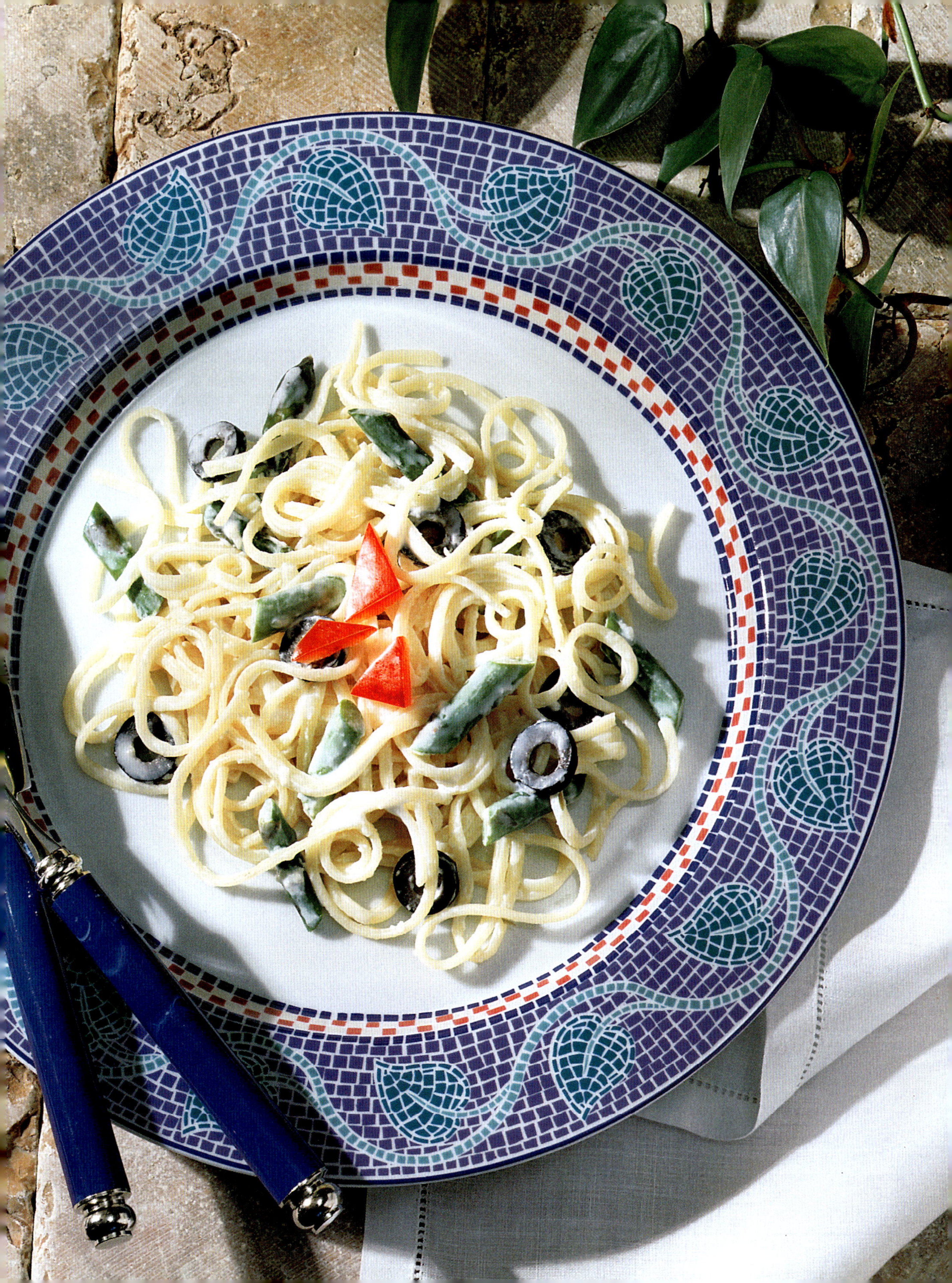

FRESH FROM THE GARDEN

238 PENNE PRIMAVERA WITH SUNDRIED TOMATO SAUCE

- 4 cups assorted cut-up vegetables (zucchini, eggplant, peppers, mushrooms)
- ½ cup GREY POUPON® Dijon Mustard, divided
- 1 tablespoon olive oil
- 1 (7-ounce) jar sun-dried tomato strips in oil, drained
- 1 clove garlic, minced
- 2 cups light cream or half-and-half
- 1 tablespoon chopped fresh basil leaves
- 1 pound penne pasta, cooked
- Grated Parmesan cheese (optional)

In large bowl, combine vegetables, 2 tablespoons mustard and oil. Place vegetables on broiler pan; broil 8 to 10 minutes or until golden and tender, stirring occasionally.

In medium saucepan, over medium heat, sauté sun-dried tomato strips and garlic 2 minutes. Reduce heat to low and stir in light cream, remaining mustard and basil; heat through.*

In large serving bowl, combine hot cooked pasta, vegetables and cream sauce, tossing to coat well. Serve immediately with Parmesan cheese and garnish, if desired.
Makes 6 servings

*If sauce thickens upon standing before tossing with pasta, thin with additional light cream.

239 LINGUINE WITH SPINACH PESTO

- 1 (10-ounce) package frozen chopped spinach, thawed and well drained
- 1 cup EGG BEATERS® Healthy Real Egg Product
- ⅓ cup PLANTER'S® Walnut Pieces
- ¼ cup grated Parmesan cheese
- 2 cloves garlic, crushed
- 1 pound thin linguine, cooked in unsalted water and drained
- ½ cup diced red bell pepper
- Additional grated Parmesan cheese (optional)

In electric blender container or food processor, blend spinach, Egg Beaters, walnuts, ¼ cup cheese and garlic until smooth. Toss with hot linguine and bell pepper. Top with additional cheese, if desired.
Makes 8 servings

Prep Time: 15 minutes
Cook Time: 10 minutes

Penne Primavera with Sundried Tomato Sauce

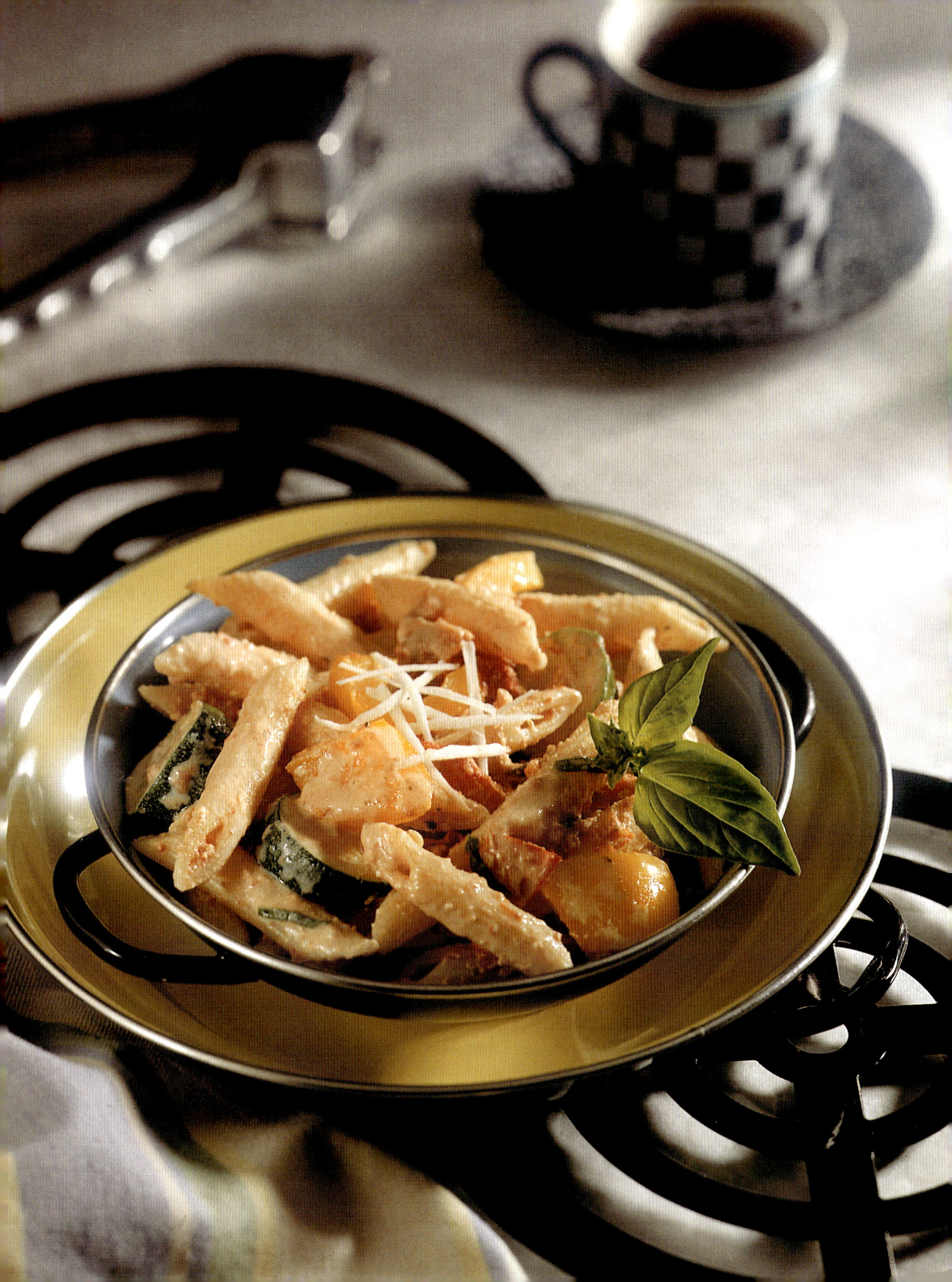

FRESH FROM THE GARDEN

240 TANGY ASPARAGUS LINGUINE

5 ounces linguine
2 tablespoons reduced-calorie margarine
¼ cup finely chopped onion
3 cloves garlic, minced
8 ounces fresh asparagus, peeled and sliced diagonally into ½-inch pieces
2 tablespoons dry white wine
2 tablespoons fresh lemon juice
Freshly ground black pepper
¼ cup (1 ounce) SARGENTO® Grated Parmesan Cheese
¾ cup (3 ounces) SARGENTO® Light Fancy Shredded Mozzarella Cheese

Cook linguine according to package directions; drain. Meanwhile, melt margarine in large skillet over medium heat. Add onion and garlic; cook and stir until tender. Add asparagus; cook and stir 2 minutes. Add wine and lemon juice; simmer 1 minute. Season with pepper to taste. Remove from heat. Add to hot pasta in large bowl with Parmesan cheese; toss lightly to coat. Remove to serving platter; top with mozzarella cheese. Garnish with strips of lemon zest, if desired. Serve immediately.

Makes 4 servings

241 FETTUCCINE WITH OLIVE PESTO

10 ounces dried fettuccine
1½ cups whole pitted California ripe olives
3 tablespoons drained capers
4 teaspoons lemon juice
1 tablespoon olive oil
2 teaspoons Dijon mustard
2 to 3 cloves garlic, peeled
¼ cup finely chopped fresh basil
¼ cup grated Parmesan cheese
Basil sprigs

Cook fettuccine according to package directions. While pasta cooks, combine olives, capers, lemon juice, oil, mustard and garlic in food processor or blender. Process until coarsely puréed. Stir in chopped basil and cheese; set aside. Drain pasta well and transfer to large warm serving bowl. Spoon pesto over pasta and mix gently. Garnish with basil sprigs.   *Makes 4 servings*

Preparation time: about 15 minutes
Cooking time: about 15 minutes

*Favorite recipe from **California Olive Industry***

FRESH FROM THE GARDEN

242 PORCINI MUSHROOM PENNE RIGATE WITH GARLIC BUTTER SAUCE

- 1 (12-ounce) package PASTA LaBELLA® Porcini Mushroom Penne Rigate
- 2 tablespoons butter
- 1 tablespoon extra-virgin olive oil
- 1½ cups chopped mushrooms
- 2 teaspoons minced garlic
- ¾ cup white wine
- 2 tablespoons lemon juice
- ¼ cup minced scallions
- 1½ tablespoons chopped fresh parsley
- ¼ cup grated Parmesan cheese

Cook pasta according to package directions. Heat butter and olive oil in large skillet; sauté mushrooms and garlic over medium heat 4 minutes. Add wine, lemon juice and scallions to skillet; simmer. Mix in hot Porcini Mushroom Penne Rigate, sprinkle with parsley and cheese; serve.

Makes 3 servings

243 SPINACH TORTELLINI WITH ROASTED RED PEPPERS

- 2 packages (9 ounces each) fresh spinach tortellini
- 1 jar (7 ounces) roasted red peppers or pimientos, drained
- 2 tablespoons butter or olive oil
- 4 cloves garlic, minced
- ¼ cup chopped fresh basil *or* 2 teaspoons dried basil leaves
- ½ cup chopped walnuts, toasted
- 1 cup prepared HIDDEN VALLEY RANCH® Original Ranch Salad Dressing
- Additional fresh basil leaves (optional)

Cook tortellini according to package directions; drain and set aside. Slice red peppers into strips; set aside. In large saucepan, melt butter; add garlic. Cook and stir about 2 minutes. Add red pepper strips, ¼ cup chopped basil and tortellini. Stir to coat; add walnuts. Stir in enough salad dressing so mixture is creamy and tortellini are coated. Garnish with additional fresh basil, if desired. Serve hot.

Makes 4 to 6 servings

FRESH FROM THE GARDEN

244 PROVENÇAL PASTA SHELLS

12 uncooked jumbo pasta shells
1 can (6 ounces) pitted black olives, drained
2 tablespoons olive oil
1 teaspoon lemon juice
½ teaspoon dried thyme leaves
1½ cups (6 ounces) shredded Gruyere or mozzarella cheese
⅓ cup herb-seasoned bread crumbs
1 teaspoon bottled minced garlic
1 jar (14 ounces) commercial chunky spaghetti sauce

1. Cook pasta according to package directions; drain. Rinse with cool water; drain again.

2. While pasta is cooking, combine olives, oil, lemon juice and thyme in food processor; cover and process until puréed. Transfer to small bowl; stir in cheese, bread crumbs and garlic.

3. Spread spaghetti sauce into 11×7×2-inch baking dish. Stuff each pasta shell with 2 tablespoons olive mixture. Arrange stuffed shells on sauce.

4. Cover with plastic wrap, turning back corner to vent. Microwave at HIGH 3 to 4 minutes or until cheese is melted and sauce is hot. *Makes 4 servings*

Prep and cook time: 30 minutes

245 PINEAPPLE–RAISIN FETTUCCINE

8 ounces crushed pineapple in natural juice
⅓ cup raisins
4 teaspoons packed brown sugar
2 tablespoons white vinegar
1 tablespoon low-sodium soy sauce
2 teaspoons cornstarch, dissolved in ¼ cup water
4 ounces fettuccine
4 teaspoons olive oil

In small saucepan, combine pineapple, raisins, brown sugar, vinegar, soy sauce and cornstarch mixture. Cook until clear and mixture thickens, about 3 to 4 minutes, stirring occasionally. Set aside.

In large pan, prepare fettuccine according to package directions. Drain; toss with olive oil, then with pineapple-raisin sauce. Warm sauce briefly, if necessary.

Makes 4 servings

Favorite recipe from **The Sugar Association**

NOTE: This sauce is especially good as an accompaniment to chicken, pork or ham.

Provençal Pasta Shells

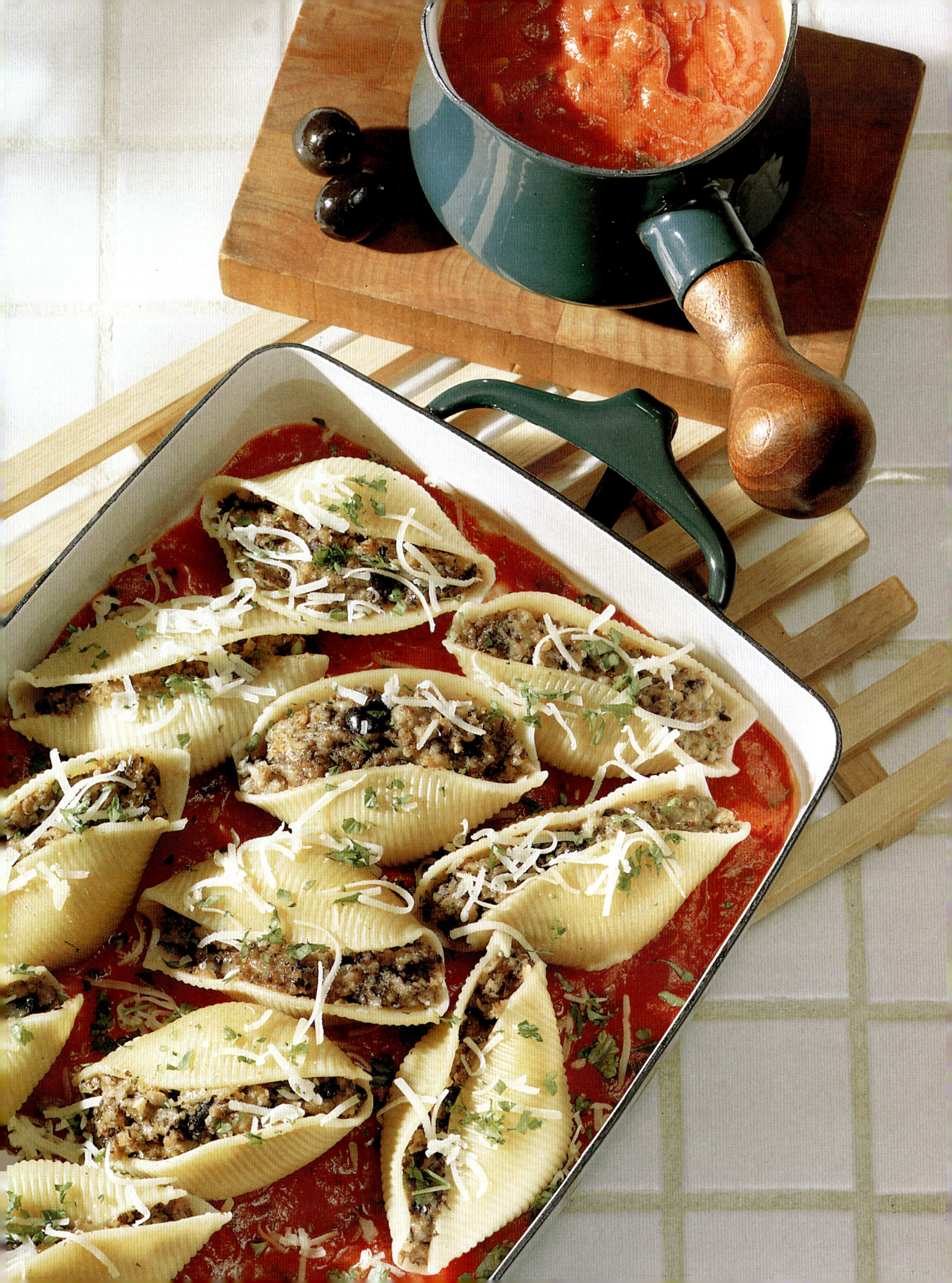

FRESH FROM THE GARDEN

246 FRESH TOMATO PASTA ANDREW

- 1 pound fresh tomatoes, cut into wedges
- 1 cup packed fresh basil leaves
- 2 cloves garlic, chopped
- 2 tablespoons olive oil
- 8 ounces Camenzola cheese *or* 6 ounces ripe Brie cheese, cut into small pieces
- 2 ounces Stilton cheese, cut into small pieces
- Salt and white pepper to taste
- 4 ounces uncooked angel hair pasta, vermicelli or other thin pasta
- Freshly grated Parmesan cheese
- Additional fresh basil leaves for garnish

1. Place tomatoes, 1 cup basil, garlic and oil in food processor or blender; process until ingredients are roughly chopped, but not puréed.

2. Combine tomato mixture with Camenzola cheese and Stilton cheese in large bowl; season with salt and pepper.

3. Cook pasta according to package directions until tender but still firm; rinse and drain.

4. Top hot pasta with tomato-cheese mixture and serve with Parmesan cheese. Garnish, if desired. *Makes 4 first-course servings*

247 LEMON PEPPER PASTA WITH PICCATTA STYLE VEGETABLES

- 1 (12-ounce) package PASTA LaBELLA® Lemon Pepper Pasta
- 1 tablespoon extra-virgin olive oil
- 2 tablespoons butter
- 1 cup julienned red onions
- 1 cup julienned carrots
- 2 teaspoons minced garlic
- 1 cup white wine
- 1½ tablespoons capers
- 1 cup julienned snow peas
- Salt and black pepper to taste
- 2 tablespoons chopped parsley
- ⅓ cup grated Parmesan cheese

Cook pasta according to package directions. In large skillet, heat olive oil and butter. Add onions, carrots and garlic; sauté 4 minutes. Add wine and capers; simmer 2 minutes. Mix in hot pasta, snow peas, salt and pepper; toss and blend well. Top with parsley and Parmesan cheese; serve.

Makes 3 servings

Fresh Tomato Pasta Andrew

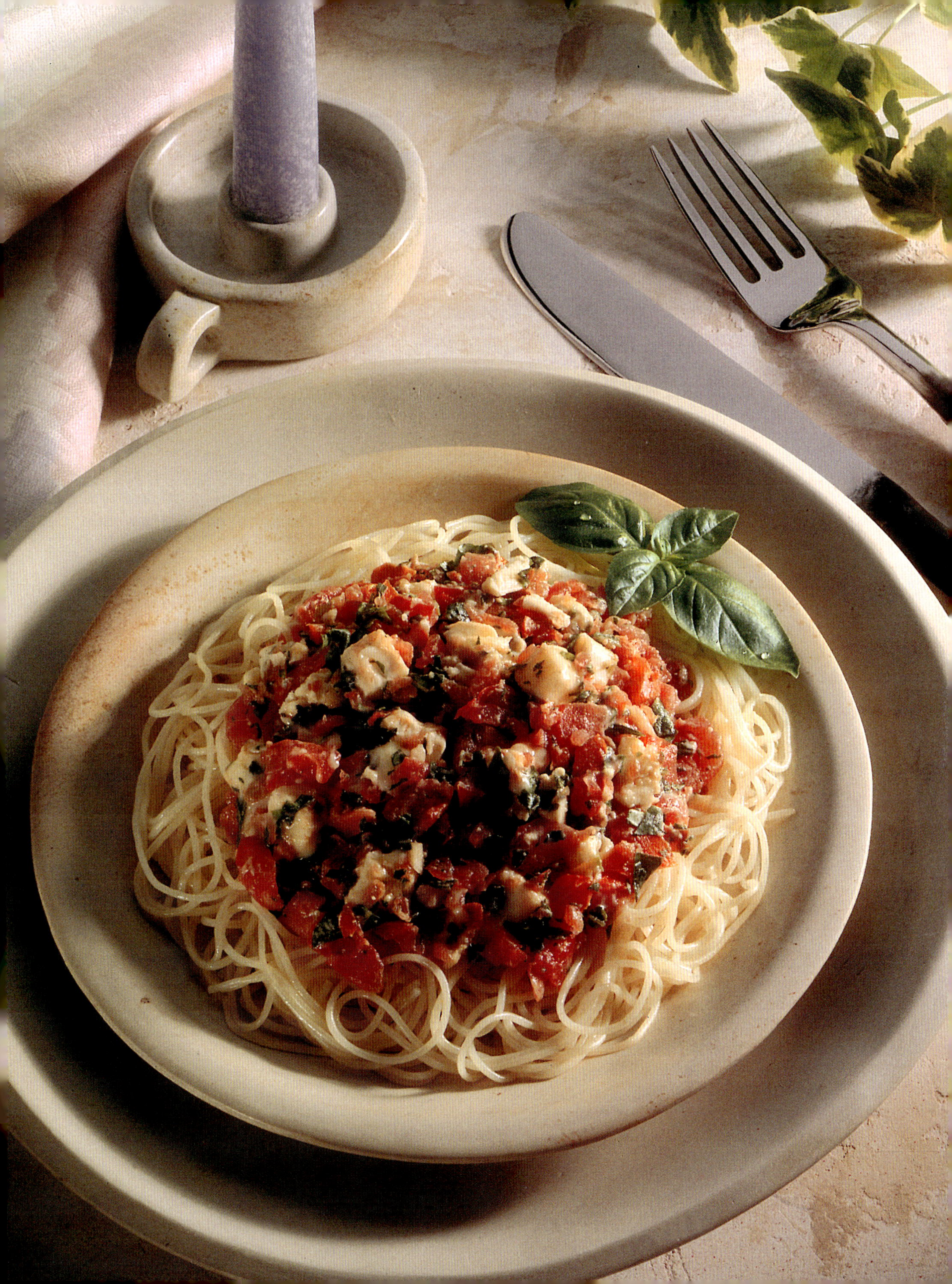

ASIAN FARE

248 VERMICELLI WITH PORK

- 4 ounces Chinese rice vermicelli or bean threads
- 32 dried mushrooms
- 3 green onions with tops, divided
- 2 tablespoons minced fresh ginger
- 2 tablespoons hot bean sauce
- 1½ cups chicken broth
- 1 tablespoon soy sauce
- 1 tablespoon dry sherry
- 2 tablespoons vegetable oil
- 6 ounces lean ground pork
- 1 small red or green hot chili pepper, seeded and finely chopped*
- Fresh cilantro leaves and hot red pepper for garnish (optional)

*Chili pepers can sting and irritate the skin; wear rubber gloves when handling peppers and do not touch eyes.

1. Place vermicelli and mushrooms in separate large bowls; cover each with hot water. Let stand 30 minutes; drain. Cut vermicelli into 4-inch pieces.

2. Squeeze out as much excess water as possible from mushrooms. Cut off and discard mushroom stems; cut caps into thin slices.

3. Cut one onion into 1½-inch slivers; reserve for garnish. Cut remaining two onions into thin slices.

4. Combine ginger and hot bean sauce in small bowl; set aside. Combine chicken broth, soy sauce and sherry in another small bowl; set aside.

5. Heat oil in wok or large skillet over high heat. Add pork; stir-fry until no longer pink, about 2 minutes. Add chili pepper, sliced onions and bean sauce mixture; stir-fry 1 minute.

6. Add chicken broth mixture, vermicelli and mushrooms. Simmer, uncovered, until most of the liquid is absorbed, about 5 minutes. Top with onion slivers. Garnish, if desired.

Makes 4 servings

Vermicelli with Pork

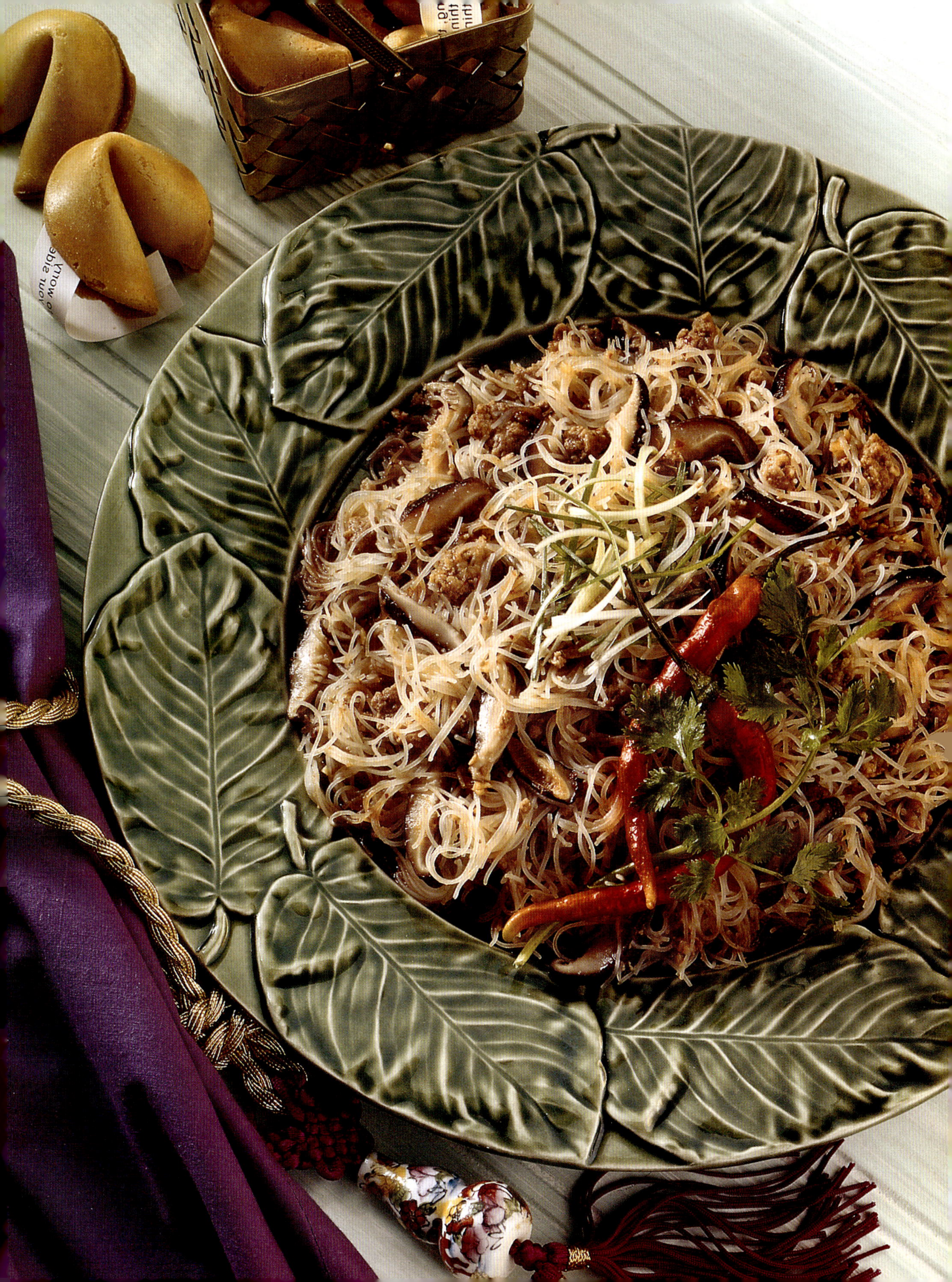

ASIAN FARE

249. THAI MEATBALLS AND NOODLES

1 pound bok choy
Thai Meatballs (recipe follows)
12 ounces uncooked egg noodles
2 cans (about 14 ounces each) reduced-sodium chicken broth
2 tablespoons packed brown sugar
2 tablespoons fish sauce or reduced-sodium soy sauce
1 small piece fresh ginger (about 1×½ inch), cut into slivers
1 medium carrot, peeled and cut into julienne strips
½ cup slivered fresh mint or basil leaves or chopped cilantro
Red pepper curls (optional)

1. Cut off root end of bok choy and discard. Separate stalks; rinse well and drain. Stack several stalks of bok choy; slice leaves and stalks crosswise into ½-inch-wide strips. Repeat with remaining stalks.

2. Prepare Thai Meatballs. Meanwhile, cook noodles according to package directions. Drain; transfer to large serving bowl.

3. Heat chicken broth in large saucepan or wok over high heat. Add brown sugar, fish sauce and ginger; stir until sugar is dissolved.

4. Add meatballs and carrot to saucepan; bring to a boil. Reduce heat to medium-low; cover and simmer 15 minutes or until meatballs are heated through.

5. Add bok choy; simmer 4 to 5 minutes or until stalks are crisp-tender. Stir in mint; pour mixture over noodles in serving bowl. Garnish with red pepper curls, if desired.

Makes 6 servings

THAI MEATBALLS

1½ pounds ground beef or pork
¼ cup chopped fresh basil leaves
¼ cup chopped fresh mint leaves
2 tablespoons finely chopped fresh ginger
4 teaspoons fish sauce
6 cloves garlic, minced
1 teaspoon ground cinnamon
½ teaspoon fennel seeds, crushed
½ teaspoon black pepper
2 tablespoons peanut oil, divided

1. Combine beef, basil, mint, ginger, fish sauce, garlic, cinnamon, fennel and pepper in large bowl; mix with hands or spoon until well blended.

2. Rub cutting board with 1 tablespoon oil. Pat meat mixture into 12×8-inch rectangle on board. Cut lengthwise into 4 strips; cut crosswise into 8 strips to form 32 squares. Shape each square into a ball.

3. Heat remaining 1 tablespoon oil in large skillet or wok over medium-high heat. Add meatballs in single layer; cook 8 to 10 minutes or until no longer pink in centers, turning to brown all sides. (Cook in several batches.)

4. Remove meatballs with slotted spoon to paper towels; drain. (Meatballs may be cooled, covered and refrigerated up to 2 days in advance or frozen for longer storage. Thaw before adding to broth.)

Makes 32 meatballs

Thai Meatballs and Noodles

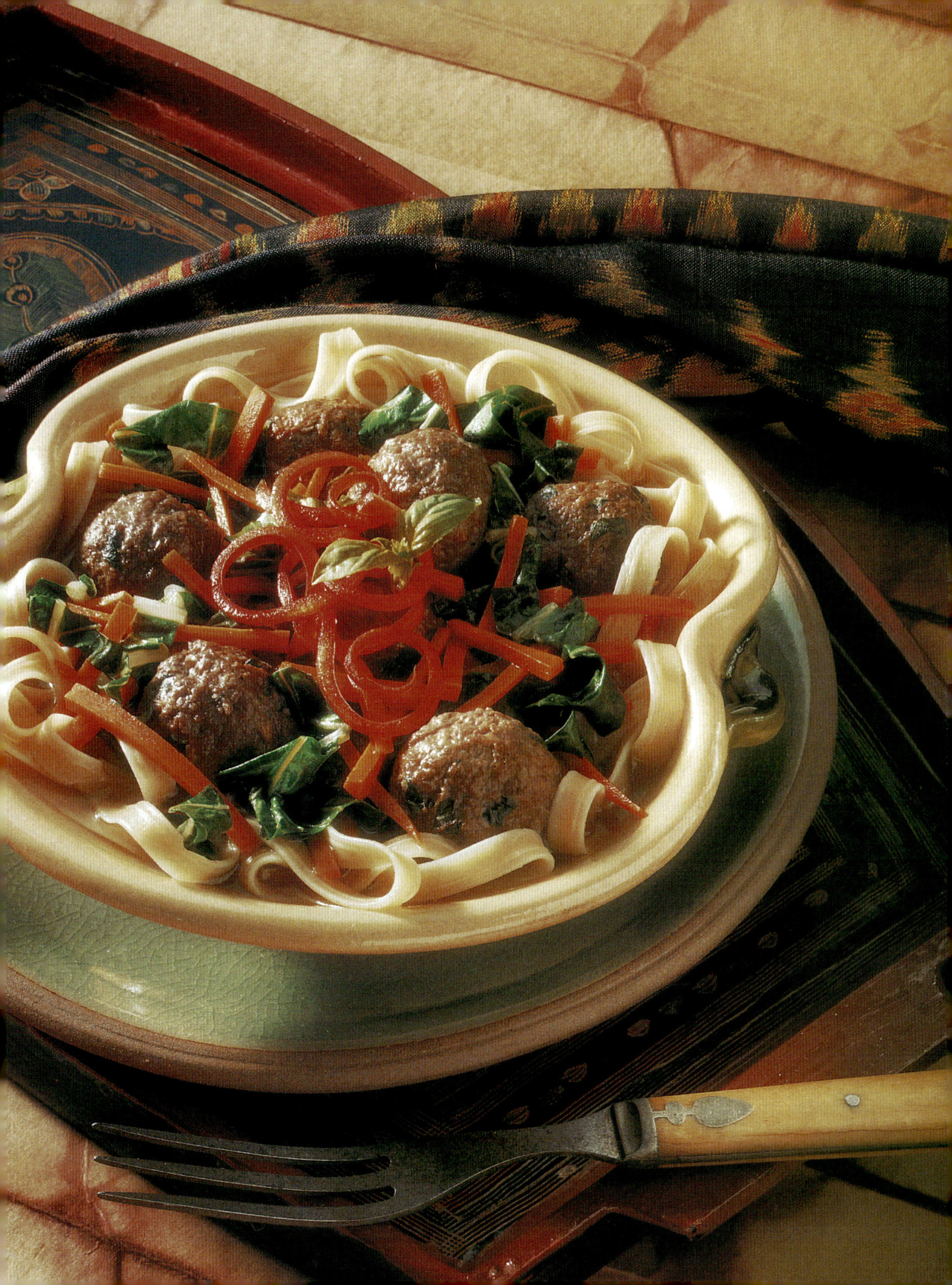

ASIAN FARE

250 LO MEIN NOODLES WITH SHRIMP

  12 ounces Chinese-style thin egg noodles
   2 teaspoons sesame oil
     Chinese chives*
  1½ tablespoons oyster sauce
  1½ tablespoons soy sauce
   ½ teaspoon sugar
   ¼ teaspoon salt
   ¼ teaspoon ground white or black pepper
   2 tablespoons vegetable oil
   1 teaspoon minced fresh ginger
   1 clove garlic, minced
   8 ounces medium shrimp, shelled and deveined
   1 tablespoon dry sherry
   8 ounces bean sprouts

Or, substitute ¼ cup domestic chives cut into 1-inch pieces and 2 green onions with tops, cut into 1-inch pieces, for the Chinese chives.

1. Add noodles to boiling water; cook according to package directions until *al dente*, 2 to 3 minutes. Drain noodles; rinse under cold running water. Drain again.

2. Combine noodles and sesame oil in large bowl; toss lightly to coat.

3. Cut enough chives into 1-inch pieces to measure ½ cup; set aside. Combine oyster sauce, soy sauce, sugar, salt and pepper in small bowl.

4. Heat vegetable oil in wok or large skillet over high heat. Add ginger and garlic; stir-fry 10 seconds. Add shrimp; stir-fry until shrimp begin to turn pink, about 1 minute. Add chives and sherry; stir-fry until chives begin to wilt, about 15 seconds. Add ½ of the bean sprouts; stir-fry 15 seconds. Add remaining bean sprouts; stir-fry 15 seconds.

5. Add oyster sauce mixture and noodles. Cook and stir until thoroughly heated, about 2 minutes. *Makes 4 servings*

251 ANGEL HAIR STIR-FRY

   1 whole chicken breast, skinned and boned
   1 tablespoon KIKKOMAN® Stir-Fry Sauce
   4 ounces angel hair pasta (capellini)
   ⅓ cup KIKKOMAN® Stir-Fry Sauce
   3 tablespoons water
   2 tablespoons vegetable oil, divided
   ¼ pound fresh snow peas, cut into julienne strips
   1 large carrot, cut into julienne strips
   ⅛ teaspoon salt
   2 teaspoons sesame seed, toasted

Cut chicken into thin strips; coat with 1 tablespoon stir-fry sauce. Let stand 30 minutes. Meanwhile, cook pasta according to package directions, omitting salt. Drain; rinse under cold water and drain thoroughly. Combine ⅓ cup stir-fry sauce and water; set aside. Heat 1 tablespoon oil in hot wok or large skillet over high heat. Add chicken and stir-fry 2 minutes; remove. Heat remaining 1 tablespoon oil in same pan; add peas and carrot. Sprinkle vegetables with salt; stir-fry 4 minutes. Add stir-fry sauce mixture, chicken, pasta and sesame seed. Cook and stir until all ingredients are coated with sauce and pasta is heated through.
Makes 4 servings

Lo Mein Noodles with Shrimp

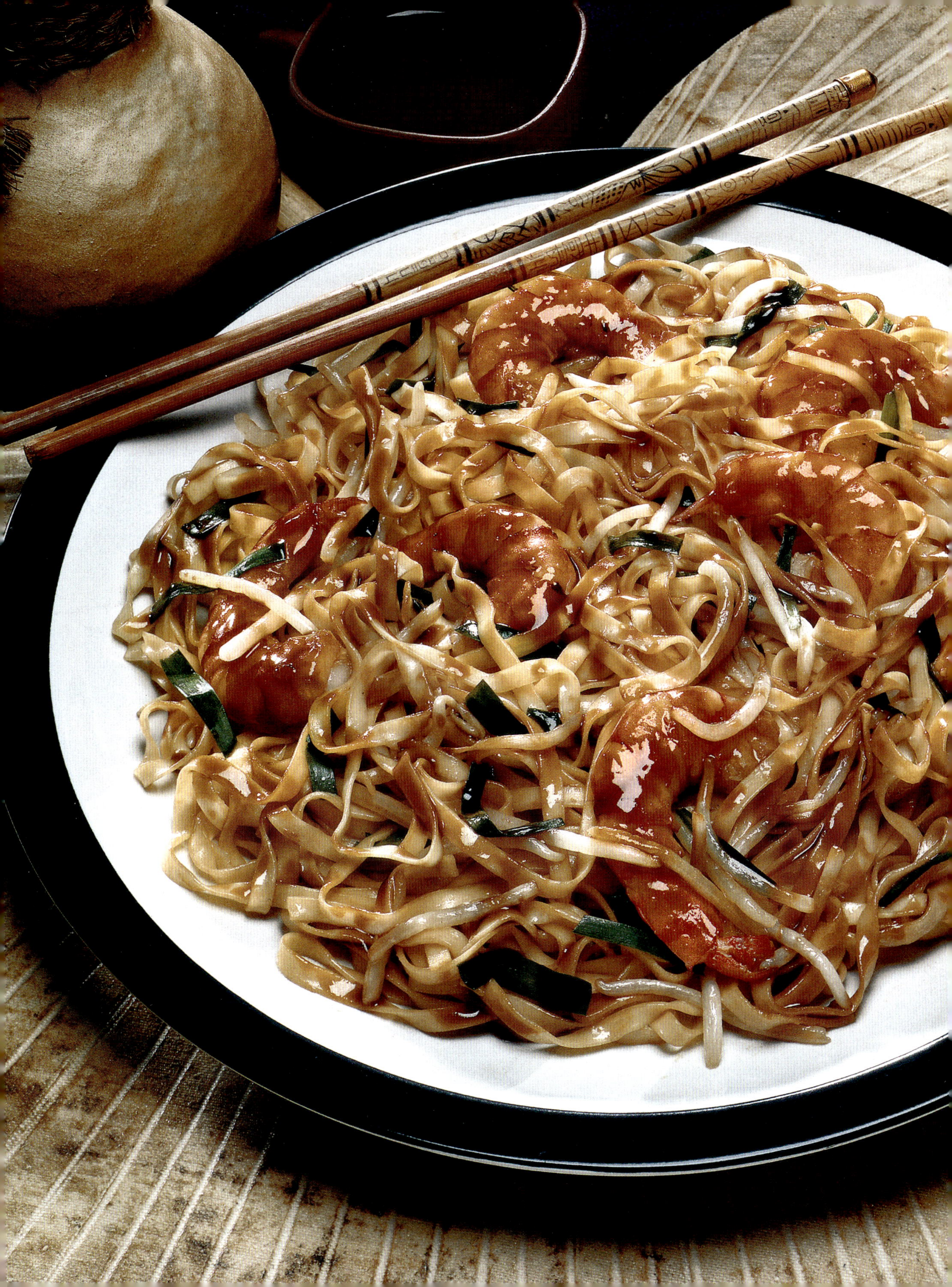

ASIAN FARE

252 CURRIED TURKEY AND COUSCOUS SKILLET

- 1 tablespoon vegetable or olive oil
- 1 small onion, chopped
- 2 cloves garlic, minced
- 1 can (10½ ounces) kosher condensed chicken broth
- ⅓ cup water
- 2 teaspoons curry powder
- ¼ teaspoon ground red pepper
- 2 cups small broccoli flowerets
- 1 cup thinly sliced carrots
- 2 packages (4 ounces each) HEBREW NATIONAL® Sliced Oven Roasted Turkey Breast, cut into ½-inch strips
- 1 cup uncooked couscous
- Chopped fresh cilantro for garnish

Heat oil in large deep nonstick skillet over medium heat. Add onion and garlic; cook 5 minutes or until onion is tender. Add broth, water, curry powder and ground red pepper to skillet; bring to a boil. Stir in broccoli and carrots. Cover; simmer 5 minutes or until vegetables are crisp-tender.

Stir turkey into broth mixture; cook until heated through. Stir in couscous, mixing well. Cover; remove from heat. Let stand 5 minutes or until liquid is absorbed. Garnish with cilantro. *Makes 4 servings*

253 NOODLES THAI STYLE

- ¼ cup ketchup
- 2 tablespoons reduced-sodium soy sauce
- 1 tablespoon sugar
- ¼ to ½ teaspoon crushed red pepper
- ¼ teaspoon ground ginger
- 2 teaspoons FLEISCHMANN'S® Margarine, divided
- 1 cup EGG BEATERS® Real Egg Product
- 8 green onions, cut into 1½-inch pieces
- 1 clove garlic, minced
- ¾ pound fresh bean sprouts, rinsed and well drained
- 8 ounces linguine, cooked and drained
- ¼ cup PLANTER'S® Dry Roasted Unsalted Peanuts, chopped

In small bowl, combine ketchup, soy sauce, sugar, pepper and ginger; set aside.

In large nonstick skillet, over medium heat, melt 1 teaspoon margarine. Pour Egg Beaters into skillet. Cook, stirring occasionally until set. Remove to another small bowl.

In same skillet, over medium heat, sauté green onions and garlic in remaining margarine for 2 minutes. Stir in bean sprouts; cook for 2 minutes. Stir in ketchup mixture. Cook until heated through. Transfer to large bowl; add eggs and linguine. Toss until combined. Top with peanuts.
Makes 6 (1-cup) servings

Prep time: 25 minutes
Cook time: 5 minutes

Curried Turkey and Couscous Skillet

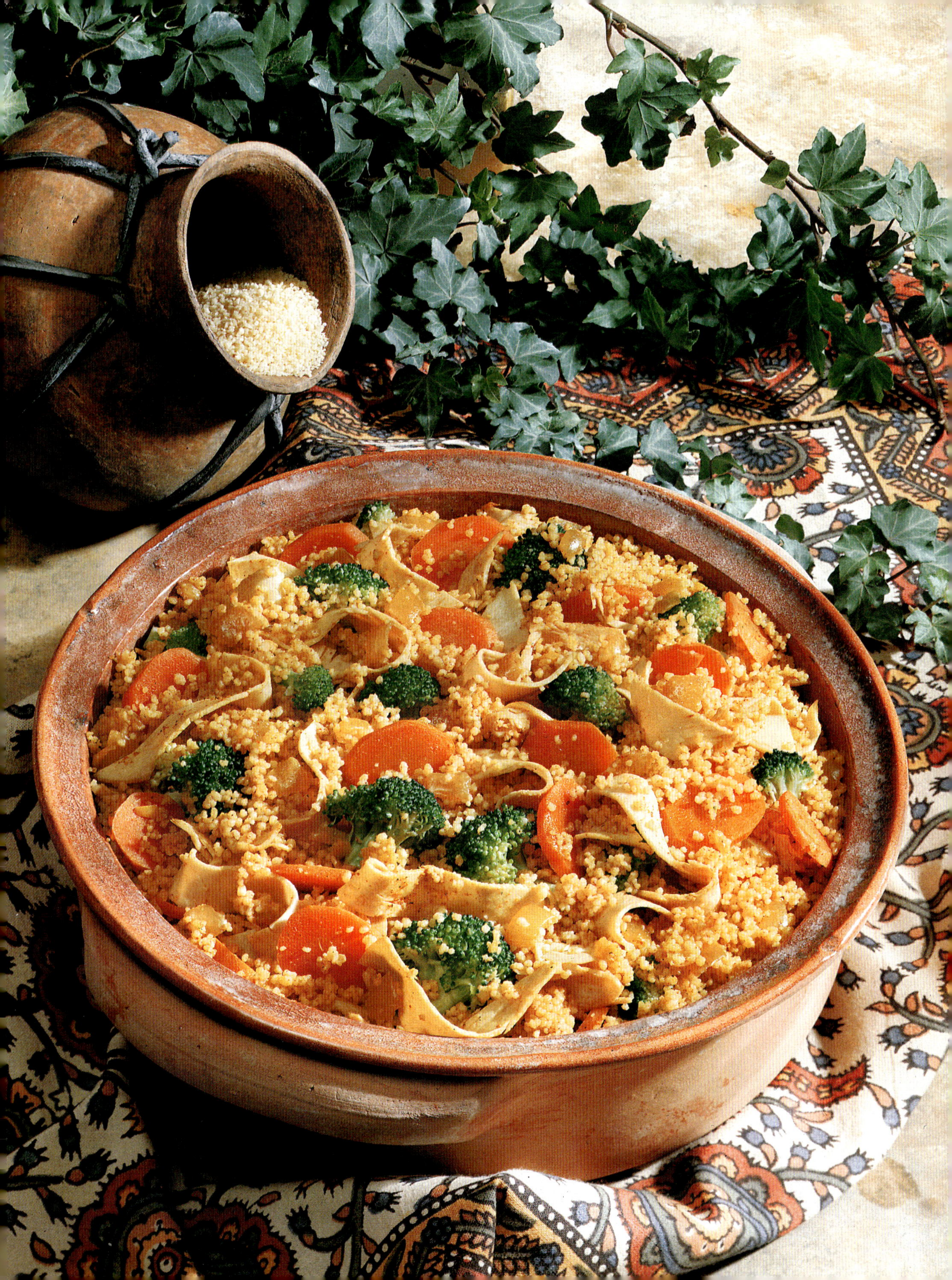

ASIAN FARE

254 CANTONESE TOMATO BEEF

1 small beef flank steak or filet mignon tail (about 1 pound)
2 tablespoons soy sauce
2 tablespoons sesame oil, divided
1 tablespoon plus 1 teaspoon cornstarch, divided
1 pound fresh Chinese-style thin wheat noodles *or* 12 ounces dry spaghetti
3 small onions (about 7 ounces), peeled
5 large ripe tomatoes (about 2 pounds), cored
1 cup beef broth
2 tablespoons packed brown sugar
1 tablespoon cider vinegar
2 tablespoons vegetable oil, divided
1 tablespoon minced fresh ginger
1 green onion with tops, diagonally cut into thin slices
Edible flowers, such as nasturtiums, for garnish

1. Trim fat from beef; discard. Cut beef lengthwise into 2 strips; cut across the grain into ¼-inch-thick slices.

2. Combine soy sauce, 1 tablespoon sesame oil and 1 teaspoon cornstarch in large bowl. Add beef slices; toss to coat. Set aside.

3. Cook noodles in large stockpot according to package directions just until tender. Cut each onion and tomato into 8 wedges. Combine broth, sugar, remaining 1 tablespoon cornstarch and vinegar in small bowl; mix well. Set aside.

4. Drain cooked noodles and return to stockpot. Add remaining 1 tablespoon sesame oil; toss. Keep warm.

5. Heat wok over high heat 1 minute or until hot. Drizzle 1 tablespoon vegetable oil into wok and heat 30 seconds. Add ginger and stir-fry about 30 seconds or until fragrant. Add beef mixture and stir-fry 5 minutes or until lightly browned. Remove beef and ginger to bowl and set aside. Reduce heat to medium.

6. Add remaining 1 tablespoon vegetable oil to wok. Add onion wedges; cook and stir about 2 minutes or until wilted. Stir in ½ of tomato wedges. Stir broth mixture and add to wok. Cook and stir until liquid boils and thickens.

7. Return beef and any juices to wok. Add remaining tomato wedges; cook and stir until heated through. Place cooked noodles in shallow serving bowl. Spoon tomato-beef mixture over noodles. Sprinkle with green onion. Garnish with edible flowers. Serve immediately. *Makes 4 servings*

Cantonese Tomato Beef

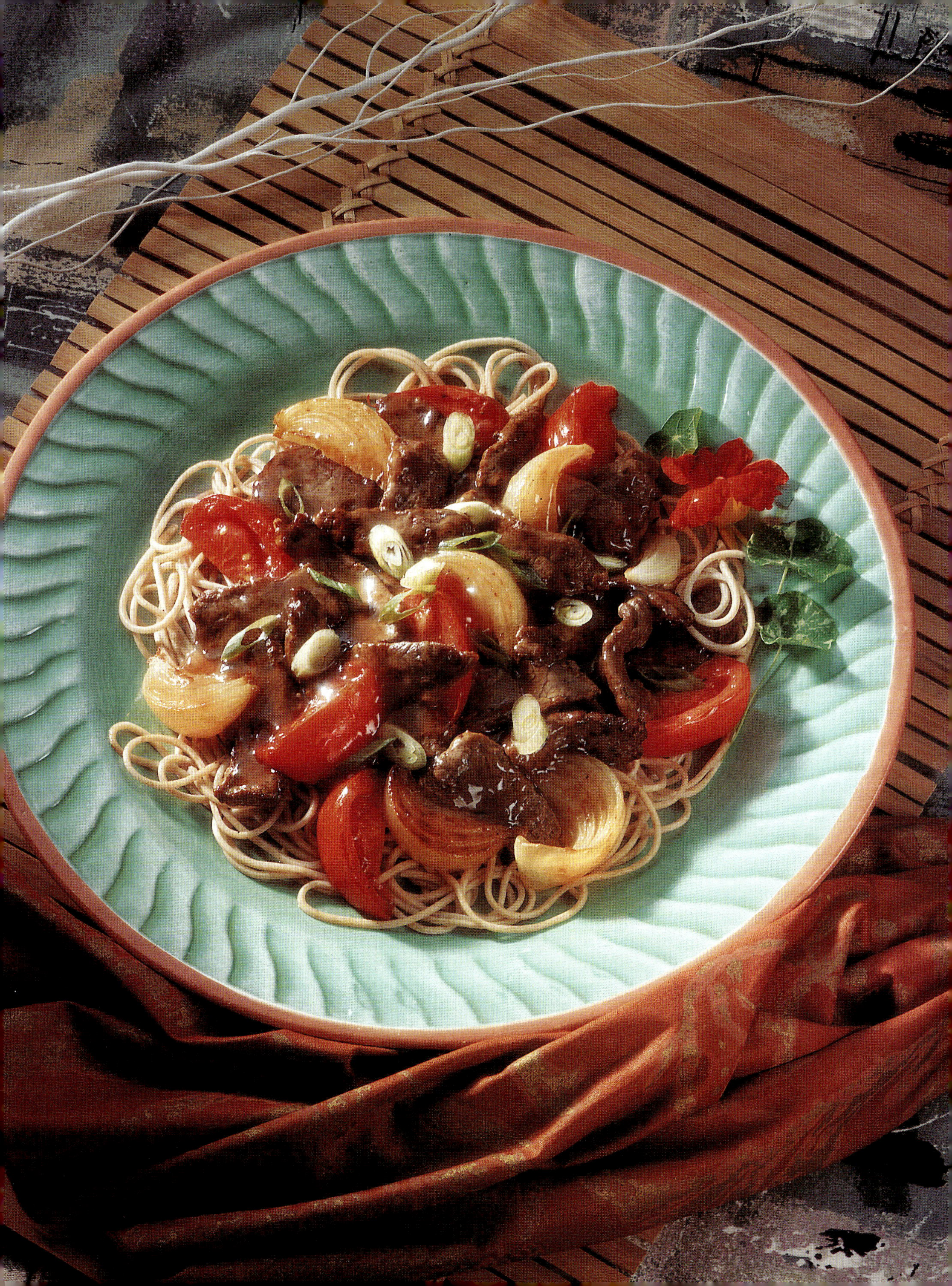

ASIAN FARE

255 LONG SOUP

- 1½ tablespoons vegetable oil
- ¼ of small head of cabbage (4 to 6 ounces), cored and shredded
- 8 ounces boneless lean pork, cut into thin strips
- 6 cups chicken broth
- 2 tablespoons soy sauce
- ½ teaspoon minced fresh ginger
- 8 green onions with tops, diagonally cut into ½-inch slices
- 4 ounces Chinese-style thin egg noodles

1. Heat oil in wok or large skillet over medium-high heat. Add cabbage and pork; stir-fry until pork is no longer pink in center, about 5 minutes.

2. Add chicken broth, soy sauce and ginger. Bring to a boil. Reduce heat to low; simmer 10 minutes, stirring occasionally. Stir in onions; add noodles.

3. Cook just until noodles are tender, 2 to 4 minutes. *Makes 4 servings*

256 BEEF WITH NOODLES

- 8 ounces Chinese-style thin egg noodles, cooked and drained
- 3 teaspoons soy sauce, divided
- ¼ teaspoon salt
- 2 teaspoons instant chicken bouillon granules
- 1 pound beef rump steak, trimmed
- 6 tablespoons vegetable oil, divided
- 6 green onions, diagonally sliced
- 1 piece fresh ginger (about 1 inch square), peeled and thinly sliced
- 2 cloves garlic, crushed

1. Place a clean towel over wire cooling racks. Spread cooked noodles evenly over towel. Let dry about 3 hours.

2. Combine ½ cup water, 2 teaspoons soy sauce, salt and bouillon granules in small bowl. Cut beef across the grain into thin slices, about 2 inches long.

3. Heat 4 tablespoons oil in wok or large skillet over high heat. Add noodles and stir-fry 3 minutes. Pour soy sauce mixture over noodles; toss until noodles are completely coated, about 2 minutes. Transfer noodles to serving plate; keep warm.

4. Heat remaining 2 tablespoons oil in same wok over high heat. Add beef, onions, ginger, garlic and remaining 1 teaspoon soy sauce. Stir-fry until beef is cooked through, about 5 minutes. Spoon meat mixture over noodles. *Makes 4 servings*

Long Soup

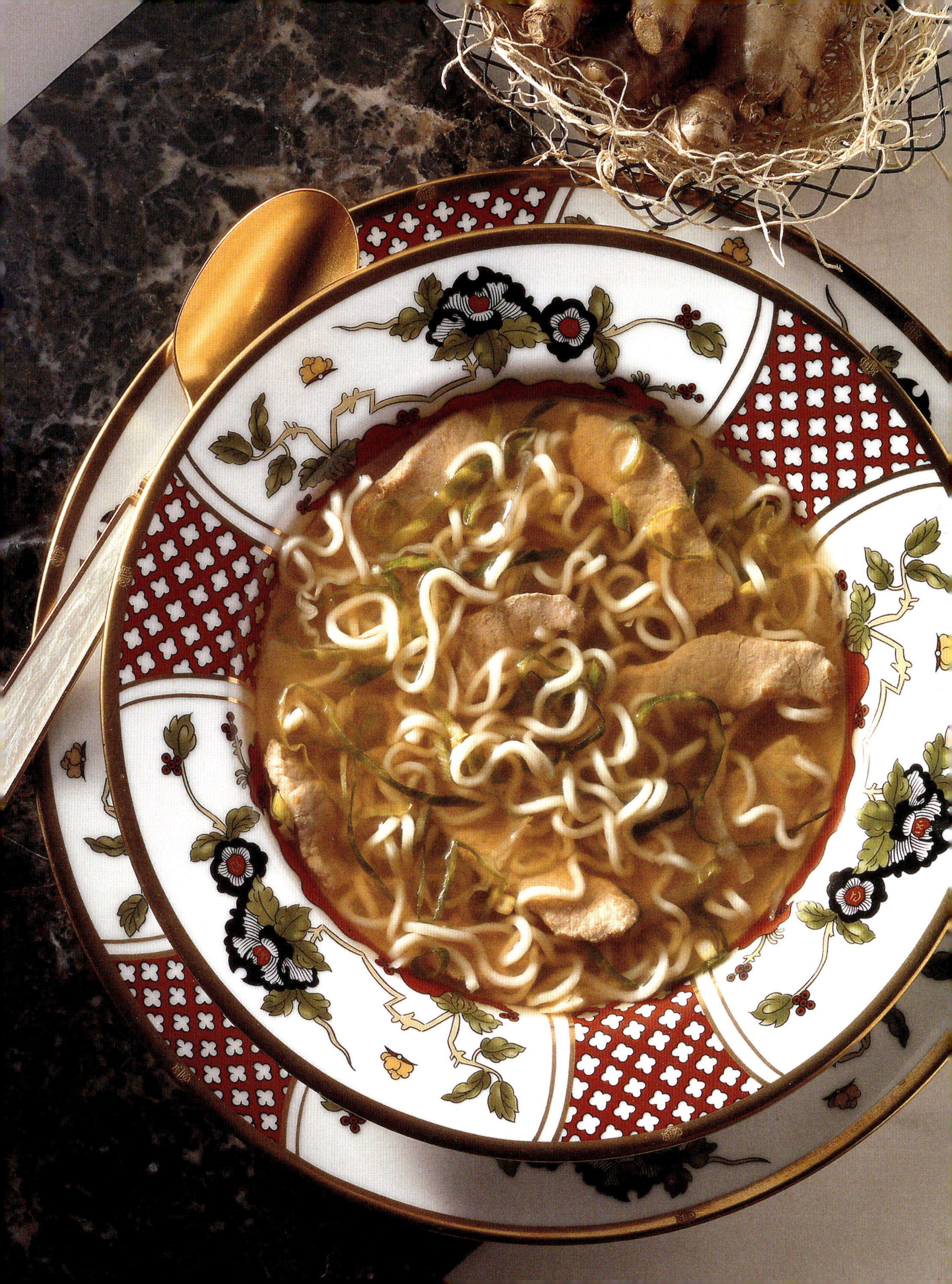

ASIAN FARE

257 SWEET & SOUR TORTELLINI

- 1 package (7 to 12 ounces) cheese-filled tortellini
- ½ pound boneless tender beef steak (sirloin, rib eye or top loin)
- 2 teaspoons cornstarch
- 2 teaspoons KIKKOMAN® Soy Sauce
- 1 small clove garlic, minced
- ½ cup KIKKOMAN® Sweet & Sour Sauce
- ⅓ cup chicken broth
- 1 tablespoon sugar
- 2 tablespoons dry sherry
- 2 tablespoons vegetable oil, divided
- 1 medium onion, chunked
- 1 small red bell pepper, chunked
- 1 small green bell pepper, chunked

Cook tortellini according to package directions, omitting salt; drain. Cut meat into thin bite-size pieces. Combine cornstarch, soy sauce and garlic in small bowl; stir in meat. Let stand 15 minutes. Meanwhile, combine sweet & sour sauce, chicken broth, sugar and sherry; set aside. Heat 1 tablespoon oil in hot wok or large skillet over high heat. Add meat mixture; stir-fry 1 minute. Remove from wok. Heat remaining 1 tablespoon oil in wok. Add onion and peppers; stir-fry 3 minutes. Add meat mixture, sweet & sour sauce mixture and tortellini. Heat thoroughly, stirring occasionally. *Makes 4 servings*

258 THAI PEANUT NOODLE STIR-FRY

- 1 cup COLLEGE INN® Chicken Broth or Lower Sodium Chicken Broth
- ½ cup GREY POUPON® Dijon Mustard
- ⅓ cup creamy peanut butter
- 3 tablespoons packed light brown sugar
- 2 tablespoons soy sauce
- 1 clove garlic, crushed
- ½ teaspoon minced fresh ginger
- 1 tablespoon cornstarch
- 4 cups cut-up vegetables (red peppers, carrots, mushrooms, green onions, pea pods)
- 1 tablespoon vegetable oil
- 1 pound linguine, cooked
  Chopped peanuts and scallion brushes for garnish

In medium saucepan, combine chicken broth, mustard, peanut butter, sugar, soy sauce, garlic, ginger and cornstarch. Cook over medium heat until mixture thickens and begins to boil; reduce heat and keep warm.

In large skillet, over medium-high heat, sauté vegetables in oil until tender, about 5 minutes. In large serving bowl, combine hot cooked pasta, vegetables and peanut sauce, tossing until well coated. Garnish with chopped peanuts and scallion brushes. Serve immediately.

Makes 4 to 6 servings

Sweet & Sour Tortellini

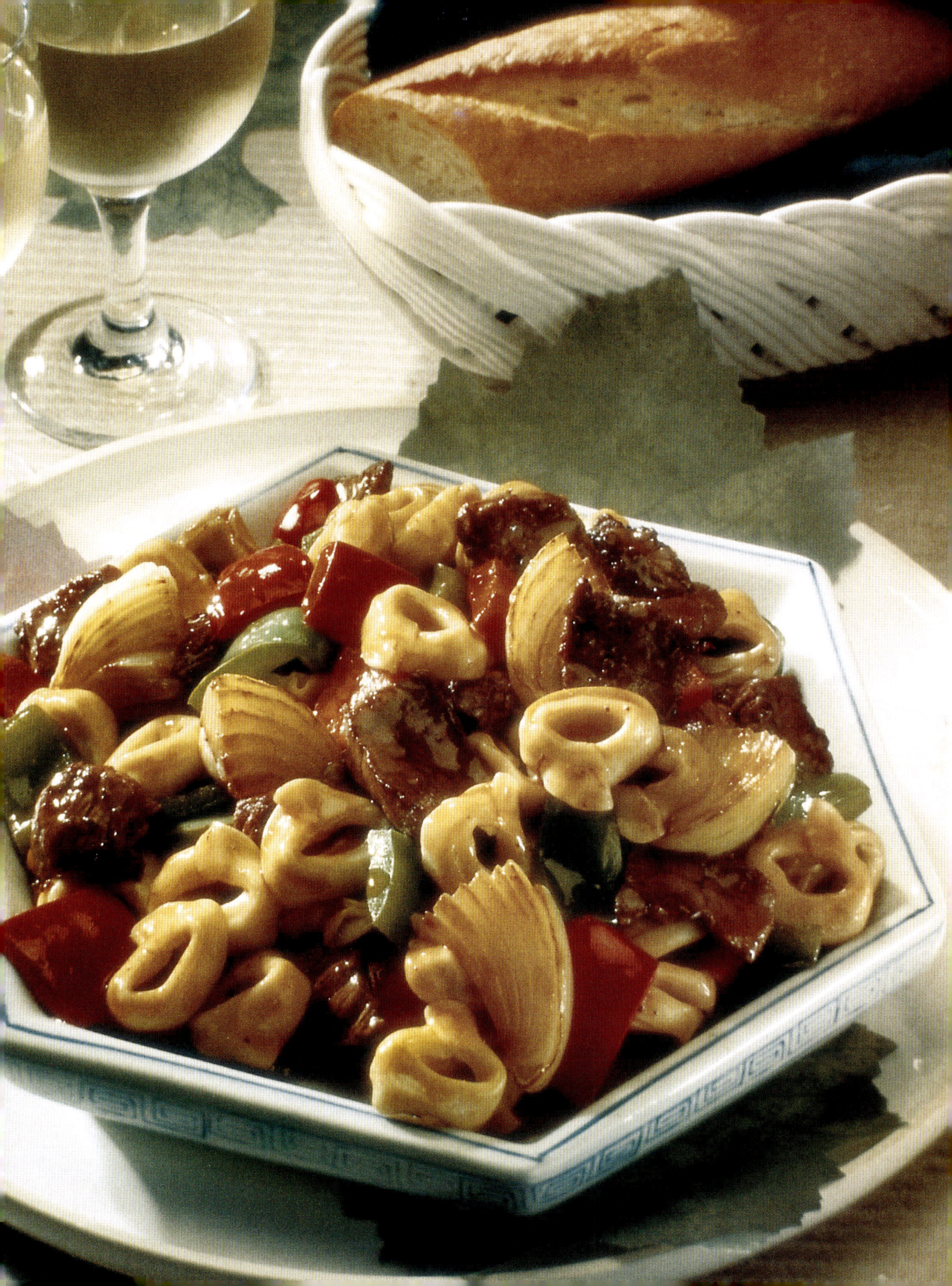

ASIAN FARE

259 MIXED VEGETABLES WITH NOODLES AND BEEF (CHAP CH'AE)

2 tablespoons dried cloud ear or other Asian mushrooms
2 tablespoons Sesame Salt (recipe follows)
5 ounces fresh spinach, washed and stemmed
4 ounces Chinese-style egg vermicelli or mung bean noodles
2 tablespoons soy sauce, divided
1 teaspoon sesame oil
2 tablespoons vegetable oil, divided
1 cup julienned carrots
1 medium onion, cut into halves and thinly sliced
1 piece fresh ginger (about 1 inch square), finely chopped
1 teaspoon minced garlic
8 ounces flank steak, cut into 2-inch-long pieces
1 teaspoon sugar
1/8 teaspoon black pepper
Chives and chive blossom for garnish

1. Place mushrooms in bowl; cover with hot water. Let stand 30 minutes or until caps are soft. Drain mushrooms; squeeze out excess water. Remove and discard stems. Cut caps into thin slices.

2. Meanwhile, prepare Sesame Salt; set aside. Bring 1 quart lightly salted water to a boil in medium saucepan over high heat. Add spinach; return to a boil. Cook 2 to 3 minutes or until crisp-tender. Drain spinach; immediately plunge into cold water to stop cooking. Place in colander to drain. Let stand until cool enough to handle. Squeeze spinach to remove excess moisture; chop finely.

3. Bring 2 quarts water to a boil in large saucepan over high heat. Add noodles; cook 2 minutes or according to package directions. Drain and immediately run cold water over noodles. Cut noodles into small strands. Return noodles to saucepan. Stir in 1 tablespoon soy sauce and sesame oil; toss to coat. Set aside and keep warm.

4. Heat 1 tablespoon vegetable oil in wok or large skillet over medium-high heat. Add carrots; stir-fry 5 minutes or until crisp-tender. Add mushrooms and onion; stir-fry 2 minutes or just until wilted. Remove vegetables from wok.

5. Heat wok over high heat 1 minute or until hot. Drizzle remaining 1 tablespoon vegetable oil into wok; heat 30 seconds. Add ginger and garlic; stir-fry 30 seconds or until fragrant.

6. Add beef to wok; stir-fry 3 to 5 minutes or until lightly browned. Remove wok from heat; stir in Sesame Salt, sugar, pepper and remaining 1 tablespoon soy sauce.

7. Return vegetables and noodles to wok; cook and stir until heated through. Add additional soy sauce to taste. Garnish with chives and chive blossom.

Makes 4 servings

SESAME SALT
1/2 cup sesame seeds
1/4 teaspoon salt

1. Heat seeds in large skillet over medium-low heat, stirring or shaking pan frequently until seeds begin to pop and turn golden, about 4 to 6 minutes. Set aside to cool.

2. Crush toasted seeds and salt with mortar and pestle or process in spice grinder. Refrigerate in covered glass jar.

Makes 1/2 cup

Mixed Vegetables with Noodles and Beef (Chap Ch'ae)

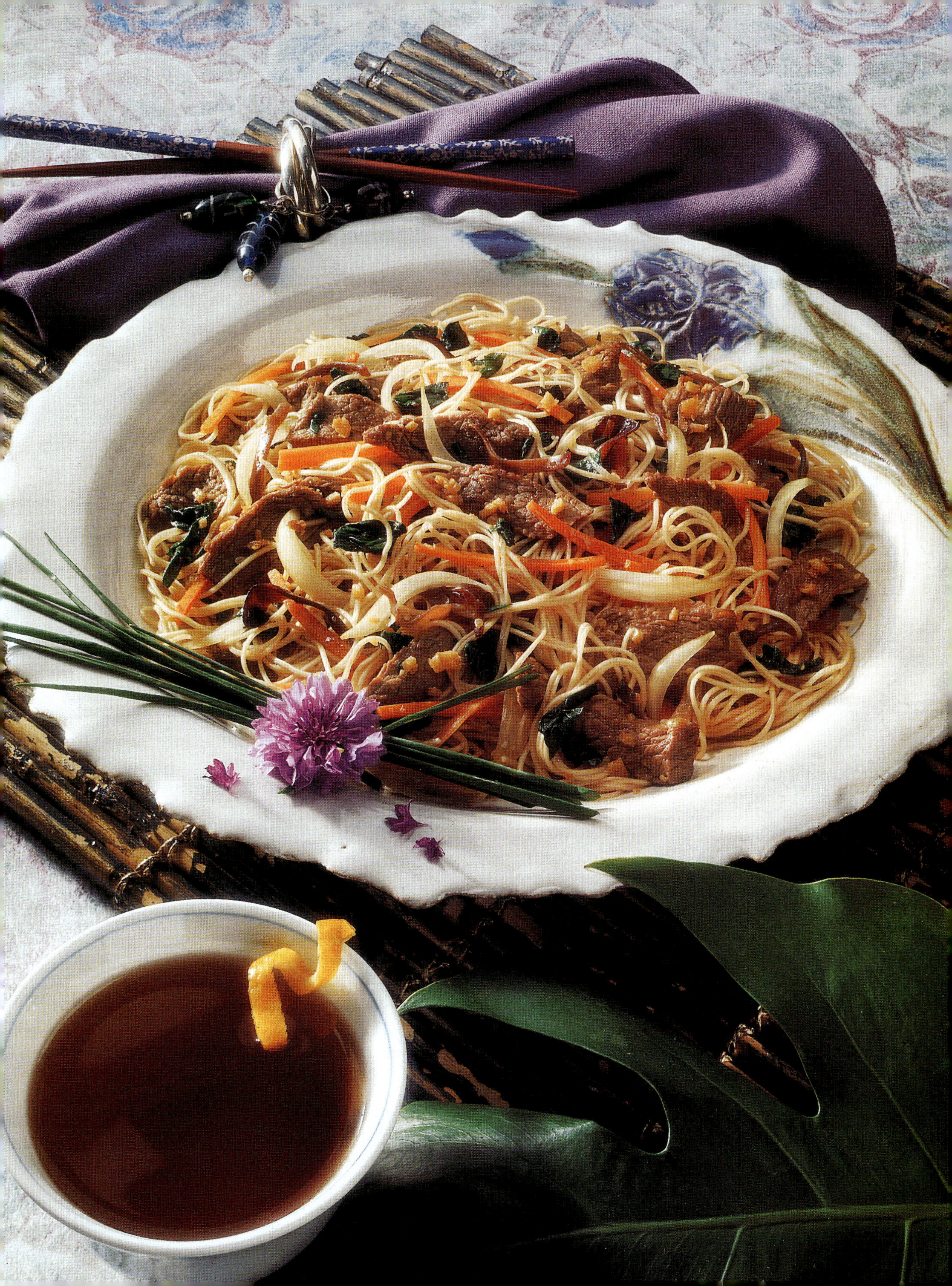

ASIAN FARE

260 CHICKEN CHOW MEIN

- 1 pound boneless skinless chicken breasts or thighs
- 2 cloves garlic, minced
- 2 tablespoons peanut or vegetable oil, divided
- ¼ cup soy sauce
- 2 tablespoons dry sherry
- 6 ounces (2 cups) fresh snow peas *or* 1 package (6 ounces) frozen snow peas, thawed, cut into halves
- 3 large green onions, cut diagonally into 1-inch pieces
- 6 ounces uncooked Chinese egg noodles or vermicelli, cooked, drained and rinsed
- 1 tablespoon dark sesame oil

1. Cut chicken crosswise into ¼-inch-thick slices; cut each slice into 1×¼-inch strips. Toss chicken with garlic in small bowl.

2. Heat wok or large skillet over medium-high heat. Add 1 tablespoon peanut oil; heat until hot. Add chicken mixture; stir-fry 3 minutes or until chicken is no longer pink. Transfer to bowl; toss with soy sauce and sherry.

3. Heat remaining 1 tablespoon peanut oil in wok. Add snow peas; stir-fry 2 minutes for fresh *or* 1 minute for frozen snow peas. Add onions; stir-fry 30 seconds. Add chicken mixture; stir-fry 1 minute.

4. Add noodles to wok; stir-fry 2 minutes or until heated through. Stir in sesame oil; serve immediately. *Makes 4 servings*

261 TASTY THAI SHRIMP & SESAME NOODLES

- 1 pound medium shrimp, shelled and deveined
- 1 (8-ounce) bottle NEWMAN'S OWN® Light Italian Dressing, divided
- 2 tablespoons chunky peanut butter
- 1 tablespoon soy sauce
- 1 tablespoon honey
- 1 teaspoon grated peeled fresh ginger
- ½ teaspoon crushed red pepper
- 1 (8-ounce) package capellini or angel hair pasta
- 2 tablespoons vegetable oil
- 1 tablespoon sesame oil
- 1 medium carrot, peeled and shredded
- 1 cup chopped green onions
- ¼ cup chopped fresh cilantro for garnish

In medium bowl, mix shrimp with ⅓ cup Newman's Own Light Italian Dressing. Cover and refrigerate 1 hour. In small bowl, with wire whisk or fork, mix peanut butter, soy sauce, honey, ginger, crushed red pepper and remaining dressing; set aside. After shrimp has marinated 1 hour, prepare capellini according to package directions; drain.

Meanwhile, in 4-quart saucepan over high heat, heat vegetable oil and sesame oil until very hot. In hot oil, cook carrot 1 minute. Drain off dressing from shrimp; discard dressing. Add shrimp and green onions to carrot and cook, stirring constantly, about 3 minutes or until shrimp turn opaque. In large bowl, toss hot capellini with dressing mixture and shrimp mixture. Sprinkle with chopped cilantro. *Makes 4 servings*

Chicken Chow Mein

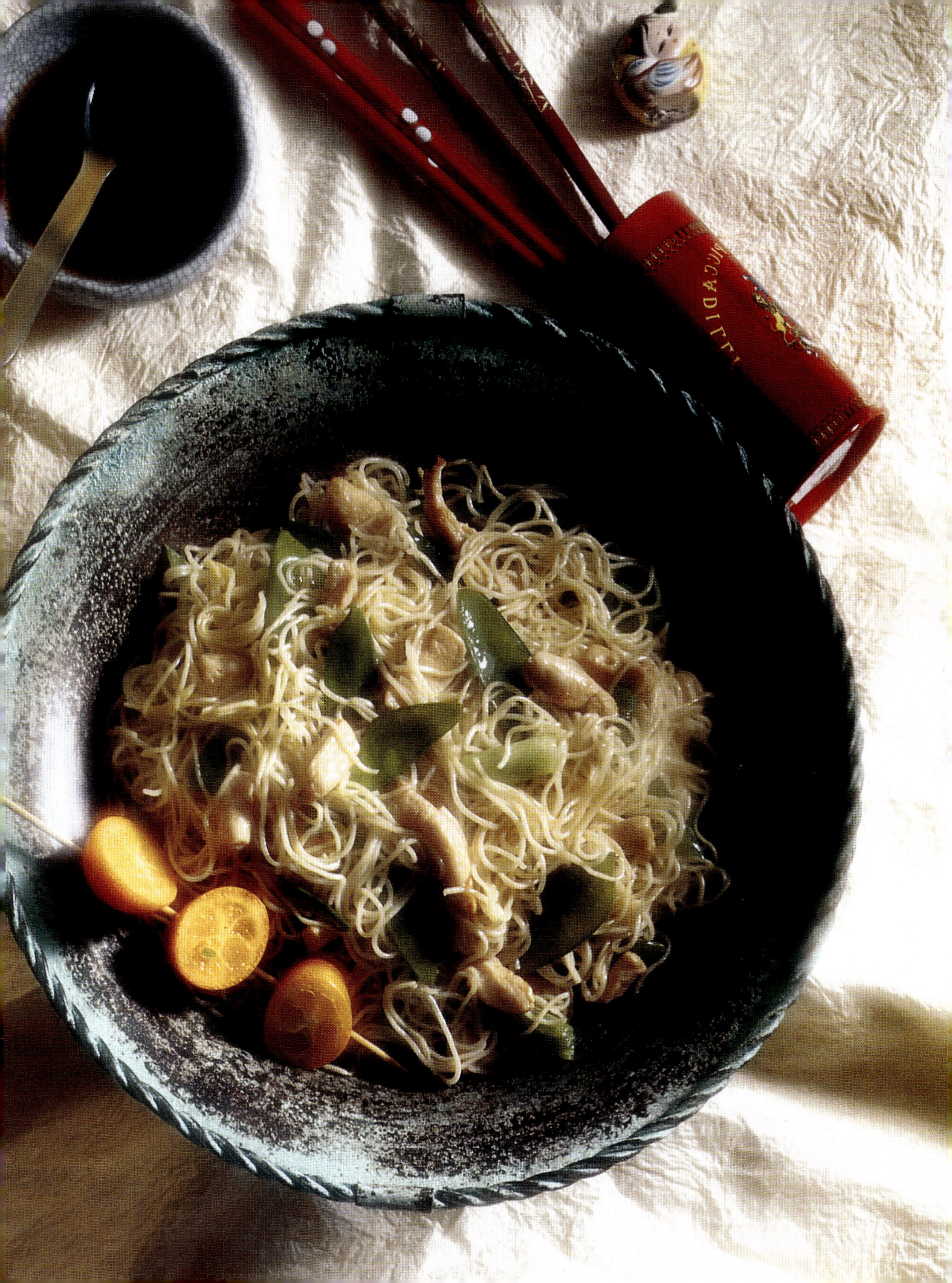

ASIAN FARE

262 BEEF SOUP WITH NOODLES

2 tablespoons soy sauce
1 teaspoon minced fresh ginger
¼ teaspoon red pepper flakes
1 boneless beef top sirloin steak, cut 1 inch thick (about ¾ pound)
1 tablespoon peanut or vegetable oil
2 cups sliced fresh mushrooms
2 cans (about 14 ounces each) beef broth
3 ounces (1 cup) fresh snow peas, cut diagonally into 1-inch pieces
1½ cups hot cooked fine egg noodles (2 ounces uncooked)
1 green onion, cut diagonally into thin slices
1 teaspoon dark sesame oil (optional)
Red bell pepper strips for garnish

1. Combine soy sauce, ginger and red pepper flakes in small bowl. Spread mixture evenly over both sides of steak. Marinate at room temperature 15 minutes.

2. Heat deep skillet over medium-high heat. Add peanut oil; heat until hot. Drain steak; reserve marinade (there will only be a small amount of marinade). Add steak to skillet; cook 4 to 5 minutes per side.* Let stand on cutting board 10 minutes.

3. Add mushrooms to skillet; stir-fry 2 minutes. Add broth, snow peas and reserved marinade; bring to a boil, scraping up browned meat bits. Reduce heat to medium-low. Stir in noodles.

4. Cut steak across the grain into ⅛-inch-thick slices; cut each slice into 1-inch pieces. Stir into soup; heat through. Stir in onion and sesame oil, if desired. Ladle into soup bowls. Garnish with red pepper strips.

Makes 4 main-dish or 6 appetizer servings (about 6 cups)

*Cooking time is for medium-rare doneness. Adjust time for desired doneness.

263 SPAGHETTI WITH BEEF AND BLACK PEPPER SAUCE

8 ounces spaghetti
5 ounces beef fillet, shredded
½ cup plus 2 tablespoons LEE KUM KEE® Black Pepper Sauce, divided
1 tablespoon vegetable oil
1 ounce onion, shredded
1 ounce green bell pepper, shredded
1 ounce red bell pepper, shredded

1. Cook spaghetti in boiling water 10 minutes. Rinse with cold water and drain.

2. Marinate beef with 2 tablespoons pepper sauce 5 minutes.

3. Heat oil in wok. Sauté onion until fragrant. Add beef and stir-fry until cooked. Add spaghetti, bell peppers and remaining ½ cup pepper sauce. Stir well and serve.

Makes 4 to 6 servings

ASIAN FARE

264 TURKEY SHANGHAI

- 1 package (1¼ pounds) PERDUE® FIT 'N EASY® Fresh Skinless and Boneless Turkey Breast Tenderloins
- ½ cup white wine, divided
- 3 tablespoons reduced-sodium soy sauce, divided
- 1 tablespoon cornstarch
  Ground black pepper to taste
- 1 tablespoon sugar
- 2 teaspoons rice vinegar or white vinegar
- 1½ tablespoons vegetable oil
- 1 clove garlic, minced
- 1 teaspoon minced fresh ginger
- 2 carrots, shredded
- ⅓ pound green beans, split lengthwise and lightly steamed
- ½ cup thinly sliced scallions
- 2 cups hot cooked Chinese noodles
  Carrots and scallions cut in flower shapes (optional)
  Cilantro sprigs (optional)

Slice turkey into thin strips; place in medium bowl. Sprinkle with ¼ cup wine, 1 tablespoon soy sauce, cornstarch and pepper; toss to coat and marinate at room temperature 15 minutes. In small bowl, combine remaining ¼ cup wine, 2 tablespoons soy sauce, sugar and vinegar; set aside.

Over medium-high heat, heat wok or large, heavy nonstick skillet. Slowly add oil; stir in garlic, ginger and turkey mixture. Stir-fry 3 to 4 minutes until turkey is cooked through. Add carrots, beans, scallions and reserved wine mixture; cook 1 to 2 minutes longer. Serve over Chinese noodles; garnish with carrot and scallion flowers and cilantro sprigs, if desired. *Makes 4 servings*

265 COLD STIRRED NOODLES

DRESSING
- 6 tablespoons soy sauce
- 2 tablespoons sesame oil
- ¼ cup red wine vinegar
- 2½ tablespoons sugar
- ¼ to ½ teaspoon chili oil

NOODLES
- 1 pound Chinese-style thin egg noodles
- 1 tablespoon sesame oil
- 2 small carrots, shredded
- 3 cups bean sprouts
- ½ large thin-skinned cucumber, shredded
- 1 bunch radishes, shredded
- 1 cup matchstick strips barbecued pork (optional)
- 4 green onions with tops, cut into 2-inch slivers
  Thin cucumber slices for garnish

1. For dressing, combine soy sauce, 2 tablespoons sesame oil, vinegar, sugar and chili oil in small bowl; mix well.

2. Cut noodles into 6-inch pieces. Cook noodles according to package directions until *al dente*, 2 to 3 minutes; drain. Rinse under cold running water; drain again.

3. Combine noodles and 1 tablespoon sesame oil in medium bowl; toss lightly to coat. Refrigerate until ready to serve.

4. Add carrots to saucepan of boiling water; cook 30 seconds. Drain. Rinse under cold running water; drain again. Repeat with bean sprouts.

5. To serve, place noodles on large platter. Top with shredded cucumber, carrots, bean sprouts, radishes and barbecued pork, if desired; sprinkle with onions. Garnish with cucumber slices. Serve with dressing.
Makes 6 to 8 servings

ASIAN FARE

266 KOREAN–STYLE BEEF AND PASTA

- ¾ pound lean beef round steak
- 2 tablespoons reduced-sodium soy sauce
- 1 tablespoon rice wine
- 2 teaspoons sugar
- Korean-Style Dressing (recipe follows)
- 1 package (6¾ ounces) rice noodles
- 2 cups thinly sliced napa cabbage
- 1¾ cups thinly sliced yellow bell peppers
- ½ cup thinly sliced radishes
- 1 medium carrot, shredded
- 2 green onions, thinly sliced

1. Freeze beef until partially firm; cut into very thin slices.

2. Combine soy sauce, rice wine and sugar in small nonmetallic bowl. Add beef slices; toss to coat evenly. Cover and refrigerate 8 hours or overnight.

3. Drain and grill beef over medium-hot coals 2 to 3 minutes or until desired doneness.

4. Meanwhile, prepare Korean-Style Dressing; set aside.

5. Cook noodles in boiling water 1 to 2 minutes or until tender; drain and rinse under cold water. Arrange noodles on platter.

6. Combine cabbage, bell peppers, radishes, carrot, onions and beef in medium bowl. Add Korean-Style Dressing; toss to coat evenly. Serve over noodles. Garnish with green onion brush and carrot ribbons, if desired. *Makes 8 (1-cup) servings*

KOREAN–STYLE DRESSING
- 2 teaspoons sesame seeds
- ⅓ cup orange juice
- 2 tablespoons rice wine
- 2 teaspoons reduced-sodium soy sauce
- 1 teaspoon dark sesame oil
- 1 teaspoon grated fresh ginger
- 1 teaspoon sugar
- 1 clove garlic, minced
- ⅛ teaspoon red pepper flakes

1. Place sesame seeds in small nonstick skillet. Cook and stir over medium heat until lightly browned and toasted, about 5 minutes. Cool completely.

2. Crush sesame seeds using mortar and pestle or with wooden spoon; transfer to small bowl.

3. Add orange juice, rice wine, soy sauce, sesame oil, ginger, sugar, garlic and red pepper flakes. Blend well.

Korean-Style Beef and Pasta

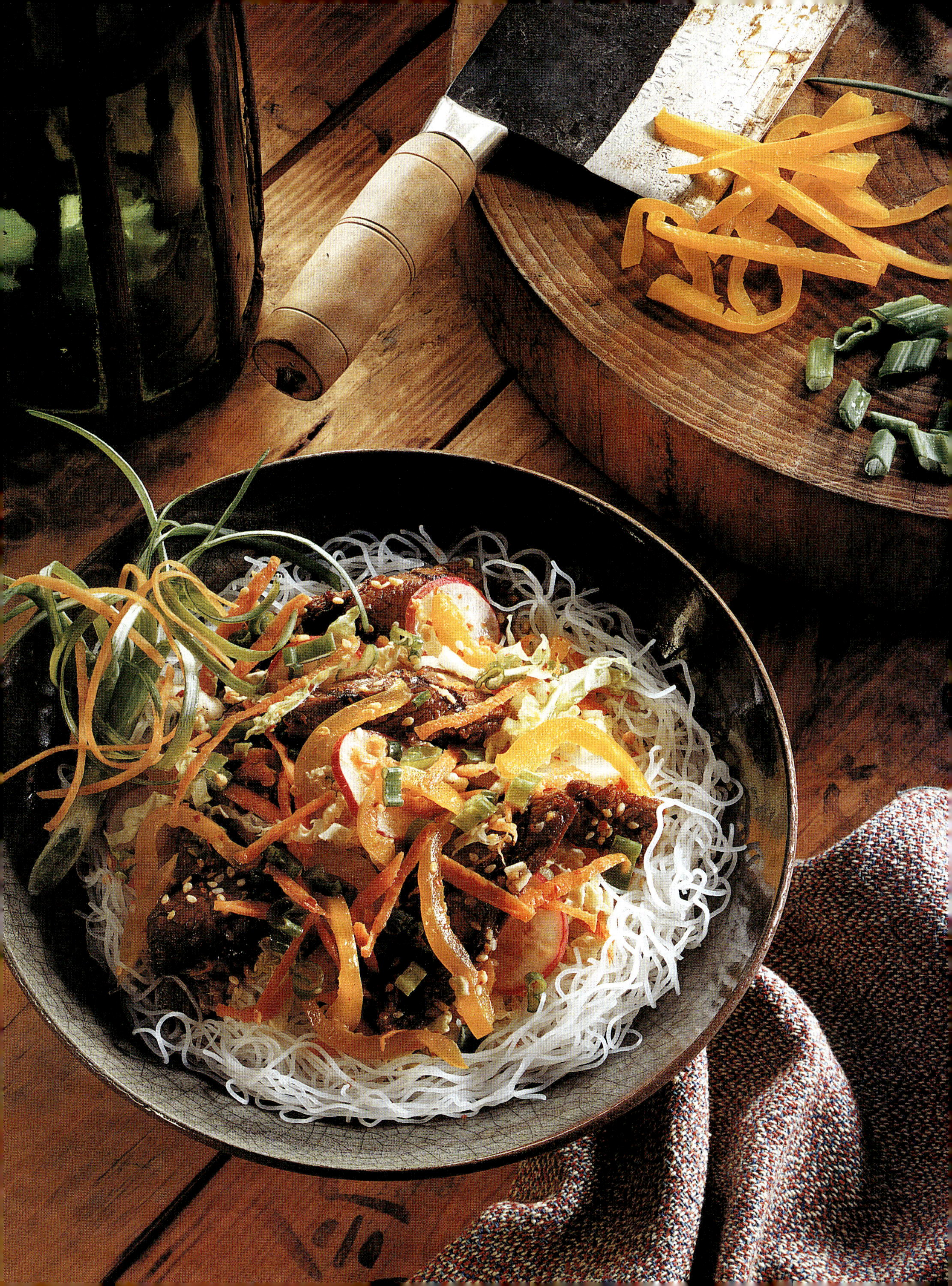

ASIAN FARE

267 INDIAN CHICKEN WITH COUSCOUS

- 1 pound boneless skinless chicken breasts
- 2 teaspoons olive oil
- 1 cup chopped onion
- 1 cup chopped green bell pepper
- 1 teaspoon chili powder
- 1 teaspoon curry powder
- ½ teaspoon ground red pepper
- 1 can (14½ ounces) Mexican-style stewed tomatoes, undrained
- ⅓ cup golden raisins
- 1⅓ cups ⅓-less-salt chicken broth
- 1⅓ cups uncooked quick-cooking couscous
- ½ cup plain nonfat yogurt
- ¼ cup sliced green onions

1. Cut chicken into ¼-inch-thick slices; cut each slice into 1-inch strips.

2. Heat oil in large nonstick skillet over medium-high heat until hot. Add chicken; cook and stir 5 minutes or until chicken is no longer pink. Remove chicken from skillet; set aside.

3. Add onion, bell pepper, chili powder, curry powder and ground red pepper to same skillet; cook and stir 5 minutes or until vegetables are tender.

4. Stir chicken, tomatoes with liquid and raisins into skillet; bring to a boil over high heat. Cover; reduce heat to medium-low. Simmer 15 minutes. Uncover; simmer 5 minutes, stirring occasionally.

5. Meanwhile, place chicken broth in small saucepan; bring to a boil over high heat. Stir in couscous; cover. Remove saucepan from heat; let stand 5 minutes.

6. Spoon ½ cup couscous onto each serving plate; top with ¾ cup chicken mixture, 2 tablespoons yogurt and 1 tablespoon green onions. *Makes 4 servings*

268 ASIAN TURKEY NOODLE SALAD

- ½ teaspoon sesame oil
- ½ teaspoon reduced-sodium soy sauce
- 1 package (3 ounces) chicken flavor instant oriental noodle soup mix, prepared according to package directions
- ¾ pound fully cooked oven-roasted turkey breast, cut into ¼-inch cubes
- 4 ounces water chestnuts, drained and sliced
- 2 ounces fresh snow peas, blanched*
- 2 large fresh mushrooms, sliced
- ½ cup diagonally-cut carrots
- 2 tablespoons sliced green onions

To blanch snow peas: plunge snow peas in boiling water 45 seconds. Immediately drain and plunge into ice water.

1. In small bowl, combine sesame oil, soy sauce and prepared soup mix. Cover and refrigerate.

2. In large bowl, combine turkey, water chestnuts, snow peas, mushrooms, carrots and green onions. Fold noodle mixture into turkey mixture. Cover and refrigerate 2 hours. *Makes 4 servings*

Favorite recipe from **National Turkey Federation**

Indian Chicken with Couscous

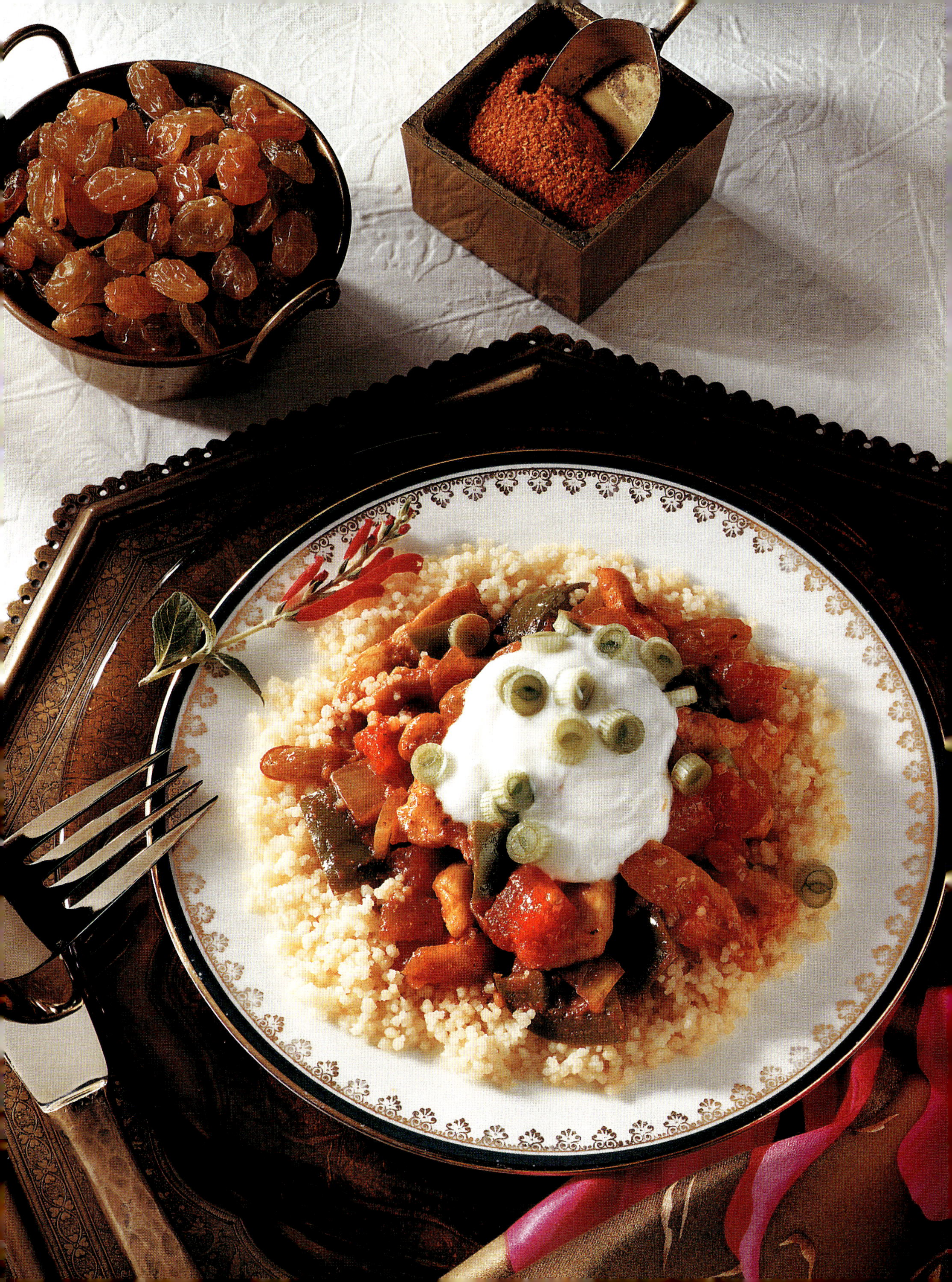

ASIAN FARE

269 SAUCY SHRIMP OVER CHINESE NOODLE CAKES

    Chinese Noodle Cakes (recipe follows)
1 teaspoon ketchup
2 tablespoons cornstarch, divided
1¼ cups water
4 tablespoons KIKKOMAN® Soy Sauce, divided
½ pound medium shrimp, peeled and deveined
2 tablespoons vegetable oil, divided
1 clove garlic, minced
1½ teaspoons minced fresh ginger root
1 green bell pepper, cut into chunks
1 medium onion, cut into chunks
2 stalks celery, cut diagonally into thin slices
2 tomatoes, cut into chunks

Prepare Chinese Noodle Cakes. Combine ketchup, 1 tablespoon cornstarch, water and 3 tablespoons soy sauce; set aside. Blend remaining 1 tablespoon *each* cornstarch and soy sauce in small bowl; stir in shrimp until coated. Heat 1 tablespoon oil in wok or large skillet over high heat. Add shrimp mixture; stir-fry 1 minute. Remove shrimp from wok; set aside. Heat remaining 1 tablespoon oil in wok. Add garlic and ginger; stir-fry until fragrant. Add bell pepper, onion and celery; stir-fry 4 minutes. Stir in soy sauce mixture, shrimp and tomatoes. Cook and stir until sauce boils and thickens. Cut Chinese Noodle Cakes into squares. Serve with shrimp mixture. *Makes 6 servings*

CHINESE NOODLE CAKES: Cook 8 ounces capellini (angel hair pasta) according to package directions. Drain; rinse under cold water and drain thoroughly. Heat 1 tablespoon vegetable oil in large nonstick skillet over medium-high heat. Add ½ of capellini; spread slightly to cover bottom of skillet to form noodle cake. Cook 5 minutes, without stirring, or until golden on bottom. Lift cake with wide spatula. Add 1 tablespoon vegetable oil to skillet; turn cake over. Cook 5 minutes or until golden brown, shaking skillet occasionally to brown evenly; remove to rack and keep warm in 200°F oven. Repeat with remaining capellini.

270 ASIAN CHILI PEPPER LINGUINE

1 (12-ounce) package PASTA LaBELLA® Chili Pepper Linguine
¼ cup vegetable oil
1 small carrot, julienned
1 small yellow squash, julienned
1 medium Spanish onion, chopped
2 cloves garlic, crushed
2 tablespoons roasted sesame seeds
2 tablespoons soy sauce
    Salt and black pepper to taste

Cook pasta according to package directions. In large skillet, heat oil. Add carrot, squash, onion and garlic; sauté 4 minutes. Add sesame seeds and soy sauce; simmer 2 minutes. Season with salt and pepper to taste. Serve over hot chili pepper linguine.
Makes 3 main-dish servings

Saucy Shrimp over Chinese Noodle Cakes

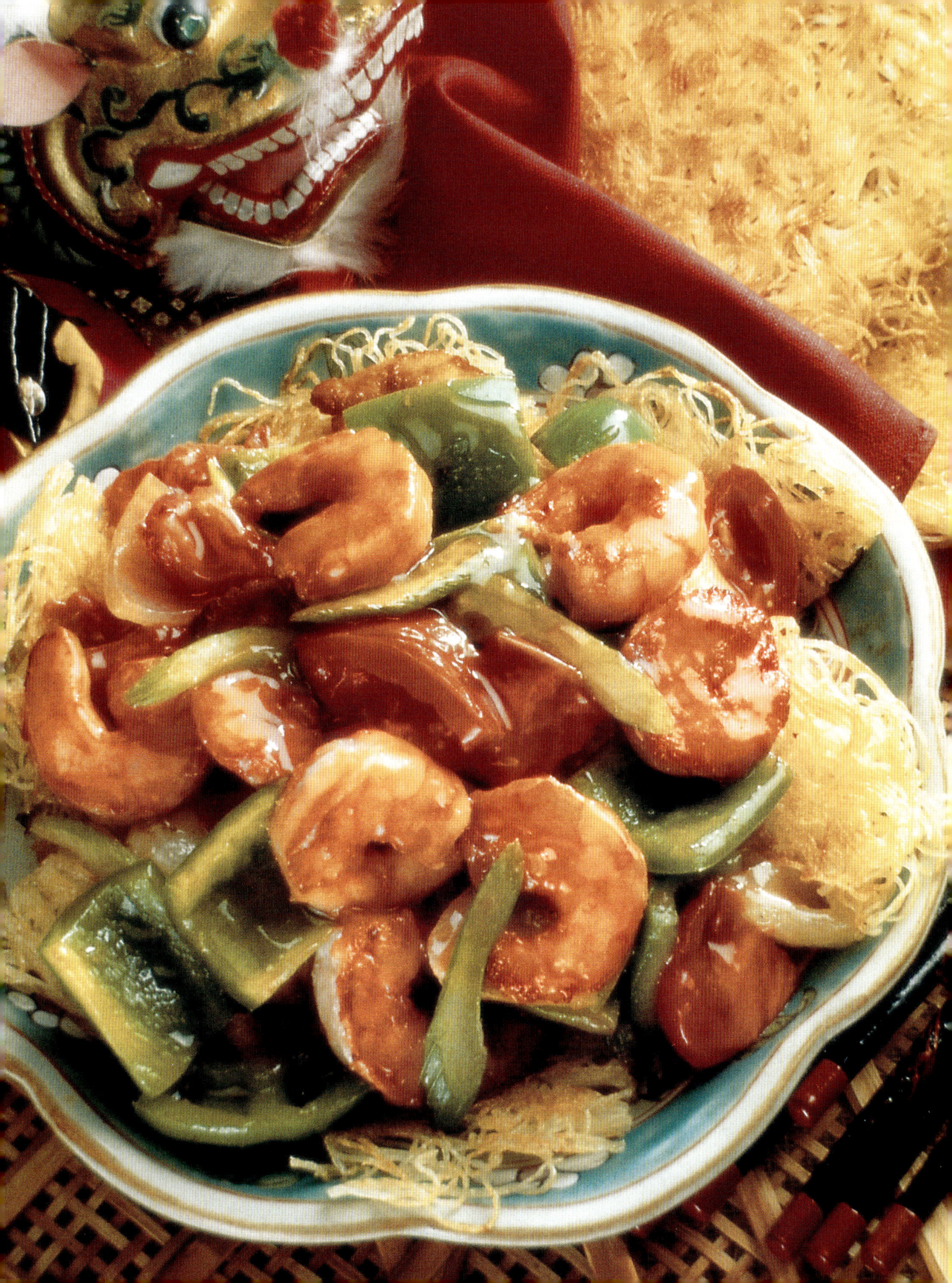

ASIAN FARE

271 SOBA STIR-FRY

8 ounces uncooked soba noodles (Japanese buckwheat pasta)
1 tablespoon light olive oil
2 cups sliced fresh shiitake mushrooms
1 medium red bell pepper, cut into thin strips
2 whole dried red peppers *or* ¼ teaspoon red pepper flakes
1 clove garlic, minced
2 cups shredded napa cabbage
½ cup ⅓-less-salt chicken broth
2 tablespoons reduced-sodium tamari or soy sauce
1 tablespoon rice wine or dry sherry
2 teaspoons cornstarch
1 package (14 ounces) firm tofu, drained and cut into 1-inch cubes
2 green onions, thinly sliced

1. Cook noodles according to package directions, omitting salt. Drain and set aside.

2. Heat oil in large nonstick skillet or wok over medium heat. Add mushrooms, bell pepper, dried peppers and garlic. Cook 3 minutes or until mushrooms are tender.

3. Add cabbage; cover. Cook 2 minutes or until cabbage is wilted.

4. Combine chicken broth, tamari, rice wine and cornstarch in small bowl. Stir sauce into vegetable mixture. Cook 2 minutes or until sauce is bubbly.

5. Stir in tofu and noodles; toss gently until heated through. Sprinkle with green onions. Serve immediately.

Makes 4 (2-cup) servings

272 ROASTED VEGETABLES WITH NOODLES

5 tablespoons soy sauce, divided
3 tablespoons peanut or vegetable oil
2 tablespoons rice vinegar
2 cloves garlic, minced
½ pound large fresh mushrooms
4 ounces shallots
1 medium zucchini, cut into 1-inch pieces, each piece cut into halves
1 medium yellow crookneck squash, cut into 1-inch pieces, each piece cut into halves
1 red bell pepper, cut into 1-inch pieces
1 yellow bell pepper, cut into 1-inch pieces
2 small Asian eggplants, cut into ½-inch slices *or* 2 cups cubed eggplant
8 ounces Chinese egg noodles or vermicelli, hot cooked, drained
1 tablespoon dark sesame oil

1. Preheat oven to 425°F. Combine 2 tablespoons soy sauce, peanut oil, vinegar and garlic in small bowl; mix well.

2. Combine vegetables in shallow roasting pan (do not line pan with foil). Toss with soy sauce mixture to coat well.

3. Roast vegetables 20 minutes or until browned and tender, stirring well after 10 minutes.

4. Place noodles in large bowl. Toss hot noodles with remaining 3 tablespoons soy sauce and sesame oil.

5. Toss roasted vegetables with noodle mixture; serve warm or at room temperature.

Makes 6 servings

Soba Stir-Fry

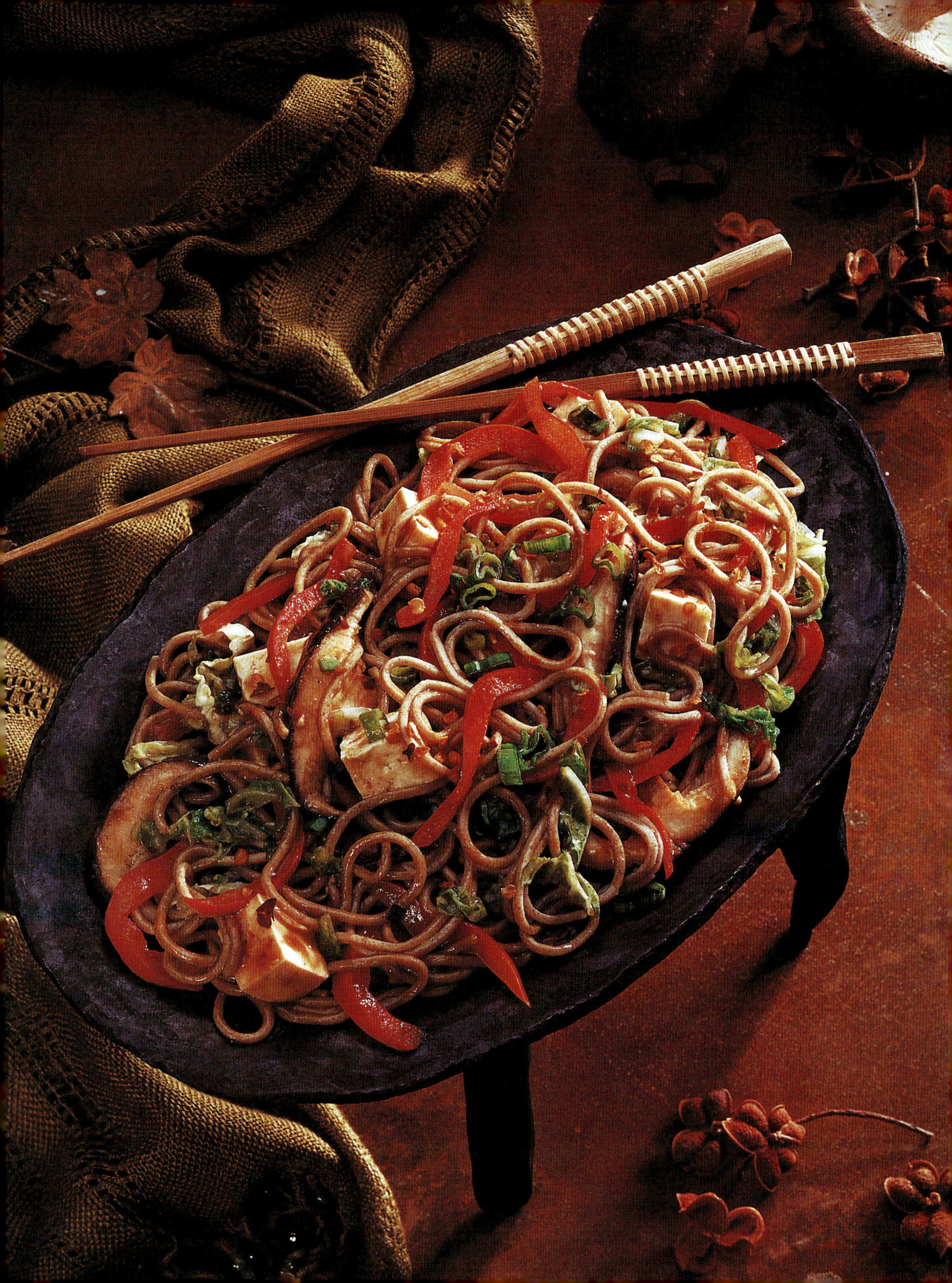

ASIAN FARE

273 THAI CHICKEN FETTUCCINE SALAD

6 ounces uncooked fettuccine
1 cup salsa
¼ cup chunky peanut butter
2 tablespoons honey
2 tablespoons orange juice
1 teaspoon soy sauce
½ teaspoon ground ginger
2 tablespoons vegetable oil
3 boneless skinless chicken breast halves (about 15 ounces), cut into 1-inch pieces
    Lettuce or savoy cabbage leaves (optional)
¼ cup coarsely chopped cilantro
¼ cup peanut halves
¼ cup thin red pepper strips, cut into halves
    Additional salsa (optional)

1. Cook pasta according to package directions; drain.

2. While pasta is cooking, combine 1 cup salsa, peanut butter, honey, orange juice, soy sauce and ginger in small saucepan. Cook and stir over low heat until blended and smooth. Reserve ¼ cup salsa mixture.

3. Place pasta in large bowl. Pour remaining salsa mixture over pasta; toss gently to coat.

4. Heat oil in large skillet over medium-high heat until hot. Cook and stir chicken in hot oil about 5 minutes until chicken is no longer pink in center. Add reserved salsa mixture; mix well.

5. Arrange lettuce leaves on serving platter, if desired. Arrange pasta on lettuce. Place chicken mixture on pasta. Top with cilantro, peanut halves and pepper strips.

6. Refrigerate until mixture is cooled to room temperature. Serve with additional salsa, if desired. *Makes 4 servings*

274 ORIENTAL MACARONI

3 cups uncooked macaroni
2 pounds ground steak or pork
1 medium onion, finely chopped
2 cloves garlic, minced
1½ cups hot water
    Salt and pepper
1 can (10 ounces) cream of tomato soup
2 tablespoons GRANDMA'S® molasses (Gold Label)

A. Cook macaroni. Drain and rinse.

B. Mix all other ingredients in medium saucepan, except soup and Grandma's molasses. Cook over medium heat about 45 minutes.

C. Add soup and Grandma's molasses; cook another 30 minutes. Mix in cooked macaroni. *Makes 5 servings*

MICROWAVE DIRECTIONS

Follow above directions with these modifications:

A. Bring 8 cups hot water to a boil at HIGH. Add macaroni and cook, uncovered, 15 minutes. Stir halfway through. Drain and rinse macaroni.

B. Cook 30 minutes at MEDIUM (70%) power.

C. Cook 10 minutes at MEDIUM power.

Thai Chicken Fettuccine Salad

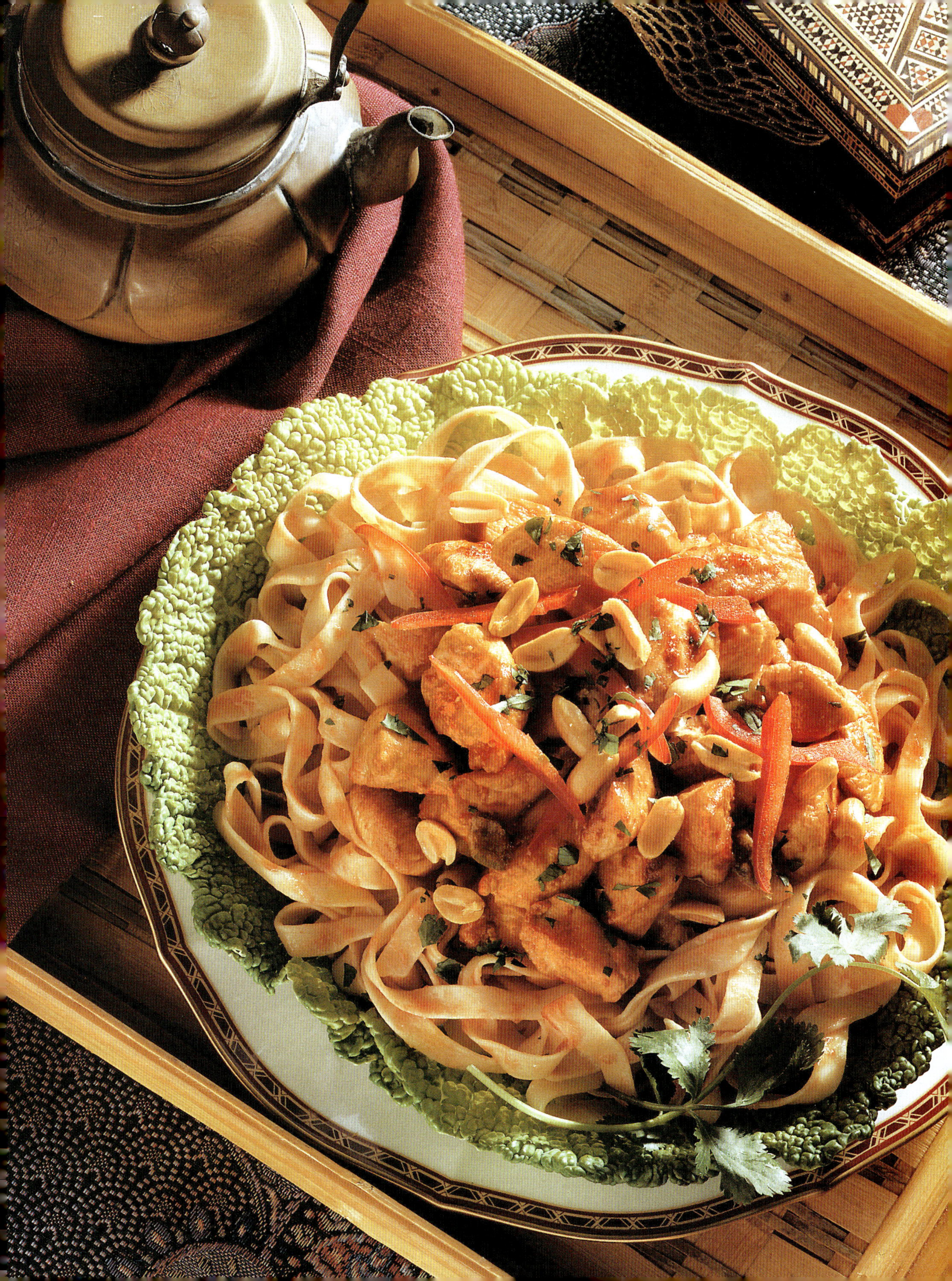

ASIAN FARE

275 TURKEY SHANGHAI

Nonstick cooking spray
12 ounces turkey breast tenderloin, thinly sliced
1 cup thinly sliced carrots
½ cup sliced green onions
3 cloves garlic, minced
4 cups ⅓-less-salt chicken broth
6 ounces uncooked angel hair pasta
2 cups frozen French-style green beans
¼ cup plus 2 tablespoons stir-fry sauce
1 teaspoon dark sesame oil

1. Spray large nonstick skillet with cooking spray; heat over medium heat until hot. Add turkey and carrots; cook and stir 5 minutes or until turkey is no longer pink. Stir in onions and garlic; cook and stir 2 minutes.

2. Add chicken broth to skillet; bring to a boil over high heat. Stir in pasta. Return to a boil. Reduce heat to low. Simmer, uncovered, 5 minutes, stirring frequently.

3. Stir green beans into skillet. Simmer 2 to 3 minutes or until pasta is just tender, stirring occasionally. Remove from heat. Stir in stir-fry sauce and sesame oil. Let stand 5 minutes. Garnish as desired.

Makes 6 servings

276 CLAMS IN BLACK BEAN SAUCE

24 small hard-shell clams
1½ tablespoons fermented, salted black beans
2 cloves garlic, minced
1 teaspoon minced fresh ginger
2 tablespoons vegetable oil
2 green onions, thinly sliced
1 cup chicken broth
2 tablespoons dry sherry
1 tablespoon soy sauce
1½ to 2 cups Chinese-style thin egg noodles, cooked and drained
3 tablespoons chopped fresh cilantro or parsley

1. Scrub clams under cold running water with stiff brush. (Discard any shells that refuse to close when tapped.)

2. Place beans in sieve and rinse under cold running water. Coarsely chop beans. Combine beans with garlic and ginger; finely chop all three together.

3. Heat oil in 5-quart pot over medium heat. Add black bean mixture and onions; stir-fry 30 seconds. Add clams and stir to coat.

4. Add chicken broth, sherry and soy sauce to pot. Bring to a boil; reduce heat, cover and simmer until clam shells open, 5 to 8 minutes. (Discard any clams that do not open.)

5. To serve, divide noodles equally among 4 large bowls. Arrange clams on top. Ladle broth over clams. Garnish each serving with cilantro.

Makes 4 servings

Turkey Shanghai

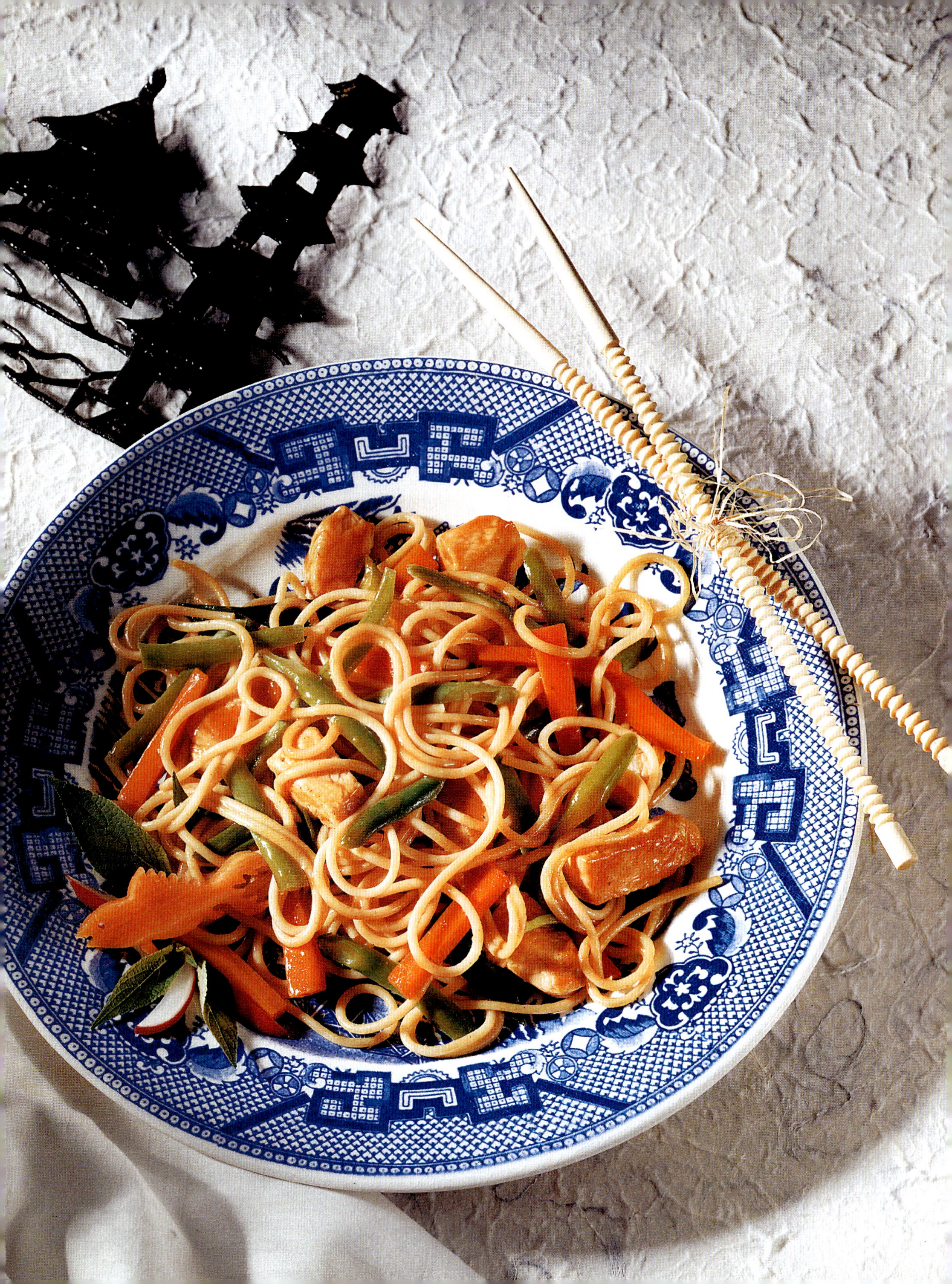

New Creations

277 SWEET POTATO RAVIOLI WITH ASIAGO CHEESE SAUCE

- ¾ pound sweet potato
- 2 tablespoons plain nonfat yogurt
- 1 teaspoon minced fresh chives
- 1 tablespoon plus ¼ teaspoon minced fresh sage, divided
- 24 wonton wrappers
- 1 tablespoon reduced-calorie margarine
- 1 tablespoon plus 2 teaspoons all-purpose flour
- ½ cup skim milk
- ½ cup ⅓-less-salt chicken broth
- ½ cup (2 ounces) shredded Asiago or Cheddar cheese
- ¼ teaspoon ground nutmeg
- ¼ teaspoon ground white pepper
- ⅛ teaspoon ground cinnamon

1. Preheat oven to 350°F. Bake sweet potato 40 to 45 minutes or until tender. Cool completely. Peel potato and mash pulp. Stir in yogurt, chives and ¼ teaspoon sage.

2. Place wonton wrappers on counter. Spoon 1 rounded teaspoon potato mixture in center of each wonton. Spread filling flat leaving ½-inch border. Brush edges lightly with water. Fold wontons in half diagonally, pressing lightly to seal. Place filled wontons on baking sheet and cover loosely with plastic wrap.

3. Bring 1½ quarts water to a boil in large saucepan. Reduce heat to medium. Add a few ravioli at a time. (Do not overcrowd.) Cook until tender, about 9 minutes. Transfer to platter with slotted spoon.

4. Melt margarine in small saucepan. Stir in flour; cook 1 minute, stirring constantly. Gradually stir in milk and chicken broth. Cook and stir until slightly thickened, about 4 minutes. Stir in cheese, nutmeg, white pepper and cinnamon.

5. Spoon 3 tablespoons sauce onto individual plates. Place 3 ravioli onto each plate. Sprinkle with remaining sage.

Makes 8 servings

Sweet Potato Ravioli with Asiago Cheese Sauce

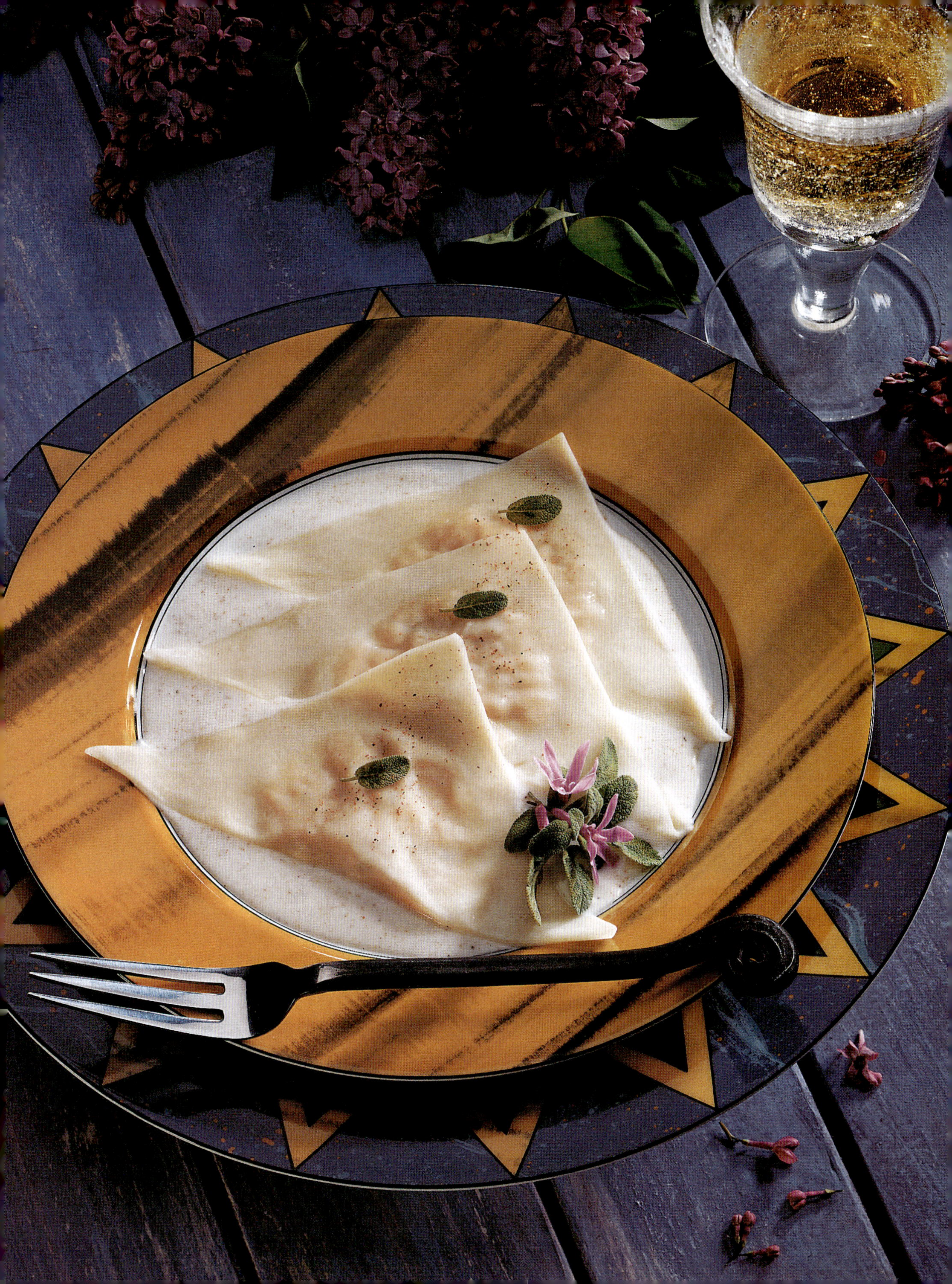

NEW CREATIONS

278 TORTELLINI KABOBS

2 tablespoons olive oil
1 large clove garlic, minced
1 can (15 ounces) CONTADINA® Tomato Sauce
2 tablespoons rinsed capers
2 tablespoons chopped fresh basil leaves
1 teaspoon Italian herb seasoning
¼ teaspoon red pepper flakes
6 cups of the following kabob ingredients: cooked drained meat- or cheese-filled tortellini, cocktail franks, cooked shrimp, whole button mushrooms, bell pepper chunks, cooked broccoli, cooked cauliflowerets, onion pieces

Heat oil in medium saucepan over medium-high heat. Add garlic; cook and stir until lightly browned. Stir in tomato sauce, capers, basil, Italian seasoning and red pepper flakes. Bring to a boil. Reduce heat to low; simmer 5 to 10 minutes, stirring occasionally.

Combine kabob ingredients in medium bowl; cover with tomato sauce mixture. Marinate in refrigerator 15 minutes or longer, if desired, stirring occasionally. Place on skewers. Broil 5 inches from heat source until heated through, turning once during cooking and brushing with any remaining tomato sauce mixture.

Makes 12 appetizer servings

279 VEGETABLE PASTA ITALIANO

½ pound lean ground turkey
1 DOLE® Red Bell Pepper, seeded, sliced
1 tablespoon paprika
1 can (14½ ounces) crushed tomatoes
1 can (14½ ounces) reduced-sodium chicken broth
2 cups uncooked bow tie pasta
2 cups DOLE® Broccoli Florettes
1 cup DOLE® Cauliflower Florettes
Savory Topping (recipe follows)

• In 12-inch nonstick skillet, brown turkey 2 minutes.

• Stir in red pepper strips and paprika. Reduce heat to low, stirring 2 minutes longer.

• Stir in tomatoes, chicken broth and pasta. Bring to a boil. Reduce heat to low, cover and simmer 15 minutes. Arrange broccoli and cauliflower on top. Cover, simmer 10 minutes or until pasta is soft.

• Sprinkle with Savory Topping. Let stand 3 minutes before serving.

Makes 6 servings

SAVORY TOPPING
¼ cup seasoned dry bread crumbs
¼ cup grated Parmesan cheese
¼ cup minced parsley

Combine all ingredients.

Tortellini Kabobs

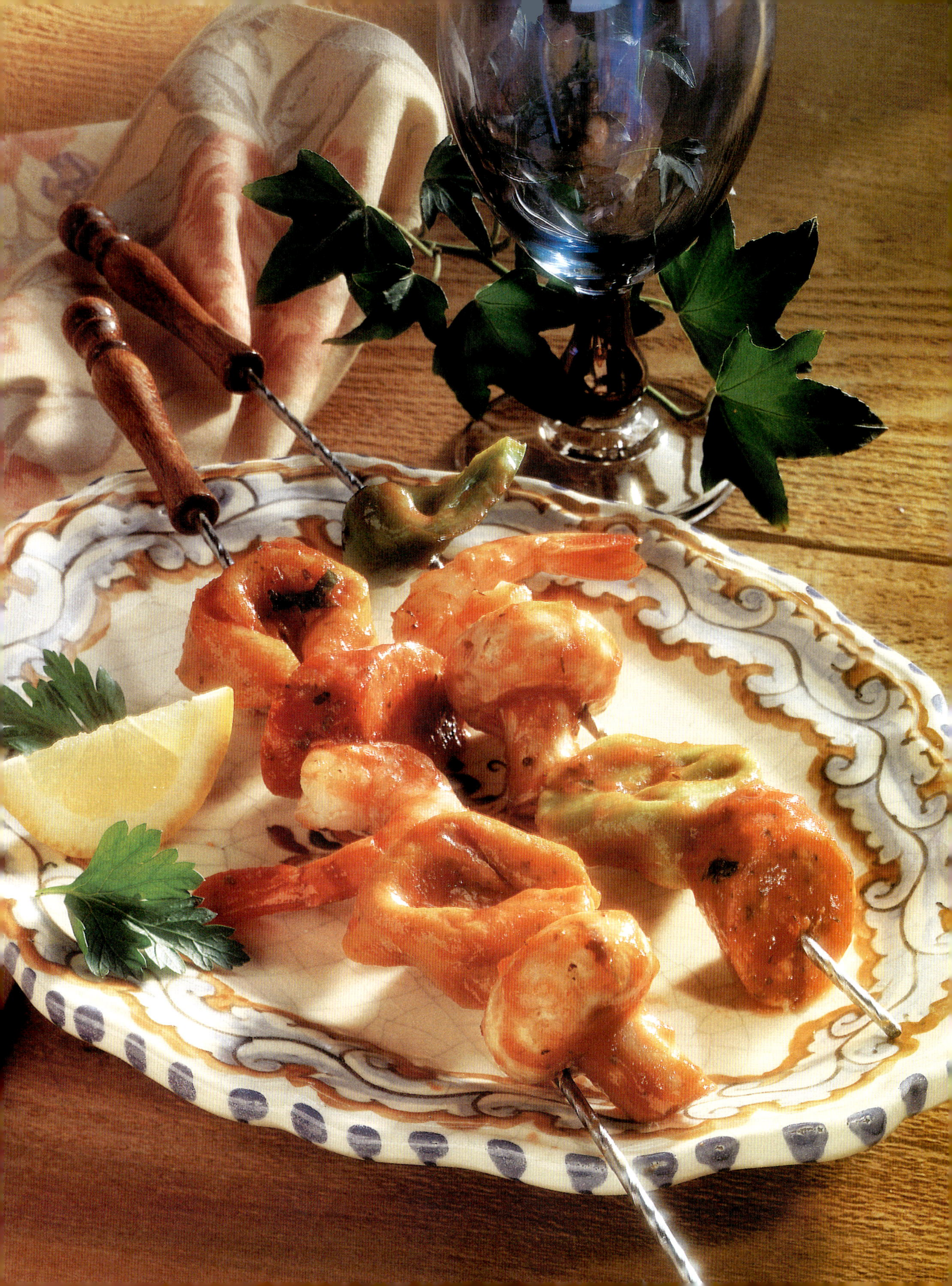

NEW CREATIONS

280 SOUTHERN GREENS AND PASTA

- 2 teaspoons olive oil
- 1 cup chopped green bell pepper
- ½ cup chopped onion
- ½ cup peeled and chopped jicama
- ⅓ cup chopped celery
- 1 clove garlic, minced
- 1 can (about 14 ounces) ⅓-less-salt chicken broth
- 2 tablespoons tomato paste
- 1 teaspoon dried oregano leaves
- ¼ teaspoon ground black pepper
- 1 package (10 ounces) frozen black-eyed peas
- 4 ounces uncooked radiatore or other medium-shape pasta
- 1 head chicory, mustard greens or kale, washed, ribs removed, thinly sliced
- 2 to 3 drops hot pepper sauce

1. Heat oil in large saucepan. Add bell pepper, onion, jicama, celery and garlic. Cook over medium heat 3 minutes. Stir in chicken broth, tomato paste, oregano and black pepper. Bring to a boil; stir in peas. Cover and simmer over low heat 20 minutes or until peas are tender.

2. Cook pasta according to package directions, omitting salt. Drain and set aside.

3. Add chicory to saucepan; cover and cook on low until wilted, about 3 minutes. Stir in pasta. Cook until heated through. Season to taste with red pepper sauce. Garnish as desired. *Makes 12 (½-cup) servings*

281 MINI NOODLE KUGELS WITH RASPBERRY FILLING

- 4 ounces medium or wide egg noodles, uncooked
- ½ cup egg substitute
- 3 tablespoons sugar
- ¼ teaspoon ground cinnamon
  Pinch ground nutmeg
- ½ cup low-fat cottage cheese
- ⅓ cup applesauce
- ¼ cup chopped dried apples or raisins
  Vegetable oil cooking spray
- 6 tablespoons raspberry jam

Preheat oven to 350°F. Prepare egg noodles according to package directions. While noodles are cooking, beat egg substitute, sugar, cinnamon and nutmeg in large bowl until sugar is dissolved and mixture is foamy. Fold in cottage cheese, applesauce and apples. Lightly spray muffin tin (preferably nonstick) with cooking spray. (Do not use baking cups.)

Drain noodles and immediately add them to egg mixture. Fill each muffin tin cup ½ full. Add 2 teaspoons raspberry jam to each, then fill muffin cups to full. Bake until firm and tops are golden brown, about 45 minutes. Serve warm. *Makes 9 servings*

Favorite recipe from **National Pasta Association**

Southern Greens and Pasta

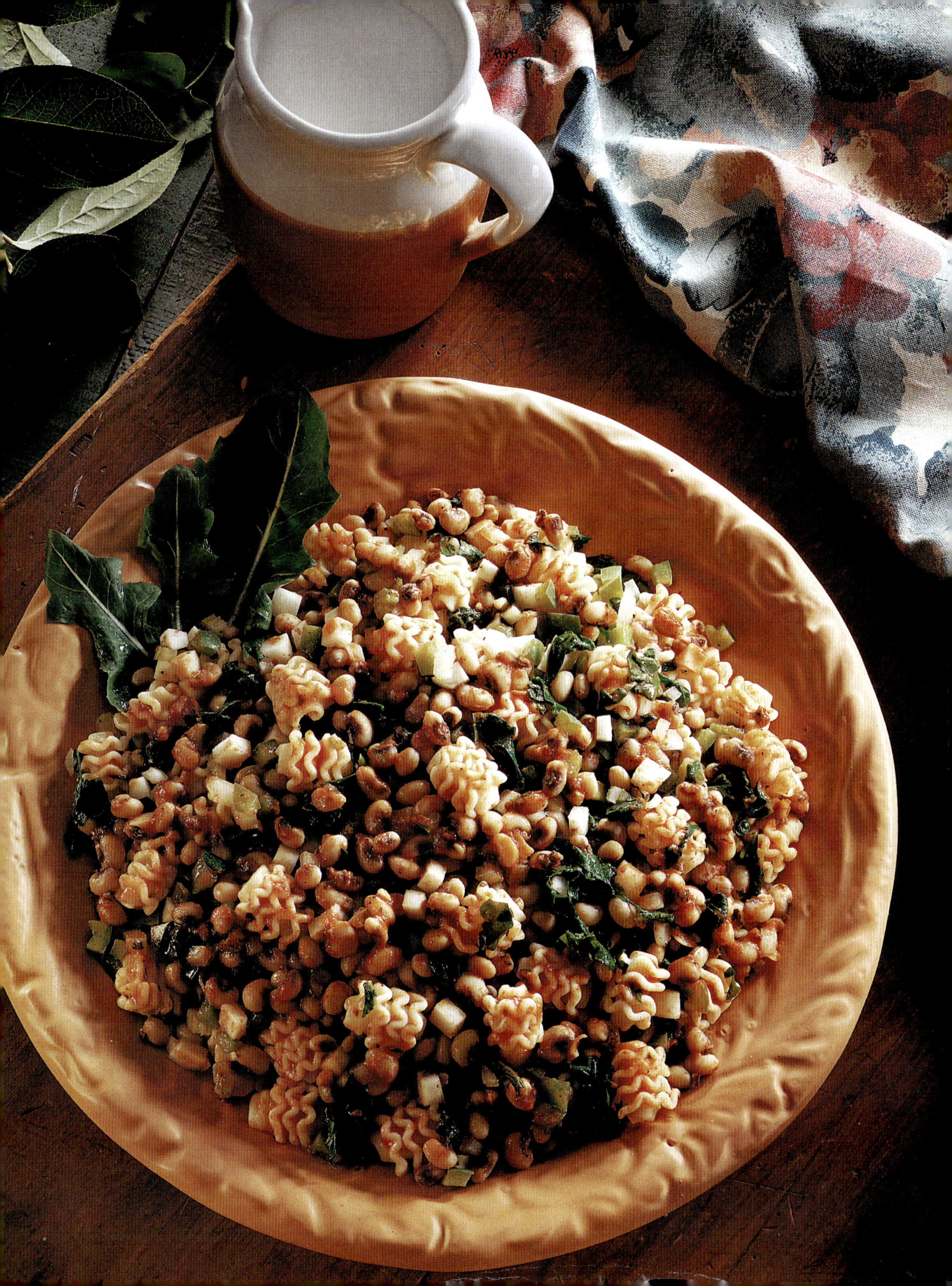

NEW CREATIONS

282 MICROWAVE PASTA PIE

- 8 ounces spaghetti, cooked and drained
- ¼ cup grated Parmesan cheese
- 1 tablespoon butter or margarine
- 1 package (1 pound) PERDUE® Fresh Sweet or Hot Italian Turkey Sausage
- ½ cup chopped onion
- 1 Italian sweet pepper, chopped
- 1 can (15 ounces) herbed tomato sauce
- 1 clove garlic, minced
- 1 tablespoon chopped fresh parsley
- ½ teaspoon dried basil leaves
- ½ teaspoon dried oregano leaves
- 1 package (4 ounces) shredded mozzarella cheese

In 10-inch microwave-safe pie plate, place spaghetti. Add Parmesan cheese and butter; toss until evenly coated. Arrange pasta on bottom and up side of plate to form pasta crust; cover with aluminum foil and set aside.

In 2½-quart microwave-safe dish, arrange sausage; cover with waxed paper. Microwave at HIGH 4 minutes. Cut sausage into thin slices. Stir in onion and sweet pepper; cover with waxed paper and microwave at HIGH 3 to 4 minutes, stirring twice. Drain off pan juices.

Stir tomato sauce, garlic, parsley, basil and oregano into meat mixture; pour into pasta shell. Sprinkle mozzarella cheese in circle over sauce. Microwave uncovered at HIGH 1 to 2 minutes until cheese is melted. Cover with foil and let stand 5 minutes.

Makes 4 to 6 servings

283 TOMATO BASIL LINGUINE MODENA STYLE

- 1 (12-ounce) package PASTA LaBELLA® Tomato Basil Linguine
- ¼ cup extra-virgin olive oil
- ½ cup julienned red onion
- ½ cup julienned yellow bell pepper
- ½ cup julienned eggplant
- ½ cup julienned zucchini
- ¼ cup chopped fresh basil
- 1 teaspoon dried oregano leaves
- ½ teaspoon garlic powder
- ½ teaspoon onion powder
- ¼ teaspoon salt
- ¼ teaspoon black pepper
- ¼ cup balsamic vinegar
- ⅓ cup chicken broth
- 1½ tablespoons butter
- ¼ cup grated Parmesan cheese

Cook pasta according to package directions. Meanwhile, heat olive oil in large pot over medium heat. Add all vegetables and spices to olive oil. Stir and sauté 7 minutes. Add vinegar and chicken broth; simmer 3 minutes. Mix in butter and hot *al dente* pasta; toss well. To finish, portion pasta into bowls, top with Parmesan cheese and serve.

Makes 3 main-dish servings

NEW CREATIONS

284 FRESH APRICOT–PASTA SALAD

2½ cups California fresh apricots (about 1 pound), cut into sixths, divided
2 tablespoons white wine vinegar
¼ cup olive oil
1 tablespoon chopped fresh basil leaves *or* 1 teaspoon dried basil leaves
Salt and fresh ground black pepper to taste
2 cups cooked spiral-shaped pasta (fusilli)
2 small zucchini, julienned
1 whole chicken breast, cooked, skinned, boned and shredded
1 red bell pepper, julienned

Place ½ cup apricots and vinegar in food processor or blender container; cover. Process until smooth. Gradually add oil, while processing, until dressing thickens. Stir in basil. Season with salt and black pepper to taste; set aside. Combine remaining 2 cups apricots, pasta, zucchini, chicken and bell pepper in large bowl. Add dressing; toss to coat.   *Makes 6 servings*

Favorite recipe from **California Apricot Advisory Board**

285 CHICKEN SIESTA TWIST

1 pound rotini pasta
1 teaspoon garlic powder
1 packet taco seasoning, divided
2 to 3 boneless skinless chicken breasts, cut into cubes
½ green or red bell pepper, sliced
1 (10-ounce) can tomatoes with green chilies
Sour cream or low-fat sour cream
Chopped green onions

Cook pasta according to package directions; drain and keep warm. Mix garlic powder and all but 1 teaspoon taco seasoning in small bowl; toss garlic-taco mixture with chicken. Spray medium skillet with cooking spray. Brown chicken over medium-high heat; add bell pepper and tomatoes. Cover and simmer 10 to 15 minutes. Toss pasta with remaining taco seasoning. Place on large serving plate. Top with chicken mixture, sour cream and chopped green onions.

Makes 4 to 5 servings

Favorite recipe from **North Dakota Wheat Commission**

NEW CREATIONS

286 PASTA WITH FRESH VEGETABLES IN GARLIC SAUCE

3 medium carrots
2 small zucchini
¼ cup butter or margarine
1 large onion, chopped
4 cloves garlic, minced
½ cup chicken broth
½ cup heavy cream
½ teaspoon salt
½ teaspoon dried tarragon leaves
¼ teaspoon black pepper
2 cups hot, cooked, drained pasta (fettuccine, ziti or shells)

Cut carrots and zucchini lengthwise into thin slices with vegetable peeler. Bring 1 inch water to a boil in medium saucepan; add carrots and zucchini. Cook until crisp-tender. Remove from saucepan and drain; set aside. Melt butter in same saucepan over medium heat. Add onion and garlic; cook until tender. Gradually stir in broth, cream, salt, tarragon and pepper; simmer 5 minutes or until sauce is slightly thickened. Add vegetables; heat thoroughly, stirring occasionally. Add vegetables and sauce to hot cooked pasta; toss lightly.

Makes 4 servings

287 TURKEY AND AVOCADO IN ORANGE SAUCE

1 pound turkey cutlets, cut into ½-inch strips
2 cloves garlic, minced
1 tablespoon margarine
3 ounces frozen orange juice concentrate, thawed
½ cup reduced-sodium chicken bouillon
2 teaspoons hot sauce
1½ teaspoons Worcestershire sauce
2 tablespoons packed brown sugar
1 tablespoon cornstarch
2 tablespoons water
1 avocado, peeled and cubed
1 can (11 ounces) mandarin oranges
8 ounces linguine, cooked
4 tablespoons almonds, toasted (optional)

1. In large skillet, over medium heat, sauté turkey and garlic in margarine 2 to 3 minutes or until turkey is no longer pink.

2. Stir in orange juice concentrate, bouillon, hot sauce, Worcestershire sauce and brown sugar; bring to boil. Reduce heat and simmer 4 to 5 minutes.

3. In small bowl, combine cornstarch and water; stir into turkey mixture. Cook and stir mixture until slightly thickened. Gently fold in avocado and oranges. Heat 1 minute.

4. To serve, spoon turkey mixture over linguine. Top with almonds, if desired.

Makes 4 servings

Favorite recipe from **National Turkey Federation**

Pasta with Fresh Vegetables in Garlic Sauce

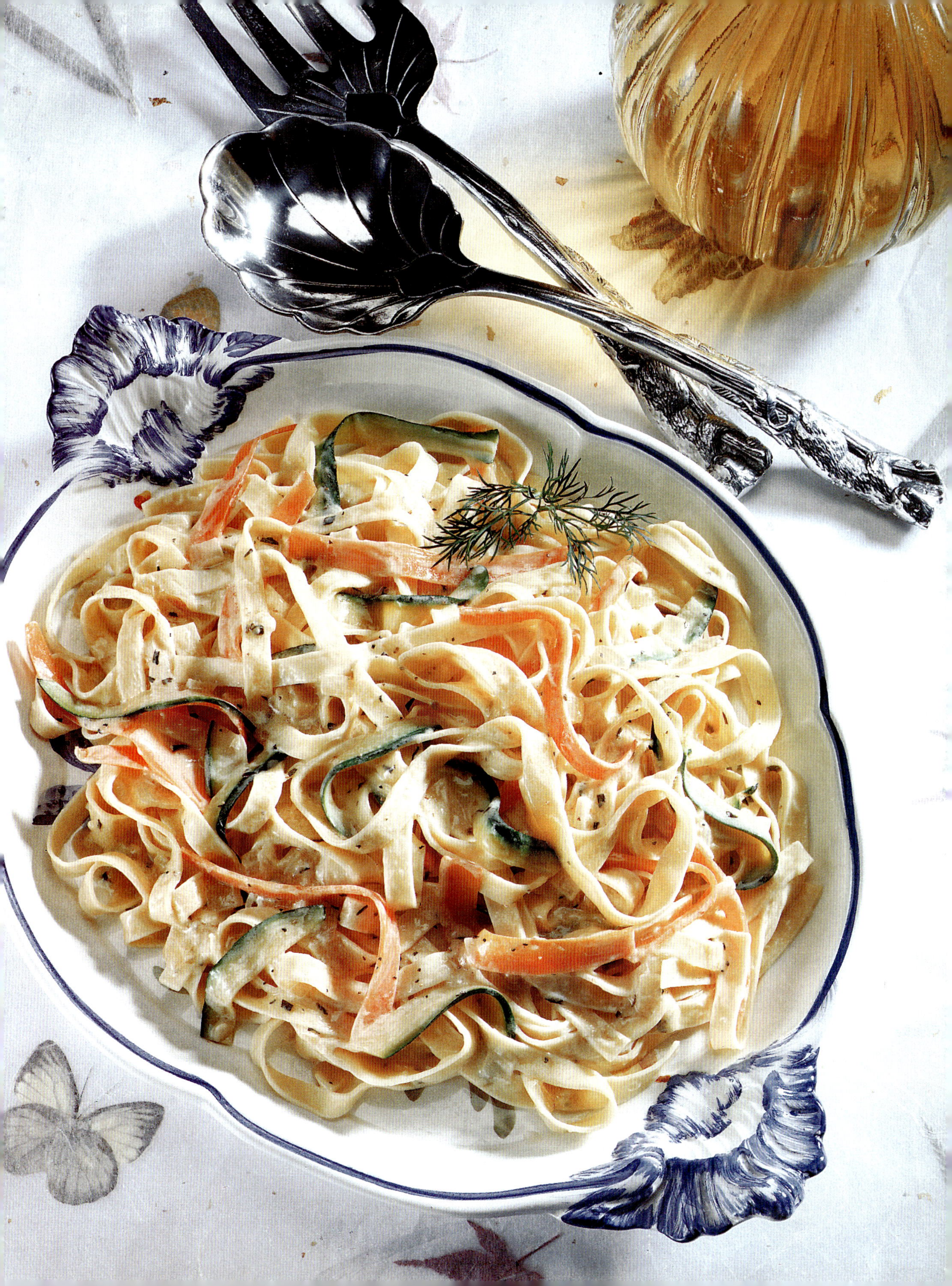

NEW CREATIONS

288 PASTA WITH ONIONS AND GOAT CHEESE

- 2 teaspoons olive oil
- 4 cups thinly sliced sweet onions
- ¾ cup (3 ounces) goat cheese
- ¼ cup skim milk
- 6 ounces uncooked baby bow tie or other small pasta
- 1 clove garlic, minced
- 2 tablespoons dry white wine or fat-free reduced-sodium chicken broth
- 1½ teaspoons chopped fresh sage *or* ½ teaspoon dried sage leaves
- ½ teaspoon salt
- ¼ teaspoon black pepper
- 2 tablespoons chopped toasted walnuts

Heat oil in large nonstick skillet over medium heat. Add onions; cook slowly until golden and caramelized, about 20 to 25 minutes, stirring occasionally.

Combine goat cheese and milk in small bowl; stir until well blended. Set aside.

Cook pasta according to package directions, omitting salt. Drain and set aside.

Add garlic to onions in skillet; cook until softened, about 3 minutes. Add wine, sage, salt and pepper; cook until moisture is evaporated. Remove from heat; add pasta and goat cheese mixture, stirring to melt cheese. Sprinkle with walnuts.

Makes 8 (½-cup) servings

289 SOUTHWEST SPAGHETTI PIE

- 8 ounces spaghetti or linguine, cooked and drained
- 1 egg
- ½ cup skim milk
- ½ pound ground pork
- 1 medium onion, chopped
- 1 medium green bell pepper, chopped
- 1 jalapeño pepper, minced
- 1 large clove garlic, minced
- 1 can (16 ounces) tomato sauce
- 1 tablespoon chili powder
- ½ teaspoon ground cumin
- ½ teaspoon dried oregano leaves
- ½ teaspoon salt
- ¼ teaspoon freshly ground black pepper
- 1 cup (4 ounces) shredded Monterey Jack cheese
- 1 cup (4 ounces) shredded Cheddar cheese

Beat egg and milk in large bowl. Add hot pasta; toss lightly to coat. Spread evenly into 13×9-inch casserole sprayed with vegetable spray. In large skillet over medium heat, brown pork with onion, bell pepper, jalapeño pepper and garlic, stirring occasionally to separate meat. Drain off excess fat. Stir in tomato sauce and seasonings. Reduce heat to low; simmer 5 minutes, stirring occasionally. Spread meat mixture over spaghetti mixture. Sprinkle with cheeses. Bake at 425°F 15 minutes or until cheese is melted and mixture is hot and bubbly. Let stand 5 minutes before cutting to serve.

Makes 4 to 6 servings

Favorite recipe from **National Pasta Association**

Pasta with Onions and Goat Cheese

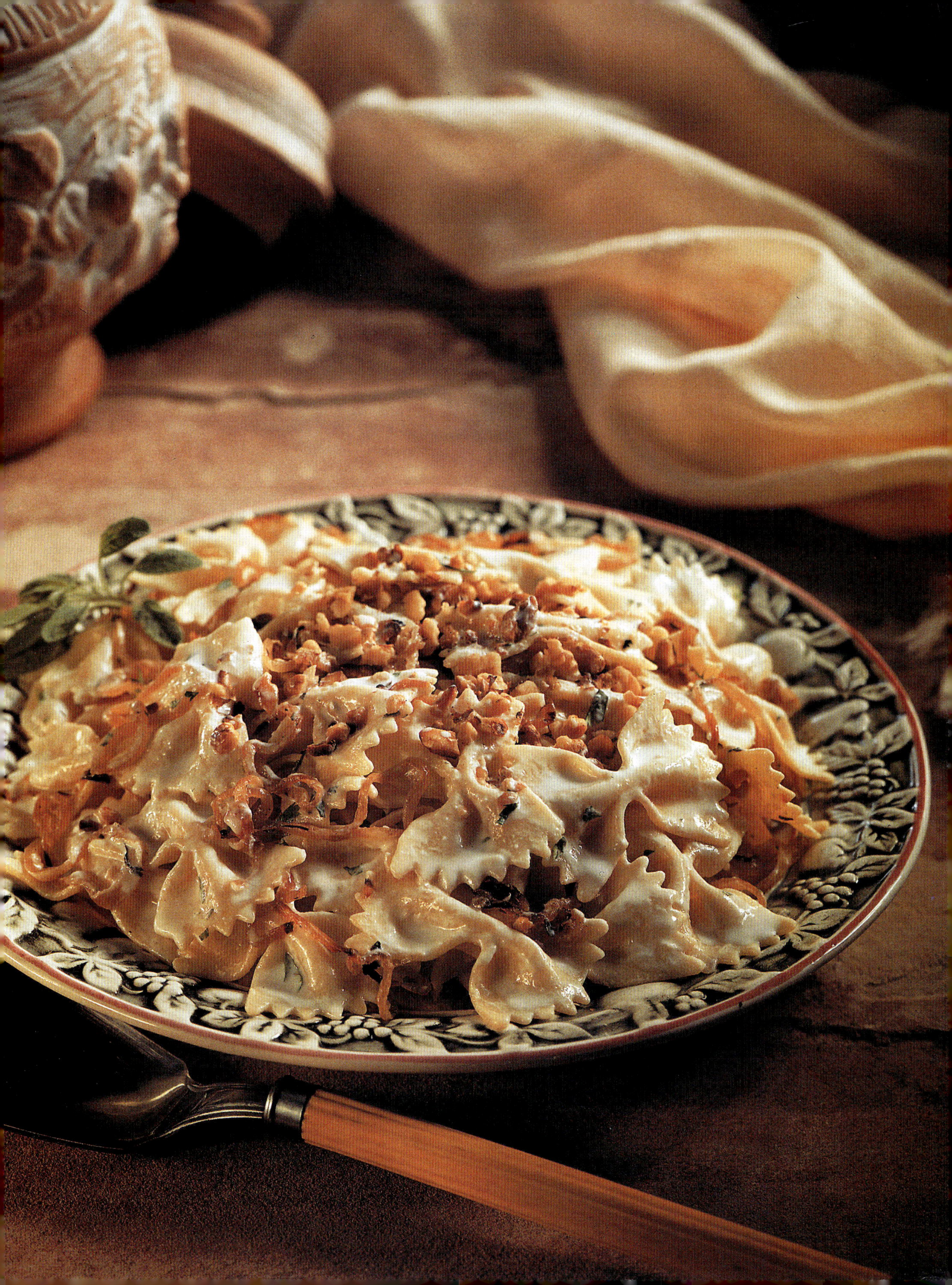

NEW CREATIONS

290 TURKEY MEATBALLS IN A PASTA CROWN

- 1 pound ground turkey
- 1 cup finely chopped onion
- 1 clove garlic, minced
- 3 tablespoons dried parsley, divided
- ½ cup seasoned bread crumbs
- ¼ cup grated Parmesan cheese
- ½ teaspoon salt
- ¼ teaspoon black pepper
- 1 tablespoon vegetable oil
- 3 cups spaghetti sauce
- 8 ounces thin spaghetti
- ½ teaspoon Italian seasoning
- ½ cup shredded mozzarella cheese

1. In medium bowl, combine turkey, onion, garlic, 1 tablespoon parsley, bread crumbs, Parmesan cheese, salt and pepper. Shape mixture into 12 meatballs.

2. In large skillet, over medium-high heat, sauté meatballs in oil. Reduce heat to medium-low, cover skillet and cook 6 to 8 minutes or until meatballs are no longer pink in centers.

3. In large saucepan, over low heat, warm spaghetti sauce.

4. Prepare spaghetti according to package directions; drain, do not rinse. Return spaghetti to cooking pan. Stir in remaining parsley, Italian seasoning and mozzarella cheese.

5. Arrange meatballs on bottom of lightly greased 7-cup ring mold. Top with spaghetti, pressing firmly to mold spaghetti around meatballs. Allow mold to stand 1 to 2 minutes.

6. Invert mold onto large platter. Spoon spaghetti sauce into center of pasta crown.
Makes 6 servings

Favorite recipe from **National Turkey Federation**

291 QUICK TORTELLINI WITH ARTICHOKES

- 1 package (9 ounces) DiGIORNO® Cheese Tortellini or Mozzarella Garlic Tortelloni, cooked, drained
- 1 can (14 ounces) artichoke hearts, drained, quartered
- ½ red bell pepper, cut into thin strips
- 1 green onion, thinly sliced
- 1 package (7 ounces) DiGIORNO® Pesto Sauce or Olive Oil and Garlic Sauce

PLACE all ingredients except pesto sauce in large bowl.

STIR sauce. Add to pasta mixture; toss lightly. Serve immediately or refrigerate. Let refrigerated mixture stand at room temperature 30 minutes before serving; toss before serving. *Makes 4 servings*

Prep time: 15 minutes

NEW CREATIONS

292 MINI MEATBALLS WITH PASTA AND APPLE PESTO

PESTO
- 2 cups fresh basil leaves
- 1 Granny Smith apple, peeled, cored and cut into large chunks
- ½ cup grated Parmesan cheese
- ½ cup walnuts
- 1 clove garlic
- 1 teaspoon TABASCO® pepper sauce
- ¼ teaspoon salt
- ¼ cup olive oil
- 8 ounces bow tie pasta

MEATBALLS
- ½ pound lean ground beef
- ½ pound ground turkey
- 1 egg
- ¼ cup dry seasoned bread crumbs
- ¼ cup club soda
- 1 tablespoon TABASCO® pepper sauce
- ½ cup water
- ½ cup roasted red peppers, cut into strips

• In food processor or blender, process basil, apple, cheese, walnuts, garlic, 1 teaspoon TABASCO sauce and salt. Gradually add oil until mixture is smooth.

• Prepare bow tie pasta according to package directions. Drain.

• Meanwhile, in large bowl, combine ground beef, turkey, egg, bread crumbs, club soda and 1 tablespoon TABASCO sauce until well mixed. Shape tablespoonfuls of meat mixture into balls.

• In 12-inch nonstick skillet over medium-high heat, cook meatballs until well browned on all sides, turning frequently. Add water to skillet; over high heat, heat to boiling. Reduce heat to low; cover and simmer 10 minutes.

• In large bowl, toss cooked pasta, pesto sauce, meatballs with their liquid and red peppers until well mixed. Serve immediately.
Makes 6 servings

293 GORGONZOLA CREAM SAUCE WITH TOMATO BASIL PASTA

- 1 package (8 ounces) dry CONTADINA® Dalla Casa Buitoni Tomato Basil Fusilli, cooked, drained, kept warm
- 1 teaspoon cornstarch
- ½ cup whipping cream
- ½ cup (2½ ounces) crumbled Gorgonzola cheese
- ¼ teaspoon salt
- 2 tablespoons chopped walnuts (optional)

Place cornstarch in small saucepan; stir in small amount of cream until smooth. Stir in remaining cream, cheese and salt. Heat over medium-low heat until mixture comes to a boil. Reduce heat; cook 1 minute.

Toss sauce with pasta in large bowl. Sprinkle with walnuts before serving, if desired.
Makes 4 servings

NEW CREATIONS

294 SWEET PEPPERED PASTA

- 3 tablespoons MAZOLA® Corn Oil
- ½ cup finely chopped onion
- ½ cup minced red bell pepper
- ½ cup minced yellow bell pepper
- 3 large cloves garlic, minced
- ⅓ cup water
- 2 tablespoons chopped fresh basil
- 1 chicken-flavored bouillon cube
- ¼ teaspoon crushed red pepper
- 7 ounces MUELLER'S® Pasta Ruffles, hot cooked and drained
- Salad greens (optional)

In large skillet, heat corn oil over medium-high heat. Add onion, red and yellow bell peppers and garlic; cook and stir 4 minutes. Stir in water, basil, bouillon cube and crushed red pepper. Bring to a boil,stirring occasionally. Reduce heat to low; simmer 4 minutes. Spoon over pasta in large bowl; toss to coat well. Serve on assorted salad greens, if desired. *Makes 6 servings*

295 PASTA WITH HEARTS

- 8 ounces mostaccioli, rotini or other medium-shape pasta, uncooked
- 1 (8-ounce) jar roasted red peppers, drained
- ¼ teaspoon red pepper flakes
- 4 to 6 drops red pepper sauce
- 2 cloves garlic
- 2 teaspoons balsamic vinegar
- 4 teaspoons vegetable or olive oil
- ¼ cup white wine
- ½ cup nonfat plain yogurt
- 8 ounces shrimp, shelled and steamed or boiled
- 1 (8½-ounce) can artichoke hearts, drained

Cook pasta according to package directions; drain.

In food processor or blender, combine red peppers with red pepper flakes, pepper sauce, garlic and vinegar. Purée until smooth.

Transfer the mixture to small skillet; heat through. Add oil; stir to combine. Add wine and simmer until mixture reduces. Just before serving, stir in yogurt until warmed through. Remove from heat. In large mixing bowl, toss together cooked pasta, shrimp, artichoke hearts and yogurt dressing. Serve immediately. *Makes 4 servings*

Favorite recipe from **National Pasta Association**

Sweet Peppered Pasta

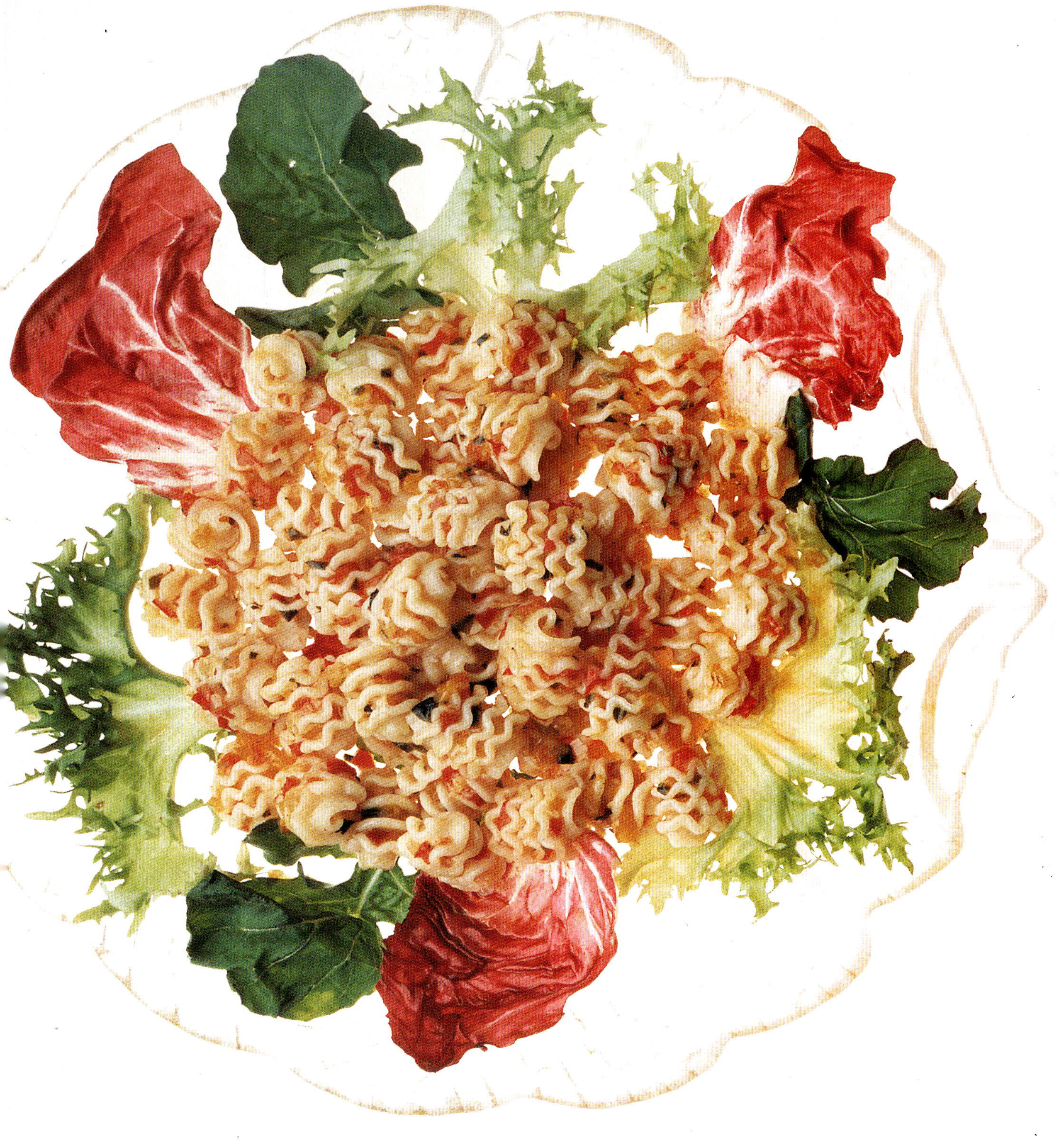

NEW CREATIONS

296 ALMOND CRUNCH MACARONI CUSTARD

CUSTARD
- 2 eggs
- 1 cup milk
- ½ cup packed brown sugar
- ¼ cup all-purpose flour
- ¼ cup butter, softened
- 1½ teaspoons almond extract
- ½ cup uncooked ring macaroni, cooked and drained

ALMOND TOPPING
- ½ cup slivered almonds
- ⅓ cup packed brown sugar
- 2 tablespoons butter, softened
- 1 tablespoon milk

For custard, combine all custard ingredients except macaroni in covered blender. Blend at medium speed 2 minutes. Fold macaroni into egg mixture in large bowl. Spoon into greased and floured 8-inch square pan. Bake in preheated 350°F oven 40 to 45 minutes or until set.

For almond topping, mix all topping ingredients in small bowl. Spread over custard. Broil 2 to 3 minutes or until topping is bubbly and golden brown. Garnish as desired. *Makes 9 servings*

Favorite recipe from **North Dakota Wheat Commission**

297 PASTA "PIZZA"

- 2 cups corkscrew macaroni, cooked and drained
- 3 eggs, lightly beaten
- ½ cup milk
- ½ cup (2 ounces) shredded Wisconsin Cheddar cheese
- ¼ cup finely chopped onion
- 1 pound lean ground beef
- 1 can (15 ounces) tomato sauce
- 1 teaspoon dried basil leaves
- 1 teaspoon dried oregano leaves
- ½ teaspoon garlic salt
- 1 medium tomato, thinly sliced
- 1 green bell pepper, sliced into rings
- 1½ cups (6 ounces) shredded Wisconsin Mozzarella cheese

Combine eggs and milk in small bowl. Add to hot macaroni; mix lightly to coat. Stir in Cheddar cheese and onion; mix well. Spread macaroni mixture onto bottom of well-buttered 14-inch pizza pan. Bake at 350°F 25 minutes. Meanwhile, in large skillet over medium-high heat, brown meat, stirring occasionally to separate meat; drain. Stir in tomato sauce, basil, oregano and garlic salt. Spoon over macaroni crust. Arrange tomato slices and pepper rings on top. Sprinkle with Mozzarella cheese. Continue baking 15 minutes or until cheese is bubbly.
Makes 8 servings

Prep time: 50 minutes

Favorite recipe from **Wisconsin Milk Marketing Board**

Almond Crunch Macaroni Custard

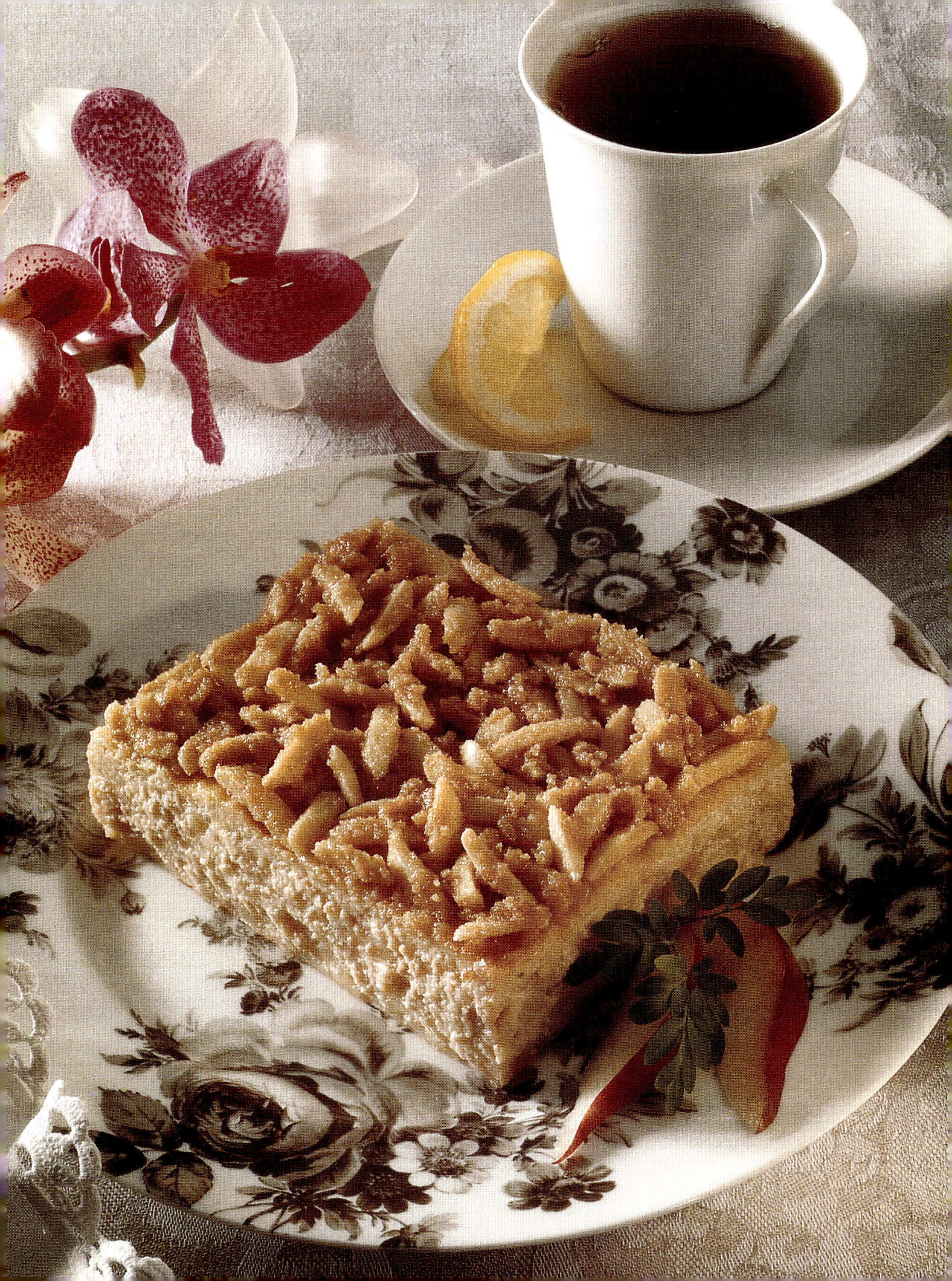

NEW CREATIONS

298 MICRO–MEATBALL RIGATONI

1 package (about 1¼ pounds) PERDUE® Fresh Ground Chicken or Turkey
¾ cup finely chopped onion
½ cup seasoned dry bread crumbs
    Grated Parmesan cheese
1 can (6 ounces) tomato paste, divided
1 teaspoon dried Italian seasoning
1 jar (30 ounces) chunky vegetable spaghetti sauce
8 ounces small rigatoni, cooked and drained

In medium bowl, mix chicken, onion, bread crumbs, ¼ cup cheese, 3 tablespoons tomato paste and Italian seasoning. Shape mixture into 12 meatballs. In 10-inch microwave-safe pie plate, arrange meatballs in a circle; cover with waxed paper. Microwave at HIGH 6 minutes. Rearrange and turn meatballs. Re-cover and microwave at HIGH 4 to 6 minutes longer.

Meanwhile, in medium bowl, combine spaghetti sauce and remaining tomato paste; add cooked meatballs. Discard juices from pie plate. Place rigatoni in plate; spoon in meatballs and sauce to combine. Cover with waxed paper. Microwave at HIGH 5 minutes or until sauce is bubbly. Sprinkle with additional Parmesan cheese; cover and let stand 5 minutes before serving.

Makes 4 to 6 servings

NOTE: Bitty Burgers (meatballs) can be made from almost any burger or meatloaf mixture. Microwave as above or roll into 24 meatballs and pan-fry or broil until meatballs are firm and spring back to the touch. **Pan-fry:** In large, lightly oiled or nonstick skillet over medium-high heat, brown meatballs 2 minutes. Reduce heat to medium-low and cook 5 to 8 minutes longer, turning occasionally. **Broil:** Place meatballs in lightly oiled broiling pan. Broil 5 to 6 inches from heat 8 to 10 minutes, turning occasionally.

299 CHILI PEPPER PASTA WITH JALAPEÑO BUTTER SAUCE

1 (12-ounce) package PASTA LaBELLA® Chili Pepper Pasta
4½ tablespoons sweet cream butter
¼ cup diced jalapeño peppers
½ teaspoon minced garlic
1½ cups diced tomatillo tomatoes
2 tablespoons chopped fresh cilantro
½ cup white wine
3 tablespoons fresh lime juice
    Salt and black pepper to taste
¼ cup grated Romano cheese

Cook pasta according to package directions. Over medium heat, melt butter in large skillet. Add jalapeños, garlic and tomatillos; sauté 3 to 4 minutes. Add cilantro, wine, lime juice, salt and pepper. Simmer sauce 2 to 3 minutes and toss in hot Chili Pepper Pasta. Mix well and portion into bowls. Top with cheese and serve.

Makes 4 servings

NEW CREATIONS

300 SPINACH TORTELLINI WITH BEL PAESE®

- 2 tablespoons butter
- 4 ounces BEL PAESE® Cheese,* cut into small chunks
- ¾ cup half-and-half
- 3 ounces chopped GALBANI® Prosciutto di Parma
- Pepper
- 8 ounces spinach tortellini

Remove wax coating and moist, white crust from cheese.

In small saucepan, melt butter over low heat. Add Bel Paese® cheese and half-and-half; cook until smooth, stirring constantly. Stir in Galbani® Prosciutto di Parma; sprinkle with pepper to taste. Remove from heat; set aside.

In large saucepan of boiling water, cook tortellini until *al dente* (tender but still firm); drain. Place in serving bowl. Pour sauce over pasta; toss to coat. Serve immediately.

Makes 2 servings

301 CRISPY TORTELLINI BITES

- ⅓ cup grated Parmesan cheese
- 1 teaspoon dried basil, crushed
- ½ teaspoon LAWRY'S® Seasoned Pepper
- ⅛ teaspoon cayenne pepper
- 1 package (8 or 9 ounces) cheese tortellini
- ⅓ cup vegetable oil
- 1 cup dairy sour cream
- ¾ to 1 teaspoon LAWRY'S® Garlic Powder with Parsley

In medium bowl, combine cheese, basil, Seasoned Pepper and cayenne; set aside. Cook tortellini according to package directions, omitting salt. Run cold water over tortellini; drain. In large skillet, heat oil. Fry cooled tortellini in oil until golden-crisp; drain. Toss cooked tortellini with cheese-spice mixture. In small bowl, blend sour cream and Garlic Powder with Parsley. Serve tortellini with sour cream mixture for dipping.

Makes 6 servings

PRESENTATION: Serve with frill toothpicks or mini skewers.

HINT: Can also be served with prepared LAWRY'S® Extra Rich & Thick Spaghetti Sauce.

NEW CREATIONS

302 PASTA IN THE SPRINGTIME

1¼ cups vegetable broth, divided
2 tablespoons cornstarch
¼ cup rice vinegar
¼ cup soy sauce
3 cloves garlic, minced
1 tablespoon sugar
1 tablespoon minced fresh ginger
1 tablespoon lemon juice
2 teaspoons sesame oil
2 teaspoons hot pepper sauce
1 teaspoon black pepper
½ pound cooked chicken breast, cut into matchstick-size strips
2 carrots, peeled and cut into matchstick-size strips
¼ pound asparagus, diagonally sliced into 1-inch pieces
1 cup packed chopped spinach
1 pound linguine, cooked and drained

1. Combine ¼ cup vegetable broth and cornstarch in small bowl; set aside.

2. Combine remaining 1 cup vegetable broth, vinegar, soy sauce, garlic, sugar, ginger, lemon juice, sesame oil, pepper sauce and black pepper in medium saucepan. Bring to a boil over high heat. Gradually add cornstarch mixture to saucepan, stirring constantly. Bring to a boil, stirring constantly. Reduce heat; simmer 2 to 3 minutes.

3. Add chicken, carrots, asparagus and spinach to saucepan; increase heat to medium. Cook 3 minutes. Combine sauce with linguine in large bowl; stir gently.

Makes 6 servings

303 FETTUCCINE ROMANO ALDANA

6 ounces plain fettuccine, cooked and drained
6 ounces spinach fettuccine, cooked and drained
¾ cup butter, divided
8 ounces mushrooms, sliced
⅔ cup chopped green onions with tops
2½ cups heavy cream, divided
1½ cups (6 ounces) grated Wisconsin Romano cheese, divided
¼ teaspoon ground nutmeg
⅓ pound prosciutto ham, julienned
White pepper to taste

Melt ¼ cup butter in large skillet over medium-high heat. Add mushrooms and onions; cook and stir until tender. Remove from skillet; set aside. Add remaining ½ cup butter to skillet; heat until lightly browned. Add 1 cup cream; bring to a boil. Reduce heat to low; simmer until slightly thickened, about 5 minutes. Add pasta, 1 cup cream, 1 cup cheese and nutmeg; mix lightly. Combine remaining cream and cheese with mushroom mixture and prosciutto. Pour over hot pasta mixture; toss lightly. Season with pepper to taste.

Makes 4 to 6 servings

Favorite recipe from **Wisconsin Milk Marketing Board**

Pasta in the Springtime

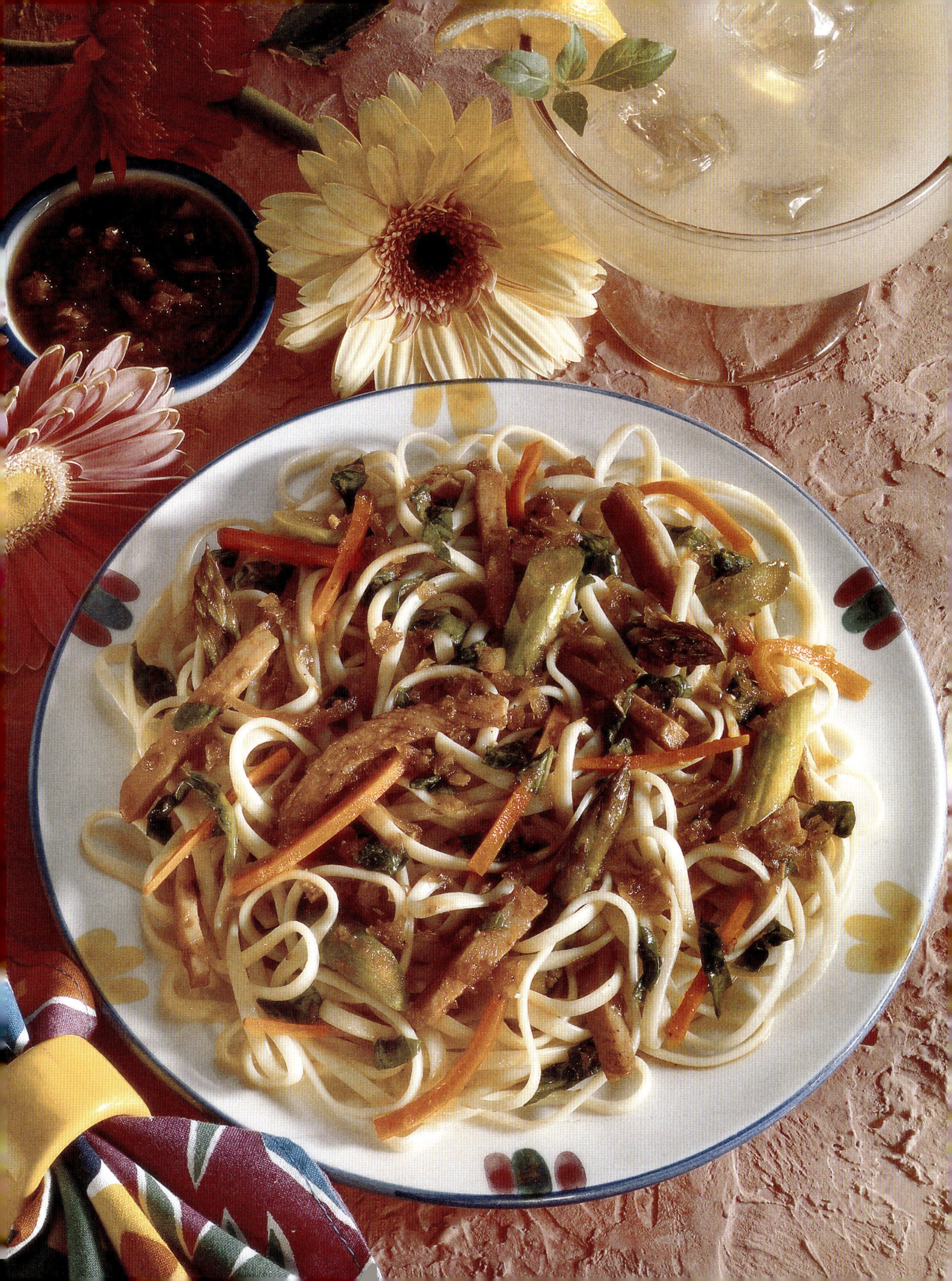

NEW CREATIONS

304 TORTELLINI WITH PUMPKIN RED PEPPER SAUCE

- 2 packages (9 ounces each) CONTADINA® Refrigerated Cheese Tortellini, cooked, drained and kept warm
- 1 cup (1 medium) chopped onion
- 2 cloves garlic, finely chopped
- 1¼ cups (1 large) chopped red bell pepper
- 1 tablespoon butter or vegetable oil
- 1¾ cups (15- or 16-ounce can) LIBBY'S® Solid Pack Pumpkin
- 1¾ cups (14½-ounce can) CONTADINA® Recipe Ready Diced Tomatoes, undrained
- 1¼ cups chicken broth
- 1 teaspoon dried basil leaves, crushed
- 1 teaspoon salt
- ½ teaspoon ground black pepper

COOK onion, garlic and bell pepper in butter in medium saucepan over medium-high heat 3 to 5 minutes or until soft. Add pumpkin, tomatoes, chicken broth, basil, salt and black pepper; stir. Bring to a boil. Reduce heat; cook gently over medium heat for 5 minutes. Serve over pasta.

Makes 4 to 6 servings

305 PINEAPPLE NOODLE PUDDING

- 1¼ cups cooked macaroni
- 1 cup canned unsweetened pineapple chunks, undrained
- ¾ cup low-fat cottage cheese
- ¼ cup imitation sour cream
- 1 egg white
- 3 tablespoons packed dark brown sugar
- ¼ cup wheat flakes
- 1 tablespoon granulated sugar
- ¼ teaspoon ground cinnamon

Preheat oven to 350°F. Spray 1-quart casserole dish with cooking spray. Reserve juice from canned pineapple. In large bowl, mix macaroni, pineapple, ¼ cup reserved juice, cottage cheese, sour cream, egg white and brown sugar. Pour into casserole dish. In small bowl, mix flakes, granulated sugar and cinnamon. Sprinkle flake mixture over noodle mixture. Bake, uncovered, 25 minutes or until bubbly.

Makes 6 servings

Favorite recipe from **The Sugar Association**

NEW CREATIONS

306 ALFREDO WITH ROASTED RED PEPPERS

- 1 package (10 ounces) DiGIORNO® Alfredo Sauce
- 1 jar (7 ounces) roasted red peppers, drained, sliced
- 1/3 cup toasted chopped walnuts
- 1 package (9 ounces) DiGIORNO® Four Cheese Ravioli, cooked, drained

HEAT sauce, peppers and walnuts in saucepan on medium heat.

TOSS with hot ravioli. Sprinkle with additional toasted chopped walnuts and chopped fresh parsley.

Makes 3 to 4 servings

Prep time: 10 minutes
Cook time: 10 minutes

307 TAGLIATELLE WITH CREAMY SAUCE

- 7 to 8 ounces tagliatelle pasta, cooked, drained
- 1 cup GALBANI® Mascarpone cheese
- 1 package (10 ounces) frozen peas, cooked, drained
- 2 ounces (1/2 cup) finely chopped prosciutto
- 1 1/2 cups (6 ounces) shredded mozzarella cheese
-   Butter or margarine

Layer 1/2 of the tagliatelle in buttered 9×9-inch baking dish. Spoon 1/2 of the Mascarpone onto tagliatelle. Sprinkle with 1/2 of the peas and 1/2 of the prosciutto. Top with 1/2 of the mozzarella. Repeat layers. Dot with butter. Bake in preheated 350°F oven 20 minutes or until heated through.

Makes 4 to 6 servings

*Favorite recipe from **Bel Paese Sales Co., Inc.***

308 JARLSBERG PASTA PIE

- 3 cups cooked thin spaghetti
- 1 1/2 cups shredded Jarlsberg cheese, divided
- 1 egg, lightly beaten
- 1 pound ground beef
- 2 cups sliced zucchini
- 1 cup chopped onion
- 1 medium clove garlic, minced
- 1 teaspoon dried basil leaves
- 1 can (16 ounces) stewed tomatoes, undrained
- 1 can (8 ounces) tomato sauce

In large bowl, blend pasta, 1 cup cheese and egg. Line bottom and side of 10-inch pie plate with mixture; set aside. In large skillet, brown beef; pour off fat. Add zucchini, onion, garlic and basil; cook until vegetables are tender. Blend in tomatoes with juice and tomato sauce. Spoon into pasta mixture in pie plate. Bake at 350°F for 30 minutes. Sprinkle with remaining 1/2 cup cheese. Bake an additional 10 minutes.

Makes 6 to 8 servings

*Favorite recipe from **Norseland Inc.***

NEW CREATIONS

309 TEX–MEX NOODLE CAKE

- 8 ounces uncooked angel hair pasta
- ½ cup finely chopped red bell pepper
- 1 egg plus 1 egg white
- 2 tablespoons skim milk
- 3 tablespoons grated Asiago or Parmesan cheese
- 2 teaspoons chili powder
- ½ teaspoon cumin
- ¼ teaspoon ground black pepper
- Plain nonfat yogurt
- Minced fresh cilantro

1. Cook pasta according to package directions, omitting salt. Drain and cool slightly, but do not rinse. Place pasta in medium bowl with bell pepper.

2. Combine egg, egg white, milk, cheese, chili powder, cumin and black pepper in small bowl; pour over pasta, tossing to coat evenly.

3. Spray large nonstick skillet with nonstick cooking spray. Add pasta mixture, spreading evenly and pressing firmly. Cook over medium-low heat until bottom is golden brown, about 7 to 8 minutes.

4. Slide noodle cake onto large plate, invert and return noodle cake to skillet. Cook until brown, 3 to 5 minutes.

5. Cut into wedges; serve warm, topped with yogurt and cilantro. *Makes 6 servings*

310 SANTA FE PASTA

- 8 ounces dried pasta, cooked, drained and kept warm
- 1 tablespoon vegetable oil
- ½ cup (about 6) sliced green onions
- 1 clove garlic, finely chopped
- 8 ounces (about 2) boneless, skinless chicken breast halves, cut into 2-inch strips
- 1 cup (1 large) green bell pepper strips
- 1 cup (1 large) red bell pepper strips
- ½ teaspoon salt
- ½ teaspoon chili powder
- ½ teaspoon ground black pepper
- Dash cayenne pepper
- 1½ cups (12-fluid ounce can) CARNATION® Evaporated Lowfat Milk
- 1 tablespoon cornstarch
- ¼ cup fresh cilantro leaves

HEAT oil in large skillet over medium-high heat. Add green onions and garlic; cook, stirring constantly, 1 to 2 minutes. Add chicken, bell peppers, salt, chili powder, black pepper and cayenne pepper; cook, stirring occasionally, 4 to 5 minutes or until chicken is no longer pink in center.

COMBINE small amount of evaporated milk and cornstarch in small bowl. Add to skillet; gradually stir in remaining evaporated milk and cilantro.

COOK, stirring occasionally, over medium-high heat 2 to 3 minutes or until mixture is slightly thickened. Serve over pasta.

Makes 6 servings

Tex-Mex Noodle Cake

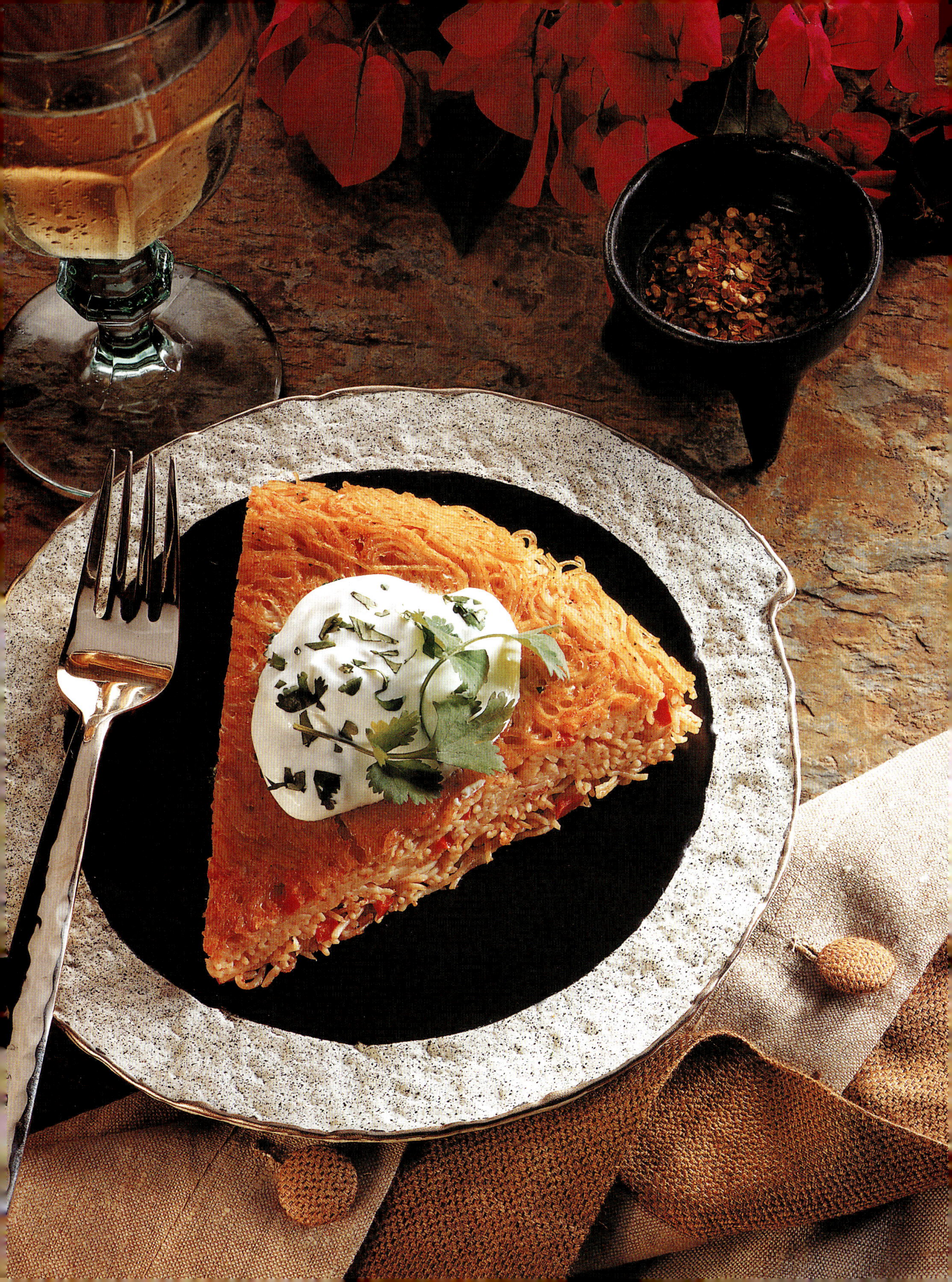

NEW CREATIONS

311 CALIFORNIA WALNUT NOODLES

DRESSING
- ½ cup plain nonfat yogurt
- ½ cup orange juice
- 3 tablespoons balsamic vinegar or wine vinegar
- 2 tablespoons packed brown sugar
- 2 teaspoons sesame oil
- 1½ teaspoons grated fresh ginger *or* ½ teaspoon ground ginger
- ½ teaspoon red pepper flakes (optional)
- 2 cloves garlic, minced
- Salt to taste (optional)

NOODLES
- 12 ounces uncooked spaghetti or linguine
- 2 cups cooked, diced skinless chicken breasts
- 1 red or green bell pepper, thinly sliced
- 1 cucumber, halved, seeded and thinly sliced
- ½ cup chopped green onions
- 2 teaspoons minced jalapeño pepper or other hot chili pepper
- 2 tablespoons chopped fresh cilantro (optional)
- ⅔ cup Savory California Walnut Sprinkles (recipe follows)

For dressing, whisk together yogurt, orange juice, vinegar, sugar, oil, ginger, red pepper flakes, garlic and salt, if desired, in large bowl. Set aside.

Cook pasta according to package directions. Drain and rinse well; drain. Toss pasta and ¾ cup dressing in large bowl. Combine chicken, bell pepper, cucumber, green onions, jalapeño pepper and cilantro with remaining dressing. Arrange pasta on large platter or in shallow bowl. Spoon chicken mixture down center. Just before serving, top with walnut sprinkles.

Makes 4 servings

SAVORY CALIFORNIA WALNUT SPRINKLES
- 4 ounces (1 cup) chopped California walnuts
- ½ cup fresh white bread crumbs
- 1 tablespoon paprika
- ¼ teaspoon cayenne pepper
- ¼ teaspoon salt (optional)

Preheat oven to 325°F. In food processor, process walnuts until finely ground; transfer to small bowl. Add bread crumbs; stir to combine. Spread mixture in even layer on ungreased baking sheet. Bake 15 minutes, stirring frequently, until mixture is golden brown and crisp. Stir in paprika, cayenne pepper and salt, if desired. Cool to room temperature.

Makes 1¼ cups

Favorite recipe from **Walnut Marketing Board**

California Walnut Noodles

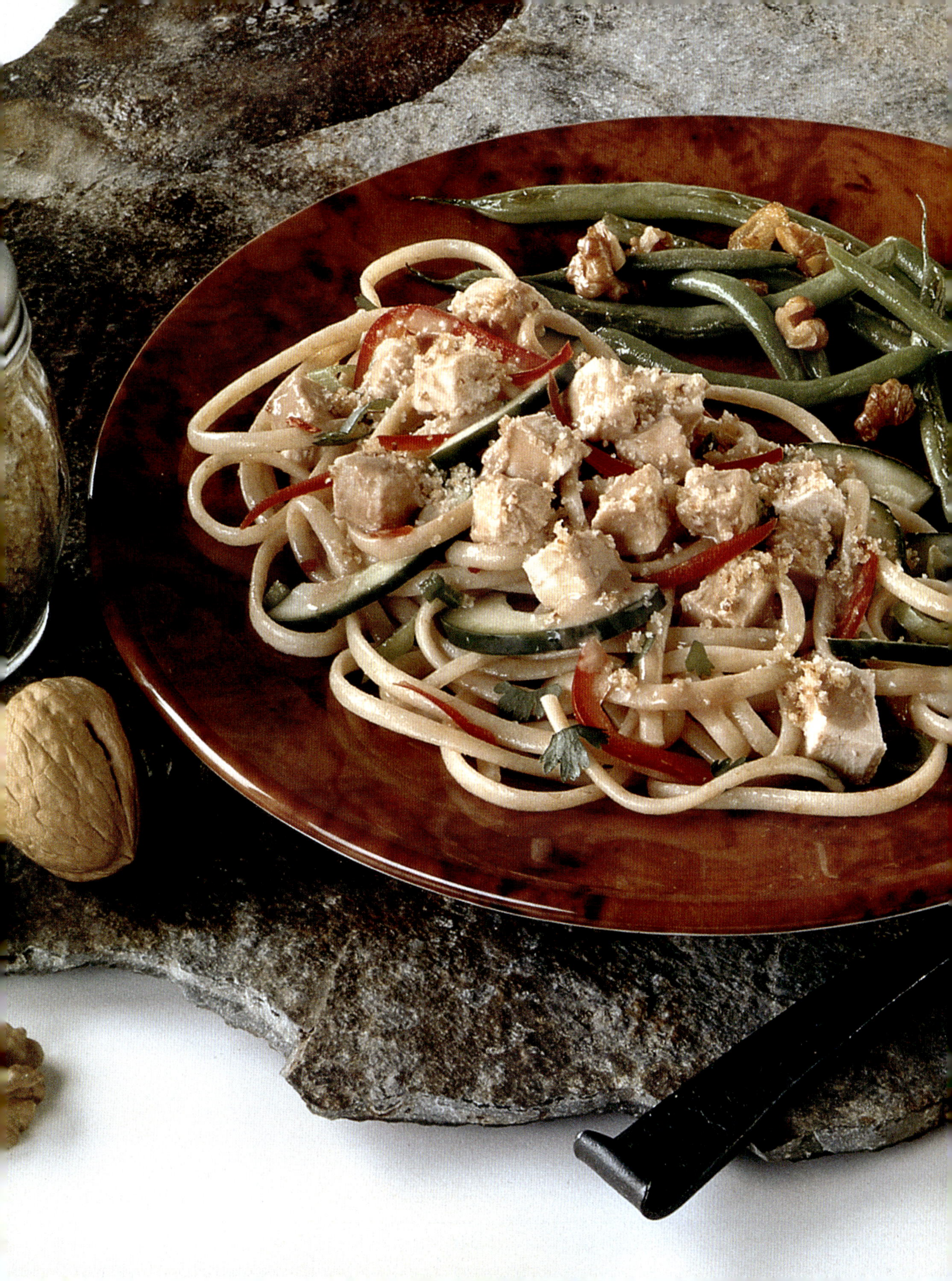

NEW CREATIONS

312 PASTA AND BROCCOLI

- 1 bunch broccoli
- 1 package (16 ounces) ziti pasta
- 2 tablespoons olive oil
- 1 clove garlic, minced
- ¾ cup (3 ounces) shredded American or mozzarella cheese
- ½ cup grated Parmesan cheese
- ¼ cup butter
- ¼ cup chicken broth
- 3 tablespoons white wine

1. Trim leaves from broccoli stalks. Trim ends of stalks. Cut broccoli into florets. Peel stalks, then cut into 1-inch pieces.

2. To steam broccoli, bring 2 inches of water in large saucepan to a boil over high heat. Place broccoli in metal steamer into saucepan. Water should not touch broccoli. Cover pan; steam 10 minutes until broccoli is tender. Add water, as necessary, to prevent pan from boiling dry.

3. Cook pasta according to package directions; drain.

4. Heat oil in large skillet over medium-high heat. Cook and stir garlic in hot oil until golden.

5. Add broccoli; cook and stir 3 to 4 minutes. Add American cheese, Parmesan cheese, butter, broth and wine; stir. Reduce heat to low. Simmer until cheese melts.

6. Pour sauce over pasta in large bowl; toss gently to coat. Garnish as desired.

Makes 6 to 8 servings

313 LINGUINE WITH PUMPKIN PORK SAUCE

- 1¼ pounds boneless pork loin chops, sliced in ¼-inch strips
- 2 tablespoons all-purpose flour
- ½ cup thinly sliced green onions
- 2 to 3 tablespoons vegetable oil
- 2½ cups (1 large) green apple, peeled, cored and thinly sliced
- 3 tablespoons maple syrup
- 1 cup chicken broth
- 1 cup LIBBY'S® Solid Pack Pumpkin
- ½ cup CARNATION® Lowfat or Lite Evaporated Skimmed Milk
- ½ teaspoon dried tarragon
- ½ teaspoon salt
- ¼ teaspoon ground black pepper
- ¼ cup Dijon mustard
- ¾ pound dry linguine, cooked, drained and kept warm

DUST pork with flour in plastic bag. Sauté pork with onions in oil in large skillet until pork is no longer pink. Remove from pan; keep warm. Add apple and maple syrup to pan and cook 1 to 2 minutes or until apple is tender. Remove; keep warm.

ADD broth and pumpkin to same pan; mix well. Slowly add evaporated milk. Mix in tarragon, salt and pepper. Remove from heat; gradually add mustard. Return pork and apple to pan; mix well. Serve over linguine.

Makes 4 to 6 servings

Pasta and Broccoli

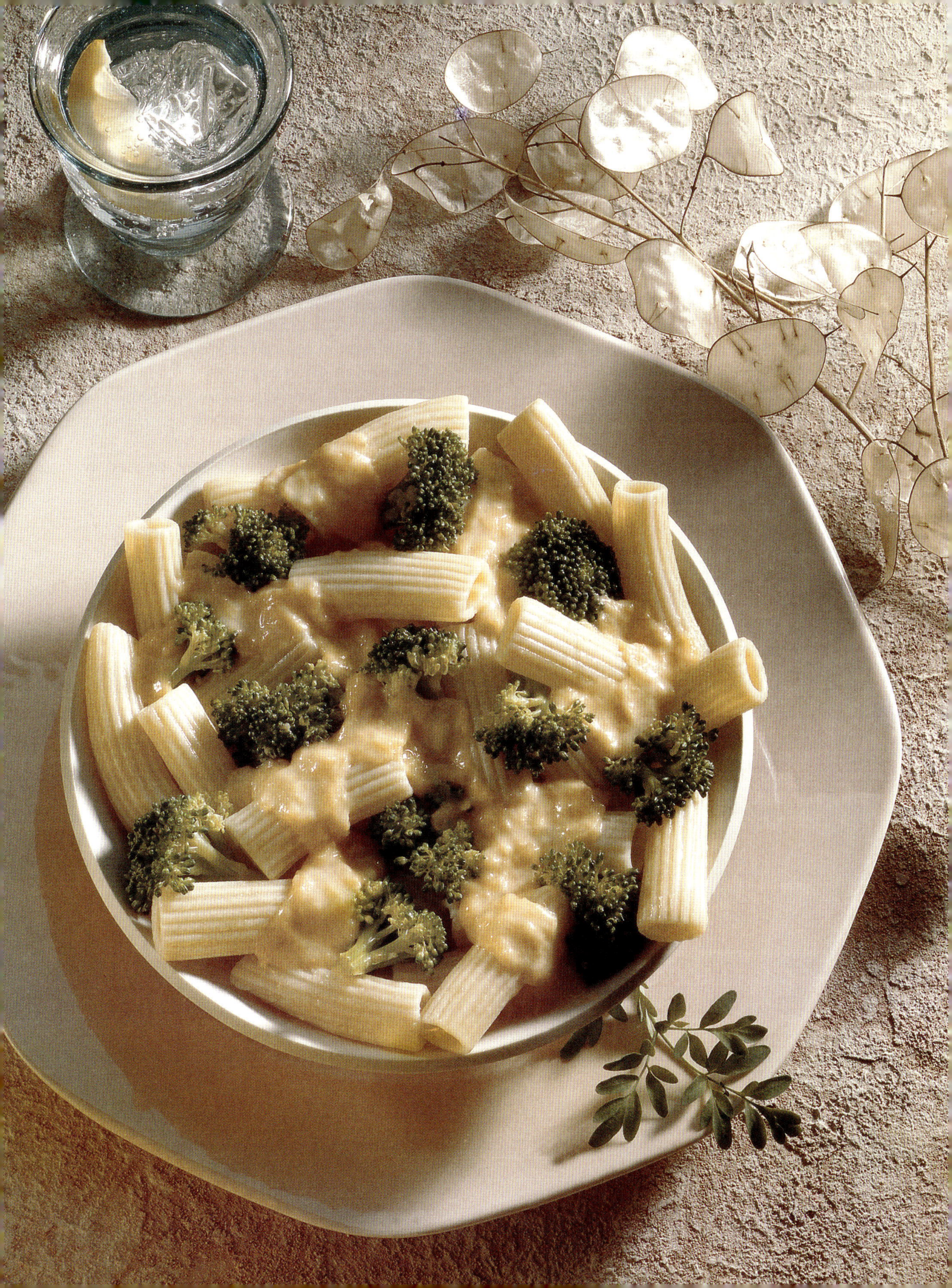

NEW CREATIONS

314 SPAM® & PASTA STUFFED TOMATOES

- 1 (7¼-ounce) package macaroni and cheese
- 8 medium tomatoes
- 1 (12-ounce) can SPAM® Luncheon Meat, cubed
- 2 tablespoons chopped fresh chives *or* 1 tablespoon dried chives
- 1 tablespoon chopped fresh basil *or* 1 teaspoon dried basil leaves
- ½ teaspoon onion powder
- ¼ teaspoon black pepper

Prepare macaroni and cheese according to package directions. Meanwhile, cut tops off tomatoes; scoop out pulp. Place tomatoes, cut side down, onto paper towels to drain. Heat oven to 350°F. In large bowl, combine prepared macaroni and cheese, SPAM®, chives and basil; mix well. In small bowl, combine onion powder and pepper; sprinkle inside of drained tomatoes with onion powder mixture. Spoon macaroni and cheese mixture into tomatoes. Place filled tomatoes in lightly greased 13×9-inch baking pan. Cover. Bake 20 to 25 minutes or until tomatoes are tender and thoroughly heated. *Makes 8 servings*

315 SUN–DRIED TOMATO LINGUINE

- 6 sun-dried tomato halves, not packed in oil
- Nonstick olive oil cooking spray
- 1 cup sliced mushrooms
- 3 cloves garlic, minced
- 1 tablespoon minced fresh parsley
- ¾ teaspoon dried rosemary
- 1 can (about 14 ounces) low-sodium chicken broth, defatted
- 2 tablespoons cornstarch
- 1 package (9 ounces) linguine, cooked in salted water, drained, hot

Place sun-dried tomatoes in small bowl; pour hot water over to cover. Let stand 10 to 15 minutes or until tomatoes are soft. Drain well; cut tomatoes into quarters. Spray medium nonstick skillet with cooking spray; heat over medium heat until hot. Add mushrooms and garlic; cook and stir about 5 minutes or until tender. Add sun-dried tomatoes, parsley and rosemary; cook and stir 1 minute.

Stir chicken broth into vegetable mixture; heat to a boil. Combine cornstarch and ¼ cup cold water in small bowl; stir into chicken broth mixture. Boil 1 to 2 minutes, stirring constantly. Pour mixture over linguine; toss. *Makes 6 servings*

SPAM® & Pasta Stuffed Tomatoes

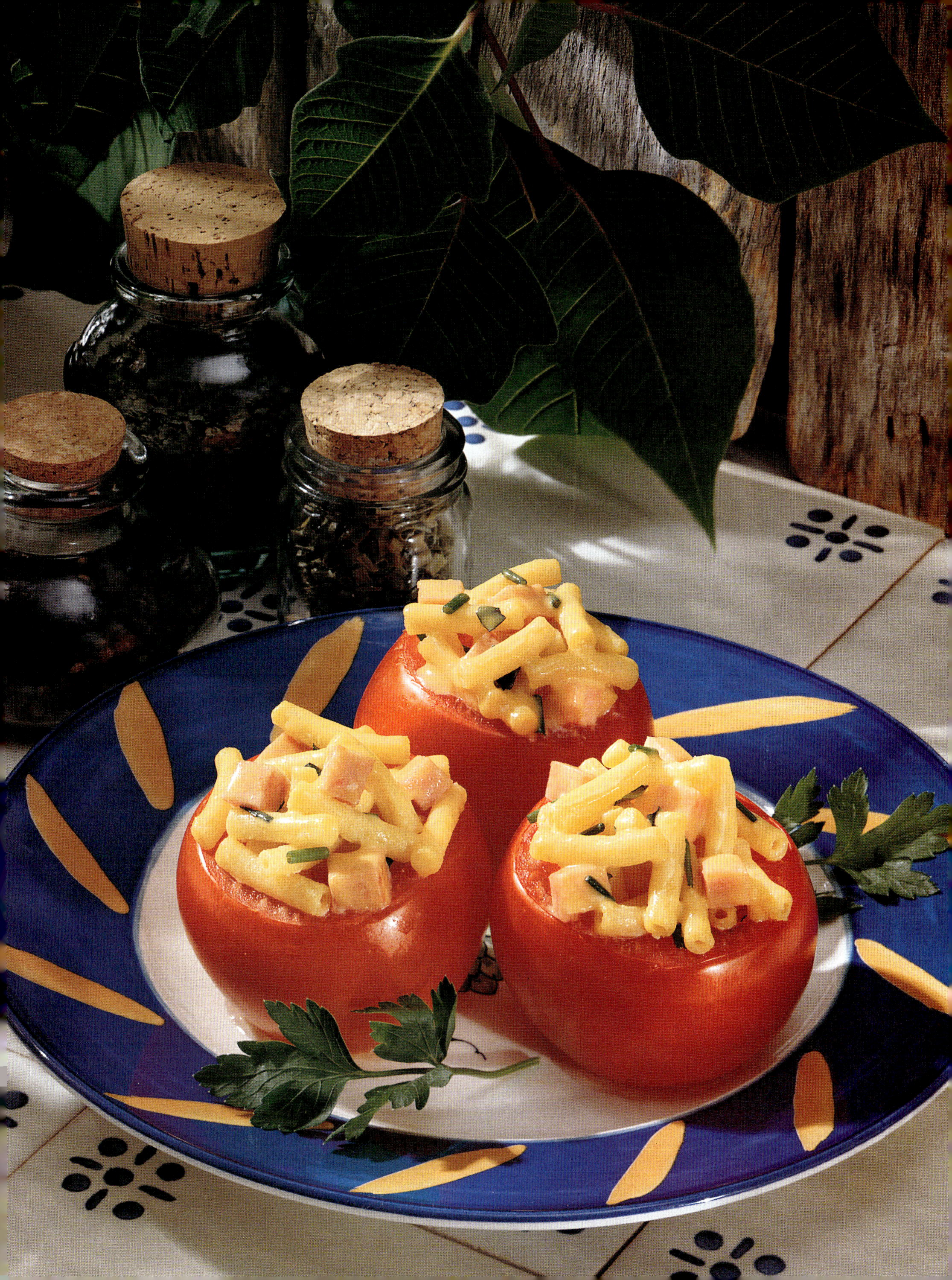

NEW CREATIONS

316 TORTELLONI WREATH WITH PESTO DIP

- 1 package (9 ounces) DiGIORNO® Mushroom Tortelloni
- 1 package (9 ounces) DiGIORNO® Hot Red Pepper Cheese Tortelloni
- 1 container (8 ounces) PHILADELPHIA BRAND® Soft Cream Cheese
- 1 package (7 ounces) DiGIORNO® Pesto Sauce
- 1 teaspoon lemon juice

ADD both packages of tortelloni to 4 quarts boiling water. Boil gently, uncovered, 6 minutes, stirring frequently. Drain; rinse with cold water.

MIX cream cheese, sauce and juice. Place in small round bowl.

PLACE bowl in middle of platter; arrange tortelloni in wreath shape around bowl. Garnish with green and red bell peppers and pitted ripe olives. *Makes 24 servings*

PREP TIME: 10 minutes
COOK TIME: 6 minutes

317 FLASH PRIMAVERA

- 1 pound mostaccioli, ziti or other medium-shape pasta, uncooked
- 1 head broccoli or cauliflower, cut into small florets
- 1 tablespoon cornstarch
- 3 cloves garlic, minced
- 1 (15½-ounce) can low-sodium chicken broth
- 1 (10-ounce) package frozen mixed vegetables
- 1 (10-ounce) package frozen chopped spinach, thawed
  Salt and black pepper to taste
- 1 cup grated Parmesan cheese

Prepare pasta according to package directions. Three minutes before pasta is done, stir in broccoli. Drain pasta and vegetables; transfer to large bowl.

In small bowl, dissolve cornstarch in ¼ cup water. Combine garlic and chicken broth in large saucepan. Simmer over medium heat 3 minutes. Whisk in cornstarch mixture. Stir in mixed vegetables and spinach; cook about 5 minutes or until heated through. Toss sauce and vegetable mixture with pasta. Season with salt and pepper and sprinkle with Parmesan cheese; serve.

Makes 6 servings

Favorite recipe from **National Pasta Association**

Tortelloni Wreath with Pesto Dip

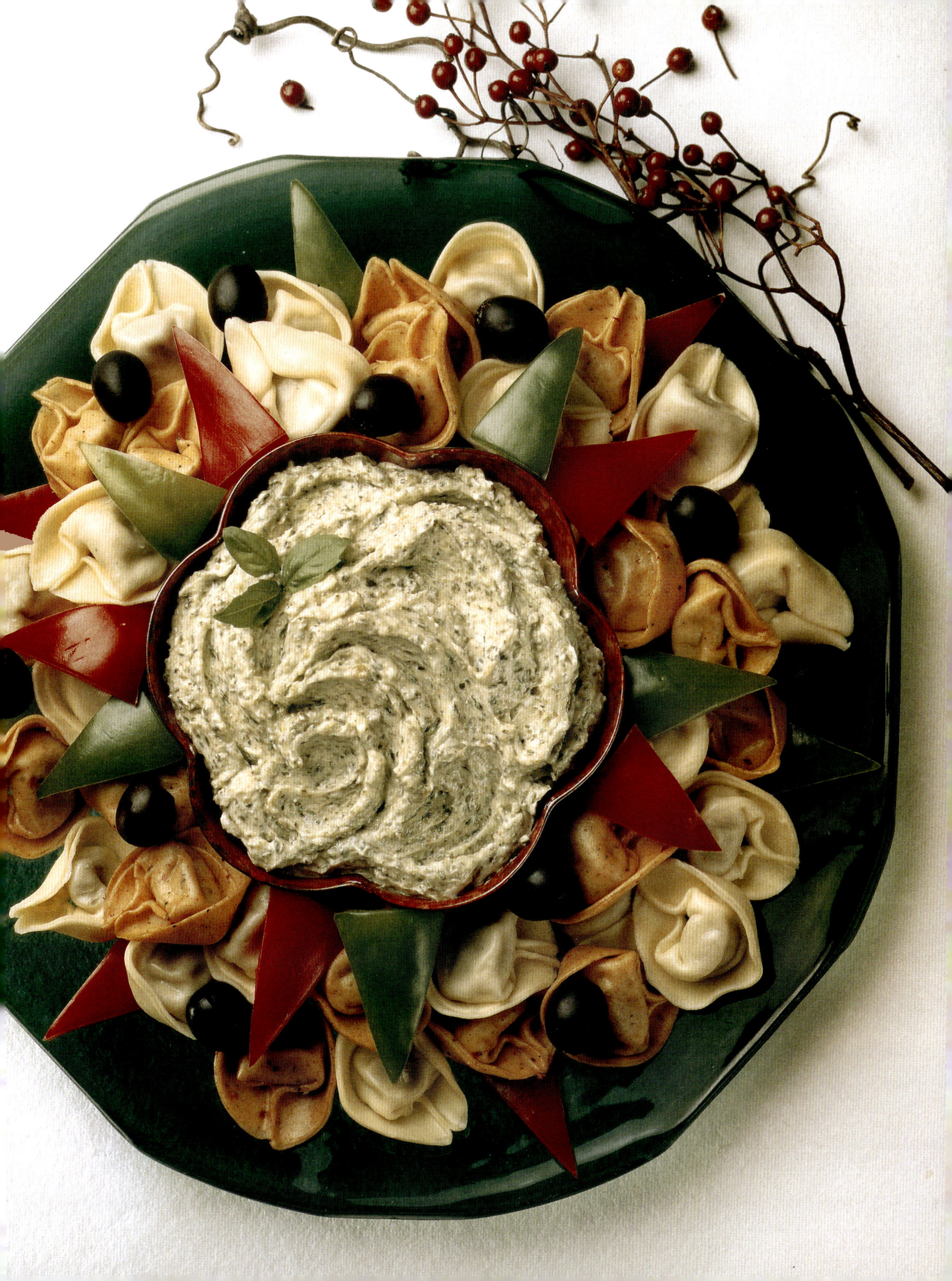

OLD FAVORITES

318 SPAGHETTI ALLA BOLOGNESE

2 tablespoons olive oil
1 medium onion, chopped
1 pound ground beef
½ small carrot, finely chopped
½ rib celery, finely chopped
1 cup dry white wine
½ cup milk
⅛ teaspoon ground nutmeg
1 can (14½ ounces) whole peeled tomatoes, undrained
1 cup beef broth
3 tablespoons tomato paste
1 teaspoon salt
1 teaspoon dried basil leaves
½ teaspoon dried thyme leaves
⅛ teaspoon black pepper
1 bay leaf
1 pound uncooked dry spaghetti
1 cup freshly grated Parmesan cheese (about 3 ounces)
Fresh thyme sprig for garnish

1. Heat oil in large skillet over medium heat. Cook and stir onion until soft. Crumble beef into onion mixture. Brown 6 minutes, stirring to separate meat, or until meat just loses its pink color. Spoon off and discard fat.

2. Stir carrot and celery into meat mixture; cook 2 minutes over medium-high heat. Stir in wine; cook 4 to 6 minutes or until wine has evaporated. Stir in milk and nutmeg; reduce heat to medium and cook 3 to 4 minutes until milk has evaporated. Remove from heat.

3. Press tomatoes and juice through sieve into meat mixture; discard seeds.

4. Stir beef broth, tomato paste, salt, basil, thyme, pepper and bay leaf into tomato-meat mixture. Bring to a boil over medium-high heat; reduce heat to low. Simmer, uncovered, 1 to 1½ hours until most of liquid has evaporated and sauce thickens, stirring frequently. Remove and discard bay leaf.

5. To serve, cook spaghetti in large pot of boiling salted water 8 to 12 minutes just until *al dente*; drain well. Combine hot spaghetti and meat sauce in serving bowl; toss lightly. Sprinkle with cheese. Garnish, if desired.
Makes 4 to 6 servings

Spaghetti alla Bolognese

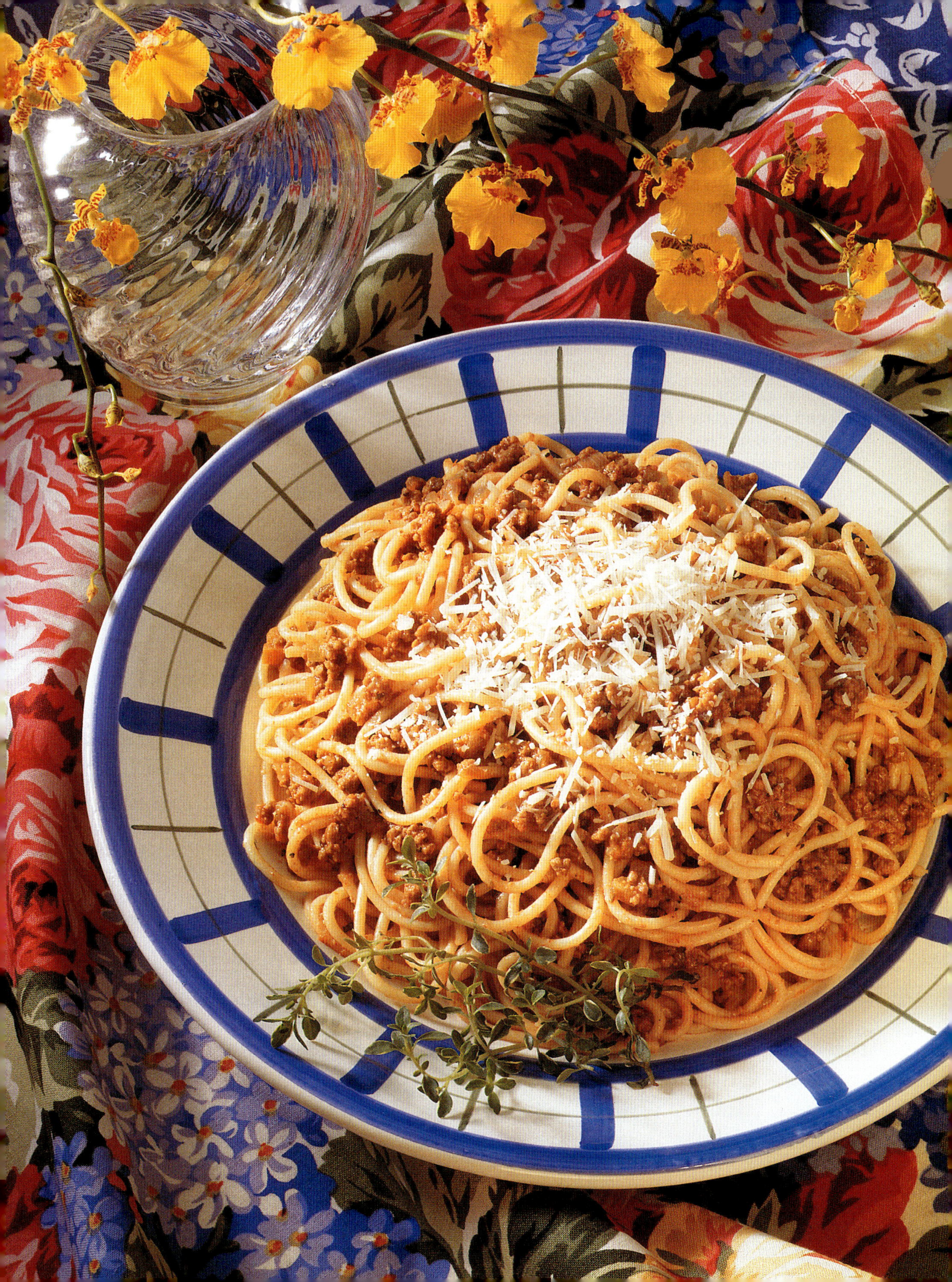

OLD FAVORITES

319 CLASSIC PESTO WITH LINGUINE

- ¾ pound dry uncooked linguine
- 2 tablespoons butter or margarine
- ¼ cup plus 1 tablespoon olive oil, divided
- 2 tablespoons pine nuts
- 1 cup tightly packed fresh (not dried) basil leaves, rinsed, drained and stemmed
- 2 cloves garlic
- ¼ teaspoon salt
- ¼ cup freshly grated Parmesan cheese
- 1½ tablespoons freshly grated Romano cheese
- Fresh basil leaves for garnish

1. Prepare linguine according to package directions; drain. Toss with butter in large serving bowl; set aside and keep warm.

2. Heat 1 tablespoon oil in small saucepan or skillet over medium-low heat. Add pine nuts; cook and stir 30 to 45 seconds until light brown, shaking pan constantly. Remove with slotted spoon; drain on paper towels.

3. Place toasted pine nuts, basil leaves, garlic and salt in food processor or blender. With processor running, add remaining ¼ cup oil in slow steady stream until evenly blended and pine nuts are finely chopped.

4. Transfer basil mixture to small bowl. Stir in Parmesan and Romano cheeses.*

5. Combine hot, buttered linguine and pesto sauce in large serving bowl; toss until well coated. Garnish, if desired. Serve immediately.
Makes 4 servings (about ¾ cup pesto sauce)

*Pesto sauce can be stored at this point in airtight container; pour thin layer of olive oil over pesto and cover. Refrigerate up to 1 week. Bring to room temperature. Proceed as directed in step 5.

320 PASTA CARBONARA

- ½ cup sliced California ripe olives
- ½ cup sliced mushrooms
- ½ cup crumbled cooked bacon
- ¼ cup minced green onions with tops
- ½ teaspoon coarsely ground black pepper
- 3 tablespoons margarine
- 1 cup whipping cream
- ¾ cup grated Parmesan cheese
- 3 eggs, lightly beaten
- 7 ounces linguine, cooked, drained, kept warm

Combine olives, mushrooms, bacon, onions and pepper in small bowl; set aside.

Melt margarine in 2-quart microwavable casserole at HIGH 1 minute. Stir in olive mixture. Microwave at HIGH 1 minute. Add whipping cream, cheese and eggs; mix well. Microwave at HIGH 3 to 5 minutes, stirring every minute or until sauce is thickened. Pour over linguine; toss well.
Makes 6 servings

Favorite recipe from **California Olive Industry**

Classic Pesto with Linguine

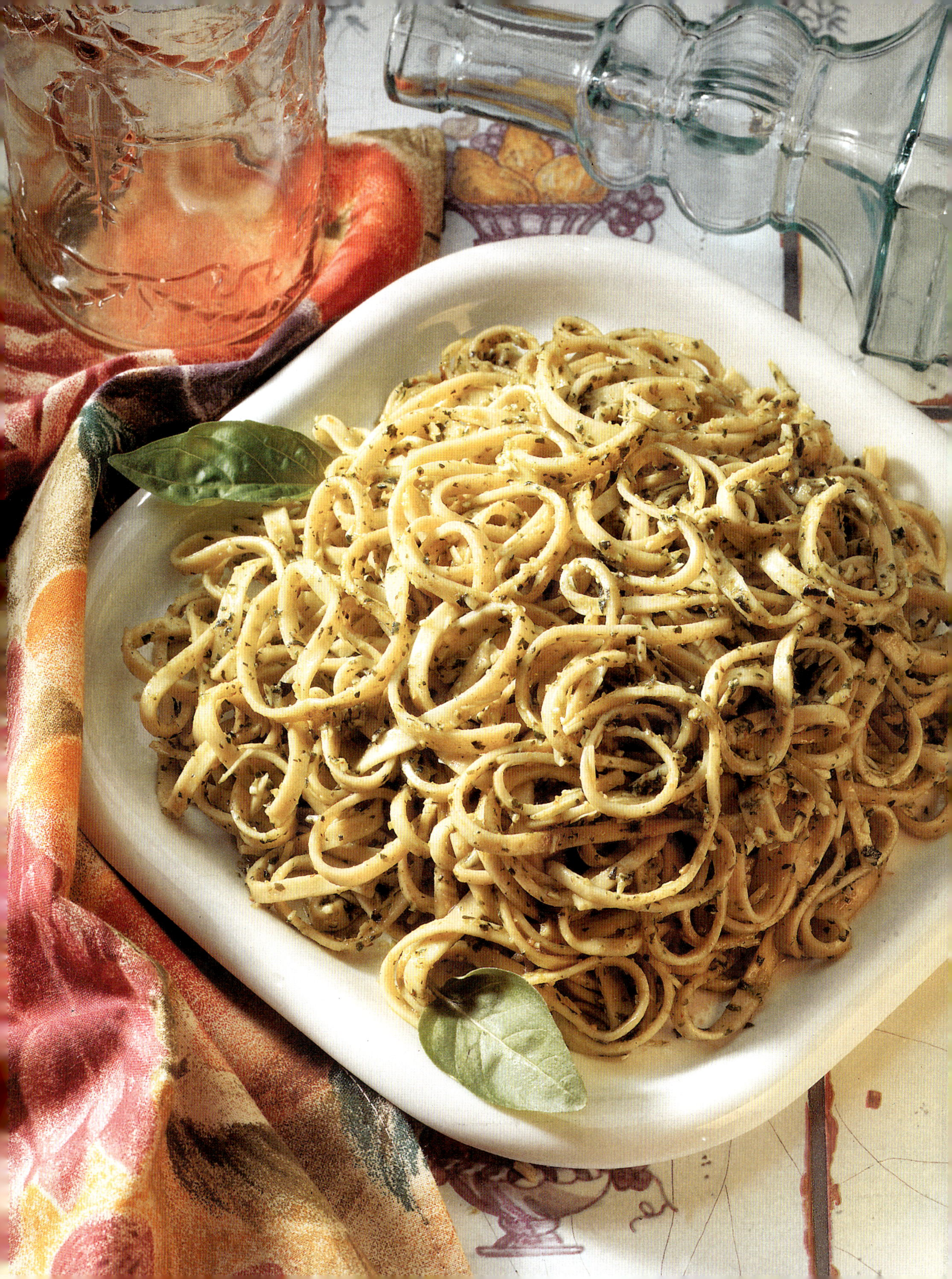

OLD FAVORITES

321 RIGATONI WITH CREAMY TOMATO SAUCE

- 8 ounces dry pasta (rigatoni or penne), cooked, drained and kept warm
- 1 tablespoon olive oil
- ½ cup diced onion
- 2 tablespoons dry vermouth or white wine
- 1¾ cups (14½-ounce can) CONTADINA® Pasta Ready™ Chunky Tomatoes, Primavera
- ½ cup heavy cream
- 1 cup California ripe olives, halved
- ½ cup grated Parmesan cheese
- ¼ cup sliced green onions

In large skillet, heat oil; add onion and sauté 4 to 5 minutes. Add vermouth; cook 1 minute. Stir in tomatoes and juice, cream, pasta, olives and Parmesan cheese; toss well. Sprinkle with green onions.

Makes 4 servings

322 CLASSIC MACARONI AND CHEESE

- 2 cups elbow macaroni
- 3 tablespoons butter or margarine
- ¼ cup chopped onion (optional)
- 2 tablespoons all-purpose flour
- ½ teaspoon salt
- ⅛ teaspoon black pepper
- 2 cups milk
- 2 cups (8 ounces) SARGENTO® Classic or Fancy Shredded Mild Cheddar Cheese, divided

Cook macaroni according to package directions; drain. In medium saucepan, melt butter and cook onion, if desired, about 5 minutes or until tender. Stir in flour, salt and pepper. Gradually add milk and cook, stirring occasionally, until thickened. Remove from heat. Add 1½ cups Cheddar cheese and stir until cheese melts. Combine cheese sauce with cooked macaroni. Place in 1½-quart casserole; top with remaining ½ cup Cheddar cheese. Bake at 350°F 30 minutes or until bubbly and cheese is golden brown.

Makes 6 servings

323 SPAGHETTI WITH GARLIC

- 12 ounces uncooked spaghetti
- 4½ teaspoons FILIPPO BERIO® Olive Oil
- 1 clove garlic, sliced
- Salt and freshly ground black pepper to taste
- Grated Parmesan cheese

Cook pasta according to package directions until *al dente* (tender but still firm). Drain; transfer to large bowl. In small skillet, heat olive oil over medium heat until hot. Add garlic; cook and stir 2 to 3 minutes or until golden. Discard garlic. Pour oil over hot pasta; toss until lightly coated. Season to taste with salt and pepper. Top with cheese.

Makes 4 servings

Rigatoni with Creamy Tomato Sauce

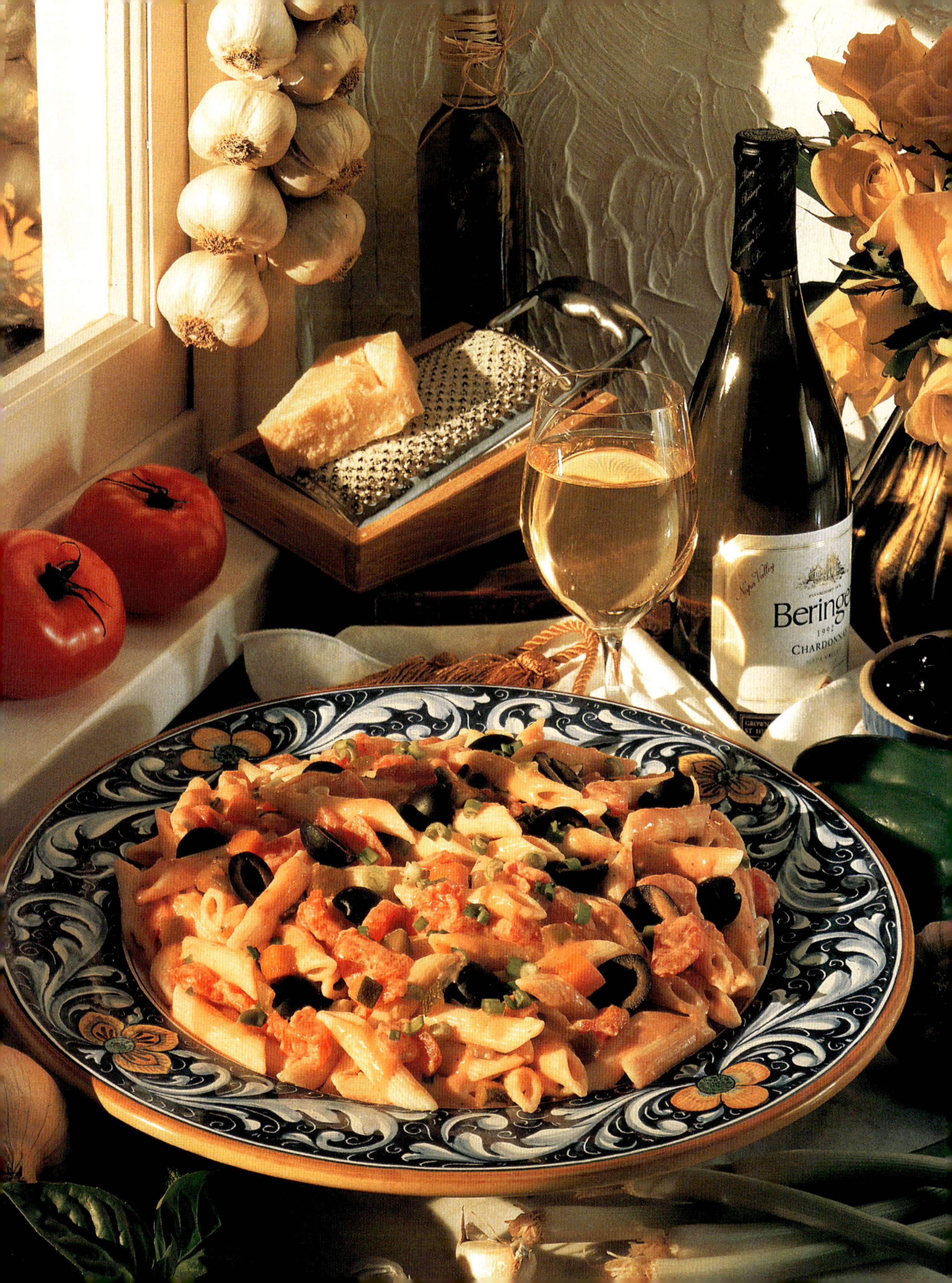
Napa Valley
Beringer
1992
CHARDONNAY

OLD FAVORITES

324 TETRAZZINI PASTA SUPPER

- 6 quarts salted water
- 1 package (16 ounces) tubular pasta, such as ziti or penne
- 2 tablespoons butter or margarine
- 3 scallions, minced
- 2 cloves garlic, minced
- 1 pound fresh shiitake mushrooms, stems removed and caps sliced, or fresh domestic mushrooms, sliced
- 3 tablespoons dry sherry
- ½ teaspoon dried tarragon leaves
- Salt and ground black pepper
- 2 to 3 cups coarsely chopped cooked PERDUE® Chicken or Turkey
- 1½ cups part-skim ricotta cheese
- ¾ cup freshly grated Parmesan cheese

In large saucepan over high heat, bring water to boil. Cook pasta according to package directions until tender. Reserve 1 cup cooking water from pasta. Drain pasta and place in large serving bowl.

Meanwhile, in large skillet over low heat, melt butter. Add scallions and garlic; cook about 1 minute or until tender, stirring constantly. Increase heat to high; add mushrooms, sherry, tarragon and ¼ teaspoon *each* salt and pepper. Cook about 5 minutes or until liquid is evaporated and mushrooms are browned, stirring constantly. Add chicken; cook 1 minute longer or until heated through.

To serve, pour warm chicken mixture over hot pasta. Add ricotta and Parmesan cheeses with about ⅓ cup reserved hot cooking water. Toss and add additional cooking water, if necessary, to make a creamy sauce. Season with additional salt and pepper; serve immediately.

Makes 4 to 6 servings

325 CLASSIC FETTUCCINE ALFREDO

- ¾ pound uncooked dry fettuccine
- 6 tablespoons unsalted butter
- ⅔ cup heavy or whipping cream
- ½ teaspoon salt
- Generous dash ground white pepper
- Generous dash ground nutmeg
- 1 cup freshly grated Parmesan cheese (about 3 ounces)
- 2 tablespoons chopped fresh parsley
- Fresh Italian parsley sprig for garnish

1. Cook fettuccine in large pot of boiling salted water 6 to 8 minutes just until *al dente*; remove from heat. Drain well; return to dry pot.

2. Place butter and cream in large, heavy skillet over medium-low heat. Cook and stir until butter melts and mixture bubbles. Cook and stir 2 minutes more. Stir in salt, pepper and nutmeg. Remove from heat. Gradually stir in cheese until thoroughly blended and smooth. Return briefly to heat to blend cheese completely if necessary. (Do not let sauce bubble or cheese will become lumpy and tough.)

3. Pour sauce over fettuccine in pot. Stir and toss with 2 forks over low heat 2 to 3 minutes until sauce is thickened and fettuccine is evenly coated. Sprinkle with chopped parsley. Garnish, if desired. Serve immediately.

Makes 4 servings

Classic Fettuccine Alfredo

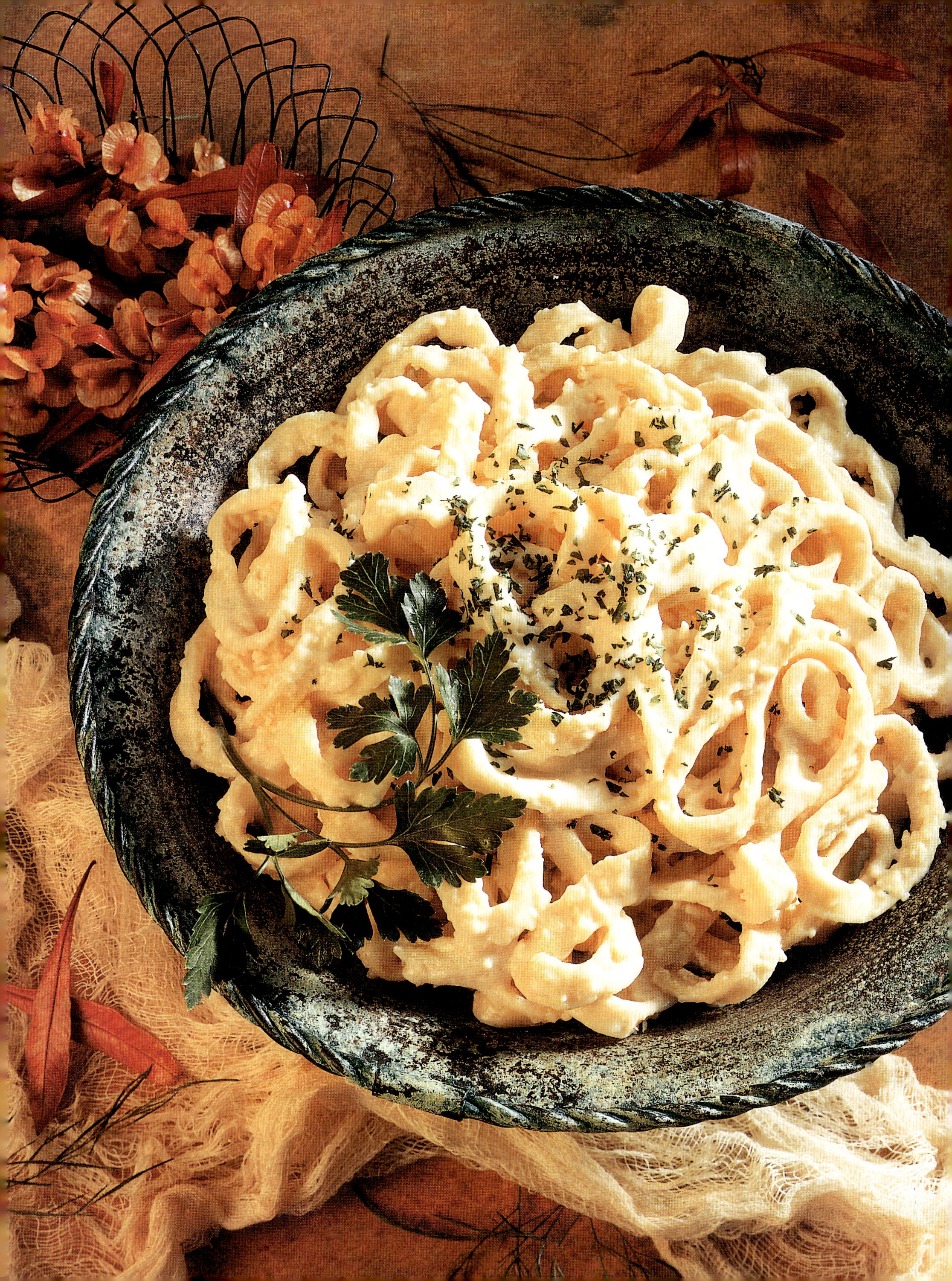

OLD FAVORITES

326 RAVIOLI WITH HOMEMADE TOMATO SAUCE

- 3 cloves garlic
- ½ cup fresh basil
- 3 cups seeded, peeled tomatoes, cut into quarters
- 2 tablespoons tomato paste
- 2 tablespoons commercial fat-free Italian salad dressing
- 1 tablespoon balsamic vinegar
- ¼ teaspoon ground black pepper
- 1 package (9 ounces) refrigerated reduced-fat cheese ravioli
- 2 cups shredded spinach leaves
- 1 cup (4 ounces) shredded part-skim mozzarella cheese

1. To prepare tomato sauce, process garlic in food processor until coarsely chopped. Add basil; process until coarsely chopped. Add tomatoes, tomato paste, salad dressing, vinegar and pepper; process using on/off pulsing action until tomatoes are chopped.

2. Spray 9-inch square microwavable dish with nonstick cooking spray. Spread 1 cup tomato sauce in dish. Layer half of ravioli and spinach over tomato sauce. Repeat layers with 1 cup tomato sauce and remaining ravioli and spinach. Top with remaining 1 cup of tomato sauce.

3. Cover with plastic wrap; refrigerate 1 to 8 hours. Vent plastic wrap. Microwave at MEDIUM (50%) 20 minutes or until pasta is tender and hot. Sprinkle with cheese. Microwave at HIGH 3 minutes or just until cheese melts. Let stand, covered, 5 minutes before serving. *Makes 6 servings*

327 SPAGHETTI PUTTANESCA

- 5 tablespoons olive oil
- 4 anchovy fillets, coarsely chopped
- 2 cloves garlic, minced
- 1 can (28 ounces) whole plum tomatoes, drained and chopped
- 2 tablespoons tomato paste
- 2 tablespoons capers, rinsed and drained
- ¾ teaspoon TABASCO® pepper sauce
- ¾ teaspoon dried oregano leaves
- ½ cup Italian or Greek cured black olives, pitted and slivered
- 2 tablespoons chopped fresh parsley
- 12 ounces spaghetti, cooked according to package directions and drained

Heat oil in large skillet; add anchovies and garlic. Cook and stir 3 minutes. Stir in tomatoes, tomato paste, capers, TABASCO sauce and oregano; simmer, uncovered, 5 minutes, stirring occasionally. Stir in olives and parsley; simmer, uncovered, 2 minutes. Pour over hot spaghetti in serving bowl; toss gently to coat. Serve with additional TABASCO sauce, if desired.

Makes 4 servings

Ravioli with Homemade Tomato Sauce

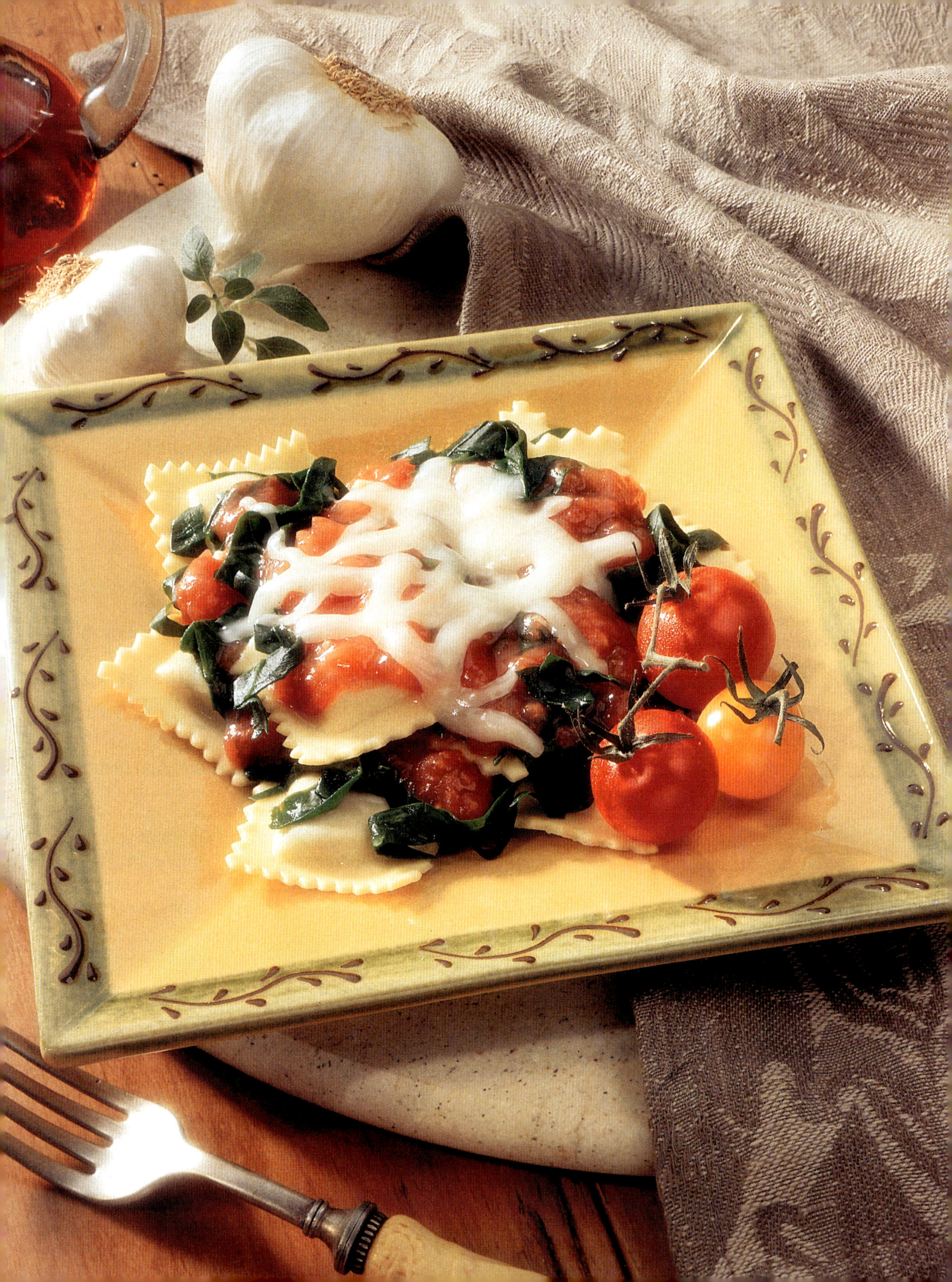

OLD FAVORITES

328 SENSATIONAL SPAGHETTI AND MEATBALLS

SAUCE
- 2 tablespoons margarine or butter
- ½ cup chopped onion
- 1 cup chicken broth
- ½ cup HOLLAND HOUSE® White Cooking Wine
- 1 (28-ounce) can plum tomatoes, puréed, strained
- 1 (6-ounce) can tomato paste
- 3 tablespoons chopped fresh basil *or* 3 teaspoons dried basil leaves
- ½ teaspoon sugar
- 1 cup whipping cream

MEATBALLS
- ¾ pound bulk Italian sausage
- ¾ pound ground beef
- ¼ cup dry bread crumbs
- ¼ cup grated Parmesan cheese
- ¼ cup HOLLAND HOUSE® Red Cooking Wine with Italian Seasonings
- 1 egg, beaten

1 pound spaghetti, cooked, drained

Melt margarine in medium saucepan. Add onion; cook until tender. Add chicken broth and cooking wine. Bring to a boil; boil until liquid is reduced to about ¾ cup. Add puréed tomatoes, tomato paste, basil and sugar. Bring to a boil; reduce heat. Simmer 30 to 45 minutes or until thickened, stirring occasionally. Gradually stir in whipping cream.

While sauce is cooking, prepare meatballs. Heat oven to 350°F. In medium bowl, combine all meatball ingredients; shape into ¾-inch balls. Place meatballs in 15×10×1-inch baking pan. Bake at 350°F for 20 minutes or until brown. Top cooked spaghetti with meatballs and sauce.

Makes 8 servings

329 PASTA PEPERONATA

- Nonstick olive oil cooking spray
- 4 cups sliced green, red and yellow bell peppers (about 1 large pepper of each color)
- 4 cups sliced onions
- 3 cloves garlic, minced
- 1 teaspoon dried basil leaves
- ½ teaspoon dried marjoram leaves
- Salt and black pepper to taste (optional)
- 4 ounces spaghetti or linguine, cooked and kept warm
- 4 teaspoons grated Parmesan cheese

1. Spray large skillet with cooking spray. Heat over medium heat until hot. Add bell peppers, onions, garlic, basil and marjoram; cook, covered, 8 to 10 minutes or until vegetables are wilted. Uncover; cook and stir 20 to 30 minutes or until onions are caramelized and mixture is soft and creamy. Season to taste with salt and black pepper, if desired.

2. Spoon pasta onto plates; top with peperonata and cheese. Garnish with fresh basil, if desired.

Makes 6 side-dish servings

Pasta Peperonata

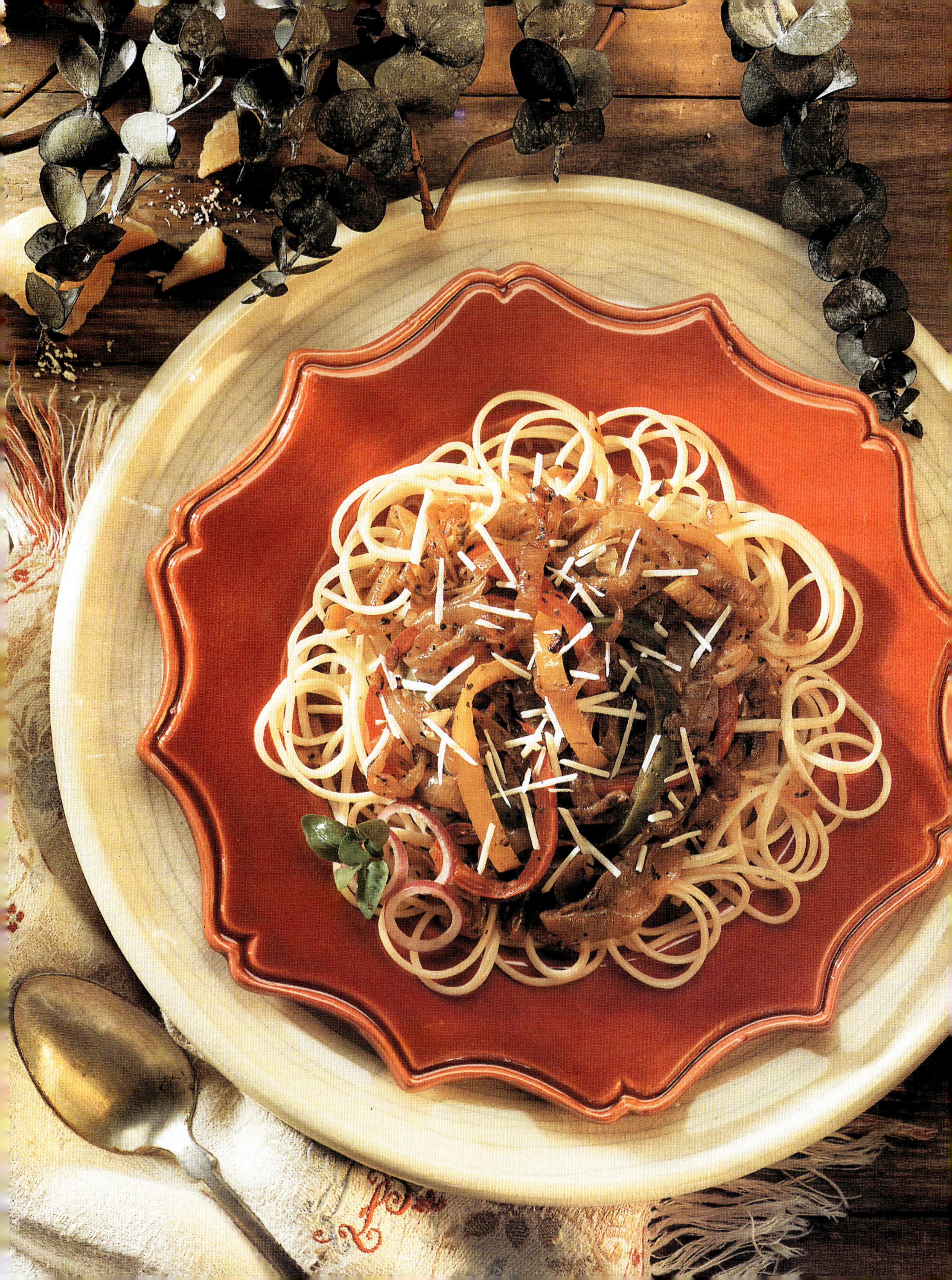

OLD FAVORITES

330 SPÄTZLE WITH MUSHROOMS

- 3 tablespoons butter, divided
- 4 ounces shiitake or button mushrooms, sliced
- 1¼ cups all-purpose flour
- ½ teaspoon salt
- ¼ teaspoon ground nutmeg
- ¾ cup milk
- 1 egg, lightly beaten
- Flat-leaf parsley for garnish

1. Melt 1 tablespoon butter in large nonstick skillet over medium-high heat. Add mushrooms; cook and stir 5 minutes or until softened. Remove from heat.

2. To prepare spätzle, combine flour, salt and nutmeg in medium bowl. Combine milk and egg in small bowl; stir milk mixture into flour mixture.

3. Bring salted water in Dutch oven to a boil. Rest colander over Dutch oven; pour batter into colander. Press batter through holes with rubber spatula.

4. Stir spätzle to separate. Cook 5 minutes or until tender, yet firm *(al dente)*. Drain spätzle.

5. Add remaining 2 tablespoons butter to skillet with mushrooms. Heat over medium heat until butter melts. Pour drained spätzle into skillet; toss with mushrooms and butter. Garnish, if desired. *Makes 4 servings*

331 TURKEY TETRAZZINI

- ½ pound fresh mushrooms, sliced
- ¼ cup sliced green onions
- 1 tablespoon margarine
- 2 tablespoons all-purpose flour
- ¼ teaspoon black pepper
- 1 (12-ounce) can light evaporated skim milk
- ⅓ cup low-sodium chicken broth
- 2 tablespoons sherry (optional)
- 8 ounces spaghetti
- 1 (8-ounce) package HEALTHY CHOICE® Fat Free natural shredded Mozzarella Cheese
- 1 pound turkey breast, cooked, cut into strips

Heat oven to 375°F. Cook mushrooms and green onions in margarine, stirring occasionally, until mushrooms are tender, about 7 minutes. Stir in flour and pepper. Cook and stir 1 minute. Add evaporated milk, chicken broth and sherry. Cook, stirring occasionally until sauce is thickened. Remove from heat. Cook spaghetti according to package directions. Drain, rinse and keep spaghetti warm. In 2-quart casserole sprayed with nonstick cooking spray, layer half of cooked spaghetti, cheese, turkey strips and sauce. Repeat layers with remaining ingredients. Bake at 375°F for 25 to 30 minutes or until bubbly and hot. *Makes 6 servings*

Spätzle with Mushrooms

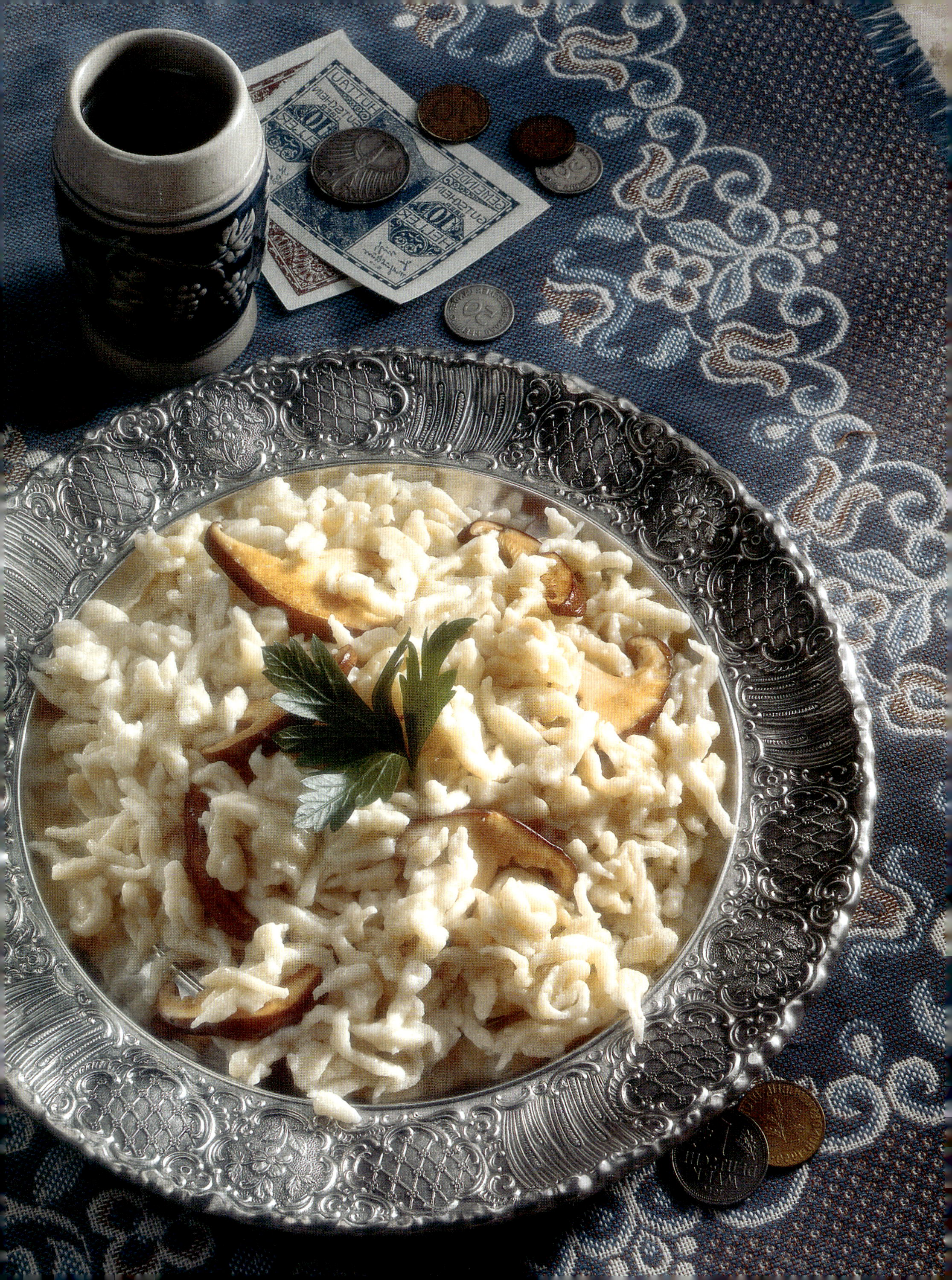

OLD FAVORITES

332 PASTA E FAGIOLI

10 ounces (1¼ cups) dry Navy or Cranberry Beans, sorted and rinsed
3¾ cups cold water
1½ teaspoons salt
⅔ cup plus 3 tablespoons vegetable oil, divided
1 bay leaf
2 to 3 whole cloves garlic, peeled
3 carrots, diced
2 ribs celery, sliced
1 large onion, chopped
1 to 2 cloves garlic, crushed
1 teaspoon dried oregano leaves
½ teaspoon dried basil leaves
Black pepper
6 to 7 tomatoes, peeled, coarsely chopped
8 ounces shell-shaped pasta

1. Place beans in Dutch oven; add cold water. Soak beans at room temperature 6 to 8 hours or overnight.

2. Add salt, ⅔ cup oil, bay leaf and whole garlic cloves to soaked beans. Simmer gently until beans are tender, 2 to 3 hours, stirring occasionally. Drain beans; reserve 1½ cups cooking liquid. Remove and discard bay leaf and garlic.

3. Heat remaining 3 tablespoons oil in large skillet. Add carrots, celery and onion; cook until soft. Add crushed garlic and seasonings; simmer 30 minutes. Add tomatoes; cook 10 minutes.

4. Cook pasta in boiling water until just tender; drain. Combine beans, vegetables, pasta and reserved cooking liquid. Cover; simmer 10 minutes, stirring occasionally.

5. Garnish with chopped fresh parsley; serve with grated Parmesan cheese.

Makes 6 to 8 servings

Favorite recipe from **Michigan Bean Commission**

333 CHICKEN WITH PASTA AND PUTTANESCA SAUCE

8 ounces uncooked ziti or other medium-sized pasta
1 package (1½ to 1¾ pounds) GALIL® Chicken Breast Cutlets, split
¼ teaspoon freshly ground black pepper
2 tablespoons olive oil
3 cloves garlic, minced
1 can (14½ ounces) diced tomatoes in juice, undrained
2 tablespoons tomato paste
1 tablespoon drained capers (optional)
1½ teaspoons dried basil leaves
¼ teaspoon crushed red pepper
10 kalamata olives, pitted
3 tablespoons chopped fresh Italian parsley (optional)

Cook pasta according to package directions. Do not drain. Set aside. Sprinkle chicken with black pepper. Heat oil in large deep nonstick skillet over medium-high heat. Add garlic and chicken. Cook chicken 2 minutes each side or until browned. Reduce heat to medium; add tomatoes with juice, tomato paste, capers, if desired, basil and crushed pepper. Simmer, uncovered, 12 to 15 minutes or until chicken is no longer pink in center. Coarsely chop olives; stir into sauce.

Transfer chicken to serving platter. Drain pasta; add to skillet. Toss well. Serve pasta with chicken. Garnish with fresh parsley, if desired.

Makes 4 servings

Chicken with Pasta and Puttanesca Sauce

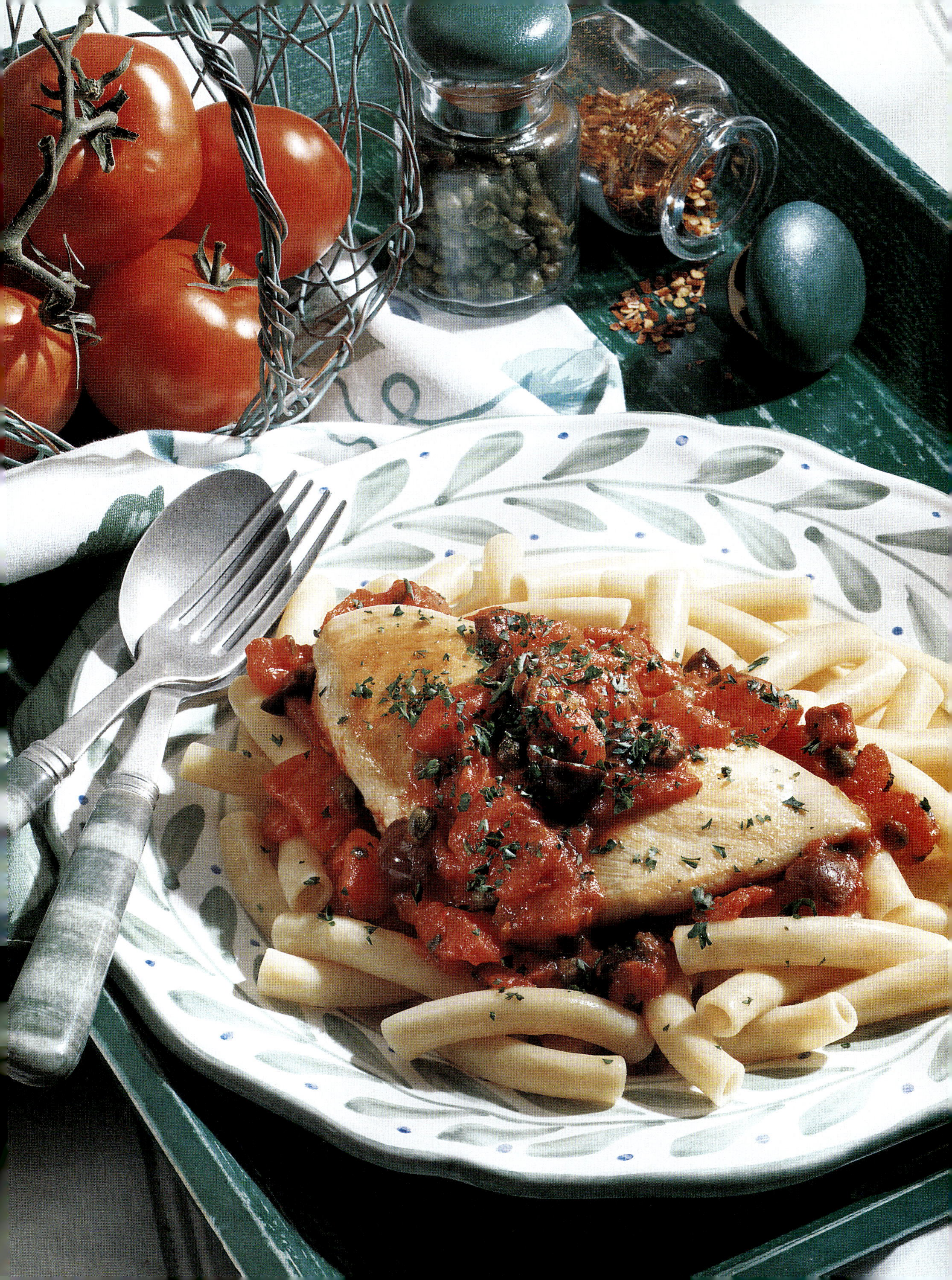

334 FETTUCCINE ALLA CARBONARA

- ¾ pound uncooked dry fettuccine or spaghetti
- 4 ounces pancetta (Italian bacon) or lean American bacon, cut into ½-inch-wide strips
- 3 cloves garlic, cut into halves
- ¼ cup dry white wine
- ⅓ cup heavy or whipping cream
- 1 egg
- 1 egg yolk
- ⅔ cup freshly grated Parmesan cheese (about 2 ounces), divided
- Generous dash ground white pepper
- Fresh oregano leaves for garnish

1. Cook fettuccine in large pot of boiling salted water 6 to 8 minutes just until *al dente;* remove from heat. Drain well; return to dry pot.

2. Cook and stir pancetta and garlic in large skillet over medium-low heat 4 minutes or until pancetta is light brown. Reserve 2 tablespoons drippings in skillet with pancetta. Discard garlic and remaining drippings.

3. Add wine to pancetta mixture; cook over medium heat 3 minutes or until wine is almost evaporated. Stir in cream; cook and stir 2 minutes. Remove from heat.

4. Whisk egg and egg yolk in top of double boiler. Place top of double boiler over simmering water, adjusting heat to maintain simmer. Whisk ⅓ cup cheese and pepper into egg mixture; cook and stir until sauce thickens slightly.

5. Pour pancetta mixture over fettuccine in pot; toss to coat. Heat over medium-low heat until heated through. Stir in egg mixture. Toss to coat evenly. Remove from heat. Serve with remaining ⅓ cup cheese. Garnish, if desired.   *Makes 4 servings*

335 HUNT'S® LINGUINE WITH RED CLAM SAUCE

- 1 tablespoon olive oil
- ¾ cup finely chopped onion
- ½ teaspoon fresh minced garlic
- 1 (15-ounce) can HUNT'S® Tomato Sauce
- 1 (10-ounce) can whole baby clams, reserve ¼ cup clam juice
- 1 tablespoon chopped fresh parsley
- 1 teaspoon dried basil leaves
- ½ teaspoon dried oregano leaves
- ⅛ teaspoon black pepper
- ¾ pound linguine, cooked and drained
- Grated Parmesan cheese

In large saucepan, heat oil; sauté onion and garlic until tender. Stir in tomato sauce, clams, clam juice, parsley, basil, oregano and pepper. Simmer, uncovered, 10 to 15 minutes; stir occasionally. Serve over linguine and top with Parmesan cheese.
Makes 4 servings

Fettuccine alla Carbonara

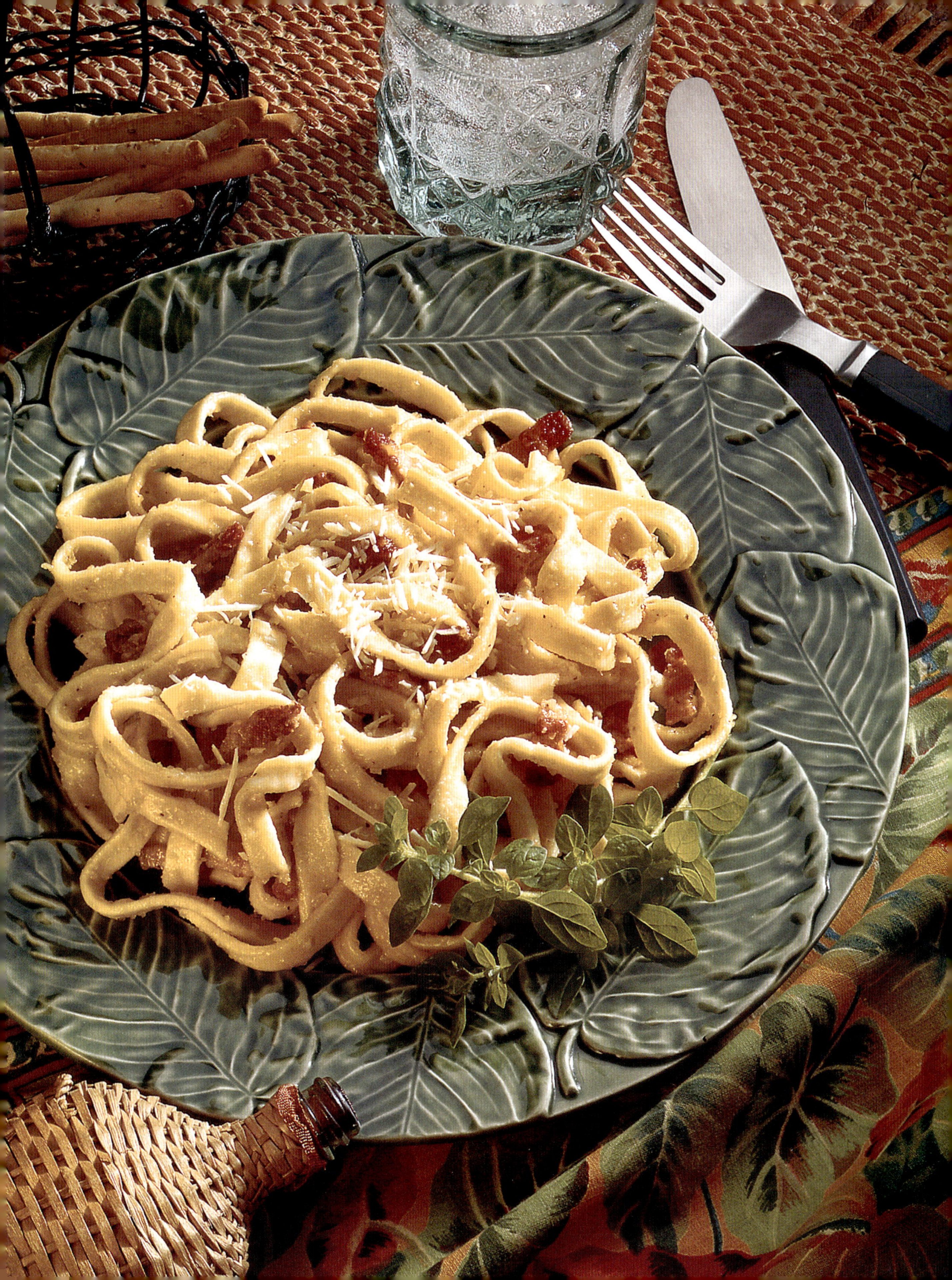

OLD FAVORITES

336 LOW–FAT MACARONI AND CHEESE

- 8 ounces uncooked macaroni
- 1 cup fat-free reduced-sodium chicken broth
- 1 shallot, finely minced
- 1 tablespoon all-purpose flour mixed with 2 tablespoons water
- ½ teaspoon dry mustard
- ⅛ teaspoon white pepper
- 1¾ cups (7 ounces) shredded reduced-fat mild Cheddar cheese, divided
- 1 cup nonfat ricotta cheese
- 1 tablespoon minced fresh parsley (optional)

1. Cook macaroni according to package directions, omitting salt. Drain; set aside.

2. Combine chicken broth and shallot in medium saucepan; bring to a boil over high heat. Cover; reduce heat to low and simmer 5 minutes. Stir in flour mixture. Cook and stir 3 to 5 minutes or until slightly thickened. Add mustard, pepper, 1 cup Cheddar cheese and ricotta cheese. Continue stirring until cheeses are completely melted. Stir in cooked pasta; mix well.

3. Remove pasta mixture from heat; stir in remaining ¾ cup Cheddar cheese and parsley, if desired. Garnish with fresh parsley sprigs, if desired. Serve immediately.
Makes 4 servings

337 CREAMY FETTUCCINE ALFREDO

- 1 (8-ounce) package PHILADELPHIA BRAND® Cream Cheese, cubed
- ¾ cup (3 ounces) KRAFT® 100% Grated Parmesan Cheese
- ½ cup butter or margarine
- ½ cup milk
- 8 ounces uncooked fettuccine, hot cooked and drained

In large saucepan, combine cream cheese, Parmesan cheese, butter and milk; stir over low heat until smooth. Add fettuccine; toss lightly.
Makes 4 servings

338 TOMATO BASIL PASTA POMADORO STYLE

- 1 (12-ounce) package PASTA LaBELLA® Tomato Basil Pasta
- ¼ cup extra-virgin olive oil
- 2½ cups diced tomatoes
- ¼ cup chopped fresh basil
- 2 teaspoons minced garlic
- Salt and black pepper to taste
- ¾ cup chicken broth
- ¼ cup grated Parmesan cheese

Cook pasta according to package directions. Heat olive oil, tomatoes, basil and garlic in large skillet. Season with salt and pepper; sauté 4 minutes. Add chicken broth and simmer 2 minutes. Mix sauce with hot Tomato Basil pasta, sprinkle with cheese and serve.
Makes 3 main-dish servings

Low-Fat Macaroni and Cheese

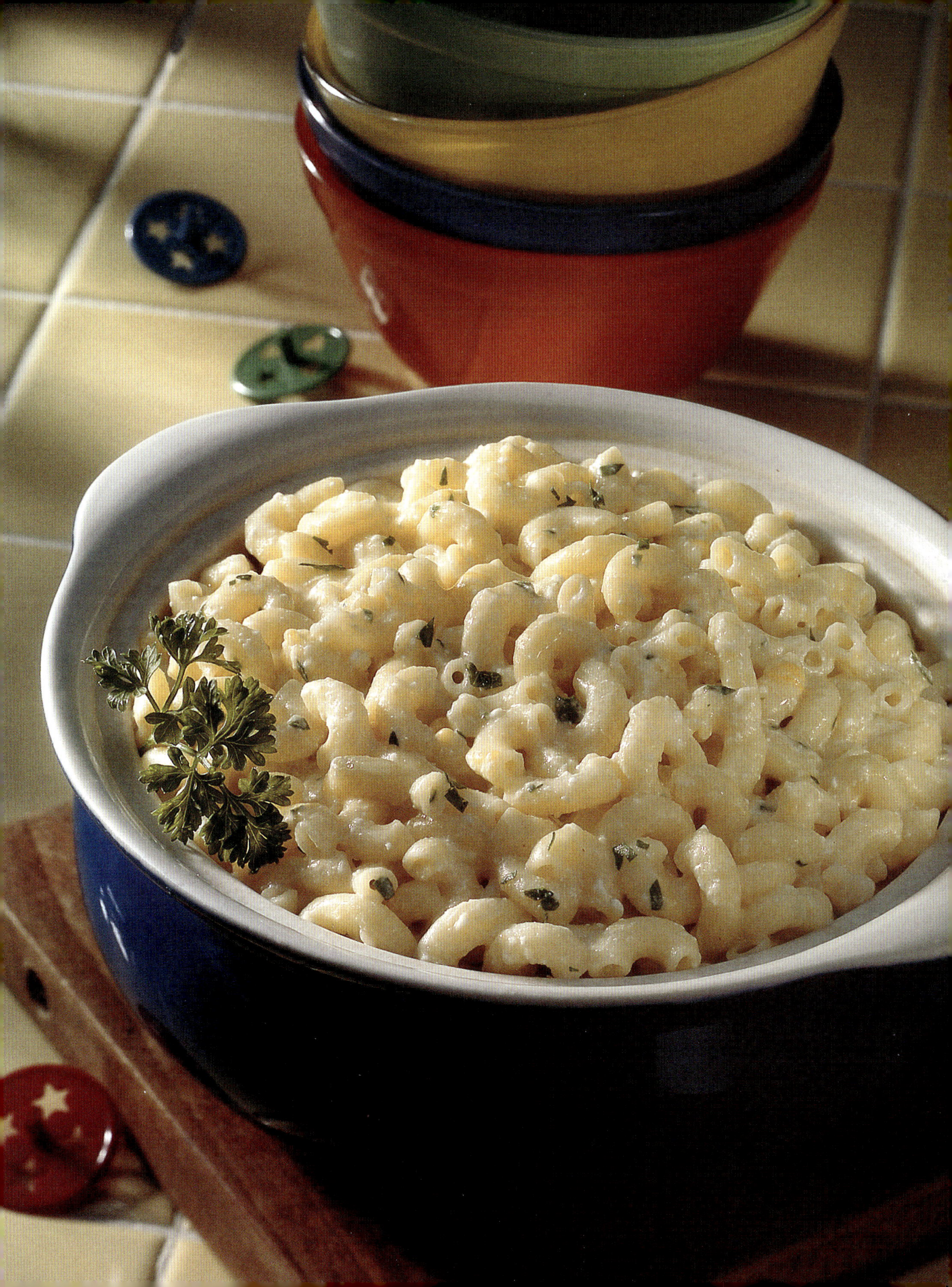

SPECTACULAR SAUCES

339 GIARDINIERA SAUCE

- 1 tablespoon olive or vegetable oil
- 2 cups sliced fresh mushrooms
- 1 cup chopped onion
- ½ cup sliced green bell pepper
- 2 cloves garlic, minced
- 1¾ cups (14½-ounce can) CONTADINA® Stewed Tomatoes, undrained
- ½ cup chicken broth
- ⅓ cup (½ 6-ounce can) CONTADINA® Tomato Paste
- 2 teaspoons Italian herb seasoning
- ½ teaspoon salt (optional)
- 1 pound dry pasta, cooked, drained, kept warm

In large skillet, heat oil. Add mushrooms, onion, bell pepper and garlic; sauté 3 to 4 minutes or until vegetables are tender. Stir in tomatoes and juice, chicken broth, tomato paste, Italian seasoning and salt, if desired. Bring to a boil. Reduce heat to low; simmer, uncovered, 10 minutes, stirring occasionally. Serve over pasta. *Makes 8 servings*

340 PIZZAIOLA SAUCE

- 1 tablespoon olive oil
- 2 cloves garlic, cut into halves
- 1 can (28 ounces) Italian plum tomatoes, undrained
- ¾ teaspoon dried marjoram leaves
- ½ teaspoon salt
- ⅛ teaspoon black pepper
- 2 tablespoons minced fresh parsley

Heat oil in medium saucepan over medium heat. Cook and stir garlic in hot oil 2 to 3 minutes until garlic is golden, but not brown. Remove and discard garlic. Press tomatoes and juice through sieve into garlic-flavored oil; discard seeds. Stir in marjoram, salt and pepper. Bring to a boil over high heat; reduce heat to medium-low. Cook, uncovered, 30 to 40 minutes until sauce is reduced to 2 cups, stirring frequently. Stir in parsley. *Makes 2 cups*

Giardiniera Sauce

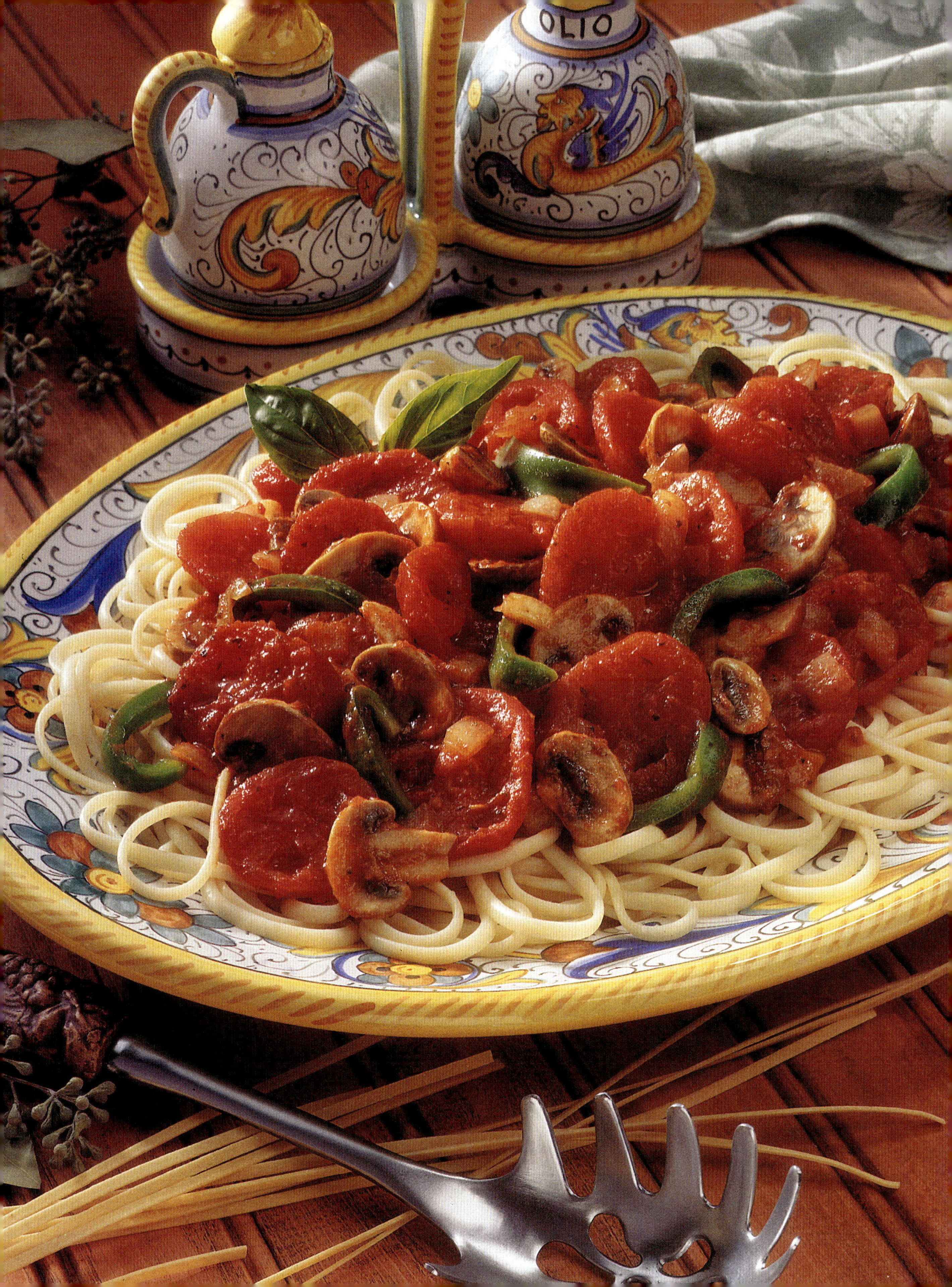
OLIO

SPECTACULAR SAUCES

341 SPINACH PESTO

- 1 bunch fresh spinach, washed, dried and chopped
- 1 cup fresh parsley
- 2/3 cup grated Parmesan cheese
- 1/2 cup walnut pieces
- 6 cloves fresh garlic, crushed
- 4 flat anchovy fillets
- 1 tablespoon dried tarragon leaves
- 1 teaspoon dried basil leaves
- 1 teaspoon salt
- 1/2 teaspoon black pepper
- 1/4 teaspoon anise or fennel seeds
- 1 cup olive oil
  Pasta twists, spaghetti or shells, cooked, drained, kept warm
  Mixed salad (optional)

Place spinach, parsley, cheese, walnuts, garlic, anchovies, tarragon, basil, salt, pepper and anise in food processor. Process until smooth. With motor running, add oil in thin stream. Adjust seasonings, if desired. Pour desired amount of sauce over pasta; toss gently to coat. Serve with salad, if desired. Garnish as desired.

Makes 2 cups sauce

NOTE: Keep any remaining sauce covered in refrigerator for up to 1 week.

Favorite recipe from **Christopher Ranch Garlic**

342 FRESH HERB SAUCE

- 1 cup whipping cream
- 1/4 cup HOLLAND HOUSE® Vermouth Cooking Wine
- 3 green onions, chopped
- 1 clove garlic, crushed
- 2 teaspoons chopped fresh basil
- 1 teaspoon chopped fresh thyme

Bring whipping cream and cooking wine to a boil in small saucepan. Reduce heat; simmer 10 minutes. Add remaining ingredients; simmer 5 minutes or until slightly thickened.

Makes 1 1/3 cups

343 FRESH TOMATO, BASIL AND RICOTTA SAUCE

- 3 cups chopped ripe tomatoes
- 1/2 cup chopped fresh basil
- 2 tablespoons minced red onion
- 1 clove garlic, chopped
- 1 cup ricotta cheese
- 1/4 cup FILIPPO BERIO® Olive Oil
  Salt and black pepper to taste
- 1 pound pasta (such as rotelle, fusilli, ziti, penne or tubetti), cooked according to package directions, drained, kept warm

Combine tomatoes, basil, onion and garlic in large bowl. Stir in ricotta cheese, olive oil and salt and pepper to taste. Add pasta; toss well. Serve immediately.

Makes 3 cups sauce

Spinach Pesto

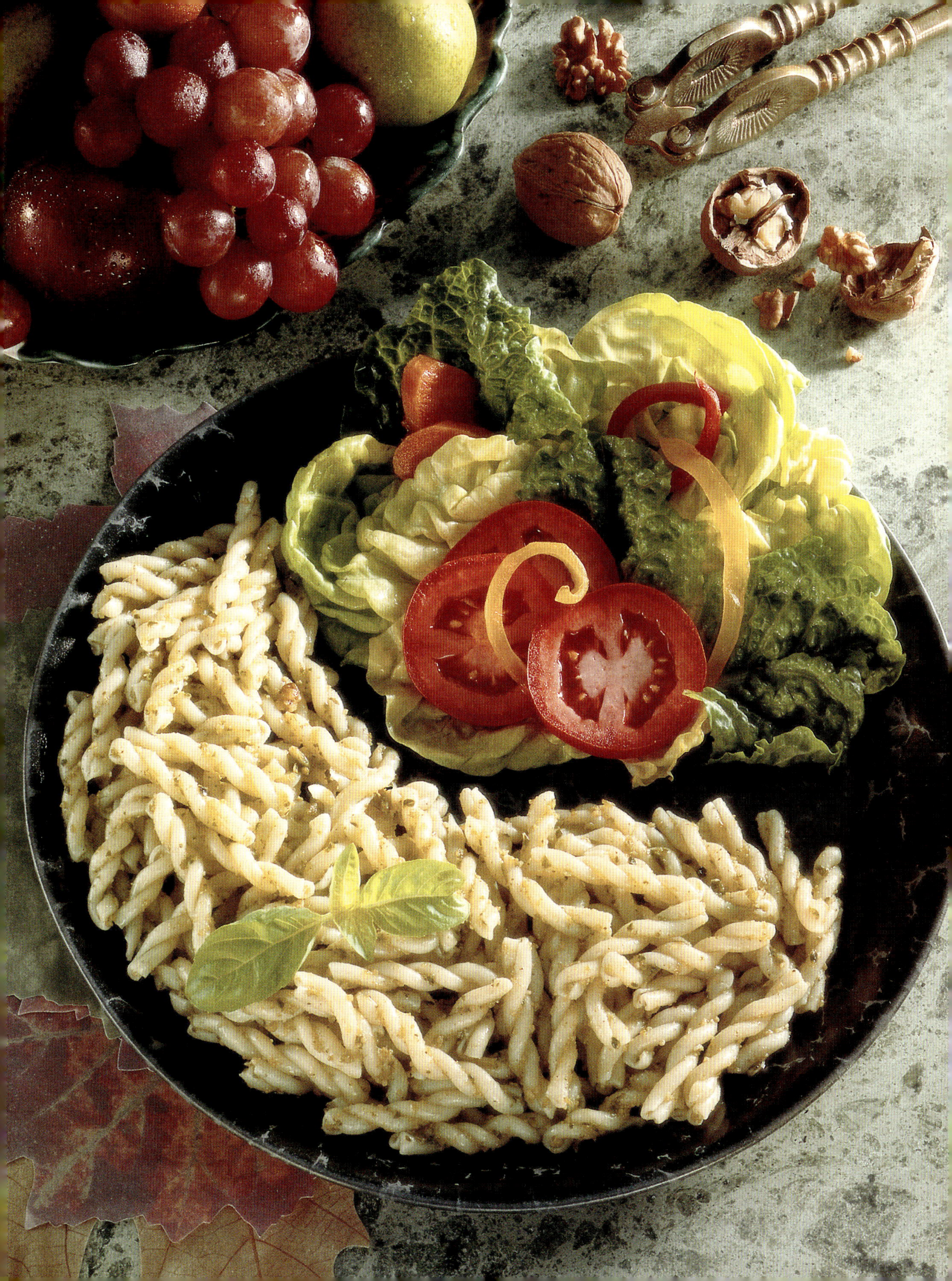

SPECTACULAR SAUCES

344 CHUNKY PASTA SAUCE WITH MEAT

- 6 ounces ground beef
- 6 ounces mild or hot Italian sausage, sliced
- ½ medium onion, coarsely chopped
- 1 clove garlic, minced
- 2 cans (14½ ounces each) DEL MONTE® Chunky Pasta Recipe Stewed Tomatoes, undrained
- 1 can (8 ounces) DEL MONTE® Tomato Sauce
- ¼ cup red wine (optional)
   Hot cooked pasta
   Grated Parmesan cheese

In large saucepan, brown beef and sausage; drain all but 1 tablespoon drippings. Add onion and garlic; cook until tender. Add stewed tomatoes with juice, tomato sauce and wine. Boil, uncovered, 15 minutes, stirring frequently. Serve over pasta; top with Parmesan cheese.

Makes 4 servings (4 cups sauce)

VARIATION: Serve sauce over vegetables, omelets or frittatas.

345 VEAL SAUCE LUCIA

- 2 tablespoons vegetable oil
- 1½ pounds veal stew meat, cut into small cubes
- 1 medium onion, chopped
- 1 medium carrot, grated
- ¾ teaspoon dried basil leaves
- ¾ teaspoon LAWRY'S® Garlic Powder with Parsley
- 1 package (1.42 ounces) LAWRY'S® Extra Rich & Thick Spaghetti Sauce Spices & Seasonings
- 1¾ cups water
- 1 can (6 ounces) tomato paste
- ½ cup frozen peas
- 8 ounces linguine or other pasta, cooked and drained

In Dutch oven, heat oil. Brown veal; drain fat. Add onion, carrot, basil and Garlic Powder with Parsley; sauté 5 minutes. Add Extra Rich & Thick Spaghetti Sauce Spices & Seasonings, water and tomato paste; blend well. Bring to a boil. Reduce heat; simmer, covered, 30 minutes. Add peas; simmer 5 minutes.

Makes 4 servings

PRESENTATION: Ladle sauce over cooked linguine and serve with a Caesar salad and garlic bread.

Chunky Pasta Sauce with Meat

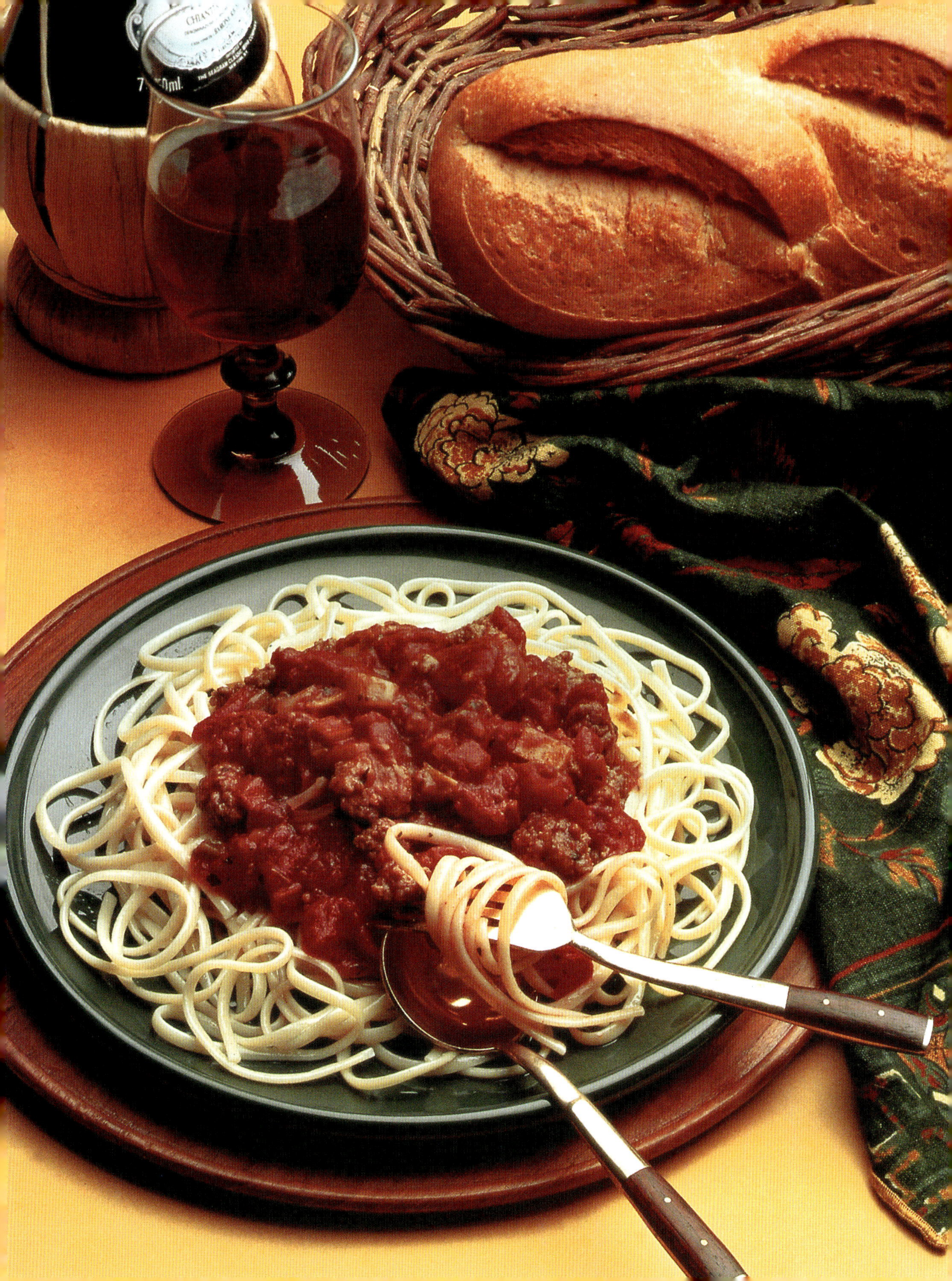

SPECTACULAR SAUCES

346 AN UNCOMMON PASTA SAUCE

- 2 tablespoons olive oil
- 1 medium onion, chopped
- 3 cups boiling water
- 1 package (3 ounces) *or* 2 cups SONOMA dried tomato halves, cut into quarters
- 1 large clove garlic, cut into quarters
- 2 tablespoons chopped parsley
- 1 tablespoon chopped fresh basil *or* 1 teaspoon dried basil leaves
- 2 teaspoons chopped fresh oregano *or* ¾ teaspoon dried oregano leaves
- 2 teaspoons lemon juice
- 1 teaspoon salt
- ¼ teaspoon black pepper
- Pasta, cooked, drained, kept warm
- Grated Parmesan cheese (optional)

Heat oil in large skillet over medium heat. Add onion; sauté 5 minutes. Combine boiling water and tomato halves in medium bowl; set aside 2 to 3 minutes. Drain well.

Place ⅔ of rehydrated tomato halves and garlic in blender or food processor; process until smooth. Add to onion in skillet. Stir in remaining ⅓ rehydrated tomato halves. Bring to a boil; reduce heat. Simmer, uncovered, 10 minutes.

Stir in parsley, basil, oregano, lemon juice, salt and pepper; simmer 1 minute. Remove from heat. Serve over pasta. Sprinkle with cheese, if desired. *Makes 2½ to 3 cups*

347 ANCHOVY–OLIVE PASTA SAUCE

- 4 tablespoons extra-virgin olive oil
- 1 (2-ounce) can anchovies in olive oil, undrained
- 2 cloves garlic, minced
- 1 medium onion, finely chopped
- 1 (4¼-ounce) can chopped black olives, drained
- 20 green olives, sliced
- 2 tablespoons capers, drained
- 1 teaspoon dried basil leaves
- 2 teaspoons dried Italian seasoning
- ½ teaspoon freshly ground black pepper
- 1 (16-ounce) can tomatoes
- 1 (6-ounce) can tomato paste
- ¾ cup water
- ½ cup marsala or other red wine
- TABASCO® pepper sauce to taste

In medium saucepan, combine olive oil and anchovies. Cook over medium heat, stirring to purée anchovies, 3 to 5 minutes. Add garlic and onion; cook 5 minutes or until tender.

Stir in remaining ingredients and simmer, uncovered, 15 minutes. *Makes 4 cups*

An Uncommon Pasta Sauce

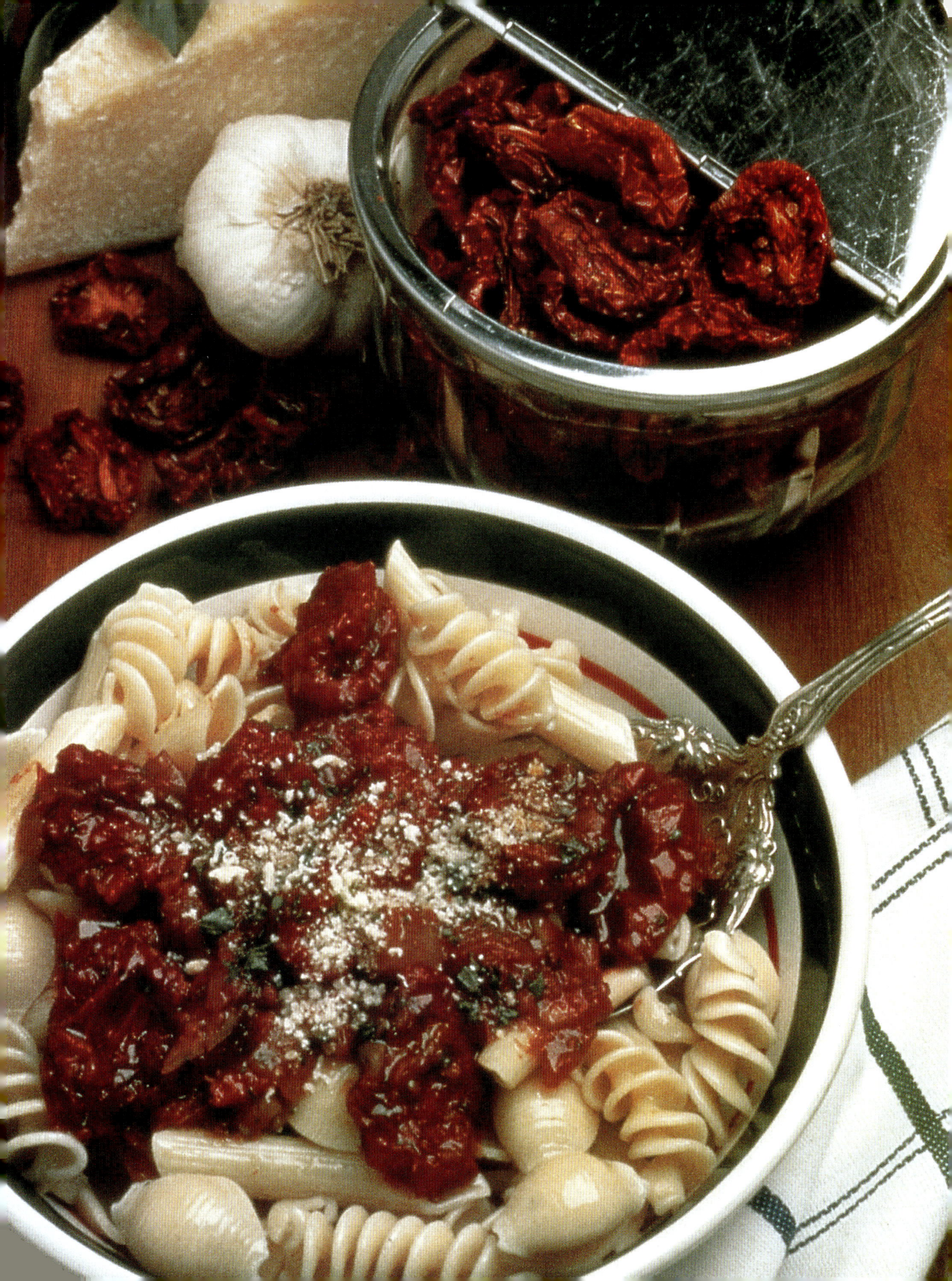

SPECTACULAR SAUCES

348 HUNT'S® SPAGHETTI SAUCE

- ½ pound ground beef
- ¼ cup chopped onion
- 2 (8-ounce) cans HUNT'S® Tomato Sauce
- ¾ teaspoon sugar
- ½ teaspoon dried basil leaves
- ¼ teaspoon dried oregano leaves
- ¼ teaspoon garlic powder

Brown beef with onion in medium saucepan over medium-high heat until no longer pink; drain. Stir in tomato sauce, sugar, basil, oregano and garlic powder. Simmer, covered, 10 minutes; stir occasionally.

Makes 2 cups

349 PINE NUT AND CILANTRO PESTO

- 1 cup pine nuts
- ½ cup cilantro leaves
- ½ teaspoon LAWRY'S® Garlic Powder with Parsley
- ¼ teaspoon LAWRY'S® Seasoned Salt
- 2 tablespoons water
- 1 tablespoon vegetable oil

In food processor, combine pine nuts, cilantro, Garlic Powder with Parsley and Seasoned Salt. Process until smooth. Add water and oil. Process until well blended.

Makes 2 servings

350 RED PEPPER & WHITE BEAN PASTA SAUCE

- 12 ounces uncooked penne or ziti pasta
- 1 teaspoon olive oil
- 3 cloves garlic, chopped
- 1 jar (11½ ounces) GUILTLESS GOURMET® Roasted Red Pepper Salsa
- ¾ cup canned cannellini beans (white kidney beans), rinsed well
- ½ cup low-sodium chicken or vegetable broth, defatted
- ⅓ cup chopped fresh cilantro
- ¼ cup crumbled feta cheese
- Fresh thyme sprigs (optional)

Cook pasta according to package directions. Drain and keep warm.

Meanwhile, heat oil in medium nonstick skillet over medium-high heat until hot. Add garlic; cook and stir 30 seconds or until softened. *Do not brown.* Add salsa, beans, broth and cilantro; bring just to a boil, stirring occasionally. (If mixture appears too thick, add water, 1 tablespoon at a time, to desired consistency.) To serve, place pasta in large serving bowl. Add salsa mixture; toss to coat well. Sprinkle with feta cheese. Garnish with thyme, if desired.

Makes 4 servings

Left to right: *Tomato Sauce with Ricotta & Herbs (page 322), Garden Tomato Sauce and Warm Tomato-Pepper Sauce (page 318)*

351 GARDEN TOMATO SAUCE

  5 cups chopped onions
  ¼ cup olive oil
  4 cans (28 ounces each) whole California tomatoes, undrained
  2 quarts cubed zucchini
  1 quart corn kernels
  1 tablespoon minced garlic
  2 teaspoons salt
  1 teaspoon red pepper flakes
  2 tablespoons sugar
  1⅓ cups chopped fresh basil

1. Sauté onions in olive oil in large skillet over medium heat until soft.

2. Stir in canned tomatoes and liquid and remaining ingredients, except basil. Cook 10 to 15 minutes, stirring occasionally, until thickened.

3. Stir in basil.   *Makes 24 servings*

Favorite recipe from **California Tomato Commission**

SPECTACULAR SAUCES

352 FIRST–CLASS PASTA SAUCE

- 1 pound lean ground beef
- 1 cup chopped onion
- 1 clove garlic, minced
- 3½ cups (28-ounce can) CONTADINA® Whole Peeled Tomatoes, cut up, undrained
- 1⅓ cups (12-ounce can) CONTADINA® Tomato Paste
- 1 cup water
- 1 cup sliced fresh mushrooms
- 1 bay leaf
- 1 teaspoon salt
- 1 teaspoon dried oregano leaves
- ½ teaspoon dried basil leaves
- ⅛ teaspoon black pepper
- 1 pound dry pasta, cooked, drained and kept warm
- ½ cup grated Parmesan cheese

Brown ground beef with onion and garlic over medium-high heat in large saucepan; drain. Add tomatoes and juice, tomato paste, water, mushrooms, bay leaf, salt, oregano, basil and pepper. Bring to a boil. Reduce heat to low. Simmer, uncovered, 30 minutes, stirring occasionally. Remove bay leaf. Serve over hot cooked pasta. Sprinkle with Parmesan cheese. *Makes 8 cups*

353 RED CHILI SAUCE

- 6 tablespoons butter or margarine
- 2 small red hot chili peppers, seeded and finely chopped*
- 4 green onions, thinly sliced
- ½ medium red bell pepper, minced
- 3 cloves garlic, minced
- 3 tablespoons minced fresh parsley
- ½ teaspoon salt
- ⅛ teaspoon black pepper

*Chili peppers can sting and irritate the skin; wear rubber gloves when handling peppers and do not touch eyes.

1. Heat butter in large skillet over medium-high heat. Add chili peppers, onions, bell pepper and garlic. Cook and stir 2 minutes or until onions are soft.

2. Remove from heat. Stir in parsley, salt and black pepper. *Makes about ¾ cup*

Red Chili Sauce

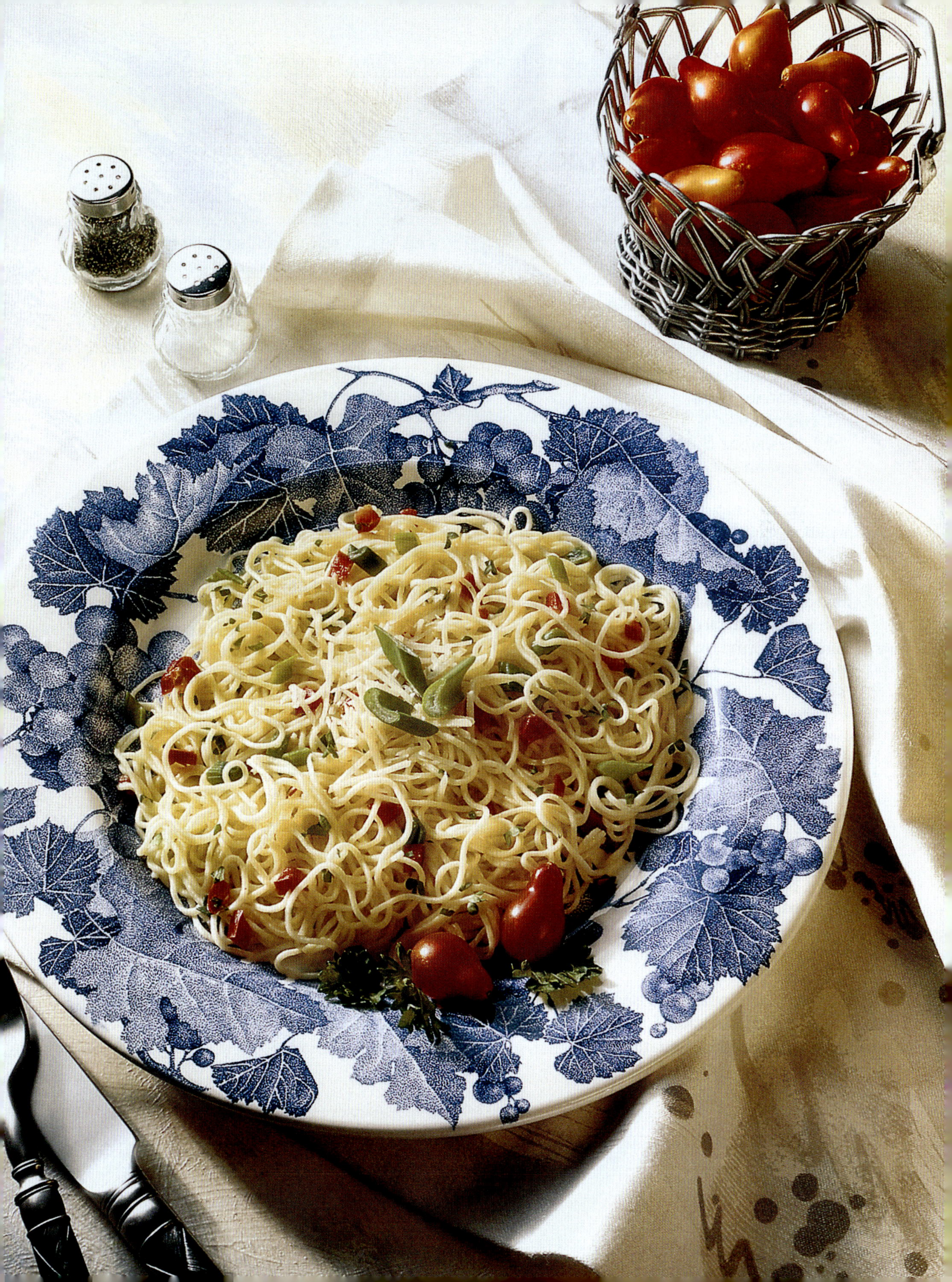

SPECTACULAR SAUCES

354 ZESTY ARTICHOKE BASIL SAUCE

- ¾ cup (6-ounce jar) marinated artichoke hearts, drained and marinade reserved
- 1 cup slivered onion
- 1 large clove garlic, minced
- 1¾ cups (14½-ounce can) CONTADINA® Whole Peeled Tomatoes, undrained
- ⅔ cup (6-ounce can) CONTADINA® Tomato Paste
- 1 cup water
- 2 tablespoons chopped fresh basil
- ½ teaspoon salt

In 2½-quart saucepan, heat reserved artichoke marinade. Cook and stir onion and garlic in marinade 2 to 3 minutes or until tender. Chop artichoke hearts; add to onion mixture with tomatoes and juice, tomato paste, water, basil and salt. Break up tomatoes. Bring to a boil; reduce heat to low. Simmer, uncovered, 15 to 20 minutes.

Makes 4 cups

355 ITALIAN SPAGHETTI SAUCE

- 1 package (12 ounces) JONES® Hot Roll Sausage
- 1 medium onion, finely chopped
- 2 cloves garlic, minced
- 1 can (6 ounces) tomato paste
- 1 cup water
- 1 can (16 ounces) pear-shaped tomatoes, cut up, undrained
- 1 can (8 ounces) tomato sauce
- 2 bay leaves
- ½ teaspoon sugar

Brown sausage in large skillet over medium-high heat, stirring occasionally to separate sausage; drain. Add onion and garlic; cook and stir until tender. Add tomato paste; mix well. Stir in water. Reduce heat to low; simmer 10 minutes, stirring occasionally.

In medium or large saucepan, heat tomatoes over medium heat. Stir in sausage mixture, tomato sauce, bay leaves and sugar. Reduce heat to low; simmer 1 to 2 hours or to desired consistency. Remove bay leaves just before serving. *Makes 4 servings*

356 WARM TOMATO–PEPPER SAUCE

- 2½ quarts chopped red bell peppers
- 5 cups thinly sliced green onions
- 3 tablespoons minced garlic
- ⅓ cup olive oil
- 8 quarts California tomatoes, seeded and diced
- 1⅔ cups grated Parmesan cheese
- 1 cup chopped fresh parsley
- 2½ teaspoons black pepper
- ¾ teaspoon cayenne pepper

1. Sauté bell peppers, onions and garlic in oil in large skillet over medium-high heat until vegetables are crisp-tender.

2. Stir in tomatoes; cook over high heat until sauce thickens, 10 to 15 minutes.

3. Stir in remaining ingredients.

Makes 24 servings

Favorite recipe from **California Tomato Commission**

Zesty Artichoke Basil Sauce

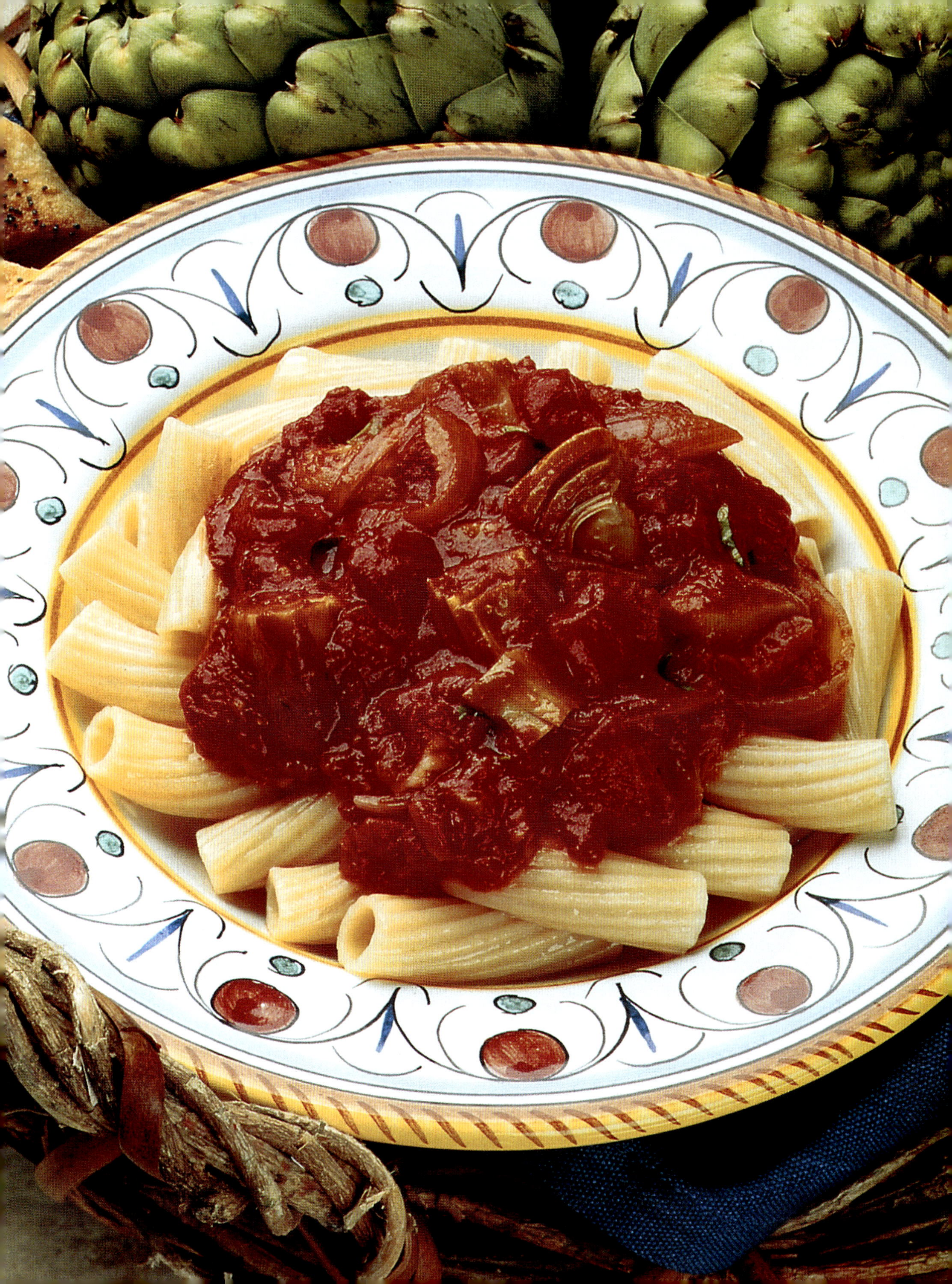

SPECTACULAR SAUCES

357 NEAPOLITAN SAUCE

- 2 tablespoons butter or margarine
- 1 tablespoon olive oil
- 1 can (28 ounces) Italian plum tomatoes, undrained
- 1 teaspoon dried basil leaves
- ½ teaspoon salt
- ⅛ teaspoon black pepper
- 3 tablespoons chopped fresh parsley

Heat butter and oil in medium saucepan over medium heat. Press tomatoes and juice through sieve into hot butter mixture; discard seeds. Stir in basil, salt and pepper. Bring to a boil over high heat; reduce heat to medium-low. Cook, uncovered, 30 to 40 minutes until sauce is reduced to 2 cups, stirring frequently. Stir in parsley.

Makes 2 cups

358 SQUID MEDITERRANEAN

- 2 pounds cleaned, whole squid (body and tentacles)
- 1 tablespoon olive oil
- ¾ cup finely chopped onion
- 1 clove garlic, minced
- 2 (16-ounce) cans Italian-style tomatoes, drained and chopped
- 3 tablespoons sliced black olives
- 1 tablespoon capers
- ½ teaspoon dried oregano leaves
- ¼ teaspoon dried marjoram leaves
- ⅛ teaspoon red pepper flakes

Cut body of squid into ½-inch slices; set aside. Heat olive oil in large skillet; add onion and garlic. Cook until onion is tender. Add squid and remaining ingredients. Bring to a boil. Cover, reduce heat and simmer 30 minutes or until squid is tender.

Makes 4 servings

Preparation time: about 45 minutes

Favorite recipe from **National Fisheries Institute**

359 SAVORY CAPER AND OLIVE SAUCE

- 1 cup chopped onion
- 1 large clove garlic, minced
- 2 tablespoons olive oil
- ¾ cup sliced, quartered zucchini
- 1¾ cups (14½-ounce can) CONTADINA® Whole Peeled Tomatoes, cut up, undrained
- 1 cup water
- ⅔ cup (6-ounce can) CONTADINA® Tomato Paste
- ½ teaspoon salt
- 1 can (2¼ ounces) sliced pitted ripe olives, drained
- 2 tablespoons drained capers

In medium saucepan, cook and stir onion and garlic in olive oil over medium heat 2 to 3 minutes. Add zucchini, tomatoes and juice, water, tomato paste, salt, olives and capers. Bring to a boil. Reduce heat to low; simmer, uncovered, 20 minutes, stirring occasionally.

Makes 4 cups

Neapolitan Sauce

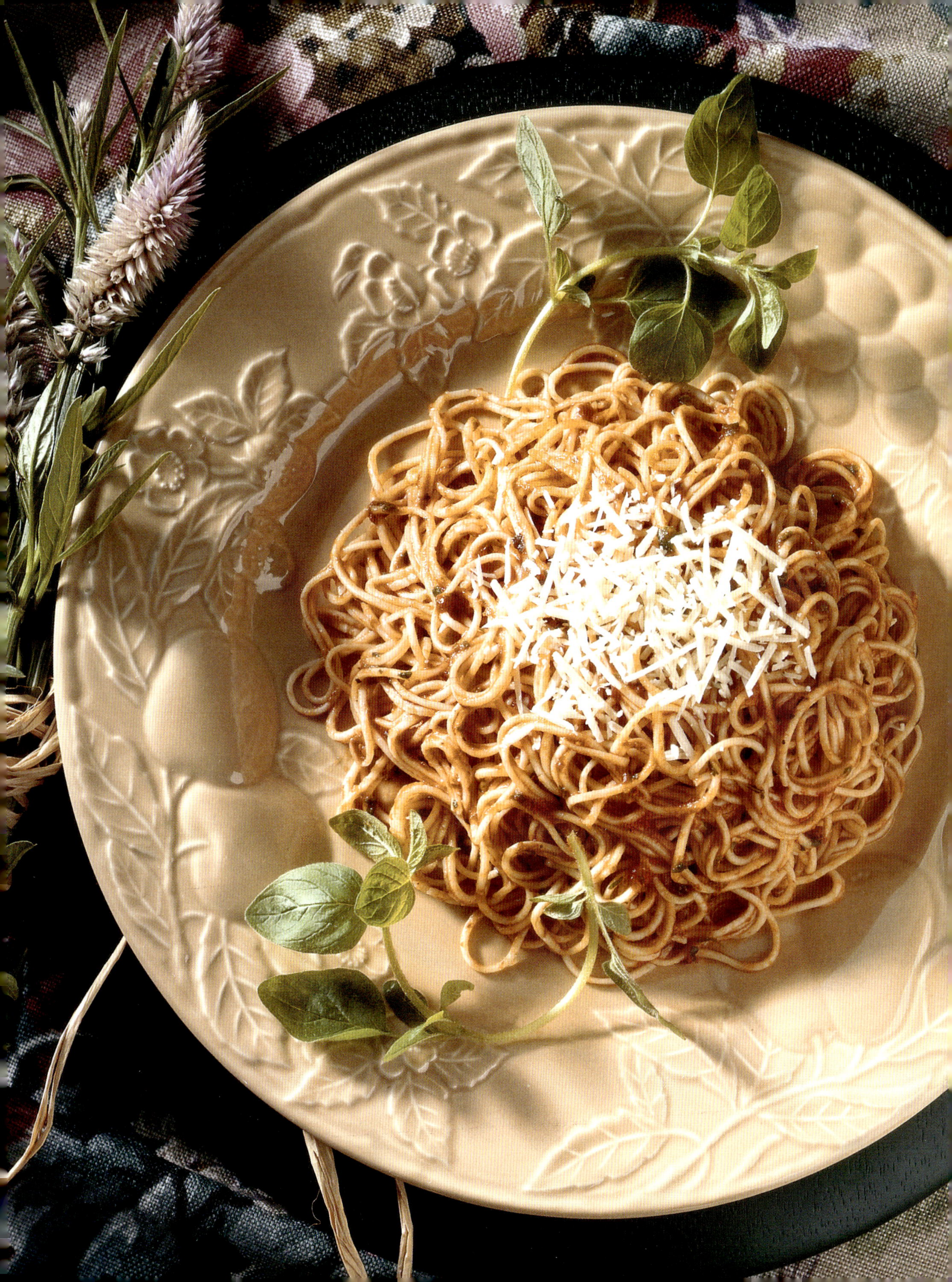

SPECTACULAR SAUCES

360 SWEETY MEATY SAUCE FOR ZITI

- 2 tablespoons CHEF PAUL PRUDHOMME'S® Poultry Magic®, divided
- 1 pound ground turkey
- 2 tablespoons olive oil
- 2 tablespoons margarine
- 1 cup chopped onion
- 1 cup chopped green bell pepper
- 2 cups canned crushed tomatoes
- 1 cup tomato purée
- ¾ cup diced carrots
- 1½ cups chicken stock or water, divided
- 1 tablespoon granulated sugar
- ½ teaspoon salt
- 1 tablespoon dark brown sugar (optional)
- 12 ounces ziti pasta, cooked and drained

Mix 1 tablespoon plus 2 teaspoons Poultry Magic® with turkey, working it in well with your hands; set aside.

Heat oil and margarine in 3½-quart saucepan over medium-high heat 1 minute or until margarine has melted and mixture begins to sizzle. Add turkey; cook, stirring occasionally to separate chunks, until turkey is no longer pink, about 6 minutes. Add onion and bell pepper; cook and stir 3 to 4 minutes or until tender. Add remaining 1 teaspoon Poultry Magic®, tomatoes, tomato purée, carrots, ½ cup stock, granulated sugar and salt; mix well. (If you like a sweeter sauce, add the brown sugar.) Cook, stirring occasionally, 3 to 4 minutes or until mixture comes to a boil. Reduce heat to low; cover. Simmer 30 minutes, stirring occasionally. Stir in remaining 1 cup stock; cover. Simmer an additional 20 minutes or until sauce has thickened and has changed from bright red to dark red in color, stirring occasionally. Remove from heat. Serve over hot pasta. *Makes 4 servings*

361 TOMATO SAUCE WITH RICOTTA & HERBS

- 8 cups chopped onions
- 2 tablespoons minced garlic
- 6 tablespoons olive oil
- 9 quarts California tomatoes, peeled, seeded and diced
- 6 tablespoons chopped fresh marjoram*
- 4 teaspoons chopped fresh rosemary
- 1 tablespoon salt
- 1 tablespoon sugar
- 2 teaspoons black pepper
- 1½ cups ricotta cheese

Or, use 2 tablespoons dried oregano leaves and 1 teaspoon dried rosemary.

1. Sauté onions and garlic in oil in large skillet over medium-high heat until softened.

2. Stir in remaining ingredients except cheese. Cook over medium-high heat, stirring frequently, 10 to 15 minutes, or until sauce thickens.

3. Top each serving with 1 tablespoon ricotta cheese. *Makes 24 servings*

Favorite recipe from **California Tomato Commission**

SPECTACULAR SAUCES

362 BASIC TOMATO SAUCE

1 teaspoon vegetable oil
1 medium onion, chopped
2 cloves garlic, chopped
2 (28-ounce) cans whole tomatoes
1 (6-ounce) can tomato paste
2 teaspoons dried Italian seasoning
2 bay leaves
Salt and black pepper to taste

In medium heavy saucepan, stir together oil, onion and garlic. Cook over low heat, stirring often, until onion is very soft and aromatic, about 6 to 8 minutes. In food processor or blender, purée tomatoes. Add tomatoes, tomato paste, Italian seasoning and bay leaves to saucepan and bring to a simmer over medium-high heat. Reduce heat to very low and let sauce simmer slowly for 30 minutes, stirring often to prevent burning. If adding meatballs, do so at this time, and simmer them in the sauce 20 minutes, stirring often. If not adding meatballs, simmer sauce for another 20 minutes (50 minutes total). Season to taste with salt and pepper. Remove bay leaves before serving. *Makes 4 servings*

Favorite recipe from **National Pasta Association**

363 TRADITIONAL SPAGHETTI SAUCE

1 pound mild pork, turkey or chicken Italian sausage, casing removed
½ cup chopped onion
2 cloves garlic, minced
1¾ cups (14½-ounce can) CONTADINA® Pasta Ready Chunky Tomatoes with Olive Oil, Garlic and Spices, undrained
1 cup water or chicken broth
⅔ cup (6-ounce can) CONTADINA® Tomato Paste
1 tablespoon chopped fresh parsley
12 ounces dry spaghetti, cooked, drained and kept warm

COOK sausage in large skillet over medium-high heat 3 to 5 minutes or until no longer pink, stirring to break up sausage.

ADD onion and garlic; cook 2 to 3 minutes. Drain.

STIR in Pasta Ready Tomatoes and juice, water, tomato paste and parsley. Bring to a boil. Reduce heat; simmer 10 to 15 minutes. Serve over hot cooked spaghetti.
Makes 4 to 6 servings

SPECTACULAR SAUCES

364 TUNA IN RED PEPPER SAUCE

- 2 cups chopped red bell peppers (about 2 peppers)
- ½ cup chopped onion
- 1 clove garlic, minced
- 2 tablespoons vegetable oil
- ¼ cup dry red or white wine
- ¼ cup chicken broth
- 2 teaspoons sugar
- ¼ teaspoon pepper
- 1 red bell pepper, slivered and cut into ½-inch pieces
- 1 yellow or green bell pepper, slivered and cut into ½-inch pieces
- ½ cup julienne-strip carrots
- 1 can (9¼ ounces) STARKIST® Tuna, drained and broken into chunks
- Hot cooked pasta or rice

In skillet, sauté chopped bell peppers, onion and garlic in oil for 5 minutes, or until vegetables are very tender. In blender container or food processor bowl, place vegetable mixture; cover and process until puréed. Return to pan; stir in wine, chicken broth, sugar and pepper. Keep warm. In 2-quart saucepan, steam bell pepper pieces and carrot over simmering water for 5 minutes. Stir steamed vegetables into sauce with tuna; cook for 2 minutes, or until heated through. Serve tuna mixture over pasta. *Makes 4 to 5 servings*

Preparation time: 20 minutes

365 BELL PEPPER AND MUSHROOM PASTA SAUCE

- 1 tablespoon WESSON® Vegetable Oil
- 2 cups julienne-cut green bell peppers
- 1 cup chopped onion
- 1 teaspoon minced fresh garlic
- 1 can (15 ounces) HUNT'S® Tomato Sauce
- 1 can (14½ ounces) HUNT'S® Whole Tomatoes, cut up, undrained
- 1 can (4 ounces) sliced mushrooms, drained
- 1 teaspoon dried basil leaves
- ½ teaspoon dried oregano leaves
- ¼ teaspoon black pepper
- 2 tablespoons grated Parmesan cheese
- 4 cups mostaccioli, cooked and drained

In medium saucepan, heat oil over medium-high heat. Add green peppers, onion and garlic; cook and stir until crisp-tender. Add all remaining ingredients except Parmesan cheese and mostaccioli. Reduce heat to medium. Simmer, uncovered, 20 minutes. Stir in Parmesan cheese; serve over hot mostaccioli. *Makes 4 to 6 servings*

Tuna in Red Pepper Sauce

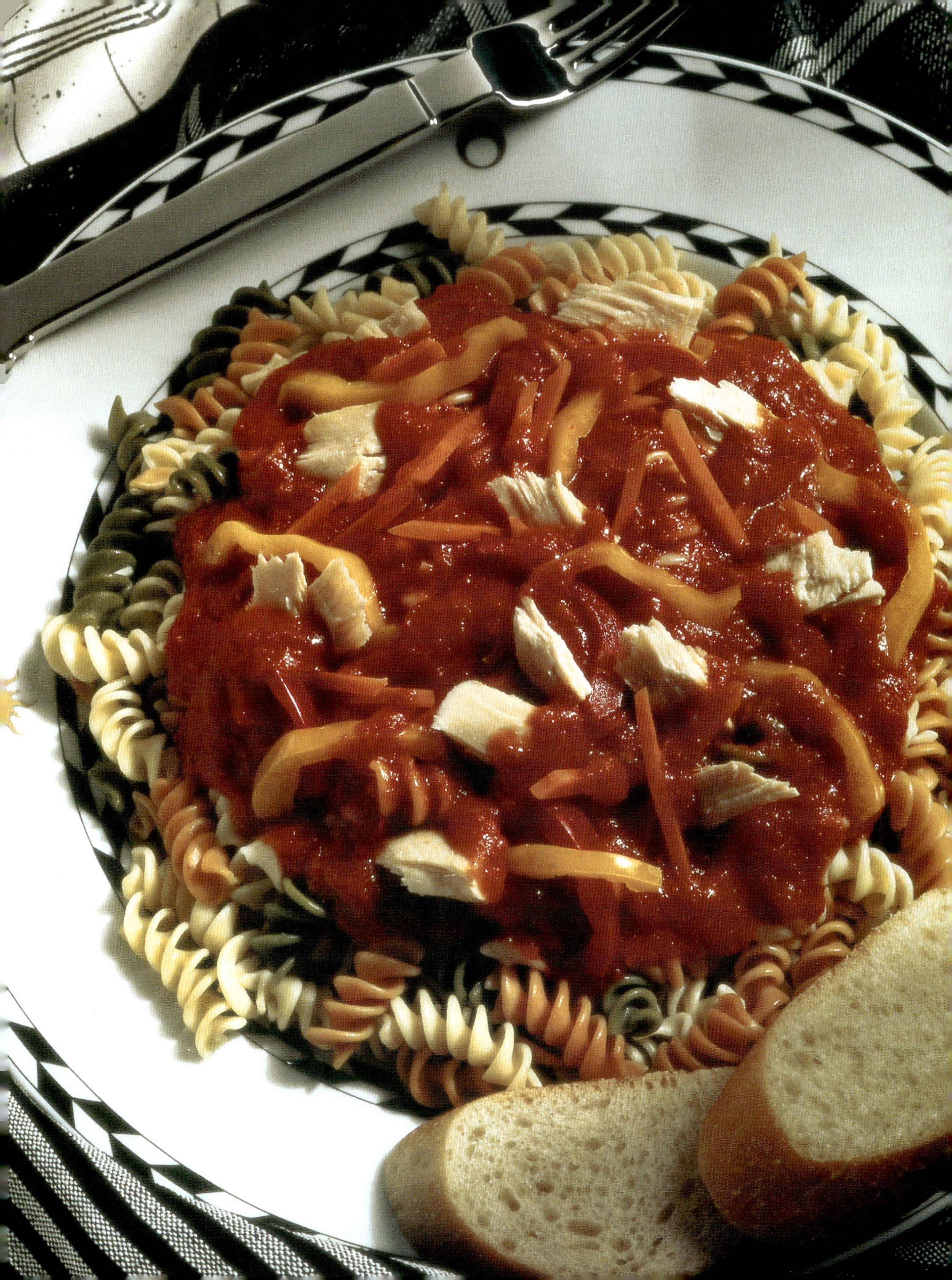

ACKNOWLEDGMENTS

The publisher would like to thank the companies and organizations listed below for the use of their recipes and photos in this publication.

American Italian Pasta Company
American Lamb Council
BelGioioso® Cheese, Inc.
Best Foods, a Division of CPC International Inc.
Black-Eyed Pea Jamboree–Athens, Texas
Blue Diamond Growers
Bob Evans Farms®
California Apricot Advisory Board
California Olive Industry
California Poultry Industry Federation
California Table Grape Commission
California Tomato Commission
Canned Food Information Council
Castroville Artichoke Festival
Chef Paul Prudhomme's® Magic Seasoning Blends®
Cherry Marketing Institute, Inc.
Christopher Ranch Garlic
Cucina Classica Italiana, Inc.
Delmarva Poultry Industry, Inc.
Del Monte Corporation
Dole Food Company, Inc.
Filippo Berio Olive Oil
The Fremont Company, Makers of Frank's & SnowFloss Kraut and Tomato Products
Golden Grain/Mission Pasta
Grandma's Molasses, a division of Cadbury Beverages Inc.
Guiltless Gourmet, Incorporated
Healthy Choice®
Holland House, a division of Cadbury Beverages Inc.
Hormel Foods Corporation
The HVR Company
Jones Dairy Farm
Kikkoman International Inc.
Kraft Foods, Inc.
Lawry's® Foods, Inc.
Lee Kum Kee (USA) Inc.
Louis Rich Company
McIlhenny Company
Michigan Bean Commission
MOTT'S® Inc., a division of Cadbury Beverages Inc.
Nabisco, Inc.
National Cattlemen's Beef Association
National Fisheries Institute
National Foods, Inc.
National Pasta Association
National Sunflower Association
National Turkey Federation
Nestlé Food Company
New Jersey Department of Agriculture
Newman's Own, Inc.®
Norseland, Inc.
North Atlantic Sardine Council
North Dakota Beef Commission
North Dakota Wheat Commission
Oscar Mayer Foods Corporation
Perdue® Farms
The Procter & Gamble Company
The Quaker® Oatmeal Kitchens
Reckitt & Colman Inc.
Sargento Foods Inc.®
Sonoma Dried Tomato
Southeast United Dairy Industry Association, Inc.
StarKist® Seafood Company
The Sugar Association, Inc.
Surimi Seafood Education Center
USA Dry Pea & Lentil Council
Walnut Marketing Board
Washington Apple Commission
Wesson/Peter Pan Foods Company
Wisconsin Milk Marketing Board

INDEX

A
Aegean Pasta Salad, 28
Albacore Salad Puttanesca with Garlic Vinaigrette, 26
Alfredo with Roasted Red Peppers, 275
Almond Crunch Macaroni Custard, 268
Amish Vegetable and Noodle Soup, 11
Anchovy-Olive Pasta Sauce, 312
Angel Hair Chicken-Olive Salad, 16
Angel Hair Stir-Fry, 224
Antipasto Salad, 48
Apple Lasagna, 60
Apples
  Apple Lasagna, 60
  Centennial Apple Pasta Salad, 24
  Golden Apple-Salmon Pasta, 174
  Linguine with Pumpkin Pork Sauce, 280
  Mini Meatballs with Pasta and Apple Pesto, 265
  Pasta and Walnut Fruit Salad, 22
  Turkey Fruited Bow Tie Salad, 32
Artichoke-Olive Chicken Bake, 70
Artichokes
  Artichoke-Olive Chicken Bake, 70
  New Orleans Sausage and Noodles, 136
  Pasta Salad in Artichoke Cups, 6
  Pasta with Hearts, 266
  Penne with Artichokes, 188
  Primavera Sauce with Artichoke and Shrimp, 168
  Quick Tortellini with Artichokes, 264
  Zesty Artichoke Basil Sauce, 318
Asian Chili Pepper Linguine, 244
Asian Turkey Noodle Salad, 242
Asparagus
  Angel Hair Chicken-Olive Salad, 16
  Dijon Asparagus Chicken Salad, 18
  Golden Apple-Salmon Pasta, 174
  Linguine with Asparagus and Asiago, 210
  Pasta in the Springtime, 272
  Sausage & Pasta Primavera, 142
  Skillet Shrimp with Rotelle, 160
  Spicy Grape Pasta Salad, 50
  Springtime Pasta Salad, 17
  Tangy Asparagus Linguine, 214

Avocados
  San Marcos Chili Pepper Penne Salad, 16
  Turkey and Avocado in Orange Sauce, 260

B
Bacon
  Cajun Shrimp Fettuccine, 172
  Chicken Ragout with Orzo, 116
  Fettuccine alla Carbonara, 302
  Harvest Drums, 125
  Italian Sausage with Kraut and Fettuccine, 124
  Pasta Carbonara, 288
  Warm Pasta and Spinach Salad, 8
Baked Cheesey Rotini, 92
Basic Tomato Sauce, 323
Basil, Fresh
  Basil Vinaigrette Dressing, 6
  Bow Ties alle Portofino, 150
  Cheese Stuffed Shells with Basil, 56
  Classic Pesto with Linguine, 288
  Colorful Pepper Fusilli, 200
  Crab Basil Fettuccine, 156
  Egg Noodles and Vegetables with Pesto, 198
  Fettuccine with Pesto, 192
  Fresh Tomato, Basil and Ricotta Sauce, 308
  Fresh Tomato Pasta Andrew, 218
  Garden Tomato Sauce, 315
  Mini Meatballs with Pasta and Apple Pesto, 265
  Pasta, Chicken & Broccoli Pesto Toss, 10
  Pasta Verde de Mar, 166
  Pesto Lasagna Rolls, 62
  Pesto Pasta, 184
  Ravioli with Homemade Tomato Sauce, 294
  Thin-Sliced Panzanella, 114
  Turkey Pesto Meatballs with Zucchini and Pasta, 134
  Winter Pesto Pasta with Shrimp, 170
Basil Vinaigrette Dressing, 6
Beans, Black
  Caribbean Pasta Salad with Tropical Island Dressing, 42
  Sweet Dijon Pasta Salad, 4
Beans, Cannellini
  Red Pepper & White Bean Pasta Sauce, 314
  Sausage Minestrone Soup, 22

Beans, Green
  Angel Hair Chicken-Olive Salad, 16
  Chicken and Pasta Soup, 17
  Turkey 'n Spaghetti Summer Salad, 40
  Turkey Shanghai, 239, 250
Beans, Kidney
  Minute Lamb Minestrone, 36
  Pasta Fazool, 26
  Zesty Romaine and Pasta Salad, 18
Beef (see also Beef, Ground; Salami)
  Beef Soup with Noodles, 238
  Beef with Noodles, 230
  Burgundy Beef Pasta, 142
  Cantonese Tomato Beef, 228
  Classic Meatball Soup, 44
  Fajita Stuffed Shells, 86
  Korean-Style Beef and Pasta, 240
  Mixed Vegetables with Noodles and Beef (Chap Ch'ae), 234
  Pasta Paprikash, 118
  Reuben Noodle Bake, 82
  Spaghetti with Beef and Black Pepper Sauce, 238
  Speedy Stroganoff, 117
  Sweet & Sour Tortellini, 232
Beef, Ground
  Baked Cheesey Rotini, 92
  Chili Wagon Wheel Casserole, 62
  Chunky Pasta Sauce with Meat, 310
  Classic Meatball Soup, 44
  First-Class Pasta Sauce, 316
  HUNT'S® Spaghetti Sauce, 314
  Jarlsberg Pasta Pie, 275
  Lasagna Supreme, 54
  Mafalda and Meatballs, 108
  Manicotti Parmigiana, 97
  Mini Meatballs with Pasta and Apple Pesto, 265
  Oriental Macaroni, 248
  Pasta "Pizza," 268
  Quick Beef Soup, 34
  Sensational Spaghetti and Meatballs, 296
  Spaghetti alla Bolognese, 286
  Spetzque, 90
  Thai Meatballs, 222
  Thai Meatballs and Noodles, 222
  Twisty Beef Bake, 76
  Zucchini Pasta Bake, 64
Bell Pepper and Mushroom Pasta Sauce, 324
Black-Eyed Peas
  Plentiful "P's" Salad, 20
  Seafood Pea-Ista Salad, 36
  Southern Greens and Pasta, 256

INDEX

Bow Tie Pasta with Chicken and Roast Garlic, 126
Bow Ties alle Portofino, 150
Broccoli
  Curried Turkey and Couscous Skillet, 226
  Egg Noodles and Vegetables with Pesto, 198
  Flash Primavera, 284
  Italian Antipasto Bake, 68
  Italian Pasta Salad, 28
  Pasta, Chicken & Broccoli Pesto Toss, 10
  Pasta and Broccoli, 280
  Pasta Primavera Salad, 24
  Pasta with Roasted Peppers and Broccoli, 196
  Pesto Linguine Tossed with Olive Oil and Broccoli, 188
  Quick Turkey Tortelloni, 117
  Rigatoni with Broccoli, 210
  Rotini with Summer Vegetables, 180
  Seafood Lasagna with Spaghetti Squash and Broccoli, 69
  Seafood Pea-Ista Salad, 36
  SPAM™ Fettuccini Primavera, 130
  Springtime Pasta Salad, 17
  Tortellini Kabobs, 254
  Vegetable Pasta Italiano, 254
  Zesty Romaine and Pasta Salad, 18
Burgundy Beef Pasta, 142
Butterflied Shrimp and Vermicelli Salad, 30

C

Cacciatore Pineapple Chicken, 130
Cajun Pork with Pasta Salad, 52
Cajun Shrimp Fettuccine, 172
Cajun Spice Rub, 52
California Walnut Noodles, 278
Cannelloni with Tomato-Eggplant Sauce, 92
Cantonese Tomato Beef, 228
Caribbean Pasta Salad with Tropical Island Dressing, 42
Catalonian Stew, 12
Cauliflower
  Cheesy Pasta Swirls, 78
  Egg Noodles and Vegetables with Pesto, 198
  Rotini with Cauliflower and Prosciutto, 114
  SPAM™ Fettuccini Primavera, 130
  Tortellini Kabobs, 254
  Vegetable Pasta Italiano, 254

Centennial Apple Pasta Salad, 24
Cheese Stuffed Shells with Basil, 56
Cheesy Pasta Swirls, 78
Chicken
  Amish Vegetable and Noodle Soup, 11
  Angel Hair Chicken-Olive Salad, 16
  Angel Hair Stir-Fry, 224
  Artichoke-Olive Chicken Bake, 70
  Bow Tie Pasta with Chicken and Roast Garlic, 126
  Cacciatore Pineapple Chicken, 130
  California Walnut Noodles, 278
  Catalonian Stew, 12
  Chicken and Pasta in Cream Sauce, 140
  Chicken and Pasta Soup, 17
  Chicken Chow Mein, 236
  Chicken Marsala, 64
  Chicken Noodle Soup, 51
  Chicken Pasta Salad Supreme, 20
  Chicken Ragout with Orzo, 116
  Chicken Siesta Twist, 259
  Chicken Stroganoff, 124
  Chicken with Pasta and Puttanesca Sauce, 300
  Creamy Chicken and Red Pepper Pasta, 106
  Creamy Herbed Chicken, 120
  Delicious Chicken Pasta, 132
  Dijon Asparagus Chicken Salad, 18
  Fiesta Chicken Breasts, 138
  Fresh Apricot-Pasta Salad, 259
  Harvest Drums, 125
  He-Man Stew, 137
  Indian Chicken with Couscous, 242
  Italian Antipasto Bake, 68
  Jerk Chicken and Pasta, 122
  Lasagne Rolls, 80
  Manicotti alla Perdue, 60
  Micro-Meatball Rigatoni, 270
  Pasta, Chicken & Broccoli Pesto Toss, 10
  Pasta Chicken Breast Salad, 34
  Pasta in the Springtime, 272
  Pasta with Chicken and Peppers, 110
  Pepper Chicken, 141
  Pesto Chicken Pasta, 108
  Pizza Chicken Bake, 94
  Quick Chicken Marinara, 134
  Santa Fe Pasta, 276
  Scalloped Chicken & Pasta, 118

Chicken (continued)
  Shaker Chicken and Noodle Soup, 14
  Spicy Grape Pasta Salad, 50
  Super Simple Chicken Soup, 52
  Tetrazzini Pasta Supper, 292
  Thai Chicken Fettuccine Salad, 248
  Thin-Sliced Panzanella, 114
Chickpeas
  Chickpea & Pasta Soup, 46
  Hearty Fettuccine, Ham and Bean Soup, 48
Chile Cheese Macaroni, 86
Chili Pepper Pasta with Jalapeño Butter Sauce, 270
Chili Peppers
  Chile Cheese Macaroni, 86
  Chili Pepper Pasta with Jalapeño Butter Sauce, 270
  Pepper Chicken, 141
  Red Chili Sauce, 316
  San Marcos Chili Pepper Penne Salad, 16
  Southwest Ruffle Salad, 46
  Southwest Spaghetti Pie, 262
  Vermicelli with Pork, 220
Chili Wagon Wheel Casserole, 62
Chilled Seafood Lasagna with Herbed Cheese, 84
Chinese Noodle Cakes, 244
Chunky Pasta Sauce with Meat, 310
Clams
  Clams in Black Bean Sauce, 250
  HUNT'S® Linguine with Red Clam Sauce, 302
  Linguine with White Clam Sauce, 162
  Spicy Pasta del Mar, 153
  Up-to-the-Minute Linguine with Clam Sauce, 176
Classic Fettuccine Alfredo, 292
Classic Macaroni and Cheese, 290
Classic Meatball Soup, 44
Classic Pesto with Linguine, 288
Cold Stirred Noodles, 239
Colorful Grape, Pepper and Pasta Salad, 14
Colorful Pepper Fusilli, 200
Colorful Turkey Pasta Salad, 50
Corn
  Garden Tomato Sauce, 315
  Mexican Turkey Chili Mac, 4
  Quick Beef Soup, 34
  SPAM™ Confetti Pasta, 110
  Spetzque, 90
  Veggie Lasagne, 202

INDEX

Cottage Cheese
  Italian Lasagna Rolls, 96
  Lasagna Supreme, 54
  Luscious Vegetarian Lasagna, 186
  Macaroni Italiano, 66
  Seafood Lasagna, 72
  Shells Florentine, 102
  Turkey Noodle Dandy (An All-American Favorite), 100
Country Noodles and Ham, 125
Country Style Cracked Black Pepper Fettuccine, 116
Couscous
  Curried Turkey and Couscous Skillet, 226
  Indian Chicken with Couscous, 242
  Many Peppered Fillets, 128
Crab Basil Fettuccine, 156
Crabmeat
  Crab Basil Fettuccine, 156
  Crabmeat with Herbs and Pasta, 154
  Creamy "Crab" Fettuccine, 98
  Jumbo Shells Seafood Fancies, 172
  Low-Fat Seafood Fettuccine, 154
  Seafood Pea-Ista Salad, 36
  Seafood Supreme Pasta Pie, 159
Cream Cheese
  Chicken Ragout with Orzo, 116
  Creamy Fettuccine Alfredo, 304
  Creamy Herbed Chicken, 120
  Creamy Orzo with Prosciutto, 133
  Fettuccine with Sun-Dried Tomato Cream, 190
  Italian Lasagna Rolls, 96
  Salmon Tortellini, 166
  Seafood Lasagna, 72
  Tortellini Primavera, 182
  Tortelloni Wreath with Pesto Dip, 284
  Turkey Noodle Dandy (An All-American Favorite), 100
Creamy Chicken and Red Pepper Pasta, 106
Creamy "Crab" Fettuccine, 98
Creamy Fettuccine Alfredo, 304
Creamy Herbed Chicken, 120
Creamy Italian Pasta Salad, 24
Creamy Orzo with Prosciutto, 133
Creamy Seafood Pasta, 146
Creamy Vinaigrette, 51
Crispy Tortellini Bites, 271
Cucumbers
  Aegean Pasta Salad, 28
  California Walnut Noodles, 278
  Cold Stirred Noodles, 239
Curried Turkey and Couscous Skillet, 226
Curry Sauce, 156

D
Deep Fried Stuffed Shells, 148
Delicious Chicken Pasta, 132
Desserts
  Almond Crunch Macaroni Custard, 268
  Apple Lasagna, 60
  Mini Noodle Kugels with Raspberry Filling, 256
  Pineapple Noodle Pudding, 274
Dijon Asparagus Chicken Salad, 18
Ditalini with Zucchini, 192
Double Spinach Bake, 88
Dressings
  Basil Vinaigrette Dressing, 6
  Creamy Vinaigrette, 51
  Garlic Vinaigrette Dressing, 26
  Korean-Style Dressing, 240
  Mustard Vinaigrette, 14
  Sesame Vinaigrette, 12
  Spicy Asian Dressing, 50

E
Easy Cheese & Tomato Macaroni, 182
Easy Cheesy Lasagna, 104
Easy Macaroni and Cheese, 98
Easy Pasta Primavera, 200
Egg Noodles and Vegetables with Pesto, 198
Eggplant
  Cannelloni with Tomato-Eggplant Sauce, 92
  Easy Pasta Primavera, 200
  Hearty Italian Medley, 138
  Penne Primavera with Sundried Tomato Sauce, 212
  Penne with Eggplant and Turkey Sausage, 132
  Roasted Vegetables with Noodles, 246
  Sesame Pasta Salad, 12
  Tomato-Eggplant Sauce, 92
  Turkey Stuffed Pasta Italiano, 80
Elaine's Tuna Tetrazzini, 148

F
Fajita Stuffed Shells, 86
Fast-Track Fettuccine, 204
Feta Cheese
  Aegean Pasta Salad, 28
  Red Pepper & White Bean Pasta Sauce, 314

Feta Cheese *(continued)*
  Sausage & Feta Strata, 113
  Scallops with Linguine and Spinach, 160
Fettuccine à la Tuna, 164
Fettuccine alla Carbonara, 302
Fettuccine Romano Aldana, 272
Fettuccine with Fresh Herb and Parmesan Sauce, 196
Fettuccine with Olive Pesto, 214
Fettuccine with Pesto, 192
Fettuccine with Sun-Dried Tomato Cream, 190
Fiesta Chicken Breasts, 138
First-Class Pasta Sauce, 316
Fish *(see also* **Salmon; Tuna***)*
  Anchovy-Olive Pasta Sauce, 312
  Chilled Seafood Lasagna with Herbed Cheese, 84
  Pasta Puttanesca with Sardines, 159
  Pasta Verde de Mar, 166
  Pick of the Crop Sardine Pasta, 169
  Seafarers' Supper, 158
  Seafood Lasagna, 72, 90
  Seafood Lasagna with Spaghetti Squash and Broccoli, 69
  Skate Noodle Casserole, 68
  Spaghetti Puttanesca, 294
  Spaghetti with Seafood Marinara Sauce, 162
  Spinach Pesto, 308
  Squid Mediterranean, 320
Flash Primavera, 284
Four-Pepper Penne, 198
Fresh Apricot-Pasta Salad, 259
Fresh Herb Sauce, 308
Fresh Tomato, Basil and Ricotta Sauce, 308
Fresh Tomato Pasta Andrew, 218
Fruit and Pasta Refresher, 10
Fusilli with Broccoli Rabe, 206

G
Garden Linguine, 190
Garden Tomato Sauce, 315
Garlic Vinaigrette Dressing, 26
Giardiniera Sauce, 306
Golden Apple-Salmon Pasta, 174
Gorgonzola Cream Sauce with Tomato Basil Pasta, 265
Grapes
  Butterflied Shrimp and Vermicelli Salad, 30
  Colorful Grape, Pepper and Pasta Salad, 14

INDEX

Grapes *(continued)*
   Fruit and Pasta Refresher, 10
   Pasta and Walnut Fruit Salad, 22
   Pasta Chicken Breast Salad, 34
   Spicy Grape Pasta Salad, 50
   Sweet and Smoky Pasta Salad, 28
   Turkey Fruited Bow Tie Salad, 32
Green and Gold Fettuccine with Salmon, 170

H
Ham
   Country Noodles and Ham, 125
   Country Style Cracked Black Pepper Fettuccine, 116
   Hearty Fettuccine, Ham and Bean Soup, 48
   Spicy Ham & Cheese Pasta, 112
   Sweet and Smoky Pasta Salad, 28
   Swissed Ham and Noodles Casserole, 84
Harvest Drums, 125
Hearty Fettuccine, Ham and Bean Soup, 48
Hearty Italian Medley, 138
He-Man Stew, 137
Herbed Tomato Sauce, 202
Hombre Shrimp and Fettuccine with Salsa Pesto, 153
HUNT'S® Linguine with Red Clam Sauce, 302
HUNT'S® Spaghetti Sauce, 314

I
Indian Chicken with Couscous, 242
Italian Antipasto Bake, 68
Italian Delight, 94
Italian Lasagna Rolls, 96
Italian Pasta Salad, 28
Italian Sausage with Kraut and Fettuccine, 124
Italian Spaghetti Sauce, 318
Italian Three-Cheese Macaroni, 56

J
Jarlsberg Pasta Pie, 275
Jerk Chicken and Pasta, 122
Jerk Sauce, 122
Jumbo Shells Seafood Fancies, 172

K
Korean-Style Beef and Pasta, 240
Korean-Style Dressing, 240

L
Lamb and Spaghetti Primavera, 137
Lamb and Spinach Manicotti, 70

Lasagna
   Apple Lasagna, 60
   Chilled Seafood Lasagna with Herbed Cheese, 84
   Easy Cheesy Lasagna, 104
   Italian Lasagna Rolls, 96
   Luscious Vegetarian Lasagna, 186
   Pesto Lasagna Rolls, 62
   Seafood Lasagna, 72, 90
   Seafood Lasagna with Spaghetti Squash and Broccoli, 69
   SPAM™ Lasagna, 78
   Spetzque, 90
   Three Cheese Vegetable Lasagna, 96
   Tomato Pesto Lasagna, 82
   Veggie Lasagne, 202
Lemon Pepper Pasta with Piccata Style Vegetables, 218
Lemon-Tossed Linguine, 204
Lemony Dill Salmon and Shell Casserole, 58
Light Tomato Sauce, 97
Linguine with Asparagus and Asiago, 210
Linguine with Fresh Tomato Basil Sauce, 203
Linguine with Pumpkin Pork Sauce, 280
Linguine with Spinach Pesto, 212
Linguine with White Clam Sauce, 162
Lo Mein Noodles with Shrimp, 224
Long Soup, 230
Low-Fat Macaroni and Cheese, 304
Low-Fat Seafood Fettuccine, 154
Luscious Vegetarian Lasagna, 186

M
Macaroni Italiano, 66
Mafalda and Meatballs, 108
Manicotti, Stuffed
   Lamb and Spinach Manicotti, 70
   Manicotti alla Perdue, 60
   Manicotti Florentine, 74
   Manicotti Parmigiana, 97
   Spicy Manicotti, 66
   Spinach Stuffed Manicotti, 100
   Tuna & Zucchini-Stuffed Manicotti, 81
Manicotti alla Perdue, 60
Manicotti Florentine, 74
Manicotti Parmigiana, 97
Many Peppered Fillets, 128
Mayonnaise
   Aegean Pasta Salad, 28
   Creamy "Crab" Fettuccine, 98

Mayonnaise *(continued)*
   Creamy Italian Pasta Salad, 24
   Dijon Asparagus Chicken Salad, 18
   Warm Pasta and Spinach Salad, 8
Melon
   Fruit and Pasta Refresher, 10
   Sweet and Smoky Pasta Salad, 28
Mexican Eye-Opener with Chili Pepper Pasta, 122
Mexican Turkey Chili Mac, 4
Micro-Meatball Rigatoni, 270
Microwave Pasta Pie, 258
Microwave Recipes
   Cheesy Pasta Swirls, 78
   Italian Antipasto Bake, 68
   Manicotti Florentine, 74
   Microwave Pasta Pie, 258
   Oriental Macaroni, 248
   Tomato Pesto Lasagna, 82
   Twisty Beef Bake, 76
Midsummer's Night Split Peas & Pasta, 32
Mini Meatballs with Pasta and Apple Pesto, 265
Mini Noodle Kugels with Raspberry Filling, 256
Minute Lamb Minestrone, 36
Mixed Vegetables with Noodles and Beef (Chap Ch'ae), 234
Mustard Vinaigrette, 14

N
Neapolitan Sauce, 320
New Orleans Sausage and Noodles, 136
Noodles Thai Style, 226
Nuts
   Alfredo with Roasted Red Peppers, 275
   Almond Crunch Macaroni Custard, 268
   Angel Hair Chicken-Olive Salad, 16
   California Walnut Noodles, 278
   Centennial Apple Pasta Salad, 24
   Classic Pesto with Linguine, 288
   Colorful Grape, Pepper and Pasta Salad, 14
   Creamy Chicken and Red Pepper Pasta, 106
   Fettuccine with Pesto, 192
   Hombre Shrimp and Fettuccine with Salsa Pesto, 153
   Linguine with Spinach Pesto, 212
   Macaroni Italiano, 66
   Mini Meatballs with Pasta and Apple Pesto, 265

365 Favorite Brand Name Pasta Recipes

INDEX

Nuts *(continued)*
Noodles Thai Style, 226
Pasta, Chicken & Broccoli Pesto Toss, 10
Pasta and Walnut Fruit Salad, 22
Pasta with Onions and Goat Cheese, 262
Pasta with Sausage and Mustard Sauce, 140
Pesto Pasta, 184
Pine Nut and Cilantro Pesto, 314
Ravioli with Roasted Red Pepper Alfredo Sauce, 208
Savory California Walnut Sprinkles, 278
Spicy Tuna and Linguine with Garlic and Pine Nuts, 152
Spinach Pesto, 308
Spinach Tortellini with Roasted Red Peppers, 215
Thai Chicken Fettuccine Salad, 248
Thai Peanut Noodle Stir-Fry, 232

O

Olives
Aegean Pasta Salad, 28
Albacore Salad Puttanesca with Garlic Vinaigrette, 26
Anchovy-Olive Pasta Sauce, 312
Angel Hair Chicken-Olive Salad, 16
Antipasto Salad, 48
Artichoke-Olive Chicken Bake, 70
Cacciatore Pineapple Chicken, 130
Catalonian Stew, 12
Chicken with Pasta and Puttanesca Sauce, 300
Creamy Chicken and Red Pepper Pasta, 106
Creamy Italian Pasta Salad, 24
Fast-Track Fettuccine, 204
Fettuccine with Olive Pesto, 214
Italian Delight, 94
Italian Pasta Salad, 28
Linguine with Asparagus and Asiago, 210
Midsummer's Night Split Peas & Pasta, 32
Orzo Salad, 51
Pasta Carbonara, 288
Pasta Primavera with Italian Sausage, 133
Pasta Puttanesca with Sardines, 159
Pesto Pasta, 184

Olives *(continued)*
Provençal Pasta Shells, 216
Rigatoni with Creamy Tomato Sauce, 290
Saucy Mediterranean Frittata, 208
Savory Caper and Olive Sauce, 320
Skillet Shrimp with Rotelle, 160
Smoked Salmon and Olive Pasta, 169
Spaghetti Puttanesca, 294
Spetzque, 90
Squid Mediterranean, 320
Summer Spaghetti, 193
Tangy Tortellini Salad, 11
Tasara Style Cavatappi Pasta Salad, 33
Turkey 'n Spaghetti Summer Salad, 40

Oranges
Butterflied Shrimp and Vermicelli Salad, 30
Caribbean Pasta Salad with Tropical Island Dressing, 42
Pasta and Walnut Fruit Salad, 22
Turkey and Avocado in Orange Sauce, 260
Turkey Fruited Bow Tie Salad, 32
Oriental Macaroni, 248
Orzo Risotto with Shrimp and Vegetables, 146
Orzo Salad, 51

P

Party Pasta Salad, 33
Pasta, Chicken & Broccoli Pesto Toss, 10
Pasta and Broccoli, 280
Pasta and Walnut Fruit Salad, 22
Pasta Carbonara, 288
Pasta Chicken Breast Salad, 34
Pasta e Fagioli, 300
Pasta Fazool, 26
Pasta from the Garden, 206
Pasta in the Springtime, 272
Pasta Paprikash, 118
Pasta Peperonata, 296
Pasta "Pizza," 268
Pasta Primavera Salad, 24
Pasta Primavera with Italian Sausage, 133
Pasta Puttanesca with Sardines, 159
Pasta Salad in Artichoke Cups, 6
Pasta Verde de Mar, 166
Pasta with BELGIOIOSO® Gorgonzola Sauce, 194
Pasta with Chicken and Peppers, 110

Pasta with Fresh Vegetables in Garlic Sauce, 260
Pasta with Hearts, 266
Pasta with Onions and Goat Cheese, 262
Pasta with Roasted Peppers and Broccoli, 196
Pasta with Salmon and Dill, 76
Pasta with Sausage and Mustard Sauce, 140
Pasta with Spinach-Cheese Sauce, 203
Pasta with Sunflower Kernels, 192
Peas
Cheesy Pasta Swirls, 78
Country Noodles and Ham, 125
Creamy Herbed Chicken, 120
Creamy Orzo with Prosciutto, 133
Lemony Dill Salmon and Shell Casserole, 58
Macaroni Italiano, 66
Orzo Salad, 51
Quick Beef Soup, 34
Spetzque, 90
Springtime Pasta Salad, 17
Straw and Hay Fettuccine, 206
Super Simple Chicken Soup, 52
Tagliatelle with Creamy Sauce, 275
Penne Pasta with Shrimp & Roasted Red Pepper Sauce, 164
Penne Primavera with Sundried Tomato Sauce, 212
Penne with Artichokes, 188
Penne with Eggplant and Turkey Sausage, 132
Pepper Chicken, 141
Pepperoni
Catalonian Stew, 12
Pizza Pasta Salad, 40
Tasara Style Cavatappi Pasta Salad, 33
Peppery Pasta Toss, 186
Pesto
Classic Pesto with Linguine, 288
Egg Noodles and Vegetables with Pesto, 198
Fettuccine with Olive Pesto, 214
Fettuccine with Pesto, 192
Hombre Shrimp and Fettuccine with Salsa Pesto, 153
Linguine with Spinach Pesto, 212
Mini Meatballs with Pasta and Apple Pesto, 265
Pasta, Chicken & Broccoli Pesto Toss, 10
Pine Nut and Cilantro Pesto, 314

INDEX

Pesto *(continued)*
    Quick Tortellini with Artichokes, 264
    Spinach Pesto, 308
    Tomato Pesto Lasagna, 82
    Tortelloni Wreath with Pesto Dip, 284
    Turkey Pesto Meatballs with Zucchini and Pasta, 134
    Winter Pesto Pasta with Shrimp, 170
Pesto Linguine Tossed with Olive Oil and Broccoli, 188
Pick of the Crop Sardine Pasta, 169
Pineapple
    Cacciatore Pineapple Chicken, 130
    Caribbean Pasta Salad with Tropical Island Dressing, 42
    Fruit and Pasta Refresher, 10
    Hearty Italian Medley, 138
    Pineapple Noodle Pudding, 274
    Pineapple-Raisin Fettuccine, 216
    Sweet and Smoky Pasta Salad, 28
Pine Nut and Cilantro Pesto, 314
Pizza Chicken Bake, 94
Pizzaiola Sauce, 306
Pizza Pasta Salad, 40
Plentiful "P's" Salad, 20
Poppy Noodles, 117
Porcini Mushroom Penne Rigate with Garlic Butter Sauce, 215
Pork *(see also **Bacon; Ham; Prosciutto; Salami; Sausage**)*
    Cajun Pork with Pasta Salad, 52
    Linguine with Pumpkin Pork Sauce, 280
    Long Soup, 230
    Southwest Spaghetti Pie, 262
    Vermicelli with Pork, 220
Potatoes
    Amish Vegetable and Noodle Soup, 11
    Sesame Pasta Salad, 12
    Sweet Potato Ravioli with Asiago Cheese Sauce, 252
Primavera Sauce with Artichoke and Shrimp, 168
Prosciutto
    Creamy Orzo with Prosciutto, 133
    Fettuccine Romano Aldana, 272
    Rotini with Cauliflower and Prosciutto, 114
    Spinach Tortellini with BEL PAESE®, 271
    Tagliatelle with Creamy Sauce, 275

Provençal Pasta Shells, 216
Pumpkin
    Linguine with Pumpkin Pork Sauce, 280
    Tortellini with Pumpkin Red Pepper Sauce, 274

Q
Quick Beef Soup, 34
Quick Chicken Marinara, 134
Quick Tortellini with Artichokes, 264
Quick Turkey Tortelloni, 117

R
Ravioli
    Alfredo with Roasted Red Peppers, 275
    Ravioli with Homemade Tomato Sauce, 294
    Ravioli with Roasted Red Pepper Alfredo Sauce, 208
    Shrimp Ravioli with Curry Sauce, 156
    Sweet Potato Ravioli with Asiago Cheese Sauce, 252
Red Chili Sauce, 316
Red Pepper & White Bean Pasta Sauce, 314
Reuben Noodle Bake, 82
Ricotta Cheese
    Apple Lasagna, 60
    Cannelloni with Tomato-Eggplant Sauce, 92
    Cheese Stuffed Shells with Basil, 56
    Chilled Seafood Lasagna with Herbed Cheese, 84
    Double Spinach Bake, 88
    Easy Cheesy Lasagna, 104
    Fresh Tomato, Basil and Ricotta Sauce, 308
    Lamb and Spinach Manicotti, 70
    Low-Fat Macaroni and Cheese, 304
    Manicotti alla Perdue, 60
    Pasta with Spinach-Cheese Sauce, 203
    Pesto Lasagna Rolls, 62
    Spicy Ham & Cheese Pasta, 112
    Spicy Manicotti, 66
    Spinach-Cheese Pasta Casserole, 74
    Tetrazzini Pasta Supper, 292
    Three Cheese Vegetable Lasagna, 96
    Tomato Pesto Lasagna, 82

Ricotta Cheese *(continued)*
    Tomato Sauce with Ricotta & Herbs, 322
    Tortellini with Three-Cheese Tuna Sauce, 178
    Tuna & Zucchini-Stuffed Manicotti, 81
    Turtle Shells, 88
    Veggie Lasagne, 202
Rigatoni, 126
Rigatoni with Broccoli, 210
Rigatoni with Creamy Tomato Sauce, 290
Roasted Vegetables Provençal, 194
Roasted Vegetables with Noodles, 246
Rotini and Turkey Mozzarella, 129
Rotini with Cauliflower and Prosciutto, 114
Rotini with Summer Vegetables, 180

S
Salami
    Antipasto Salad, 48
    Plentiful "P's" Salad, 20
    Tangy Tortellini Salad, 11
Salmon
    Golden Apple-Salmon Pasta, 174
    Green and Gold Fettuccine with Salmon, 170
    Lemony Dill Salmon and Shell Casserole, 58
    Pasta with Salmon and Dill, 76
    Salmon, Fettuccine & Cabbage, 168
    Salmon Pasta with Peppered Cream Sauce, 177
    Salmon Tortellini, 166
    Smoked Salmon and Olive Pasta, 169
Salsa
    Hombre Shrimp and Fettuccine with Salsa Pesto, 153
    Penne Pasta with Shrimp & Roasted Red Pepper Sauce, 164
    Thai Chicken Fettuccine Salad, 248
San Marcos Chili Pepper Penne Salad, 16
Santa Fe Pasta, 276
Saucy Mediterranean Frittata, 208
Saucy Shrimp over Chinese Noodle Cakes, 244
Sauerkraut
    Italian Sausage with Kraut and Fettuccine, 124
    Reuben Noodle Bake, 82

INDEX

Sausage
  Chicken Ragout with Orzo, 116
  Chunky Pasta Sauce with Meat, 310
  Hearty Italian Medley, 138
  Italian Delight, 94
  Italian Sausage with Kraut and Fettuccine, 124
  Italian Spaghetti Sauce, 318
  Lasagna Supreme, 54
  Mexican Eye-Opener with Chili Pepper Pasta, 122
  Microwave Pasta Pie, 258
  New Orleans Sausage and Noodles, 136
  Pasta Primavera with Italian Sausage, 133
  Pasta with Sausage and Mustard Sauce, 140
  Penne with Eggplant and Turkey Sausage, 132
  Rigatoni, 126
  Sausage & Feta Strata, 113
  Sausage & Pasta Primavera, 142
  Sausage Minestrone Soup, 22
  Savory Sausage & Spinach Penne, 120
  Sensational Spaghetti and Meatballs, 296
  Spicy Manicotti, 66
  Tomato Pesto Lasagna, 82
  Tortellini Kabobs, 254
  Traditional Spaghetti Sauce, 323
  Turkey and Bow Tie Pasta, 141
  Turkey Franks and Pasta Salad, 42
Savory California Walnut Sprinkles, 278
Savory Caper and Olive Sauce, 320
Savory Sausage & Spinach Penne, 120
Savory Topping, 254
Scalloped Chicken & Pasta, 118
Scallops
  Creamy Seafood Pasta, 146
  Seafood Lasagna, 72
  Seafood Lasagna with Spaghetti Squash and Broccoli, 69
  Seafood Supreme Pasta Pie, 159
  Spaghetti with Seafood Marinara Sauce, 162
Seafarers' Supper, 158
Seafood Lasagna, 72, 90
Seafood Lasagna with Spaghetti Squash and Broccoli, 69
Seafood Orzo Salad, 38
Seafood Pea-Ista Salad, 36
Seafood Supreme Pasta Pie, 159
Seaside Squash Spaghetti, 150
Sensational Spaghetti and Meatballs, 296
Sesame Pasta Salad, 12
Sesame Salt, 234
Sesame Vinaigrette, 12
Shaker Chicken and Noodle Soup, 14
Shells, Stuffed
  Cheese Stuffed Shells with Basil, 56
  Deep Fried Stuffed Shells, 148
  Fajita Stuffed Shells, 86
  Jumbo Shells Seafood Fancies, 172
  Provençal Pasta Shells, 216
  Shells Florentine, 102
  Turkey Stuffed Pasta Italiano, 80
  Turtle Shells, 88
Shells Florentine, 102
Shrimp
  Bow Ties alle Portofino, 150
  Butterflied Shrimp and Vermicelli Salad, 30
  Cajun Shrimp Fettuccine, 172
  Creamy Seafood Pasta, 146
  Hombre Shrimp and Fettuccine with Salsa Pesto, 153
  Jumbo Shells Seafood Fancies, 172
  Lo Mein Noodles with Shrimp, 224
  Low-Fat Seafood Fettuccine, 154
  Orzo Risotto with Shrimp and Vegetables, 146
  Pasta with Hearts, 266
  Penne Pasta with Shrimp & Roasted Red Pepper Sauce, 164
  Primavera Sauce with Artichoke and Shrimp, 168
  Saucy Shrimp over Chinese Noodle Cakes, 244
  Seafood Lasagna, 72, 90
  Seafood Orzo Salad, 38
  Seafood Supreme Pasta Pie, 159
  Seaside Squash Spaghetti, 150
  Sesame Pasta Salad, 12
  Shrimp Creole Pronto, 152
  Shrimp Fettuccine Primavera, 178
  Shrimp Marinara with Pasta, 177
  Shrimp Pasta Medley, 174
  Shrimp Ravioli with Curry Sauce, 156
  Shrimp with Pasta, 158
  Skillet Shrimp with Rotelle, 160
  Spaghetti with Seafood Marinara Sauce, 162
  Spicy Pasta del Mar, 153
Shrimp *(continued)*
  Tasty Thai Shrimp & Sesame Noodles, 236
  Tortellini Kabobs, 254
  Winter Pesto Pasta with Shrimp, 170
Skate Noodle Casserole, 68
Skillet Shrimp with Rotelle, 160
Smoked Salmon and Olive Pasta, 169
Smoked Turkey and Pepper Pasta Salad, 38
Snow Peas
  Angel Hair Chicken-Olive Salad, 16
  Angel Hair Stir-Fry, 224
  Asian Turkey Noodle Salad, 242
  Beef Soup with Noodles, 238
  Chicken Chow Mein, 236
  Chicken Pasta Salad Supreme, 20
  Garden Linguine, 190
  Lemon Pepper Pasta with Piccata Style Vegetables, 218
  Shrimp Pasta Medley, 174
  Thai Peanut Noodle Stir-Fry, 232
Soba Stir-Fry, 246
SONOMA Fettuccine Alfredo, 184
Soups
  Amish Vegetable and Noodle Soup, 11
  Beef Soup with Noodles, 238
  Chicken and Pasta Soup, 17
  Chicken Noodle Soup, 51
  Chickpea & Pasta Soup, 46
  Classic Meatball Soup, 44
  Hearty Fettuccine, Ham and Bean Soup, 48
  Long Soup, 230
  Minute Lamb Minestrone, 36
  Pasta e Fagioli, 300
  Pasta Fazool, 26
  Quick Beef Soup, 34
  Sausage Minestrone Soup, 22
  Shaker Chicken and Noodle Soup, 14
  Super Simple Chicken Soup, 52
  Tortellini Soup, 30
  Zucchini-Tomato-Noodle Soup, 8
Sour Cream
  Apple Lasagna, 60
  Creamy "Crab" Fettuccine, 98
  Crispy Tortellini Bites, 271
  Pasta Paprikash, 118
  Speedy Stroganoff, 117
  Swissed Ham and Noodles Casserole, 84
  Veal 'n' Spaghetti Casserole, 113

365 Favorite Brand Name Pasta Recipes

INDEX

Southern Greens and Pasta, 256
Southwest Ruffle Salad, 46
Southwest Spaghetti Pie, 262
Spaghetti alla Bolognese, 286
Spaghetti Puttanesca, 294
Spaghetti with Beef and Black Pepper Sauce, 238
Spaghetti with Garlic, 290
Spaghetti with Seafood Marinara Sauce, 162
SPAM® & Pasta Stuffed Tomatoes, 282
SPAM™ Confetti Pasta, 110
SPAM™ Fettuccini Primavera, 130
SPAM™ Lasagna, 78
Spätzle with Mushrooms, 298
Speedy Stroganoff, 117
Spetzque, 90
Spicy Asian Dressing, 50
Spicy Grape Pasta Salad, 50
Spicy Ham & Cheese Pasta, 112
Spicy Manicotti, 66
Spicy Pasta del Mar, 153
Spicy Tuna and Linguine with Garlic and Pine Nuts, 152
Spinach
   Cannelloni with Tomato-Eggplant Sauce, 92
   Double Spinach Bake, 88
   Egg Noodles and Vegetables with Pesto, 198
   Flash Primavera, 284
   Hombre Shrimp and Fettuccine with Salsa Pesto, 153
   Italian Lasagna Rolls, 96
   Lamb and Spinach Manicotti, 70
   Lasagne Rolls, 80
   Linguine with Spinach Pesto, 212
   Macaroni Italiano, 66
   Manicotti alla Perdue, 60
   Manicotti Florentine, 74
   Mixed Vegetables with Noodles and Beef (Chap Ch'ae), 234
   Pasta Chicken Breast Salad, 34
   Pasta in the Springtime, 272
   Pasta with Spinach-Cheese Sauce, 203
   Ravioli with Homemade Tomato Sauce, 294
   Savory Sausage & Spinach Penne, 120
   Scallops with Linguine and Spinach, 160
   Shells Florentine, 102
   Spinach-Cheese Pasta Casserole, 74
   Spinach Pesto, 308

Spinach *(continued)*
   Spinach Stuffed Manicotti, 100
   Three Cheese Vegetable Lasagna, 96
   Tortellini Primavera, 182
   Tortellini Soup, 30
   Turtle Shells, 88
   Veggie Lasagne, 202
   Warm Pasta and Spinach Salad, 8
Spinach Tortellini with BEL PAESE®, 271
Spinach Tortellini with Roasted Red Peppers, 215
Springtime Pasta Salad, 17
Squash
   Asian Chili Pepper Linguine, 244
   Roasted Vegetables Provençal, 194
   Roasted Vegetables with Noodles, 246
   Seafood Lasagna with Spaghetti Squash and Broccoli, 69
   Seaside Squash Spaghetti, 150
   Turkey Franks and Pasta Salad, 42
   Winter Primavera, 193
Squid Mediterranean, 320
Straw and Hay Fettuccine, 206
Summer Spaghetti, 193
Sun-Dried Tomato Linguine, 282
Super Simple Chicken Soup, 52
Sweet and Smoky Pasta Salad, 28
Sweet & Sour Tortellini, 232
Sweet Dijon Pasta Salad, 4
Sweet Peppered Pasta, 266
Sweet Potato Ravioli with Asiago Cheese Sauce, 252
Sweety Meaty Sauce for Ziti, 322
Swiss Cheese
   Jumbo Shells Seafood Fancies, 172
   Reuben Noodle Bake, 82
   Seafood Supreme Pasta Pie, 159
   Swissed Ham and Noodles Casserole, 84
   Swissed Ham and Noodles Casserole, 84

T

Tagliatelle with Creamy Sauce, 275
Tangy Asparagus Linguine, 214
Tangy Tortellini Salad, 11
Tasara Style Cavatappi Pasta Salad, 33
Tasty Thai Shrimp & Sesame Noodles, 236
Tetrazzini Pasta Supper, 292

Tex-Mex Noodle Cake, 276
Thai Chicken Fettuccine Salad, 248
Thai Meatballs and Noodles, 222
Thai Peanut Noodle Stir-Fry, 232
Thin-Sliced Panzanella, 114
Three Cheese Vegetable Lasagna, 96
Tomato Basil Linguine Modena Style, 258
Tomato Basil Pasta Pomadoro Style, 304
Tomato-Eggplant Sauce, 92
Tomatoes, Cherry
   Chicken Pasta Salad Supreme, 20
   Creamy Italian Pasta Salad, 24
   Egg Noodles and Vegetables with Pesto, 198
   Pasta Primavera Salad, 24
   Pasta Verde de Mar, 166
   Pick of the Crop Sardine Pasta, 169
   Pizza Pasta Salad, 40
   Skillet Shrimp with Rotelle, 160
   Turkey Franks and Pasta Salad, 42
   Turkey 'n Spaghetti Summer Salad, 40
Tomatoes, Dried
   Bow Ties alle Portofino, 150
   Fast-Track Fettuccine, 204
   Fettuccine with Sun-Dried Tomato Cream, 190
   Pasta Verde de Mar, 166
   Penne Primavera with Sundried Tomato Sauce, 212
   Penne with Artichokes, 188
   Savory Sausage & Spinach Penne, 120
   SONOMA Fettuccine Alfredo, 184
   Sun-Dried Tomato Linguine, 282
   Super Simple Chicken Soup, 52
   Uncommon Pasta Sauce, An, 312
Tomatoes, Stewed
   Burgundy Beef Pasta, 142
   Cacciatore Pineapple Chicken, 130
   Cajun Shrimp Fettuccine, 172
   Chili Wagon Wheel Casserole, 62
   Chunky Pasta Sauce with Meat, 310
   Giardiniera Sauce, 306
   Indian Chicken with Couscous, 242
   Jarlsberg Pasta Pie, 275
   Mafalda and Meatballs, 108
   Mexican Turkey Chili Mac, 4
   Sausage Minestrone Soup, 22
   Seafarers' Supper, 158
   Tomato Pesto Lasagna, 82
   Tortellini Soup, 30
Tomato Pesto Lasagna, 82

INDEX

Tomato Sauce, 208
Tomato Sauce with Ricotta & Herbs, 322
Tortellini
  Chickpea & Pasta Soup, 46
  Crispy Tortellini Bites, 271
  Pesto Chicken Pasta, 108
  Quick Tortellini with Artichokes, 264
  Quick Turkey Tortelloni, 117
  Salmon Tortellini, 166
  Spinach Tortellini with BEL PAESE®, 271
  Spinach Tortellini with Roasted Red Peppers, 215
  Sweet & Sour Tortellini, 232
  Tortellini Kabobs, 254
  Tortellini Primavera, 182
  Tortellini Soup, 30
  Tortellini with Pumpkin Red Pepper Sauce, 274
  Tortellini with Three-Cheese Tuna Sauce, 178
  Tortelloni Wreath with Pesto Dip, 284
Traditional Spaghetti Sauce, 323
Tuna
  Albacore Salad Puttanesca with Garlic Vinaigrette, 26
  Deep Fried Stuffed Shells, 148
  Elaine's Tuna Tetrazzini, 148
  Fettuccine à la Tuna, 164
  Spicy Tuna and Linguine with Garlic and Pine Nuts, 152
  Tortellini with Three-Cheese Tuna Sauce, 178
  Tuna & Zucchini-Stuffed Manicotti, 81
  Tuna in Red Pepper Sauce, 324
  Tuna Linguine, 176
  Tuna Noodle Casserole, 102
Turkey (see also **Turkey, Ground**)
  Asian Turkey Noodle Salad, 242
  Colorful Turkey Pasta Salad, 50
  Curried Turkey and Couscous Skillet, 226
  Many Peppered Fillets, 128
  Midsummer's Night Split Peas & Pasta, 32
  Quick Turkey Tortelloni, 117
  Rotini and Turkey Mozzarella, 129
  Smoked Turkey and Pepper Pasta Salad, 38
  Turkey and Avocado in Orange Sauce, 260
  Turkey Fruited Bow Tie Salad, 32

Turkey (continued)
  Turkey 'n Spaghetti Summer Salad, 40
  Turkey Orzo Italiano, 129
  Turkey Shanghai, 239, 250
  Turkey Stuffed Pasta Italiano, 80
  Turkey Tetrazzini, 298
Turkey, Ground
  Italian Delight, 94
  Mafalda and Meatballs, 108
  Mexican Turkey Chili Mac, 4
  Microwave Pasta Pie, 258
  Mini Meatballs with Pasta and Apple Pesto, 265
  New Orleans Sausage and Noodles, 136
  Penne with Eggplant and Turkey Sausage, 132
  Sweety Meaty Sauce for Ziti, 322
  Turkey and Bow Tie Pasta, 141
  Turkey Meatballs in a Pasta Crown, 264
  Turkey Noodle Dandy (An All-American Favorite), 100
  Turkey Pesto Meatballs with Zucchini and Pasta, 134
  Vegetable Pasta Italiano, 254
Turtle Shells, 88
Twisty Beef Bake, 76

U
Uncommon Pasta Sauce, An, 312
Up-to-the-Minute Linguine with Clam Sauce, 176

V
Veal 'n' Spaghetti Casserole, 113
Veal Sauce Lucia, 310
Vegetable Pasta Italiano, 254
Veggie Lasagne, 202
Vermicelli with Pork, 220

W
Warm Pasta and Spinach Salad, 8
Warm Tomato-Pepper Sauce, 318
Winter Pesto Pasta with Shrimp, 170
Winter Primavera, 193
Wisconsin Cheese Pasta Casserole, 58

Y
Yogurt
  Caribbean Pasta Salad with Tropical Island Dressing, 42
  Fruit and Pasta Refresher, 10

Yogurt (continued)
  Midsummer's Night Split Peas & Pasta, 32
  Pasta and Walnut Fruit Salad, 22
  Winter Pesto Pasta with Shrimp, 170

Z
Zesty Artichoke Basil Sauce, 318
Zesty Romaine and Pasta Salad, 18
Zucchini
  Creamy Seafood Pasta, 146
  Ditalini with Zucchini, 192
  Easy Cheesy Lasagna, 104
  Easy Pasta Primavera, 200
  Fresh Apricot-Pasta Salad, 259
  Garden Linguine, 190
  Garden Tomato Sauce, 315
  Harvest Drums, 125
  Hearty Italian Medley, 138
  Jarlsberg Pasta Pie, 275
  Lamb and Spaghetti Primavera, 137
  Luscious Vegetarian Lasagna, 186
  Orzo Risotto with Shrimp and Vegetables, 146
  Pasta Primavera Salad, 24
  Pasta Primavera with Italian Sausage, 133
  Pasta with Fresh Vegetables in Garlic Sauce, 260
  Penne Primavera with Sundried Tomato Sauce, 212
  Pesto Lasagna Rolls, 62
  Roasted Vegetables Provençal, 194
  Roasted Vegetables with Noodles, 246
  Rotini and Turkey Mozzarella, 129
  Sausage & Feta Strata, 113
  Seaside Squash Spaghetti, 150
  Smoked Turkey and Pepper Pasta Salad, 38
  Southwest Ruffle Salad, 46
  Three Cheese Vegetable Lasagna, 96
  Tuna & Zucchini-Stuffed Manicotti, 81
  Turkey Franks and Pasta Salad, 42
  Turkey 'n Spaghetti Summer Salad, 40
  Turkey Pesto Meatballs with Zucchini and Pasta, 134
  Winter Primavera, 193
  Zucchini Pasta Bake, 64
  Zucchini-Tomato-Noodle Soup, 8

METRIC CONVERSION CHART

VOLUME MEASUREMENTS (dry)

1/8 teaspoon = 0.5 mL
1/4 teaspoon = 1 mL
1/2 teaspoon = 2 mL
3/4 teaspoon = 4 mL
1 teaspoon = 5 mL
1 tablespoon = 15 mL
2 tablespoons = 30 mL
1/4 cup = 60 mL
1/3 cup = 75 mL
1/2 cup = 125 mL
2/3 cup = 150 mL
3/4 cup = 175 mL
1 cup = 250 mL
2 cups = 1 pint = 500 mL
3 cups = 750 mL
4 cups = 1 quart = 1 L

VOLUME MEASUREMENTS (fluid)

1 fluid ounce (2 tablespoons) = 30 mL
4 fluid ounces (1/2 cup) = 125 mL
8 fluid ounces (1 cup) = 250 mL
12 fluid ounces (1 1/2 cups) = 375 mL
16 fluid ounces (2 cups) = 500 mL

WEIGHTS (mass)

1/2 ounce = 15 g
1 ounce = 30 g
3 ounces = 90 g
4 ounces = 120 g
8 ounces = 225 g
10 ounces = 285 g
12 ounces = 360 g
16 ounces = 1 pound = 450 g

DIMENSIONS

1/16 inch = 2 mm
1/8 inch = 3 mm
1/4 inch = 6 mm
1/2 inch = 1.5 cm
3/4 inch = 2 cm
1 inch = 2.5 cm

OVEN TEMPERATURES

250°F = 120°C
275°F = 140°C
300°F = 150°C
325°F = 160°C
350°F = 180°C
375°F = 190°C
400°F = 200°C
425°F = 220°C
450°F = 230°C

BAKING PAN SIZES

Utensil	Size in Inches/Quarts	Metric Volume	Size in Centimeters
Baking or Cake Pan (square or rectangular)	8×8×2	2 L	20×20×5
	9×9×2	2.5 L	22×22×5
	12×8×2	3 L	30×20×5
	13×9×2	3.5 L	33×23×5
Loaf Pan	8×4×3	1.5 L	20×10×7
	9×5×3	2 L	23×13×7
Round Layer Cake Pan	8×1½	1.2 L	20×4
	9×1½	1.5 L	23×4
Pie Plate	8×1¼	750 mL	20×3
	9×1¼	1 L	23×3
Baking Dish or Casserole	1 quart	1 L	—
	1½ quart	1.5 L	—
	2 quart	2 L	—